P9-DUY-370

The Collected Works of St. Teresa of Avila

VOLUME TWO

The Collected Works of St. Teresa of Avila

VOLUME TWO

The Way of Perfection
Meditations on the Song of Songs
The Interior Castle

Translated by
Kieran Kavanaugh, O.C.D.
and
Otilio Rodriguez, O.C.D.

ICS Publications
Institute of Carmelite Studies
Washington, D.C.

ICS Publications
2131 Lincoln Road, NE
Washington, DC 20002-1199

www.icspublications.org

Cover: Portrait of St. Teresa of Jesus (1515–1582),
"The Ahumada Portrait," commissioned by the saint's family;
artist unknown; Real Academia de la Historia, Madrid, Spain.

ACKNOWLEDGMENT

Special thanks to the Discalced Carmelite nuns of Terre Haute, Indiana, and Baltimore and Port Tobacco, Maryland, for their assistance in providing this image and for their historical research on it.

Cover design by Say Yes Design

Typesetting by the Carmel of Indianapolis

Library of Congress Cataloging-in-Publications Data (Revised)

Teresa, Saint, 1515–1582
The collected works of St. Teresa of Avila.
Includes bibliographical references and index.
CONTENTS: v. 1. The book of her life. Spiritual testimonies. Soliloquies.—v. 2. The way of perfection. Meditations on the song of songs. The interior castle.—v. 3. The book of her foundations. Minor works.
1. Catholic Church—Collected works.
2. Theology—Collected works—16th century.
BX890.T353 1976 248 75-31305
ISBN: 0-9600876-6-4
ISBN-13: 978-0-9600876-6-2

CONTENTS

THE WAY OF PERFECTION

Introduction 15
Prologue 39
Chapter
1 The reason I founded this monastery with such strict observance. 41
2 Treats of how one should not worry about bodily needs and of the blessing there is in poverty. 43
3 Continues the subject she began to discuss in the first chapter; she urges her Sisters always to busy themselves begging God to help those who labor for the Church. The chapter ends with an earnest plea. 47
4 Urges the observance of the rule and discusses three things that are important for the spiritual life. Explains the first of these, which is love of neighbor, and how particular friendships do harm. 53
5 Continues on the subject of confessors. Speaks of the importance of their being learned. 58
6 Returns to the subject already begun, that of perfect love. 61
7 Treats of the same subject, spiritual love, and gives some advice on how to obtain it. 65
8 The great good that lies in detaching oneself inwardly and outwardly from all created things. 71
9 On how good it is for those who have left the world to flee from relatives and how they find truer friends. 73
10 How it is not enough to be detached from what was mentioned if we are not detached from ourselves, and how both this virtue of detachment and humility go together. 76
11 Continues to discuss mortification, and speaks about what must be acquired in sickness. 79
12 How the true lover of God will have little regard for his own life and honor. 81
13 Continues to discuss mortification and how one must flee from the world's maxims and rules about honor in order to arrive at true wisdom. 85

14 The importance of not allowing anyone to make profession whose spirit goes contrary to the things mentioned. 88
15 The great good that lies in not excusing oneself even when blamed without fault. 90
16 The difference that must lie between the perfection of the life of contemplatives and that of those who are simply content with the practice of mental prayer. How it is possible that God may at times raise a distracted soul to perfect contemplation and the reason for His doing so. This chapter and the following one are very noteworthy. 93
17 Not all souls are suited for contemplation, and some reach it late. The truly humble person must be content with the path along which God leads him. 98
18 Continues on the same subject and tells how the trials of contemplatives are much greater than those of persons living an active life. This chapter is very consoling for these latter. 102
19 Begins to discuss prayer. Speaks to souls unable to reason with the intellect. 106
20 How in different ways consolation is never lacking on the path of prayer. Counsels the Sisters to let their conversations deal always with prayer. 114
21 Tells how important it is to begin the practice of prayer with great determination and not pay any attention to obstacles set up by the devil. 117
22 Explains what mental prayer is. 121
23 Treats of how important it is for one who has begun the path of prayer not to turn back and speaks once more of the great value that lies in beginning with determination. 125
24 How vocal prayer must be recited with perfection, and mental prayer joined with it. 128
25 Tells how much the soul gains through a perfect recitation of vocal prayer and how God happens to raise it from this prayer to supernatural things. 131
26 Explains a method for recollecting one's mind. Sets down some ways of doing this. The chapter is very useful for beginners in prayer. 133
27 Deals with the great love our Lord showed us in the first words of the Our Father and how important it is for

those who truly want to be children of God to pay no attention whatsoever to lineage. 137

28 Explains the nature of the prayer of recollection and sets down some ways of getting accustomed to this form of prayer. 140

29 Continues to present means for obtaining this prayer of recollection. How little it should matter to us whether or not we are favored by the bishop. 145

30 The importance of understanding what is being asked for in prayer. Deals with the next words of the Our Father: *Sanctificetur nomen tuum, adveniat regnum tuum.* Applies these words to the prayer of quiet and begins to explain this kind of prayer. 149

31 Continues on the same subject. Explains the nature of the prayer of quiet. Gives some advice for those who experience it. This chapter should be carefully noted. 153

32 Discusses the words of the Our Father, *Fiat voluntas tua sicut in caelo et in terra;* the great deal a person does when he says them with full determination; and how well the Lord repays this. [So I counsel you to be attentive because the matter is very important.] 160

33 Deals with the great need we have that the Lord give us what we ask for in these words of the Our Father: *Panem nostrum quotidianum da nobis hodie.* 165

34 Continues on the same subject. The matter is very helpful with regard to the time immediately following reception of the most Blessed Sacrament. 168

35 With a prayerful exclamation to the Eternal Father concludes the subject that was begun. 174

36 Discusses these words of the Our Father: *Dimitte nobis debita nostra.* 177

37 Speaks of the excellence of this prayer, the Our Father, and of how we shall in many ways find consolation in it. 183

38 Deals with the great need we have to beseech the Eternal Father to grant us what we ask for in the words, *Et ne nos inducas in tentationem, sed libera nos a malo;* and explains some temptations. The subject matter is important. 185

39 Continues the same subject, gives advice about some different kinds of temptations, and sets down two remedies by which to free oneself from them. 189

40 Tells how by striving always to walk in the love and the fear of God we will proceed safely among so many temptations. 192
41 Speaks of the fear of God and of how we must be on guard against venial sins. 196
42 Discusses these last words of the Our Father: *Sed libera nos a malo. Amen.* But deliver us from evil. Amen. 200

MEDITATIONS ON THE SONG OF SONGS

Introduction 207
Prologue 215
Chapter
1 Treats of the veneration with which the Sacred Scriptures should be read and of the difficulty women have in comprehending them, especially the *Song of Songs.* 216
2 Treats of nine kinds of false peace presented to the soul by the world, the flesh, and the devil. Explains the holiness of the religious state. This holiness leads to the true peace desired by the bride in the *Song of Songs.* 222
3 Treats of the true peace God grants the soul and of His union with it. Gives some examples of the heroic charity of some servants of God. 236
4 Speaks of the prayer of quiet and of union and of the sweetness and delight they cause in the spirit; in comparison, earthly delights are nothing. 242
5 Continues to deal with the prayer of union and tells of the riches the soul acquires in it through the mediation of the Holy Spirit. Tells of the soul's determination to suffer trials for the Beloved. 247
6 Treats of how the benefits of this loving union surpass all the desires of the bride. Speaks of the suspension of the faculties and tells how some souls reach this sublime prayer in a short time. 250
7 Explains the bride's strong desires to suffer much for God and neighbor and the abundant fruits that come to the Church from souls favored by the divine union and detached from self-interest. 256

THE INTERIOR CASTLE

Introduction 263
[Prologue] 281

THE FIRST DWELLING PLACES

Chapter

1 Discusses the beauty and dignity of our souls. Draws a comparison in order to explain, and speaks of the benefit that comes from understanding this truth and knowing about the favors we receive from God and how the door to this castle is prayer. 283

2 Treats of how ugly a soul is when in mortal sin and how God wanted to let a certain person know something about this. Discusses, also, some matters on the theme of self-knowledge. This chapter is beneficial, for there are noteworthy points. Explains what is meant by these dwelling places. 288

THE SECOND DWELLING PLACES

Chapter

1 Discusses the importance of perseverance if one is to reach the final dwelling places; the great war the devil wages; and the importance of taking the right road from the beginning. Offers a remedy that has proved very efficacious. 297

THE THIRD DWELLING PLACES

Chapter

1 Treats of what little security we can have while living in this exile, even though we may have reached a high state, and of how we should walk with fear. This chapter has some good points. 304

2 Continues on the same topic; deals with dryness in prayer; with what, in her opinion, might take place at this stage; how it is necessary to test ourselves; and with the fact that the Lord does try those who are in these dwelling places. 309

THE FOURTH DWELLING PLACES

Chapter

1 Discusses the difference between consolations (or feelings of tenderness) in prayer and spiritual delights. Tells of her happiness on learning the difference between the mind and the intellect. This knowledge is very beneficial for anyone who is greatly distracted in prayer. 316

2 Continues on the same subject and explains through a comparison the nature of spiritual delight and how this is attained by not seeking it. 322

3 Deals with the prayer of recollection which for the most part the Lord gives before the prayer just mentioned. Tells about its effects and about those that come from that spiritual delight, given by the Lord, that was discussed in the previous chapter. 327

THE FIFTH DWELLING PLACES

Chapter

1 Begins to deal with how the soul is united to God in prayer. Tells how one discerns whether there is any illusion. 335

2 Continues on the same topic. Explains the prayer of union through an exquisite comparison. Tells about the effects it leaves in the soul. The chapter is very important. 341

3 Continues on the same subject. Tells about another kind of union the soul can reach with God's help and of how important love of neighbor is for this union. The chapter is very useful. 348

4 Continues with the same subject, explaining further this kind of prayer. Tells how important it is to walk with care because the devil himself uses a great deal of care in trying to make one turn back from what was begun. 354

THE SIXTH DWELLING PLACES

Chapter

1 Discusses how greater trials come when the Lord begins to grant greater favors. Mentions some and how those who are now in this dwelling place conduct themselves. This chapter is good for souls undergoing interior trials. 359

2 Deals with some of the ways in which our Lord awakens the soul. It seems there is nothing in these awakenings to

fear even though the experience is sublime and the favors are great. 366

3 Deals with the same subject and tells of the manner in which God, when pleased, speaks to the soul. Gives counsel about how one should behave in such a matter and not follow one's own opinion. Sets down some signs for discerning when there is deception and when not. This chapter is very beneficial. 370

4 Treats of when God suspends the soul in prayer with rapture or ecstasy or transport, which are all the same in my opinion, and how great courage is necessary to receive sublime favors from His Majesty. 378

5 Continues on the same subject and deals with a kind of rapture in which God raises up the soul through a flight of the spirit, an experience different from that just explained. Tells why courage is necessary. Explains something about this delightful favor the Lord grants. The chapter is a very beneficial one. 386

6 Tells about an effect of the prayer discussed in the previous chapter. How to understand whether this effect is true rather than deceptive. Discusses another favor the Lord grants so that the soul might be occupied in praising Him. 391

7 Discusses the kind of suffering those souls to whom God grants the favors mentioned feel concerning their sins. Tells what a great mistake it is, however spiritual one may be, not to practice keeping the humanity of our Lord and Saviour Jesus Christ present in one's mind; also His most sacred Passion and life, His glorious Mother, and the saints. The chapter is very helpful. 397

8 Discusses how God communicates Himself to the soul through an intellectual vision; gives some counsels. Tells about the effects such a vision causes if it is genuine. Recommends secrecy concerning these favors. 405

9 Treats of how the Lord communicates with the soul through an imaginative vision; gives careful warning against desiring to walk by this path and the reasons for such a warning. The chapter is very beneficial. 410

10 Tells about other favors God grants the soul, in a way different from those just mentioned, and of the great profit that comes from them. 418

11 Treats of some desires God gives the soul that are so powerful and vehement they place it in danger of death. Treats also of the benefits caused by this favor the Lord grants. 421

THE SEVENTH DWELLING PLACES

Chapter

1 Treats of the great favors God grants souls that have entered the seventh dwelling places. Tells how in her opinion there is a certain difference between the soul and the spirit, although the soul is all one. The chapter contains noteworthy doctrine. 427

2 Continues on the same subject. Explains the difference between spiritual union and spiritual marriage. Describes this difference through some delicate comparisons. 432

3 Deals with the wonderful effects of this prayer that was mentioned. It is necessary to pay attention and heed to these effects, for the difference between them and the previous ones is remarkable. 438

4 Concludes by explaining what she thinks our Lord's purpose is in granting such great favors to the soul and how it is necessary that Martha and Mary join together. This chapter is very beneficial. 444

[Epilogue] 451

NOTES

Notes to *The Way of Perfection* 455

Notes to *The Meditations on the Song of Songs* 477

Notes to *The Interior Castle* 480

INDEX 501

The Way of Perfection

THE WAY OF PERFECTION

INTRODUCTION

Origins

IN THE LAST FIVE CHAPTERS of her *Life,* St. Teresa describes the unusual events that surrounded her first foundation of a monastery for nuns. These chapters were added in her revision of this work and were written when she was already living in the new monastery called St. Joseph's.[1] Her confessor at the time was the Dominican theologian Domingo Báñez, who was a professor of theology at St. Thomas College in Avila. It was another Dominican friar, however, García de Toledo, for whom she wrote her *Life.* Because he was anxious to have it, she sent her final version to him without taking time to read it over.[2] This account of her life dealing with so many personal matters and such unusual and sublime mystical experiences passed, a few months later, into the hands of Báñez. Though the work contained excellent doctrine about contemplative prayer, he nonetheless shunned the thought of allowing it to be circulated among nuns or others interested in the subject.

Having got word of this work written by their Mother Foundress, the nuns at St. Joseph's were understandably curious and eager to read it. Teresa herself did not share her confessor's misgivings and thought the book could be read profitably by those who were favored with passive prayer.[3] But since Báñez refused to hear of this and even threatened to throw the manuscript into the fire, the nuns pressed Teresa to write another work just for them about prayer. The learned Dominican was more receptive to this idea, and he allowed Teresa to "write some things about prayer."[4] The nuns themselves, in addition to Báñez's general permission, made their own specific requests about the subject matter. Some of them were eager to learn about contemplation—and even perfect contemplation. Others, apparently frightened by the thought of such elevated topics, asked for simpler themes such as how to recite vocal prayer.[5] In any event, Teresa wrote *The Way of Perfection* for her nuns and with their requests and needs in mind; and she therefore dialogues with them throughout the work.

In Teresa's view, her response to the Sisters' urgings was like an act of obedience; "I have decided to obey them,"[6] she says. And when at different times she begins to sense the lack of order in the way she is proceeding, she comforts herself with the thought that she is writing for her Sisters, in obedience to them, and that they will not mind. At one point in the middle of her work, she moans in complete dissatisfaction over the jumbled way the material is being treated: "But what disorder in the way I write! Really, it's as though the work were done by one who doesn't know what she's doing. The fault is yours, Sisters, because you are the ones who ordered me to write this. Read it as best you can, for I am writing it as best I can. And if you find that it is all wrong, burn it. Time is necessary to do the work well, and I have so little as you see, for eight days must have gone by in which I haven't written anything. So I forget what I have said and also what I was going to say."[7]

When she comes to the conclusion of her work, Teresa summarizes briefly the subject matter she dealt with: "how one reaches this fount of living water, what the soul feels there, how God satisfies it,"[8] and so on. She then implies that she has thought of this book as an introduction to her *Life* by asserting that those who have reached the fount of living water will find her *Life* very beneficial and receive much light from it.[9]

At the outset, Teresa tells of her intention to submit her work to a theologian for censorship before turning it over to any of her nuns to read. For reasons we do not know, the censor was not Báñez, the person she mentions,[10] but García de Toledo. Less severe as a censor than his Dominican confrere would probably have been, García de Toledo nonetheless performed his task diligently, making in all about fifty corrections. Some of them concerned trifles, but others were more extensive and amounted to cancelling entire pages. He obviously had a clear grasp of the polemics underlying a number of the topics that were discussed. Though posterity can be grateful to him for not having consigned the book to the flames, as Teresa suggested he might if it did not meet with his approval, the number of corrections did call for a cautious revision of the whole work.

Leaving the prologue almost intact, including the reference to Báñez as the possible censor, Teresa amended the problematical passages and conformed them to the censor's opinion. In addition, she elaborated on some doctrinal matters and toned down many of the more spontaneous and confidential assertions and some of the subtle irony that flowed from her pen. Her second version also manifests a decided effort to write more legibly, as though the censor might have complained of difficulty in reading the text.

Teresa probably wrote her first redaction of *The Way of Perfection* in 1566, the year after she had completed her *Life*. Although some have thought the work was composed between 1562-1564, it seems from internal evidence, such as her references to Báñez and to her *Life*, the date would more likely be 1566.[11]

The year in which she actually composed her second version of *The Way of Perfection* is also a matter for debate. Almost unanimously, historians of the past set 1569 as the date of composition. They established their opinion on the testimony given by a young novice from the monastery of Toledo. The worth of this testimony has been recently challenged, and the date suggested is 1566.[12] Thus Teresa would have undertaken the task as soon as the censored manuscript had been returned to her. This opinion is based on her failure to allude to any new Carmels founded by her or to the missionary spirit she received from the enthusiastic Franciscan missionary Fr. Alonso Maldonado in the autumn of 1566 after his return from the Indies.

This second version of *The Way of Perfection* was censored

again by García de Toledo as well as by another censor whose identity is unknown. Neither of them made cancellations or observations that required any major change in the book this time. One passage of the second redaction Teresa herself later modified. It is in chapter 16. In answer to the question whether God might give mystical graces to imperfect souls, Teresa thinks that He would, so as to free them from their imperfections. But she categorically denies that contemplation would ever be granted to someone in mortal sin. In her altered view she simply says: "I want to say, then, that there are times when God will want to grant some great favor to persons who are in a bad state so as to draw them by this means out of the hands of the devil."[13]

The Autographs

Happily the two autographs of *The Way of Perfection* censored by García de Toledo are still conserved. The first is on display in the royal library of the Escorial; and the second is kept in the monastery of the Carmelite nuns in Valladolid, one of Teresa's own foundations. The first manuscript, referred to as "Escorial," begins with a prologue and continues without any division into chapters, although Teresa did indicate where she desired that a chapter begin. There are seventy-two chapters and the headings of these are written in the back of the book in Teresa's hand.

Since the length of some of the chapters in the Valladolid manuscript was increased, there are, in all, only forty-two chapters. Knowing now that this work would be read by others besides her Sisters at St. Joseph's, and also, as was said, in response to the remarks of the censors, Teresa suppressed some of the material. But in other areas she enlarged upon the matter being discussed and developed her ideas further; for example, this is seen in the important matter of the prayer of recollection and quiet.

The autograph of Valladolid is the work approved by the Dominican censor, and the text that was circulated in the new

Carmels. The copies made of Valladolid, however, were not always carefully done. Two of the copies, which were reviewed, corrected, and annotated by Teresa herself, are conserved today in the monasteries of the Carmelite nuns in Salamanca and Madrid.

Historical Context

In sixteenth-century Spain, political events were closely tied to religious ideas. What was happening in the world at large, particularly in Spain and in other parts of Europe, left its traces on Teresa's works. What was happening in the little world of the monastery of the Incarnation also left its mark on Teresa and her writings. An understanding of some of these events enlivens many of the pages of her treatises on prayer.

Reflecting on the final experiences of which Teresa writes in her *Life*, the reader is left with the notion that the Castilian Saint was living more among the Church triumphant of heaven than the Church of this earth. She beholds the glorious risen Christ, the Blessed Virgin Mary, the saints, and the angels. In an extraordinary vision of the angels, she experiences the glory of heaven within herself, though she does not see the Divinity clearly.[14] How much she was living in heaven is reflected in her following thoughts: "These revelations helped me very much, I think, in coming to know our true country and realizing that we are pilgrims here below. . . It happens to me sometimes that those who I know live there are my companions and the ones in whom I find comfort; it seems to me that they are the ones who are truly alive and that those who live here on earth are so dead that not even the whole world, I think, affords me company, especially when I experience those impulses."[15] All of this in addition to the painful longings of love that she felt caused her to surmise that she would soon die.[16]

The first chapter of *The Way of Perfection*, however, reveals a Teresa very much back on earth, keenly distraught over the afflicted Church. "At that time news reached me of the harm being done in France and of the havoc the Lutherans had caused and how much this miserable sect was growing. The news distressed me greatly, and, as though I could do something or were something, I cried to the Lord and begged Him that I might remedy so much evil."[17] What had occurred is that some harsh rumors had reached Teresa, but her remarks show that her knowledge of the facts was vague. It must be remembered that her references to the Lutherans in France represent her hazy way of speaking of Protestantism and demonstrate neither historical nor geographical precision. The unhappy news that had spread even to the enclosure of St. Joseph's concerned the religious war between the Catholics and the Huguenots. Teresa's stereotyped remarks reflect the way the ordinary people in Spain probably commented on the news. "Churches were being destroyed, the Blessed Sacrament taken away, many priests were being lost."[18]

In Teresa's mind the Church and Christianity were identical. The attack of "those Lutherans" was an attack against Christianity, she thought. Nowhere in this work does she use the qualifier "Catholic" to designate the members of the Church or the Church itself. Moreover the relationship between her mystical life and the Church, both in its ministry and its sufferings, was inseparable.

Curiously enough, despite all her locutions, visions, and communications from God, Teresa never received revelations destined for the Church as did other saints, such as Bridget of Sweden, Catherine of Siena, and Margaret Mary Alacoque. Her mystical life, rather, consisted of an inner experience of the content of Revelation. While it issued from within the faith, it also brought what was contained in that faith into sharper focus resulting for her in a convinced and powerful awareness of faith's mysteries. Understandably a love of the faith accompanied her experiences and, in addition, moved her to look to the Church and Scripture for guidance. In this respect she writes: "And with this love of the faith, which God then infuses and which is strong living faith, it always strives to proceed in conformity with what the Church holds, asking of this one and that, as one who has already made a firm assent to these truths."[19] And further on she adds: "For from what I see and know through experience, a locution bears the credentials of being from God if it is in conformity with Sacred Scripture."[20] In her mind, the faith was what the Church holds, the truths of Sacred Scripture.

Consequently, in consulting learned men and giving them an account of her spiritual life, Teresa was most of all concerned with whether or not her life and experiences were in agreement with the truths of the Sacred Scriptures. In a general manifestation of her soul, written in 1563 for García de Toledo, she explains with reference to Domingo Báñez: "He was a very spiritual man and a theologian with whom I discussed everything about my soul. And he discussed these matters with other learned men, among whom was Father Mancio. They found that none of my experiences was lacking in conformity with Sacred Scripture. This puts me very much at peace now, although I understand that as long as God leads me by this path I must not trust myself in anything. So I have always consulted others, even though I find it difficult."[21] The learned man, the theologian, is envisioned by Teresa as the spokesman for "what the Church holds," a master in "the truths of Sacred Scripture."

Not for the mere sake of fulfilling a formality, then, did Teresa submit her writings. Thus, at the beginning and end of *The Way of Perfection*, she mentions Fr. Báñez as the one who she thinks will take on the task of being her censor; and on two occasions in the course of her work she states her adherence to the faith professed by the Church.[22] An interesting aside is that only later, sometime around 1578, when reviewing her text in preparation for its publication, she added the qualifier "Roman." The attestation of faith at the beginning was also inserted at this time. Similar changes were introduced into the *Interior Castle* and the *Book of Foundations*. These factors, it would seem, point to little more than her eagerness for orthodoxy. In her simple view, she finds in "Holy Mother Church," the truths of Revelation, the sacraments, and a family of Christians.

"Don't allow any more harm to come to Christianity, Lord."[23] It was easy to speak of the Church as Christianity; just as easily did Teresa feel that what was done against the Church was done against Christ, "who is so roughly treated."[24] What might Teresa do to prevent this harm, these "great evils"? She has no use for any recourse to violence. "Human forces are not sufficient to stop the spread of this fire caused by these heretics, even though people have tried to see if with the force of arms they could remedy all the evil that is making such progress. It has seemed to me that what is necessary is a different approach. . . . For as I have said, it is the ecclesiastical, not the secular, arm that will save us."[25] Now the "ecclesiastical arm" consisted of preachers and theologians; and on the plane of knowledge, they were the ones who must through their learning and words defend the Church. This excluded Teresa. "I realized I was a woman and wretched and incapable of doing any of the useful things I desired to do in the service of the Lord."[26] The result of these reflections, though, was not a surrender to apathy but the resolve "to do the little that was in my power."[27]

This "little" developed into the Teresian ideal: a small group of Christians (in the beginning only eleven or twelve, later increased to fifteen and then to twenty-one), who would be good friends of the Lord by striving to follow the evangelical counsels as closely as possible and living a life of prayer for preachers and theologians, the defenders of the Church; thus a life in service of the Church, in service of Christ.

But a group of women dedicating themselves to a life of prayer and contemplation in that age and in those circumstances was destined to be looked upon, if not with complete distrust, then at least with caution.[28] The Spanish people in general were officially taught to follow the "level" and "safe" paths of both the ascetical life and vocal prayer and to shun the extraordinary ways of mysticism, especially its accessory phenomena of locutions, visions, and revelations.

In the case of women, the teaching was put forward with greater urgency. And the examples of false women mystics became material for small talk and subtle threat. Moreover, there were the interpretations of genetic laws which claimed that women were a mistake of nature, a kind of unfinished man. The shocking extent to which antifeminism could reach is evident in a passage from a writing by Francisco de Osuna: "Since you see your wife going about visiting many churches, practicing many devotions, and pretending to be a saint, lock the door; and if that isn't sufficient, break her leg if she is young, for she can go to heaven lame from her own house without going around in search of these suspect forms of holiness. It is enough for a woman to hear a sermon and then put it into practice. If she desires more, let a book be read to her while she spins, seated at her husband's side."[29] More than mere jest was involved in a saying of the time that a woman should be allowed to leave the house on only three occasions: once for her baptism, another in order to go to the house of the man she marries, and a third for her burial.

The scholastic theologians themselves were influenced by Aristotle's reasoning that women were guided by their passions rather than by stable judgments. In the processes for Teresa's canonization, Báñez acknowledged his unwillingness to let the writings of women be circulated.[30] And in his official judgment of Teresa's *Life*, he praises her virtues but warns against the many revelations and visions "which are always to be greatly feared, especially in women, who are more inclined to believe that these are from God and to make sanctity consist of them."[31]

The deleterious effects these attitudes may have had on women can be imagined; and as a woman Teresa indeed did feel incapable of much. Nonetheless, her defense of women was so clear and forceful in her first writing of *The Way of Perfection* that the censor intervened, and she felt obliged to omit a large portion in her revision. After pointing out that the Lord found as much love in women as in men, and more faith, while He was on this earth and that the world has so intimidated women that they do not dare do anything worthwhile in public for Him or "dare speak some truths that we lament over in secret," she concludes sharply: "Since the world's judges are sons of Adam and all of them men, there is no virtue in women that they do not hold suspect. Yes, indeed, the day will come, my King, when everyone will be known for what he is. I do not speak for myself, because the world already knows my wickedness—and I have rejoiced that this wickedness is known publicly—but because I see that these are times in which it would be wrong to undervalue virtuous and strong souls, even though they are women."[32]

Teresa's small group of women were to become good friends of the Lord, developing this friendship through a life of unceasing prayer as the Carmelite rule prescribed. But over and above their being women, the notion that they were to practice mental prayer also created problems. For both the followers of Erasmus and the *Alumbrados* went to such extremes in urging the practice of mental prayer that they manifested a certain contempt for vocal prayer, including liturgical prayer and other ceremonies and rituals. Whether or not such contempt was indeed a part of the teaching of many of the groups classified as *Alumbrados* is a matter for further research. Archbishop Carranza intimates the possibility of false accusations when he speaks of a person who was accused of being an *Alumbrado* merely for praying before a crucifix.[33] In his defense of mental prayer, Carranza holds that such prayer is more excellent than vocal prayer, but he does not condemn the latter.

Nonetheless, conservative theologians feared that in the practice of mental prayer lay the seeds of Protestantism, which was as dreaded as the plague by both the civil and the ecclesiastical rulers of Spain in the golden age. The Dominican friar Melchior Cano, a theologian at the Council of Trent and consultant to Philip II and to the Inquisition, attacked his fellow Dominican, Archbishop Carranza, and Luis de Granada for promoting the practice of mental prayer among the common people. Fernando Valdés, the Inquisitor General, complained that Luis de Granada was trying to write things about contemplation for mere carpenter's wives.[34] It was Valdés who published in 1559 an Index of forbidden books which included almost all those dealing with prayer.[35] The ordinary people were to be busy maintaining their households. For such people, Mass and vocal prayer were sufficient. Another theologian in this camp, Domingo Soto, confessed that he did not understand how those who were on their knees before the tabernacle for two hours could be thinking of God since God is invisible.[36] And Mancio de Corpus Christi, another theologian at Trent, criticized Carranza for speaking of prayer as though it were a sharing between friends.

This was the skeptical environment in which Teresa founded a monastery of women who would dedicate themselves to a life of prayer, of intimate friendship with God, of living faith and love, the most perfect exemplar of which was, for her, the Blessed Mother, a carpenter's wife. All this mistrust of women is clearly enough implied in Teresa's words: "You will hear some persons frequently making objections: there are dangers; so-and-so went astray by such means; this other one was deceived; another who prayed a great deal fell away; it's harmful to virtue; it's not for women, for they will be susceptible to illusions; it's better they stick to their sewing; they don't need these delicacies; the Our Father and the Hail Mary are sufficient."[37]

With the last statement, however, Teresa was in full agreement. If the Our Father is to be prayed in an authentic manner, it must be joined by mental prayer. Almost as if she were a mother scolding her child, she points accusingly to the senselessness of what was being urged. "Well, what is this, Christians, that you say mental prayer isn't necessary? Do you understand yourselves? Indeed, I don't think you do, and so you desire that we all be misled. You don't know what mental prayer is, or how vocal prayer should be recited, or what contemplation is, for if you did you wouldn't on the one hand condemn what on the other hand you praise."[38] Teresa, here, offers a strong defense of mental prayer, but she exalts vocal prayer joining it to mental prayer and observing that it may lead one into perfect contemplation.

While insisting that if there is any danger that danger lies in the neglect of mental prayer, she exclaims with enthusiasm: "Hold fast, daughters, for they cannot take from you the Our Father and the Hail Mary."[39] Here the censor, quick to catch the point, intervened and, going a step further from his usual method of simply crossing out a passage, wrote in the margin: "It seems she is reprimanding the Inquisitors for prohibiting books on prayer."[40]

That prayer is a work of the Church and particularly efficacious in the case of God's close friends, Teresa is convinced, even though it may be women's prayer. "I trust, my Lord, in these your servants who live here, and I know they desire and strive for nothing else than to please You. For You they renounced the little they had—and would have wanted to have more so as to serve You with it. Since You, my Creator, are not ungrateful, I think You will not fail to do what they beg of You. Nor did You, Lord, when You walked in the world despise women; rather, You always, with great compassion, helped them."[41] The petitions of these souls closely united to Christ, she further observes, are in conformity with Him and His Spirit and are granted through His own merits.[42]

This community of women that had come together to live a life of prayer could find support also in the spirit of the Carmelite rule. The hermits of the past who had spent their days in rugged solitude and contemplation on Mount Carmel were to be the group's inspiration.[43] Despite the fact that Teresa did not seem to know about the earlier Carmelite rule written for hermits and approved by Honorius III in 1226, there was for her enough of the eremitical spirit in the rule for Carmelite mendicants approved in 1247 by Innocent IV to lead her to emphasize the practice of solitude through an enclosure and withdrawal from the world greater than that which existed at the Incarnation.[44] Because of the large numbers living in the Incarnation and the penury of the community, the nuns were obliged to spend more time in the company of benefactors both in the monastery and outside in private homes. For similar reasons, in times of sickness they often had to leave their monastery and seek assistance outside. There were other motives as well for which they could easily enough obtain permission to leave the enclosure. Some nuns at the Incarnation desired a stricter observance of enclosure so as to comply with the mandate of the Council of Trent in this regard. But Teresa's appeal was to the eremitical spirit: "For the style of life we aim to follow is not just that of nuns but of hermits."[45] Solitude was important for her small community dedicated to prayer. Thus work in a common room was to be avoided;

"silence is better observed when each nun is by herself; and to get used to solitude is a great help for prayer."[46]

Though there is much evidence to attest to the fact that the community of the Incarnation was a devout and fervent one, there did exist a class structure with its varying lifestyles according to whether one was of wealthy or poor background. Individuals were able to obtain permission to keep money, from whatever source they may have received it, and some were even allowed to have an income. Thus we find references to the custom of buying and selling rooms, the better rooms, of course, going to the richer nuns. And the nuns who were poor didn't have rooms at all but slept in dormitories. The difference between the rich and the poor was indicated also in the religious garb by means of such things as pleats, colors, buckles, and so on. Some wore rings, and others owned pet dogs. There were those who, like Teresa, kept the title *doña* and had ample private quarters where members of their families could visit or stay. Some had servants or slaves. There were those who in virtue of their family rank took the first places in the choir. It might be added as well that in those times it was not unusual for many to enter a monastery as the solution to a social problem rather than in response to a religious vocation.[47]

Upon all these practices and ways of looking at religious life, Teresa turned her back. The poverty of spirit of the gospels, like a powerful magnet, drew her. "But the one who is from nobler lineage should be the one to speak least about her father. All the Sisters must be equal."[48] Poverty was to be the insignia of Teresa's nuns: "in houses, clothing, words, and most of all in thought."[49] And closely linked with detachment from money is detachment from honor because "honor and money always go together; anyone who wants honor doesn't despise money, and anyone who despises money doesn't care much about honor."[50] This life of equality and humility was meant, as Teresa envisioned it, to blossom into a life of authentic sisterly love, the love Christ insisted upon for His followers. As she puts it, "in this house where there are no more than thirteen—nor must there be any more—all must be friends, all must be loved, all must be held dear, all must be helped."[51]

The Central Theme

When Teresa revised *The Way of Perfection* after Fr. García de Toledo had examined the work, she wrote somewhat formally on the opening page: "This book deals with the advice and counsel Teresa of Jesus gives to her religious Sisters and daughters." Only later was a title given to this book of "advice and counsel," and the title was not composed by Teresa. However she knew of it and approved. The title appears in her manuscript on the opposite side of the opening page: "The book called *The Way of Perfection* written by Teresa of Jesus, a nun of the Order of our Lady of Mount Carmel." *The Way of Perfection* is therefore a practical book of advice and counsel destined to initiate the Carmelite nun into the life of prayer. Thus, Teresa is a teacher throughout the work, demonstrating how, pointing to the pitfalls, and explaining the right way from the wrong.

The Foundation of Prayer

In beginning her work, she first established the reasons behind this new manner of contemplative life. Because of her keen desire that the Lord's friends be good ones, she wanted the little community to follow Christ's counsels as perfectly as possible.[52] This implies careful observance of the rule, and for Teresa the essential element of the Carmelite rule is unceasing prayer.[53] Peace is necessary for a life of prayer. Thus Teresa avoids placing burdens on her nuns. She dwells mainly on only three practices because these will help them to possess both inwardly and outwardly the peace the Lord recommends to them and will dispose them to a life of prayer.[54] What are these three practices? Love of neighbor, detachment, and humility. Together they form a foundation for prayer. Since they touch upon the ties that are felt in one's relationship to others, to the world, and to oneself, they free the spirit.

Though admittedly there is an underlying structure and a logic in her works, Teresa makes little effort to present her ideas according to a well-ordered plan. In her characteristically simple manner, she confesses at the outset: "Since I don't know what I am about to say, I cannot say it in an orderly way."[55] It is not only in the first part of her work that she speaks of these practices that serve as a foundation for prayer, but the subjects of charity, detachment, and humility provide material for discussion again later as effects of prayer. Her digressions, too, for which she is well known, may cause readers some frustration in their efforts to follow her thought; hardly does she begin her work when she goes off into a lengthy digression (the entire second chapter) that would fit better elsewhere. Consequently, subjects treated in one section of the book will frequently be complemented by what is said on the matter in other places.

Taking up the first practice, love of neighbor, Teresa devotes four chapters to an analysis of love. Dividing love into that which is purely spiritual and that which is mixed with sensuality, she met with particular difficulty in explaining the latter. After rewriting the entire part in her revision, she then tore out the page and tried a third time.[56]

With regard to the whole subject of love, she complains that the term "love" is applied to much that has nothing to do with true and perfect love. She acknowledges the importance of friendships and of how they must grow into this perfect love and are enriched by it; but for her nuns living close together and only few in number she encourages them all to be friends. Furthermore, with her great capacity for friendship, Teresa observed that too much restraint could frighten people away from the service of God. "Our nature is such that this constraint is frightening and oppressive to others, and they flee from following the road that you are taking, even though they know clearly it is the more virtuous path."[57] Her own spontaneity and freedom from excessive constraint are noticeable in many passages of her first redaction that were censored or omitted in her revision. For example, in warning her nuns against magnificent buildings, she concluded: "And if I can say this in good conscience, may such a building fall to the ground the day you construct one." But the words used in her first writing are much stronger: ". . . may such a building fall to the ground and kill you all the day you desire one."[58]

However sublime the spirituality of which she speaks, Teresa would never want her daughters or any of her readers to lose the compassion that goes with charity. "For at times it happens that some trifle will cause as much suffering to one as a great trial will to another; little things can bring much distress to persons who have sensitive natures. If you are not like them, do not fail to be compassionate."[59]

The subject of detachment includes all that Teresa has to say through such expressions as poverty of spirit, mortification, and surrender to the will of God. What she observed in the human condition that most influenced her thinking about detachment was "how quickly all things come to an end."[60] Nor is the practice of detachment exclusively for nuns, no more than is that of charity or humility. Though Teresa wrote *The Way of Perfection* for her nuns, and it is, in a sense, a commentary on the constitutions she drafted for them, the treatise has become a popular book of spirituality since much of her advice is applicable to whoever is reading it. Remarkably, Teresa avoids any claim that nuns have a greater occasion for the practice of detachment or that their life is harder; rather, at times, she observes that married people are forced to practice greater self-discipline because of their obligations and that people living in the world have difficult trials from which the nuns are freed.[61] She states: "I do not call 'giving up everything' entering religious life, and the perfect soul can be detached and humble anywhere."[62]

The happy result of detachment is inner freedom, freedom from worry about bodily comfort, honor, and wealth. Considering the times in which she lived, the role Teresa gives to spartan fasts and penances is a small one. "But I am speaking about persons who by temperament like to be esteemed and honored and who look at the faults of others and never at their own, and other similar things that truly arise from lack of humility."[63]

Detachment and humility: so closely joined that Teresa could not speak of the one without the other; these two virtues "it seems always go together."[64] For humility implies detachment from oneself, from worry about esteem and honor. Then, just as the Virgin by humility drew the King of heaven to earth, so the soul by humility draws Love into itself. "I cannot understand how there could be humility without love or love without humility; nor are these two virtues possible without detachment from all creatures."[65]

There is that lack of self-esteem which has nothing to do with humility and is discernible through the agitation it causes. "Humility does not disturb or disquiet," Teresa writes, "however great it may be; it comes with peace, delight, and calm. . . . The pain of genuine humility doesn't agitate or afflict the soul; rather, this humility expands it and enables it to serve God more."[66]

In humility one is touched with the conviction that every good thing comes from God. If she felt great detachment from all things one day, Teresa knew through experience that on another such detachment could be taken from her; and she therefore concludes: "Now since this is true, who will be able to say of himself that he is virtuous or rich? For at the very moment when there is need of virtue one finds oneself poor."[67]

A Method of Prayer

A question often proposed is whether Teresa had a method of prayer which she taught. A popular method of prayer in her day was that of discursive meditation. And in turning her attention to the subject of prayer in the second part of her work in which she writes a commentary on the Our Father, she begins by referring to the many books of meditations. One of the most famous was the Dominican friar Luis de Granada's *Book of Prayer and Meditation*, published in 1554, a work she recommends in her constitutions. While praising these books,

Teresa adds a significant qualification: "There are so many good books written by able persons for those who have methodical minds and for souls that are experienced and can concentrate within themselves that it would be a mistake if you pay attention to what I say about prayer."[68] She, indeed, does not intend to write for those who possess these qualities. Her method is for those whose minds, similar to hers, are like "wild horses."[69] "I pity these souls greatly, for they seem to be like very thirsty persons who see water in the distance, but when they want to go there, they meet someone who prevents their passing from the beginning through the middle to the end."[70]

To these persons and to all others who cannot follow the path of discursive meditation, Teresa offers her method. In doing so, she turns to the Our Father, the prayer Christ taught us; for vocal prayer does not impede contemplation. But the recitation of this prayer must be informed by Teresa's method, which she calls the prayer of recollection. She calls it "recollection" because "the soul collects its faculties together and enters within itself to be with its God."[71] What is necessary along with this centering of attention is the realization that God is very close. She insists on the nearness of God to each one. "All the harm comes from not truly understanding that He is near."[72] Not only is He near, but He "never takes His eyes off you." And she asks: "Who can keep you from turning the eyes of your soul toward this Lord?"[73]

Her method is one of presence, of being fully present to God in our prayer, for He is fully present to us at all times. "What I'm trying to point out is that we should see and be present to the One with whom we speak without turning our back on Him."[74] Centering the attention within, being fully present, looking at, gazing upon; these are the expressions that fit her method. "I'm not asking you now that you think about Him or that you draw out a lot of concepts or make long and subtle reflections with your intellect. I'm not asking you to do anything more than look at Him."[75]

It is sufficient that one make the effort, and for that reason Teresa calls this prayer of recollection a method.[76] Understandably, the degrees of this recollection may vary, and

Teresa predicts that in the beginning it may be a little difficult, but soon "the gain will be clearly seen."[77]

This prayer of recollection, accompanied by vocal prayer, proved to be an excellent method, Teresa discovered, of disposing one for contemplative prayer. "And its divine Master comes more quickly to teach it and give it the prayer of quiet than He would through any other method it might use."[78] She claims she "never knew what it was to pray with satisfaction until the Lord taught me this method."[79] And concludes: "Therefore, Sisters, out of love for the Lord, get used to praying the Our Father with this recollection, and you will see the benefit before long. This is a manner of praying that the soul gets so quickly used to that it doesn't go astray, nor do the faculties become restless, as time will tell."[80]

Strict adherence to any one formula never became a part of Teresa's teaching. Her own spontaneity in prayer is displayed on almost every page and includes petitions, praise, adoration, offering, thanksgiving—all the forms of prayer. The opening words of the Our Father lead her into flights of her own unpremeditated prayer, and she teaches us to pray by praying herself. But the Our Father is always there to return to. In addition to this freedom from restriction, she values variety in the mode of being present to Christ: in joy, to be with Him as risen; in trial and sadness, to be with Him in His Passion. Presence to Christ within as He is shown to us in the different gospel accounts can be a further important aid, then, to the practice of recollection and of centering one's attention on Him. Although risen, He still influences us through His earthly mysteries by which He draws close to us in a more tangible way.[81]

At times during this prayer, the soul will feel a passive quieting and be drawn gradually to a greater silence. "I know there are many persons who while praying vocally, as has been already mentioned, are raised by God to sublime contemplation."[82] From this method of recollection, then, Teresa goes on to describe the prayer of quiet, the initial stage of contemplation which, in her terminology, is always passive prayer and unattainable through any human efforts. This initial stage of contemplation, in which there is not yet a complete silencing of the faculties, is followed by the prayer of union in which all the faculties come to rest in the inner silence. As contemplation begins, the recollection takes deeper hold; the words become fewer, one word uttered from time to time being sufficient. But one's own efforts are of no avail in either producing or holding on to mystical prayer. "The best way to hold on to this favor is to understand clearly that we can neither bring it about nor remove it; we can only receive it with gratitude, as most unworthy of it; and this not with many words."[83] Contemplation is like living water drunk from the fount; yet it is different from earthly water in that, while satisfying the soul's thirst, at the same time it increases that thirst.

The Lord gave the Our Father in a rather obscure form, Teresa thinks, so that each one may petition according to his own intention. As for herself, she came to the knowledge of many deep secrets unfolded before her by the Master who teaches those who say this prayer. "Certainly, it never entered my mind that this prayer contained so many deep secrets; for now you have seen the entire spiritual way contained in it, from the beginning stages until God engulfs the soul and gives it to drink abundantly from the fount of living water, which He said was to be found at the end of the way."[84]

The end of the way cannot be reached without Teresa's indomitable determination a *muy determinada determinacion.* "They must have a great and very resolute determination to persevere until reaching the end, come what may, happen what may, whatever work is involved, whatever criticism arises, whether they arrive or whether they die on the road, or even if they don't have courage for the trials that are met, or if the whole world collapses."[85]

Our Translation

Because of the demand and the lack of copies, Teresa thought, after a time, of having her book printed; but she felt the need of help for some careful editing. The unknown editor she commissioned entered unscrupulously into the delicate task. His polished text no longer bore many of the fascinating Teresian traits. She dutifully reviewed it, patiently cancelling and rewriting some of his excessive changes; and this manuscript is now conserved in the monastery of the Carmelite nuns in Toledo. It was a copy of this text that served for the first editions of *The Way of Perfection* that appeared in Evora, 1583, in Salamanca, 1585, and in Valencia, 1587. But since those acquainted with Teresa's unlabored, conversational style were unhappy with it, Fray Luis de León in his edition of Teresa's complete works chose the autograph of Valladolid as the text. The different versions of the book, however, left the matter very confused, even into our own century, until Fr. Silverio brought clarity to the entire question in his critical editions.

Our translation is of the Valladolid autograph, the work revised by Teresa and for which she received approval from Fr. García de Toledo. A translation only of the Valladolid text, however, would bring with it certain disadvantages. The lively passages and interesting variations in the Escorial text would be lost to the English-speaking reader. Many of these omissions and variations from Escorial can be inserted into the Valladolid text without seriously damaging the flow of thought. We have indicated whatever is taken from Escorial and introduced into our main text from Valladolid by enclosing it in brackets. Where there are two versions of the same passage, yet with significant differences, we give a translation of the Escorial version in a note.

The Way of Perfection may be divided as follows:

I. Purpose of the Teresian Carmel (chs. 1-3)
II. Foundations of prayer: love of neighbor, detachment, and humility (chs. 4-15)
III. Diversity of paths in contemplative communities (chs. 16-18)
IV. Prayer in general (chs. 19-26)
V. Commentary on the Our Father (chs. 27-42)
    A. Christ as Master and Guide in prayer (chs. 26-27)
    B. prayer of recollection (chs. 28-29)

C. prayer of quiet (chs. 30-31)
D. abandonment to the will of God (ch. 32)
E. the Eucharist (chs. 33-35)
F. pardon of offenses and detachment from honor and esteem (chs. 36-37)
G. deliverance from deception and illusions (chs. 38-41)
H. desires for eternal life (ch. 42)

Kieran Kavanaugh, O.C.D.
Carmelite Monastery
Brookline, Massachusetts

1979

* * * * * * *

Many have helped in the preparation of this volume and deserve to receive an expression of gratitude. Special thanks go to Padre Tomás de la Cruz (Alvarez) for allowing the translators to make use of his Spanish edition of the complete works of St. Teresa. His plentiful footnotes were indispensable to us in preparing our own notes. I would also like to thank the Carmel in Elysburg, Pennsylvania, for its important contribution of an index. Several other Carmels were helpful with some much-needed editorial assistance and proofreading, the Carmels of Danvers, Roxbury, and Indianapolis. Father Adrian Cooney assisted with some editorial advice, and Jean Mallon carefully typed the entire manuscript. Finally, I must express my appreciation to the many who have encouraged Father Otilio and me, after the appearance of volume one, to persevere translating through all the writings of this great Saint.

K. K.

THE WAY OF PERFECTION

The book called *The Way of Perfection* written by Teresa of Jesus, a nun of the Order of our Lady of Mount Carmel. This book is intended for the discalced nuns who observe the primitive rule of our Lady of Mount Carmel.

JHS

This book deals with the advice and counsel Teresa of Jesus gives to her religious Sisters and daughters who live in the monasteries that, with the help of our Lord and the glorious Virgin Mother of God, our Lady, she founded. These monasteries follow the primitive rule of our Lady of Mount Carmel. She directs her counsel particularly to the Sisters at St. Joseph's monastery in Avila, which was the first foundation and the place where she was prioress when she wrote this book.[1]

In all that I say in this book I submit to what our Mother the Holy Roman Church holds.[2] If there should be anything contrary to that, it will be due to my not understanding the matter. And so I beg the learned men who will see this work to look it over carefully and to correct any mistake there may be as to what the Church holds, as well as any other mistakes in other matters. If there should be anything good in this work, may it be for the honor and glory of God and the service of His most Blessed Mother, our Lady and Patroness, whose habit I wear despite my being very unworthy to do so.

JHS

Prologue

1. The Sisters in this monastery of St. Joseph have known that I received permission from the Father *Presentado,*[1] Friar Domingo Báñez, of the order of the glorious St. Dominic, who at present is my confessor,[2] to write some things about prayer. It seems I might be able to meet with success in doing this because I have discussed prayer with many spiritual and holy persons. The Sisters have urged me so persistently to tell them something about it that I have decided to obey them. I am aware that the great love they have for me will make what I say, so imperfectly and with such poor style, more acceptable than what is in some books that are very well written by those who know what they are writing about. And I trust in the Sisters' prayers that possibly through them the Lord will be pleased that I manage to say something about the mode and manner of life proper to this house. And if I should be mistaken, the Father *Presentado*, who will be the first to see this book, will either make corrections or burn it. I will not have lost anything by obeying these servants of God, and they will see what I have when left to myself and when His Majesty doesn't help me.

2. I am thinking of listing some remedies for certain common, small temptations of the devil, for since they are so common perhaps little attention is paid to them. And I shall write of other things as the Lord inspires me or that might come to my mind; for since I don't know what I'm going to say, I cannot say it in an orderly way. I believe this lack of order is best since writing this book is a thing already so out of order for me. May the Lord have a hand in all that I do so that it may conform to His holy will; these are my desires always, even though my works are as faulty as I am.

3. I know there is no lack of love in me and of the desire to help as much as I can that the souls of my Sisters may advance in the service of the Lord. This love together with my age and the experience I have from living in some monasteries may help me in speaking of ordinary things to be more successful than learned men. Since these learned men have other more important occupations and are strong, they don't pay so much attention to things that don't seem to amount to much in themselves. But everything can be harmful to those as weak as we women are. The wiles of the devil are many for women who live a very cloistered life, for the devil sees that new weapons are needed in order to do harm. I, as wretched as I am, have known how to defend myself only poorly. So I have desired that my Sisters might take warning from my own experience. I shall say nothing about what I have not experienced myself or seen in others [or received understanding of from our Lord in prayer.]

4. Not long ago I was ordered to write a certain account of my life, in which I also dealt with some things about prayer.[3] It could be that my confessor would not want you to see this account, and so I shall put down here something of what was said there. I shall also write of other things that to me seem necessary. May the Lord's own hand be in this work, as I have begged Him; and may He direct the work to His glory, amen.

Chapter 1

The reason I founded this monastery with such strict observance.

WHEN I BEGAN to take the first steps toward founding this monastery (for the reasons given in the book I mentioned that I wrote and also because of some great favors from the Lord through which I learned that He would be greatly served in this house), it was not my intention that there be so much external austerity or that the house have no income; on the contrary, I would have desired the possibility that nothing be lacking. In sum, my intention was the intention of the weak and wretched person that I am—although I did have some good motives besides those involving my own comfort.

2. At that time news reached me of the harm being done in France and of the havoc the Lutherans had caused and how much this miserable sect was growing. The news distressed me greatly, and, as though I could do something or were something, I cried to the Lord and begged Him that I might remedy so much evil. It seemed to me that I would have given a thousand lives to save one soul out of the many that were being lost there. I realized I was a woman and wretched and incapable of doing any of the useful things I desired to do in the service of the Lord. All my longing was and still is that since He has so many enemies and so few friends that these few friends be good ones. As a result I resolved to do the little that was in my power; that is, to follow the evangelical counsels as perfectly as I could and strive that these few persons who live here do the same. I did this trusting in the great goodness of God, who never fails to help anyone who is determined to give up everything for Him. My trust was that if these Sisters matched the ideal my desires had set for them, my faults would not have

much strength in the midst of so many virtues; and I could thereby please the Lord in some way. Since we would all be occupied in prayer for those who are the defenders of the Church and for preachers and for learned men who protect her from attack, we could help as much as possible this Lord of mine who is so roughly treated by those for whom He has done so much good; it seems these traitors would want Him to be crucified again and that He have no place to lay His head.

3. O my Redeemer, my heart cannot bear these thoughts without becoming terribly grieved. What is the matter with Christians nowadays? Must it always be those who owe You the most who afflict You? Those for whom You performed the greatest works, those You have chosen for Your friends, with whom You walk and commune by means of Your sacraments? Aren't they satisfied with the torments You have suffered for them?

4. Indeed, my Lord, one who withdraws from the world nowadays is not doing anything. Since the world so little appreciates You, what do we expect? Do we perhaps deserve to be treated better? Have we perhaps done better toward those in the world that they would keep us in their friendship? What is this? What do we now expect, those of us who through the goodness of the Lord are freed of that contagious, scabby sore, that sect whose followers already belong to the devil? Indeed, they have won punishment with their own hands and have easily earned eternal fire with their pleasures. That's their worry! Still, my heart breaks to see how many souls are lost. Though I can't grieve so much over the evil already done—that is irreparable—I would not want to see more of them lost each day.

5. O my Sisters in Christ, help me beg these things of the Lord. This is why He has gathered you together here. This is your vocation. These must be the business matters you're engaged in. These must be the things you desire, the things you weep about; these must be the objects of your petitions—not, my Sisters, the business matters of the world. For I laugh at and am even distressed about the things they come here to ask us to pray for: to ask His Majesty for wealth and money—and this is done by persons who I wish would ask Him for the grace

to trample everything underfoot. They are well intentioned, and in the end we pray for their intentions because of their devotion—although for myself I don't think the Lord ever hears me when I pray for these things. The world is all in flames; they want to sentence Christ again, so to speak, since they raise a thousand false witnesses against Him; they want to ravage His Church—and are we to waste time asking for things that if God were to give them we'd have one soul less in heaven? No, my Sisters, this is not the time to be discussing with God matters that have little importance.

6. Indeed, were I not to consider the human weakness that is consoled by receiving help in time of need (and it is good that we help in so far as we can), I'd be happy only if people understood that these are not the things they should be begging God for with so much care.

Chapter 2

Treats of how one should not worry about bodily needs and of the blessing there is in poverty.

DON'T THINK, my Sisters, that because you do not strive to please those who are in the world you will lack food. I assure you that such will not be the case. Never seek sustenance through human schemes, for you will die of hunger—and rightly so. Your eyes on your Spouse! He will sustain you. Once He is pleased, those least devoted to you will give you food even though they may not want to, as you have seen through experience. If in following this advice you should die of hunger, blessed be the nuns of St. Joseph's! For the love of the Lord, do not forget this. Since you have given up an income, give up worry about food. If you don't, everything will be lost. God wants some to have an income, and in their case it's all right for them to worry about their income since that goes with their vocation; but for us to worry, Sisters, would be absurd.

2. Worry about the financial resources of others, it seems to me, would amount to thinking about what others are enjoying.

Indeed, your worrying won't make the other change his thinking, nor will it inspire him with the idea to give alms. Leave this worrying to the One who can move all, for He is the Lord of money and of those who earn money. By His command we came here. His words are true; they cannot fail; rather, heaven and earth will fail.[1] Let us not fail Him; do not fear that He will fail you. And if some time He should fail you, it will be for a greater good. The lives of the saints failed when they were killed because of the Lord, but this happened so that through martyrdom their glory would be increased. It would be a good exchange to give up everything for the enjoyment of everlasting abundance.

3. Sisters, what I am saying is so important that I want you to remember it after my death—and that's why I'm leaving it for you in writing—for while I live I will remind you of it. I have seen by experience the great gain that comes from not worrying about such things. The less there is the more carefree I become. The Lord knows that, in my opinion, it distresses me more when we have a large surplus than when we are in need. I don't know if this is because I've experienced that the Lord immediately gives what we need. For us to worry about money would amount to deceiving the world, making ourselves poor in an exterior way but not being poor in spirit. I would feel scrupulous, so to speak, and it would seem to me as though a rich person were begging alms. Please God such may not be the case, for where there are too many cares about whether others will give us alms, sooner or later these cares will become habitual; or it could happen that we would go asking for what we have no need of, perhaps from someone more needy than we ourselves. Although those who give to us cannot lose anything but only gain, we would be losing. No, please God, my daughters! If you should start worrying like this, I would prefer that you have an income.

4. I beg you for the love of God and as an alms to me, in no way let your thoughts be taken up with these cares. If at any time such cares should be present in this house, let the youngest Sister cry out to His Majesty and bring the matter to the attention of the prioress. She may humbly tell the prioress

that the latter is mistaken, and so mistaken that little by little true poverty will be lost. I hope in the Lord that this will never happen and that He will not abandon His servants. May this book you have asked me to write, even if it do no more, serve to awaken you in these matters.

5. Believe me, my daughters, that for your good the Lord has given me a little understanding of the blessings that lie in holy poverty. Those who experience them will understand, though perhaps not as much as I. For not only had I failed to be poor in spirit, even though I professed it, but I was foolish in spirit. Poverty of spirit is a good that includes within itself all the good things of the world. [And I believe it has many of the good things contained in all the virtues. I am not saying this for certain, because I don't know the worth of each virtue. I will not speak about what in my opinion I do not understand well. But, for myself, I hold that poverty of spirit embraces many of the virtues.] In it lies great dominion. I say that it gives once again to one who doesn't care about the world's good things dominion over them all. What do kings and lords matter to me if I don't want their riches, or don't care to please them if in order to do so I would have to displease God in even the smallest thing? Nor what do I care about their honors if I have understood that the greatest honor of a poor person lies in the fact of his being truly poor?

6. In my opinion honor and money almost always go together; anyone who wants honor doesn't despise money, and anyone who despises money doesn't care much about honor. Let this be clearly understood, for it seems to me that the desire for honor always brings with it some interest in money or income. It would be a wonder if any poor person were honored in the world; on the contrary, even though he may be worthy of honor, he is little esteemed.[2] True poverty brings with it overwhelming honor. Poverty that is chosen for God alone has no need of pleasing anyone but Him. It is certain that in having need of no one a person has many friends. I have become clearly aware of this through experience.

7. So much is written about this virtue that I wouldn't know how to understand it all or still less speak of it. And so in order

not to do an injustice to this virtue by trying to praise it, I will say no more. I have only spoken of what I have seen through experience, and I confess that until now I have been so absorbed in speaking of these things that I did not realize I was doing so. But since I have written this, for the love of the Lord, keep in mind that holy poverty is our insignia and a virtue which at the beginning, when our order was founded, was so esteemed and well kept by our holy fathers. For I have been told, by someone who knows, that they did not keep anything for the next day. If exteriorly we do not carry out this practice so perfectly, let us strive to do so interiorly. Life lasts but a couple of hours; exceedingly great will be the reward. If we should do nothing else but what the Lord counseled us to do, the pay of just being able in some way to imitate Him would be great.

8. These are the insignia that must be on our coat of arms, for we must desire to observe poverty in every way: in houses, clothing, words, and most of all in thought. As long as you do this, have no fear that the religious life in this house will fail; God will help. As St. Clare said, great walls are those of poverty. She said that it was with walls like these, and those of humility, that she wanted to enclose her monasteries.[3] Surely, if poverty is truly observed, recollection and all the other virtues will be much better fortified than with very sumptuous buildings. Be careful of buildings like these; I beg you for the love of God and by His precious blood. And if I can say this in good conscience, may such a building fall to the ground the day you construct one.[4]

9. It looks very bad, my daughters, if large houses are built with money from the poor. May God not allow it. The houses must be poor and small in every way. Let us in some manner resemble our King, who had no house but the stable in Bethlehem where He was born and the cross where He died. These were houses where there was little room for recreation. Those who build large ones know what they are doing; they have other holy intentions. But for thirteen poor little women, any corner should be enough.[5] If it is necessary because of the extremely secluded life you live to have a stretch of land (and this even helps prayer and devotion) with some hermitages

where you can withdraw to pray, well and good. But no buildings, or large and ornate house. God deliver us from them! Always remember that everything will come tumbling down on the day of judgment. Who knows whether this will come soon?

10. Now it would not be right for the house of thirteen poor little women to make a loud crash when it falls; the truly poor must make no noise. They must be noiseless people so that others will take pity on them. And how they will rejoice when they see someone who was freed from hell because of the alms he gave them! That's all possible because they are much obliged to pray continually for the souls of their benefactors, since their food comes from them. The Lord also desires that, even though it comes from Him, we show gratitude to those persons through whose means He gives this food to us. Do not be negligent about showing gratitude.

11. I don't know what I began to say, for I have wandered off the subject. I believe the Lord wanted me to do so, for I never thought about saying what I have said here. May His Majesty always help us so that we never fail in the practice of poverty, amen.

Chapter 3

Continues the subject she began to discuss in the first chapter; she urges her Sisters always to busy themselves begging God to help those who labor for the Church. The chapter ends with an earnest plea.

TO RETURN TO THE MAIN REASON the Lord brought us together in this house and why I have greatly desired that we live so as to please His Majesty, I want to speak of helping to remedy the great evils I have seen. Human forces are not sufficient to stop the spread of this fire caused by these heretics, even though people have tried to see if with the force of arms they could remedy all the evil that is making such progress. It has seemed to me that what is necessary is a different approach, the approach of a lord when in time of war his land is overrun with enemies and he finds himself restricted on all sides. He withdraws to a city that he has well fortified and from there sometimes strikes his foe. Those who are in the city, being chosen people, are such that they can do more by themselves than many cowardly soldiers can. And often victory is won in this way. At least, even though victory is not won, these chosen people are not conquered. For since they have no traitor, they cannot be conquered—unless through starvation. In this example the starvation cannot be such as to force them to surrender—to die, yes; but not to surrender.

2. But why have I said this? So that you understand, my Sisters, that what we must ask God is that in this little castle where there are already good Christians not one of us will go over to the enemy and that God will make the captains of this castle or city, who are the preachers and theologians, very advanced in the way of the Lord. Since most of them belong to religious orders, ask God that they advance very far in the perfection of religious life and their vocation; this is most necessary. For as I have said, it is the ecclesiastical, not the secular, arm that will save us. Since in neither the ecclesiastical nor the secular arm can we be of any help to our King, let us strive to be the kind of persons whose prayers can be useful in helping those servants of God who through much toil have strengthened themselves with learning and a good life and have labored so as now to help the Lord.

3. You may perhaps ask why I am stressing this so much, and saying that we must help those who are better than we ourselves are. I will tell you why: it is because I don't think that as yet you understand well how much you owe the Lord for bringing you here where you are so removed from business affairs, occasions of sin, and worldly occupations. Indeed, it is a very great mercy. As for those persons I mentioned, who are not free in this way, it is good that they are not free; more so in these times than in the past. They are the persons who must strengthen people who are weak, and encourage the little ones. A fine state things would be in—soldiers without captains! These persons must live among men, deal with men, live in palaces, and even sometimes outwardly behave as such men

do. Do you think, my daughters, that little is required for them to deal with the world, live in the world, engage in its business, and, as I said, resemble it in its conversation, while interiorly remaining its strangers, its enemies; in sum, not being men but angels? For if they do not live in this way, they do not deserve to be called captains; nor may the Lord allow them to leave their cells, for they will do more harm than good. This is not the time for seeing imperfections in those who must teach.

4. And if they are not interiorly fortified through an understanding of the importance of trampling everything underfoot, of detachment from things that come to an end, and of attachment to eternal things, they will show some sign of this lack no matter how much they try to conceal it. Is it not the world they have to deal with? Have no fear that the world will forgive this deficiency; nor is there any imperfection it fails to recognize. It will overlook many good things and perhaps not even consider them good; but have no fear that it will overlook any evil or imperfect things. Now I wonder who it is that teaches people in the world about perfection, not so much that these people might seek perfection (for it doesn't seem to them they have any obligation to do this, but they think they are doing enough if they keep the commandments reasonably well), but that they might condemn others. And at times what is virtuous seems to them luxury. So, then, do not think that little help from God is necessary for this great battle these preachers and theologians are fighting; a very great deal is necessary.

5. I beg you to strive to be such that we might merit from God two things: First, that among the numerous learned men and religious there be many who will meet these requirements I mentioned that are necessary for this battle, and that the Lord may prepare those who do not meet them; one who is perfect will do much more than many who are not. Second, that after being placed in this combat, which, as I say, is not easy, they may receive protection from the Lord so as to remain free of the many perils there are in the world, and stop their ears in order not to hear the siren's song on this dangerous sea. If we can obtain some answers from God to these requests, we shall be fighting for Him even though we are very cloistered. And if

some of our requests are answered, I would consider well worthwhile the trials I have suffered in order to found this little corner, where I have also sought that this rule of our Lady and Empress be observed with the perfection with which it was observed when initiated.

6. Do not think it is useless to have these petitions[1] continually in your heart, for with some persons it seems a difficult thing for them not to be praying a great deal for their own soul. But what better prayer is there than these petitions I mentioned? If you are uneasy because you think your sufferings in purgatory will not be shortened, know that by this prayer they will be; and if you must still pay some debts, so be it. What would it matter were I to remain in purgatory until judgment day if through my prayer I could save even one soul? How much less would it matter if my prayer is to the advantage of many and for the honor of the Lord. Pay no attention to sufferings that come to an end if through them some greater service is rendered to Him who endured so many for us. Always try to be informed about what is more perfect [for as I will ask you later, and will give my reasons, you must always communicate with learned men].

So, then, I beg you for the love of the Lord to ask His Majesty to hear us in this matter. Miserable though I am, I ask His Majesty this since it is for His glory and the good of the Church; this glory and good is the object of my desires.

7. It seems bold that I think I could play some role in obtaining an answer to these petitions. I trust, my Lord, in these Your servants who live here, and I know they desire and strive for nothing else than to please You. For You they renounced the little they had—and would have wanted to have more so as to serve You with it. Since You, my Creator, are not ungrateful, I think You will not fail to do what they beg of You. Nor did You, Lord, when You walked in the world, despise women; rather, You always, with great compassion, helped them. [And You found as much love and more faith in them than You did in men. Among them was Your most blessed Mother, and through her merits—and because we wear her habit—we merit what, because of our offenses, we do not

deserve. Is it not enough, Lord, that the world has intimidated us. . . so that we may not do anything worthwhile for You in public or dare speak some truths that we lament over in secret, without Your also failing to hear so just a petition? I do not believe, Lord, that this could be true of Your goodness and justice, for You are a just judge and not like those of the world. Since the world's judges are sons of Adam and all of them men, there is no virtue in women that they do not hold suspect. Yes, indeed, the day will come, my King, when everyone will be known for what he is. I do not speak for myself, because the world already knows my wickedness—and I have rejoiced that this wickedness is known publicly—but because I see that these are times in which it would be wrong to undervalue virtuous and strong souls, even though they are women.][2] When we ask You for honors, income, money, or worldly things, do not hear us. But when we ask You for the honor of Your Son, why wouldn't You hear us, eternal Father, for the sake of Him who lost a thousand honors and a thousand lives for You? Not for us, Lord, for we don't deserve it, but for the blood of Your Son and His merits.

8. O eternal Father, see to it that so many lashes and injuries and such heavy torments are not forgotten! How then, my Creator, can a heart as loving as Yours allow that the deeds done by Your Son with such ardent love and so as to make us more pleasing to You (for You commanded that He love us) be esteemed so little? For nowadays these heretics have so little regard for the Blessed Sacrament that they take away its dwelling places by destroying churches. Was something still to be done to please You? But He did everything. Wasn't it enough, eternal Father, that while He lived He did not have a place to lay His head—[3] and always in the midst of so many trials? But now they take away the places He has at present for inviting His friends, for He realizes that we are weak and knows that the laborers must be nourished with such food. Hasn't He already paid far more than enough for the sin of Adam? Whenever we sin again must this loving Lamb pay? Don't allow this, my Emperor! Let Your Majesty be at once appeased! Do not look at our sins but behold that Your most blessed Son redeemed us,

and behold His merits and those of His glorious Mother and of so many saints and martyrs who died for You!

9. Ay, what a pity, Lord, and who has dared to make this petition on behalf of all of us? What a bad intermediary, my daughters, is she who seeks to be heard and to make such a petition for you! Indeed, this sovereign Judge should become more indignant—and rightly and justly so—at seeing me so bold! But behold, my Lord, that You are a God of mercy; have mercy on this little sinner, this little worm that is so bold with You. Behold, my God, my desires and the tears with which I beg this of You; forget my deeds because of who You are; have pity on so many souls that are being lost, and help Your Church. Don't allow any more harm to come to Christianity, Lord. Give light now to these darknesses.

10. I ask you, my Sisters, for the love of the Lord, to recommend to His Majesty this poor little thing, and beg Him to give her humility. Do this as something you are obliged to do. I am not requesting you to pray in particular for kings and prelates in the Church, especially our bishop.[4] I see you now so careful about doing so that it doesn't seem necessary for me to insist. Let those who are to come realize that if the bishop is holy the subjects will be so too; and as something very important always ask this of the Lord in your prayers. And when your prayers, desires, disciplines, and fasts are not directed toward obtaining these things I mentioned, reflect on how you are not accomplishing or fulfilling the purpose for which the Lord brought you here together. [And may the Lord because of who His Majesty is never allow you to forget this.]

Chapter 4

Urges the observance of the rule and discusses three things that are important for the spiritual life. Explains the first of these, which is love of neighbor, and how particular friendships do harm.[1]

NOW, DAUGHTERS, you have seen the great task we have undertaken [for the prelate and bishop who is your superior and for the order, already included in what was mentioned, since all is for the good of the Church; and to pray for the Church is an obligation]. What do you think we must be like if we are not to be considered very bold by God and the world? Clearly, we must work hard, and it helps a great deal to have lofty thoughts so that we will exert ourselves and make our deeds comply with our thoughts. For if we strive to observe our rule and constitutions very carefully, I hope in the Lord that our prayers will be heard. I am not beseeching you to do something new, my daughters, but only that we observe what we profess; to observe this is our vocation and obligation—although there are many degrees of observance.

2. Our primitive rule states that we must pray without ceasing.[2] If we do this with all the care possible—for unceasing prayer is the most important aspect of the rule—the fasts, the disciplines, and the silence the order commands will not be wanting. For you already know that if prayer is to be genuine, it must be helped by these other things; prayer and comfortable living are incompatible.

3. It is about prayer that you asked me to say something, and I beg you that in recompense for what I am going to say you eagerly do what I have said up until now, and read it often. Before I say anything about interior matters, that is, about prayer, I shall mention some things that are necessary for those who seek to follow the way of prayer; so necessary that even if these persons are not very contemplative, they can be far advanced in the service of the Lord if they possess these things. And if they do not possess them, it is impossible for them to be very contemplative. And if they think they are, they are being

highly deceived. May the Lord help me speak of these things, and may he teach me what I am about to say so that it may be for his glory, amen.

4. Do not think, my friends and daughters, that I shall burden you with many things; please God, we shall do what our holy fathers established and observed, for by walking this path they themselves established they merited this title we give them. It would be wrong to seek another way or try to learn about this path from anyone else. I shall enlarge on only three things, which are from our own constitutions, for it is very important that we understand how much the practice of these three things helps us to possess inwardly and outwardly the peace our Lord recommended so highly to us. The first of these is love for one another; the second is detachment from all created things; the third is true humility, which, even though I speak of it last, is the main practice and embraces all the others.

5. About the first, love for one another, it is most important that we have this, for there is nothing annoying that is not suffered easily by those who love one another—a thing would have to be extremely annoying before causing any displeasure. And if this commandment were observed in the world as it should be, I think such love would be very helpful for the observance of the other commandments. But, because of either excess or defect, we never reach the point of observing this commandment perfectly.

It may seem that having excessive love among ourselves could not be evil, but such excess carries with it so much evil and so many imperfections that I don't think anyone will believe this save the one who has been an eyewitness. The devil lays many snares here, for this excess is hardly noticed by persons having consciences that deal only roughly with pleasing God, and the excess even seems to them virtuous; but those who are interested in perfection have a deep understanding of this excessive love, because little by little it takes away the strength of will to be totally occupied in loving God.

6. I believe this excessive love must be found among women even more than among men; and the harm it does in the com-

munity is well known. It gives rise to the following: failing to love equally all the others; feeling sorry about any affront to the friend; desiring possessions so as to give her gifts; looking for time to speak with her, and often so as to tell her that you hold her dear and other trifling things rather than about your love for God. For these great friendships are seldom directed toward helping one love God more. On the contrary, I think the devil gets them started so as to promote factions in religious orders. For when love is in the service of His Majesty, the will does not proceed with passion but proceeds by seeking help to conquer other passions.

7. I should like that there be many of these friendships where there is a large community, but in this house where there are no more than thirteen—nor must there be any more[3]—all must be friends, all must be loved, all must be held dear, all must be helped. Watch out for these friendships, for love of the Lord, however holy they may be; even among brothers they can be poisonous. I see no benefit in them. And if the friends are relatives, the situation is much worse—it's a pestilence![4] And believe me, daughters, even though this kind of talk seems extreme, great perfection and great peace lie in keeping my advice; and many occasions are removed from those who are not strong. But if the will should be inclined to one more than to another (this cannot be helped, for it is natural and we are often drawn to love the worst one if that person is endowed with more natural graces), let us be careful not to allow ourselves to be dominated by that affection. Let us love the virtues and interior good, and always studiously avoid paying attention to this exterior element.

8. Let us not condescend, oh daughters, to allow our wills to be slaves to anyone, save to the One who bought it with His blood.[5] Be aware that, without understanding how, you will find yourselves so attached that you will be unable to manage the attachment. Oh, God help me, the silly things that come from such attachment are too numerous to be counted. And because these things are so minute that only the one who sees such friendship will understand and believe what is said about them, there's no reason to say any more here—except that such

a friendship is bad when found in anyone; but when found in the prioress it's a pestilence.

9. To break away from these friendships involving a particular fondness, great care is necessary at the outset of the friendship. This breaking away should be done delicately and lovingly rather than harshly. In providing a remedy it is important that the friends avoid being together and speaking to each other save at the designated hours. This would be in conformity with the custom we now follow, which is that we are not to be together but each one alone in her own cell, as the rule commands.[6] At St. Joseph's the nuns should be excused from having a common workroom, for although having one is a laudable custom, silence is better observed when each nun is by herself; and to get used to solitude is a great help for prayer. Since prayer must be the foundation of this house, it is necessary that we strive to dedicate ourselves to what most helps us in prayer.

10. Returning to the subject of our loving one another, it seems pointless to be recommending this love. For are there persons who can be so like brutes that they will not love each other even though they must always deal with and be in the company of one another and have no dealings and no recreation with persons outside the house and believe that God loves them and they Him, since for His sake they have left everything? I say this especially since virtue always inspires love, and I hope in His Majesty that those living in this house will with the help of God always be virtuous. So, in my opinion, I don't have to recommend this love a great deal.

11. What I would like to say a little about now is how this love for one another must be practiced. I would like to speak also of the nature of this virtuous love—which is the love I want practiced here—and how we know if we have this love; for our Lord recommended it so highly and so urgently to His apostles.[7] What I say will be in conformity with my dullness of mind; and if in other books you find a detailed explanation don't take anything from me, for perhaps I don't know what I'm talking about.

12. Two kinds of love are what I'm dealing with: One kind is spiritual, because it in no way seems to stir sensuality or affect

the tenderness of our nature so as to take away purity. The other is spiritual mixed with our sensuality and weakness or good love, for it seems to be licit, as is love for our relatives and friends. I have already said something about it.[8]

13. I want to speak now about the love that is spiritual, that which is not affected by any passion; where passion is present the good order is thrown into complete disorder. And if we deal with virtuous persons discreetly and moderately, especially confessors, we will benefit. But if you should become aware that the confessor is turning toward some vanity, be suspicious about everything and in no way carry on conversations with him even though they may seem to be good, but make your confession briefly and bring it to a conclusion. And it would be best to tell the prioress that your soul doesn't get on well with him and change confessors. That would be the most proper thing to do—if you can do it without hurting his reputation.

14. In similar cases and others as well, in which the devil could ensnare one in many difficulties and in which one does not know what counsel to take, the best thing to do is try to speak with some learned person; when necessary there should be the freedom to do this. Make your confession to him and do what he tells you to do about the matter; for since one must provide some remedy, one could fall into great error. How many mistakes have been made in the world by doing things without counsel, especially in matters that could be harmful to someone! Failing to provide a remedy cannot be allowed; for unless the devil is quickly cut short, the effect will not be something of minor importance when he begins to interfere. Thus what I have said about trying to speak with another confessor is what is best to do, provided that there be an opportunity; and I hope in the Lord there will be.

15. Keep in mind that this is a very important point, for such friendship is dangerous, harmful, and a hell for all the Sisters. I say that you must not wait until you recognize that serious evil is present, but you should in the beginning cut the relationship short by every possible and knowable means. In good conscience you can do so. But I hope in the Lord that He will not permit that persons who must always be engaged in

prayer will be able to love anyone who is not the Lord's great servant. That they ought not is very certain—or else they have neither the prayer nor the perfection that is in conformity with our goal here. For if they see that a person doesn't understand their language and doesn't love to speak of God, they will not be able to love him, because he will not be like them. If he is like them, since the opportunities for these servants of God to engage in such friendship are so few, he will not want to disturb them; or he will be a simpleton.

16. Now I have begun to speak about this matter because, as I have said,[9] the harm the devil can here cause is great, and only very slowly is it recognized; thus perfection can be gradually vitiated without one's knowing why. For if this confessor wants to allow room for vanity, because he himself is vain, he makes little of it even in others. May God, because of who He is, deliver us from such things. A situation like this would be enough to disturb all the nuns because their consciences tell them the opposite of what their confessor does. And if they are restricted to only one confessor, they don't know what to do or how to be at peace. For the one who should be calming them and providing a remedy is the one who is causing the harm. There must be a lot of these kinds of affliction in some places. It makes me feel great pity, and so you shouldn't be surprised if I have tried to explain this danger to you.

Chapter 5

Continues on the subject of confessors. Speaks of the importance of their being learned.

MAY THE LORD, because of who He is, not allow anyone in this house to undergo the trial that has been mentioned; that is, to find oneself in this affliction of body and soul. Nor may He allow a situation in which if the prioress gets along well with the confessor no one dares to speak either to him about her or to her about him. The result of this state of affairs will be the temptation to omit the confession of very serious sins for fear of being disturbed. O God help me, what harm the devil can cause here, and how dearly the nuns will pay for this restriction and concern about honor! For while they think that by dealing with no more than one confessor they are doing something great for religious life and the reputation of the monastery, the devil manages in this way to catch souls, since he cannot in any other. If they ask to go to another confessor, it immediately seems as if the peace and harmony of religious life will be lost. Or if the desired confessor is not from the same order, merely speaking with him, even though he may be a saint [Jerome], is taken as an affront by the others. [Praise God very much, daughters, for this freedom that you have, since you are able here to speak to others—though not too many others—besides your ordinary confessors, and these will give you light about everything.][1]

2. I ask, for the love of the Lord, that this holy freedom be allowed by the one who is superior. May she always ask permission from the bishop or the provincial that, besides speaking with the ordinary confessors, she and all the others might sometimes speak and discuss their souls with learned persons, especially if the confessors, however good, may not be learned.[2] Learning is a great help for shedding light upon every matter. It will be possible to find both learning and goodness in some persons. And the more the Lord favors you in prayer, the more necessary it will be that your prayer and good works have a good foundation.

3. You already know that the cornerstone must be a good conscience and that with all your strength you must strive to free yourselves even from venial sins and seek what is the most perfect. It will seem to you that any confessor knows this, but that is misleading. It happened to me that I spoke about matters of conscience with a confessor who had gone through the whole course of theology, and he did me a great deal of harm by telling me that some matters didn't amount to anything. I know that he didn't intend to misinform me and had no reason to, but he simply didn't know any more. And the same thing

happened to me with two or three others, besides the one I mentioned.[3]

4. Having true light at our disposal for the sake of keeping the law of God with perfection is all our good; prayer is well founded on such light. Without this strong foundation and if the Sisters are not given freedom to confess and discuss their souls with persons like those I have mentioned, the whole building will be wobbly. [Thus they must speak to spiritual and learned persons. If the appointed confessor is not spiritual and learned, they should at times seek out others. And if, perhaps, they receive orders not to confess to others, they can speak outside of confession to the kind of person I mentioned.] And I dare say more, that even if the confessor has all the qualities I mentioned, it is good sometimes to consult others because it is still possible for him to be mistaken; and it is important that not all be misled by him. One should seek always that there be nothing contrary to obedience, for there are ways and means for everything. And so it is good that in all possible ways one seek such counsel that is so valuable to souls.

5. All this that I have said should be of concern to the prioress. So I beg her again that, since no other consolation is sought here than the soul's, she should seek the soul's consolation by doing what I said. For there are different paths along which God leads souls, and one confessor perhaps will not know them all. I assure you there will not be lacking holy persons who will want to speak to you about your souls and bring you comfort—if your souls are what they should be—even though you may be poor. He who sustains your bodies will awaken someone and give him the desire to enlighten your souls and bring a remedy to this evil that I fear. For even if the devil tempts a confessor so as to deceive him about some doctrine, he will be careful and consider with caution everything he does when he knows that you speak to others.

Once this entrance has been taken away from the devil, I hope in God he will not find another one in this house. So I beg the bishop, whoever he may be, for love of the Lord, to allow the Sisters this freedom and not take it away from them when the persons they consult possess learning and goodness, a fact they can easily get to know in a city as small as this.[4]

6. I have seen and understood what I have mentioned here, and discussed it with learned and holy persons who have considered what was most suitable for this house so that there would be progress along the path of perfection. Among dangers, which are always present as long as we live, we find that this one is a lesser one. The vicar[5] should never have a free hand to come and go, nor should the confessor have this freedom. Rather, they should be protecting the recollection and decorum of the house and its progress, both interior and exterior, and should tell the bishop when there is some fault; but neither the vicar nor the confessor should be the superior.[6]

7. This is our practice at present—but not merely because of my opinion. The bishop we now have, under whose obedience we are (for many reasons obedience was not given to the order),[7] is a person fond of religious life and holiness and is a great servant of God. (His name is Don Alvaro de Mendoza; he is of high nobility and lineage and very fond of favoring this house in every way.) He gathered persons of learning, spirituality, and experience together in order to deal with this point; and freedom was decided upon. It is only right that the superiors who follow should hold to this opinion; it was decided upon by such good persons and sought from God with many prayers for enlightenment about the best thing to do. And from what has been known up until the present, this practice certainly is the best thing. May the Lord be pleased to preserve it always since it is for His greater glory, amen.

Chapter 6

Returns to the subject already begun, that of perfect love.

I HAVE DIGRESSED ENOUGH, but what was said is so important that anyone who understands it will not blame me.

Let us return now to the love that it is good for us to have, that which I say is purely spiritual.[1] I don't know if I know what I am saying. At least I don't think it's necessary to speak much about this love, because few have it. Let the one to whom the Lord has given it praise Him very much because such a person must have reached the highest perfection. Anyway, I want to say a little about this love. Doing so will perhaps be of some benefit; for when virtue is placed before our eyes, the one who desires it grows fond of it and seeks to gain it.

2. May it please God that I understand this love; and even more, that I know how to speak of it. For I don't think I know which love is spiritual, or when sensual love is mixed with spiritual love, nor do I know why I want to speak about this spiritual love. My situation is like that of one who hears others speaking in the distance but doesn't understand what they are saying. So it is that sometimes I don't think I understand what I'm saying, but the Lord wills that it be well said. If at other times what I say is nonsense, that is what is most natural to me—not being correct in anything.

3. Now it seems to me that those whom God brings to a certain clear knowledge love very differently than do those who have not reached it. This clear knowledge is about the nature of the world, that there is another world, about the difference between the one and the other, that the one is eternal and the other a dream; or about the nature of loving the Creator and loving the creature (and this seen through experience, which is entirely different from merely thinking about it or believing it); or this knowledge comes from seeing and feeling what is gained by the one love and lost by the other, and what the Creator is and what the creature is, and from many other things that the Lord teaches to anyone who wants to be taught by Him in prayer, or whom His Majesty desires to teach.

4. It may be, Sisters, that you will think it useless for me to speak of this love and that you will say everybody already knows these things I have mentioned. May it please the Lord that this be so, that you know them in such a way that they be important to you and impressed deep within your being. For if

you have this knowledge, you will see that I do not lie in saying that whoever the Lord brings to the state of perfection has this love. The persons the Lord brings to this state are generous souls, majestic souls. They are not content with loving something as wretched as these bodies, however beautiful they may be, however attractive. Yes, it pleases them to see such bodies, and they praise the Creator; but, no, they do not stop there. I mean stop in such a way that they love these things. It would seem to them that they were loving something of no substance, loving a shadow. They would feel chagrin, and they wouldn't have the courage, without great shame, to tell God they love Him.

5. You will tell me that such perfect persons do not know how to love or repay the love others have for them—at least, they care little about being loved. At times nature suddenly rejoices at being loved, but then when these persons return to themselves they see that this is foolish, unless the souls of the others will benefit either by doctrine or by prayer. All other affection wearies these persons, for they understand that no benefit comes from it and that it could be harmful. But this does not make these persons ungrateful or unwilling to repay the love of others by recommending them to God. They entrust to the Lord the care of those who love them, for they understand that the love comes from Him. It doesn't seem there is anything within themselves to love, and they immediately think they are loved because these others love God. They leave it to His Majesty to repay those who love them, and they beg Him to do so. In this way they remain free, for it seems to them that repaying the love is not their business. And, in fact, I think at times that if love does not come from those persons who can help us gain the blessings of the perfect, there would be great blindness in this desire to be loved.

6. Now, note well that when we desire love from some person, there is always a kind of seeking our own benefit or satisfaction, and these perfect persons have already trampled underfoot all the good things and comforts the world has to offer them. Their consolations are of a kind that even though they may desire them, so to speak, they cannot tolerate having

them apart from God or from speaking of Him. For what benefit can come to them from being loved?

7. Since this truth is made known to them, they laugh at themselves because of the affliction they once suffered as to whether or not their love was repaid. Although our affection is good, the desire that it be repaid is very natural. But once we receive the payment, we realize that the pay is all straw; it's all air and without substance so that the wind carries it away. No matter how much we have been loved, what is there that remains for us? As a result, you shouldn't care whether you are loved or not, unless the love is for your spiritual benefit as in the case of those perfect souls I mentioned, for they realize that our nature is such that if we are not loved we soon grow weary.

It will seem to you that such persons do not love or know anyone but God. I say, yes they do love, with a much greater and more genuine love, and with passion, and with a more beneficial love; in short, it is love. And these souls are more inclined to give than to receive. Even with respect to the Creator Himself they want to give more than to receive. I say that this attitude is what merits the name "love," for these other base attachments have usurped the name "love."

8. You will also wonder what they have affection for if they do not love because of the things they see. It is true that what they see they love and what they hear they become attached to; but the things that they see are stable. As soon as these persons love, they go beyond the bodies and turn their eyes to the soul and look to see if there is something to love in the soul. And if there isn't anything lovable, but they see some beginning and readiness so that if they love this soul and dig in this mine they will find gold, their labor causes them no pain. Nothing could be presented to them that they wouldn't eagerly do for the good of this soul, for they desire to continue loving it; but they know that if it does not love God very much and have His blessings, their loving it is impossible. And I say that this is impossible, no matter how much they are obligated to it; and even if it dies with love for them and does all the good works it can for them and possesses all natural graces combined, their wills will not have the strength to love it or make this love last. These

persons with perfect love already have experience and know what everything is; they will not be deceived. They see that they are not at one with the other and that it is impossible for the two to continue loving each other. For it is a love that must end when they die if the other is not keeping the law of God, and these persons understand that the other does not love God and that the two must then go to their different destinies.

9. And one of these persons to whom the Lord has given true wisdom cannot esteem this love, which lasts only here on earth, for more than what it is worth, or even for less. Those who like to find their pleasure in the things of the world, in its delights, honors, and riches will attribute some value to whether the other is rich or has the means to provide for diversion and recreation. But whoever has already come to abhor all of this cares little or nothing about such things.

Well now in the case of perfect love, if a person loves there is the passion to make the other soul worthy of being loved, for, as I say, this person knows that otherwise he will not continue to love the other. It is a love that costs dearly. This person does everything he can for the other's benefit; he would lose a thousand lives that a little good might come to the other soul. O precious love that imitates the Commander-in-chief of love, Jesus, our Good!

Chapter 7

Treats of the same subject, spiritual love, and gives some advice on how to obtain it.

IT'S STRANGE HOW IMPASSIONED THIS LOVE IS, the tears it costs, the penances and prayer; what concern to ask prayers for the one loved from all who it thinks can help that person toward God; what constant desire that others recommend him to God. It is not happy unless it sees that person make progress. If, on the other hand, it sees him improving and then sees him turning back somewhat, there doesn't seem to be any pleasure for it in life. It neither eats nor sleeps without this care about the other. It is always fearful lest the soul it loves so much be lost and the two be separated forever. Death here below matters nothing to it, for it doesn't want to become attached to anything that in a mere moment escapes from one's hand and cannot be grasped again. It is, as I said,[1] a love with no self-interest at all. All that it desires or wants is to see the other soul rich with heavenly blessings.

2. This is what love is, and not these other miserable earthly affections—although I don't mean evil ones, for God deliver us from them. We must never tire of condemning anything that leads to hell, for the slightest evil of hell cannot be exaggerated. We shouldn't let our mouths utter even a word about this sinful love, Sisters, nor should we think that it exists in the world. We shouldn't listen to anything said about it, whether this be done in jest or in truth. Do not allow that this type of love be spoken of or discussed in your presence. Such love has nothing good in it, and even hearing about it can be harmful. You may speak about the licit love I mentioned, which we have for one another or for relatives and friends and in which our care is that our loved ones don't die; or, if the other's head aches our souls seem to ache too, and if they suffer trials, it seems that we lose our patience; and other things like that.

3. Spiritual love is not like this. Even though some grief is at first felt through natural weakness, reason immediately considers whether the trial is good for the one loved, whether there is an enrichment in virtue and how that soul bears the suffering; it asks God to give the other patience and merit in the trials. If this love sees that the other person has patience, no distress is felt; rather it rejoices and is consoled. This love would much rather suffer the trial itself than see the other suffer it if the merit and gain that lies in suffering could be given to the other entirely—but not because this love is disquieted and disturbed.

4. I say once again[2] that spiritual love seems to be imitating that love which the good lover Jesus had for us. Hence, these lovers advance so far because they embrace all trials, and the others, without trial, receive benefit from those who love. And

believe me, either these lovers will cut off their relationship—I mean special friendship—or they will obtain from our Lord that the one loved walk along their own way toward the same goal, as did St. Monica with St. Augustine. These lovers cannot in their hearts be insincere with those they love; if they see them deviate from the path or commit some faults they immediately tell them about it. They cannot help but do so. And since they are not going to change their attitude, nor are they going to flatter or hide anything from the other, either that other person mends his ways or the friendship is broken. For these lovers cannot suffer such a thing, nor should it be suffered. There is a continual war between the two attitudes these lovers have; on the one hand they go about forgetful of the whole world, taking no account of whether others serve God or not but only keeping account of themselves; on the other hand, with their friends, they have no power to do this, nor is anything covered over; they see the tiniest speck. I say that they bear a truly heavy cross. [Oh fortunate are the souls loved by such as these! Fortunate was the day they came to know them! O my Lord, would you not be doing me a favor if there were many who so loved me? Certainly, it would be more beneficial to me than if I were loved by all the kings and lords of the world; and rightly so, for these persons strive in as many ways as they can that we ourselves be lords of that very world and that all things be subject to us.

When you know some person like this, Sisters, let the Mother prioress diligently strive that he speak with you. Love such persons as much as you like. They must be few, but the Lord does desire that it be known when someone has reached perfection. You will be immediately told that speaking with him is unnecessary, that it is enough to have God. But a good means to having God is to speak with His friends, for one always gains very much from this. I know through experience. After the Lord, it is because of persons like these that I am not in hell, for I was always very attached to their praying for me, and so I strove to get them to do this. Now let us return to our subject.]

5. This spiritual love is the kind of love I would desire us to have. Even though in the beginning it is not so perfect, the

Lord will gradually perfect it. Let us begin by using the suitable means, for even though the love bears with it some natural tenderness no harm will be done provided this tenderness is shown toward all. It is good and necessary sometimes in loving to show and also have affection, and to feel some of the trials and sicknesses of the Sisters, even though these may be small. For at times it happens that some trifle will cause as much suffering to one as a great trial will to another; little things can bring much distress to persons who have sensitive natures. [And do not be surprised, for perhaps the devil employed all his energy here, more energy than what he uses when you feel great sufferings and trials.] If you are not like them, do not fail to be compassionate. And perhaps our Lord desires to exempt us from these sufferings, whereas in other matters we will suffer. And those sufferings that for us are heavy—even if in themselves they truly are—may be light for another. So in these matters let us not judge from ourselves, nor let us think that we are at a stage in which perhaps the Lord without our own effort has made us stronger, but let us think of the stage we were at when we were weaker.

6. Consider that this advice is important for knowing how to sympathize with your neighbor in his trials, however small they may be. This is especially true in the case of those souls that were mentioned.[3] Since they desire trials they make little of everything, and it is very necessary that they take the time to remember how they themselves were once weak and that if they are not weak now, their strength doesn't come from themselves. For it could be that the devil by this means will make charity toward one's neighbor grow cold, and make us think that what in reality is a fault belongs to perfection. It is necessary to be careful and awake in everything, for he does not sleep. This is truer in the case of those advancing in perfection. The temptations are then very deceiving, since the devil wouldn't dare anything else. It doesn't seem the harm is recognized until it is already done—if, as I say, one doesn't take care. In sum, it is necessary to watch and pray always, for there is no better remedy than prayer for discovering these secret things of the devil and bringing them to light.

7. Strive also to take time for recreation with the Sisters when there is need and during the time set aside for it by custom, even though this may not be to your pleasure, for everything done with a pure intention is perfect love. [And so it is that when I desire to speak of that other love that is not so perfect, I do not find in this house any path in which I think it would be good for us to have such love. For however good this love might be, everything must hark back to its origin, which is the perfect love I spoke of. I thought of saying much about this other love, and now that I've come to discuss its fine points, I don't think it fits our way of life. So, I want to leave the matter as it stands; I hope in God that in this house there will be no opportunity for any other kind of love than perfect love, even though our love may not be entirely perfect.] Thus, it is very good that some take pity on others in their need. Let them take care that there be no lack of discretion in things that would go against obedience. Even though within yourself the prioress' commands may seem harsh, don't show this or let anyone know about it—unless, with humility, the prioress herself—for you would cause much harm. And learn how to understand which are the things one ought to feel sorry about and take pity on with regard to the Sisters. And always grieve over any fault, if it is publicly known, that you see in a Sister. Here love shows itself, and it is practiced well when you know how to suffer the fault and not be surprised; so the others will do with respect to your faults, for you may have many more than you are aware of. Recommend the Sister to God and strive yourself to practice with great perfection the virtue opposite the fault that appears in her. Make every effort to do this so that you teach that Sister in deed what perhaps through words or punishment she might not understand or profit by; and the imitation of the virtue in which one sees another excel has a great tendency to spread. This is good advice; don't forget it.

8. Oh, how good and true will be the love of the Sister who can help others by setting aside her own advantage for their sake. She will make much progress in all the virtues and keep her rule with great perfection. Better friendship will this be than all the tender words that can be uttered, for these are not

used, nor should they be used, in this house; those like, "my life," "my soul," "my only good," and other similar expressions addressed now to one, now to another, of the Sisters. Keep these words of affection for your Spouse, for you must be with Him so much and so alone that you will need to be helped by everything; His Majesty allows us to use these words with Him. But if they are used a lot among ourselves, they will not be so touching when used with the Lord. And besides, there's no reason for using them. They are very womanish, and I would not want you, my daughters, to be womanish in anything, nor would I want you to be like women but like strong men. For if you do what lies in your power, the Lord will make you so strong that you will astonish men. And how easy this is for His Majesty since He made us from nothing.

9. Another very good proof of love is that you strive in household duties to relieve others of work, and also rejoice and praise the Lord very much for any increase you see in their virtues. All these things, not to mention the great good they contain in themselves, help very much to further peace and conformity between the Sisters, as we now, by God's goodness, see through experience. May it please His Majesty that this love always continue. The contrary would be a terrible thing, and very difficult to endure: that is, few in number and disunited. God forbid.[4]

10. If by chance some little word should escape, try to remedy the matter immediately and pray intensely. And if things of this sort against charity continue, such as little factions, or ambition, or concern about some little point of honor (for I think my blood freezes when I write about this and think that at some time it could happen, because I see it is the main evil in monasteries); when these things begin to take place consider yourselves lost. Think and believe that you have thrown your Spouse out of the house and have made it necessary for Him to go in search of another dwelling, since you threw Him out of His own house. Cry out to His Majesty. Seek a remedy; for if you don't find one after such frequent confession and Communion, there is reason to fear a Judas among you.

11. Let the prioress for the love of God watch carefully that

no place be given to such concerns, and root them out from the beginning; from whether she does this or not will stem either all the harm or all the remedy. [And if love doesn't suffice to do this, let it be done with severe punishments.] And anyone found to be the cause of such disturbance should be sent to another monastery, for God will provide her with the dowry. Get rid of this pestilence; cut off the branches as best you can, and if this is not enough pull up the roots. And if that doesn't work, do not let the one who is taken up with these things leave the prison cell. That's much better than letting so incurable a pestilence infect all the nuns. Oh, how great an evil it is! God deliver us from the monastery where it enters; I would rather that the monastery catch fire and all be burned. Because I believe I shall say something about this elsewhere—since it is something so important—I'll not enlarge on it any more here.[5]

Chapter 8

The great good that lies in detaching oneself inwardly and outwardly from all created things.

NOW LET US TALK ABOUT the detachment we ought to have, for detachment, if it is practiced with perfection, includes everything. I say it includes everything because if we embrace the Creator and care not at all for the whole of creation, His Majesty will infuse the virtues. Doing little by little what we can, we will have hardly anything else to fight against; it is the Lord who in our defense takes up the battle against the demons and against the world.

Do you think, Sisters, it is a small blessing we receive in obtaining this grace to give ourselves to the All entirely and without reserve? And since in Him are all blessings, as I say, let us praise Him very much, Sisters, for having brought us together here where the only concern is to give ourselves entirely to Him. Indeed, I don't know why I am saying this because every one of you here can teach me. I confess that in this matter so important I am not as perfect as I desire or understand to be fitting. And this goes for all the virtues and all that I say here, for it is much easier to write about these things than to put them into practice. And I don't even succeed in writing about them, because sometimes knowing how to speak of them requires experience; and if I do succeed, it is perhaps by writing of the opposite of what I have practiced.

2. With regard to externals, obviously we are separated here from everything. [I think the Lord wants all of us He has gathered together in this house to withdraw from everything so that His Majesty may unite us to Himself here without any hindrance. O my Creator and Lord! When did I merit such honor? For it seems you went a roundabout way to bring us closer to Yourself. May it please Your goodness that we do not lose through our own fault this nearness to You.] O Sisters, understand, for the love of God, the great favor the Lord has granted those whom he brought here. Each of you should reflect upon this carefully, for there are only twelve here and His Majesty desired that you be one of them.[1] And how many there are who are better than I, who I know would take this place eagerly, and the Lord gave it to me who so poorly deserved it! May You be blessed, my God, and may all creatures praise You! One cannot repay You for this favor—as is likewise so for many others You have granted me—for my vocation to be a nun was a very great favor! Since I have been so miserable, You did not trust me, Lord. Instead of keeping me where there were so many living together and where my wretchedness would not have been so clearly seen during my lifetime, You have brought me to a place where, since there are so few nuns, it seems impossible for this wretchedness not to be known. That I might walk more carefully, You have removed from me all opportunities to conceal it. Now I confess there is no longer an excuse for me, Lord, and so I have greater need of Your mercy that You might pardon any fault I may have.[2]

3. What I ask of you, Sisters, is that if anyone sees within herself that she is unable to follow what is customarily practiced here she say so; there are other monasteries where the

Lord is also served. Do not disturb these few nuns brought here together by His Majesty. In other places there is the freedom to find relief by being with relatives; here if some relatives are allowed to visit, it is that they might find relief by being with us. But the nun who desires to see them for her own consolation, if these relatives are not spiritual persons, should consider herself imperfect. She ought to believe that she is not detached, not healthy; she will not possess freedom of spirit; she will not possess complete peace. She needs a doctor; and I say that if this attachment is not removed and she is not cured, she is not meant for this house.

4. The best remedy I know is that she not see them until obviously she is free and obtains this freedom from the Lord through much prayer. When it is clear that she considers these visits a cross, it will be all right for her to see them, for then she will be of benefit to her relatives and not be harmed herself. [But if she loves her relatives, if she grieves a great deal over their sufferings and eagerly listens to what they tell her about their business affairs in the world, she should believe that she will bring harm to herself and no good to them.]

Chapter 9

On how good it is for those who have left the world to flee from relatives and how they find truer friends.

OH, IF WE RELIGIOUS COULD understand the great harm that comes from having too much to do with relatives! How we would flee them! I don't know what consolation they give us (if in talking with them we leave out what pertains to God and deal only with what pertains to our comfort and rest), for we cannot enjoy their recreations, nor would this be lawful for us. Oh yes, we can grieve over their trials; in fact, we do cry over all their tribulations and sometimes more than they themselves do. Surely, if they give the body some comfort, the spirit pays well for it. You are removed from this here.

Since everything is held in common and no one can have any special comfort, the alms they give you are given in a general way; and you are freed from trying to please them on this account, for you know that it is the Lord who provides for all in common.

2. I am astonished by the harm that is caused from dealing with relatives. I don't think anyone will believe it except the one who has experienced it for himself. And how this practice of perfection seems to be forgotten nowadays in religious orders. I don't know what it is in the world that we renounce when we say that we give up everything for God if we do not give up the main thing, namely, our relatives. The situation has reached the state in which it seems to be a lack of virtue for religious not to love and talk a great deal with their relatives, and these religious are not afraid to say and even advance their reasons.

3. In this house, daughters, great care should be taken to recommend them to God; that is right. As for the rest, we should keep them out of our minds as much as possible, because it is a natural thing for the will to become attached to them more than to other persons.

I have been much loved by my relatives—according to what they have said—and I loved them so much that I didn't let them forget me. But I know through my own experience as well as that of others that in time of trial my relatives helped me least. It was the servants of God who helped me. By relatives I do not mean parents, for parents very seldom fail to help their children, and it is right for us to console them in their need. Let us not remain aloof from them if we see that communicating with them does no harm to our religious life. This communication can be carried on with detachment; and so, too, with brothers and sisters.

4. Believe, Sisters, that if you serve His Majesty as you ought, you will not find better relatives than those He sends you. I know that this is so. Convinced of that, as you are here, and understanding that in doing otherwise you would be failing your true Friend and Spouse, believe that in a very short

time you will gain this freedom. Believe that you can trust those who love you only for His sake more than you can all your relatives, and that these former will not fail you. And you will find fathers and brothers in those about whom you had not even thought. For since these seek to be repaid by God, they do things for us. Those who seek to be repaid by us soon grow tired, since they see that we are poor and unable to help them in any way. And although this may not be universally so, it is now more usually so; for, after all, the world is the world.

Do not believe whoever tells you to do something else and that it is virtue to do so. For if I should mention all the harm that this association with relatives brings in its wake, I would have to enlarge a great deal. And because others who know what they are saying better than I do have written about this, what I have said should suffice. If I who am so imperfect have understood so much about this, I wonder what those who are perfect know?

5. All that the saints counsel us about fleeing the world is clearly good. Well, believe me, our relatives are what clings to us most from the world, as I have said,[1] and the most difficult to detach ourselves from. Consequently, those who flee from their own countries do well—if it helps them, I say, for I don't think it helps to flee bodily; rather what helps is that the soul embrace the good Jesus our Lord with determination, for since in Him everything is found, in Him everything is forgotten. Yet, it is a very great help to withdraw even bodily until we have come to know this truth. For afterward it may be that the Lord will want us to have dealings with them, giving us a cross where we used to find pleasure.

Chapter 10

How it is not enough to be detached from what was mentioned if we are not detached from ourselves, and how both this virtue of detachment and humility go together.

ONCE WE HAVE DETACHED ourselves from the world and from relatives and have enclosed ourselves here under the conditions that were mentioned, it seems that we have done all there is to do and that we don't have to struggle with anything. Oh, my Sisters, do not feel secure or let yourselves go to sleep! By feeling secure you would resemble someone who very tranquilly lies down after having locked his doors for fear of thieves while allowing the thieves to remain inside the house. And you already know that there is no worse thief than we ourselves. For if you do not walk very carefully and if each Sister is not alert in going against her own will as though doing so were more important than all else, there are many things that will take away this holy freedom of spirit by which you can fly to your Maker without being held down by clay or leaden feet.

2. A great aid to going against your will is to bear in mind continually how all is vanity and how quickly everything comes to an end. This helps to remove our attachment to trivia and center it on what will never end. Even though this practice seems to be a weak means, it will strengthen the soul greatly, and the soul will be most careful in very little things. When we begin to become attached to something, we should strive to turn our thoughts from it and bring them back to God—and His Majesty helps. He has done us a great favor because in this house most of the work of detachment has been done—although this turning and being against ourselves is a difficult thing because we live very close together and love ourselves greatly.

3. Here true humility can enter the picture because this virtue and the virtue of detachment it seems to me always go together. They are two inseparable sisters. These are not the relatives I advise you to withdraw from; rather, you should em-

brace them and love them and never be seen without them. O sovereign virtues, rulers over all creation, emperors of the world, deliverers from all snares and entanglements laid by the devil, virtues so loved by our teacher Christ who never for a moment was seen without them! Whoever has them can easily go out and fight with all hell together and against the whole world and all its occasions of sin. Such a person has no fear of anyone, for his is the kingdom of heaven. He has no one to fear because he doesn't care if he loses everything, nor would he consider this a loss. The only thing he fears is displeasing his God, and he begs God to sustain him in these virtues lest they be lost through his own fault.

4. It is true that these virtues have the characteristic of so hiding themselves from the person who possesses them that he never sees them or manages to believe that he has them even though he is told he does. But he esteems them so highly that he always goes about striving to obtain them, and he gradually perfects them within himself. Yet, they are so manifest in the one who possesses them that without his desiring it, these virtues are at once recognized by others who deal with him.

But what foolishness that I should set about praising humility and mortification when they were so much praised by the King of Glory and so confirmed by His many trials. Now, my daughters, this is the work that must be done in order to escape from the land of Egypt, for in finding these virtues you will find the manna.[1] All things will taste good to you. However bad a thing may taste to those who are in the world, you will find it sweet.

5. Now, then, the first thing we must strive for is to rid ourselves of our love for our bodies, for some of us are by nature such lovers of comfort that there is no small amount of work in this area. And we are so fond of our health that it is amazing what a war our bodies cause, especially with nuns and even with those who are not. But some nuns it seems, including myself, didn't come to the monastery for any other reason than to strive not to die; each one strives for this as best she can. Here, truthfully, there is little opportunity to do this in deed, but I wouldn't want there to be even the desire. Be deter-

mined, Sisters, that you came to die for Christ, not to live comfortably for Christ. The devil suggests that you indulge yourselves so that you can keep the observance of the order; and a nun will so eagerly want to strive to care for and preserve her health for the sake of keeping the observance of the order that she dies without ever having kept this observance entirely for so much as a month, nor perhaps for even a day. Well, I don't know why we have come here!

6. Do not fear; very seldom will we lack discretion in this matter, for our confessors will at once be afraid that we may kill ourselves with penances. And the lack of such discretion is so abhorred by us that I wish we'd be so discreet in everything. I know that those who do the opposite will not care that I say this, nor do I care if they say I am judging from myself, for they would be saying the truth. I find for myself that the Lord wishes that we be sickly; at least in my case He granted me a great mercy in my being sick; for since I would have looked after my comfort anyway, He desired that there be a reason for my doing so.

Now it is amusing to see these persons and the torment they put themselves through. Sometimes they feel a desire to do penances without rhyme or reason, a desire that lasts a couple of days, so to speak; subsequently the devil makes them imagine that the penances did them harm. He makes them fear penance, and after some attempts they don't even dare carry out what the order commands.[2] We don't keep some of the very ordinary things of the rule, such as silence, which isn't going to do us any harm. Hardly does our head begin to ache than we stop going to choir, which won't kill us either. [We stay away one day because our head ached, another because it was just now aching, and three more so that it won't ache again.] And we seek to invent penances in our heads with the result that we can neither do the penances nor keep the observance. And at times the illness is slight, but we think we aren't obliged to do anything since we have done our duty by asking permission.

7. You will ask why the prioress gives it. If she knew what was going on inside us, perhaps she wouldn't give it. But since

you tell her about your need and there is no want of a doctor to side with you about the advisability of such permission, or a friend or relative to weep at your side, what can she do? She has a scruple that she might fail in charity. She would rather that you fail than that she herself fail. [And it doesn't seem to her right to judge badly of you. Oh, God help me, this complaining among nuns! May He forgive me, but I fear it has already become a custom. Once there was a nun who complained to me about a headache, and she complained a great deal about it. When it came time to examine her, the head didn't ache at all, but she felt an ache somewhere else.]

8. These are the things that can happen sometimes; that you might be on guard against them, I am putting them down here. For if the devil begins to frighten us about losing our health, we shall never do anything. May the Lord give us the light to be right about everything, amen.

Chapter 11

Continues to discuss mortification, and speaks about what must be acquired in sickness.

IT SEEMS TO ME AN IMPERFECTION, my Sisters, to be always complaining about light illnesses. If you can tolerate them, don't complain about them. When the sickness is serious, it does the complaining itself; this is different and the sickness is immediately obvious. Consider that you are few, and if one has this habit of complaining, it wears everyone out if you have love for one another and there is charity. If someone is truly sick, she should say so and take the necessary remedy. If you have lost self-love, you will feel any self-indulgence so keenly that there is no fear you will take anything without necessity or complain needlessly. If there is some need, it would be worse not to say anything than to seek your comfort without being sick, and it would be very wrong if the others did not feel compassion for you.

2. Moreover, where there's charity, and so few nuns, con-

cern about your getting well will surely never be lacking. But with regard to some of the weaknesses and little illnesses of women, forget about complaining of them, for sometimes the devil makes us imagine these pains. They are things that come and go. If you do not lose the habit of speaking and complaining about everything—unless you do so to God—you will never finish your lamenting. [I insist so much on this because I think it's very important and a reason why monasteries have mitigated their observance.] A fault this body has is that the more comfort we try to give it the more needs it discovers. It's amazing how much comfort it wants; and since in the case of health the need presents itself under the color of some good, however small it may be, the poor soul is deceived and doesn't grow.

3. Remember how many sick people there are who are poor and have no one to complain to; now it is nonsense to think one can be poor and live in comfort. Recall as well many women who are married. I know of some who are persons of high station and who have serious illnesses and heavy trials but for fear of annoying their husbands dare not complain. Well, sinner that I am! Indeed, we have not come here to receive more comfort than they! Oh, you who are free from the great trials of the world, learn how to suffer a little for love of God without having everyone know about it! If a woman in an unhappy marriage suffers much adversity without being able to receive comfort from anyone lest her husband know that she speaks and complains about it, shouldn't we suffer just between ourselves and God some of the illnesses He gives us because of our sins? And even more so because by our complaining the sickness is not alleviated.

4. In all this that I have said I am not dealing with serious illnesses, when there is great fever—although I beg for moderation and always patience—but of little ailments, that one can bear on one's feet. But what would happen if this that I'm writing were seen outside the house? What would all the nuns say about me? How willingly I would suffer their talk if someone were to make amends! For if there is but one nun like this, the situation can reach a point that for the most part no one is

believed no matter how serious her sickness may be. Let us remember our holy fathers of the past, those hermits whose lives we aim to imitate. What sufferings they endured! What solitude, cold, and hunger, and what sun and heat, without anyone to complain to but God! Do you think they were made of steel? Well, they were as delicate as we. And believe, daughters, that when we begin to conquer these wretched little bodies, we will not be so troubled by them. There will be enough Sisters to look after what is necessary; forget about yourselves except in what concerns a definite need. If we do not determine once and for all to swallow death and the lack of health, we will never do anything. Strive not to fear them; abandon yourselves totally to God, come what may. So what if we die? If our body has mocked us so often, shouldn't we mock it at least once?

5. And believe that this determination is more important than we can realize. For little by little as we grow accustomed to this attitude we shall, with the Lord's help, remain lords of our bodies. Now, then, conquering such an enemy is a very important means to enduring the battle of this life. May the Lord conquer him as He alone can. I truly believe that the benefits coming from this practice are not known except by one who already enjoys the victory. They are so great, from what I believe, that no one would feel he was undergoing trial if he could remain in this calm and dominion.

Chapter 12

How the true lover of God will have little regard for his own life and honor.

LET US GO ON to other things that are also quite important, although they may seem small. Everything seems to be a heavy burden, and rightly so, because it involves a war against ourselves. But once we begin to work, God does so much in the soul and grants it so many favors that all that one can do in this life seems little. And as nuns we do the most we can; that is, we give up our freedom for the love of God, placing it in the power of another, and undergo so many trials and fasts, so much silence, enclosure, and service in choir that however much we may want to please ourselves we can only seldom do so. And in many of the monasteries that I have seen, perhaps I am the only one who pleases herself. Why should we, then, delay in practicing interior mortification? For interior mortification makes everything else more meritorious and perfect, and afterward enables us to do the other things with greater ease and repose. This interior mortification is acquired, as I have said,[1] by proceeding gradually, not giving in to our own will and appetites, even in little things, until the body is completely surrendered to the spirit.

2. I repeat[2] that the whole matter, or a great part of it, lies in losing concern about ourselves and our own satisfaction. The least that any of us who has truly begun to serve the Lord can offer Him is our own life. Since we have given the Lord our will, what do we fear? It is clear that if someone is a true religious or a true person of prayer and aims to enjoy the delights of God, he must not turn his back upon the desire to die for God and suffer martyrdom. For don't you know yet, Sisters, that the life of a good religious who desires to be one of God's close friends is a long martyrdom? A long martyrdom because in comparison with the martyrdom of those who are quickly beheaded, it can be called long; but all life is short, and the life of some extremely short. And how do we know if ours won't be so short that at the very hour or moment we determine to serve God completely it will come to an end? This is possible. In sum, there is no reason to give importance to anything that will come to an end. And who will not work hard if he thinks that each hour is the last? Well, believe me, thinking this is the safest course.

3. So, let us try hard to go against our own will in everything. For if you are careful, as I said,[3] you will gradually, without knowing how, find yourselves at the summit. But how extremely rigorous, it seems, to say that we shouldn't please ourselves in anything when we do not also mention the pleasure and delight this going against our will carries in its wake and

what is gained by it even in this life. What security! Since all of you practice this denial here, the most is done; for you awaken and help one another. This is the practice in which each one should strive to be ahead of the others.

4. Take careful note of interior stirrings, especially if they have to do with privileges of rank. God, by His Passion, deliver us from dwelling on such words or thoughts as, "I have seniority," "I am older," "I have done more work," "the other is treated better than I." If such thoughts come they should be quickly cut off. If you dwell on them or begin to speak about them, the result is a pestilence from which great evils arise [in monasteries. Be careful, for I know a great deal about it!] If you should have a prioress who consents to this kind of thing, however small, believe that God has permitted, on account of your sins, that you have her as prioress so that you will begin to go astray; and pray hard that He will provide a remedy because you are in great danger.

5. Perhaps you will say: "Why should I give so much importance to this detachment and be so rigorous about it, for God gives consolations to those who are not so detached?" I believe He does do this, for in His infinite wisdom He sees that this is fitting so as to draw them to give up everything for Him. I do not call "giving up everything" entering religious life, for there can be impediments to entering religious life, and the perfect soul can be detached and humble anywhere; although this latter may involve greater trial, for being in a monastery is a big help. But believe me in one thing: if there is any vain esteem of honor or wealth (and this can be had inside monasteries as well as outside, although inside the occasions for it are more removed and the fault would be greater), you will never grow very much or come to enjoy the true fruit of prayer. And this is so even though you may have many years of experience in prayer—or, better, I should say reflection because perfect prayer in the end removes these bad habits.

6. Consider, Sisters, whether any of these things pertain to you; you are here for no other purpose. It will be due to your vain esteem of honor that you will not be honored. Moreover,

you will lose the benefit you could have otherwise gained; thus dishonor and loss will be joined together here.

Let each one consider how much humility she has, and she will see what progress has been made. It doesn't seem to me the devil will tempt the truly humble person about rank even with the first stirrings. Since he is so shrewd, he fears getting hurt. It is impossible for a person who is humble not to gain strength and progress in humility when the devil tempts him in this way. Clearly, a humble person will reflect on his life and consider how he has served the Lord in comparison with how the Lord ought to be served and the wonders the Lord performed in lowering Himself so as to give us an example of humility; and he will consider his sins and where he merited to be on account of them. The soul ends up with so much gain that the devil doesn't dare return another day lest he get his head crushed.

7. Take this advice from me and do not forget it; do not strive only in an interior way—for it would be a very great loss if we didn't derive some benefit from these acts of humility—but strive also in an exterior way that the Sisters draw some benefit from your temptation. If you wish to take revenge on the devil and free yourself more quickly from temptation, ask the prioress as soon as the temptation comes to give you orders to do some lowly task; or, if possible, do it on your own and go about studying how to double your willingness to do things that go contrary to your nature. The Lord will reveal these things to you, and in this way and as a result the temptation will last only a short while.[4] God deliver us from persons who are concerned about honor while trying to serve Him. Consider it an evil gain, and, as I said,[5] honor is itself lost by desiring it, especially in matters of rank. For there is no toxin in the world that kills perfection as do these things.

8. You will say that these are natural little things to which we need pay no attention. Don't fool yourselves, they increase like foam, and there is nothing so small in which there is so obvious a danger as this concern about honor and whether we have been offended. Do you know why—besides many other reasons? Perhaps this concern begins in someone as something small and amounting to hardly anything, and then the devil

stirs another to think it is something big, and this other will even think she is practicing charity by going and saying to the offended nun, "How do you put up with such an offense? God give you patience to offer it up; a saint wouldn't suffer more." The devil puts such malicious talk on the other Sister's tongue that though you barely overcome the offense, you are still tempted to vainglory, when in reality you did not suffer with the perfection with which you should have suffered.

9. And this nature of ours is so weak that merely by telling ourselves that the offense should not be tolerated, we think and believe that we have done something; how much more is this so when we see that others feel this way for us. As a result, the soul loses the occasions it had for meriting; it becomes weaker and opens the door for the devil to come again with something worse. And it could even happen, when you want to suffer the injury, that they will come to you and say: "Are you a beast or what? It's good for you to feel things." [Huh, and if one of them is a friend!] Oh, for love of God, my Sisters! May no one be moved by an indiscreet charity to show pity for another in something that touches upon these false injuries, for such pity is like that of Job's wife and friends.[6]

Chapter 13

Continues to discuss mortification and how one must flee from the world's maxims and rules about honor in order to arrive at true wisdom.

I HAVE OFTEN TOLD YOU, Sisters, and now I want to leave it in writing here so that you will not forget it, that in this house—and even in the case of any person seeking perfection—you should run a thousand miles from such expressions as: "I was right." "They had no reason for doing this to me." "The one who did this to me was wrong." God deliver us from this poor way of reasoning. Does it seem to have been right that our good Jesus suffered so many insults and was made to undergo so much injustice? I don't know why the nun who doesn't want to carry the cross, except the one that seems to her reasonable, is in the monastery. Let her return to the world, although even there they will not respect such reasonings. Could you by chance suffer as much as you deserve? What kind of reasoning is this? I certainly don't understand it.

2. Let us reason in such a way when some honor is paid to us, or when we are given some comfort or receive good treatment; for certainly it isn't right that we be so treated in this life. When wrongs are done—that's what they call them without there being any wrong done to us—I don't know what there is to talk about. Either we are brides of so great a King or we are not. If we are, what honorable woman is there who does not share in the dishonors done to her spouse even though she does not will them? In fact, both spouses share the honor and the dishonor. Now, then, to enjoy a part in His kingdom and want no part in His dishonors and trials is nonsense.

3. May God not allow us to refuse the latter; but the nun to whom it seems she is herself least of all should consider herself the most blessed of all. And she indeed is. If she bears dishonor as it must be borne, she will not be without honor either in this life or in the next. Believe me in this. But what nonsense I have spoken—that you believe me, when it has been said by true Wisdom, [who is Truth itself, and by the Queen of the angels.[1] Let us, at least, imitate His humility in some way. I say "in some way," for however much we might lower and humble ourselves, someone like myself does nothing; for because of her sins she has merited that the devils humiliate and despise her, even though she wouldn't like their doing so. For even if you may not have so many sins, seldom is there anyone who hasn't done something by which he has merited hell.]

Let us, my daughters, imitate in some way the great humility of the Blessed Virgin, whose habit we wear, for it is embarrassing to call ourselves her nuns. However much it seems to us that we humble ourselves, we fall far short of being the daughters of such a Mother and the brides of such a Spouse.

Thus, if you do not diligently put a stop to the things mentioned, what today seems to be nothing will tomorrow perhaps be a venial sin; and it is so dangerous that if you are careless about it you will suffer its ill effects, for it is something very bad for religious communities.

4. We who live in community should be very careful about it so as not to harm those who work to do good for us and give us good example. And if we could understand what great harm is done when a bad custom is begun, we would rather die than be the cause of it. For such a death would be a bodily one, but the loss of souls is a great loss, and it doesn't seem there is any end to the loss. Once some are dead, others follow after; and all, perhaps, are hurt more from a bad custom we have started than from many virtues. For the devil does not allow the bad custom to cease, but natural weakness causes the virtues to be lost.

5. Oh, what a great act of charity and what a great service to God a nun would perform if when she sees she cannot follow the customs of this house she would recognize the fact and leave! And she ought to do so if she doesn't want to go through a hell here on earth; and, please God, there won't be another in the next life,[2] for there are many reasons to fear such perdition, and perhaps neither she nor the others will understand this as I do.

6. Believe me in this matter; and if you don't, time will be my witness. For the style of life we aim to follow is not just that of nuns but of hermits, and thus you detach yourselves from every creature. I see the Lord gives this favor of detachment in a special way to the one He has chosen for this life. Even though the detachment may not be entirely perfect from the beginning, it is seen that she is advancing toward it by the great contentment and happiness she finds in not having to deal again with anything of the world and by how she relishes everything about the religious life.

I repeat that if she is inclined to the things of the world and not seen to be making progress that she should leave. If she still desires to be a nun, let her go to another monastery; and if she doesn't she will see what will happen to her. Don't let her complain about me, who started this way of life, for not having warned her.

7. This house is a heaven, if one can be had on this earth. Here we have a very happy life if one is pleased only with pleas-

ing God and pays no attention to her own satisfaction. If a nun desires something in addition to pleasing God, all will be lost because that something cannot be had. The discontented nun is like someone who feels great loathing for food; however good the food may be, it nauseates him, and the food that healthy people find great pleasure in eating is repugnant to such a person. This nun will be saved better elsewhere, and it may be that little by little she will reach the perfection that here she couldn't endure because she had to undertake it all at once. For although interiorly it takes time to become totally detached and mortified, exteriorly it must be done immediately. I fear that any nun who walks in such good company and sees that all the other nuns are detached but does not herself make progress in a year will not make more progress in many years, but less. I don't say that the detachment need be as complete as it is with the other nuns, but that you recognize that health is returning; for when the sickness is mortal, the fact becomes immediately obvious.

Chapter 14

The importance of not allowing anyone to make profession whose spirit goes contrary to the things mentioned.

I TRULY BELIEVE that the Lord highly favors the one who has real determination. Thus, the intention of the new member should be considered, lest she merely be looking for a secure future, as will be the case with many,[1] although the Lord can bring this intention to perfection if she has good intelligence; but if she doesn't, in no way should she be accepted, for neither will she understand why she is entering, nor afterward will she understand those who desire to lead her along the best spiritual path. For the most part those who have this fault always think they know more about what suits them than do those who are wiser. And the fault is an evil I consider incurable, for it would be a wonder if those having this fault ever gave up their malice. Where there are many nuns this fault could be tolerated, but where there are so few it shouldn't be allowed.

2. When a nun with good intelligence begins to grow attached to good, she takes hold of it with fortitude because she sees that doing so is most appropriate. And if her intelligence doesn't help her to attain a high degree of spirituality, it will be useful for giving good counsel and for many other services without being a bother to anyone. If this good intelligence is lacking, I don't know how she can be of any use to the community, and she could be the cause of much harm.

This lack of intelligence is not so quickly noticed. For many speak well but understand poorly; others speak little and without polish but they have the intelligence for a great deal of good. In fact, there is a holy simplicity that knows little about the affairs and style of the world but a lot about dealing with God. Hence much information is necessary before accepting new members and a long probation before admitting them to profession. Let the world understand once and for all that you have the freedom to dismiss the new members and that in a monastery where austerities are practiced, there are many occasions for doing so. And when decisions of this sort become the custom, no one will take the dismissal as an affront.

3. I say this because we are living in such miserable times and our nature is so weak that we don't want to offend relatives, and so it is not enough that we have a command from our forefathers to stop paying attention to what people nowadays take for honor. May it please God that we do not pay in the next life for the new members we admit in this life; there is never lacking a pretext for convincing ourselves that we can't do otherwise. [And in a matter so important no pretext is good, for when the bishop without attachment or passion looks after the good of the house, I don't think God will ever let him be mistaken. And I do believe that there will always be some mistake made if he is affected by such pity and foolish ideas about one's honor.]

4. And this is a matter that each one should consider, recommend to God, and encourage the prioress about, for it's something so important. Thus, I beg God to give you light. You are very fortunate that you do not receive dowries, for it can happen that in monasteries where they are accepted the nuns, so as to avoid giving back the money—which they no longer have—leave the thief in the house who steals the treasure from them; which is a great pity. In this matter you shouldn't take pity on anyone, for you would be doing harm to the person you are trying to help.

Chapter 15

The great good that lies in not excusing oneself even when blamed without fault.

[BUT WHAT DISORDER IN THE WAY I write! Really, it's as though the work were done by one who doesn't know what she's doing. The fault is yours, Sisters, because you are the ones who ordered me to write this. Read it as best you can, for I am writing it as best I can. And if you find that it is all wrong, burn it. Time is necessary to do the work well, and I have so little as you see, for eight days must have gone by in which I haven't written anything. So I forget what I have said and also what I was going to say. Now it is wrong for me to ask you to avoid doing what I have just finished doing, that is, making excuses. For I see that not making excuses for oneself is a habit characteristic of high perfection, and very meritorious; it gives great edification. And although I have often taught it to you, and by God's goodness you practice it, His Majesty has never given it to me.]

I am very embarrassed about what I am going to try to persuade you of, for I should have practiced at least something of what I am about to tell you concerning this virtue. The fact is, I confess, that I have made very little progress. It always seems to me there is some reason for my thinking it is greater virtue to make an excuse for myself. Since at times it is lawful to give an excuse and it would be wrong not to do so, I don't have the discretion or, to put it better, humility to do so when fitting. Indeed, it calls for great humility to be silent at seeing oneself condemned without fault. This is a wonderful way to imitate the Lord who took away all our faults. So, I ask you to take great care about this practice; it brings with it great benefits. I see no reason at all for us to try to excuse ourselves, unless, as I say, in some cases where not telling the truth would cause anger or scandal. When to excuse oneself will be recognized by those who have more discretion than I.

2. I believe it's very advantageous to get in the habit of practicing this virtue, or to strive to attain from the Lord the true humility that comes from it. The truly humble person must in fact desire to be held in little esteem, persecuted, and condemned without fault even in serious matters. If she desires to imitate the Lord, in what better way can she do so? For here there is no need of bodily strength or help from anyone but God.

3. I should like us, my Sisters, to strive very much for these great virtues; and let us do this penance, for you already know that I am rather strict when there is question of your doing too many penances. They can do harm to one's health if done without discretion. In this practice there is nothing to fear. However great the interior virtues may be, they do not take away the bodily strength necessary to keep the religious observance; on the contrary, they strengthen the soul. And from very little things, as I have said at other times,[1] one can gain the light so as to come out the victor in great things. [But how easily one writes of this and how poorly I practice it!] Indeed, in these great things I have not been able to test this myself, for I have never heard anything evil said of me that I didn't see that it fell short; for even though I had not failed in the things they accused me of, I have offended God in many other areas, and it seemed to me they were being quite kind by not mentioning these other offenses. I am always happier that they speak about what is not true of me than the truth.[2]

4. It is a great help to reflect upon the many things that are

gained through all the various ways and how—if we observe carefully—we are never, never blamed without there being faults on our part, for we always go about full of them since the just man falls seven times a day, and it would be a lie to say we have no sin.[3] Thus even though we are blamed for faults we haven't committed, we are never entirely without fault, as was the good Jesus.

5. O my Lord, when I think of the many ways You suffered and how You deserved none of these sufferings, I don't know what to say about myself, nor do I know where my common sense was when I didn't want to suffer, nor where I am when I excuse myself. You already know, my Good, that if I have some good it is a gift from no one else's hands but Yours. Now, Lord, what costs You more, to give much or little? If it is true that I have not merited this good, neither have I merited the favors You have granted me. Is it possible that I have wanted anyone to feel good about a thing as bad as I after so many evil things have been said about You who are the Good above all goods? Don't allow, don't allow, my God—nor would I ever want You to allow—that there be anything in Your servant that is displeasing in Your eyes. Observe, Lord, that mine are blind and satisfied with very little. Give me light and grant that I may truly desire to be abhorred by all since I have so often failed You who have loved me so faithfully.

6. What is this, my God? What do we expect to obtain from pleasing creatures? What does it matter if we are blamed a lot by all of them if in Your presence we are without fault? O my Sisters, we never completely understand this virtue; so, we are never completely perfect if we do not reflect and think a great deal upon what is and what is not. For when you have no other gain than the embarrassment of the person who after having blamed you sees that you are in fact without fault and yet allow yourself to be condemned, that gain is extremely great. At times something like this elevates a soul more than ten sermons. We must all try to be preachers through our deeds since the Apostle[4] and our incapacity prevent us from being preachers through our words.

7. However enclosed you are, never think that the good or

evil you do will remain a secret. And do you think, daughters, that when you do not excuse yourselves there will be lacking someone to defend you? Observe how the Lord answered for the Magdalene both in the house of the Pharisee and when her sister accused her.[5] He will not be as harsh with you as He was with Himself, for at the time that one of the thieves defended Him, He was on the cross.[6] So His Majesty will inspire someone to defend you; and when He doesn't, the defense won't be necessary. I have seen this, and it is true. But I wouldn't want you to be thinking about being defended, but that you rejoice in being blamed; and time will be the witness to the benefit you will see in your soul. For one begins to obtain freedom and doesn't care whether they say good or evil of him but rather thinks of what is said as though it were another's affair. The situation is like that in which we have two persons talking together but not to us; we then don't care about answering. So it is here; with the habit that has been acquired of not responding, it doesn't seem they are speaking to us.

This will seem impossible to those of us who are very sensitive and little mortified. In the beginning it is difficult; but I know that such freedom, self-denial, and detachment from ourselves can, with God's help, be attained.

Chapter 16

The difference that must lie between the perfection of the life of contemplatives and that of those who are simply content with the practice of mental prayer. How it is possible that God may at times raise a distracted soul to perfect contemplation and the reason for His doing so. This chapter and the following one are very noteworthy.[1]

[DON'T THINK THAT WHAT I HAVE SAID so far is all I have to say, for I am just setting up the game, as they say. You asked me to mention something about the foundation for prayer. Even though God did not lead me by means of this foundation, for I still don't have these virtues,[2] I know of no other. Now realize that anyone who doesn't know how to set up the pieces for a game of chess won't know how to play well. And if he doesn't know how to check his opponent's king, he won't know how to checkmate it either. Well, you will reprimand me because I am speaking about a game we do not have in this house, nor should we have it. Here you see the kind of Mother God has given you, that she even knows about this vanity; although they say that sometimes the game is permissible. And oh, how permissible this kind of game will be for us; and how quickly, if we play it often, will we checkmate this divine King, who will not be able to escape, nor will He want to.

2. The queen is the piece that can carry on the best battle in this game, and all the other pieces help. There's no queen like humility for making the King surrender. Humility drew the King from heaven to the womb of the Virgin, and with it, by one hair,[3] we will draw Him to our souls. And realize that the one who has more humility will be the one who possesses Him more; and the one who has less will possess Him less. For I cannot understand how there could be humility without love or love without humility; nor are these two virtues possible without detachment from all creatures.

3. You will ask me, daughters, why I am speaking to you about virtues when you have enough books to teach you about them, and you will say that you want to hear only about contemplation. I say that had you asked about meditation I could have spoken about it and counseled all to practice it even though they do not possess the virtues, for meditation is the basis for acquiring all the virtues, and to undertake it is a matter of life and death for all Christians. And no one, however lost he may be, should set it aside if God has awakened him to so great a good, as I have already written elsewhere[4] and as have many others who know what they are writing about; for I certainly don't know what I'm writing about—God knows.

4. But contemplation is something else, daughters. This is the mistake we all make, that if a person spends a little time each day thinking about his sins—for he is obliged to do that if

he is a Christian more than in name—they immediately say he is a very contemplative soul and they want him to possess at once virtues as great as those a very contemplative soul is obliged to have; and even the person himself wants this, but is mistaken. In the beginning he didn't know how to set up the game. He thought it was enough to know the pieces in order to checkmate the King. But that was impossible, for this King doesn't give Himself but to those who give themselves entirely to Him.]

5. Therefore, daughters, if you desire that I tell you about the way that leads to contemplation, you will have to bear with me if I enlarge a little on some other matters even though they may not seem to you so important; for in my opinion they are. And if you don't want to hear about them or put them into practice, stay with your mental prayer for your whole life, for I assure you and all persons who aim after true contemplation (though I could be mistaken since I am judging by myself for whom it took twenty years) that you will not thereby reach it.

6. I now want to explain—because some of you don't know—what mental prayer is, and please God we shall practice this as it ought to be practiced. But I fear that mental prayer also involves much labor if the virtues are not obtained—although it's not necessary that they be possessed in as high a degree as is required for contemplation. I say that the King of glory will not come to our soul—I mean to be united with it—if we do not make the effort to gain the great virtues. I want to explain this because if you should catch me saying something that isn't true you wouldn't believe anything, and you would be right if I did so knowingly; but God forbid! If I should say something that isn't true, it would be a matter of my not knowing more or not understanding. I want to say, then, that there are times when God will want to grant some great favor to persons who are in a bad state so as to draw them by this means out of the hands of the devil.[5]

7. O my Lord, how often do we make You fight the devil in arm to arm combat! Isn't it enough that You allowed him to take You in his arms when he carried You to the pinnacle of

the temple[6] so that You might teach us how to conquer him? But what would it be like, daughters, to see him, with his darknesses, next to the Sun. And what fear that unfortunate one must have borne without knowing why, for God didn't allow him to understand it.[7] Blessed be such compassion and mercy. What shame we Christians ought to have for making Him wrestle arm to arm, as I have said, with so foul a beast. It was truly necessary, Lord, that you have such strong arms. But how is it that they didn't weaken by the many torments You suffered on the cross? Oh, how everything that is suffered with love is healed again! And so I believe that had You survived, the very love You have for us would have healed Your wounds, for no other medicine was necessary. [It seems I am speaking nonsense, but I'm not; for divine love can do greater things than these. But to avoid seeming strange—which I really am—and so as not to give you bad example, I'll say no more.] O my God, grant that I might put medicine like this in everything that causes me pain and trial! How eagerly I would desire these if I could be sure that I'd be healed with so soothing a balm!

8. To return to what I was saying,[8] there are souls that God thinks He can win to Himself by these means. Since He sees they are completely lost, His Majesty desires that nothing be wanting on His part. And even though they are in a bad state and lacking in virtue, He gives them spiritual delight, consolation, and tenderness that begin to stir the desires. And He even places them in contemplation sometimes, though He does so rarely and it lasts only a short while. He does this, as I say, so as to try them to see if with that favor they will want to prepare themselves to enjoy Him often. But if they don't prepare themselves—pardon me; or better, may You pardon us, Lord, for it is a great evil when after You bring a soul like this to Yourself it approaches and becomes attached to some earthly thing.

9. For myself I hold that there are many to whom our Lord God gives this test, but few who prepare themselves for the enjoyment of the favor of contemplation. When the Lord grants it and we do not fail on our part, I hold as certain that He

never ceases to give until we reach a very high degree. When we do not give ourselves to His Majesty with the determination with which He gives Himself to us, He does a good deal by leaving us in mental prayer and visiting us from time to time like servants in His vineyard.[9] But these others are favored children. He would not want them to leave His side, nor does He leave them, for they no longer want to leave Him. He seats them at His table, He shares with them His food even to the point of taking a portion from His own mouth to give them.

10. Oh, blessed care, my daughters! Oh, blessed renunciation of things so small and so base that reaches so high a state. What would it matter, when you are in the arms of God, if the whole world blamed you! He has the power to free you from everything, for once He commanded that the world be made, it was made; His will is the deed. Now do not fear that He will allow others to speak against you except for the benefit of one who loves Him. His love for those who love Him is not so small. Well why, my Sisters, shouldn't we show our love for Him as much as we can? Behold it is a beautiful exchange to give our love for His. Consider that He can do all things, and we can't do anything here below but what He enables us to do. Well, what is this that we do for You, Lord, our Maker? It amounts to almost nothing, just a little determination. Well, if from that which is nothing His Majesty desires us to merit everything, let's not be foolish.

11. O Lord, how true that all harm comes to us from not keeping our eyes fixed on You; if we were to look at nothing else but the way, we would soon arrive. But we meet with a thousand falls and obstacles and lose the way because we don't keep our eyes—as I say—on the true way. It seems so new to us that you would think we had never walked on it. It's certainly something to excite pity, that which sometimes happens. [I say that it doesn't seem we are Christians or that we ever in our lives read the Passion. God help me, if I neglect a little rule concerning someone's honor! If anyone tells you not to worry about your honor, he at once seems to be unchristian. I laughed to myself—or rather was distressed—at what I sometimes saw in the world and even, because of my sins, in religious com-

munities.] For any slight loss in one's honor is not tolerated, nor does it seem that such a loss should be tolerated. They immediately say:"We're not saints."

12. God deliver us, Sisters, when we do something imperfect, from saying: "We're not angels, we're not saints." Consider that even though we're not, it is a great good to think that if we try we can become saints with God's help. And have no fear that He will fail if we don't fail. Since we have not come here for any other thing, let us put our hands to the task, as they say. May we presume to use everything we learn about greater service of the Lord in His favor. The presumption I would like to see present in this house, for it always makes humility grow, is to have a holy daring; for God helps the strong and He shows no partiality.[10]

13. I have digressed a good deal. I want to return to what I was saying,[11] that is, explaining the nature of mental prayer and of contemplation. It may seem impertinent for me to be doing that, but for you everything is acceptable. It may be that you will understand the matter better through my rough style than through other more elegant styles. May the Lord help me, amen.

Chapter 17

Not all souls are suited for contemplation, and some reach it late. The truly humble person must be content with the path along which God leads him.

IT SEEMS I AM ALREADY DEALING with prayer. But something still remains to be said that is very important because it pertains to humility and is necessary in this house[1] where the main occupation is prayer. And, as I have said,[2] it is only right that you should try to understand how to train yourselves a great deal in humility. In fact, this is an important aspect of prayer and indispensable for all persons who practice it. How could a truly humble person think he is as good as those who are contemplatives? Yes, it is true, God can make you a contemplative—through His goodness and mercy; but, in my opinion, one should always take the lowest place, for this is what the Lord told us to do[3] and taught us in deed. Prepare yourself so that God may lead you along this path if He so desires. When He doesn't, you can practice humility, which is to consider yourself lucky to serve the servants of the Lord and praise His Majesty because He brought you among them and drew you away from the devils in hell where you deserved to be a slave of these devils.

2. I don't say this without serious cause, because, as I have said,[4] it is important to understand that God doesn't lead all by one path, and perhaps the one who thinks she is walking along a very lowly path is in fact higher in the eyes of the Lord.

So, not because all in this house practice prayer must all be contemplatives; that's impossible. And it would be very distressing for the one who isn't a contemplative if she didn't understand the truth that to be a contemplative is a gift from God; and since being one isn't necessary for salvation, nor does God demand this, she shouldn't think anyone will demand it of her. So, you will not fail to be very perfect if you do what has been mentioned. Indeed, it could be that a Sister will gain much more merit because she must work harder and the Lord leads her as one who is strong, saving for her what she doesn't enjoy here below so as to give it to her all at once. Not for this reason should she grow fainthearted or give up prayer or what all the other Sisters are doing, for sometimes the Lord comes very late and pays just as well, and all at once, what He was giving to others in the course of many years.

3. I spent fourteen years never being able to practice meditation without reading. There will be many persons of this sort, and others who will be unable to meditate even with the reading but able only to pray vocally, and in this vocal prayer they will spend most of their time. There are minds so active they cannot dwell on one thing but are always restless, and to such an extreme that if they want to pause to think of God, a thousand absurdities, scruples, and doubts come to mind.

I know an elderly person who lives a good life, is penitential and an excellent servant of God, who has spent many hours for many years in vocal prayer, but in mental prayer she's helpless; the most she can do is go slowly in reciting the vocal prayers.[5] There are a number of other persons of this kind. If humility is present, I don't believe they will be any the worse off in the end but will be very much the equals of those who receive many delights; and in a way they will be more secure, for we do not know if the delights are from God or from the devil. Now if the delights are not from God, there is greater danger because the work of the devil here is to instigate pride. But if they are from God, there is nothing to fear; they bring with them humility, as I have written very much at length in another book.[6]

4. Those who do not receive these delights walk with humility, suspecting that this lack is their own fault, always concerned about making progress. They don't see anyone shed a tear without thinking that if they themselves don't shed any they are very far behind in the service of God. And perhaps they are much more advanced, for tears, even though they be good, are not all perfect. In humility, mortification, detachment, and the other virtues there is always greater security. There is nothing to fear; don't be afraid that you will fail to reach the perfection of those who are very contemplative.

5. St. Martha was a saint, even though they do not say she was contemplative. Well now, what more do you want than to be able to resemble this blessed woman who merited so often to have Christ our Lord in her home, give Him food, serve Him, and eat at table with Him [and even from His plate]?[7] If she had been enraptured like the Magdalene, there wouldn't have been anyone to give food to the divine Guest. Well, think of this congregation as the home of St. Martha and that there must be people for every task. And those who are led by the active life shouldn't complain about those who are very much absorbed in contemplation, for these active ones know that the Lord will defend the contemplatives, even though these latter are silent[8] since for the most part contemplation makes one forgetful of self and of all things.

6. Let them recall that it is necessary for someone to prepare His meal and let them consider themselves lucky to serve with

Martha. Let them consider how true humility consists very much in great readiness to be content with whatever the Lord may want to do with them and in always finding oneself unworthy to be called His servant. If contemplating, practicing mental and vocal prayer, taking care of the sick, helping with household chores, and working even at the lowliest tasks are all ways of serving the Guest who comes to be with us and eat and recreate, what difference does it make whether we serve in the one way or the other?

7. I don't say that we shouldn't try; on the contrary, we should try everything. What I am saying is that this is not a matter of your choosing but of the Lord's. If after many years He should give to each a certain task, it would be a nice kind of humility for you to want to choose for yourselves. Leave it up to the Lord of the house; He is wise, He is mighty, He understands what is suitable for you and what is suitable for Him as well. Be sure that if you do what lies in your power, preparing yourselves for contemplation with the perfection mentioned, and that if He doesn't give it to you (and I believe He will give it if detachment and humility are truly present), He will save this gift for you so as to grant it to you all at once in heaven. And, as I have said before,[9] He wants to lead you as though you were strong, giving you the cross here below, something that His Majesty always had. What better friendship than that He desire for you what He desired for Himself? And it could be that you would not have received so great an award in contemplation. The judgments are His, there's no reason for us to become involved in them. It is good that the choice is not up to us, for then—since contemplation seems a more restful path—we would all be great contemplatives.

O wonderful gain, not to want to gain from following our own judgment lest we suffer any loss! God, in fact, never permits any loss to come to a person truly mortified save for a greater gain.

Chapter 18

Continues on the same subject and tells how the trials of contemplatives are much greater than those of persons living an active life. This chapter is very consoling for these latter.

NOW, DAUGHTERS, I TELL THOSE OF YOU whom God does not lead by this path that from what I have seen and understood concerning the lives of those who do walk along it, contemplatives do not bear a lighter cross; and you would be surprised at the ways and modes in which God gives them crosses. I know both paths, and I know clearly that the trials God gives to contemplatives are intolerable. These trials are of such a kind that if He didn't give that food with its delights, these persons wouldn't be able to endure the trials. And it is clear that since God wants to lead those whom He greatly loves by the path of tribulation—and the more He loves them the greater the tribulation—there is no reason to think that He despises contemplatives, for with His own mouth He praises them and considers them His friends.[1]

2. Well, to think that He admits into His intimate friendship people who live in comfort and without trials is foolish. I am very certain that God gives contemplatives much greater trials. Thus, since He leads them along a rough and uneven path and at times they think they are lost and must return to begin again, His Majesty needs to give them sustenance, and not water but wine so that in their inebriation they will not understand what they are suffering and will be able to endure it. So, I see few true contemplatives who are not courageous and determined to suffer, for the first thing the Lord does, if they are weak, is to give them courage and make them unafraid of trials.

3. I believe that when those of the active life see the contemplative favored a little, they think there is nothing else to the contemplative's life than receiving favors. Well, I say that perhaps these active persons couldn't endure one day of the kind the contemplative endures. Thus, since the Lord knows

what each one is suited for, He gives to each person a proper task, one that He sees as appropriate for that person's soul, for the service of the Lord Himself and for the good of neighbor. And if you have done what you can to be prepared, do not fear that your effort will be lost. Keep in mind that I say we should all try to be contemplatives, since we are not here for any other reason. And we should try not for just a year, nor for only two, nor even for just ten; otherwise we leave the impression that we are giving up as cowards; and it is good for the Lord to know we are doing our best. We must be like soldiers who even though they may not have served a great deal must always be ready for any duty the captain commands them to undertake, since it is he who gives them their salary. And how much better the pay our King gives than the pay of earthly kings.[2]

4. Since the captain sees his soldiers present and eager to serve and has understood the capability of each one, he distributes the duties according to the strengths he sees. And if these soldiers were not present, he wouldn't give them anything, nor would he command them to serve.

So it is with us, Sisters; let us give ourselves to mental prayer. And let whoever cannot practice it turn to vocal prayer, reading, and colloquy with God, as I shall say afterward.[3] Do not abandon the hours of prayer we have in common;[4] you don't know when the Spouse[5] will call—let not what happened to the foolish virgins happen to you.[6] He may want to give more work, disguised in delight. If He doesn't, you should understand that this delight is not meant for you, that it is fitting for you to go without it. And here is where meriting through humility enters; one truly believes that he isn't even capable of doing the little he does.

5. You should be happy to serve in what they command you to do, as I have said.[7] And if this humility is true, blessed be such a servant in the active life, for she will not complain but of herself. [I would much rather be like her than like some contemplatives.] Let the others fight their own war, which is not small. Even though the standard-bearer doesn't fight in the battle, he doesn't for that reason fail to walk in great danger; and interiorly he must do more work than anyone. Since he

carries the flag, he cannot defend himself; and even though they cut him to pieces he must not let it out of his hands. So it is with contemplatives: they must keep the flag of humility raised and suffer all the blows they receive without returning any. Their duty is to suffer as Christ did, to hold high the cross, not to let it out of their hand whatever the dangers they see themselves in, nor let any weakness in suffering be seen in them; for this reason they are given so honorable an office. The contemplative must be careful about what he is doing, for if he lets go of the flag the battle will be lost. Thus, I believe that great harm is done to those who are not so advanced when they see that the deeds of those they consider to be captains already and friends of God are not in conformity with this office.

6. The other soldiers advance as best they can, and sometimes they retreat from where they see greater danger; and no one notices this, nor do these soldiers lose honor. As for the former ones, the eyes of all are upon them; they cannot stir. So their office is a good one, and the king does a great honor and favor to the one he gives it to, but the obligation in accepting it is not a small one.

So, Sisters, we don't know what we are asking for. Let us leave it to the Lord. [For He knows us better than we do ourselves. And true humility is content with what is received.] There are some persons who demand favors from God as though these were due them in justice. That's a nice kind of humility! Thus, He who knows all very seldom grants such persons favors, and rightly so. He sees clearly that they are not ready to drink from the chalice.[8]

7. What each of you will understand, daughters, if you are advanced, will be that you are the most wretched of all. And this understanding will be manifested in deeds done for your own spiritual growth and for the good of others, and not in having more delights and raptures in prayer, or visions, or favors of this kind that the Lord grants; for we shall have to wait for the next world to see the value of such experiences. This understanding is like current coin, like unfailing revenue, like having a perpetual annuity and not a sum that's paid only once; for these other experiences come and go. This attitude

includes the great virtues of humility and mortification, careful obedience by not in any way going against what the superior commands, for you truly know that God, in whose place the superior stands, commands it.

It is into this obedience that you must put the most effort; and, in my opinion, where there is no obedience there are no nuns. I am not saying anything about this virtue because I am speaking with nuns and, I think, good ones—at least they desire to be good. In a matter of such wisdom and importance, no more than a word so that it won't be forgotten.

8. I say that I don't know why a nun under obedience by vow is in the monastery if she doesn't make every effort to practice this obedience with greater perfection. At least I can assure her that as long as she fails in obedience she will never attain to being a contemplative, nor will she even be a good active Sister; and I hold this as very, very certain. Even though a person may not have this obligation of the vow, if he desires or aims after contemplation, it is necessary for him in order to proceed correctly to give up his will, with complete determination, to a confessor, who must be the kind [that will understand him.] Since this practice is something already well known—for there is more progress made in this way in one year than without it in many—and it is not necessary for you, there's no need to talk of it.

9. I conclude by saying that these are the virtues I desire you to have, my daughters, the ones you must strive for and about which you should have holy envy. As for those other devotions, there's no need to be sorry about not having them; having them is an uncertain matter. It could be that in other persons they may be from God, whereas in your case His Majesty may permit them to be an illusion of the devil and that you be deceived by him, as were other persons [for in women this is something dangerous]. Why desire to serve the Lord in a doubtful way when you have so much that is safe? Who places you in these dangers?

10. I have enlarged so much on this subject because I know it is important; for this nature of ours is weak, and His Majesty will strengthen anyone to whom He wishes to give contempla-

tion. I have paused to give these counsels to those to whom He doesn't give contemplation. By practicing them, the contemplatives, also, may humble themselves. [If, daughters, you say that you don't need them, perhaps someone else will come along who will be pleased to have them.]

May the Lord, because of who He is, give us light to follow His will in everything, and there will be nothing to fear.

Chapter 19

Begins to discuss prayer. Speaks to souls unable to reason with the intellect.

SO MANY DAYS HAVE GONE BY since I wrote the above, days in which I haven't had time to return to it, that if I don't reread it I won't know what I was saying. So as not to take up time, I'll have to let this work turn out in whatever way it does, without any order. There are so many good books written by able persons for those who have methodical minds and for souls that are experienced and can concentrate within themselves that it would be a mistake if you paid attention to what I say about prayer. As I say, there are books in which the mysteries of the Lord's life and Passion are divided according to the days of the week, and there are meditations about judgement, hell, our nothingness, and the many things we owe God together with excellent doctrine and method concerning the beginning and end of prayer.[1] There is nothing for me to say to anyone who can form the habit of following this method of prayer, or who has already formed it, for by means of so good a path the Lord will draw him to the haven of light. And through such a good beginning the end will be reached. All who are able to walk along this path will have rest and security, for when the intellect is bound one proceeds peacefully.

But what I would like to speak about and offer a remedy for, if the Lord should will that I succeed—and if I don't, at least you will understand that there are many souls who undergo this trial, and those of you who suffer it will not grow weary—is the following.

2. There are some souls and minds so scattered they are like wild horses no one can stop. Now they're running here, now there, always restless. [And if the rider is skillful, there is not always a danger—just sometimes. But even though his life is in no danger, he is not free from some dishonor in mounting the wild horse; and there is always some hardship.] This restlessness is either caused by the soul's nature or permitted by God. I pity these souls greatly, for they seem to be like very thirsty persons who see water in the distance, but when they want to go there, they meet someone who prevents their passing from the beginning through the middle to the end. It happens that after they have conquered the first enemy through their labor—and through a great deal of labor—they let themselves be conquered by the second; they would rather die of thirst than drink water so costly. Their efforts cease, their courage fails. And when some have the courage to conquer the second class of enemy as well, their strength gives way when they meet the third, and perhaps they were no more than two steps from the fount of living water, of which the Savior said to the Samaritan woman, "whoever drinks of it will never thirst."[2] How right and true, as words coming from the mouth of Truth Itself, that such a person will not thirst for anything in this life—although thirst for the things of the next life increases much more than can ever be imagined through natural thirst! How thirsty one becomes for this thirst! The soul understands the great value of this thirst, and even though the thirst is a most painful, wearying one, it brings with it the very satisfaction by which it is assuaged, in such a way that it is a thirst unquenchable except in earthly things. Indeed, this thirst slakes in such a way that when God satisfies the thirst, the greatest favor He can grant the soul is to leave in it this same need—and a greater one—to drink the water again.

3. Water has three properties that I now recall as applicable to our subject, for it must have many more. The first is that it refreshes; for, no matter how much heat we may experience, as soon as we approach the water the heat goes away. If there is a

great fire, it is extinguished by water—unless the fire burns from pitch; then it is enkindled more. Oh, God help me, what marvels there are in this greater enkindling of the fire by water when the fire is strong, powerful, and not subject to the elements. For this water doesn't impede the fire, though it is fire's contrary, but rather makes the fire increase! It would be a great help here to be able to speak with someone who knows philosophy, for in knowing the properties of things he would be able to explain to me what I enjoy thinking about but don't know how to speak of or even perhaps understand.

4. Those of you, Sisters, who drink this water and you others, once the Lord brings you to drink, will enjoy it and understand how the true love of God—if it is strong, completely free of earthly things, and if it flies above them—is lord of all the elements and of the world. And since water flows from the earth, don't fear that it will extinguish this fire of the love of God; such a thing does not lie within its power. Even though the two are contraries, this fire is absolute lord; it isn't subject to water. Hence do not be surprised, Sisters, about the many things I have written in this book so that you might obtain this liberty. Isn't it wonderful that a poor nun of St. Joseph's can attain dominion over all the earth and the elements? No wonder the saints, with the help of God, were able to do with the elements whatever they wanted. Fire and water obeyed St. Martin; even the birds and the fish, St. Francis; and so it was with many other saints. There was clear evidence that they had dominion over all worldly things because they labored to take little account of them and were truly subject with all their strength to the Lord of the world. So, as I say, the water that rises from the earth has no power over the love of God; the flames of this love are very high, and the source of it is not found in anything so lowly.

There are other little fires of love of God that any event will extinguish. But extinguish this fire? No, not at all! Even though a whole sea of temptations comes, the fire will not be put out and thereby made to lose control over these temptations.[3] [For with the help of God and doing what lies in their power, men can almost seek this love by right. Do you think that because the Psalmist says that all things are subject to man and put under his feet that it is so with all men? Not at all! On the contrary, I see many of them subject to and trampled upon by things. In fact, I knew a gentleman who was killed in a quarrel over a few dimes. What a miserable price he was subject to. There are many things you will see every day from which you will know that I am speaking the truth. If the psalmist couldn't lie—for what he says is from the Holy Spirit—it seems to me that the saying, "they will rule over all earthly things," pertains to the perfect. It could be that I don't understand and am foolish, but I have read this.[4]]

5. Well, if it is water that rains from heaven, so much less will it extinguish this fire; the two are not contraries but from the same land. Have no fear that the one element will do harm to the other; rather, they help each other produce their effect. For the water of true tears, those that flow in true prayer, readily given by the King of heaven, helps the fire burn more and last longer; and the fire helps the water bring refreshment. Oh, God help me, what a beautiful and marvelous thing, that fire makes one feel cooler! Yes, and it even freezes all worldly attachments when it is joined to the living water from heaven. Heaven is the source of the tears that were mentioned, for they are given and not acquired through our own efforts. Therefore, this living water will certainly not let the heat from worldly things detain the soul—unless to allow the soul to communicate this fire to others. For by its nature this fire is not content with little; it would burn up the whole world if it could.

6. Another property of water is that it cleans dirty things. What would the world be like if there were no water for washing? Do you know how clean this water is, this heavenly water, this clear water, when it isn't cloudy, when it isn't muddy, but falls from heaven? Once this water has been drunk, I am certain that it leaves the soul bright and cleansed of all faults. Since this divine union is something very supernatural, it is not a matter of our own choosing. As I have written,[5] God doesn't permit a soul to drink this water unless to cleanse it and leave it clean and free from all the mud and misery in which,

through its own faults, it was stuck. Other delights that come through the medium of the intellect, however much they may accomplish, come from water running on the ground; they do not come from drinking at the fount. There is never a lack of muddy things to detain one on this path, and the water is not so pure and clean. Living water is not what I call this prayer in which, as I say, there is reasoning with the intellect; I mean from the way I understand things. For something from the road that we don't want will stick to our soul and be helped to cling there by our body and natural lowliness, however much we may want to avoid this.

7. Let me explain myself further: suppose that in order to despise the world we are thinking about its nature and how all things come to an end. Almost without our realizing it we find ourselves thinking about the things we like in the world; and in desiring to flee them, we are at least hindered a little by thinking about how they were and how they will be and what we will do; in order to think of what we must do to free ourselves, we place ourselves in danger again. Not that this reasoning must be abandoned, but one must be fearful; it's necessary to proceed with care.

By means of this living water the Lord Himself takes up these cares, for He doesn't want to entrust them to us.[6] He so esteems our soul that He doesn't allow it to be occupied with things that can harm it during the time He wishes to favor it. Rather, He immediately places it near Himself and shows it in an instant more truths, and gives it clearer understanding of what everything is, than we could have here below in many years. For our eyes don't see clearly; the dust blinds us as we walk. By this living water the Lord brings us to the end of the journey without our understanding how.

8. The other property of water is that it satisfies to the full and takes away thirst. To me it seems that thirst signifies the desire for something of which we are in great want, so that if the thing is completely lacking its absence will kill us. How strange that if water is lacking, this lack kills us; and if there is too much, we die, as is seen through the many who drown. O my Lord, and who will find himself so immersed in this living

water that he will die! But, is this possible? Yes, because the love of God and desire for Him can increase so much that the natural subject is unable to endure it, and so there have been persons who have died from love. I know of one who would have died if God hadn't succored her immediately with such an abundance of this living water, for she was almost carried out of herself with raptures.[7] I say that she was almost carried out of herself because in this water the soul finds rest. It seems that while she is drowning from not being able to endure the world, she is revived in God; and His Majesty enables her to enjoy what in herself she couldn't without dying.

9. It should be understood here that since there can be nothing imperfect in our supreme Good, everything He gives is for our good; and however great the abundance of this water He gives, there cannot be too much in anything of His. If He gives a great deal, He gives the soul, as I said,[8] the capacity to drink much; like a glassmaker who makes the vessel a size he sees is necessary in order to hold what he intends to pour into it.

In desiring this water there is always some fault, since the desire comes from ourselves; if some good comes, it comes from the Lord who helps. But we are so indiscreet that since the pain is sweet and delightful, we never think we can have enough of this pain. We eat without measure, we foster this desire as much as we can, and so sometimes it kills. How fortunate such a death! But perhaps by continuing to live we can help others die of desire for this death. And I believe the devil causes this desire for death, for he understands the harm that can be done by such a person while alive; and so at this stage he tempts one to perform indiscreet penances so that one's health will be lost, which would be no small gain for the devil.

10. I say that anyone who reaches the experience of this thirst that is so impelling should be very careful because I believe he will have this temptation. And although he may not die of thirst, his health will be lost and he will give exterior manifestations of this thirst, even though he may not want to; these manifestations should be avoided at all costs. Sometimes our diligence is of little avail, for we will be unable to hide everything we would like to hide. But when these impulses that

so greatly increase this desire to die come, we should be careful not to add to the desire, but gently cut the thread with another consideration. For our nature at times can be as much at work as the love; there are persons who will vehemently desire anything, even if it is bad. I don't believe these persons will be very mortified, for mortification helps in everything. It seems foolish to cut short something so good; but it isn't. For I do not say that the desire is taken away, but that it is cut short, and perhaps by another desire as meritorious as the former.

11. I wish to say something in order to explain myself better: a great desire is given to see oneself with God and to be loosed from this prison, like the desire St. Paul had.[9] Pain for a reason like this must in itself be very delightful; no small amount of mortification is needed to break it off, and one will be unable to do so completely. Sometimes the pain is seen to afflict so much that it almost takes away one's reason. Not long ago I saw a person of an impetuous nature who, even though she was experienced in going against her will—I think she had already lost it, as was seen in other things—was deranged for a while by the great pain and the effort that was made to conceal this pain. I hold that in so extreme a case, even though the experience may come from the Spirit of God, the humble thing is to be fearful, for we shouldn't think we have so much charity that it will put us in such straits.

12. If a person is able—for perhaps he will not always be able—I say that I wouldn't consider it wrong if he were to remove the desire by the thought that if he lives he will serve God more and enlighten some soul that would have been lost, and that by serving more he will merit the capacity to enjoy God more. And let him fear the little that he has served. These consoling thoughts are good for so great a work. His affliction will be mitigated, and he will gain very much. For in order to serve the Lord Himself, one should desire to suffer here below and live with the Lord's affliction. It's as when one has a great trial or a heavy sorrow; you comfort him by telling him to be patient and leave it in the hands of God and that the Lord's will is being done by it, for in every event the best we can do is leave ourselves in the hands of God.

13. It would be possible for the devil in some way to foster such a great desire. The account is given, I believe in Cassian, of a hermit who lived a most austere life. The devil made him think that by throwing himself into a well he would see God more quickly.[10] I truly believe that this hermit could not have served with humility or goodness; for the Lord is faithful, and His Majesty would not consent that one be blinded in a matter so obvious. But clearly, if the desire were from God, it wouldn't cause any harm: such a desire bears light, discretion, and measure. But this adversary and enemy of ours tries to cause harm wherever he can; and since he doesn't go about carelessly, neither should we. This is an important point for many reasons. Thus the time of prayer should be shortened, however delightful the prayer may be, when it is seen that the bodily energies are failing or that the head might suffer harm. Discretion is very necessary in all.

14. Why do you think, daughters, that I have tried to explain the goal and show you the reward before the battle, by telling you about the good that comes from drinking of this heavenly fount, of this living water? So that you will not be dismayed by the trial and contradiction there is along the way, and advance with courage and not grow weary. For, as I have said,[11] it can happen that after having arrived you will have nothing left to do but stoop and drink from the fount; and yet you will abandon everything and lose this good, thinking that you have not the strength to reach it and that you are not meant for it.

15. Behold, the Lord invites all. Since He is truth itself, there is no reason to doubt. If this invitation were not a general one, the Lord wouldn't have called us all, and even if He called all, He wouldn't have promised, "I will give you to drink."[12] He could have said, "Come all of you, for in the end you won't lose anything, and to those whom I choose I will give to drink." But since He spoke without this condition to all, I hold as certain that all those who do not falter on the way will drink this living water. May the Lord, because of who He is, give us the grace to seek this living water as it should be sought, for He promises it.

Chapter 20

How in different ways consolation is never lacking on the path of prayer. Counsels the Sisters to let their conversations deal always with prayer.

IT SEEMS I CONTRADICTED in the previous chapter what I had said before. When I was consoling those who were not contemplatives,[1] I said that the Lord had different paths by which to go to Him just as there are many dwelling places.[2] So I repeat it now. Since His Majesty has understood our weakness, He has provided after the manner of who He is. But He did not say: "some come by this path, and others by another." Rather, His mercy was so great He excluded no one from striving to come to this fount of life to drink. May He be blessed forever! And how rightly might He have excluded me!

2. Now, since He didn't stop me when I started to walk along this path, nor order me to be thrown into the abyss, surely He excludes no one; rather, He calls us publicly, crying aloud.[3] But since He is so good, He does not force us; on the contrary, in many ways He gives drink to those who wish to follow Him so that no one will go without consolation or die of thirst. Rivers stream from this overflowing fount, some large, others small; and sometimes little pools for children—for that is enough for them, and moreover it would frighten them to see a lot of water. These children are the ones who are at the beginning. So, Sisters, do not fear that you will die of thirst on this road. Never is the lack of consoling water such that it cannot be endured. Since this is so, take my advice and do not stop on the road but, like the strong, fight even to death in the search, for you are not here for any other reason than to fight. You must always proceed with this determination to die rather than fail to reach the end of the journey. If even though you so proceed, the Lord should lead you in such a way that you are left with some thirst in this life, in the life that lasts forever He will give you to drink in great plenty and you will have no fear of being without water. May it please the Lord that we ourselves do not fail, amen.

3. Now, that you might so walk along this path of prayer that you do not go astray at the beginning, let us deal a little with how this journey must begin; for the beginning is the more important part—indeed it is the most important part for everything. I don't say that if a person doesn't have the determination of which I shall speak here, he should stop trying; for the Lord will continue perfecting him. And if that person should do no more than take one step, the step will contain in itself so much power that he will not have to fear losing it, nor will he fail to be very well paid.

This situation can be compared to that of a person who uses beads to count indulgenced prayers. If he uses them once, he gains the indulgences; if he uses them more often, he gains more; but if he never uses them, keeping them rather in a chest, it would be better for him not to have them. So it is here: even though afterward a person may not continue on the same road, the little progress he may have made on it will have provided him with light so that he may walk well on other paths; and the greater the progress, the more light. In sum, even if later he gives up, he may be certain that it will not have done him any harm to have begun; for good never produces evil.

Thus, daughters, in reference to all the persons who speak with you, if they are disposed and there is some friendship, try to remove any fear they may have of beginning to use so great a good. And for the love of God I beg you that your conversation always be directed toward bringing some good to the one with whom you are speaking, for your prayer must be for the benefit of souls. And since the good of souls is what you must always beg the Lord for, it would seem wrong, Sisters, if you did not strive for this in every way.

4. If you want to be a good relative, this desire to be of benefit to the relative is where true friendship lies; if you want to be a good friend, know that you cannot be one save by this path. Let truth dwell in your hearts, as it should through meditation, and you will see clearly the kind of love we are obliged to have for our neighbor.

There's no longer time, Sisters, for children's games, for

these worldly friendships, even though they may be good, seem to be nothing else. Unless there is a very good reason and it is for the benefit of that soul, don't let your conversation be of the sort in which you ask, "Do you like me?" or "Don't you like me?" It can happen that in order that your relative or brother or a similar person listen to a truth you want to point out and admit it you will have to dispose him by means of these words and demonstrations of love that are always pleasing to sensuality. It will happen that a good word, as these are called, will do more and dispose one more than will many about God so that afterward these latter may be accepted. And thus if you use them knowingly for the benefit of others, I do not forbid them. But if they are not used for this reason, they will be of no avail and may do harm without your realizing it. Others already know that you are religious and that your business is prayer. Don't think to yourself that you don't want them to consider you good, for what they see in you is to the benefit or harm of all. And it is a serious wrong for those who have so great an obligation to speak of God, as do nuns, to think that it is good for them to hide their feelings about God; although they may be allowed to do this sometimes for a greater good. God is your business and language. Whoever wants to speak to you must learn this language; and if he doesn't, be on your guard that you don't learn his; it will be a hell.

5. If they should think you're unsophisticated, what does it matter? If they take you for hypocrites, it matters even less. You will gain in that no one will want to see you except the one who understands this language. There wouldn't be much reason for anyone who doesn't know Arabic to enjoy speaking a great deal with one who knows only that language. And so, neither will they make you weary or do you harm, for to begin to speak a new language would cause no small amount of harm, and all your time would be spent in learning it. And you cannot know as I do, for I have experience of it, the great evil this new language is for the soul; in order to know the one, the other is forgotten. The new language involves a constant disturbance from which you ought to flee at all costs, for what is very suited to this path that we are beginning to discuss is peace and tranquillity of soul.

6. If those who speak with you wish to learn your language, though it is not your business to teach anyone, you can tell about the riches that are gained in learning it since telling of this is beneficial to the other, and when he learns about the great gain that is to be had, he may go and seek out a master who will teach him. It would be no small favor from the Lord if you were to succeed in awakening some soul to this good.

But how many things come to mind in beginning to discuss this path, even to the mind of one who has walked it as poorly as I. [Would that I had many hands with which to write so that while putting down some of these things I wouldn't forget the others.] May the Lord be pleased, Sisters, that I know how to speak of it better than I have practiced it, amen.

Chapter 21

Tells how important it is to begin the practice of prayer with great determination and not pay any attention to obstacles set up by the devil.

DO NOT BE FRIGHTENED, daughters, by the many things you need to consider in order to begin this divine journey which is the royal road to heaven. A great treasure is gained by traveling this road; no wonder we have to pay what seems to us a high price. The time will come when you will understand how trifling everything is next to so precious a reward.

2. Now returning to those who want to journey on this road[1] and continue until they reach the end, which is to drink from this water of life,[2] I say that how they are to begin is very important—in fact, all important.[3] They must have a great and very resolute determination to persevere until reaching the end, come what may, happen what may, whatever work is involved, whatever criticism arises, whether they arrive or whether they die on the road, or even if they don't have courage for the trials that are met, or if the whole world col-

lapses. You will hear some persons frequently making objections: "there are dangers"; "so-and-so went astray by such means"; "this other one was deceived"; "another who prayed a great deal fell away"; "it's harmful to virtue"; "it's not for women, for they will be susceptible to illusions"; "it's better they stick to their sewing"; "they don't need these delicacies"; "the Our Father and the Hail Mary are sufficient."

3. This last statement, Sisters, I agree with. And indeed they are sufficient! It is always good to base your prayer on prayers coming from the mouth of the Lord. In this matter those who warn us are right, for if our nature were not so weak and our devotion so lukewarm there wouldn't be any need to compose other prayers, nor would there be need for other books. As I say,[4] I am speaking to souls that cannot recollect their minds in the thought of other mysteries because they think some kind of skill is needed, and there are some minds so ingenious that they're never satisfied with any of their thoughts. So it seems to me now that I should proceed by setting down some points here about the beginning, the means, and the end of prayer. I shall not take time to dwell on more sublime things. No one will be able to take from you these books (the Our Father and the Hail Mary), and if you are eager to learn you won't need anything else provided you are humble.[5] I have always been fond of the words of the Gospels [that have come from that most sacred mouth in the way they were said] and found more recollection in them than in very cleverly written books. I especially had no desire to read these books if the author was not well approved. If, then, I draw near to this Master of wisdom, He will perhaps teach me some worthwhile thoughts that will please you.

I don't say that I'm going to write a commentary on these divine prayers,[6] for I wouldn't dare. Many commentaries have been written; and even if they hadn't been, it would be absurd for me to write one. But I will mention some thoughts on the words of the Our Father. For sometimes, with regard to many books, it seems we lose devotion in the very exercise in which it is so important for us to have devotion. Clearly, when a master teaches something he gets to love his disciple and is pleased if that which he teaches satisfies his pupil, and he helps him a great deal to learn the material. The heavenly Master will do the same with us.

5. Hence, don't pay any attention to the fears they raise or to the picture of the dangers they paint for you. Wouldn't it be nice if while desiring to procure a great treasure I should want to walk without danger along a path where there are so many robbers. It would be a pleasant world if they would let you get the treasure in peace. But for a penny's worth of self-interest they will go many nights without sleep and disturb you in body and soul. For when you are about to gain the treasure – or steal it, since the Lord says that the violent take it away[7] – by a royal road and by a safe road, the road chosen by our King and all His elect and saints, they will tell you that there are so many dangers and so many things to fear. How many more dangers are there for those who think they obtain this good without following a road?

6. Oh, my daughters! There are incomparably more dangers for such persons, but people don't know about them until they bump blindly into the true danger when there is no one to give them a hand; and they lose the water entirely without drinking either little or much – neither from a small pool nor from a stream.

So you see, how will one journey without a drop of this water on a road where there are so many struggles? It is clear that when it is needed most they will not have it and will die of thirst. Because whether we like it or not, my daughters, we must all journey toward this fount, even though in different ways. Well, believe me; and don't let anyone deceive you by showing you a road other than that of prayer.

7. I am not speaking now about whether the prayer should be mental or vocal for everyone. In your case, I say that you need both. Such is the duty of religious. Should anyone tell you that prayer is dangerous, consider him the real danger and run from him. Don't forget this counsel, for perhaps you will need it. There will be danger in not having humility and the other virtues. But that the way of prayer be a way of danger – God

would never will that. It seems the devil has invented these fears, and so he has been skillful, apparently, in making some who have practiced prayer fall away.

8. And see how blind the world is, for they fail to consider the many thousands who have fallen into heresies and great evils because they didn't practice prayer but engaged in distractions. And if in order to carry on his work better the devil has caused, among this multitude of persons, some of those who practiced prayer to fall, he has caused as much fear in others about virtuous things. Those who take this reasoning as a refuge in order to free themselves should be on their guard, for they are running away from good in order to free themselves from evil. Never have I seen such a wicked contrivance; it really seems to come from the devil. O my Lord, defend Yourself! See how they understand Your words in reverse. Don't permit such weaknesses in Your servants. [Hold fast, daughters, for they cannot take from you the Our Father and the Hail Mary.][8]

9. There's one great blessing: you will always find some who will help you, because this is a characteristic of the real servant of God to whom His Majesty has given light concerning the true way; in the midst of these fears the desire not to give up increases within him. He understands clearly where the devil is going to strike, flees from him and crushes his head. The devil feels more regret over this than he does satisfaction over the many pleasures that others give him. In a time of disturbance, of discord caused by the devil—for it seems all are following him half blind because they do so under the guise of zeal—God will raise up someone to open the eyes of these half-blind people and tell them that the devil has placed a cloud in front of them to prevent their seeing the way. Oh, the greatness of God, for sometimes one or two men alone can do more when they speak the truth than many together! Little by little, souls discover again the way; God gives them courage. If they are told there is danger in prayer, one of these servants of God will strive, if not in words then in deeds, to make known how good prayer is. If they are told that frequent Communion is not good, he will receive more frequently. Thus, since there are

one or two who fearlessly do what is best, the Lord at once begins to win back gradually the ground that was lost.

10. Therefore, Sisters, give up these fears; never pay attention in like matters to the opinion of the crowd. Behold, these are not the times to believe everyone; believe only those who you see are walking in conformity with Christ's life. Try to preserve a pure conscience, humility, and contempt for all worldly things; believe firmly what Holy Mother Church holds, and you can be sure you will be walking along a good path.

Leave aside, as I said,[9] your fears where there is no reason for fear. If someone should raise these fears to you, humbly explain the path to him. Tell him you have a rule that commands you to pray unceasingly—for that's what it commands us[10]—and that you have to keep it. If they tell you that the prayer should be vocal, ask, for the sake of more precision, if in vocal prayer the mind and heart must be attentive to what you say. If they answer "yes"—for they cannot answer otherwise—you will see how they admit that you are forced to practice mental prayer and even experience contemplation if God should give it to you by such a means.

Chapter 22

Explains what mental prayer is.

REALIZE, DAUGHTERS, that the nature of mental prayer isn't determined by whether or not the mouth is closed. If while speaking I thoroughly understand and know that I am speaking with God and I have greater awareness of this than I do of the words I'm saying, mental and vocal prayer are joined. If, however, others tell you that you are speaking with God while you are reciting the Our Father and at the same time in fact thinking of the world, then I have nothing to say. But if you are to be speaking, as is right, with so great a Lord, it is good that you consider whom you are speaking with as well as who you are, at least if you want to be polite. How can you call the king "your highness" or know the ceremonies to be observed in addressing a highest ranking nobleman if you do not clearly understand what his position is and what yours is? For it is in conformity with these facts that you must show respect, and in conformity with custom—because you also need to know even the customs. If you don't know them, you will be sent away as a simpleton and will fail to negotiate anything. [And what's more, if you don't know these things well, you will need to find out and even rehearse what you must say. Once it happened to me[1] that, not having been accustomed to speaking with lords and ladies I had to speak with someone who was to be addressed as your ladyship; and so they had to show me how to say it. Since I am dull and was not used to these titles, I didn't get it right when the time came. I decided to tell her what happened and, laughing at myself, asked her to allow me to address her with the ordinary form "you"; and so I did.]

Well, what is this, my Lord? What is this, my Emperor? How can it be tolerated? You are King forever, my God; Your kingdom is not a borrowed one. When in the Creed the words, "and His kingdom will have no end," are said, it is almost always a special delight for me. I praise You, Lord, and bless You forever; in sum, Your kingdom will last forever. Well then, may You never permit, Lord, that anyone who is about to speak to You consider it good to do so only vocally.

2. What is this, Christians, that you say mental prayer isn't necessary? Do you understand yourselves?[2] Indeed, I don't think you do, and so you desire that we all be misled. You don't know what mental prayer is, or how vocal prayer should be recited, or what contemplation is, for if you did you wouldn't on the one hand condemn what on the other hand you praise.

3. I shall always have to join mental prayer to vocal prayer—when I remember—so that others don't frighten you, daughters. I know how this criticism of mental prayer will end up, for I have suffered some trials in this matter, and thus I wouldn't want anyone to disturb you. It is harmful to walk on this road with fear. It is very important for you to know that you are on the right road. When a traveler is told that he has

made a mistake and lost his way, he is made to go from one end to another, and all his searching for the way tires him, and he wastes time and arrives late.

Who can say that it is wrong, when we begin to recite the Hours or the rosary, to consider whom we are going to speak with, and who we are, so as to know how to speak with Him? Now I tell you, Sisters, if before you begin your vocal prayer you do the great deal that must be done in order to understand these two points well, you will be spending a good amount of time in mental prayer. Yes, indeed, for we must not approach a conversation with a prince as negligently as we do one with a farm worker, or with some poor thing like ourselves for whom any manner of address is all right.

4. It is only right that we consider these two points since, because of his humility, this King listens to me and lets me approach Him; and His guards do not throw me out, even though as an uneducated person I don't know how to speak to Him. The angels who assist Him know well the attitude of their King, for He delights more in the unpolished manners of a humble shepherd who He realizes would say more if he knew more than He does in the talk of very wise and learned men, however elegant their discourse, if they don't walk in humility. But just because He is good doesn't mean that we should be rude. At least, in order to thank Him for the bad odor He must endure in consenting to allow one like myself to come near Him, we should strive to be aware of His purity and of who He is. It's true that upon approaching Him one understands immediately, just as with lords here below; for when they tell us who their father was and about the millions they get in rent and of their title of dignity, there's no more to know. In fact, here below people in paying honor don't take into account the persons themselves, however much these persons may deserve the honor, but their wealth.

5. O miserable world! Praise God very much, daughters, because you have left something so wretched, where men pay attention not to what they have within themselves but to what their tenant farmers and vassals have; and if these men lack subordinates then no honor is paid them. It's something amus-

ing to relax over when you all have to take some recreation. For this is a good pastime: to notice how blindly those who are in the world spend their time.

6. Oh, our Emperor, supreme Power, supreme Goodness, Wisdom itself, without beginning, without end, without any limit to Your works; they are infinite and incomprehensible, a fathomless sea of marvels, with a beauty containing all beauty, strength itself! Oh, God help me, who might possess here all human eloquence and wisdom together in order to know how to explain clearly—insofar as is possible here below, because in this case all knowledge is equivalent to knowing nothing—a number of the many things we can consider in order to have some knowledge of who this Lord and Good of ours is!

7. Yes, bring yourselves to consider and understand whom you are speaking with, or, as you approach, with whom you are about to speak. In a thousand lives we would never completely understand the way in which this Lord deserves that we speak with Him, for the angels tremble before Him. He commands all; He can do all; for Him, to will is to do. Well then, it is only right, daughters, that we try to delight in these grandeurs our Spouse possesses and that we understand whom we are wedded to and what kind of life we must live. Oh, God help me, here below before getting married a person will know the other party, who he is and what he possesses. We are already betrothed and before the wedding must be brought to His house. Here below they don't try to make those who are betrothed renounce such thoughts. Why should they try to prevent us from thinking about who this man is, who His Father is, what country He is going to bring me to, what good things He promises to give me, what His status is, how I can make Him happy, and in what ways I can please Him, and from studying how I can conform my way of life to His? Now if a woman is to be happily married, she must, according to the advice she receives, strive for this conformity even though her husband is a man of lowly estate.

8. Well, my Spouse, must they in everything pay less attention to You than to men? If paying more attention to You doesn't seem right to them, let them at least leave Your brides

alone, for these latter must live their lives with You. Indeed, their life is a good one. If a spouse is so jealous that he doesn't want his bride to talk to anyone, it would be a fine thing if she didn't think about how she might please him in this matter and the reason she has for putting up with this jealousy and for wanting to avoid speaking with another since in him she has all that she could want!

This is mental prayer, my daughters: to understand these truths. If you should want to grow in understanding these things and pray vocally, well and good. You should not be thinking of other things while speaking with God, for doing so amounts to not knowing what mental prayer is. I believe the matter has been explained. May it please the Lord that we know how to put it into practice. Amen.[3]

Chapter 23

Treats of how important it is for one who has begun the path of prayer not to turn back and speaks once more of the great value that lies in beginning with determination.

WELL NOW, I SAY there are so many reasons why it is extremely important to begin with great determination that I would have to go on at much length if I mentioned them all. Sisters, I want to mention only two or three.

One is that if we resolve to give something, that is, this little care, to someone who has given so much to us and continually gives—giving this little care is certainly to our advantage and we thereby gain so many wonderful things—there is no reason for failing to give with complete determination. There's no reason for being like the lender who gives something with the intention of getting it back again. Lending doesn't seem to me to amount to giving; rather, there is always some displeasure felt by the borrower when the object is taken back, especially if he needs it and has already used it as his own, or if the lender is his friend, or if the borrower has given the lender many gifts without any self-seeking. The borrower would rightly think there was very little love in the lender who won't even let him keep a little thing, not even as a sign of love.

2. What bride is there who in receiving many valuable jewels from her bridegroom will refuse to give him even a ring, not because of what it is worth, for everything belongs to him, but to give it as a pledge that she will be his until death? Does this Lord deserve less, that we should mock Him by giving and then taking back the trifle that we gave Him? But this little bit of time that we resolve to give Him, which we spend on ourselves and on someone who will not thank us for it, let us give to Him, since we desire to do so, with our thoughts free of other things and unoccupied by them. And let us be wholly determined never to take it back from Him, neither because of trials on this account, nor because of contradictions, nor because of dryness. I should consider the time of prayer as not belonging to me and think that He can ask it of me in justice when I do not want to give it wholly to Him.

3. In saying "wholly," I do not mean that abandoning it for a day or for a few days on account of some just occupations or because of some indisposition is the equivalent of taking it back. Let the intention be firm; my God is not at all touchy; He doesn't bother about trifling things. Thus you will have something to be grateful for; this intention amounts to giving something. As for others, for anyone who is not generous but so stingy that he doesn't have the spirit of giving, it is enough for them to lend. In the end, one who lends does do something, and this Lord of ours takes everything into account. He adjusts Himself to our way of giving. In taking account of us, He is not at all petty, but generous. However great our debt may be, He finds it easy to pardon; but when there is a question of His repaying us, He's so careful that you need have no fear. Just the raising of our eyes in remembrance of Him will have its reward.

4. Another reason for beginning with determination is that the devil will not then have so free a hand to tempt. He's extremely afraid of determined souls, for he has experienced the

great harm they do him. And all the harm he plans to do them turns out to their benefit and to that of others as well; and he comes out with a loss. But we should not be careless or trust in this fact, for we are dealing with traitors, and they don't dare attack so often those who are well prepared; they are very cowardly. But if the devil should see carelessness, he would do great harm. And if he knows that someone is changeable and unstable in being good and not strongly determined to persevere, he will keep after him day and night; he will cause fears and never-ending obstacles. I know this very well through experience, and that's why I'm able to say, and do say, that no one knows how important determination is.

5. The other reason for beginning with determination is—and it is very much to the point—that the person who does so struggles more courageously. He knows that come what may he will not turn back. As in the case of one who is in a battle, he knows that if he is conquered they won't spare him his life and that if he doesn't die in battle he will die afterward. He struggles with greater determination and wants to fight like a desperado—as they say—and he doesn't fear the blows so much, because he is convinced of how important victory is and that for him to conquer is to live. It's also necessary to begin with the assurance that if we don't let ourselves be conquered, we will obtain our goal; this without a doubt, for no matter how small the gain, one will end up being very rich. Don't be afraid that the Lord will leave you to die of thirst, for He calls us to drink from this fount.[1] I have already said this[2] and would like to say it many times, for the devil intimidates persons who don't yet fully know the goodness of the Lord through experience, even though they know it through faith. But it is a great thing to have experienced the friendship and favor He shows toward those who journey on this road and how He takes care of almost all the expenses.

6. I'm not surprised that those who have not experienced this want the assurance of some gain for themselves. Well, you already know there is the hundredfold even in this life[3] and that the Lord says, "ask, and you will receive."[4] If you don't believe His Majesty in the sections of His gospel that insure this

gain, it will be of little benefit, Sisters, for me to break my head in trying to tell you about it. Nevertheless, I say that should anyone have some doubt little would be lost in trying the journey of prayer; for this journey brings with it the following good: more is given than is asked for, beyond what we could desire. This is absolutely true; I know. And those of you who know it by experience, through the goodness of God, can be my witnesses.[5]

Chapter 24

How vocal prayer must be recited with perfection, and mental prayer joined with it.

NOW, THEN, LET US SPEAK AGAIN[1] to those souls I mentioned that cannot recollect or tie their minds down in mental prayer or engage in reflection. Let's not mention here by name these two things, since you are not meant to follow such a path. As a matter of fact there are many persons seemingly terrified by the mere term "mental prayer" or "contemplation," and perhaps one of these might come to this house, for as I have also said[2] not everyone walks by the same path.

2. Well what I now want to counsel you about (I can even say teach you, because as a Mother, having the office of prioress, I'm allowed to teach) is how you must pray vocally, for it's only right that you should understand what you're saying. And because it can happen that those who are unable to think about God may also find long prayers tiring, I don't want to concern myself with these. But I will speak of those prayers we are obliged as Christians to recite (such as, the Our Father and the Hail Mary) so that people won't be able to say of us that we speak and don't understand what we're speaking about—unless we think it is enough for us to follow the practice in which merely pronouncing the words is sufficient. I'm not concerned with whether this is sufficient or not; learned men

will explain [the matter to those persons to whom God gives light to ask the question. And I'm not meddling with what doesn't belong to our state.] What I would like us to do, daughters, is refuse to be satisfied with merely pronouncing the words. For when I say, "I believe," it seems to me right that I should know and understand what I believe. And when I say, "Our Father," it will be an act of love to understand who this Father of ours is and who the Master is who taught us this prayer.

3. If you reply that you already know this and that there is no reason to recall it, you are wrong. There is a large difference in teachers; but it is even a great misfortune if we forget those who teach us here below. Especially, if they are saints and spiritual masters and we are good disciples, it is impossible to forget them [but we love them very much and even take pride in them and often speak of them.] Well, God never allows us to forget the Master who taught us this prayer, and with so much love and desire that it benefit us. He wants us to remember Him often when we say the prayer, even though because of our weakness we do not remember Him always.

4. Now with regard to vocal prayer you already know that His Majesty teaches that it be recited in solitude.[3] This is what He always did when He prayed,[4] and not out of any need of His own but for our instruction. It has already been mentioned[5] that one cannot speak simultaneously to God and to the world; this would amount to nothing more than reciting the prayer while listening to what is being said elsewhere or to letting the mind wander and making no effort to control it. There can be exceptions at times either because of bad humors—especially if the person is melancholic—or because of faint feelings in the head so that all efforts become useless. Or it can happen that God will permit days of severe temptation in his servants for their greater good. And though in their affliction they are striving to be quiet, they cannot even be attentive to what they are saying, no matter how hard they try; nor will the intellect settle down in anything, but by the disordered way it goes about, it will seem to be in a frenzy.

5. Whoever experiences the affliction these distractions

cause will see that they are not his fault; he should not grow anxious, which makes things worse, or tire himself trying to put order into something that at the time doesn't have any, that is, his mind. He should just pray as best he can; or even not pray, but like a sick person strive to bring some relief to his soul; let him occupy himself in other works of virtue. This advice now is for persons who are careful and who have understood that they must not speak simultaneously to both God and the world.

What we ourselves can do is to strive to be alone; and please God it will suffice, as I say, that we understand to whom we are speaking and the answer the Lord makes to our petitions. Do you think He is silent? Even though we do not hear Him, He speaks well to the heart when we beseech Him from the heart.

And it is good for us to consider that He taught this prayer to each of us and that He is showing it to us; the teacher is never so far from his pupil that he has to shout, but he is very close. I want you to understand that it is good for you, if you are to recite the Our Father well, to remain at the side of the Master who taught this prayer to you.

6. You will say that doing so involves reflection and that you neither can nor want to pray any other way but vocally; for there are also impatient persons who like to avoid any suffering. Since such individuals do not have the habit, it is difficult for them to recollect their minds in the beginning; and so as to avoid a little fatigue, they say they neither can nor know how to do anything else than pray vocally.

You are right in saying that this vocal prayer is now in fact mental prayer. But I tell you that surely I don't know how mental prayer can be separated from vocal prayer if the vocal prayer is to be recited well with an understanding of whom we are speaking to. It is even an obligation that we strive to pray with attention. Please God that with these remedies we shall recite the Our Father well and not end up in some other irrelevant thing. I have experienced this sometimes, and the best remedy I find is to strive to center the mind upon the one to whom the words are addressed. So, be patient and strive to make a habit out of something that is so necessary [if you are to be good nuns, and even pray as good Christians, in my opinion.]

Chapter 25

Tells how much the soul gains through a perfect recitation of vocal prayer and how God happens to raise it from this prayer to supernatural things.

TO KEEP YOU FROM THINKING that little is gained through a perfect recitation of vocal prayer, I tell you that it is very possible that while you are reciting the Our Father or some other vocal prayer, the Lord may raise you to perfect contemplation. By these means His Majesty shows that He listens to the one who speaks to Him. And it is His grandeur that speaks to the soul, suspending one's intellect, binding one's imagination, and, as they say, taking the words from one's mouth; for even though the soul may want to do so, it cannot speak unless with great difficulty.

2. The soul understands that without the noise of words this divine Master is teaching it by suspending its faculties, for if they were to be at work they would do harm rather than bring benefit. They are enjoying without understanding how they are enjoying. The soul is being enkindled in love, and it doesn't understand how it loves. It knows that it enjoys what it loves, but it doesn't know how. It clearly understands that this joy is not a joy the intellect obtains merely through desire. The will is enkindled without understanding how. But as soon as it can understand something, it sees that this good cannot be merited or gained through all the trials one can suffer on earth. This good is a gift from the Lord of earth and heaven, who, in sum, gives according to who He is. What I have described, daughters, is perfect contemplation.

3. Now you will understand the difference that lies between perfect contemplation and mental prayer. Mental prayer consists of what was explained: being aware and knowing that we are speaking, with whom we are speaking, and who we ourselves are who dare to speak so much with so great a Lord. To think about this and other similar things, of how little we have served Him and how much we are obliged to serve Him, is

mental prayer. Don't think it amounts to some other kind of gibberish, and don't let the name frighten you.

To recite the Our Father or the Hail Mary or whatever prayer you wish is vocal prayer. But behold what poor music you produce when you do this without mental prayer. Even the words will be poorly pronounced at times. In these two kinds of prayer we can do something ourselves, with the help of God. In the contemplation I now mentioned, we can do nothing; His Majesty is the one who does everything, for it is His work and above our nature.

4. Since I explained contemplation very much at length and as best I could in the account of my life that I said I wrote for my confessors[1]—for they had ordered me to write that account—I will not speak of contemplation here or do any more than touch upon it. Those of you who have been so fortunate as to be brought by the Lord to the state of contemplation may, if you can get that account, find there some advice and counsel which God granted that I be able to give; it will be very consoling and beneficial to you. This is what I think, and so do some of those who have seen it—for they have the account in order to make a judgment about it. What shame I feel in telling you that you should pay attention to something I have done, and the Lord knows the embarrassment with which I write much of what I write. May He be blessed for so putting up with me! Those of you who, as I say, experience supernatural prayer may obtain that account after my death; those of you who do not, need not worry about obtaining it but only about striving after what is contained in this present book and leave the rest to God; for it is He who must bestow supernatural prayer, and He will grant it to you if you do not stop short on the road but try hard until you reach the end.[2]

Chapter 26

Explains a method for recollecting one's mind. Sets down some ways of doing this. The chapter is very useful for beginners in prayer.

NOW THEN LET US RETURN to our vocal prayer that it may be so recited that, without our being aware of the fact, God may grant us everything together and also enable us to say vocal prayers as we should, as I have mentioned.[1]

As is already known, the examination of conscience, the act of contrition, and the sign of the cross must come first. Then, daughters, since you are alone, strive to find a companion. Well what better companion than the Master Himself who taught you this prayer? Represent the Lord Himself as close to you and behold how lovingly and humbly He is teaching you. Believe me, you should remain with so good a friend as long as you can. If you grow accustomed to having Him present at your side, and He sees that you do so with love and that you go about striving to please Him, you will not be able—as they say—to get away from Him; He will never fail you; He will help you in all your trials; you will find Him everywhere. Do you think it's some small matter to have a friend like this at your side?

2. O Sisters, those of you who cannot engage in much discursive reflection with the intellect or keep your mind from distraction, get used to this practice! Get used to it! See, I know that you can do this; for I suffered many years from the trial—and it is a very great one—of not being able to quiet the mind in anything. But I know that the Lord does not leave us so abandoned; for if we humbly ask Him for this friendship, He will not deny it to us. And if we cannot succeed in one year, we will succeed later. Let's not regret the time that is so well spent. Who's making us hurry? I am speaking of acquiring this habit and of striving to walk alongside this true Master.

3. I'm not asking you now that you think about Him or that you draw out a lot of concepts or make long and subtle reflec-

tions with your intellect. I'm not asking you to do anything more than look at Him. For who can keep you from turning the eyes of your soul toward this Lord, even if you do so just for a moment if you can't do more? You can look at very ugly things; won't you be able to look at the most beautiful thing imaginable? Well now, daughters, your Spouse never takes His eyes off you. He has suffered your committing a thousand ugly offenses and abominations against Him, and this suffering wasn't enough for Him to cease looking at you. Is it too much to ask you to turn your eyes from these exterior things in order to look at Him sometimes? Behold, He is not waiting for anything else, as He says to the bride,[2] than that we look at Him. In the measure you desire Him, you will find Him. He so esteems our turning to look at Him that no diligence will be lacking on His part.

4. They say that for a woman to be a good wife toward her husband she must be sad when he is sad, and joyful when he is joyful, even though she may not be so. (See what subjection you have been freed from, Sisters!) The Lord, without deception, truly acts in such a way with us. He is the one who submits, and He wants you to be the lady with authority to rule; He submits to your will. If you are joyful, look at Him as risen. Just imagining how He rose from the tomb will bring you joy. The brilliance! The beauty! The majesty! How victorious! How joyful! Indeed, like one coming forth from a battle where he has gained a great kingdom! And all of that, plus Himself, He desires for you. Well, is it such a big thing that from time to time you turn your eyes to look upon one who gives you so much?

5. If you are experiencing trials or are sad, behold Him on the way to the garden: what great affliction He bore in His soul; for having become suffering itself, He tells us about it and complains of it. Or behold Him bound to the column, filled with pain, with all His flesh torn in pieces for the great love He bears you; so much suffering, persecuted by some, spit on by others, denied by His friends, abandoned by them, with no one to defend Him, frozen from the cold, left so alone that you can console each other. Or behold Him burdened with the cross, for they didn't even let Him take a breath. He will look at you

with those eyes so beautiful and compassionate, filled with tears; He will forget His sorrows so as to console you in yours, merely because you yourselves go to Him to be consoled, and you turn your head to look at Him.

6. O Lord of the world, my true Spouse! (You can say this to Him if He has moved your heart to pity at seeing Him thus, for not only will you desire to look at Him but you will also delight in speaking with Him, not with ready-made prayers but with those that come from the sorrow of your own heart, for He esteems them highly.) Are You so in need, my Lord and my Love, that You would want to receive such poor company as mine, for I see by Your expression that You have been consoled by me? Well then, how is it Lord that the angels leave You and that even Your Father doesn't console You? If it's true, Lord, that You want to endure everything for me, what is this that I suffer for You? Of what am I complaining? I am already ashamed, since I have seen You in such a condition. I desire to suffer, Lord, all the trials that come to me and esteem them as a great good enabling me to imitate You in something. Let us walk together, Lord. Wherever You go, I will go;[3] whatever you suffer, I will suffer.

7. Take up that cross, daughters. Don't mind at all if the Jews trample upon you, if His trial can thereby be lessened. Pay no attention to what they say to you, be deaf to their gossip. In stumbling, in falling with your Spouse, do not withdraw from the cross or abandon it. Consider carefully the fatigue with which He walks and how much greater His trials are than those trials you suffer, however great you may want to paint them and no matter how much you grieve over them. You will come out consoled because you will see that they are something to be laughed at when compared to those of the Lord.

8. You will ask, Sisters, how you can do this, saying that if you had seen His Majesty with your bodily eyes at the time He walked in this world that you would have looked at Him very willingly and done so always. Don't believe it. Whoever doesn't want to use a little effort now to recollect at least the sense of sight and look at this Lord within herself (for one can do so

without danger but with just a little care) would have been much less able to stay at the foot of the cross with the Magdalene, who saw His death with her own eyes. But how much the glorious Virgin and this blessed saint must have suffered! How many threats, how many wicked words, how much shoving about and rudeness! For the people around them were not exactly what we would call courteous! No, they were people from hell, ministers of the devil. Indeed, what these two suffered must have been terrible; but in the presence of another greater affliction they didn't feel their own.

So, Sisters, don't think you are capable of such great trials if you are not capable of such little ones. By exercising yourselves in these little trials, you will come to be able to suffer other greater ones. [And believe that I am speaking the truth in saying that you can speak with Him, for I have passed through this difficulty.]

9. What you can do as a help in this matter is try to carry about an image or painting of this Lord that is to your liking, not so as to carry it about on your heart and never look at it but so as to speak often with Him; for He will inspire you with what to say. Since you speak with other persons, why must words fail you more when you speak with God? Don't believe they will; at least I will not believe they will if you acquire the habit. Otherwise, the failure to communicate with a person causes both estrangement and a failure to know how to speak with him. For it seems then that we don't know him, even if he may be a relative; family ties and friendship are lost through a lack of communication.

10. It is also a great help to take a good book written in the vernacular in order to recollect one's thoughts and pray well vocally, and little by little accustom the soul with coaxing and skill not to grow discouraged. Imagine that many years have passed since the soul left the house of its Spouse and that until it returns to this house there's a great need that it know how to deal with Him. For so we sinners are: our soul and our thoughts are so accustomed to wandering about at their own pleasure—or grief, to put it better—that the poor soul doesn't understand itself. In order that it get to love remaining at

home once again, a great deal of skill is necessary. If little by little this is not accomplished, we shall never do anything.

And I again assure you that if with care you grow accustomed to what I have said[4] your gain will be so great that even if I wanted to explain this to you I wouldn't know how. Draw near, then, to this good Master with strong determination to learn what He teaches you, and His Majesty will so provide that you will turn out to be good disciples. He will not abandon you if you do not abandon Him. Consider the words that divine mouth speaks, for in the first word you will understand immediately the love He has for you; it is no small blessing and gift for the disciple to see that his Master loves him.

Chapter 27

Deals with the great love our Lord showed us in the first words of the Our Father and how important it is for those who truly want to be children of God to pay no attention whatsoever to lineage.

OUR FATHER WHO ART IN HEAVEN.[1] O my Lord, how You do show Yourself to be the Father of such a Son; and how Your Son does show Himself to be the Son of such a Father! May You be blessed forever and ever! This favor would not be so great, Lord, if it came at the end of the prayer. But at the beginning, You fill our hands and give a reward so large that it would easily fill the intellect and thus occupy the will in such a way one would be unable to speak a word.

Oh, daughters, how readily should perfect contemplation come at this point! Oh, how right it would be for the soul to enter within itself in order to rise the better above itself[2] that this holy Son might make it understand the nature of the place where He says His Father dwells, which is in the heavens. Let us go forth from the earth, my daughters, for there is no reason that a favor like this should be so little esteemed, that after we have understood how great it is, we should still want to remain on earth.

2. O Son of God and my Lord! How is it that You give so much all together in the first words? Since You humble Yourself to such an extreme in joining with us in prayer and making Yourself the Brother of creatures so lowly and wretched, how is it that You give us in the name of Your Father everything that can be given? For You desire that He consider us His children, because Your word cannot fail.[3] You oblige Him to be true to Your word, which is no small burden since in being Father He must bear with us no matter how serious the offenses. If we return to Him like the prodigal son, He has to pardon us.[4] He has to console us in our trials. He has to sustain us in the way a father like this must. For, in effect, He must be better than all the fathers in the world because in Him everything must be faultless. And after all this He must make us sharers and heirs with You.[5]

3. Behold, my Lord, that since with the love You bear us and with Your humility, nothing will stop you . . . in sum, Lord, You are on earth and clothed with it. Since You possess our nature, it seems You have some reason to look to our gain. But behold, Your Father is in heaven. You Yourself said so. It is right that You look to His honor. Since You have vowed to undergo disgrace for us, leave Your Father free. Don't oblige Him to do so much for a people so wretched, like myself, who will not thank You properly [and there are no others who will do better.]

4. O good Jesus! How clearly You have shown that You are one with Him, and that Your will is His and His, Yours![6] How clear your declaration, my Lord! How magnificent it is, the love You bear us! You made use of roundabout ways, hiding from the devil the fact that You are the Son of God; and with the great desire You have for our good, nothing was able to stop You from granting us so very great a favor. Who could have done it but You, Lord? I don't know how the devil failed to understand in these words who You were, and had doubts about it. At least I see it clearly, my Jesus. You have spoken, as a favored son, for Yourself and for us; and You are powerful enough so that what You say on earth will be done in heaven.

May You be blessed forever, my Lord, for You are so willing to give that nothing will stop You from doing so.

5. Well, daughters, doesn't it seem to you that this Master is a good one, since in order to make us grow fond of learning what He teaches us He begins by granting us so wonderful a favor? Does it seem right to you now that even though we recite these first words vocally we should fail to let our intellects understand and our hearts break in pieces at seeing such love? What son is there in the world who doesn't strive to learn who his father is when he knows he has such a good one with so much majesty and power? If our Father had not so much majesty, it wouldn't surprise me if we refused to be known as His children. The world has come to such a state that if the father is of a lower status than his son, the son doesn't feel honored in recognizing him as his father.

6. Such an attitude doesn't belong here. In this house, please God, may there never be any thought about such a thing; it would be a hell. But the one who is from nobler lineage should be the one to speak least about her father. All the Sisters must be equal.

O college of Christ, where St. Peter, being a fisherman, had more authority—and the Lord wanted it so—than St. Bartholomew, who was a king's son![7] His Majesty knew what would take place in the world where people dispute over lineage. These disputes in reality amount to nothing much more than a debate about whether the mud is better for making bricks or adobes. God help me, what a great trial we bear! God deliver us, Sisters, from similar disputes, even though they be in jest; I hope in His Majesty that He will do so. When this concern about lineage is noticed in a Sister, apply a remedy at once and let her fear lest she be Judas among the apostles. Give her penances until she understands that she doesn't deserve to be thought of as made from even a very wretched kind of mud.[8]

You have a good Father, for He gives you the good Jesus. Let no one in this house speak of any other father but Him. And strive, my daughters, so to behave that you will deserve to find your delight in Him; and cast yourselves into His arms. You already know that He will not reject you if you are good daughters. Who, then, would fail to strive so as not to lose such a Father?

7. Oh, God help me! How much there is in these words to give you consolation. So as not to enlarge any more on this matter, I want to leave it to your own reflection. For no matter how unruly one's mind may be, the truth is—leaving aside our gain in having so good a Father—that the Holy Spirit must be present between such a Son and such a Father, and He will enkindle your will and bind it with a very great love.

Chapter 28

Explains the nature of the prayer of recollection and sets down some ways of getting accustomed to this form of prayer.

NOW CONSIDER WHAT YOUR MASTER SAYS: *Who art in heaven.*[1] Do you think it's of little importance to know what heaven is and where you must seek your most sacred Father? Well, I tell you that for wandering minds it is very important not only to believe these truths but to strive to understand them by experience. Doing this is one of the ways of greatly slowing down the mind and recollecting the soul.

2. You already know that God is everywhere. It's obvious, then, that where the king is there is his court; in sum, wherever God is, there is heaven. Without a doubt you can believe that where His Majesty is present, all glory is present. Consider what St. Augustine says, that he sought Him in many places but found Him ultimately within himself.[2] Do you think it matters little for a soul with a wandering mind to understand this truth and see that there is no need to go to heaven in order to speak with one's Eternal Father or find delight in Him? Nor is there any need to shout. However softly we speak, He is near enough to hear us. Neither is there any need for wings to go to find Him.[3] All one need do is go into solitude and look at Him

within oneself, and not turn away from so good a Guest but with great humility speak to Him as to a father. Beseech Him as you would a father; tell Him about your trials; ask Him for a remedy against them, realizing that you are not worthy to be His daughter.

3. Leave aside any of that faintheartedness that some persons have and think is humility. You see, humility doesn't consist in refusing a favor the King offers you but in accepting such a favor and understanding how bountifully it comes to you and being delighted with it. What a nice kind of humility! I have the Emperor of heaven and earth in my house (for He comes to it in order to favor me and be happy with me), and out of humility I do not want to answer Him or stay with Him or take what He gives me, but I leave Him alone. Or, while He is telling me and begging me to ask Him for something, I do not do so but remain poor; and I even let Him go, for He sees that I never finish trying to make up my mind.

Have nothing to do with this kind of humility, daughters, but speak with Him as with a father, or a brother, or a lord, or as with a spouse; sometimes in one way, at other times in another; He will teach you what you must do in order to please Him. Don't be foolish; take Him at His word. Since He is your Spouse, He will treat you accordingly. [Consider that it is well worthwhile for you to have understood this truth: that the Lord is within us, and that there we must be with Him.]

4. The intellect is recollected much more quickly with this kind of prayer even though it may be vocal; it is a prayer that brings with it many blessings. This prayer is called "recollection," because the soul collects its faculties together and enters within itself to be with its God. And its divine Master comes more quickly to teach it and give it the prayer of quiet than He would through any other method it might use. For centered there within itself, it can think about the Passion and represent the Son and offer Him to the Father and not tire the intellect by going to look for Him on Mount Calvary or in the garden or at the pillar.

5. Those who by such a method can enclose themselves

within this little heaven of our soul, where the Maker of heaven and earth is present, and grow accustomed to refusing to be where the exterior senses in their distraction have gone or look in that direction should believe they are following an excellent path and that they will not fail to drink water from the fount; for they will journey far in a short time. Their situation is like that of a person who travels by ship; with a little wind he reaches the end of his journey in a few days. But those who go by land take longer. [It's the path of heaven. I say "of heaven," because they are there in the palace of the King; they are not on earth and are more secure against many occasions.]

6. Those who know how to recollect themselves are already out to sea, as they say. For even though they may not have got completely away from land, they do what they can during that time to get free from it by recollecting their senses within. If the recollection is true, it is felt very clearly; for it produces some effect in the soul. I don't know how to explain it. Whoever has experienced it will understand; the soul is like one who gets up from the table after winning a game, for it already sees what the things of the world are. It rises up at the best time, as one who enters a fortified castle to be safe from enemies. There is a withdrawing of the senses from exterior things and a renunciation of them in such a way that, without one's realizing it, the eyes close so as to avoid seeing them and so that the sight might be more awake to things of the soul.

So, anyone who walks by this path keeps his eyes closed almost as often as he prays. This is a praiseworthy custom for many reasons. It is a striving so as not to look at things here below. This striving comes at the beginning; afterward, there's no need to strive; a greater effort is needed to open the eyes while praying. It seems the soul is aware of being strengthened and fortified at the expense of the body, that it leaves the body alone and weakened, and that it receives in this recollection a supply of provisions to strengthen it against the body.

7. And even though it isn't aware of this at the beginning, since the recollection is not so deep—for there are greater and lesser degrees of recollection—the soul should get used to this recollection; although in the beginning the body causes dif-

ficulty because it claims its rights without realizing that it is cutting off its own head by not surrendering. If we make the effort, practice this recollection for some days, and get used to it, the gain will be clearly seen; we will understand, when beginning to pray, that the bees are approaching and entering the beehive to make honey. And this recollection will be effected without our effort because the Lord has desired that, during the time the faculties are drawn inward, the soul and its will may merit to have this dominion. When the soul does no more than give a sign that it wishes to be recollected, the senses obey it and become recollected. Even though they go out again afterward, their having already surrendered is a great thing; for they go out as captives and subjects and do not cause the harm they did previously. And when the will calls them back again, they come more quickly, until after many of these entries the Lord wills that they rest entirely in perfect contemplation.

8. May what has been said be well understood; even though it seems obscure, it will be understood by anyone who desires to practice it.

Therefore, those who know how to recollect themselves are like those who travel by sea; and since it is important for us not to proceed so slowly, let us speak a little about how we should get accustomed to a method that's so good. These souls are safer from many occasions. The fire of divine love is more quickly enkindled when they blow a little with their intellects. Since they are close to the fire, a little spark will ignite and set everything ablaze. Because there is no impediment from outside, the soul is alone with its God; it is well prepared for this enkindling. [I would like you to understand clearly this manner of prayer, which, as I have said, is called recollection.]

9. Well, let us imagine that within us is an extremely rich palace, built entirely of gold and precious stones; in sum, built for a lord such as this. Imagine, too, as is indeed so, that you have a part to play in order for the palace to be so beautiful; for there is no edifice as beautiful as is a soul pure and full of virtues. The greater the virtues the more resplendent the jewels. Imagine, also, that in this palace dwells this mighty King who has been gracious enough to become your Father;

and that He is seated upon an extremely valuable throne, which is your heart.

10. This may seem trifling at the beginning; I mean, this image I've used in order to explain recollection. But the image may be very helpful—to you especially—for since we women have no learning, all of this imagining is necessary that we may truly understand that within us lies something incomparably more precious than what we see outside ourselves. Let's not imagine that we are hollow inside. And please God it may be only women that go about forgetful of this inner richness and beauty. I consider it impossible for us to pay so much attention to worldly things if we take the care to remember we have a Guest such as this within us, for we then see how lowly these things are next to what we possess within ourselves. Well, what else does an animal do upon seeing what is pleasing to its sight than satisfy its hunger by taking the prey? Indeed, there should be some difference between them and us.

11. You will laugh at me, perhaps, and say that what I'm explaining is very clear, and you'll be right; for me, though, it was obscure for some time. I understood well that I had a soul. But what this soul deserved and who dwelt within it I did not understand because I had covered my eyes with the vanities of the world. For, in my opinion, if I had understood as I do now that in this little palace of my soul dwelt so great a King, I would not have left Him alone so often. I would have remained with Him at times and striven more so as not to be so unclean. But what a marvelous thing, that He who would fill a thousand worlds and many more with His grandeur would enclose Himself in something so small! [And so He wanted to enclose Himself in the womb of His most Blessed Mother.] In fact, since He is Lord He is free to do what He wants, and since He loves us He adapts Himself to our size.

12. So that the soul won't be disturbed in the beginning by seeing that it is too small to have something so great within itself, the Lord doesn't give it this knowledge until He enlarges it little by little and it has the capacity to receive what He will place within it. For this reason I say He is free to do what He wants since He has the power to make this palace a large one.

The whole point is that we should give ourselves to Him with complete determination, and we should empty the soul in such a way that He can store things there or take them away as though it were His own property. And since His Majesty has the rights of ownership, let us not oppose Him. [Even here below guests in the house are a bother when we cannot tell them to leave.] And since He doesn't force our will, He takes what we give Him; but He doesn't give Himself completely until we give ourselves completely.

This fact is certain; and because it is so important, I bring it to your minds so often. He never works in the soul as He does when it is totally His without any obstacle, nor do I see how He could. He is the friend of all good order. Now, then, if we fill the palace with lowly people and trifles, how will there be room for the Lord with His court? He does enough by remaining just a little while in the midst of so much confusion.

13. Do you think, daughters, that He comes alone? Don't you see that His Son says, "who art in heaven"? Well, since He is such a King, certainly His court attendants would never leave Him alone, but they will always be with Him; and they beseech Him on our behalf since they are full of charity. Don't think that things in heaven are like they are here below; for if here below a lord or prelate, because of certain of his own aims or because he wants to, favors someone, the envy of others is immediately stirred, and that poor person is hated without having done anything against them.

Chapter 29

Continues to present means for obtaining this prayer of recollection. How little it should matter to us whether or not we are favored by the bishop.

FOR THE LOVE OF GOD, daughters, don't bother about being favored by lords or prelates. Let each nun strive to do what she ought; if the bishop doesn't show gratitude for what she does, she can be sure that the Lord will repay and be grateful for it. Indeed, we have not come here to seek a reward in this life. Let us always direct our thoughts to what is lasting and pay no attention to things here below, for even though our lives are short these preferences do not last for us. Today the bishop will favor one Sister, and tomorrow he will favor you if he sees one virtue more in you; and if he doesn't favor you, it matters little. Give no room to these thoughts. Sometimes they begin in a small way, but they can become very disturbing to you. Cut them off with the thought that your kingdom is not here below and of how quickly all things come to an end.

2. But even this kind of remedy is a lowly one and not indicative of great perfection. It is better that this disfavor of your superior continue, that you be unappreciated and humbled, and that you accept this for the Lord who is with you. Turn your eyes inward and look within yourself, as has been said.[1] You will find your Master, for He will not fail you; rather, the less you have of exterior consolation the more He will favor you. He is very merciful, and He never fails persons who are afflicted and despised if they trust in Him alone. So, David says that the Lord is with the afflicted.[2] Either you believe this or you don't. If you believe it, then why are you killing yourselves?

3. O my Lord, if we truly knew You we wouldn't care at all about anything, for You give much to those who sincerely want to trust in You! Believe, my friends, that it is a great thing to have knowledge of this truth so that you can then see that all favors here below are a lie when they divert the soul somewhat from entering within itself. Oh, God help me, who will make you understand this! Certainly, not I; for I know that I, who more than anyone should understand, have not succeeded in understanding it as it should be understood.

4. Now to return to what I was saying.[3] I would like to know a way of explaining how this holy fellowship with our Companion, the Saint of saints, may be experienced without any hindrance to the solitude enjoyed between the soul and its Spouse when the soul desires to enter this paradise within itself to be with its God and close the door to all the world. I say

"desires" because you must understand that this recollection is not something supernatural, but that it is something we can desire and achieve ourselves with the help of God—for without this help we can do nothing,[4] not even have a good thought. This recollection is not a silence of the faculties; it is an enclosure of the faculties within the soul.

5. The soul gains from this recollection in many ways as is written in some books [on mental prayer.[5] Since I'm speaking only of how vocal prayer should be recited well, there's no reason to say so much. What I'm trying to point out is that we should see and be present to the One with whom we speak without turning our backs on Him, for I don't think speaking with God while thinking of a thousand other vanities would amount to anything else but turning our backs on Him. All the harm comes from not truly understanding that He is near, but in imagining Him as far away. And indeed how far, if we go to heaven to seek Him! Now, is Your face such, Lord, that we would not look at it when You are so close to us? If people aren't looking at us when we speak, it doesn't seem to us that they are listening to what we say. And do we close our eyes to avoid seeing that You, Lord, are looking at us? How will we know whether You've heard what we're saying to You? This alone is what I want to explain: that in order to acquire the habit of easily recollecting our minds and understanding what we are saying, and with whom we are speaking, it is necessary that the exterior senses be recollected and that we give them something with which to be occupied. For indeed we have heaven within ourselves since the Lord of heaven is there.]

We must, then, disengage ourselves from everything so as to approach God interiorly and even in the midst of occupations withdraw within ourselves. Although it may be for only a moment that I remember I have that Company within myself, doing so is very beneficial. In sum, we must get used to delighting in the fact that it isn't necessary to shout in order to speak to Him, for His Majesty will give the experience that He is present.

6. With this method we shall pray vocally with much calm, and any difficulty will be removed. For in the little amount of

time we take to force ourselves to be close to this Lord, He will understand us as if through sign language. Thus if we are about to say the Our Father many times, He will understand us after the first. He is very fond of taking away our difficulty. Even though we may recite this prayer no more than once in an hour, we can be aware that we are with Him, of what we are asking Him, of His willingness to give to us, and how eagerly He remains with us. If we have this awareness, He doesn't want us to be breaking our heads trying to speak a great deal to Him. [Therefore, Sisters, out of love for the Lord, get used to praying the Our Father with this recollection, and you will see the benefit before long. This is a manner of praying that the soul gets so quickly used to that it doesn't go astray, nor do the faculties become restless, as time will tell. I only ask that you try this method, even though it may mean some struggle; everything involves struggle before the habit is acquired. But I assure you that before long it will be a great consolation for you to know that you can find this holy Father, whom you are beseeching, within you without tiring yourself in seeking where He is.]

7. May the Lord teach this recollection to those of you who don't know about it, for I confess that I never knew what it was to pray with satisfaction until the Lord taught me this method. And it is because I have always found so many benefits from this habit of recollection that I have enlarged so much upon it.

I conclude by saying that whoever wishes to acquire it—since, as I say, it lies within our power—should not tire of getting used to what has been explained. It involves a gradual increase of self-control and an end to vain wandering from the right path; it means conquering, which is a making use of one's senses for the sake of the inner life. If you speak, strive to remember that the One with whom you are speaking is present within. If you listen, remember that you are going to hear One who is very close to you when He speaks. In sum, bear in mind that you can, if you want, avoid ever withdrawing from such good company; and be sorry that for a long time you left your Father alone, of whom you are so much in need. If you can, practice this recollection often during the day; if not, do so a few times. As you become accustomed to it you will experience the benefit, either sooner or later. Once this recollection is given by the Lord, you will not exchange it for any treasure.

8. Since nothing is learned without a little effort, consider, Sisters, for the love of God, as well employed the attention you give to this method of prayer. I know, if you try, that within a year, or perhaps half a year, you will acquire it, by the favor of God. See how little time it takes for a gain as great as is that of laying a good foundation. If then the Lord should desire to raise you to higher things He will discover in you the readiness, finding that you are close to Him. May it please His Majesty that we not consent to withdrawing from His presence. Amen. [Perhaps all of you know what I've explained, but someone may come along who will not know it. For that reason don't be annoyed that I've mentioned it here. Now let us come to learn how our good Master continues and begins to petition His holy Father for us; it is good that we understand what He asks.]

Chapter 30

The importance of understanding what is being asked for in prayer. Deals with the next words of the Our Father: Sanctificetur nomen tuum, adveniat regnum tuum. *Applies these words to the prayer of quiet and begins to explain this kind of prayer.*

IS THERE ANYONE, however foolish, who when he is about to ask for something from an important person doesn't think over how he should go about asking? He must find favor with this person and not seem rude. He thinks about what he should ask for and why he needs it, especially if he is asking for something significant, which is what our good Jesus teaches us to ask for. There is something it seems to me that should be noted: Couldn't You, my Lord, have concluded the Our Father with the words: "Give us, Father, what is fitting for us"? It doesn't seem there would have been need to say anything else to One who understands everything so well.

2. O Eternal Wisdom! Between You and Your Father these words would have sufficed. Your petition in the garden was like this. You manifested Your own desire and fear, but You abandoned them to His will.[1] Yet, You know us, my Lord, that we are not as surrendered to the will of Your Father as You were. You know that it was necessary for You to make those specific requests so that we might pause to consider if what we are seeking is good for us, so that if it isn't we won't ask for it. If we aren't given what we want, being what we are, with this free will we have, we might not accept what the Lord gives. For although what He gives is better, we don't think we'll ever become rich, since we don't at once see the money in our hand.

3. Oh, God help me! What a pity to have so unawakened a faith that we never come to understand fully the certainty of both punishment and reward! As a result it is good, daughters, that you understand what you are asking for in the Our Father so that if the Eternal Father should offer it to you, you will not scoff at it. And consider very carefully whether what you ask for is good for you; if it isn't, don't ask for it, but ask His Majesty to give you light. For we are blind and feel loathing for the food that will give us life; we want the food that will bring us death. And what a death! So dangerous and so everlasting!

4. Well, Jesus says that we may recite these words in which we ask for a kingdom like His to come within us: "Hallowed be Your name, Your kingdom come within us."[2]

Now behold, daughters, how great the wisdom of our Master is. I am reflecting here on what we are asking for when we ask for this kingdom, and it is good that we understand our request. But since His Majesty saw that we could neither hallow, nor praise, nor extol, nor glorify this holy name of the Eternal Father in a fitting way, because of the tiny amount we ourselves are capable of doing, He provided for us by giving us here on earth His kingdom. That is why Jesus put these two petitions next to each other. I want to tell you here, daughters, what I understand so that we may know what we are asking for and the importance of our begging persistently for it, and do as much as we can so as to please the One who is to give it to us. If I do not satisfy you, you can think up other reflections yourselves. Our Master will allow us to make these reflections provided that we submit in all things to what the Church[3] holds, as I do [always. And I will not even give you this to read until learned persons have seen it. At least, if there is anything incorrect, the error will not be done through malice but for my not knowing any better.]

5. Now, then, the great good that it seems to me there will be in the kingdom of heaven, among many other blessings, is that one will no longer take any account of earthly things, but have a calmness and glory within, rejoice in the fact that all are rejoicing, experience perpetual peace and a wonderful inner satisfaction that comes from seeing that everyone hallows and praises the Lord and blesses His name and that no one offends Him. Everyone loves Him there, and the soul itself doesn't think about anything else than loving Him; nor can it cease loving Him, because it knows Him. And would that we could love Him in this way here below, even though we may not be able to do so with such perfection or stability. But if we knew Him we would love in a way very different from that in which we do love Him.

6. It seems I'm saying that we would have to be angels in order to make this petition and recite well our vocal prayers. Our divine Master would truly desire this since He asks us to make so lofty a petition, and certainly He doesn't tell us to ask for impossible things. The above would be possible, through the favor of God, for a soul placed in this exile, but not with the perfection of those who have gone forth from this prison; for we are at sea and journeying along this way. But there are times when, tired from our travels, we experience that the Lord calms our faculties and quiets the soul. As though by signs, He gives us a clear foretaste of what will be given to those He brings to His kingdom. And to those to whom He gives here below the kingdom we ask for, He gives pledges so that through these they may have great hope of going to enjoy perpetually what here on earth is given only in sips.

7. If you wouldn't say that I'm treating of contemplation, this petition would provide a good opportunity for speaking a little about the beginning of pure contemplation; those who ex-

perience this prayer call it the prayer of quiet. But since, as I say, I'm dealing with vocal prayer, it may seem to anyone who doesn't know about the matter that vocal prayer doesn't go with contemplation; but I know that it does. Pardon me, but I want to say this: I know there are many persons who while praying vocally, as has already been mentioned,[4] are raised by God to sublime contemplation [without their striving for anything or understanding how. It's because of this that I insist so much, daughters, upon your reciting vocal prayer well.] I know a person[5] who was never able to pray any way but vocally, and though she was tied to this form of prayer she experienced everything else. And if she didn't recite vocal prayer her mind wandered so much that she couldn't bear it. Would that our mental prayer were as good! She spent several hours reciting a certain number of Our Fathers, in memory of the times our Lord shed His blood, as well as a few other vocal prayers. Once she came to me very afflicted because she didn't know how to practice mental prayer nor could she contemplate; she could only pray vocally. I asked her how she was praying, and I saw that though she was tied to the Our Father she experienced pure contemplation and that the Lord was raising her up and joining her with Himself in union. And from her deeds it seemed truly that she was receiving such great favors, for she was living a very good life. So I praised the Lord and envied her for her vocal prayer.

If this account is true, as it is, those of you who are the enemies of contemplatives should not think that you are free from being a contemplative if you recite your vocal prayers as they should be recited, with a pure conscience. [And so I will speak of this again. Whoever doesn't want to hear it may pass on.]

Chapter 31

Continues on the same subject. Explains the nature of the prayer of quiet. Gives some advice for those who experience it. This chapter should be carefully noted.

WELL, DAUGHTERS, I NONETHELESS want to explain this prayer of quiet. I have heard talk about it, or the Lord has given me understanding of it, perhaps, that I might tell you of it [and that others may praise Him; although since I have written about it elsewhere, as I said, I will not give lengthy explanations but just say something.] In this prayer it seems the Lord begins, as I have said,[1] to show that He hears our petition. He begins now to give us His kingdom here below so that we may truly praise and hallow His name and strive that all persons do so.

2. This prayer is something supernatural, something we cannot procure through our own efforts. In it the soul enters into peace or, better, the Lord puts it at peace by His presence, as He did to the just Simeon,[2] so that all the faculties are calmed. The soul understands in another way, very foreign to the way it understands through the exterior senses, that it is now close to its God and that not much more would be required for it to become one with Him in union. This is not because it sees Him with the eyes either of the body or of the soul. The just Simeon didn't see any more than the glorious, little, poor child. For by the way the child was clothed and by the few people that were in the procession, Simeon could have easily judged the babe to be the son of poor people rather than the Son of our heavenly Father. But the child Himself made Simeon understand. And this is how the soul understands here, although not with as much clarity. For the soul, likewise, fails to understand how it understands. But it sees it is in the kingdom, at least near the King who will give the kingdom to the soul. And seemingly the soul has so much reverence that it doesn't even dare ask for this. The state resembles an interior and exterior swoon; for the exterior man (or so that you will understand me better, I mean the body [for some simpleton will come along who won't know what "interior" and "exterior" means])

doesn't want any activity. But like one who has almost reached the end of his journey he wants to rest so as to be better able to continue; in this rest his strength for the journey is doubled.

3. A person feels the greatest delight in his body and a great satisfaction in his soul. He feels so happy merely with being close to the fount that he is satisfied even without drinking. It doesn't seem there is anything else for him to desire. The faculties are still; they wouldn't want to be busy; everything else seems to hinder them from loving. But they are not completely lost; they can think of who it is they are near, for two of them are free. The will is the one that is captive here. If there is some sorrow that can be experienced while in this state, that sorrow comes from a realization that the will must return to the state of being free. The intellect wouldn't want to understand more than one thing; nor would the memory want to be occupied with anything else. Persons in this prayer see that only this one thing is necessary, and everything else disturbs them. They don't want the body to move because it seems they would thereby lose that peace; thus they don't dare stir. It pains them to speak; in their saying "Our Father" just once a whole hour passes. They are so close that they see they are understanding as though through signs. They are within the palace, near the King, and they see that He is beginning to give them here His kingdom. It doesn't seem to them that they are in the world, nor would they want to see or hear about anything other than their God. Nothing pains them, nor does it seem anything ever will. In sum, while this prayer lasts they are so absorbed and engulfed with the satisfaction and delight they experience within themselves that they do not remember there is more to desire; they would eagerly say with St. Peter: "Lord, let us build three dwelling places here."[3]

4. Sometimes in this prayer of quiet the Lord grants another favor which is very difficult to understand if there is not a great deal of experience. But if there is some experience, the one who receives it will immediately understand. It will be a great consolation for you to know what it is, and I believe God often grants this favor together with the other one. When this quiet is great and lasts for a long while, it seems to me that the will

wouldn't be able to remain so long in that peace if it weren't bound to something. For it may happen that we will go about with this satisfaction for a day or two and will not understand ourselves—I mean those who experience it—and they definitely see that they are not wholly in what they are doing, but that the best part is lacking, that is, the will. The will, in my opinion, is then united with its God, and leaves the other faculties free to be occupied in what is for His service—and they then have much more ability for this. But in worldly matters, these faculties are dull and at times as though in a stupor.

5. This is a great favor for those to whom the Lord grants it; the active and the contemplative lives are joined. The faculties all serve the Lord together: the will is occupied in its work and contemplation without knowing how; the other two faculties serve in the work of Martha. Thus Martha and Mary walk together.

I know someone whom the Lord often placed in this state. She didn't know what to make of it and asked a great contemplative. He answered that the experience was very possible, that it had happened to him.[4] Thus, I think that because the soul is so satisfied in this prayer of quiet the faculty of the will remains more continually united with Him who alone can satisfy it.

6. I think it would be good here to give some counsels for those of you, Sisters, whom the Lord, solely through His goodness, has brought here, for I know there are some of you.

The first is that since they see themselves in that contentment and do not know how it came on them—at least they see they cannot obtain it by themselves—they experience this temptation: they think they'll be able to hold on to that satisfaction and they don't even dare take a breath. This is foolish, for just as there's nothing we can do to make the sun rise, there's little we can do to keep it from setting. This prayer is no longer our work, for it's something very supernatural and something very much beyond our power to acquire by ourselves. The best way to hold on to this favor is to understand clearly that we can neither bring it about nor remove it; we can only receive it with gratitude, as most unworthy of it; and this not with many words, but by raising our eyes to Him, as the publican did.[5]

7. It is good to find more solitude so as to make room for the Lord and allow His Majesty to work as though with something belonging to Him. At most, a gentle word from time to time is sufficient, as in the case of one who blows on a candle to enkindle it again when it begins to die out. But if the candle is burning, blowing on it will in my opinion serve no other purpose than to put it out. I say that the blowing should be gentle lest the will be distracted by the intellect busying itself with many words.

8. And note well, friends, this counsel that I now wish to give, for you'll often see that you'll be unable to manage these other two faculties.[6] It happens that the soul will be in the greatest quiet and the intellect will be so distracted that it won't seem that the quiet is present in the intellect's house. It seems to the intellect, during that time, that it is nowhere else than in a stranger's house, as a guest, and seeking other dwelling places because the house it's in doesn't satisfy it and it knows little about how to remain stable. Perhaps it's only my intellect that's like this, and others' intellects are not. I am speaking about myself, for sometimes I want to die in that I cannot cure this wandering of the intellect. At other times I think it takes up residence in its own house and accompanies the will. It's a wonderful thing when all three faculties are in accord. It's like what happens between two married people: if they love each other, the one wants what the other wants. But if the husband is unhappily married, it's easy to see what disturbance he'll cause his wife. Thus when the will finds itself in this quiet [and note well this counsel, for the matter is important], it shouldn't pay any more attention to the intellect than it would to a madman. For should it want to keep the intellect near itself, it will necessarily have to be somewhat disturbed and disquieted. And in this state of prayer everything will then amount to working without any further gain but with a loss of what the Lord was giving the will without its own work.

9. And notice carefully this comparison [for the Lord put it in my mind while I was at prayer]; it seems to me very ap-

propriate: the soul is like an infant that still nurses when at its mother's breast, and the mother without her babe's effort to suckle puts the milk in its mouth in order to give it delight. So it is here; for without effort of the intellect the will is loving, and the Lord desires that the will, without thinking about the matter, understand that it is with Him and that it does no more than swallow the milk His Majesty places in its mouth, and enjoy that sweetness. For the will knows that it is the Lord who is granting that favor. And the will rejoices in its enjoyment. It doesn't desire to understand how it enjoys the favor or what it enjoys; but it forgets itself during that time, for the One who is near it will not forget to observe what is fitting for it. If the will goes out to fight with the intellect so as to give a share of the experience, by drawing the intellect after itself, it cannot do so at all; it will be forced to let the milk fall from its mouth and lose that divine nourishment.

10. This is the way this prayer of quiet is different from that prayer in which the entire soul is united with God, for then the soul doesn't even go through the process of swallowing this divine food. Without its understanding how, the Lord places the milk within it. In this prayer of quiet it seems that He wants it to work a little, although so gently that it almost doesn't feel its effort. [Whoever experiences this prayer will understand clearly what I'm saying if after having read this he reflects on it carefully; and let him consider how important the matter is. If he doesn't experience the prayer, this will seem like gibberish.] That which torments the will is the intellect. The intellect doesn't cause this torment when there is union of all three faculties, for He who created them suspends them. With the joy He gives them He keeps them all occupied without their knowing or understanding how. Thus, as I say, they feel this prayer within themselves, a quiet and great contentment of the will, without being able to discern what it is specifically. Yet the soul easily discerns that it is far different from earthly satisfactions and that ruling the world with all its delights wouldn't be enough to make the soul feel that delight within itself. The delight is in the interior of the will, for the other consolations of life, it seems to me, are enjoyed in the exterior of the will, as in the outer bark, we might say. When the will

sees itself in this degree of prayer so sublime (for the prayer is, as I have already said,[7] very recognizably supernatural), it laughs at the intellect as at a fool when this intellect—or mind, to explain myself better—goes off to the more foolish things of the world. The will remains in its quietude, for the intellect will come and go. In this prayer the will is the ruler and the powerful one. It will draw the intellect after itself without your being disturbed. And if the will should desire to draw the intellect by force of arms, the strength it has against the intellect will be lost. This strength comes from eating and receiving that divine food. And neither the will nor the intellect will gain anything, but both will lose. As the saying goes, whoever tries to grasp too much loses everything; this it seems to me is what will happen here. Experience will enable one to understand, for I wouldn't be surprised if to anyone who doesn't have this experience what I've said would seem very obscure and unnecessary. But I've already mentioned[8] that with a little experience one will understand it, be able to benefit from it, and will praise the Lord because He was pleased that I managed to explain it here.

11. Now, then, let's conclude by saying that to the soul placed in this prayer it seems the Eternal Father has already here below granted its petition for His kingdom. Oh, blessed request, in which, without realizing it, we ask for so much good! What a blessed way of asking! For this reason, Sisters, I want us to look at how we recite this prayer, the Our Father, and all other vocal prayers. For when this favor is granted by God, we shall forget the things of the world; when the Lord of the world arrives He casts out everything else. I don't say that all those who experience this prayer must by necessity be completely detached from the world. At least, I would like them to know what is lacking and that they humble themselves and try to go on detaching themselves from everything; if they don't, they will remain in this state. A soul to whom God gives such pledges has a sign that He wants to give it a great deal; if not impeded through its own fault, it will advance very far. But if the Lord sees that after He places the kingdom of heaven in the soul's house this soul turns to earthly things, He will not only fail to

show it the secrets there are in His kingdom but will seldom grant it this favor, and then for just a short space of time.

12. Now it could be that I am mistaken in this matter, but I see and know that this is what happens, and in my opinion this is why there are not many more spiritual persons. When individuals do not respond by service that is in conformity with so great a favor, when they do not prepare themselves to receive it again, but take back their wills from the hands of the Lord who already possesses these wills as His own, and set them upon base things, the Lord goes in search of those who do love Him so as to give more to them. Yet He doesn't take away entirely what He has given, when one lives with a pure conscience. But there are persons—and I have been one of them—who make themselves deaf when the Lord, taking pity on them, gives them holy inspirations and light concerning the nature of things, and, in sum, gives this kingdom and places them in this prayer of quiet. For they are so fond of speaking and reciting many vocal prayers very quickly, like one who wants to get a job done, since they oblige themselves to recite these every day, that even though, as I say, the Lord places His kingdom in their hands, they do not receive it. But with their vocal prayers they think they are doing better, and they distract themselves from the prayer of quiet.

13. Do not do this, Sisters, but be on your guard when the Lord grants you this favor. Consider that you are losing a great treasure and that you do much more by saying one word of the Our Father from time to time than by rushing through the entire prayer many times. You are very close to the One you petition; He will not fail to hear you. And believe that herein lies the true praise and hallowing of His name. For now, as one who is in His house, you glorify the Lord and praise Him with more affection and desire; and it seems that you cannot fail to serve Him. [Thus I counsel you to be very careful in this matter because it is extremely important.]

Chapter 32

Discusses the words of the Our Father, Fiat voluntas tua sicut in caelo et in terra; *the great deal a person does when he says them with full determination; and how well the Lord repays this. [So I counsel you to be attentive because the matter is very important.]*

NOW THAT OUR GOOD MASTER has asked, and taught us to ask, for something so highly valuable that it includes everything we can desire here below and that He has granted us so wonderful a favor as to make us His brothers, let us see what He desires us to give His Father, and how He offers this gift for us and what He asks of us. For it is right that we somehow serve Him in return for such great favors. O good Jesus! What You give on our behalf in return for what You requested for us is no small thing, although it really amounts to nothing when compared to the greatness of the Lord and what we owe Him. But certainly, my Lord, You do not leave us empty-handed when we give You everything we can—I mean if we really give it, as we say we will.

2. "Your will be done on earth as it is in heaven." You did well, good Master of ours, to make this petition so that we might accomplish what You give on our behalf. For certainly, Lord, if You hadn't made the petition, the task would seem to me impossible. But when Your Father does what You ask Him by giving us His kingdom here on earth, I know that we shall make Your words come true by giving what You give for us. For once the earth has become heaven, the possibility is there for Your will to be done in me. But if the earth hasn't—and earth as wretched and barren as mine—I don't know, Lord, how it will be possible. It is indeed a great thing, that which You offer!

3. When I think of this, I am amused by persons who don't dare ask for trials from the Lord, for they suppose that in doing so they will be given them at once. I'm not speaking of those who fail to do so out of humility, thinking they will be incapable of suffering them; although I myself hold that He, who gives these persons the love to ask for these means, which are so

harsh, in order that they may show their love, will give them the capacity to suffer them. I would like to question those who fear to ask for trials, lest these be given them at once, about what they say when they beseech the Lord to do His will in them. Perhaps they say the words just to say what everyone else is saying but not so that His will be done. To do this, Sisters, would not be right. Consider that Jesus acts here as our ambassador and that He has desired to intervene between us and His Father, and at no small cost of His own. It would not be right for us to fail to do what He has offered on our behalf; if we don't want to do it we shouldn't say these words.

4. Now let me put it in another way. Look, daughters, His will must be done whether we like this or not, and it will be done in heaven and on earth. Believe me, take my advice, and make a virtue of necessity. O my Lord, what a great comfort this is for me, that you didn't want the fulfillment of Your will to depend on a will as wretched as mine! May You be blessed forever, and may all things praise You! Your name be glorified forever! I'd be in a fine state, Lord, if it were up to me as to whether or not Your will were to be done! Now I freely give mine to You, even though I do so at a time in which I'm not free of self-interest. For I have felt and have had great experience of the gain that comes from freely abandoning my will to Yours. O friends, what a great gain there is here! Oh, what a great loss there is when we do not carry out what we offer to the Lord in the Our Father!

5. Before I tell you about what is gained, I want to explain the great deal you offer so that afterward you won't take back what you gave, claiming that you hadn't understood. Don't be like some religious who do nothing but promise; and when we don't follow through, we make an excuse saying we didn't understand what we were promising. And this could be so, because to say that we abandon our will to another's will seems very easy until through experience we realize that this is the hardest thing one can do if one does it as it should be done. But superiors are not always strict in leading us since they see we are weak. And at times they lead both the weak and the strong in the same way. With the Lord, such is not the case; He knows

what each one can suffer. He does not delay in doing His will in anyone He sees has strength.[1]

6. Well, I want to advise you and remind you what His will is. Don't fear that it means He will give you riches, or delights, or honors, or all these earthly things. His love for you is not that small, and He esteems highly what you give Him. He wants to repay you well, for He gives you His kingdom while you are still alive. Do you want to know how He answers those who say these words to Him sincerely? Ask His glorious Son, who said them while praying in the Garden.[2] Since they were said with such determination and complete willingness, see if the Father's will wasn't done fully in Him through the trials, sorrows, injuries, and persecutions He suffered until His life came to an end through death on a cross.

7. Well, see here, daughters, what He gave to the one He loved most. By that we understand what His will is. For these are His gifts in this world. He gives according to the love He bears us: to those He loves more, He gives more of these gifts; to those He loves less, He gives less. And He gives according to the courage He sees in each and the love each has for His Majesty. He will see that whoever loves Him much will be able to suffer much for Him; whoever loves Him little will be capable of little. I myself hold that the measure for being able to bear a large or small cross is love. So, Sisters, if you love Him, strive that what you say to the Lord may not amount to mere polite words; strive to suffer what His Majesty desires you to suffer. For, otherwise, when you give your will, it would be like showing a jewel to another, making a gesture to give it away, and asking that he take it; but when he extends his hand to accept it, you pull yours back and hold on tightly to the jewel.

8. This is no way to mock Him who was the butt of so much mockery for our sakes. Even if there were no other reason, it would not be right to mock Him so often; the number of times we say the Our Father is not small. Let's give Him the jewel once and for all, no matter how many times we have tried to give it before. The truth is that He rewards us beforehand so that we might give it to Him. [Oh, God help me, how obvious it is that my good Jesus knows us! For He doesn't say at the outset

that we should give this will to the Lord, but first reveals that we will be well paid for this little service and that the Lord wants us to benefit a great deal by it. Even in this life He begins to reward us, as I shall now say.] Those in the world will be doing enough if they truly have the determination to do His will. You, daughters, will express this determination by both saying and doing, by both words and deeds, as indeed it seems we religious do. But at times we not only commit ourselves to giving the jewel but place it in His hand, only to take it back again. We are quick to be generous, but afterward so stingy that it would have been more fruitful, in part, if we had delayed in giving.

9. Because everything I have advised you about in this book is directed toward the complete gift of ourselves to the Creator, the surrender of our wills to His, and detachment from creatures—and you have understood how important this is—I'm not going to say any more about the matter; but I will explain why our good Master teaches us to say the words mentioned above, as one who knows the many things we gain by rendering this service to His eternal Father. For we are preparing ourselves that we may quickly reach the end of our journey and drink the living water from the fount we mentioned.[3] Unless we give our wills entirely to the Lord so that in everything pertaining to us He might do what conforms with His will, we will never be allowed to drink from this fount. Drinking from it is perfect contemplation, that which you told me to write about.

10. In this contemplation, as I have already written,[4] we don't do anything ourselves. Neither do we labor, nor do we bargain, nor is anything else necessary—because everything else is an impediment and hindrance—than to say *fiat voluntas tua:* Your will, Lord, be done in me in every way and manner that You, my Lord, want. If You want it to be done with trials, strengthen me and let them come; if with persecutions, illnesses, dishonors, and a lack of life's necessities, here I am; I will not turn away, my Father, nor is it right that I turn my back on You. Since Your Son gave You this will of mine in the name of all, there's no reason for any lack on my part. But

grant me the favor of Your kingdom that I may do Your will, since He asked for this kingdom for me, and use me as You would Your own possession, in conformity with Your will.

11. O my Sisters, what strength lies in this gift! It does nothing less, when accompanied by the necessary determination, than draw the Almighty so that He becomes one with our lowliness, transforms us into Himself, and effects a union of the Creator with the creature. Behold whether or not you are well paid and have a good Master; since He knows how the love of His Father can be obtained, He teaches us how and by what means we must serve Him.

12. And the more our deeds show that these are not merely polite words, all the more does the Lord bring us to Himself and raise the soul from itself and all earthly things so as to make it capable of receiving great favors, for He never finishes repaying this service in the present life. He esteems it so highly that we do not ourselves know how to ask for ourselves, and His Majesty never tires of giving. Not content with having made this soul one with Himself, He begins to find His delight in it, reveal His secrets, and rejoice that it knows what it has gained and something of what He will give it. He makes it lose these exterior senses so that nothing will occupy it. This is rapture. And He begins to commune with the soul in so intimate a friendship that He not only gives it back its own will but gives it His. For in so great a friendship the Lord takes joy in putting the soul in command, as they say, and He does what it asks since it does His will. And He does this even better than the soul itself could, for He is powerful and does whatever He wants and never stops wanting this.

13. The poor soul cannot do what it desires even though it may want to; nor can it give anything save what is given. This is its greatest wealth: the more it serves, the more indebted it remains. It often grows weary seeing itself subject to so many difficulties, impediments, and fetters, which result from dwelling in the prison of this body. It would want to repay something of what it owes. To grow weary is quite foolish; for even though one does what's in one's power, what can those of us repay who, as I say, don't have anything save what we have received? All

we can do is know ourselves and what we are capable of, which is to give our will, and give it completely. Everything else encumbers the soul brought here by the Lord and causes it harm rather than benefit. Only humility can do something, a humility not acquired by the intellect, but by a clear perception that comprehends in a moment the truth one would be unable to grasp in a long time through the work of the imagination about what a trifle we are and how very great God is.

14. I give you one counsel: that you don't think that through your own strength or efforts you can arrive, for reaching this stage is beyond our power; if you try to reach it, the devotion you have will grow cold. But with simplicity and humility, which will achieve everything, say: *fiat voluntas tua.*

Chapter 33

Deals with the great need we have that the Lord give us what we ask for in these words of the Our Father: Panem nostrum quotidianum da nobis hodie.

AS I HAVE SAID,[1] Jesus understands what a difficult thing it is He offers for us. He knows our weakness, that we often show we do not understand what the Lord's will is. We are weak and He is merciful. He knows that a means was necessary. He saw it would not be in any way to our benefit if we failed to give what He gave, because all our gain lies in giving this. He saw that doing the Father's will was difficult. If we tell a rich person living in luxury that it is God's will that he be careful and use moderation at table so that others might at least have bread to eat, for they are dying of hunger, he will bring up a thousand reasons for not understanding this save in accordance with his own selfish purposes. If we tell a backbiter that it is God's will that he love his neighbor as himself, he will become impatient and no reason will suffice to make him understand. We can tell a religious who has grown accustomed to freedom and comfort that he should remember his obligation to give good example and keep in mind that when he says these words they be not just words but be put into practice since he has promised them under oath; and that it is God's will that he be faithful to his vows and that he should note that if he gives scandal he is acting very contrary to them, even though he may not be breaking them entirely; and that since he has promised poverty, he should observe it without subterfuge, for this is what the Lord wills. But it is just useless to insist nowadays with some of them. What would happen if the Lord had not provided for us with the remedy He gave? There would have been only a very few who would have carried out these words He spoke for us to the Father, *fiat voluntas tua*.

Now then, once Jesus saw the need, He sought out a wonderful means by which to show the extreme of His love for us, and in His own name and in that of His brothers He made the following petition: "Give us this day, Lord, our daily bread."

Let us understand, Sisters, for the love of God, what our good Master is asking for; it is a matter of life and death not to pass over these words hastily. Consider what you have given as very little since you will receive so much.

2. Now I think—unless one has a better opinion—that Jesus observed what He had given for us, how important it was that we in turn give this, and the great difficulty there is in our doing so, as was said,[2] since we are the way we are: inclined to base things and with so little love and courage that it was necessary for us to see His love and courage in order to be awakened—and not just once but every day. After He saw all this, He must have resolved to remain with us here below. Since to do this was something so serious and important, He desired that it come from the hand of the Eternal Father. For even though they are one and He knew that what He did on earth God would do in heaven and consider good—since His will and that of His Father were one—the humility of Jesus was such that He wanted, as it were, to ask permission. He already knew that His Father loved Him and took His delight in Him.[3] He well understood that He was asking for more in this request than He was in the others, for He knew beforehand the death they would make Him die and the dishonors and insults He would suffer.

3. Well, what father could there be, Lord, who in having given us his son, and a son like this who receives such treatment, would consent that he remain among us every day to suffer? Certainly no father, Lord, but Yours. You well know whom You are petitioning.

Oh, God help me, what great love from the Son and what great love from the Father! Yet I am not so surprised about Jesus, for since He had already said, *fiat voluntas tua*, He had to do that will, being who He is. Yes, for He is not like us! Since, then, He knows that He does it by loving us as Himself, He went about looking for ways of doing it with greater perfection, even though His fulfillment of this commandment was at a cost to Himself. But You, Eternal Father, how is it that You consented? Why do You desire to see Your Son every day in such wretched hands? Since You have already desired to see Him in these hands and given Your consent, You have seen how they treated Him. How can You in Your compassion now see Him insulted day after day? And how many insults will be committed today against this Most Blessed Sacrament! In how many enemies' hands must the Father see Him! How much irreverence from these heretics!

4. O eternal Lord! Why do You accept such a petition? Why do You consent to it? Don't look at His love for us, because in exchange for doing Your will perfectly, and doing it for us, He allows Himself to be crushed to pieces each day. It is for You, my Lord, to look after Him, since He will let nothing deter Him. Why must all our good come at His expense? Why does He remain silent before all and not know how to speak for Himself, but only for us? Well, shouldn't there be someone to speak for this most loving Lamb? [Allow me, Lord, to speak—since You have willed to leave Him to our power—and to beseech You since He so truly obeyed You and with so much love gave Himself to us.] I have noticed how in this petition alone He repeats the words: first He says and asks the Father to give us this daily bread, and then repeats, "give it to us this day, Lord," invoking the Father again.[4] It's as though Jesus tells the Father that He is now ours since the Father has given Him to us to die for us; and asks that the Father not take Him

from us until the end of the world; that He allow Him to serve each day. May this move your hearts, my daughters, to love your Spouse, for there is no slave who would willingly say he is a slave, and yet it seems that Jesus is honored to be one.

5. O Eternal Father! How much this humility deserves! What treasure do we have that could buy Your Son? The sale of Him, we already know, was for thirty pieces of silver.[5] But to buy Him, no price is sufficient. Since by sharing in our nature He has become one with us here below—and as Lord of His own will—He reminds the Father that because He belongs to Him the Father in turn can give Him to us. And so He says, "our bread." He doesn't make any difference between Himself and us, but we make one by not giving ourselves up each day for His Majesty.

Chapter 34

Continues on the same subject. The matter is very helpful with regard to the time immediately following reception of the most Blessed Sacrament.

IN THIS PETITION THE WORD "DAILY" seems to mean forever. Reflecting upon why after the word "daily" the Lord said "give us this day, Lord," that is, be ours every day, I've come to think that it is because here on earth we possess Him and also in heaven we will possess Him if we profit well by His company.[1] He, in fact, doesn't remain with us for any other reason than to help, encourage, and sustain us in doing this will that we have prayed might be done in us.

2. In saying "this day," it seems to me, He is referring to one day: that which lasts as long as the world and no longer. And one day indeed! With regard to the unfortunate ones who will be condemned (who will not enjoy Him in the next life), it will not be the Lord's fault if they let themselves be conquered.[2] He doesn't stop encouraging them until the battle is over. They will have no excuse or complaint to make to the Father for tak-

ing Him away when they most need Him. So the Son tells His Father that because there is no more than one day the Father should let Him pass it in servitude. Since the Father has already given us His Son and, just because He wanted to, sent Him into the world, the Son, just because He wants to, desires not to abandon us but to remain here with us, to the greater glory of His friends and the affliction of His enemies. He asks again for no more than to be with us this day only, because it is a fact that He has given us this most sacred bread forever. His Majesty gave us, as I have said, the manna and nourishment of His humanity that we might find Him at will and not die of hunger,[3] save through our own fault. In no matter how many ways the soul may desire to eat, it will find delight and consolation in the most Blessed Sacrament. [I don't want to think the Lord had in mind the other bread that is used for our bodily needs and nourishment; nor would I want you to have that in mind. The Lord was in the most sublime contemplation (for whoever has reached such a stage has no more remembrance that he is in the world than if he were not, however much there may be to eat), and would He have placed so much emphasis on the petition that He as well as ourselves eat? It wouldn't make sense to me. He is teaching us to set our wills on heavenly things and to ask that we might begin enjoying Him from here below; and would He get us involved in something so base as asking to eat? As if He didn't know us! For once we start worrying about bodily needs, those of the soul will be forgotten! Well, we are such temperate people that we are satisfied by little and ask for little! On the contrary, the more He gives us the more we think we are lacking everything, even water. Let those, my daughters, who want more than is necessary ask for this material bread.] There is no need or trial or persecution that is not easy to suffer if we begin to enjoy the delight and consolation of this sacred bread.

3. Ask the Father, daughters, together with the Lord, to give you your Spouse "this day" so that you will not be seen in this world without Him. To temper such great happiness it's sufficient that He remain disguised in these accidents of bread and wine. This is torment enough for anyone who has no other love

than Him nor any other consolation. Beg Him not to fail you, and to give you the dispositions to receive Him worthily.

4. Don't worry about the other bread, those of you who have sincerely surrendered yourselves to the will of God. I mean during these times of prayer when you should be dealing with more important things; there are other times for working and for earning your bread. [Have no fear that you will be in want of bread if you are not wanting in what you have said about the surrender of yourselves to God's will. And indeed, daughters, I say for myself, if I should maliciously fail in this surrender, as I have many other times, I would not beg that He give me this bread or anything else to eat. Let me die of hunger; why should I want life if with it I am daily gaining more of eternal death?] Carefully avoid wasting your thoughts at any time on what you will eat. Let the body work, for it is good that you work to sustain yourselves; let your soul be at rest. Leave this care, as has been amply pointed out,[4] to your Spouse; He will care for you always.

5. Your attitude should be like that of a servant when he begins to serve. His care is about pleasing his master in everything. But the master is obliged to provide his servant with food as long as the servant is in the house and serves him, unless the master is so poor that he doesn't have enough either for himself or for his servant. In our case this isn't so; the Master always is, and will be, rich and powerful. Well, it wouldn't be right for the servant to go about asking for food when he knows that the master of the house takes care of providing it for him, and must do so. The master would rightly tell his servant to be occupied in serving and seeking ways to please the master, for the servant, by worrying about what isn't his own business, would be doing everything wrong.

Thus, Sisters, let whoever wants be concerned with asking for this bread. As for ourselves, let us ask the Eternal Father that we might merit to receive our heavenly bread in such a way that the Lord may reveal Himself to the eyes of our soul and make Himself thereby known since our bodily eyes cannot delight in beholding Him, because He is so hidden. Such knowledge is another kind of satisfying and delightful sustenance that maintains life. [In order to sustain life we will be desiring that other bread more often than we want and asking for it even without realizing we're doing so. There's no need to stir ourselves to ask for it; for our wretched tendency toward base things will awaken us, as I say, more often than we may desire. But let us watch so that we don't advertently place our care on anything other than begging the Lord for what I have mentioned; in having this, we will have everything.]

6. Do you think this heavenly food fails to provide sustenance, even for these bodies, that it is not a great medicine even for bodily ills? I know that it is. I know a person[5] with serious illnesses, who often experiences great pain, who through this bread had them taken away as though by a gesture of the hand and was made completely well. This is a common experience, and the illnesses are very recognizable, for I don't think they could be feigned. And because the wonders this most sacred bread effects in those who worthily receive it are well known, I will not mention many that could be mentioned regarding this person I've spoken of. I was able to know of them, and I know that this is no lie. But the Lord had given her such living faith that when she heard some persons saying they would have liked to have lived at the time Christ our Good walked in the world, she used to laugh to herself. She wondered what more they wanted since in the most Blessed Sacrament they had Him just as truly present as He was then.

7. But I know that for many years, when she received Communion, this person, though she was not very perfect, strove to strengthen her faith so that in receiving her Lord it was as if, with her bodily eyes, she saw Him enter her house. Since she believed that this Lord truly entered her poor home, she freed herself from all exterior things when it was possible and entered to be with Him. She strove to recollect the senses so that all of them would take notice of so great a good, I mean that they would not impede the soul from recognizing it. She considered she was at His feet and wept with the Magdalene, no more nor less than if she were seeing Him with her bodily

eyes in the house of the Pharisee.[6] And even though she didn't feel devotion, faith told her that He was indeed there.

8. If we don't want to be fools and blind the intellect there's no reason for doubt. Receiving Communion is not like picturing with the imagination, as when we reflect upon the Lord on the cross or in other episodes of the Passion, when we picture within ourselves how things happened to Him in the past. In Communion the event is happening now, and it is entirely true. There's no reason to go looking for Him in some other place farther away. Since we know that Jesus is with us as long as the natural heat doesn't consume the accidents of bread, we should approach Him. Now, then, if when He went about in the world the mere touch of His robes cured the sick,[7] why doubt, if we have faith, that miracles will be worked while He is within us and that He will give what we ask of Him, since He is in our house? His Majesty is not accustomed to paying poorly for His lodging if the hospitality is good.

9. If it pains you not to see Him with your bodily eyes, consider that seeing Him so is not fitting for us. To see Him in His glorified state is different from seeing Him as He was when He walked through this world. On account of our natural weakness there is no person capable of enduring such a glorious sight, nor would anyone in the world want to continue in it. In seeing this Eternal Truth one would see that all the things we pay attention to here below are lies and jokes. And in beholding such great Majesty, how would a little sinner like myself who has so much offended Him remain so close to Him? Beneath that bread He is easy to deal with. If a king were disguised it wouldn't matter to us at all if we conversed with him without so many gestures of awe and respect. It seems he would be obliged to put up with this lack since he is the one who disguised himself. Who would otherwise dare approach so unworthily, with so much lukewarmness, and with so many imperfections!

10. Oh, how we fail to know what we are asking for;[8] and how His wisdom provided in a better way! He reveals Himself to those who He sees will benefit by His presence. Even though they fail to see Him with their bodily eyes, He has many

methods of showing Himself to the soul, through great interior feelings and through other different ways. Be with Him willingly; don't lose so good an occasion for conversing with Him as is the hour after having received Communion.[9] If obedience should command something, Sisters, strive to leave your soul with the Lord. If you immediately turn your thoughts to other things, if you pay no attention and take no account of the fact that He is within you, how will He be able to reveal Himself to you? This, then, is a good time for our Master to teach us, and for us to listen to Him, kiss His feet because He wanted to teach us, and beg Him not to leave.[10]

11. If you have to pray to Him by looking at His picture, it would seem to me foolish. You would be leaving the Person Himself in order to look at a picture of Him. Wouldn't it be silly if a person we love very much and of whom we have a portrait came to see us and we stopped speaking with him so as to carry on a conversation with the portrait? Do you want to know when it is very good to have a picture of Christ and when it is a thing in which I find much delight? When He himself is absent, or when by means of a great dryness He wants to make us feel He is absent. It is then a wonderful comfort to see an image of One whom we have so much reason to love.[11] Wherever I turn my eyes, I would want to see His image. With what better or more pleasing thing can our eyes be occupied than with One who loves so much and who has in Himself all goods. Unfortunate are those heretics who through their own fault have lost this consolation among others.

12. But after having received the Lord, since you have the Person Himself present, strive to close the eyes of the body and open those of the soul and look into your own heart. For I tell you, and tell you again, and would like to tell you many times that you should acquire the habit of doing this every time you receive Communion and strive to have such a conscience that you will be allowed to enjoy this blessing frequently. Though He comes disguised, the disguise as I have said,[12] does not prevent Him from being recognized in many ways, in conformity with the desire we have to see Him. And you can desire to see Him so much that He will reveal Himself to you entirely.

13. On the other hand, if we pay no attention to Him but after receiving Him leave Him and go seeking after other base things, what is there for Him to do? Must He force us to see Him, since He wants to reveal Himself to us? No, for they didn't treat Him so well when He let Himself be seen openly by all and told them clearly who He was; very few were those who believed Him. So His Majesty is being merciful enough to all of us who love Him, by letting us know that it is He who is present in the most Blessed Sacrament. He doesn't want to show Himself openly, communicate His grandeurs, and give His treasures except to those who He knows desire Him greatly; these are His true friends. I tell you that whoever is not His true friend and does not draw near to receive Him as such, by doing what lies in her power, will never trouble Him with requests that He reveal Himself. Such a person will hardly have fulfilled what the Church requires when she will leave and quickly forget what took place. Thus, such a person hurries on as soon as she can to other business affairs, occupations, and worldly impediments so that the Lord of the house may not occupy it.

Chapter 35

With a prayerful exclamation to the Eternal Father concludes the subject that was begun.

BECAUSE THIS MATTER is so important I have greatly enlarged upon it, even though in discussing the prayer of recollection I spoke of the significance of entering within ourselves to be alone with God. When you do not receive Communion, daughters, but hear Mass, you can make a spiritual communion. Spiritual communion is highly beneficial; through it you can recollect yourselves in the same way after Mass, for the love of this Lord is thereby deeply impressed on the soul. If we prepare ourselves to receive Him, He never fails to give in many ways which we do not understand. It is like approaching a fire; even though the fire may be a large one, it will not be able to warm you well if you turn away and hide your hands, though you will still get more heat than you would if you were in a place without one. But it is something else if we desire to approach Him. If the soul is disposed (I mean, if it wants to get warm), and if it remains there for a while, it will stay warm for many hours.

2. Now then, Sisters, consider that if in the beginning you do not fare well (for it could be that the devil will make you feel afflicted and constrained in heart since he knows the great damage that will be caused him by this recollection), the devil will make you think you find more devotion in other things and less in this recollection after Communion. Do not abandon this practice; the Lord will see in it how much you love Him. Remember that there are few souls who accompany Him and follow Him in trials. Let us suffer something for Him; His Majesty will repay you for it. Remember also how many persons there are who not only refuse to remain with Him but rudely reject Him. Well, we have to suffer something that He may understand we desire to see Him. And since He suffers and will suffer everything in order to find even one soul that will receive Him and lovingly keep Him within, let your desire be to do this. If there isn't anyone who will do it, the Eternal Father will rightly refuse to let Him remain with us. But the Father is so fond of friends and so much the Lord of His servants that in seeing the will of His good Son He doesn't want to hinder this excellent work; in it the Son's love for Him is fully demonstrated [by the invention of this admirable means in which He shows how much He loves us and helps us suffer our trials.]

3. Well, holy Father in heaven, since You desire and accept this work, and it is clear that You will not deny us anything that is good for us, there has to be someone, as I said in the beginning,[1] who will speak for Your Son since He never looks out for Himself. Let us be the ones, daughters, even though the thought is a bold one, we being who we are. But obeying and trusting in the Lord's command to us that we ask,[2] let us beseech His Majesty in the name of Jesus that, since nothing remained for Him to do and He left sinners a gift as great as this one, He might in His compassion desire and be pleased to pro-

vide a remedy that His Son may not be this badly treated. Let us beseech Him that, since His Son provided a means so good that we may offer Him many times in sacrifice, this precious gift may avail; that there'll be no advance made in the very great evil and disrespect committed and shown in places where this most Blessed Sacrament is present among those Lutherans, where churches are destroyed, so many priests lost, and the sacraments taken away.[3]

4. Well, what is this, my Lord and my God! Either bring the world to an end or provide a remedy for these very serious evils. There is no heart that can suffer them, not even among those of us who are wretched. I beseech You, Eternal Father, that You suffer them no longer. Stop this fire, Lord, for if You will You can. Behold that Your Son is still in the world. Through His reverence may all these ugly and abominable and filthy things cease. In His beauty and purity He doesn't deserve to be in a house where there are things of this sort. Do not answer for our sakes, Lord; we do not deserve it. Do it for Your Son's sake. We don't dare beseech You that He be not present with us; what would become of us? For if something appeases You, it is having a loved one like this here below. Since some means must be had, my Lord, may Your Majesty provide it.

5. O my God, would that I might have begged You much and served You diligently so as to be able to ask for this great favor in payment for my services, since You don't leave anyone without pay! But I have not done so, Lord; rather, perhaps I am the one who has angered You so that my sins have caused these many evils to come about. Well, what is there for me to do, my Creator, but offer this most blessed bread to You, and even though You have given it to us, return it to You and beg You through the merits of Your Son to grant me this favor since in so many ways He has merited that You do so? Now, Lord, now; make the sea calm! May this ship, which is the Church, not always have to journey in a tempest like this. Save us, Lord, for we are perishing.[4]

Chapter 36

Discusses these words of the Our Father: Dimitte nobis debita nostra.

SINCE OUR GOOD MASTER SAW that with this heavenly bread everything is easy for us, save through our own fault, and that we can carry out very well what we have said about the Father's will being done in us, He now tells the Father to forgive us our debts since we ourselves forgive. Thus, He says, going on with the prayer He teaches us, "And forgive us, Lord, our debts as we forgive our debtors."[1]

2. Let us observe, Sisters, that He doesn't say "as we will forgive." We can thereby understand that whoever asks for a gift as great as the one last mentioned and whoever has already surrendered his will to God's will should have already forgiven. So, He says, "as we forgive." Thus, whoever may have said sincerely to the Lord *fiat voluntas tua* should have done that will entirely; at least have had the resolve to.

You see here why the saints were pleased with the wrongs and persecutions they suffered; they then had something to offer the Lord when they prayed to Him. What will someone as poor as I do, who has had so little to pardon and so much to be pardoned for?

This is a matter, Sisters, that we should reflect upon very much: that something so serious and important, as that our Lord forgive us our faults, which deserve eternal fire, be done by means of something so lowly as our forgiving others. And I have so little opportunity to offer even this lowly thing, that the Lord has to pardon me for nothing. [What can be said against someone like myself, or what wrong can be done to her who has deserved to be always mistreated by the demons? If the world were to treat me very badly, such mistreatment would be just. In sum, my Lord, I have nothing as a result to give You by means of which I may ask You to forgive my debts. May Your Son pardon me; no one has done me an injustice, and so I have nothing to pardon for your sake, unless, Lord, You accept my desire. It seems to me that anything I might forgive I would forgive in order that You would forgive me, or to do Your will unconditionally. Yet I don't know what I would do actually if I were condemned without fault. Now I see myself so deserving of blame in Your presence that everyone falls short with respect to blaming me; although those who do not know what I am, as You know, think they are offending me.] Here Your mercy fits in well. May You be blessed for putting up with one so poor as I. What Your Son says in the name of all has to exclude me because of what I am and because I am so penniless.

3. But, my Lord, are there some persons in my company who have not understood this? If there are, I beg them in Your name to remember this and pay no attention to the little things they call wrongs. It seems that, like children, we are making houses out of straw with these ceremonious little rules of etiquette. Oh, God help me, Sisters, if we knew what honor is and what losing honor consists in! Now I am not speaking of ourselves, for it would be quite bad for us not to have understood this yet, but of myself at the time when I prized honor without understanding what it was. I was following the crowd [through what I heard.] Oh, by how many things was I offended! I am ashamed now. Yet, I wasn't at that time one of those who pay close attention to these little rules of etiquette. But neither was I careful about the main rule, because I didn't consider or pay any heed to the honor that is beneficial; that is, the honor that benefits the soul. And how well it was said by whoever said it that honor and profit don't go together; although I don't know if it was said with this purpose in mind. But it is right to the point because the soul's profit and what the world calls honor can never go together. It's a frightful thing; the world moves in the opposite direction. Blessed be the Lord who drew us out of it. [May it please His Majesty that such a concept of honor always be as far from this house as it is now. God deliver us from monasteries where they pay attention to these ceremonious little rules. He is never much honored in such monasteries. God help me, what great foolishness, that religious seek honor in such trifles; I am astonished! You don't

know about this, Sisters, but I want to tell you about it so that you will guard yourselves against it.]

4. But consider, Sisters, that the devil hasn't forgotten us. He also invents his own honors in monasteries and establishes his own laws. There, people ascend and descend in rank just as in the world. Those with degrees must follow in order, according to their academic titles. Why? I don't know. The one who has managed to become professor of theology must not descend to professor of philosophy, for it is a point of honor that he must ascend and not descend. Even if obedience should command, he would consider the change an affront. And there will always be someone standing by to defend him and tell him that it's an insult; then the devil at once discloses reasons why even according to God's law this thinking seems right. Well, now, among ourselves: the one who has been prioress must remain ineligible for any lower office; a preoccupation about who the senior is—for we never forget this—and we even think at times we gain merit by such concern because the order commands it.

5. One doesn't know whether to laugh or to cry; the latter would be more fitting. The order doesn't command us to lack humility. It commands that there be a balanced arrangement of things, but I don't have to be so careful about this arrangement when it comes to matters of self-esteem that I am as concerned about these little ceremonious rules as about other practices that perhaps we observe imperfectly. All of our perfection doesn't consist in the observance of what has to do with our honor. Others will look after me if I forget about myself. The fact is that since we are inclined to ascend—even though we will not ascend to heaven by such an inclination—there must be no descending. O Lord, Lord! Are You our Model and Master? Yes, indeed! Well then, what did Your honor consist of, You who honored us? Didn't you indeed lose it in being humiliated unto death? No, Lord, but You won it for all.

6. Oh, for the love of God, Sisters, how we get lost on the road because we start out wrong from the beginning.[2] Please God no soul will be lost because it keeps these miserable little

rules of etiquette without understanding what honor consists in. And then we shall reach the point of thinking that we have done a great deal if we pardon one of these little things that was neither an offense, nor an injury, nor anything. Like someone who has accomplished something, we shall think that the Lord pardons us because we have pardoned others. Help us understand, my God, that we do not know ourselves and that we come to You with empty hands; and pardon us through Your mercy. [Indeed, You are always the wronged and the offended one.] Truly, Lord, since all things come to an end, but the punishment is without end, I don't see anything that would give us a reason to remind You to grant us so great a favor; unless You would grant it because of Your Son who asks it of You.

7. But yet, how the Lord must esteem this love we have for one another! Indeed, Jesus could have put other virtues first and said: forgive us, Lord, because we do a great deal of penance or because we pray much and fast or because we have left all for You and love You very much. He didn't say forgive us because we would give up our lives for You, or, as I say, because of other possible things. But He said only, "forgive us because we forgive." Perhaps He said the prayer and offered it on our behalf because He knows we are so fond of this miserable honor and that to be forgiving is a virtue difficult for us to attain by ourselves but most pleasing to His Father.

8. Well, consider carefully, Sisters, that He says, "as we forgive," as though it were something already being done, as I have mentioned.[3] And pay very close attention, for when among the favors God grants in the prayer of perfect contemplation that I mentioned[4] there doesn't arise in the soul a very resolute desire to pardon any injury however grave it may be and to pardon it in deed when the occasion arises, do not trust much in that soul's prayer. And I don't refer to these nothings that they call injuries. For the soul God brings to Himself in so sublime a contemplation is not touched by these wrongs nor does it care at all whether it is esteemed or not. I didn't say this well, "nor does it care at all," for it is much more afflicted by honor than by dishonor and by a lot of ease and

rest than by trials. For when truly the Lord has given His kingdom here below, the soul no longer desires honor in this world. And so as to reign more sublimely it understands that the above-mentioned way is the true way; it has already seen through experience the great gain and progress that comes to it by suffering for God. Very seldom does God give such great gifts, save to persons who have willingly undergone many trials for Him. As I have said in another part of this book,[5] the trials of contemplatives are great, and so the Lord looks for contemplatives among people who have been tested.

9. Now then, Sisters, realize that since these contemplatives already know what everything is worth, they are not long delayed by a passing thing. If at first a great affront or trial causes pain, their reason comes to their rescue, before the pain is fully felt, with another consideration as if to raise the banner and almost annihilate the pain by means of joy. This joy comes from their seeing that the Lord has placed in their hands something by which they will gain more graces and perpetual favors from His Majesty than they would in ten years through trials they might wish to undertake on their own. This is very common from what I understand, for I have dealt with many contemplatives and am certain that this is what happens. Just as others prize gold and jewels, they prize trials and desire them; they know that these latter are what will make them rich.

10. Self-esteem is far removed from these persons. They like others to know about their sins and like to tell about them when they see themselves esteemed. The same is true in matters concerning their lineage. They already know that in the kingdom without end they will have nothing to gain from this. If they should happen to be pleased to be of good descent, it's when this would be necessary in order to serve God. When it isn't, it grieves them to be taken for more than what they are; and without any grief at all but gladly they disillusion others. So it is with those to whom God grants the grace of this humility and great love for Himself. In what amounts to His greater service, they are already so forgetful of self that they can't even believe that others feel some things and consider them an affront.

11. These effects I just mentioned are found in persons who are closer to perfection and whom the Lord very habitually favors by bringing to Himself through perfect contemplation. But of the first effect, which is the resolve to suffer wrongs and suffer them even though this may be painful, I say that it will soon be possessed by anyone who has from the Lord this favor of the prayer of union. If one doesn't experience these effects and come away from prayer fortified in them, one may believe that the favor was not from God but an illusion, or the devil's gift bestowed so that we might consider ourselves more honored.

12. It can happen that in the beginning when the Lord grants these favors the soul will not immediately experience this fortitude. But I say that in a short while if He continues to grant them, it will have fortitude in this virtue of forgiving others even though it may not have fortitude in other virtues. I cannot believe that a person who comes so close to Mercy itself, where he realizes what he is and the great deal God has pardoned him of, would fail to pardon his offender immediately, in complete ease, and with a readiness to remain on very good terms with him. Such a person is mindful of the gift and favor granted by God, by which he saw signs of great love; and he rejoices that an opportunity is offered whereby he can show the Lord some love.

13. I repeat that I know many persons whom the Lord has favored by raising to supernatural things, giving them this prayer or contemplation that was mentioned and, even though I see other faults and imperfections in them, I have never seen anyone with this one; nor do I believe that such a fault will be present if the favors are from God, as I have said.[6] The one who receives greater favors should observe whether these effects are increasing within him. If he doesn't see any increase, he should be afraid and refuse to believe that these gifts are from God, as I have said. For God's favor always enriches the soul it reaches. This is certain. Although the favor and gift passes quickly, it is gradually recognized through the benefits the soul receives. Since Jesus knows this well, He says resolutely to His holy Father that "we pardon our debtors."

Chapter 37

Speaks of the excellence of this prayer, the Our Father, and of how we shall in many ways find consolation in it.

WE OUGHT TO GIVE GREAT PRAISE to the Lord for the sublime perfection of this evangelical prayer. Each of us, daughters, can apply the prayer to her own needs since it was composed by such a good Master. I marvel to see that in so few words everything about contemplation and perfection is included; it seems we need to study no other book than this one. Up to now the Lord has taught us the whole way of prayer and of high contemplation, from the beginning stages to mental prayer, to the prayer of quiet, and to that of union; so much so that, if I knew how to explain the matter, a large book on prayer could be written based on this genuine foundation.[1] From here on, the Lord begins to teach us about the effects of His favors, as you have seen.

2. I have wondered why His Majesty did not explain more about these sublime and obscure things that we might all know about them. It has seemed to me that since this prayer was intended for general use so that each one could petition according to his own intention, be consoled, and think that he has a good understanding of the prayer, the Lord left it in this obscure form. Contemplatives and persons already very much committed to God, who no longer desire earthly things, ask for the heavenly favors that can, through God's goodness, be given on earth. Those who still live on earth, and it is good that they live in conformity with their state in life, may ask also for bread. They must be sustained and must sustain their households. Such a petition is very just and holy, and so also is their petition for other things according to their needs.

3. But both should consider that two of the things mentioned pertain to all: giving Him our will and forgiving others. True, there is a more and a less in the degree to which this is done, as has been said.[2] The perfect will give their will in the way perfect souls do and forgive with that perfection that was

mentioned. We, Sisters, will do what we can; the Lord receives everything.[3] It seems that on our behalf He makes a kind of pact with His Eternal Father, like one who says: "You do this, Lord, and My brothers will do that." Well, surely He doesn't fail to do His part. Oh, oh, how well He pays! And He pays without measure!

4. We can say this prayer only once in such a way that the Lord will enrich us since He sees that we do so sincerely and are determined to do what we say. He likes us to be truthful with Him. If we speak plainly and clearly so that we don't say one thing and then act differently, He always gives more than what we ask of Him.

Our good Master knows this well. He knows that those who ask with perfection will be filled with such favors from His Father that they will reach a high state. In fact, those who are already perfect or those who are approaching it are not afraid of anything, nor should they be, since they have trampled the world underfoot, as the saying goes. The Lord of the world is pleased with them, and they have the greatest hope of this in the effects of the favors He grants them. Absorbed in these delights they don't want to remember even that there is a world or that they have enemies.

5. O Eternal Wisdom! O good Teacher! What a wonderful thing it is, daughters, to have a wise and cautious teacher who foresees the dangers. This is the entire good that a spiritual soul can desire here below because it provides great security. One could not exaggerate the importance of this. Thus since the Lord sees that it is necessary to awaken and remind us that we have enemies, that it is very dangerous to be negligent with regard to these enemies, and that we need much more help from the Eternal Father because our fall will be from a higher place, and so that we do not go about mistaken and without self-knowledge, He makes the following petitions so necessary for all as long as we live in this exile: "And lead us not, Lord, into temptation; but deliver us from evil."

Chapter 38

Deals with the great need we have to beseech the Eternal Father to grant us what we ask for in the words, Et ne nos inducas in tentationem, sed libera nos a malo; *and explains some temptations. The subject matter is important.*

WE HAVE GREAT THINGS to think about and understand here, Sisters, because these things are what we are asking for. Now see, I am certain that those who reach perfection do not ask the Lord to free them from trials or temptations or persecutions or struggles. This is another very great and certain effect of the contemplation and the favors His Majesty gives, and of the Lord's Spirit rather than of an illusion. On the contrary, as I have said a little while ago,[1] these persons desire, ask for, and love trials. They are like soldiers who are happier when there are more wars because they then hope to earn more. If there is no war, they receive their wages but realize they won't get rich.

2. Believe, Sisters, that the soldiers of Christ, those who experience contemplation and engage in prayer, are eager to fight. They never fear public enemies very much; they already recognize them and know that these enemies have no power against the strength the Lord gives and that they themselves always come out the victors and with much gain. They never turn from these enemies. Those whom they fear—and it is right they fear and always ask the Lord to be freed from them—are the traitorous enemies, the devils who transfigure themselves into angels of light,[2] who come disguised. Not until they have done much harm to the soul do they allow themselves to be recognized. They suck away our blood and destroy our virtues, and we go about in the midst of the same temptation but do not know it. With regard to these enemies, daughters, let us ask and often beg the Lord in the Our Father to free us and not let us walk into temptation, so that they will not draw us into error or hide the light and truth from us, that the poison will be discovered. Oh, how rightly does our good Master ask this for us and teach us to ask for it.

3. Consider, daughters, the many ways these enemies can cause harm. Don't think they do so only by making us suppose that the delights and consolations they can feign in us are from God. This seems to me the least harm—in part—they can cause; rather, it could be that by means of this they will make one advance more quickly. For, in being fed on that delight, such a person will spend more hours in prayer. Since he doesn't know that the delight is from the devil and since he sees he is unworthy of those consolations, he doesn't stop thanking God. He will feel greater obligation to serve Him and, thinking the favors come from the hand of the Lord, he will strive to dispose himself so that God will grant him more.

4. Strive always, Sisters, for humility and to see that you are unworthy of these favors; do not seek them. I hold that the devil loses many souls who strive for this humility. He thinks he is going to bring them to perdition, but the Lord draws good from the evil the devil aims at. His Majesty looks at our intention, which is to please and serve Him and remain with Him in prayer; and the Lord is faithful.[3] It's good to be on one's guard lest there be a break in humility, or some vainglory emerge. If you beseech the Lord to free you from this, do not fear, daughters, that His Majesty will allow you to be favored very much by anyone other than Himself.

5. The way the devil can do a great deal of harm, without our realizing it, is to make us believe we have virtues when we do not. This is a pestilence.[4] In regard to the delights and consolations, it seems merely that we are receiving and that we have the greater obligation to serve. In regard to our thinking we are virtuous, it seems we are serving and giving and that the Lord is obliged to pay. Thus little by little this latter notion does great harm. On the one hand it weakens humility, and on the other hand we grow careless about acquiring that virtue we think we have already acquired. Well, what is the remedy, Sisters? That which seems best to me is what our Master teaches us: prayer and supplication to the Eternal Father not to let us enter into temptation.[5]

6. I also want to tell you something else. If it seems the Lord

has already given us virtue, let us understand that actually it has been received and that He can take it away, as in fact often happens, but not without His wonderful providence. Haven't you ever seen this for yourselves, Sisters? I have. Sometimes I think I am very detached; and as a matter of fact when put to the test, I am. At another time I will find myself so attached, and perhaps to things that the day before I would have made fun of, that I almost don't know myself. At other times I think I have great courage and that I wouldn't turn from anything of service to God; and when put to the test, I do have this courage for some things. Another day will come in which I won't find the courage in me to kill even an ant for God if in doing so I'd meet with any opposition. In like manner it seems to me that I don't care at all about things or gossip said of me; and when I'm put to the test this is at times true—indeed I am pleased about what they say. Then there come days in which one word alone distresses me, and I would want to leave the world because it seems everything is a bother to me. And I am not alone in this. I have noticed it in many persons better than I, and know that it so happens.

7. Now since this is true, who will be able to say of himself that he is virtuous or rich? For at the very moment when there is need of virtue one finds oneself poor. No, Sisters; but let us always think we are poor, and not go into debt when we do not have the means with which to repay. The treasure will have to come from elsewhere, and we do not know when the Lord will want to leave us in the prison of our misery without giving us anything. And if others in thinking that we are good, bestow favor and honor on us—which is the borrowing I mentioned—both they and we ourselves will have been fooled. True, if we serve with humility, the Lord in the end will succor us in our needs; but if this poverty of spirit is not genuinely present at every step, as they say, the Lord will abandon us. And this abandonment by the Lord is one of His greatest favors, for He does it so that we might be humble and understand in truth that we have nothing we haven't received.

8. Now, then, take note of some other advice: the devil

makes us think we have a virtue, let's say of patience because we resolve and make very frequent acts of willingness to suffer much for God, and it seems to us as a matter of fact that we would suffer much; so we are very satisfied, for the devil helps us to believe this. I advise you not to pay any attention to these virtues; let us neither think we know them other than by name nor, until we see the proof, think the Lord has given them to us. For it will happen that with one displeasing word spoken to you, your patience will go tumbling to the ground. When you suffer often, praise God that He is beginning to teach you this virtue of patience and strive to endure, for the suffering is a sign that in this way He wants you to pay for the virtue. He gives it to you, and you do not possess it save as though on deposit, as has already been said.[6]

9. The devil brings about another temptation. We think we are very poor in spirit and have the habit of saying that we don't desire anything or that we couldn't care less about anything. But hardly does the occasion arise to receive a gift—even if it would be more than we need—than our poverty of spirit is completely ruined. So often do we say we have this virtue that we end up believing we have it.

Great is the importance of always being careful to understand this temptation, both in the things I have mentioned as well as in many others. For when the Lord truly gives one of these solid virtues, it seems it carries all the others in its wake. This is something felt very clearly. But I again warn you that even though it seems you possess it, you should fear lest you be mistaken. The truly humble person always walks in doubt about his own virtues, and usually those he sees in his neighbors seem more certain and more valuable.

Chapter 39

Continues the same subject, gives advice about some different kinds of temptations, and sets down two remedies by which to free oneself from them.

NOW BE ALSO ON YOUR GUARD, daughters, against some types of humility given by the devil in which great disquiet is felt about the gravity of our sins. This disturbance can afflict in many ways even to the point of making one give up receiving Communion and practicing private prayer.[1] These things are given up because the devil makes one feel unworthy. And when such persons approach the Blessed Sacrament, the time they used to spend in receiving favors is now spent in wondering whether or not they are well prepared. The situation gets so bad that the soul thinks God has abandoned it because of what it is; it almost doubts His mercy. Everything it deals with seems dangerous, and what it uses, however good, seems fruitless. It feels such distrust of itself that it folds its arms and remains idle; what is good in others seems evil when the soul sees it within its own self.

2. Consider carefully, daughters, the matter I'm going to speak to you about, for sometimes it will be through humility and virtue that you hold yourselves to be so wretched, and at other times it will be a gross temptation. I know of this because I have gone through it. Humility does not disturb or disquiet or agitate, however great it may be; it comes with peace, delight, and calm. Even though a person upon seeing himself so wretched understands clearly that he merits to be in hell, suffers affliction, thinks everyone should in justice abhor him, and almost doesn't dare ask for mercy, his pain, if the humility is genuine, comes with a sweetness in itself and a satisfaction that he wouldn't want to be without. The pain of genuine humility doesn't agitate or afflict the soul; rather, this humility expands it and enables it to serve God more. The other type of pain disturbs everything, agitates everything, afflicts the entire soul, and is very painful. I think the devil's aim is to make us think

we are humble and, in turn, if possible, make us lose confidence in God.

When you find yourselves in this condition, stop thinking about your misery, insofar as possible, and turn your thoughts to the mercy of God, to how He loves us and suffered for us. And if you are undergoing a temptation, you will not even be able to do this, for the devil will not let you quiet your mind or concentrate on anything unless so as to tire you all the more. It will be enough if you recognize that this is a temptation.[2]

Likewise he tempts us in regard to excessive penances so that we might think we are more penitential than others and are doing something. If you hide them from your confessor or prioress, or if when told to stop you do not do so, you are clearly undergoing a temptation. Strive to obey, even if this may be more painful for you, since the greatest perfection lies in obedience.

4. The devil sets up another dangerous temptation: self-assurance in the thought that we will in no way return to our past faults and worldly pleasures: "for now I have understood the world and know that all things come to an end and that the things of God give me greater delight." If this self-assurance is present in beginners, it is very dangerous because with it a person doesn't take care against entering once more into the occasions of sin, and he falls flat; please God the relapse will not bring about something much worse. For since the devil sees that he is dealing with a soul that can do him harm and bring profit to others, he uses all his power so that it might not rise.

Thus, however many delights and pledges of love the Lord gives you, never proceed with such self-assurance that you stop fearing lest you fall again; and be on guard against the occasions of sin.

5. Strive, without hiding anything, to discuss these favors and consolations with someone who will enlighten you. And take care about this: however sublime the contemplation, let your prayer always begin and end with self-knowledge. And if the favor is from God, even though you may not want to follow the advice, you will still follow it most of the time because

God's favor brings humility and always leaves greater light that we may understand the little that we are.

I don't want to enlarge on this any more, for you will find many books with such advice. I have said what I did because I have experienced it and found myself in trouble at times. All that we say, however much it is, cannot give us complete security.

6. Thus, Eternal Father, what can we do but have recourse to You and pray that these enemies of ours not lead us into temptation? Let public enemies come, for by Your favor we will be more easily freed. But these other treacheries; who will understand them, my God? We always need to pray to You for a remedy. Instruct us, Lord, so that we may understand ourselves and be secure. You already know that few take this path; but if they have to travel it with so many fears, many fewer will take it.

7. What a strange thing! It's as though the devil tempts only those who take the path of prayer. And everyone is more surprised by a mistake of one of those who are nearing perfection than by the public mistakes and sins of a hundred thousand others. With these latter mistakes there is no need to consider whether they are good or bad, for from a thousand-leagues distance one recognizes that they come from Satan.

As a matter of fact people are right in being surprised, for among those who recite the Our Father as was explained there are so very few deceived by the devil that as something new and unusual their mistake causes surprise. It is something very common among mortals that they pass over easily what they continually see, and wonder about what seldom or almost never happens. And the devil himself causes them to be surprised, for this surprise is to his advantage; he loses many souls through one who reaches perfection. [And I say that this is so surprising I do not marvel that others are surprised. Unless it is very much due to their own fault, souls who practice prayer walk so much more securely than those who take another road. They are like those in the stands watching the bull in comparison with one who is right in front of its horns. I have heard this comparison, and it seems to me true to the letter.

Do not fear, Sisters, to travel these paths, for in prayer there are many. Some souls profit by one path, and others by another, as I have said. Prayer is a safe road; you will be more quickly freed from temptation when close to the Lord than when far. Beseech Him and ask Him to deliver you from evil as you do so often each day in the Our Father.]

Chapter 40

Tells how by striving always to walk in the love and the fear of God we will proceed safely among so many temptations.

NOW THEN, GOOD MASTER, teach us how to live without any sudden assault in so dangerous a war. What we can have, daughters, and what His Majesty gave us are love and fear. Love will quicken our steps; fear will make us watch our steps to avoid falling along the way. On this way there are many stumbling blocks for all of us who are alive and continue our journey. With this fear we will be secure against being deceived.

2. You will ask me how you can tell if you have these two virtues which are so great; and you are right in doing so, for you cannot be very certain and definite about them. If we possess love, we are certainly in the state of grace. But reflect, Sisters, that there are some signs that even the blind, it seems, see. They are manifest signs, though you may not want to recognize them. They cry out loudly, for not many possess them perfectly; and hence these signs are more obvious. Love and fear of God: what more could you ask for! They are like two fortified castles from which one can wage war on the world and the devils.

3. Those who truly love God, love every good, desire every good, favor every good, praise every good. They always join, favor, and defend good people. They have no love for anything but truth and whatever is worthy of love. Do you think it is possible for a person who really loves God to love vanities? No, indeed, he cannot; nor can he love riches, or worldly things, or

delights, or honors, or strife, or envy. All of this is so because he seeks only to please the Beloved. These persons go about dying so that their Beloved might love them, and thus they dedicate their lives to learning how they might please Him more. Hide itself? Oh, with regard to the love of God—if it is genuine love—this is impossible. If you don't think so, look at St. Paul or the Magdalene. Within three days the one began to realize that he was sick with love; that was St. Paul. The Magdalene knew from the first day; and how well she knew! Love has this characteristic: it can be greater or lesser in degree. Thus, the love makes itself known according to its intensity. When slight, it shows itself but slightly; when strong, it shows itself strongly. But where there is love of God, whether little or great, it is always recognized.

4. However, the things with which we are now dealing more specifically, the deceptions and illusions the devil brings on contemplatives, are not few. With contemplatives there is always much love, or they wouldn't be contemplatives; and so their love is clearly recognized and in many ways. It is a great fire; it cannot but shine brightly. And if this splendor is not present, they should walk with serious misgivings; they should believe that they indeed have many reasons for fear; they should strive to understand these; they should pray, walk with humility, and beseech the Lord not to lead them into temptation. For certainly if this sign isn't present, I fear we may walk into temptation. But if one proceeds with humility, strives to know the truth, is subject to a confessor, and communicates with him openly and truthfully, it will come about, as has been said,[1] that the things by which the devil intends to cause death will cause life, however many the haunting illusions he wants to scare you with.

5. But if you feel this love of God I've mentioned and the fear I shall now speak of,[2] rejoice and be at peace. In order to disturb your soul so that you will not enjoy these wonderful blessings the devil will set a thousand false fears before you and strive that others do so. Since he cannot win us over, he can at least try to make us lose something. He may strive to make souls lose when they might have gained a great deal by thinking that

his favors are from God and are bestowed on creatures as wretched as themselves and that it is possible for God to grant favors—for it seems sometimes we have forgotten about the Lord's ancient mercies.[3]

6. Do you think it matters little to the devil to set up these fears? No, it matters a great deal, for he causes two kinds of harm. First, those who listen to him are struck with a terror of approaching prayer, for they think they will be deceived. Second, if it were not for these fears many more would come closer to God in seeing that He is so good, as I have said,[4] and that it is possible for Him now to communicate so much with sinners. They covet these favors. And they are right, for I know some persons who were encouraged by such favors and began prayer; and in a short while the favors became authentic, and the Lord granted them great ones.

7. So, Sisters, when you see among yourselves someone to whom the Lord gives favors, praise the Lord very much but don't think she is for this reason safe; rather help her with more prayer. No one can be safe while living and engulfed in the dangers of this tempestuous sea.

You will not fail to recognize this love where it is present, nor do I know how it can be concealed.[5] If we love creatures here on earth, it's impossible, we are told, to hide this, and the more we do to hide it the more it is revealed (and it is something so lowly that it doesn't merit the name "love," for it is grounded on nothing). And could one conceal a love that is so strong and just that it always increases and sees no reason to stop since its foundation is made from the cement of being repaid by another love? This other love can no longer be doubted since it was shown so openly and with so many sufferings and trials, and with the shedding of blood even to the point of death in order that we might have no doubt about it. Oh, God help me, how different must the love of God be from the love of creatures for whoever has experienced the former!

8. May it please His Majesty to give us His love before He takes us out of this life, for it will be a great thing at the hour of death to see that we are going to be judged by the One whom we have loved above all things. We shall be able to proceed

securely with the judgment concerning our debts. It will not be like going to a foreign country but like going to our own, because it is the country of one whom we love so much and who loves us. [In this love—besides everything else—there is greater security than with earthly loves; in loving God we are certain that He loves us.] Remember here, my daughters, the gain there is in this love, and the loss in not having it. Such a loss puts us in the hands of the enemy, in hands so cruel, hands so hostile toward everything good, and so fond of everything bad.

9. What will become of the poor soul that, after being freed from the sufferings and trials of death, falls immediately into these hands? What terrible rest it receives! How mangled as it goes to hell! What a multitude of different kinds of serpents! What a terrifying place! What a wretched inn! If it is hard for a self-indulgent person (for such are the ones who will be more likely to go there) to spend one night in a bad inn, what do you think that sad soul will feel at being in this kind of inn forever, without end?

Let us not desire delights, daughters; we are well-off here; the bad inn lasts for only a night. Let us praise God; let us force ourselves to do penance in this life. How sweet will be the death of one who has done penance for all his sins, of one who won't have to go to purgatory! Even from here below you can begin to enjoy glory! You will find no fear within yourself but complete peace.

10. As long as we have not reached this state, Sisters, let us beseech God that if therefore we are to receive sufferings, they will be received here below. For, with the hope of being freed from them, we can bear them here willingly, and we will not lose His friendship and grace. Let us beseech Him to give us His grace in this life so that we will not walk unawares into temptation.[6]

Chapter 41

Speaks of the fear of God and of how we must be on guard against venial sins.

HOW LENGTHY I HAVE BEEN! But not as lengthy as I wanted to be, for it is a delight to speak about the love of God. What will it be like to possess it? May the Lord give it to me because of who His Majesty is. [Let me not leave this life, O my Lord, until I no longer desire anything in it; neither let me know any love outside of You, Lord, nor let me succeed in using this term "love" for anyone else. Everything is false since the foundation is false, and so the edifice doesn't last. I don't know why we are surprised. I laugh to myself when I hear it said: "That person repaid me badly." "This other one doesn't love me." What does anyone have to repay you for, or why should anyone love you? This experience will show you what the world is, for your very love for it will afterward punish you. And this is what wears you down: you realize you have let your affection become involved like children in their games.][1]

Now let us deal with the fear of God.[2] This trait is also something easily recognized by the person who has it as well as by those who approach him. But I want you to understand that in the beginning it is not so developed, unless in some persons to whom, as I have said,[3] the Lord grants great favors, for in a short time He makes them rich in virtue. Hence this fear isn't discernible in everyone—at the outset, I mean. It goes on increasing in strength each day. But it is soon recognized because in the beginning one starts to turn away from sin and its occasions and from bad companions; and other signs as well are seen. But once the soul has reached contemplation—which is what we are now dealing with most—the fear of God also, as with love, becomes very manifest; it doesn't disguise itself even exteriorly. Despite the fact that you may watch these persons very carefully, you will not see them become careless. For no matter how long we observe them, the Lord keeps them in such a way that even if a thing very much to their own interest comes along, they will not advertently commit a venial sin;

mortal sins they fear like fire. And illusions involving sin are the ones I would want us, Sisters, to be very much afraid of. Let us beseech God always that the temptation may not be so strong as to make us offend Him, that its strength might not outweigh the fortitude He gives us to conquer it. This fear is what is important; it is what I desire may never be taken from us, for it is what will help us.

2. Oh, what a great thing it is to have resisted offending the Lord so that His slaves and servants in hell may be bound; for in the end all must serve Him despite themselves. But those in hell do so by force, whereas we do so willingly. Therefore, if we please the Lord, those in hell will be kept bound; they will not do anything that may be harmful to us however much they might draw us into temptation and set secret snares for us.

3. Be careful and attentive—this is very important—until you see that you are strongly determined not to offend the Lord, that you would lose a thousand lives rather than commit a mortal sin, and that you are most careful not to commit venial sins—that is, advertently; for otherwise, who can go without committing many? But there is an advertence that is very deliberate; another that comes so quickly that committing the venial sin and adverting to it happen almost together in such a way that we don't first realize what we are doing. But from any very deliberate sin, however small it be, may God deliver us. [I don't know how we could be so bold as to go against such a great Lord, even though it be in something very small.] What's more, there is nothing small if it goes against His immense Majesty and we see He is looking at us. It seems to me a sin is very deliberate when, for example, one says: "Lord, although this grieves You, I will do it; I'm already aware that You see it, and I know You do not want it, and I understand this; but I want to follow my whim and appetite more than Your will." It doesn't seem to me possible that something like this can be called little, however light the fault; but it's serious, very serious. [For the love of God, daughters, never become careless in this regard; now—glory be to the Lord—you are not.]

4. Consider, Sisters, for the love of God, if you want to gain

this fear of the Lord, that it is very helpful to understand the seriousness of an offense against God and to reflect on this frequently in your thoughts; for it is worth our life and much more to have this virtue rooted in our souls. And until you have it, you must always proceed carefully and turn from every occasion and companion who does not help you come closer to God. We should take great care in everything we do to bend our will, and take care that our speech be edifying; we must flee those places where conversations are not of God.

It's very necessary that this fear be deeply impressed within the soul. Such fear is easy to obtain if there is true love together with a great inner determination, as I have said,[4] not to commit an offense against God for any created thing, even though afterward the soul may sometimes fall because we are weak and have no reason to trust ourselves. When we are more determined we are less confident of ourselves, for confidence must be placed in God. When we understand this that I said about ourselves, there will be no need to go about so tense and constrained; the Lord will protect us, and the habit acquired will now be a help against offending Him. The need instead will be to go about with a holy freedom, conversing with those who are good even though they may be somewhat worldly. For those who, before you possessed this authentic fear of God, were a poison and a means of killing the soul will afterward often be a help to your loving and praising God more because He has freed you from that which you recognize as a glaring danger. If previously you played a part in contributing to their weaknesses, now by your mere presence you contribute to their restraint; this happens without their having any idea of paying you honor.

5. I often praise the Lord, thinking how it comes about that often a servant of God, without uttering a word, prevents things from being said against God. This must happen for the same reason that something similar happens here below: there is always some restraint so as not to offend an absent person in the presence of someone known to be his friend. So it is with a servant of God: his friendship with God wins him respect no matter how lowly his status, and others avoid afflicting him in

a matter they so well realize would grieve him; that is, they avoid offending God in his presence. The fact is that I don't know the reason for this, but I do know that it's a common occurrence. So do not be tense, for if you begin to feel constrained, such a feeling will be very harmful to everything good, and at times you will end up being scrupulous and become incapable of doing anything for yourself or for others. And if you don't end up being scrupulous, this constraint will be good for you but it will not bring many souls to God, because they will see so much repression and tenseness. Our nature is such that this constraint is frightening and oppressive to others, and they flee from following the road that you are taking, even though they know clearly that it is the more virtuous path.

6. Another harm derives from this attitude; it is that of judging others. There are those who advance with greater holiness and in order to be of benefit to their neighbor speak with him freely and without this constraint; but since they do not journey by your path they at once seem to you to be imperfect. If they have a holy joy, it will seem to be dissipation, especially to those of us who have no learning or knowledge of what one can speak about without sinning. This constraint is a very dangerous thing; it means going about in continual temptation and it bears ill effects; it is detrimental to your neighbor. To think that if all do not proceed as you do, in this constrained way, they are not proceeding well is extremely wrong.

And there is another harm: in some things of which you must speak, and it is right that you speak, you don't dare do so for fear of going to extremes; rather, perhaps, you speak well of something that it would be very good for you to abhor.

7. So, Sisters, strive as much as you can, without offense to God, to be affable and understanding in such a way that everyone you talk to will love your conversation and desire your manner of living and acting, and not be frightened and intimidated by virtue. This is very important for religious; the holier they are the more sociable they are with their Sisters. And even though you may feel very distressed if all your Sisters' conversations do not go as you would like them to, never turn

away from them if you want to help your Sisters and be loved. This is what we must strive for earnestly, to be affable, agreeable, and pleasing to persons with whom we deal, especially our Sisters.

8. Thus, my daughters, strive to think rightly about God, for He doesn't look at trifles as much as you think, and don't lose your courage or allow your soul to be constrained, for many blessings could be lost. Have the right intention, a resolute will, as I have said,[5] not to offend God. Don't let your soul withdraw into a corner, for instead of obtaining sanctity you will obtain many imperfections that the devil in other ways will place before you; and, as I have said,[6] you will not be of as much benefit to yourself or to others as you could have been.

9. Here you see how, with these two virtues—love and fear of God—you can advance on this road calmly and quietly, but not carelessly since fear must always take the lead. As long as we live, we will never have complete security; that would be a great danger. And this is what our Teacher understood when at the end of this prayer He spoke these words to His Father as one who well understood they were necessary.[7]

Chapter 42

Discusses these last words of the Our Father: Sed libera nos a malo. Amen. But deliver us from evil. Amen.

IT SEEMS TO ME JESUS WAS RIGHT to include Himself in this petition, for we already see how tired He was of this life when He said to His Apostles at the last supper: *I have greatly desired to eat this supper with you.*[1] Here we see how weary He must have been of living. Nowadays people don't tire of living even if they go on to be a hundred, but always want to live longer. True, we don't suffer in life as much evil and as many trials as His Majesty suffered, nor such poverty. What was His whole life if not a continual death, in which He always saw beforehand that most cruel death they were going to inflict on Him? And this was the least of His sufferings; but how many offenses committed against His Father and what a multitude of souls that were lost! If one who possesses charity here on earth finds all this a great torment, what must have been the Lord's torment, with His boundless and immeasurable charity? And what a good reason He had to beseech the Father to free Him finally from so many evils and trials and bring Him to rest forever in the Father's kingdom, since He was its true inheritor!

2. *Amen.* By the "amen" I understand that since with this word all things come to an end, the Lord asks likewise that we be freed from all evil forever. [It is useless, Sisters, to think that while we live we can be free of many temptations and imperfections and even sins, for it is said that whoever thinks he is without sin deceives himself[2] — and this is true. Now, if we turn to bodily ailments and hardships, who is without very many and in many ways? Nor is it good that we ask to be without them.

Well, then, let us understand what we are asking for here since it seems impossible to say "from all evil," whether of the body or, as I have said, of imperfections and faults in the service of God. I am not speaking about the saints — they can do everything in Christ, as St. Paul said[3] — but sinners like myself. I see myself closed in by weakness, lukewarmness, and a lack of mortification, and many other things. I see that it behooves me to ask the Lord for a remedy. You, daughters, ask according to what you think. I do not find this remedy while living, and so I ask the Lord to deliver me from all evil forever. What good do we find in this life, Sisters, since we lack so much good and are absent from Him?

Deliver me, Lord, from this shadow of death, deliver me from so many trials, deliver me from so many sufferings, deliver me from so many changes, from so many compliments that we are forced to receive while still living, from so many, many, many things that tire and weary me, that would tire anyone reading this if I mentioned them all. There's no longer anyone who can bear to live. This weariness must come to me because I have lived so badly, and from seeing that the way I live now is still not the way I should live since I owe so much.] Thus I beseech the Lord to deliver me from all evil forever since I do not make up for what I owe; it could be that perhaps each day I become more indebted. And what is unendurable, Lord, is not to know for certain that I love You or that my desires are acceptable before You. O my Lord and my God, deliver me now from all evil and be pleased to bring me to the place where all blessings are. What do they still hope for here, those to whom You have given knowledge of what the world is, and those who have a living faith concerning what the Eternal Father has kept for them?

3. To ask for these blessings with great desire and complete determination is a clear sign for contemplatives that the favors they receive in prayer are from God. Thus those who have this sign should esteem their prayer highly. In the case of my asking for these things the same is not true; I mean that it shouldn't be interpreted as a sign of divine favors; but since I have lived so badly, I fear living still longer; and so many trials weary me. It is no surprise that those who have a share in the consolations of God desire to be there where they will enjoy them more than in mere sips, that they do not want to remain in a life where there are these many obstacles to the enjoyment of so much good, and that they desire to be where the Sun of justice[4] does not set. Everything they afterward see here below will be completely dark to them, and I marvel at how they live. They could not live with any contentment if they have received and already begun to enjoy the Lord's kingdom here below. And such a person must not live for his own will but for the will of his King.

4. Oh, how different this life would have to be in order for one not to desire death! How our will deviates in its inclination from that which is the will of God. He wants us to love truth; we love the lie. He wants us to desire the eternal; we, here below, lean toward what comes to an end. He wants us to desire sublime and great things; we, here below, desire base and earthly things. He would want us to desire only what is secure; we, here below, love the dubious. Everything is a mockery, my daughters, except beseeching God to free us from these dangers forever and draw us at last away from every evil. Even though our desire may not be perfect, let us force ourselves to make the request. What does it cost us to ask for a

great deal? We are asking it of One who is powerful. But in order to be right, let us leave the giving to His will since we have already given Him our own. His name be forever hallowed in heaven and on earth, and may His will be always done in me. Amen.

[Here you see, friends, what it means to pray vocally with perfection. It means that you be aware of and understand whom you are asking, who it is that is asking, and what you are asking for. When they tell you that it isn't good to practice any other kind of prayer than vocal prayer, do not be distressed. Read this very carefully, and what you do not understand about prayer, beseech the Lord to teach you. For no one can take vocal prayer from you or make you recite the Our Father hastily and without understanding it. If some person should take it from you or counsel you to give it up, do not believe him. Believe that he is a false prophet and consider that in these times of ours you don't have to believe everybody. Even though there is nothing to fear from those who can counsel you now, we don't know what will come in the future.

I have also thought of saying something to you about how to recite the Hail Mary. But I have been so lengthy that I have to let it go. It is enough for you to have understood how to recite the Our Father well in order to know how to recite all the vocal prayers you must recite.]

5. Now see, Sisters, how the Lord by giving me understanding of the great deal we ask for when reciting this evangelical prayer has removed the difficulty involved in my teaching you and myself the path that I began to explain to you. May He be blessed forever! Certainly, it never entered my mind that this prayer contained so many deep secrets; for now you have seen the entire spiritual way contained in it, from the beginning stages until God engulfs the soul and gives it to drink abundantly from the fount of living water, which He said was to be found at the end of the way.[5] [And having come out of it—I mean of this prayer—I don't know how to go any further.]

It seems the Lord has desired to give us understanding, Sisters, of the great consolation contained in this prayer. It is highly beneficial to persons who don't know how to read. If they understand this prayer, they can draw a lot of doctrine from it and find consolation there. [And when books are taken away from us, this book cannot be taken away, for it comes from the mouth of Truth itself, who cannot err. And since, as I have said, we recite the Our Father so many times in a day, let us delight in it and strive to learn from so excellent a Master the humility with which He prays and all the other things that were mentioned.]

6. Sisters, beg this good Master to pardon me, for I have been bold to speak of such sublime things. His Majesty knows well that my intellect would not have been capable of it if He had not taught me what I have said. Be grateful to Him, Sisters, for He must have done so because of the humility with which you asked me and desired to be taught by someone so miserable.

[Well, Sisters, it now seems the Lord doesn't want me to say any more, for I don't know what to say; although I thought of going on. The Lord has taught you and me the path that I have described in the book I said I wrote,[6] how one reaches this fount of living water, what the soul feels there, how God satisfies it, takes away thirst for earthly things, and makes it grow in the things pertaining to the service of God. Those who have reached this fount will find that book very beneficial and receive much light from it. You may get it from Father Domingo Báñez, a *presentado* of the Order of St. Dominic, who as I said is my confessor and the one to whom I'll give this book. If this one is all right for you to see and he gives it to you, he'll also give you that other one.]

7. If he thinks this book will be helpful and gives it to you, I will be consoled that you are consoled. If it should be such that no one may see it, you can accept my good will, for by this work I have obeyed your command. I consider myself well paid for the trouble involved in writing it, for there has been no trouble at all in thinking out what I have said.

May the Lord be blessed and praised; from Him comes every good we speak of, think about, and do. Amen.

Meditations on the Song of Songs

MEDITATIONS ON THE SONG OF SONGS

INTRODUCTION

ALTHOUGH AT BOTH the beginning and the end of these meditations Teresa says she wrote them out of obedience, the obviously main motivating force was her desire to share with her Sisters the delight and the understanding she experienced in the *Song of Songs*. Her hope was that her daughters would receive some of the consolation and knowledge given to her when she heard those mysterious words of love.[1] Thus Teresa does not begin this work reluctantly or as a sacrifice of obedience as she did some of her other writings. Rather, she admits that "it consoles me to tell my meditations to my daughters."[2] Even if she fails to explain the understanding of them that was given to her mystically, she reasons that her time will have been well spent in reflecting on such sublime themes.[3] Furthermore, she felt that the Lord's love is so poorly understood that people refuse to think of the mysteries contained in these words "spoken by the Holy Spirit."[4] "I know someone who for a number of years had many fears, and nothing gave her assurance, but the Lord was pleased that she hear some words from the *Song of Songs*, and through them she understood that her soul was being well guided. As I have said, she understood that it was possible for a soul in love with its Spouse to experience all these favors, swoons, deaths, afflictions, delights, and joys in relation to Him."[5] Teresa reasoned that it was wrong that women were being prevented from enjoying the riches contained in God's words and works.[6]

Historical Context

The daring behind her *Meditations* can only be grasped somewhat if we consider the prevalent attitude in Spain at the time with regard to the Scriptures. The vernacular versions of the Bible were neither as numerous nor as important as in other countries of Europe, for the Spanish Inquisition acted as a tight check on them. There is an example of the seriousness of the situation in the life of Fray Luis de León who made a literal prose translation of the *Song of Songs*; the circulation of this version in manuscript form was one of the charges brought against him by the Inquisition and led to his imprisonment from 1572-1576.

In the fourth session of the Council of Trent in 1546, the suitability of translating the Bible into the language of the people was debated. The Spanish theologians were opposed; and though the Council in the end made no legislation about the matter, Spain, on its own, included vernacular versions of the Bible in its indexes of forbidden books. The reasoning behind this prohibition is expressed by Archbishop Carranza when he points to particular cases of error that arose because simple and unlearned people read parts of Scripture without understanding them. The prohibitions affected mainly women and unlearned people because they were the ones, it was thought, who could more easily fall into error through the free examen of the Sacred text.

The Spanish indexes that would have affected Teresa were those of the Inquisitor, Fernando Valdés, published in 1551, 1554, and 1559. In them, both the publication and the reading of Sacred Scripture in the vernacular were forbidden. It was permissible, however, to provide translations of Scriptural passages in spiritual books. The spiritual writers as a result made such ample use of this permission that the claim has been made that a Bible in the vernacular could have been constructed from the Scriptural citations that filled the pages of these works.

In light of such facts, Teresa could not have had access to

the Bible in the vernacular; and therefore she could not have used a Bible for her meditations. With respect to the verses from the *Song of Songs* that she uses, there are a number of ways in which she may have come to know them and cite them in her own tongue.

We know she read verses in Latin in the breviary and understood the meaning despite her lack of knowledge of Latin. She tells us this herself: "For a number of years now the Lord has given me great delight each time I hear or read some words from Solomon's *Song of Songs*. The delight is so great that without understanding the vernacular meaning of the Latin, my soul is stirred and recollected more than by devotional books written in the language I understand. And this happens almost all the time, and even when the Latin words were translated for me into the vernacular I did not understand the text any more."[7]

It is possible that she may have used a translation from some Office of the Blessed Virgin, from one of the many copies of the Spanish *Book of Hours*. She suggests this possibility when she says: "And thus you can see, daughters, in the Office of our Lady which we recite each week, how much in its antiphons and readings is taken from this *Song of Songs*."[8]

She may have asked some learned man or confessor for a translation. This possibility is indicated in her statement that she questioned learned men about what the Holy Spirit meant by the verses.[9] And it is possible she may have gotten the passages from some spiritual book.

The Word of God

A study of Teresa's life shows clearly enough that she received no education in Sacred Scripture. Nonetheless, one is amazed by her knowledge and use of the Scriptures despite this lack of formal training and the limited access she had to the contents of the Bible. Without any previous understanding of the meaning of a passage, without a knowledge even of the exact meaning of the words, the text being in Latin, she would suddenly penetrate, through mystical experience, to the deepest sense contained there and taste and enjoy it. "And, in fact, it has happened to me that while in this quietude, and understanding hardly anything of the Latin prayers, especially of the psalter, I have not only understood how to render the Latin verse in the vernacular but have gone beyond to rejoicing in the meaning of the verse."[10] The obstacle to an understanding of this kind is not lack of learning but sin. "Since such persons have no love, they can easily read the *Song of Songs* every day and not themselves become involved with the words; nor would they even dare take these words on their lips."[11]

By all of this Teresa did not mean that her experience was the criterion for judging Scripture; the contrary was true. She recognized that there are those who by profession have the obligation to explain the Scriptures and are thus required to work hard at their task; and she believed that much could be gained through their careful studies. Yet even these learned masters of the Scriptures whom she humbly consulted admitted to her with respect to the *Song of Songs* that the doctors had written many commentaries and had never finished explaining the words.[12] Understanding the awesomeness of the task of interpreting the Scriptures, Teresa at one point exclaims: "For one word of His will contain within itself a thousand mysteries, and thus our understanding is only very elementary."[13] The attitude, then, that must accompany anyone's approach to the Bible is humility. The supreme example of this humility is found in the Blessed Virgin Mary. Once the angel had responded to her question and told her how the word of God would be accomplished, "she engaged in no further discussion." And then, in an occurrence rare in her writings, Teresa expresses displeasure with some learned men and sharply observes: "She did not act as do some learned men (whom the Lord does not lead by this mode of prayer and who haven't begun a life of prayer), for they want to be so rational about things and so precise in their understanding that it doesn't seem anyone else but they with their learning can understand the grandeurs of God. If only they could learn something from the humility of the most Blessed Virgin!"[14]

In keeping with the custom followed by spiritual writers and preachers in her day, Teresa often uses Scripture in an accommodated sense. On the other hand an abundance of instances can be cited in which her use of Scripture corresponds generally with the literal meaning. Through her mystical experience, moreover, she was able to penetrate to the deepest content of the Biblical texts; and this is especially true when these texts center on such themes as: God's truth and fidelity;[15] the indwelling of the Blessed Trinity;[16] union with Christ in both His humanity and divinity;[17] and the peace of Christ.[18]

Justifiably, the *Song of Songs* may be applied, as it has been in Christian tradition, to the mutual love between Christ and His Church, the Blessed Virgin Mary, or the individual soul. Generally speaking, there can be noted in the *Song* a crescendo in both the love and the intimacy between bride and bridegroom. The culmination, at least according to a large number of exegetes, lies in the total gift of marriage. If this is applied to an individual member of Christ's Church, then who better than a soul that has experienced them can understand the "favors, swoons, deaths, afflictions, delights, and joys" that accompany the ascent to total union with God?

In her reflections on the *Song*, Teresa covers only a few verses of the entire text. While admitting their perfect application to the Blessed Virgin Mary,[19] she chooses to concentrate on an interpretation that speaks of the love between Christ and the soul.

Copies and Date of Composition

Jerome Gratian, who edited and published this work for the first time in Brussels in 1611, gives the reason the autograph has been lost to posterity. It seems that though Teresa wrote her *Meditations* with the approval of her confessor, a later confessor, upon hearing of the existence of so daring a work, became frightened. Gratian says that this later confessor thought it a dangerous novelty for a woman to write on the *Song of Songs* and "moved with zeal by the words of St. Paul that women should be silent in the Church," ordered Teresa to burn it. Gratian's account goes on to say that at the moment Teresa was told to do so, she threw the book in the fire. Through witnesses in the process for beatification and canonization, we know that this cautious director was the Dominican preacher, theologian, and writer, Diego de Yanguas.[20] But since the incident took place as late as 1580, copies of these meditations were already in circulation and carefully guarded by persons who valued them as spiritual treasures.

The Discalced Carmelite nuns in Alba de Tormes hid their copy in the monastery. When Fr. Yanguas ordered that the copies they possessed be burned "not because the work was bad but because he didn't think it was proper for a woman to explain the *Song of Songs*," the nuns demonstrated their expertise in casuistry by giving the manuscript away, to the Duchess of Alba, who they knew would value and guard it safely.[21]

Four copies of this work are extant. We can distinguish two groups based on different renderings: the copy of Alba de Tormes (the most complete) and that of Baeza; and the copies of Consuegra and Las Nieves. The copy of Alba is the one approved by Domingo Báñez, June 10, 1575. All four are conserved in the *Biblioteca Nacional de Madrid.*

From the manner in which these meditations end, it is generally supposed that we possess the complete text excepting some lines in the prologue. These lines are missing because of the deterioration of the copy of Alba, the only one that contains the prologue.

Although none of the manuscripts contains chapter divisions, Gratian in his edition divided the work into seven chapters and composed headings for each. He, too, is the author of the frequently used title of the work, *Conceptos del amor de Dios*, rendered in English as *Conceptions of the Love of God*. But since this title is not Teresa's and she herself refers to the work more simply as "my meditations,"[22] a number of editors have changed Gratian's title to *Meditations on the Song of Songs*. Although somewhat misleading since Teresa reflects on only a few verses of the *Song*, this is the title we have chosen for this edition.

Establishing the date of composition has required a study of evidence internal to the text since no definite external testimony remains. The reference to Friar Alonso de Cordobilla, his visit and later death, indicates that Teresa possibly wrote the work at St. Joseph's in Avila before making her next foundation in August of 1567, for this friar died in October 1566.[23] Still, her reference in the prologue to "these monasteries" indicates that more monasteries had been founded and thus some later date. More specifically, in this line, she speaks of a personal experience of hers which took place at Easter in 1571.[24] The latest date that could be mentioned is August 10, 1575, when Bañez gave his approval to the writing. With respect to the earliest date, the work could not have been written before 1566 because she speaks of two books she had already written: her *Life* and the *Way of Perfection*.[25] The apparent contradiction in this evidence has led scholars to conclude that the work was drafted at least twice. The first draft would have been written at Avila in late 1566, or the first part of 1567; and the second rendered sometime between 1572 and 1575.

Our translation is made from the copy of Alba, the one preferred by Spanish editors; but the chapter divisions and headings are taken from Gratian's edition. Those important additions not found in Alba but in the copies of Consuegra and Las Nieves are indicated in our translation by the use of brackets.

Though small in size, these *Meditations* are both fascinating and fresh in insight. They merit all the attention given to other Teresian works.[26] The content may be generally divided as follows:

I. Mystical experience of "some words from Solomon's *Song of Songs*" (Prologue and ch. 1, nos. 1-7)
II. Purpose in writing (ch. 1, nos. 8-12)
III. The kiss: symbol of peace and friendship
   A. false peace

III. (continued)

- a. from friendship with the devil (ch. 2, nos. 1-6)
- b. from the world and the flesh
  - from riches (ch. 2, nos. 8-10)
  - from honors (ch. 2, nos. 11-13)
  - from comforts (ch. 2, nos. 14-15)

B. peace from friendship with the Lord (ch. 2, nos. 16-18)

- a. imperfect kinds of friendship with Him (ch. 2, nos. 19-30)
- b. the peace of union and its signs (ch. 3)

IV. Communion in friendship

A. prayer of quiet and of union (chs. 4-6)

B. effects of this prayer: the desire to serve; union of both the active and the contemplative life (ch. 7)

K.K.

Prologue

I HAVE SEEN THE MERCIES our Lord grants souls He has brought to these monasteries which observe the primitive rule of our Lady of Mount Carmel and which have been founded through His Majesty's good pleasure. For so many are the favors our Lord grants to some of the Sisters in particular that only souls who know about the need there is for an explanation of some of the things that pass between the soul and our Lord will be able to see the trial that is suffered in not having light. For a number of years now the Lord has given me great delight each time I hear or read some words from Solomon's *Song of Songs*. The delight is so great that without understanding the vernacular meaning of the Latin my soul is stirred and recollected more than by devotional books written in the language I understand. And this happens almost all the time, and even when the Latin words were translated for me into the vernacular I did not understand the text any more. . .[1]

2. For about two years, more or less, it seems to me the Lord has been giving me, for the sake of my purpose in writing this work, some understanding of the meaning of certain words, and I think these words will bring consolation to the Sisters our Lord leads by this path and also to me. For at times the Lord gives understanding of so much that I find myself hoping I won't forget, but I didn't dare put anything in writing.

3. Now in accord with the opinion of persons whom I'm obliged to obey, I shall write something about the understanding the Lord gives me of what is contained in the words that bring delight to my soul about this path of prayer. As I have said, it is along this path that the Lord leads these Sisters, and my daughters, in these monasteries. If this writing is such that you may see it, accept this poor little gift from one who desires for you as well as for herself all the gifts of the Holy Spirit, in whose name I begin. If I succeed in saying something worthwhile, the success will not be from me. May it please the divine Majesty. . .[2]

Chapter 1

Treats of the veneration with which the Sacred Scriptures should be read and of the difficulty women have in comprehending them, especially the Song of Songs.

> *Let the Lord kiss me with the kiss of His mouth, for Your breasts are better than wine, etc. . . . (Sg. 1:2)*

I HAVE CAREFULLY NOTED that it seems from what is manifested here that the soul is speaking with one person and asking peace from another. It says: *Let Him kiss me with the kiss of His mouth;* and next, seemingly, it speaks to someone whom it is with: *Your breasts are better.*

I don't understand why this is; and that I don't understand gives me great delight. Indeed, daughters, the soul will not have to reflect upon the things it seems we can grasp with our lowly intellects here below as intensely as it will upon those that can in no way be understood; nor will the former make it respect God as much as do His mysteries. Thus I highly recommend that when you read some book or hear a sermon or think about the mysteries of our sacred faith you avoid tiring yourselves or wasting your thoughts in subtle reasoning about what you cannot properly understand. Many things are not meant for women to understand, nor even for men.

2. When the Lord desires to give understanding, His Majesty does so without our effort. I am saying this to women, and also to men who aren't obliged to defend the truth through their learning. For those whom the Lord has called to explain the Scriptures to us must understandably work, and they will gain much from their work. But we should accept with simplicity whatever the Lord gives us; and what He doesn't we shouldn't tire ourselves over, but rejoice in considering what a

great Lord and God we have. For one word of His will contain within itself a thousand mysteries, and thus our understanding is only very elementary. That we do not understand His words when they are written in Latin or Hebrew or Greek is no surprise. But even in our own language; how many things there are in the psalms of the glorious King David that after being translated into the vernacular for us remain as obscure as they were in Latin! Thus always guard against wasting your thoughts on these things or tiring yourselves, for women have need of no more than what is sufficient for their meditations. With this, God will favor them. When His Majesty desires to give us understanding of the words, without worry or work on our part, we shall surely find it. As for the rest, let us humble ourselves and, as I have said, rejoice that we have such a Lord, that even words of His spoken in our own language cannot be understood.

3. It will seem to you that there are some words in the *Song of Songs* that could have been said in another style. In light of our dullness such an opinion doesn't surprise me. I have heard some persons say that they avoid listening to them. Oh, God help me, how great is our misery! Just as poisonous creatures turn everything they eat into poison, so do we. From favors as great as those the Lord gives us here in revealing what is possessed by the soul who loves Him and in encouraging it to speak with His Majesty and find delight in Him, we have to create fears and give opinions that manifest the small degree of love of God we have.

4. O my Lord, how poorly we profit from the blessing You grant us! You seek ways and means and you devise plans to show Your love for us; we, inexperienced in loving You, esteem this love so poorly that our minds, little exercised in love, go where they always go and cease to think of the great mysteries this language, spoken by the Holy Spirit, contains within itself. What more was necessary than this language in order to enkindle us in His love and make us realize that not without good reason did He choose this style.

5. Indeed, I recall hearing a priest who was a religious preach a very admirable sermon, most of which was an ex-

planation of those loving delights with which the bride communed with God. And there was so much laughter, and what he said was so poorly taken, that I was shocked. He was speaking about love since the sermon was on Maundy Thursday,[1] when one shouldn't be speaking of anything else. And I see clearly that the reason for not understanding is the one I mentioned (that we practice so poorly the love of God), for it doesn't seem to us possible for a soul to commune in such a way with God. These people did not benefit, surely because they did not understand, nor, I believe, did they think anything but that the preacher made the sermon up in his own head. Yet, I know other persons who have drawn out great good, delight, and security against fears, so much so that they had to offer special praise to our Lord. He has left a salutary remedy to souls that love Him with a fervent love because they understand and see that it is possible for God to humble Himself so much. For experience was not enough to keep them from fearing when the Lord granted them great favors. What they see represented here makes them feel secure.

6. I know someone who for a number of years had many fears, and nothing gave her assurance, but the Lord was pleased that she hear some words from the *Song of Songs,* and through them she understood that her soul was being well guided. As I have said,[2] she understood that it was possible for a soul in love with its Spouse to experience all these favors, swoons, deaths, afflictions, delights, and joys in relation to Him. It does so after it has left all the world's joys out of love for Him and is completely given over and abandoned into His hands, and when it has done this not just in words, as happens with some, but in all truth, confirmed with works.

Oh, my daughters, how well God repays! You have a Lord and Spouse with whom nothing takes place without His seeing and understanding it! Thus, even though the things be very small, do not fail to do what you can for love of Him. His Majesty will repay for them; He looks only at the love with which you do them.

7. Hence, I conclude this matter by saying that you should never dwell on what you do not understand in Sacred Scripture

or the mysteries of our faith more than I have said, nor should you be startled by the lofty words that take place between God and the soul. Being what we are, the love that He had and has for us surprises and bewilders me more; for knowing that He has such love I already understand that there is no exaggeration in the words by which He reveals it to us, for He has shown this love even more through his deeds. But when you reach this place in my writing, I ask you that for love of me you pause a little to think upon what He has shown us and what He has suffered for us, observing clearly that a love so powerful and strong that it made Him suffer so much could not reveal itself in words that should be any surprise to us.

8. Well now, to return to what I began saying,[3] these words must contain great things and mysteries since they are of such value that when I asked learned men to explain what the Holy Spirit meant by them and what the true meaning was they answered that the doctors wrote many commentaries and yet never finished explaining the words fully. Since this is so, it will seem to be excessive pride on my part to want to explain something about them for you. It is not my intention, however little my humility, to think that I can get to the truth of them. What I do intend is that, just as I delight in what the Lord gives me understanding of when I hear some passage from the *Song of Songs*, you will perhaps find consolation in it, as I do, if I tell you. And I interpret the passage in my own way, even though my understanding of it may not be in accord with what is meant. For if we do not depart from what the Church and the saints hold (which is why learned men who understand the matter will examine this carefully before you see it), the Lord gives us license—from what I think—just as He does when we think of the Passion and consider many more things about the anguish and torments the Lord must have suffered than the Evangelists record. And if we do not indulge in curiosity, as I said at the beginning,[4] but accept the understanding His Majesty gives us, I hold it as certain that we do not offend Him when we find delight and consolation in His words and works. A king would be happy and pleased if he saw a little shepherd he loved looking spellbound at the royal brocade and wonder-

ing what it is and how it was made. Nor must we make women stand so far away from enjoyment of the Lord's riches. If they argue and teach and think they are right without showing their writings to learned men; yes, that would be wrong. Consequently, I am not thinking I am right in what I say—the Lord knows this well. But as with this little shepherd I mentioned, it consoles me to tell my meditations to my daughters; and what I tell will contain plenty of foolishness. Thus I begin with the favor of my divine King and with the permission of my confessor. May it please His Majesty that as He has wanted me to succeed in explaining other things for you[5]—and perhaps He did so because they were for you—I might succeed in explaining these. If I don't, I will consider the time well spent that I occupy in writing and reflecting upon material so divine that I haven't deserved to hear it.

9. It seems to me from what she says in the beginning that she is speaking with a third person; and she herself makes it known that there are in Christ two natures, one divine and the other human. I'm not going to dwell on this, because my intention is to speak about what I think can be beneficial to us who engage in prayer; although everything is beneficial for the encouragement and admiration of a soul that ardently loves the Lord. His Majesty knows well that even though at times—and these were few—I have heard explanations of some of these words and have been told their meaning when I asked, I don't remember the explanations at all, for I have a very poor memory. Thus, I shall be able to say only what the Lord teaches me and what serves my purpose; and I don't remember ever having heard anything about this first verse.

Let Him kiss me with the kiss of His mouth.

10. O my Lord and my God, and what words are these that a worm speaks them to its Creator! May You be blessed, Lord, for in so many ways have You taught us! But who will dare, my King, utter these words without Your permission? The thought is frightening, and so it will be frightening that I tell anyone to utter them. People will say I am a fool, that the words don't mean this, that they have many meanings, that obviously we must not speak such words to God, that for this reason it is

good that simple people do not read these things. I confess that the passage has many meanings. But the soul that is enkindled with a love that makes it mad desires nothing else than to say these words. Indeed, the Lord does not forbid her to say them.

God help me! Why are we surprised? Isn't the deed more admirable? Do we not approach the most Blessed Sacrament? And I was even wondering if the bride was asking for this favor that Christ afterward gave us. I also wondered whether she was asking for that union so great that God became man, for that friendship that he effected with the human race. Obviously a kiss is the sign of great peace and friendship among two persons. May the Lord help us understand how many kinds of peace there are.

11. Before I go any further, and so as not to forget, I want to say one thing—very important in my opinion—although the matter would fit better at another time. I hold as certain that there are many persons who approach the most Blessed Sacrament (and please the Lord I be lying) with serious mortal sins. Yet, if such persons were to hear a soul dying with love of its God say these words, they would be surprised and consider it great boldness. At least I am sure they themselves would not say them, for these words and other similar ones in the *Song of Songs* are said by love. Since such persons have no love, they can easily read the *Song of Songs* every day and not themselves become involved with the words; nor would they even dare take the words on their lips. For truly even hearing them makes one fear, for these words bear in themselves great majesty. How much majesty You bear, my Lord, in the most Blessed Sacrament. But since these persons do not have a living faith but a dead one, You do not speak to them when they see You so humble under the species of bread. They do not deserve to hear—and thus they are not so daring.

12. As a result these words in themselves, taking them only literally, would truly cause fear if the one uttering them were in his senses. But the one whom Your love, Lord, has drawn out of himself, You will truly pardon if he says them and also others, even though to say them is daring. And my Lord, if the kiss signifies peace and friendship why shouldn't souls ask You

for this kiss? What better thing can we ask for than what I ask You for, my Lord; that You give me this peace "with the kiss of Your mouth"? This, daughters, is a lofty petition, as I shall tell you afterward.[6]

Chapter 2

Treats of nine kinds of false peace presented to the soul by the world, the flesh, and the devil. Explains the holiness of the religious state. This holiness leads to the true peace desired by the bride in the Song of Songs.

GOD DELIVER YOU from the peace of many kinds that worldly people have. May He never allow us to try it, for it brings perpetual war. When such persons of the world remain quiet, while going about in serious sin, and so tranquil about their vices, for their consciences don't feel remorseful about anything, their peace, you have read, is a sign that they and the devil are friends. While they live, the devil does not wage war against them. For bad as they are they would then return to God somewhat, not out of love for Him but so as to flee from this war. Those who would act in such a way would never persevere in serving God. Soon, since the devil understands this, he would again give them delight in their pleasure and they would return to their friendship with him, until he has them in that place where he shows them how false their peace was. There is no reason to speak of these persons here; let them worry about it, for I hope in the Lord that so much evil will not be found among you. But the devil could begin to offer you another peace in small things, and always, while we live, daughters, we must fear.

2. When a Sister begins to grow lax in things that in themselves seem small, persisting in them for a long time without feeling any remorse of conscience, the resulting peace is bad. And consequently the devil can draw her into a thousand evils. Examples of these little things would be an infrac-

tion of something in the constitutions, which in itself would not be a sin, or being careless, even though without malice, about what the bishop commands (in fact he stands in God's place, and it is good always—for this reason we have come here—to consider what he desires), and many other little things that come along and which in themselves do not appear to be sins. In sum, there are faults and always will be, for we are miserable creatures. I don't say that there are not; what I say is that these faults should be felt when they are committed and that the soul should understand that there was a fault. For if the soul doesn't, the devil, as I say, can rejoice and gradually make it insensible to these little things. I tell you, daughters, that when the devil attains this, he has attained no small thing, for I fear he will go further. Hence, for love of God be very careful. There must be war in this life.[1] In the face of so many enemies it's not possible for us to sit with our hands folded; there must always be this care about how we are proceeding interiorly and exteriorly.

3. I tell you that even though in prayer the Lord grants you favors and gives you what I shall speak of later,[2] when you leave prayer you will meet with a thousand little obstacles, a thousand little occasions to break one rule carelessly, or not to carry out another well, interior disturbances and temptations. I don't say that this war must be going on always or habitually; but it is a wonderful favor from the Lord. By this means the soul advances. It's impossible for us to be angels here below because such is not our nature. In fact, a soul doesn't disturb me when I see it with great temptations. If love and fear of our Lord are present, the soul will gain very much; I'm certain of that. If I see a soul always quiet and without any war—for I've run into some like this—I always fear even if I do not see it offending the Lord. Never do I finish seeking to assure myself; and trying and tempting such persons, if I can, since the devil doesn't do so, in order that they may know themselves. I have met a few; to be without war is possible, once the Lord has brought the soul to an abundance of contemplation.

4. There is a variety of ways to proceed in prayer. These souls I am referring to remain in an habitual and interior hap-

piness. Yet, I think they do not understand themselves. And after I take a careful look I see that sometimes they have their little wars, though these are few. But it is a fact that I do not envy these souls. I have considered the matter attentively and see that those who have to fight the war that was mentioned advance much further in the things pertaining to perfection, without experiencing such abundant prayer, than we can understand here below. Let us exclude souls that are far advanced and very mortified after having endured this war for many years. Since they are already dead to the world, our Lord ordinarily gives them peace, but not in such a way that they don't deplore a fault they may commit and experience deep sorrow over it.

5. Thus, daughters, the Lord leads souls along many paths. But always fear, as I have said,[3] when some fault you commit does not grieve you. For in regard to sin, even venial, you already know that the soul must feel deep sorrow, and, glory to God, I believe and see that you do feel it now.

Note one thing, and remember this for love of me: if a person is alive, doesn't he feel a tiny pinprick or a thorn however small? Well then, if our souls are not dead but alive in the love of God, isn't it a great favor to feel any little thing we do against our obligations or what we have professed? Oh, His Majesty is making a bed of roses and flowers for Himself in the soul to whom He gives this care, and it is impossible that He fail to come and favor it, even though late. God help me, what are we religious doing in the monastery? Why did we leave the world? For what reason did we come? In what better way could we be occupied than to prepare rooms within our souls for our Spouse and reach the stage in which we can ask Him to give us the kiss of His mouth? Happy will be the soul that makes this request and whose lamp will not be out when the Lord comes,[4] otherwise the Lord will grow tired of knocking, and turn away. Oh, my daughters! What a great state of life we are in, for no one but we ourselves can keep us from saying these words to our Spouse since we took Him for our Spouse when we made our professions.

6. Let scrupulous souls understand me, for I am not speak-

ing of some fault that is committed occasionally or of faults that cannot be recognized or always felt by everyone, but of one who commits faults habitually without paying any attention to them, thinking they are trifles, and without any remorse, and who does not strive to make amends. I repeat that peace of this sort is dangerous and you should be warned about it. Well now, what will be the peace of those who are very lax about the observance of their rule? (Please God there will be none.) In many ways the devil will give them peace, for God permits him to do so on account of our sins. There is no reason to discuss the matter. I wanted to warn you with this small comment. Let us go on to the peace and friendship the Lord begins to show us in prayer, and I will tell what His Majesty makes known to me.

7. But before I do, I think it will be good to tell you a little about the peace the world and our own sensuality give. Even though in many books this topic has been discussed better than I'm capable of doing, perhaps you will not have money to buy books, for you are poor, or have any benefactor to give them to you. Whereas this writing of mine will remain in the house, and you will have all the material together. Souls could in many ways be deceived by the peace the world gives. From some of these ways that I shall mention you will deduce the rest.

8. Oh, as for riches! If people have easily what they need and a lot of money in their coffers and guard against committing serious sins, they think everything is done. They enjoy what they have. They give an alms from time to time. They do not reflect that their riches are not their own but given by the Lord so that they, as His stewards, may share their wealth among the poor, and that they must give a strict account for the time they keep a surplus in their coffers while delaying and putting off the poor who are suffering. This topic is not pertinent to us except that you beg the Lord to give rich people light that they may not continue in this daze and have happen to them what happened to the covetous rich man,[5] and that you praise His Majesty because He has made you poor, and that you accept poverty as a particular favor from Him.

9. Oh, my daughters, what a great relief it is, even with respect to our tranquillity here below, not to have these burdens; as for the final day, you can't imagine. The rich are the slaves and you are the masters. By the following example you will see this clearly. Who is more at rest? A gentleman who has all he needs to eat on the table and all his clothing laid out for him or his steward who must render him an account of every penny? The gentleman spends without measure since all belongs to him. The poor steward is the one who suffers for it. And the more wealth there is the more vigilant the steward has to be, for he has to give an accounting. He will especially have a large balance to make up if he has held the office for many years and has been a little careless. I don't know how he stays calm. Don't read this, daughters, without praising our Lord very much, and always go forward doing what you are now doing in not having any possessions in particular. For without worry we eat what the Lord sends since His Majesty takes care that we lack nothing. We don't have to give an account of what is left over because His Majesty provides in such a way that what is left is so small that we are not obliged to share it with others.

10. What is necessary, daughters, is that we be content with little. We must not want as much as those who give a strict accounting, as any rich person will have to give, even though he may not have to do so here on earth but receives it from his stewards. And how strict an accounting he will have to give! If he understood he would not eat so happily nor would he spend what he has on vanities and trivialities. As for you, daughters, look always for the poorest things, which will be enough to get by on; in clothing as well as in food. If you don't, you will find yourselves frustrated because God is not going to give you more, and you will be unhappy. Strive always to serve His Majesty in such a way that you do not eat the food of the poor without serving Him for it; although one can only poorly repay in service for the calm and repose the Lord gives when there is no obligation to account for riches. I well know that you understand, but it's necessary that at times you give special thanks to His Majesty for riches.

11. Concerning the peace the world gives through honors, I

don't think I have to say anything for you; the poor are never honored very much. What can do you great harm is praise—for once it starts it never ends—if you are not careful, so as to humble yourselves more afterward. The most common way will be by telling you that you are saints, in such exaggerated terms that it seems the devil teaches these words. And indeed he must sometimes. For if the words were spoken in the person's absence, they could be tolerated. But spoken in the person's presence, what fruit can they bear? Only harm, if you are not very cautious.

12. For love of God I ask you that you never seek peace for yourselves through these words of praise, for little by little they could do you harm and make you believe that the truth was spoken or make you think that now everything is accomplished and that you have done your part. You should never let a word of praise pass without it moving you to wage war interiorly, for this is easily done if you acquire the habit. Remember how the world treated Christ, our Lord, and how they exalted Him on Palm Sunday. Look at the esteem it had for St. John the Baptizer, for they wanted to take him for the Messiah, and how and why they beheaded him.

13. Never does the world exalt without putting down, if the exalted are the sons of God. I have a lot of experience of this. It used to afflict me to see so much blindness in these praises, and now I laugh to myself as though someone crazy were speaking. Remember your sins, and if in some matters people speak the truth in praising you, note that the virtue is not yours and that you are obliged to serve more. Awaken fear in your soul so that you do not rest in the kiss of this false peace given by the world; think that it is a kiss from Judas. Although some do not praise you with such an intention, the devil is watching to see how he can take away the spoils if you do not defend yourselves against him. Believe that you have to stand here with a sword in the hand of your thoughts. Although you think the praise does you no harm, do not trust it. Remember how many were at the top and are now at the bottom. There is no security while we are alive. For love of God, Sisters, always wage an interior war against these praises, for thus you will come away from them

with the gain of humility, and the devil and the world who are on the lookout for you will be abashed.

14. Concerning the peace and harm that this security can cause in your own flesh, there would be much to say. I shall mention some points, and from them, as I have said,[6] you can go on to deduce the rest. The flesh is very fond of comfort—you have already seen this. If we could understand we would realize that to seek one's peace in comforts is very dangerous. I often think about the matter and cannot understand how there can be so much peace and calm in persons who live very comfortably. Does the most sacred body of our Model and Light perhaps deserve less comfort than our own bodies? What did the Lord do to suffer so many trials? Have we read in the lives of the saints, those who we know for sure are in heaven, that they had a comfortable life? Where does this tranquillity in comfort come from? Who has told us that comfortable living is good? What is this, that some persons spend their days eating well and sleeping and seeking recreations and all the rest they can? I'm stunned when I consider this. It doesn't seem to them there will be another world and they think that the things mentioned are the least dangerous of this present world.

15. Oh, daughters, if you knew what great evil lies enclosed here. The body grows fat and the soul weakens. If we were to see the soul, we would think it about ready to expire. In many books you will find doctrine written about the great evil found in seeking one's peace in comforts, for if we understand that to do so is wrong, we will have hope for a remedy. But I fear that the thought doesn't pass through peoples' minds. I'm not surprised since the evil is so common. I tell you that even though through comforts a person's flesh is at rest, in a thousand ways there will be war if such a person is going to be saved. And it would be more valuable for souls to understand themselves and take up gradually the penance that otherwise will come to them all at once. I have said this that you might fervently praise God, daughters, that you are in a place where your flesh cannot find peace in comforts even though it may want to. Such craving for comfort could harm you without your being aware, that is, under the excuse of sickness. You need to be

very careful about this. For one day it will hurt you to take the discipline[7] and eight days later perhaps not. Another day or number of days you will be unable to bear the coarse tunics,[8] but this won't be permanent. Some days eating fish may hurt you, but once your stomach gets used to it, it will not harm you. Another time you will think you are so weak that you'll be unable to go without eating meat,[9] but by not fasting for one day you will overcome this weakness. Of these things and of much more, I have experience. It shouldn't be thought that these things involve serious fault, but that there may not be much need for them. What I am saying is that we must not find our rest in being lax, but must test ourselves sometimes. I know that this flesh is very deceptive and that we need to understand it. May the Lord out of His goodness give us light for everything. Discretion is very important, as is also trust in our superiors rather than in ourselves.

16. To return to our topic;[10] since the bride indicates the peace she is seeking by saying, *Let Him kiss me with the kiss of His mouth,* we have a sign that the Lord has other ways of bestowing peace and showing friendship. I now want to explain some to you so that you will see the kind of lofty petition this is and the difference that lies between these two types of peace.

O great God and Lord of ours, what profound wisdom! Well could the bride have said, *let Him kiss me,* and, it seems, have concluded her petition in fewer words. Why does she specify, *with the kiss of His mouth?* Surely, there is not a letter too many. I don't know the reason, but I shall say something about this. It matters little if what I say is not what the passage means provided, as I said,[11] we benefit from the thoughts. Now then, in many ways does our King offer souls peace and friendship, as we see each day both in prayer and outside of it; but our friendship with His Majesty is only skin-deep, as the saying goes. You will observe, daughters, the degree of love you have reached in that you will be able to ask for that which the bride does if the Lord brings you to Himself. If He doesn't do so, do not become discouraged; whatever the friendship you have with God, you will be very rich if there is no fault on your part. But we should grieve and be very sorry that through our own fault we do not reach this excellent friendship and that we are happy with little.

17. O Lord, why is it that we do not remember that the reward is great and everlasting, and that once we have reached such close friendship here below the Lord gives us the reward, and that many remain at the foot of the mount who could ascend to the top? In other little things I have written for you[12] I have often mentioned this, and now I repeat and ask that you always have courageous thoughts. As a result of them the Lord will give you grace for courageous deeds. Believe that these brave thoughts are important. There are some persons who have already attained friendship with the Lord because they have confessed their sins well and have repented, but two days don't pass before they return to them. Indeed, that is not the friendship the bride is asking for. Always strive, O daughters, so that you don't go to the confessor each time to confess the same fault.

18. It's true that we cannot live without faults, but at least there should be some change so that they don't take root. If they take root, they will be harder to eradicate and even many others could arise from them. If we plant an herb or small tree and water it each day, it grows so strong that afterward you need a shovel and a pickax to get it out by the roots. Committing the same fault each day, however small, if we do not make amends for it, is like watering a plant each day. And if one day it is planted and ten more pass by, it can still be easily rooted out. In prayer you must ask help from the Lord, for we of ourselves can do little; rather, we add faults instead of taking them away. Reflect that in that frightful judgment at the hour of death we shall see that this was no small matter especially for those the Judge took for His brides in this life.

19. Oh, great dignity, worthy of awakening us that we might try diligently to please this Lord and King of ours! But how badly these persons repay this friendship since they turn so quickly into mortal enemies! Indeed, how great is the mercy of God. Where would we find a friend so patient? And even if a friend commits one fault, it is never erased from the other's memory, nor do the two manage to have a friendship as

trusting as before. Now then, how often will souls similarly fail in their friendship with our Lord, and how many years He waits for us in this way? May You be blessed, Lord, my God, for You show us so much pity that it seems You forget Your greatness so as not to punish—as would be right—a betrayal as treacherous as this. I think this infidelity is a dangerous state, for even though the mercy of God is what it is we also frequently see people dying in this state without confession. May His Majesty deliver us, because of who He is, daughters, from being in so dangerous a state.

20. There is another kind of friendship, stronger than this, had by persons who guard themselves against offending the Lord mortally. Those who have reached this stage have attained much, the world being what it is. These persons even though they guard themselves against sinning mortally do not fail to fall now and again, from what I believe. For they care little about venial sins; they commit many daily, and thus they are very close to committing mortal sins. They will ask: "Do you pay attention to that?" Many others I have heard say: "That's why we have holy water and the remedies of our holy Mother the Church." Such remarks are certainly something to grieve over very much. For love of God, take great care never to grow careless about venial sin, however small, by recalling that we have a remedy. It is not right that something good be the occasion for doing wrong. To be mindful of this remedy after the fact and to strive to use it at once is, of course, good.

21. It is a very important thing always to have a conscience so pure that nothing hinders you from asking our Lord for the perfect friendship the bride asks for. At least, the kind of friendship we just mentioned is not the one the bride asks for. That friendship just mentioned is truly suspect for many reasons. And those given over to comforts and prepared for much lukewarmness will not know clearly whether what they do is a venial or mortal sin. God deliver us from this lukewarmness. Since it seems to them that they do not commit the serious sins they see in others—and such is not the state of perfect humility—they judge these others to be wicked. It could be that these latter are much better because they weep over their

sins with deep repentance and, perhaps, with a better purpose of amendment, which will result in their never offending the Lord in little or much. Those doing the judging, since it seems to them they don't do any of these bad things, give themselves greater latitude for their enjoyments. For the most part, they will recite their vocal prayers, but not very well, because their consciences are not so delicate.

22. There is another kind of friendship and peace our Lord begins to give some persons who are totally committed to not offending Him in anything, although they don't withdraw so much from the occasions. They have their times for prayer. Our Lord gives them tenderness and tears. Yet, they do not want to give up the enjoyments of this life. They want to live a good and well-ordered life, for they think it is beneficial for them to live here below with tranquillity. Life bears with it many changes. They will be doing enough if they continue in the practice of virtue. But if they don't withdraw from the satisfactions and pleasures of the world, they will soon grow lax again in walking the Lord's path; there are great enemies we must defend ourselves against. Such, daughters, is not the friendship the bride desires; neither should you desire it. Turn away always from any little occasion, however small, if you want the soul to grow and live securely.

23. I don't know why I'm saying these things to you unless so that you will understand the dangers that lie in not turning resolutely from all worldly things. For if we do turn from them we will spare ourselves many faults and trials. There are so many ways in which our Lord begins to exchange friendship with souls that I don't think I would ever finish recounting the ones I've recognized, even though I am a woman. What would confessors or those who deal with them more particularly have to say? Indeed, some of those persons bewilder me, for it seems they have everything that is required for them to be friends of God. I shall tell you about one lady in particular, for it is not long ago that I spoke with her in a special way. She was very fond of receiving Communion frequently, never said anything bad about anyone, experienced devotion in her prayer, and

lived in constant solitude because she was in her house by herself. She was so mild in her temperament that nothing said to her ever made her angry or say any bad word, for she was quite perfect. She had never married, nor was she now at an age in which she could, and she had undergone many contradictions along with having this peace. Since I saw all these virtues, it seemed to me they were effects of a very advanced soul and of deep prayer. And I esteemed this lady highly at the beginning because I didn't see her offend God and understood that she guarded against doing so.

24. After getting to know her I began to understand that all was peaceful as long as her self-interest was not affected. But when her own interests were at stake, her conscience was not so delicate, but actually easygoing. I learned that although she would suffer all the things that were said against her, she would not tolerate anything said against her reputation even in some tiny point concerning her honor or the esteem she thought was her due. She was so overcome by this misery, so eager to know everything that was said against these and so fond of her comfort that I was amazed how such a person could live even an hour. She embellished all this in such a way that it appeared free from sin. And taking into account the reasons she gave to justify some of her actions I think I would have tried to defend her if someone had blamed her. In other things it was quite obvious that she was wrong though perhaps this judgment came from not understanding her motives well. I was really bewildered. Almost everyone considered her to be a saint, although I observed that she must have been somewhat at fault for the persecutions she underwent. And I did not envy her manner of living and sanctity. Rather, she and two other souls that I have seen in this life—for now I recall them[13]—who were saints in their own opinion, caused me more fear, after I spoke with them, than all the sinners I have seen. I beg the Lord to give us light.

25. Praise Him, daughters, very much for He brought you to the monastery where, however much the devil may do, we cannot be deceived as much as can those who live in their own homes. There are souls whom, it seems, nothing keeps from fly-

ing off to heaven; they seek perfection in everything—in their opinion. But there is no one to inform them of their faults. In monasteries I have never seen this lack, for souls must do, not what they want, but what they are told. Instead, people living in their own homes cannot know their faults, even though they would like to because they want to please the Lord. For, in the end, what they do is their own will. And even though they may go against their own will sometimes, they do not exercise themselves so much in mortification. Let us exclude some persons to whom our Lord has given light for many years, for these persons seek someone who will inform them of their faults and to whom they may submit, and their great humility leads them to have little confidence in themselves, however learned they may be.

26. There are others who have left everything for the Lord and have neither house nor possessions, nor do they take pleasure in comfort—on the contrary, they are penitential—or in the things of the world, because the Lord has already given them light about how miserable these things are. But they are too attached to their honor. They would not want to do anything that was not really acceptable to men as well as to the Lord; great discretion and prudence. It is not always easy to reconcile these two, for the trouble is that without one's being aware the interests of the world almost always gain more than do those of God. These souls, for the most part, grieve over anything said against them. They do not embrace the cross but drag it along, and so it hurts and wearies them and breaks them to pieces. However, if the cross is loved, it is easy to bear; this is certain.

27. No, neither is this the friendship the bride seeks. As a result, my daughters, since you have done what I mentioned here first, be careful not to let yourself be overcome by the second thing.[14] Everything should be wearisome to you; if you have given up the most (you have left the world, its comforts, joys, and riches, which, even though false, in the end are pleasing) what do you fear? Look how you fail to understand, for in order to free yourselves from some bitterness a word can cause you, you burden yourselves with a thousand worries and

obligations. There are so many of these, if we want to please those who are in the world, that one can't bear mentioning them all or enlarging upon them, nor would I even know how.

28. There are other souls, and in speaking of them I'm going to conclude, for if you pay attention to what I have said you will understand many ways by which they begin to make progress and then falter on the road. I say "there are other souls," because no longer are they concerned about what people say or about their own honor. But these souls are not exercised in mortification and in denying their own will, and so they never get over their fear. Since they are determined to suffer everything, it may seem that the job is done. But in serious matters concerning the honor of the Lord their concern for their own honor revives. Yet, they don't seem to understand. They think they don't fear the world but fear God. They figure out how dangers might arise in that virtuous deeds could result in much evil. It seems the devil teaches them; a thousand years in advance they prophesy what could come, if doing so is necessary.

29. These are not souls of the kind that would do what St. Peter did, by throwing himself into the sea,[15] or what many other saints did. In their calm they will draw souls to the Lord, but not by putting themselves in dangers. Nor does the faith they have do much for them in their efforts to carry out their resolutions with deeds. One thing I have noticed; we see few in the world, outside of religious life, entrust their livelihood to God. I know only two persons. In religious life it is already known that there will be no lack—although whoever truly enters for God alone, I believe, will not think of this. But how many there are, daughters, who will not give up what they have unless it be with security! In other writings where I have given you advice, I have spoken much about these pusillanimous souls and mentioned the harm their faintheartedness does them and how good it is for them to have great desires since they cannot do great works.[16] I don't say any more about these, although I would never tire of doing so. Once the Lord brings them to so great a state, let them serve Him through it, and not be shy. For even if someone who is a religious—especially a woman—cannot help her neighbor, her

prayer will be powerful if she has strong determination and ardent desires for souls. Even, perhaps, the Lord will desire that either in life or in death she will help others, as the holy friar Diego does now.[17] He was a lay brother and did nothing more than serve; and after his death, so many years ago, his memory is revived by the Lord that he might be an example to us. Let us praise His Majesty!

30. Thus, my daughters, if the Lord has brought you to this state, little is lacking for you to receive the peace and friendship the bride asks for. Don't fail to beg the Lord for it with continual tears and desires. Do what you can for your part that He might give it to you. Realize that the religious state itself is not the peace and friendship the bride asks for, even though the Lord grants a great favor to the one He has brought to it. For only after one has been occupied in much prayer, penance, humility, and many other virtues, will that peace come. May the Lord always be praised for He gives all, amen.

Chapter 3

Treats of the true peace God grants the soul and of His union with it. Gives some examples of the heroic charity of some servants of God.

> *Let Him kiss me with the kiss of His mouth. (Sg. 1:2)*

O HOLY BRIDE, let us turn to what you ask for: that holy peace which makes the soul, while remaining itself completely secure and tranquil, venture out to war against all worldly kinds of peace. Oh, how happy will be the lot of one who obtains this favor since it is a union with the will of God; such a union that there is no division between Him and the soul, but one same will. It is a union not based on words or desires alone, but a union proved by deeds. Thus, when the bride knows she is serving the Bridegroom in something, there is so much love and desire to please Him that she doesn't listen to the reasons the intellect will give her or to the fears it will propose. But she lets faith so work that she doesn't look for her own profit or rest; rather, she succeeds now in understanding that in this service lies all her profit.

2. It will seem to you, daughters, that this way of acting is not advisable, since doing things with discretion is so praiseworthy a practice. You must keep in mind one point: the Lord has heard your petition (from what you can understand, I mean, for one cannot know with certainty) that He kiss you with the kiss of His mouth. For if you know this through the effects of His having done so, there is no reason to delay in anything; but forget yourselves so as to please this most sweet Bridegroom. His Majesty gives many signs of Himself to those who enjoy this favor. One sign is contempt for all earthly things, in which they are judged to be as little as they in fact are. Another, not desiring one's own good, because one's own vanity is already understood. A third, not rejoicing except with those who love their Lord. Life becomes wearisome to these persons; their esteem is for the riches they merit. And there are other similar signs that He who placed them in this state teaches.

3. Once the soul has arrived here, it has nothing to fear except that God may not make use of it by giving it trials and the occasions for serving Him even at a great cost to itself. Hence, as I've said,[1] love and faith are at work. And the soul does not want to benefit by what the intellect teaches it, for this union between the bride and Bridegroom has taught it other things the intellect cannot attain to, and the soul tramples the intellect underfoot.

Let us draw a comparison so that you may understand. There is a captive in the land of the Moors whose father is poor, but who has a good friend. If this friend doesn't ransom him, the captive has no means of liberation. What his friend possesses is not enough to pay the ransom, but the friend will have to go to serve in the captive's place. The great love the friend has makes him want freedom for the captive more than for himself. But then discretion comes along with many reasons and tells the friend that he is more obligated to himself and that he perhaps has less fortitude than the one who is now in captivity and that the Moors will make him lose his faith, that it is not good to place oneself in this danger, and many other things.

4. Oh, strong love of God! And how true it is that nothing seems impossible to the one who loves! Oh, happy the soul that has obtained this peace from its God, for it is master over all the trials and dangers of the world, fears no one provided it serves so good a Spouse and Lord. Its reason to love Him is far greater than the reason the father and friend have for loving the captive. Well, daughters, you've already read about a saint who when a widow came to him in desolation went to the land of the Moors to exchange himself for her son.[2] He did this not for a son or for a friend but because he must have truly arrived at this blessed state in which God must have given him this peace and so that he could please His Majesty and somehow imitate Him. You've also read how things turned out and how spiritually enriched this saint was when he returned from captivity.

5. [I would think that his mind did not fail to come up with some more reasons besides those I mentioned, because he was a bishop and would have had to abandon his flock, and perhaps he would have had fears. Consider one thing that comes to me now and is appropriate for those who are pusillanimous and weak in spirit—for the most part they will be women. Although in truth their souls may have reached this state, their weak nature fears. It's necessary for us to be on guard because this natural weakness will make us lose a great crown. When you feel this pusillanimity, have recourse to faith and humility, and don't fail to go on fighting with faith, for God can do all. Thus He was able to give fortitude to many saintly girls, and He gave it so that they were able to suffer many torments, since they were determined to suffer for Him.

6. By means of this determination in the soul, the Lord desires to make it master of its own free will, for in no way does He need our strength. Rather, His Majesty enjoys having His works shine forth in weak people, for in them there is more room for His power to work and fulfill the desire He has to grant us favors. As a result, the virtues God has given you will

help you act with determination and forget the reasons the intellect presents and your own weakness. These virtues will prevent this weakness from increasing when there are thoughts about what will or will not happen or thoughts, perhaps, that because of my own sins I will not deserve that He give me the fortitude He has given others. This isn't the time to think about your sins; leave them aside, as I have said. Such humility is inopportune right now and comes at the worst moment.

7. When others desire to give you something very honorable or when the devil incites you to a comfortable life or to other similar things, be afraid lest because of your sins you will not be able to bear these things with rectitude. And when you have to suffer something for our Lord or for your neighbor, do not be afraid of your sins. You could perform one of these works with so much charity that all your sins would be pardoned. The devil fears this, and that's why he reminds you of your sins at such a time. Be certain that the Lord will never fail His lovers, when they take a risk for Him alone. What they should watch out for are other selfish intentions, for I am not speaking except of those who aim after pleasing the Lord with the greatest perfection.]

8. And now in our times, I know a person—and you have seen him for he came to see me—who was moved by the Lord with such great charity that it cost him many tears not to be able to go in exchange for a captive. He spoke of the matter to me—he was one of the discalced followers of Friar Peter of Alcántara—and after many urgent entreaties got the permission from his Father General. And when he was four leagues from Argel—about to realize his good desire—the Lord brought him to Himself.[3] Surely he received a good reward. Well now how many discreet persons there were who told him his idea was crazy! For those of us who have not reached such love of God, it may seem so. And how much crazier it will be to come to the end of the dream that is this life with so much common sense! Please God we will merit to enter heaven; and, what is more, to be numbered among those who have advanced so far in the love of God.

9. Now I realize that God's great help is necessary for things

like this. Consequently, I counsel you, daughters, always to ask with the bride for this peace that is so delightful. With it the soul will reign over all these little fears of the world. And peacefully and quietly the soul will conquer the world. Isn't it clear that the soul to whom God grants so great a favor as to join it with Himself in a friendship like this will be left truly rich in His blessings? For certainly these things cannot be ours. We can ask and desire that He grant us this favor—and even the asking is done with His help. As for the rest, what power has a worm? Sin keeps it so cowardly and miserable that all the virtues we can imagine are appraised according to our lowly nature.

Well then, what is the remedy, daughters? To ask for what the bride asks for. If a peasant girl should marry the king and have children, don't the children have royal blood? Well, if our Lord grants so much favor to our soul that He joins Himself to it in this inseparable way, what desires, what effects, what heroic deeds will be born from it as offspring, if the soul be not at fault!

10. [Hence I repeat that in similar cases if the Lord should grant you the favor of offering you something to be done for Him that you pay no attention to the fact that you have been sinners. It is necessary here that faith master our misery and that you be not frightened if at the beginning in making the resolution, and even afterward, you feel fear and weakness. Pay no attention to these except to encourage yourselves more; don't interfere with the flesh. Behold what the good Jesus says in His prayer in the garden, *the flesh is weak;*[4] and remember His admirable and sorrowful sweat. Now then, if His Majesty says that the divine and sinless flesh is weak, how is it we desire our flesh to be so strong that it doesn't feel the persecutions and the trials that can come to it? And in these very trials the flesh will be as though subject to the spirit. When the soul's will is joined to the will of God, the flesh does not complain.

11. The thought comes to me now that our good Jesus showed us the weakness of His humanity previous to the trials, and when He was in the abyss of His sufferings showed such great fortitude that He not only did not complain but did

nothing that would make it appear He was suffering with weakness. When He went to the garden, He said: *My soul is sorrowful even to death.*[5] Yet, while on the cross, for He was already suffering death, He did not complain. Nor did He do so when in the prayer of the garden He went to awaken His apostles. With greater reason might He have complained to His Mother and our Lady when she was at the foot of the cross, and not asleep but suffering in her most holy soul and dying a harsh death; it always consoles us more to complain to those who we know feel our trials and love us more.

12. So, let's not complain of fears or become discouraged at seeing our nature weak and without strength. Let us strive to strengthen ourselves with humility and understand clearly the little we ourselves can do and that if God does not favor us, we are nothing. Let us distrust completely our own strength and confide in His mercy, and until we attain this mercy our weakness will persist. Not without reason did our Lord show us His weakness, for it is clear that He was not weak since He was fortitude itself. But He did so for our consolation and that we might understand how it is fitting for us to carry out our desires with deeds. Let us observe that when the soul begins to mortify itself, everything is painful to it. If it begins to give up comforts, it grieves; if it must give up honor, it feels torment; and if it must suffer an offensive word, the hurt becomes intolerable for it. In sum, there are never lacking sorrows for it until death. But as it succeeds in its determination to die to the world, it will find itself freed of these sufferings; and, on the contrary, there will be no fear of its complaining any longer, for the peace the bride asks for will have been attained.]

13. Certainly, I think that if we were to approach the most Blessed Sacrament with great faith and love, once would be enough to leave us rich. How much richer from approaching so many times as we do. The trouble is we do so out of routine, and it shows. O miserable world, you have so covered the eyes of those who live in you that they do not see the treasures by which they could win everlasting riches!

14. O Lord of heaven and earth, how is it possible that even while in this mortal life one can enjoy You with so special a

friendship, that the Holy Spirit says this so clearly in these words, and that still we do not want to understand that these are the delights You share with souls in this *Song of Songs!* What endearing words! What sweetness! One of these words would have been enough for us to be dissolved in You. May You be blessed, Lord, because we don't lose anything through Your fault. Along how many paths, in how many ways, by how many methods You show us love! With trials, with a death so harsh, with torments, suffering offenses every day and then pardoning; and not only with these deeds do You show this love, but with words so capable of wounding the soul in love with You that You say them in this *Song of Songs* and teach the soul what to say to You. For I don't know how the words can be endured if You do not help the one who hears them to bear them—because of our weakness, not because of what the words deserve.

15. Hence, my Lord, I do not ask You for anything else in life but that *You kiss me with the kiss of Your mouth,* and that You do so in such a way that although I may want to withdraw from this friendship and union, my will may always, Lord of my life, be subject to Your will and not depart from it; that there be nothing to impede me from being able to say: "My God and my Glory, indeed *Your breasts are better and more delightful than wine.*"[6]

Chapter 4

Speaks of the prayer of quiet and of union and of the sweetness and delight they cause in the spirit; in comparison, earthly delights are nothing.

> *Your breasts are better than wine, and give forth the most sweet fragrance. (Sg. 1:2-3)*

OH, MY DAUGHTERS, what deep secrets there are in these words! May the Lord give us experience of them, for they are very difficult to explain.

When His Majesty, through His mercy, desires to answer the petition of the bride, He begins to commune with the soul in so friendly a way that only those who experience this friendship will understand it, as I say. I have written much about this in two books[1] (which, if the Lord is pleased, you will see after my death) in a very detailed way and at length, for I see that you will need them. Thus, I will do no more here than touch upon the matter. I don't know whether I will succeed in using the same words by which the Lord wished to explain the matter there.

2. In the interior of the soul a sweetness is felt so great that the soul feels clearly the nearness of its Lord. This experience is not merely one of devotion moving a person to shed many tears—which give satisfaction—either by thinking of the Passion of the Lord or of our sins. In this prayer of which I speak, that I call "quiet" because of the calm caused in all the faculties (for it seems the person has them well under control—although sometimes the experience is not like this, because the soul is not so absorbed in this sweetness), it seems that the whole man interiorly and exteriorly is comforted. It's as though there were poured into the marrow of one's bones a sweet ointment with a powerful fragrance. If we were suddenly to enter a place where this fragrance was strong and not from one thing but from many, and we did not know what it was or where it came from except that it permeated everything, we would have some idea of this most sweet love of our God. He enters the soul and does so with wonderful sweetness. He pleases and makes it happy, and it cannot understand how or from where that blessing enters. It would not want to lose that good; it would not want to stir or speak or even look lest the blessing go away.

3. [And this is what the bride says here according to my interpretation, that the breasts of the Bridegroom give forth fragrance greater than that of precious ointments.]

In these books I mentioned[2] I spoke of what the soul must do in order to make progress, and my purpose here is solely to explain the type of prayer I am dealing with. Thus, I do not want to enlarge any more than to say that in this friendship (for the

Lord now shows the soul that He loves it in so particular a way that there is nothing separating the two) great truths are communicated to the soul. For this light that dazzles the soul, since it is not understood, makes one see the vanity of the world. The soul doesn't see the good Master who teaches it, although it understands that He is with it. But it is left so well instructed, with such great effects and fortitude in the virtues, that it doesn't know itself afterward; nor would it want to do or say anything other than praise the Lord. While in this joy it is so enwrapped and absorbed that it doesn't seem to be within itself but in a kind of divine intoxication so that it doesn't know what it wants or what it says or what it asks for. In sum, it doesn't know itself; but it isn't outside itself to the extent that it fails to understand something of what is going on.

4. But when this most wealthy Bridegroom desires to enrich and favor the soul more, He changes it into Himself to such a point that, just as a person is caused to swoon from great pleasure and happiness, it seems to the soul it is left suspended in those divine arms, leaning on that sacred side and those divine breasts. It doesn't know how to do anything more than rejoice, sustained by the divine milk with which its Spouse is nourishing it and making it better so that He might favor it, and it might merit more each day.

When it awakens from that sleep and that heavenly inebriation, it remains as though stupefied and dazed and with a holy madness. It seems to me it can say these words: *Your breasts are better than wine.*

While it was in that intoxication, the soul thought it had no farther to ascend. But when it saw itself in a higher degree and completely drenched in the countless grandeurs of God, and sustained in this way, it makes a delicate comparison and says: *Your breasts are better than wine.*

An infant doesn't understand how it grows nor does it know how it gets its milk, for without its sucking or doing anything, often the milk is put into its mouth.[3] Likewise, here, the soul is completely ignorant. It knows neither how nor from where that great blessing came to it, nor can it understand. It knows that the blessing is the greatest that can be tasted in life, even if all the delights and pleasures of the world were joined together. It sees that it is nourished and made better and doesn't know when it deserved this. It is instructed in great truths without seeing the Master who teaches it; fortified in virtues and favored by One who knows it well and can do these things for it. It doesn't know what to compare His grace to, unless to the great love a mother has for her child in nourishing and caressing it.

5. [This comparison is appropriate. For the soul is so elevated and beyond the ability to benefit from its intellect, that it is, in part, like an infant that delights in a caress but doesn't have an intellect by which to understand how that good comes. For in the sleep coming from the divine inebriation the soul is still functioning because it understands and does something. It understands that it is near its God, and thus it has reason for saying: *Your breasts are better than wine.*

6. Great is this favor, my Spouse; a pleasing feast. Precious wine do You give me, for with one drop alone You make me forget all of creation and go out from creatures and myself, so that I will no longer want the joys and comforts that my sensuality desired up until now. Great is this favor; I did not deserve it.

After His Majesty granted it a greater favor and brought it closer to Himself, it rightly says: *Your breasts are better than wine.* The past favor was a great one, my God, but much greater is this one because I do less in it, and thus it is in every way better. The joy and delight of the soul are great when it arrives here.]

7. Oh, my daughters, may our Lord give us understanding or, to put it better, a taste—for there is no other way of being able to understand—of what the soul's joy is in this state. Let worldly people worry about their lordships, riches, delights, honors, and food, for even if a person were able to enjoy all these things without the accompanying trials—which is impossible—he would not attain in a thousand years the happiness that in one moment is enjoyed by a soul brought here by the Lord. St. Paul says, *all the trials of the world are not worthy to be compared with the glory which we await.*[4] I say that

in addition they are not worthy nor can they merit even one hour of this satisfaction, joy, and delight given here by God to the soul. There is no comparison between this delight and the baseness of worldly things, in my opinion. Nor can one merit so delightful a favor from our Lord, so intimate a union, or a love so destined to be experienced and felt. How ridiculous it would be to compare the trials of worldly people with those suffered here by the soul. If trials are not suffered for God, they are worth nothing; if they are suffered for Him, His Majesty adapts them to our strength. Thus, if we are so afraid of them it is because we are fainthearted and miserable.

8. Oh, Christians and my daughters! Let us now, for love of the Lord, awake from this sleep and behold that He does not keep the reward of loving Him for the next life alone. The pay begins in this life. O my Jesus, who could explain the benefit that lies in throwing ourselves into the arms of this Lord of ours and making an agreement with His Majesty that *I look at my Beloved, and my Beloved at me,*[5] and that He look after my things and I look after His![6] Let's not, as the saying goes, love ourselves to death. I repeat, my God, and beg You through the blood of your Son that You grant me this favor: *Let Him kiss me with the kiss of His mouth*, for without You, what am I, Lord? If I am not close to You, what am I worth? If I stray a little from Your Majesty, where will I end up?

9. Oh, my Lord, my Mercy, and my Good! And what greater good could I want in this life than to be so close to You, that there be no division between You and me? With this companionship, what can be difficult? What can one not undertake for You, being so closely joined? What is there in me to be grateful for, my Lord? Rather, I must blame myself very much for my failure to serve You. And thus I beg You, with St. Augustine, and with full determination, that You "give me what You command and command what You will."[7] Never, with Your favor and help, will I turn my back on You.

10. Now I see, my Bridegroom, that *You are mine.*[8] I cannot deny it. You came into the world for me; for me You underwent severe trials; for me You suffered many lashes; for me You remain in the most Blessed Sacrament; and now You

grant me so many wonderful favors. Well then, O most holy bride, with what ardor I have said what you say: "What can I do for my Spouse?"

11. [Indeed, Sisters, I don't know how to go on from here. How can I be Yours, my God? What can one who has used so unskillfully the favors You have granted do for You? What can be expected of her services? Since with Your help she does something, consider what a poor worm will be able to do. Why does a Lord so powerful need her? Oh, love! How I would want to say this word everywhere because love alone is that which can dare say with the bride, *I am my Beloved's.* He gives us permission to think that He, this true Lover, my Spouse and my Good, needs us.

12. Since He gives us permission, let us repeat, daughters, *my Beloved is mine and I am my Beloved's.* You are mine, Lord? If You come to me, why do I doubt that I will be able to serve You? From here on, Lord, I want to forget myself and look only at how I can serve You and have no other desire than to do Your will. But my desire is not powerful, my God; You are the powerful One. What I can do is be determined; thus from this very moment I am determined to serve You through deeds.]

Chapter 5

Continues to deal with the prayer of union and tells of the riches the soul acquires in it through the mediation of the Holy Spirit. Tells of the soul's determination to suffer trials for the Beloved.

> *I sat down under the shadow of Him whom I desired and His fruit is sweet to my taste. (Sg. 2:3)*

NOW LET US question the bride. Let us learn from this blessed soul that has approached the divine mouth and been sustained by these heavenly breasts; and we shall learn from it further what we must do, how we must act, what we must say if the Lord is to bring us sometime to the experience of this wonderful favor.

2. What she tells us is: *I sat down under the shadow of Him whom I desired and His fruit is sweet to my taste. The King brought me into the wine cellar and set charity in order in me.*[1] She says, *I sat down under the shadow of Him whom I desired.* God help me, how exposed to the sun, and burned by it, is the soul! She says she sat under the shadow of Him whom she desired. Here she compares Him to the apple tree, and she says its fruit is sweet to her taste. O souls that practice prayer, taste all these words! How many ways there are of thinking about our God. How different the kinds of food we can make from Him! He is manna, for the taste we get from Him conforms to the taste we prefer.[2] Oh, what heavenly shade this is! And who could say what the Lord reveals from it! I recall what the angel said to the most Blessed Virgin, our Lady: *the power of the Most High will overshadow you.*[3] How fortified will a soul be when the Lord places it in this grandeur! Rightly can it sit down and be assured.

3. Now note that for the most part, and almost always, God gives these sublime gifts and great favors to persons who have labored much in His service and desired His love and striven to prepare themselves so that in all things they might be agreeable to His Majesty. There may be some exception when the Lord wishes to give some person a special call, as He did St. Paul, for He brought him at once to the peak of contemplation and appeared to him and spoke in such a way that immediately that saint was truly exalted.[4] But when souls are worn out from many years of meditation and of having sought this Bridegroom, and most weary of worldly things, they sit under the shadow of Truth, they do not seek their comfort or calm or rest anywhere except where they understand they can truly have it. They place themselves under the protection of the Lord; they desire no other. And how well they are acting by trusting in His Majesty; for just as they have desired, they sit under His shadow. Fortunate is the soul that merits to remain under this shadow even from the viewpoint of things that can be seen here below! In regard to things the soul alone can

understand—that's something else as I have often realized.

4. It seems that while the soul is in this delight that was mentioned it feels itself totally engulfed and protected in this shadow and kind of cloud of the Divinity. From it come inspirations and a delightful dew which indeed rightly takes away the weariness that worldly things have caused the soul. The soul feels there a kind of repose that will even make breathing wearisome to it. And the faculties are so quiet and calm that the will would not want them to admit any thoughts, even good ones, nor does it admit any by way of inquiry or striving after them. There's no need to move the hand or raise it—I'm referring to reflection—for anything, for the Lord gives from the apple tree (to which she compares her Beloved) the fruit already cut, cooked, and even chewed. So she says that *His fruit is sweet to her taste.* For in this prayer all the soul does is taste, without any work on the part of the faculties; and present in this shadow of the Divinity—well does she say "shadow," since we cannot see It clearly here below but only under this cloud—is that brilliant Sun. This Sun sends, by means of love, the knowledge that His Majesty is indescribably close. I know that anyone who has undergone this experience will understand how truly this meaning can be given to these words spoken by the bride.

5. It seems to me the Holy Spirit must be a mediator between the soul and God, the One who moves it with such ardent desires, for He enkindles it in a supreme fire, which is so near. O Lord, how great are these mercies You show to the soul here! May You be blessed and praised forever, for You are so good a Lover. O my God and my Creator! Is it possible that there is no one who loves You? Oh, alas, and how often it is I who do not love You! Why didn't I merit to know You? How low do the branches of this divine apple tree reach, so that at times the soul may take hold of them by reflecting upon the grandeurs and multitude of mercies shown to it, and that it might see and enjoy the fruit that Jesus Christ, our Lord, drew from His Passion, watering this tree with His precious blood, with so admirable a love.

Previously, the soul says, it enjoyed sustenance from his divine breasts. As a beginner in receiving these favors the soul was nourished by the Bridegroom. Now it is growing, and He is enabling it to receive more. He nourishes it with apples.[5] He wants it to understand how it is obliged to serve and suffer. And the Lord is not content with all this—something marvelous, worthy of careful attention—for He understands that the soul is totally His, without any other interests. This means that things must not move it because of what they are, but that it be moved because of who its God is and out of love for Him, since He never ceases to commune with it in so many ways and manners, as One who is Wisdom itself.

6. In the first kind of peace, it seemed that no more could be given, yet this favor that was just mentioned is a much more sublime one. It is badly explained because my only intention is to note it briefly. In the book I mentioned to you,[6] daughters, you will find—if the Lord wills that it be published—the favor explained much more clearly. Well now, what more could we desire than this favor just mentioned? Oh, God help me, how little we desire to reach Your grandeurs, Lord! How miserable we would remain if Your giving were in conformity with our asking! Now let us consider what the bride said further on.

Chapter 6

Treats of how the benefits of this loving union surpass all the desires of the bride. Speaks of the suspension of the faculties and tells how some souls reach this sublime prayer in a short time.

The King brought me into the wine cellar and set charity in order within me. (Sg. 2:4)

WELL, NOW THAT THE SOUL is resting under the longed-for shadow,[1] and rightly so, what is left for it to desire unless that it never lack this good? It doesn't think there is anything more to desire. But our most sacred King has still much to give. He would never want to do anything else than give if He could find receivers. And as I have said often—I want you never to forget, daughters — the Lord is never content with giving us as little as we desire; I have seen it here.[2] He grants the soul in answer to some of its petitions an opportunity to merit and suffer something for Him, whereas the soul's intention was to suffer only what its strength could bear. Since His Majesty can make one's strength increase in payment for the little that one determines to do for Him, He will give so many trials and persecutions and illnesses that a poor man won't know himself.

2. This happened to me when I was quite young. Sometimes I would say, "Oh, Lord, I didn't want so much." But His Majesty gave strength and patience in such a way that even now I am amazed at how I was able to suffer, and I would not exchange those trials for all the world's treasures.

The bride says: *The King brought me.* How appropriate this name, "powerful King," is, for the Lord has no superior, nor will His reign ever end. Surely the soul in such a state will understand much about the greatness of this King; but not everything since that is impossible in this mortal life.

3. She says: *He brought me into the wine cellar; set charity in order within me.* I understand from these words the grandeur of this favor. For a greater or less amount can be given a person to drink, a good or a better wine, and the wine will leave him more or less inebriated and intoxicated. So with the favors of the Lord; to one He gives a little wine of devotion, to another more, with another He increases it in such a way that the person begins to go out from himself, from his sensuality, and from all earthly things; to some He gives great fervor in His service; to others, impulses of love; to others, great charity toward their neighbors. These gifts are given in such a way that these persons go about so stupefied they do not feel the great trials that take place here. But much is contained in what the bride says. He brings her into the wine cellar so that she may come out more abundantly enriched. It doesn't seem the King wants to keep anything from her. He wants her to drink in conformity with her desire and become wholly inebriated, drinking of all the wines in God's storehouse. Let the soul rejoice in these joys. Let it admire God's grandeurs.

Let it not fear to lose its life from drinking so much beyond what its natural weakness can endure. Let it die in this paradise of delights. Blessed be such a death that so makes one live! And truly this is what it makes the soul do. For the marvels the soul understands are so great—without its understanding how it understands—that it remains outside itself. The bride refers to this in saying: *He set charity in order within me.*

4. Oh, words that should never be forgotten by the soul to whom the Lord gives delight! Oh, sovereign favor! How impossible it is to deserve if the Lord does not give the wealth required for it. Indeed the soul does not even find itself awake in order to love. But blessed sleep, happy inebriation that makes the Bridegroom supply for what the soul cannot do; that is, set up so wonderful an order. For while the faculties are dead or asleep, love remains alive. And the Lord ordains that the soul function so wonderfully, without its understanding how, that it is made one, in great purity, with the very Lord of love, who is God. For no one hinders the soul, neither senses nor faculties (I mean intellect and memory), nor is the will aware of itself.

5. I was wondering now whether there is some difference between the will and love. And it seems to me there is. I don't know whether or not I'm speaking foolishly. But it seems to me that love is like an arrow sent forth by the will. If it travels with all the force that the will has, freed from all earthly things, and directed to God alone, it truly must wound His Majesty. Thus, fixed in God Himself, who is love, it is brought back from there with the greatest gain, as I shall say. I have been informed by some persons whom our Lord has brought to this great favor in prayer that He brings them to this holy inebriation with a suspension and that even exteriorly one can see they are not in themselves. When I ask what they feel, they are completely unable to explain; nor could they know how to do so, nor would they be able to understand anything of how love works there.

6. The tremendous gain drawn from this kind of prayer is clearly recognized through the effects, the virtues, the living faith and the contempt for the world left in the soul. But since

these blessings and what the soul enjoys here are gifts, nothing is understood—except at the beginning—for the sweetness is very great. Thus what the bride says is clear: that is, the wisdom of God supplies here for the soul, and He ordains the way in which it gains these marvelous favors during that time. Since it is so outside itself and so absorbed that it can do nothing with the faculties, how can it merit? Well, is it possible for God to grant it a favor so great that it wastes time and gains nothing in Him? No, I don't think so.

7. Oh, secrets of God! Here there is no more to do than surrender our intellects and reflect that they are of no avail when it comes to understanding the grandeurs of God. It is good to recall here how God acted with the Blessed Virgin, our Lady. In spite of all her wisdom she asked the angel: *How can this be?* But after he answered, *The Holy Spirit will come upon you; the power of the Most High will overshadow you,*[3] she engaged in no further discussion. As one who had such great faith and wisdom, she understood at once that if these two intervened, there was nothing more to know or doubt. She did not act as do some learned men (whom the Lord does not lead by this mode of prayer and who haven't begun a life of prayer), for they want to be so rational about things and so precise in their understanding that it doesn't seem anyone else but they with their learning can understand the grandeurs of God. If only they would learn something from the humility of the most Blessed Virgin!

8. O Blessed Lady, how perfectly we can apply to you what takes place between God and the bride according to what is said in the *Song of Songs*. And thus you can see, daughters, in the Office of our Lady, which we recite each week, how much in its antiphons and readings is taken from this *Song of Songs*. As for other souls, each one can understand according to the understanding God wants to give him, for he will see very clearly if he is receiving some of these favors, similar to what the bride says: *He set charity in order within me.* For souls that receive this favor do not know where they were, or how through a delight so sublime they could have pleased the Lord, or what they were doing since they did not give Him thanks for it.

9. O soul, beloved of God! Do not be anxious when His Majesty brings you here and speaks so endearingly; as you will see in many words that He says to the bride in the *Song of Songs*, such as: *You are all beautiful, my love,*[4] and many others, as I say. By these He shows He is happy with her. Thus you should believe that He will not consent to your being displeasing to Him at that time, but He will help you in what you might not have known so that He may be more pleased with you. He sees the soul lost to itself, transported so as to love Him, and that love's very force has taken away the intellect in order that the soul may love more. Indeed, His Majesty is not wont to fail nor can He fail to give Himself to the one who has given Him everything, nor could He endure not doing so.

10. It seems to me His Majesty is embellishing with His gifts this gold He has prepared and tested so as to see how many carats the soul's love is. These gifts are bestowed in a thousand ways and modes of which only the soul having arrived here will be able to speak. This soul, which is the gold, no more moves or works during this time than if it were in fact gold. And divine Wisdom, happy to see it thus (since there are so few who love Him with this strength) makes a thousand designs in the gold with inlays of precious stones and enamels.

11. Well now, this soul, what does it do at this time? This is what cannot be understood or known beyond what the bride says: *He set charity in order within me.* The soul, at least if it loves, does not know how nor does it understand what it loves. The King's most intense love, which has brought the soul to this high state, must have joined this soul's love to itself in such a way that the intellect does not deserve to understand; but these two loves become one again. Since the soul's love is brought so truly close to the love of God, how can the intellect reach that far? The intellect loses sight at that time, for the union never lasts long, but is brief. And there God sets love in order in such a way that it then knows well how to please His Majesty and even afterward, without understanding on the part of the intellect, as was said. But the intellect understands well afterward when it sees this soul with the enamel and inlays of precious stones and pearls of virtue, for it is amazed and can

say: *Who is this that is as bright as the sun?*[5]

O true King, and how right the bride was in giving You this name! For in a moment You can give riches and place them in a soul that they may be enjoyed forever. How well ordered love is in this soul!

12. I shall be able to give good examples of this because I have met some persons in this stage of prayer. I now remember one of them. Within three days the Lord gave her such blessings that were it not for my experience with her for some years and my seeing her always improve, I would not have believed the blessings possible. And I saw Him do the same for another within three months; and both were quite young. Others I have seen to whom God grants this favor after a long time. I have mentioned these two—and I could mention some others—because I have written here that few are those to whom our Lord grants these favors without their having undergone many years of trials, and thus it may be understood that there are some exceptions. One must not place limits on a Lord so great and desirous to grant favors. I am speaking of true favors from God, not of illusions or of the results of melancholy or of our own natural efforts. Only time will tell where the favors come from. When they are from God the virtues grow so strong and love becomes so enkindled that there's no concealing the two. Even without any specific desire on the part of the soul, they always bring profit to other souls.

13. *The King set charity in order within me,* set it in order so well that the love the soul had for the world is taken away; the soul's love of itself turns to disregard; its love for its relatives is such that it loves them solely for God; its love for its neighbors and its enemies is unbelievable unless experienced—a very strong love; its love of God is boundless, for sometimes the love impels it so much that its lowly nature cannot endure the love. And since the soul sees that it is now growing weak and about to die, it says: *Sustain me with flowers; surround me with apples for I am dying with the sickness of love.*[6]

Chapter 7

Explains the bride's strong desires to suffer much for God and neighbor and the abundant fruits that come to the Church from souls favored by the divine union and detached from self-interest.

Sustain me with flowers and surround me with apples, for I am dying of love. (Sg. 2:5)

OH, HOW WELL this divine language applies to what I want to speak of here! Holy bride, how is it that this sweetness slays you! From what I have known, sometimes the delight is so excessive that it seems to dissolve the soul in such a way that there is no longer any desire to live. And do you ask for flowers? What flowers will these be? Flowers will provide no remedy unless you ask for them so as to die, for in truth nothing else is desired when the soul arrives here. But this interpretation doesn't fit well because the bride says: *sustain me with flowers.* Asking to be sustained doesn't seem to me to involve a request for death but for life and the desire to serve in some way the One to whom she sees she owes so much.

2. Don't think, daughters, there is any exaggeration in saying that she dies. As I have said, it indeed happens that love sometimes operates with such force that it rules over all the powers of the natural subject. Thus, I know a person who while in this kind of prayer heard someone, with a beautiful voice, singing; and she certifies that, in her opinion, if the singing had not stopped the soul would have gone out of itself on account of the great delight and sweetness the Lord gave it to enjoy. His Majesty provided that the singing stop, for the one who was in this suspension could easily have died. But because she was powerless to stir or make any exterior movement, she couldn't tell the one singing to stop. And she was clearly aware of the danger she was in, but her state resembled that of someone in a deep sleep who is unable to come out of it and speak even though he may want to.[1]

3. In this suspension the soul would not want to come out of this sleep, nor would death be painful to it but great happiness, for this is what it desires. And how happy a death it would be, at the hands of this love! But sometimes His Majesty gives it light to see that living is good for it. However, the soul sees that its natural weakness will not be able to suffer that good for long if the delight lasts, and begs Him for another good so as to escape from that one that is so extraordinary, and thus it says: *sustain me with flowers.*

The fragrance of these flowers is different from the fragrance of flowers we smell here below. I understand by these words that the soul is asking to perform great works in the service of our Lord and of its neighbor. For this purpose it is happy to lose that delight and satisfaction. Although a person's life will become more active than contemplative, and one will seemingly lose if the petition is granted, Martha and Mary never fail to work almost together when the soul is in this state. For in the active—and seemingly exterior—work the soul is working interiorly. And when the active works rise from this interior root, they become lovely and very fragrant flowers. For they proceed from this tree of God's love and are done for Him alone, without any self-interest. The fragrance from these flowers spreads to the benefit of many. It is a fragrance that lasts, not passing quickly, but having great effect.

4. I want to explain myself further so that you understand. Someone preaches a sermon with the intention of benefitting souls, but he is not so detached from human considerations that he doesn't make some attempt to please, or to gain honor or credit; or he has his mind set on receiving some canonry for having preached well. There are also other things people do for their neighbor's benefit—many things—and with a good intention, but with much care not to lose anything through them and not to displease. They fear persecution; they want to be pleasing to kings, lords, and the people; they proceed with the discretion the world so much honors. This discretion is a shelter for many imperfections; they call it "discretion," and please God it will be.

5. These persons will serve His Majesty, and they profit

much. But, in my opinion, such are not the works and flowers asked for by the bride; she looks only for the honor and glory of God in everything. Truly, I don't believe that souls brought to this state by the Lord, from what I have understood of some, think of themselves, and of whether they will lose or gain, any more than if they did not exist. They look only at serving and pleasing the Lord. And because they know the love He has for His servants, they like to leave aside their own satisfaction and good so as to please Him and serve and tell souls beneficial truths by the best means they can. Nor do they, as I say, think about whether or not they will themselves lose. They keep before their minds the benefit of their neighbor, nothing else. So as to please God more, they forget themselves for their neighbor's sake, and they lose their lives in the challenge, as did many martyrs. They are not aware of the words they say while enveloped in so sublime a love of God, in their inebriation from that heavenly wine. And if they are aware, they don't care if they displease men. These souls do much good.

6. I recall now what I have often thought concerning that holy Samaritan woman,[2] for she must have been wounded by this herb. How well she must have taken into her heart the words of the Lord, since she left the Lord for the gain and profit of the people of her village. This explains well what I am saying. And in payment for her great charity, she merited to be believed and to see the wonderful good our Lord did in that village.[3]

It seems to me that one of the greatest consolations a person can have on earth must be to see other souls helped through his own efforts. Then, it seems to me, one eats the delicious fruit of these flowers. Happy are those to whom the Lord grants these favors. These souls are indeed obligated to serve Him. This holy woman, in that divine intoxication, went shouting through the streets. What amazes me is to see how the people believed her—a woman. And she must not have been well-off since she went to draw water. Indeed she was very humble because when the Lord told her faults to her she didn't become offended (as the world does now, for the truth is hard to bear), but she told Him that He must be a prophet. In sum, the people believed her; and a large crowd, on her word alone, went out of the city to meet the Lord.

7. So I say that much good is done by those who, after speaking with His Majesty for several years, when receiving His gifts and delights, want to serve in laborious ways even though these delights and consolations are thereby hindered. I say that the fragrance of these flowers and works produced and flowing from the tree of such fervent love lasts much longer. One of these souls does more good with its words and works than do many others whose works carry the dust of our sensuality and some self-interest.

8. From these flowers comes the fruit, the apples of which the bride then says: *Surround me with apples.* Give me trials, Lord; give me persecutions. And truly this soul desires them and indeed passes through them well. For since it no longer looks to its own satisfaction but to what pleases God, its pleasure is in somehow imitating the laborious life that Christ lived.

By the "apple tree," I understand the tree of the cross because it is said in another verse in the *Song of Songs: under the apple tree I raised you up.*[4] And a soul that is surrounded by crosses, trials, and persecutions has a powerful remedy against often continuing in the delight of contemplation. It finds great delight in suffering; but suffering doesn't consume it and waste its strength, as would this suspension, if very frequent, of the faculties in contemplation. And the soul also has another reason for making this request, for it must not be always enjoying without serving and working in something. I notice in some persons—there are not many because of our sins—that the more they advance in this kind of prayer and the gifts of our Lord the more attention they pay to the needs of their neighbor, especially to the needs of their neighbors' souls. For to draw one soul away from mortal sin it seems such persons would give many lives, as I said at the beginning.

9. Who will make those to whom our Lord begins to give these delights believe this? But perhaps it will seem to them that such persons are not making good use of their lives and that to remain in a corner enjoying this delight is what is im-

portant. It belongs to the Lord's providence, in my opinion, that these beginners do not understand where these other souls are because with this initial fervor they would immediately want to leap forward to that stage. But such a quick move ahead does not suit them, for they are still not weaned. It's necessary that they be nourished some days more with the milk I mentioned at the beginning.[5] Let them remain close to those divine breasts, for the Lord will take care, when they are strong, to bring them further. Otherwise, they would not do the good they think; rather they would harm themselves. Since in the book I mentioned[6] you will find very detailed explanations about when a soul may go out to benefit others and about the danger that lies in going out ahead of time, I do not want to mention the matter here or enlarge upon this any more. When I began, my intention was simply to explain how you can find comfort when you hear some words from the *Song of Songs*, and how, even though they are obscure to your understanding, you can reflect upon the profound mysteries contained in them. It would be bold of me to go on at any greater length.

10. May it please the Lord that what I have said may not have been bold. The work has been done to obey the one who commanded me to do it. May His Majesty be served in everything. If something good is here, you can indeed believe that it does not come from me; the Sisters here with me have seen that because of my many occupations I have written this hastily. Beseech His Majesty that I may understand through experience what has been said. Any Sister who thinks she has some experience of these delights should praise our Lord and ask Him for the latter-mentioned works and trials so that the gain will not be just for herself.

May it please our Lord to keep us in His hands and teach us always how to carry out His will, amen.

The Interior Castle

THE INTERIOR CASTLE

INTRODUCTION

IN THE WAY OF PERFECTION, Teresa assures her readers that the prayer of the Our Father leads to the fount of living waters. She then refers them to her *Life*, the book she had written in which she describes what the soul feels when it drinks this living water, how God satisfies and takes away thirst for earthly things.

Some ten or so years later, after she had labored much and increased the number of her new Carmels to twelve, she was speaking again, on May 28, 1577, for basically the same reasons, of what was contained in her *Life*. But this time the result was the command to write another book since the *Life* was then in the scrupulously cautious hands of the Inquisition. The scene of the fateful incident took place at Toledo at the Carmel founded by Teresa. Fr. Gratian, her confessor and also enthusiastic supporter as a Carmelite friar in her reform, has left us his account of the event: "What happened with regard to the book of the *Dwelling Places* is that while I was superior and speaking with her once in Toledo of many things concerning her spirit, she said to me: 'Oh, how well this point was described in the book about my life which is in the Inquisition!' I answered: 'Since we cannot have it, recall what you can and other things and write another book, but put down the doctrine in a general way without naming the one to whom the things you mentioned there happened.' And thus I ordered her to write this book of the *Dwelling Places*."[1]

Now sixty-two years old, Teresa had for five years been aware of the depth of spiritual life she describes as the ultimate stage of the mystical journey. She had come, then, to an experiential grasp of so much more than what she had written previously in her *Life*. In evidence of this, toward the outset of her *Interior Castle* she admits: "And although in other things I've written the Lord has given me some understanding, I know there were certain things I had not understood as I have come to understand them now, especially certain more difficult things."[2]

"Business Matters and Poor Health"

If from the viewpoint of her own more evolved experience and understanding the command to undertake such a task again seemed well advised, from the standpoint of her physical sufferings and the external problems and trials that were being heaped upon her at this time the mere thought of writing a new book was painful to her. The prologue begins in complaint. Not many things that obedience had asked of her — and obedience had asked many difficult things — were as difficult as the chore of writing at this time yet another book. "I have been experiencing now for three months," she wearily reports, "such great noise and weakness in my head that I've found it a hardship even to write concerning necessary business matters."[3]

In addition to this miserable health, the year was a troublesome and discouraging one; what she had struggled for zealously over the previous fifteen years could now be suppressed by the new authorities. Her work had become the center of a conflict that raged between Madrid and Rome. The jurisdictional complexities became so tangled and the misunderstandings, rivalries, and calumnies so much a part of everyday life that historians today find it difficult to judge objectively.[4]

In 1576 Fr. Jerónimo Tostado arrived in Spain with the faculties of visitator, reformer, and commissary general of the Spanish provinces and with the responsibility of carrying out the decrees of the order's chapter at Piacenza which had directed that the houses opened in Andalusia against the will of the general be abandoned. The "contemplative," or "primitive," fathers were forbidden to form a province or a congregation separate from the province of Castile. Mother Teresa was not to leave her monastery. The unpleasant rumor was that Tostado had come to quash Teresa's work; and his presence was the cause of considerable disquiet. But the papal nuncio in Spain, Nicolás Ormaneto, who favored Teresa and her foundation, advised Tostado to postpone his visit of Andalusia (where Gratian, under an assignment of the nuncio, was on a mission of reform among the Carmelites there) and to pass instead on to Portugal. In a letter dated September 7, 1576, Teresa thus wrote to María de San José: "But, as God has delivered us from Tostado, I hope His Majesty will help us in everything. You are not maligning him in describing how he has worked against the discalced Fathers and against me, for he has given clear indications of having done so."

In June of 1577, Ormaneto died, and without the nuncio's favor Teresa's followers now felt lost. With the death of Ormaneto, the Mother foundress thought it would be better to return to her monastery of St. Joseph in Avila and to remain there, "as a kind of prisoner" in accordance with the order of the general definitory. To make matters worse, Ormaneto's successor, Felipe Sega, whose reference to Teresa as a "restless gadabout" at least demonstrated a lack of firsthand information, immediately set out with his new authority to discard the plans of reform sponsored by Ormaneto.

About this time, as well, there appeared a scurrilous pamphlet denouncing Teresa and calumniating Gratian with a number of crimes, some too foolish and lurid to be believed but yet sufficient to arouse at least faint suspicions. Again in October of 1577 Teresa was once more elected prioress of the Incarnation; she felt nothing but aversion toward taking up again such a responsibility. When this election became known, Tostado unwittingly came to Teresa's rescue and gave orders to annul the valid election. The nuns persisting to vote for Teresa in a second election were duly excommunicated. Though happy to be left in peace, Teresa protested the injustice: "Learned men declare that they are not excommunicated at all and that the friars are going against the Council in declaring anyone elected prioress who has a minority of votes. . . . Everyone is shocked to see something like this, so offensive to everyone."[5]

It was while she was in the midst of all these unpleasant and disturbing events that Teresa was engaged in writing her sublime book on prayer. The work was begun, appropriately, on the feast of the Holy Trinity, June 2, 1577. Within little more than a month, she had proceeded as far as the fifth dwelling place. We may suppose this from the copy made in Toledo and ending with chapter two of the fifth dwelling place when Teresa departed for Avila in mid-July. Already in chapter two of the fourth dwelling place she had alluded to the inconvenience of interruptions: "God help me with what I have undertaken! I've already forgot what I was dealing with, for business matters and poor health have forced me to set this work aside just when I was at my best; and since I have a poor memory everything will come out confused because I can't go back to read it over."[6]

Nothing more was done on the work until the beginning of November, as she asserts at the outset of chapter four of the fifth dwelling place: "About five months have passed since I began, and because my head is in no condition to read over what I've written, everything will have to continue without order, and perhaps some things will be said twice."[7] She completed the remaining large section, more than half the work, by November 29, within less than a month. Thus the actual time spent on this spiritual masterpiece was a mere two months.

Inspiration

Despite her trials and ill health, Teresa held firmly to her belief that "obedience usually lessens the difficulty of things that seem impossible."[8] She prayed when beginning: "May He, in whose mercy I trust and who has helped me in other more difficult things so as to favor me, do this work for me."[9] Her prayer was heard. By the time she had reached the epilogue, her mood was entirely changed: "Although when I began writing this book I am sending you I did so with the aversion I mentioned in the beginning, now that I am finished I admit the work has brought me much happiness, and I consider the labor, though I confess it was small, well spent."[10]

At times she seemed to feel special inspiration, and that a work of such brilliance was brought to a conclusion so quickly is itself extraordinary. In one instance she wrote: "If what I have said up to now about this prayer is worthwhile, I know clearly that I'm not the one who has said it."[11] When she turns to the topic of mystical prayer she prays: "In order to speak of the fourth dwelling places I really need to entrust myself, as I've already done, to the Holy Spirit and beg Him to speak for me from here on that I may say something about the remaining rooms in a way that you will understand."[12] Among those who actually saw Teresa writing this book was María del Nacimiento who gave the following testimony: "When the said Mother Teresa of Jesus wrote the book called *The Dwelling Places*, she was in Toledo, and this witness saw that it was after Communion that she wrote this book, and when she wrote she did so very rapidly and with such great beauty in her countenance that this witness was in admiration, and she was so absorbed in what she was writing that even if some noise was made there, it did not hinder her; wherefore this witness understood that in all that which she wrote and during the time she was writing she was in prayer."[13]

The Image of a Castle

The *Interior Castle* has come to be regarded as Teresa's best synthesis. In it the spiritual doctrine is presented through the unifying outline of seven dwelling places among which there is a division into two sections. The first three groups of dwelling places speak of what is achievable through human efforts and the ordinary help of grace. The remaining four groups deal with the passive, or mystical, elements of the spiritual life. By the term "supernatural prayer" (contemplation), Teresa refers to the whole series of forms and degrees of infused or mystical prayer. By the term "perfect contemplation," she refers only to those pure forms of contemplation found in the fifth, sixth, and seventh dwelling places.

The question has been raised, as one would expect in academics, as to how Teresa conceived the notion of using the castle as a symbol for the interior life. What she reveals leaves room for interpretation: "Today while beseeching our Lord to speak for me because I wasn't able to think of anything to say, nor did I know how to begin to carry out this obedience, there came to my mind what I shall now speak about, that which will provide us with a basis to begin with. It is that we consider our soul to be like a castle made entirely out of a diamond or of very clear crystal, in which there are many rooms, just as in heaven there are many dwelling places."[14] Previously, in the *Way of Perfection*, with similar thoughts, Teresa had advised: "Well, let us imagine that within us is an extremely rich palace, built entirely of gold and precious stones; in sum, built for a Lord such as this... Imagine, also, that in this palace dwells this mighty King."[15]

In an interesting account, one of her early biographers, Fr. Diego de Yepes, testifies that Teresa told him that on the eve of Trinity Sunday, 1577, God showed her in a flash the whole book. There was "a most beautiful crystal globe like a castle in which she saw seven dwelling places, and in the seventh, which was in the center, the King of Glory dwelt in the greatest splendor. From there He beautified and illumined all those dwelling places to the outer wall. The inhabitants received more light the nearer they were to the center. Outside of the castle all was darkness, with toads, vipers, and other poisonous vermin. While she was admiring this beauty which the grace of God communicates to souls, the light suddenly disappeared and, although the King of Glory did not leave the castle, the crystal was covered with darkness and was left as ugly as coal and with an unbearable stench, and the poisonous creatures outside the wall were able to get into the castle. Such was the state of a soul in sin."[16] This was told to Yepes, a former confessor of Teresa's, when she met him by chance one snowy day in an inn in Arévalo either in 1579 or 1580. Yepes also adds with a certain self-satisfaction that "although in the *Book of Her Life* and the *Dwelling Places* she mentions this, she doesn't in either of them communicate this vision as specifically as she did to me."[17] But if this vision came to Teresa in 1577, we are left wondering both how she could have referred to it in her *Life*, written in the 1560's, and about the value of Diego de Yepes' testimony. Nonetheless, Teresa's vague expression "there came to my mind" (*se me ofreció*) does not rule out the possibility of a vision as a basis of her symbol.

As described in her *Life*, she once did receive a mystical vision of God's presence and what it is for a soul to be in mortal sin: "Once while I was reciting with all the Sisters the hours of the Divine Office, my soul suddenly became recollected; and it seemed to me to be like a brightly polished mirror, without any part on the back or sides or top or bottom that wasn't totally clear. In its center Christ, our Lord, was shown to me . . . I was given understanding of what it is for a soul to be in mortal sin. It amounts to clouding this mirror with mist and leaving it black; and thus this Lord cannot be revealed or seen even though He is always present giving us being."[18] Later in the same chapter it seems from her reference that this experience influenced her thinking when she compares the Divinity to a very clear diamond in which everything is visible including sin with all its ugliness.[19]

Whatever the speculation on matters like the above, the point must be made that the *Interior Castle* is principally the fruit of her own experience, and though Teresa makes the effort to hide her identity by referring to this other person she knows, her talents for concealing her identity were abysmally poor.

The Synthesis

Although the outer wall of the castle (the body) is ordinary, it nonetheless may lure the soul's attention from the inner brilliant castle.[20] Inside the castle are many dwelling places, above, below, and to the sides. In other words, the spiritual life that goes on within the castle is a complex matter involving the individual's capacities, the diversity of ways, and differing spiritual depths. The seven stages represent only types and allow for a wide range of variations. In speaking of the seven dwelling places, we must keep in mind that "in each of these there are many others, below and above and to the sides, with lovely gardens and fountains and labyrinths, such delightful things that you would want to be dissolved in praises of the great God who created the soul in His own image and likeness."[21] At the center of the castle is God's dwelling place.

The gate of entry is prayer.[22] Prayer is a door that opens up into the mystery of God and at the same time a means of communing with Him. It actuates the personal relationship with the Lord present in the very depths of the spirit.

The first dwelling places. Setting aside those souls outside the castle, paralysed and crippled, in need of special healing from the Lord Himself if they are to enter,[23] Teresa turns her attention to those who have entered the first area. Little of the glowing light from the King's royal chamber filters into these first dwelling places. Too many things entice and distract souls here and thus prevent them from taking the time to search for the true light. "So, I think, must be the condition of the soul. Even though it may not be in a bad state, it is so involved in worldly things and so absorbed with its possessions, honor, or business affairs, as I have said, that even though as a matter of fact it would want to see and enjoy its beauty these things do not allow it to; nor does it seem that it can slip free from so many impediments."[24] Such people do have some good desires, however; and they even pray on occasion. Their need, as is true of everyone, is for self-knowledge and for knowledge of the beauty of a soul in grace and of the ugliness of one in sin; in a word, for some insight into the Christian mystery of sin and grace. Self-knowledge and humility grow as the soul moves onward through the castle toward the center.

The second dwelling places. Here we have rooms set apart

for those who have taken some first steps in the practice of prayer, who are more receptive to the promptings and invitations of Christ's grace which comes especially through external means such as books, sermons, good friendships, and through trials. The struggle with the forces of evil is now more keenly felt, and the time is ripe for the characteristically Teresian determination to persevere convinced that the spiritual life cannot be grounded on consolations. Conformity with God's will must be the goal of one's strivings.

The third dwelling places. To persevere in prayer and the struggle involved is to go forward.[25] Those who have come to this stage begin to long not to offend His Majesty; they guard against venial sin, are fond of both ascetical practices and periods of recollection, seek to use their time well, practice charity toward their neighbor, and maintain balance in the use of speech and dress and in the management of their household. They are good Christians, and the Lord will not deny these souls entrance into the final dwelling place if they so desire.[26] Like the young man in the Gospel, however, they could turn away upon hearing the requirements for becoming perfect. Any threat to wealth or honor will quickly uncover their attachments to these; and they are excessively discreet about their health—to the point of fearing everything.[27] In addition to their reluctance to part with wealth and honor, they have a tendency to be too easily shocked by the faults of others and quickly distraught by a little dryness.[28] Though these persons find more consolation in the spiritual life than they do in material comforts and distractions, they seldom receive the deeper, more delectable peace and quiet of contemplation except occasionally as an invitation to prepare better for what lies ahead.[29] They need someone who is free of the world's illusions with whom they might speak.

Dealing less extensively with these first three dwelling places, Teresa says little about prayer; nor does she give advice about methods. The impression left on her reader is that she is anxious to advance quickly to the part that deals more immediately with what God does; and she complains that while we are admonished to pray, only what we can do ourselves is explained and little said of what the Lord does, "I mean about the supernatural."[30] It is in response to this need souls have of knowing about passive prayer that Teresa felt she could contribute.

The question might be raised here: is it not useless for people to read about mystical prayer and favors when they do not themselves, for whatever reason, experience the same things? In answer to this, Teresa replies that learning about God's work will lead a receptive person to the prayer of praise. Characteristically, she reasons that if she who was so wretched was led to this praise when she read of such things, how much more will good and humble souls praise Him upon learning of them. Also, she thinks that these favors superabound with love and fortitude enabling a person to do more good and to journey with less toil. Knowledge of these favors will make the readers aware of how much they may lose through their own fault. Furthermore, the testimony she gives of her contemplative experience, in which so many aspects of the Christian faith are illumined, provides the theologian with a rich abundance of material for reflection.[31]

The fourth dwelling places. The beginning of the supernatural or mystical marks off this section and presents Teresa with the problem of how to explain infused prayer.[32] She first seeks a solution through an analysis of the difference between consolations (*contentos*) and spiritual delight (*gustos*); she notes that the former have their beginning in our human nature and end in God while the latter have their beginning in God and overflow to human nature.[33] The consolations, then, result from our own efforts accompanied by God's grace; the spiritual delight is received not through human efforts but passively. In this dwelling place the first degrees of infused prayer are discussed. Though there are no rules about the length of time required to reach this point, "the important thing is not to think much but to love much; and so do that which best stirs you to love."[34] In Teresa's thinking, love "doesn't consist in great delight but in desiring with strong determination to please God in everything, in striving, insofar as possible, not to offend Him, and in asking Him for the advancement of the honor and glory of His Son."[35]

This contemplative prayer begins with a passive experience of recollection, a gentle drawing of the faculties inward; it is different from recollection achieved at the cost of human effort.[36] This prayer of infused recollection is a less intense form of initial contemplation or, as called by Teresa, the prayer of quiet. While the will finds rest in the prayer of quiet, in the peace of God's presence, the intellect (in Teresa's terminology) continues to move about. One should let the intellect go and surrender oneself into the arms of love,[37] for distractions, the wandering mind, are a part of the human condition and can no more be avoided than can eating and sleeping.

In a further effort to explain the difference between acquired and infused prayer, she turns to another analogy: the different ways in which two water troughs are filled. One trough is filled with water channelled through aqueducts, by the exercise of a great deal of ingenuity while the other is filled by a spring bubbling up from the very spot where the trough is. However, the worth of one's prayer is not judged by its passive character; rather, "it is in the effects and deeds following afterward that one discerns the true value of prayer."[38]

Finally, in this dwelling place since the passive prayer is in its beginning stages, the natural (active) and the supernatural (passive) are joined. It is not unusual for souls to enter here.

The fifth dwelling places. The prayer of union characterizes these rooms, an experience in which the faculties become completely silent, or, in Teresa's words, are suspended, and which leaves a certitude that the soul "was in God and God was in it."[39] Such certitude is not present when the union is merely partial as in the previous dwelling place.[40]

Here Teresa, never wanting in her attempts to find the best explanation, turns to another analogy. Leaving aside the castle and the troughs of water, she finds an unusual comparison as an example for explaining what is in her mind: the silkworm. Through the image of the silkworm she speaks ingeniously of death and of new life in Christ. In this prayer of union, God Himself becomes the dwelling place or cocoon in which a person dies. Once a soul is indeed dead to itself and its attachments, it breaks forth from the cocoon transformed as does a small white butterfly.[41]

Having made the point of the soul's death in Christ, Teresa introduces her final analogy which serves to lead her readers through the remaining dwelling places to the center of the castle: marriage and its preparatory stages. In her day, before two people became engaged, they progressed through certain stages by which they sought to know first if there was any likeness between them and then whether there was any chance for love. If these were affirmatively established, they shared in additional meetings so as to deepen their knowledge of each other. In these experiences of union, then, His Majesty is desirous that the soul may get to know Him better.[42]

Teresa makes a final plea that love be not idle. One so intimate with His Majesty must walk with special care and attentiveness in the exercise of virtue and with particular emphasis on love of neighbor, humility (the desire to be considered the least), and the faithful performance of ordinary tasks.[43]

The sixth dwelling places. The longest section of the *Interior Castle* is devoted to this stage of the inward journey. Teresa deals here with many extraordinary mystical phenomena. Though the spiritual betrothal takes place in these rooms, the desires of the soul at a cost to itself must first increase.[44] Through both vehement desires for God and the sufferings these desires cause, the Lord enables the soul to have the courage to be joined with Him and take Him as its Spouse.[45] Aware that readers will wonder why all this courage is necessary for something that should be looked upon as an attractive opportunity, Teresa asserts strongly: "I tell you there is need for more courage than you think."[46] Without the courage, which must be given by God, such a union would be impossible. This fortitude comes through many trials both exterior and interior: opposition from others; praise (itself becoming a trial); severe illnesses; inner sufferings, fears, and misunderstanding on the part of the confessor and the consequent anxiety that God will allow one to be deceived; and a feeling of unbearable inner oppression and even of being rejected by God.[47]

Other preparations for the betrothal come in the form of certain spiritual awakenings and impulses deep within the soul.

These are of many kinds and include the woundings of love that can cause at one and the same time both pain and delight.[48]

The betrothal itself takes place when His Majesty "gives the soul raptures that draw it out of its senses. For if it were to see itself so near this great majesty while in its senses, it would perhaps die."[49] Though the soul in ecstasy is without consciousness in its outward life, it was never before so awake to the things of God nor did it ever before have so deep an enlightenment and knowledge of God.[50]

Besides locutions from God with their beneficial effects, the soul may now also begin to receive through intellectual and imaginative visions understanding about the divine mysteries.[51] The Lord shows it heavenly secrets. Some are so sublime that it is incapable of explaining anything about them; others can be explained to some extent. The supernatural realities that became the objects of Teresa's mystical experience were so varied and complex that the scholar is left disconcerted in his efforts to categorize them. Accompanying the discussion of these diverse favors are also many sharp analyses and keenly perceptive rules for discerning authentic mystical experiences from pseudo-mystical phenomena. The effects the authentic favors leave in the soul are like the jewels the Spouse gives to the betrothed; they are knowledge of the grandeur of God, self-knowledge together with humility, and rejection of earthly things except of those that can be used in the Lord's service.[52] Finally, joy will reach such an excess that the soul will want to be a herald to the entire world that all might help it praise the Lord.[53]

When speaking of the intellectual and imaginative visions of Christ, Teresa pauses to make some firm assertions about the human and divine Christ present throughout one's spiritual pilgrimage. He is the one through whom all blessings come. No state is so sublime that a person must always be occupied with divinity and thus obliged to empty the mind of all reference to the human Christ. "Life is long, and there are in it many trials, and we need to look at Christ our model, how He suffered them, and also at His apostles and saints, so as to bear these trials with perfection. Jesus is too good a companion for us to turn away from Him."[54] And here Teresa makes an important distinction between discursive meditation about Christ and contemplative presence to Him. The inability of contemplative souls to engage in discursive thought about the mysteries of the Passion and life of Christ in their prayer is very common, she holds. But contemplating these mysteries, "dwelling on them with a simple gaze," in Teresa's words, "will not impede the most sublime prayer."[55] On the contrary, an effort to forget Christ and live in continual absorption in the Divinity will result in a failure to enter the last two dwelling places. Teresa is most insistent on this. The purification of the person is realized not merely through the sufferings inherent to the human condition but especially through contact with the person of Christ in his humanity and divinity.

Through these many favors and purifications, the desires of love are always increasing and the flight of the butterfly ever more restless. These desires reach a point of extreme spiritual torment causing the soul a final purification of the spirit before entering the seventh dwelling place, "just as those who will enter heaven must be cleansed in purgatory."[56] Not only can this intense spiritual torment cause ecstasy, as can intense spiritual joy, but also it can place one in danger of death.[57] Nonetheless, the soul is aware that this spiritual suffering is a precious favor.

The seventh dwelling places. On account of these moments of great illumination, Teresa is able to teach that there are no closed doors between the sixth and the seventh dwelling places. If she divides them, it is "because there are things in the last that are not revealed to those who have not yet reached it."[58] In the prayer of union explained in the fifth dwelling place and the raptures of the sixth, the Lord makes the soul blind and deaf as was St. Paul in his conversion. When God joins the soul to Himself, it doesn't understand anything of the nature and kind of favor enjoyed.[59] But in the seventh dwelling place the union is wrought differently: "Our good God now desires to remove the scales from the soul's eyes and let it see and understand, although in a strange way, something of the favor He grants it."[60] Now fortified, a person lifted up to these exalted mysteries no longer loses equilibrium or falls into ecstasy, but rather experiences them as a proper object, as connatural.

Entry into these last and most luminous dwelling places takes place through an amazing intellectual vision of the Most Blessed Trinity. Teresa places much emphasis on the depth at which this experience occurs, a spiritual profundity previously unrevealed, in "the extreme interior, in some place very deep within itself."[61] Though the presence of the Trinity remains and is felt habitually, it is not revealed in the fullness of light as at first or sometimes afterward when the Lord "desires that the window of the intellect be opened."[62] What seems awesome is that the habitual intellectual vision of the Trinity does not interfere with multiple and diverse daily duties carried out as acts of service.

The grace of spiritual marriage, of perfect union, is bestowed also in this center dwelling place and occurs through an imaginative vision of the Lord's most sacred humanity "so that the soul will understand and not be ignorant of receiving this sovereign gift."[63] The vision was so much at variance with previous ones that it left Teresa "stupefied," for, as does the vision of the Trinity, this takes place in that most interior depth of the spirit. In successive experiences of this grace, which is repeatable, the vision is an intellectual one. Suggesting the trait of inseparability, the term "marriage" designates the union and the degree of His Majesty's love. It is so great and reaches such a point that the spirit is made one with God "just as those who are married cannot be separated."[64] With no allowance for division, as there is in spiritual betrothal (likened to the joining and separation of the two candles), the union of spiritual marriage makes Teresa think of the rain that has fallen into a river, or of a stream that enters the sea, or of the beams of light entering a room through different windows and becoming one.[65]

At this point the butterfly dies with the greatest joy because its new life is Christ. In St. Paul's words: "He that is joined or united to the Lord becomes one spirit with Him," and "for me to live is Christ."[66] The ultimate goal, then, of Teresa's journey, the spiritual marriage, is a union with Christ, now no longer living as the divine Logos but as the Word incarnate, risen and connotated by the attributes of His earthly adventure, especially those of His resurrection. With the passing of time, the soul understands more clearly that its life is Christ.

Having examined the effects of this union, Teresa in the final chapter explains that the purpose of all these splendid favors is that one might live like Christ and that the fruit of the spiritual marriage must be good works. The interior calm fortifies these persons so that they may endure much less calm in the exterior events of their lives, that they might have the strength to serve.[67] The works of service may be outstanding ones, as in Teresa's case, but they need not be. One must concentrate on serving those who are in one's company. "The Lord doesn't look so much at the greatness of our works as at the love with which they are done." His Majesty will join our sacrifice with that which He offered for us. "Thus even though our works are small they will have the value our love for Him would have merited had they been great."[68]

In the prologue Teresa states her intention to write about prayer, and anyone reading the *Interior Castle* would probably agree that it is indeed a book about prayer and its stages. But in a letter dated December 7, 1577, a week after completion of her manuscript, Teresa refers to her book and speaks of its theme differently. She says the book is about God ("it treats only of what He is"). This remark illustrates well how for Teresa the journey in prayer through the interior castle to the center room is nothing else than the magnificent work of God's love.[69]

The Autograph

The *Interior Castle* was not revised, although the manuscript does contain the marks of censors. Between June 13 and July 6, 1580 at the monastery of Carmelite nuns in Segovia, Fr. Gratian and the Dominican Fr. Diego de Yanguas went over the work with Teresa pointing out their difficulties, cancelling passages, and making corrections. Many of

Gratian's corrections annoyed Teresa's Jesuit biographer Ribera, leading him to write on the opening page of the autograph a strong rebuke against censors of the work.[70] José Vicente Rodríguez surmises that Gratian was just killing time since he was in that part of Spain waiting for a Brief to come from Rome.[71]

Teresa gave the new book to Gratian to guard, for her *Life* was still at the Inquisition. Gratian brought the work to Seville in 1580 and entrusted it for safekeeping to María de San José. Sometime between 1582 and 1585, while he was still provincial, Gratian gave the work as a gift to Don Pedro Cerezo Pardo who was a generous benefactor of the Discalced Carmelites. Between 1586 and 1588 the autograph was in the hands of Fray Luis de León who was at the time preparing the first edition of Teresa's works; and it was then returned to Don Pedro Cerezo. In 1618 Don Pedro's daughter, Doña Constancia de Ayala made her profession of vows in the monastery of the Discalced Carmelite nuns in Seville. She had brought with her to the Carmel the autograph of the *Interior Castle*, and it has remained with the nuns in Seville ever since, with one exception. In 1961 it was brought to Rome for repair, and in the following year, beautifully restored, the spiritual masterpiece was returned to the Carmelites in Seville. The red-bound book, referred to by its author as a jewel, is now set like a ruby in a reliquary that has walls like those of Avila and in the shape of a castle surrounding and protecting it.

K. K.

THE INTERIOR CASTLE

Teresa of Jesus, a nun of Our Lady of Mount Carmel, wrote this treatise called the Interior Castle for her Sisters and daughters, the Discalced Carmelite nuns.

JHS

[Prologue]

NOT MANY THINGS that I have been ordered to do under obedience have been as difficult for me as is this present task of writing about prayer. First, it doesn't seem the Lord is giving me either the spirit or the desire to undertake the work. Second, I have been experiencing now for three months such great noise and weakness in my head that I've found it a hardship even to write concerning necessary business matters. But knowing that the strength given by obedience usually lessens the difficulty of things that seem impossible, I resolved to carry out the task very willingly, even though my human nature seems greatly distressed. For the Lord hasn't given me so much virtue that my nature in the midst of its struggle with continual sickness and duties of so many kinds doesn't feel strong aversion toward such a task. May He, in whose mercy I trust and who has helped me in other more difficult things so as to favor me, do this work for me.

2. Indeed, I don't think I have much more to say than what I've said in other things they have ordered me to write;[1] rather, I fear that the things I write about will be nearly all alike. I'm, literally, just like the parrots that are taught to speak; they know no more than what they hear or are shown, and they often repeat it. If the Lord wants me to say something new, His Majesty will provide. Or, He will be pleased to make me remember what I have said at other times, for I would be happy even with this. My memory is so poor that I would be glad if

I could repeat, in case they've been lost, some of the things which I was told were well said.[2] If the Lord doesn't make me remember, I will gain just by tiring myself and getting a worse headache for the sake of obedience—even if no one draws any benefit from what I say.

3. And so I'm beginning to comply today, the feast of the most Blessed Trinity, in the year 1577, in this Carmelite monastery of St. Joseph in Toledo where I am at present.[3] In all that I say I submit to the opinion of the ones who ordered me to write, for they are persons of great learning.[4] If I should say something that isn't in conformity with what the holy Roman Catholic Church holds, it will be through ignorance and not through malice. This can be held as certain, and also that through the goodness of God I always am, and will be, and have been subject to her. May He be always blessed and glorified, amen.

4. The one who ordered me to write told me that the nuns in these monasteries of our Lady of Mt. Carmel need someone to answer their questions about prayer and that he thought they would better understand the language used between women, and that because of the love they bore me they would pay more attention to what I would tell them. I thus understood that it was important for me to manage to say something. So, I shall be speaking to them while I write; it's nonsense to think that what I say could matter to other persons. Our Lord will be granting me favor enough if some of these nuns benefit by praising Him a little more. His Majesty well knows that I don't aim after anything else. And it should be very clear that if I manage to say something well the Sisters will understand that this does not come from me since there would be no foundation for it, unless the Lord gave it to me; otherwise they would have as little intelligence as I little ability for such things.

THE FIRST DWELLING PLACES

Contains Two Chapters

Chapter 1

Discusses the beauty and dignity of our souls. Draws a comparison in order to explain, and speaks of the benefit that comes from understanding this truth and knowing about the favors we receive from God and how the door to this castle is prayer.

TODAY WHILE BESEECHING our Lord to speak for me because I wasn't able to think of anything to say nor did I know how to begin to carry out this obedience, there came to my mind what I shall now speak about, that which will provide us with a basis to begin with. It is that we consider our soul to be like a castle made entirely out of a diamond or of very clear crystal, in which there are many rooms, just as in heaven there are many dwelling places.[1] For in reflecting upon it carefully, Sisters, we realize that the soul of the just person is nothing else but a paradise where the Lord says He finds His delight.[2] So then, what do you think that abode will be like where a King so powerful, so wise, so pure, so full of all good things takes His delight? I don't find anything comparable to the magnificent beauty of a soul and its marvelous capacity. Indeed, our intellects, however keen, can hardly comprehend it, just as they cannot comprehend God; but He Himself says that He created us in His own image and likeness.[3]

Well if this is true, as it is, there is no reason to tire ourselves in trying to comprehend the beauty of this castle. Since this castle is a creature and the difference, therefore, between it and God is the same as that between the Creator and His creature, His Majesty in saying that the soul is made in His own image makes it almost impossible for us to understand the sublime dignity and beauty of the soul.

2. It is a shame and unfortunate that through our own fault we don't understand ourselves or know who we are. Wouldn't it show great ignorance, my daughters, if someone when asked who he was didn't know, and didn't know his father or mother or from what country he came? Well now, if this would be so extremely stupid, we are incomparably more so when we do not strive to know who we are, but limit ourselves to considering only roughly these bodies. Because we have heard and because faith tells us so, we know we have souls. But we seldom consider the precious things that can be found in this soul, or who dwells within it, or its high value. Consequently, little effort is made to preserve its beauty. All our attention is taken up with the plainness of the diamond's setting or the outer wall of the castle; that is, with these bodies of ours.

3. Well, let us consider that this castle has, as I said,[4] many dwelling places: some up above, others down below, others to the sides; and in the center and middle is the main dwelling place where the very secret exchanges between God and the soul take place.

It's necessary that you keep this comparison in mind. Perhaps God will be pleased to let me use it to explain something to you about the favors He is happy to grant souls and the differences between these favors. I shall explain them according to what I have understood as possible. For it is impossible that anyone understand them all since there are many; how much more so for someone as wretched as I. It will be a great consolation when the Lord grants them to you if you know that they are possible; and for anyone to whom He doesn't, it will be a great consolation to praise His wonderful goodness. Just as it doesn't do us any harm to reflect upon the things there are in heaven and what the blessed enjoy—but rather we rejoice and strive to attain what they enjoy—it doesn't do us any harm to see that it is possible in this exile for so great a God to commune with such foul-smelling worms; and, upon seeing this, come to love a goodness so perfect and a mercy so immeasurable. I hold as certain that anyone who might be harmed by knowing that God can grant this favor in this exile would be very much lacking in humility and love of neighbor. Otherwise, how could we fail to be happy that God grants these favors to our brother? His doing so is no impediment toward His granting them to us, and His Majesty can reveal His grandeurs to whomever He wants. Sometimes He does so merely to show forth His glory, as He said of the blind man whose sight He restored when His apostles asked Him if the blindness resulted from the man's sins or those of his parents.[5] Hence, He doesn't grant them because the sanctity of the recipients is greater than that of those who don't receive them but so that His glory may be known, as we see in St. Paul and the Magdalene, and that we might praise Him for His work in creatures.

4. One could say that these favors seem to be impossible and that it is good not to scandalize the weak. Less is lost when the weak do not believe in them than when the favors fail to benefit those to whom God grants them; and these latter will be delighted and awakened through these favors to a greater love of Him who grants so many gifts and whose power and majesty is so great. Moreover, I know I am speaking to those for whom this danger does not exist, for they know and believe that God grants even greater signs of His love. I know that whoever does not believe in these favors will have no experience of them, for God doesn't like us to put a limit on His works. And so, Sisters, those of you whom the Lord doesn't lead by this path should never doubt His generosity.

5. Well, getting back to our beautiful and delightful castle we must see how we can enter it. It seems I'm saying something foolish. For if this castle is the soul, clearly one doesn't have to enter it since it is within oneself. How foolish it would seem were we to tell someone to enter a room he is already in. But you must understand that there is a great difference in the ways one may be inside the castle. For there are many souls who are in the outer courtyard—which is where the guards

stay—and don't care at all about entering the castle, nor do they know what lies within that most precious place, nor who is within, nor even how many rooms it has. You have already heard in some books on prayer that the soul is advised to enter within itself;[6] well that's the very thing I'm advising.

6. Not long ago a very learned man told me that souls who do not practice prayer are like people with paralysed or crippled bodies; even though they have hands and feet they cannot give orders to these hands and feet.[7] Thus there are souls so ill and so accustomed to being involved in external matters that there is no remedy, nor does it seem they can enter within themselves. They are now so used to dealing always with the insects and vermin that are in the wall surrounding the castle that they have become almost like them. And though they have so rich a nature and the power to converse with none other than God, there is no remedy. If these souls do not strive to understand and cure their great misery, they will be changed into statues of salt, unable to turn their heads to look at themselves, just as Lot's wife was changed for having turned her head.[8]

7. Insofar as I can understand the door of entry to this castle is prayer and reflection. I don't mean to refer to mental more than vocal prayer, for since vocal prayer is prayer it must be accompanied by reflection. A prayer in which a person is not aware of whom he is speaking to, what he is asking, who it is who is asking and of whom, I do not call prayer however much the lips move. Sometimes it will be so without this reflection, provided that the soul has these reflections at other times. Nonetheless, anyone who has the habit of speaking before God's majesty as though he were speaking to a slave, without being careful to see how he is speaking, but saying whatever comes to his head and whatever he has learned from saying at other times, in my opinion is not praying. Please God, may no Christian pray in this way. Among yourselves, Sisters, I hope in His Majesty that you will not do so, for the custom you have of being occupied with interior things is quite a good safeguard against falling and carrying on in this way like brute beasts.

8. Well now, we are not speaking to these crippled souls, for

if the Lord Himself doesn't come to order them to get up—as He did the man who waited at the side of the pool for thirty years[9]—they are quite unfortunate and in serious danger. But we are speaking to other souls that, in the end, enter the castle. For even though they are very involved in the world, they have good desires and sometimes, though only once in a while, they entrust themselves to our Lord and reflect on who they are, although in a rather hurried fashion. During the period of a month they will sometimes pray, but their minds are then filled with business matters which ordinarily occupy them. They are so attached to these things that where their treasure lies their heart goes also.[10] Sometimes they do put all these things aside, and the self-knowledge and awareness that they are not proceeding correctly in order to get to the door is important. Finally, they enter the first, lower rooms. But so many reptiles get in with them that they are prevented from seeing the beauty of the castle and from calming down; they have done quite a bit just by having entered.

9. You may have been thinking, daughters, that this is irrelevant to you since by the Lord's goodness you are not among these people. You'll have to have patience, for I wouldn't know how to explain my understanding of some interior things about prayer if not in this way. And may it even please the Lord that I succeed in saying something, for what I want to explain to you is very difficult to understand without experience. If you have experience you will see that one cannot avoid touching upon things that—please God, through His mercy—do not pertain to us.

Chapter 2

Treats of how ugly a soul is when in mortal sin and how God wanted to let a certain person know something about this. Discusses, also, some matters on the theme of self-knowledge. This chapter is beneficial, for there are noteworthy points. Explains what is meant by these dwelling places.

BEFORE GOING ON I want to say that you should consider what it would mean to this so brilliantly shining and beautiful castle, this pearl from the Orient, this tree of life planted in the very living waters of life[1] —that is, in God—to fall into mortal sin; there's no darker darkness nor anything more obscure and black. You shouldn't want to know anything else than the fact that, although the very sun that gave the soul so much brilliance and beauty is still in the center, the soul is as though it were not there to share in these things. Yet, it is as capable of enjoying His Majesty as is crystal capable of reflecting the sun's brilliance. Nothing helps such a soul; and as a result all the good works it might do while in mortal sin are fruitless for the attainment of glory. Since these works do not proceed from that principle, which is God, who is the cause of our virtue being really virtue, and are separated from Him, they cannot be pleasing in His sight. Since, after all, the intention of anyone who commits a mortal sin is to please the devil, who is darkness itself, not God, the poor soul becomes darkness itself.

2. I know a person to whom our Lord wanted to show what a soul in mortal sin was like.[2] That person says that in her opinion if this were understood it would be impossible to sin, even though a soul would have to undergo the greatest trials imaginable in order to flee the occasions. So the Lord gave her a strong desire that all might understand this. May He give you, daughters, the desire to beseech Him earnestly for those who are in this state, who have become total darkness, and whose works have become darkness also. For just as all the streams that flow from a crystal-clear fount are also clear, the works of

a soul in grace, because they proceed from this fount of life, in which the soul is planted like a tree, are most pleasing in the eyes of both God and man. There would be no freshness, no fruit, if it were not for this fount sustaining the tree, preventing it from drying up, and causing it to produce good fruit. Thus in the case of a soul that through its own fault withdraws from this fount and plants itself in a place where the water is black and foul-smelling, everything that flows from it is equally wretched and filthy.

3. It should be kept in mind here that the fount, the shining sun that is in the center of the soul, does not lose its beauty and splendor; it is always present in the soul, and nothing can take away its loveliness. But if a black cloth is placed over a crystal that is in the sun, obviously the sun's brilliance will have no effect on the crystal even though the sun is shining on it.[3]

4. O souls redeemed by the blood of Jesus Christ! Understand and take pity on yourselves. How is it possible that in realizing these things you don't strive to remove the pitch from this crystal? See that if your life comes to an end you will never again enjoy this light. O Jesus, how sad a thing it is to see a soul separated from this light! How miserable is the state of those poor rooms within the castle! How disturbed the senses are, that is, the people who live in these rooms! And in the faculties, that is, among the custodians, the stewards, and the chief waiters, what blindness, what bad management! In sum, since the tree is planted where the devil is, what fruit can it bear?

5. I once heard of a spiritual man who was not surprised at things done by a person in mortal sin, but at what was not done. May God in His mercy deliver us from so great an evil. There is nothing, while we are living, that deserves this name "evil," except mortal sin, for such sin carries in its wake everlasting evils. This, daughters, is what we must go about in fear of and what we must ask God in our prayers to protect us against. For if He doesn't guard the city, our labor will be in vain[4] since we are vanity itself.

That person I mentioned[5] said she received two blessings from the favor God granted her: the first, an intense fear of offending Him, and so in seeing such terrible dangers she always went about begging Him not to let her fall; the second, a mirror for humility, in which she saw how none of our good deeds has its principle from ourselves but from this fount in which the tree, symbolizing our souls, is planted and from this sun that gives warmth to our works. She says that this truth was represented to her so clearly that in doing something good, or seeing it done, she gave heed to the source and understood how without this help we could do nothing. As a result she would begin immediately to praise God and usually not think of herself in any good thing that she did.

6. The time you spend in reading this, or I in writing it, Sisters, would not be lost if we were left with these two blessings. Learned and wise men know about these things very well, but everything is necessary for our womanly dullness of mind; and so perhaps the Lord wills that we get to know comparisons like these. May it please His goodness to give us grace to profit by them.

7. These interior matters are so obscure for our minds that anyone who knows as little as I will be forced to say many superfluous and even foolish things in order to say something that's right. Whoever reads this must have patience, for I have to have it in order to write about what I don't know. Indeed, sometimes I take up the paper like a simpleton, for I don't know what to say or how to begin. I understand well that it's important for you that I explain some things about the interior life as best I can. We always hear about what a good thing prayer is, and our constitutions oblige us to spend so many hours in prayer.[6] Yet only what we ourselves can do in prayer is explained to us; little is explained about what the Lord does in a soul, I mean about the supernatural.[7] By speaking about this heavenly interior building and explaining and considering it in many ways we shall find great comfort. It is so little understood by mortals, even though many walk through it. And although in other things I've written the Lord has given me some understanding,[8] I know there were certain things I had not understood as I have come to understand them now, especially certain more difficult things. The trouble is that before discussing them, as I have said,[9] I will have to repeat matters

that are well known; on account of my stupidity things can't be otherwise.

8. Well now let's get back to our castle with its many dwelling places. You mustn't think of these dwelling places in such a way that each one would follow in file after the other; but turn your eyes toward the center, which is the room or royal chamber where the King stays, and think of how a palmetto[10] has many leaves surrounding and covering the tasty part that can be eaten. So here, surrounding this center room are many other rooms; and the same holds true for those above. The things of the soul must always be considered as plentiful, spacious, and large; to do so is not an exaggeration. The soul is capable of much more than we can imagine, and the sun that is in this royal chamber shines in all parts. It is very important for any soul that practices prayer, whether little or much, not to hold itself back and stay in one corner. Let it walk through these dwelling places which are up above, down below, and to the sides, since God has given it such great dignity. Don't force it to stay a long time in one room alone. Oh, but if it is in the room of self-knowledge! How necessary this room is—see that you understand me—even for those whom the Lord has brought into the very dwelling place where He abides. For never, however exalted the soul may be, is anything else fitting for it; nor could it be even were the soul to so desire. For humility, like the bee making honey in the beehive, is always at work. Without it, everything goes wrong. But let's remember that the bee doesn't fail to leave the beehive and fly about gathering nectar from the flowers. So it is with the soul in the room of self-knowledge; let it believe me and fly sometimes to ponder the grandeur and majesty of its God. Here it will discover its lowliness better than by thinking of itself, and be freer from the vermin that enter the first rooms, those of self-knowledge. For even though, as I say, it is by the mercy of God that a person practices self-knowledge, that which applies in lesser matters applies so much more in greater ones, as they say. And believe me, we shall practice much better virtue through God's help than by being tied down to our own misery.

9. I don't know if this has been explained well. Knowing

ourselves is something so important that I wouldn't want any relaxation ever in this regard, however high you may have climbed into the heavens. While we are on this earth nothing is more important to us than humility. So I repeat that it is good, indeed very good, to try to enter first into the room where self-knowledge is dealt with rather than fly off to other rooms. This is the right road, and if we can journey along a safe and level path, why should we want wings to fly? Rather, let's strive to make more progress in self-knowledge. In my opinion we shall never completely know ourselves if we don't strive to know God. By gazing at His grandeur, we get in touch with our own lowliness; by looking at His purity, we shall see our own filth; by pondering His humility, we shall see how far we are from being humble.

10. Two advantages come from such activity. First, it's clear that something white seems much whiter when next to something black, and vice versa with the black next to the white. The second is that our intellects and wills, dealing in turn now with self now with God, become nobler and better prepared for every good. And it would be disadvantageous for us never to get out of the mire of our miseries. As we said of those who are in mortal sin, that their streams are black and foul-smelling, so it is here; although not entirely—God deliver us—for we are just making a comparison. If we are always fixed on our earthly misery, the stream will never flow free from the mud of fears, faintheartedness, and cowardice. I would be looking to see if I'm being watched or not; if by taking this path things will turn out badly for me; whether it might be pride to dare begin a certain work; whether it would be good for a person so miserable to engage in something as lofty as prayer; whether I might be judged better than others if I don't follow the path they all do. I'd be thinking that extremes are not good, even in the practice of virtue; that, since I am such a sinner, I might have a greater fall; that perhaps I would not advance and would do harm to good people; that someone like myself has no need of anything special.

11. Oh, God help me, daughters, how many souls must have been made to suffer great loss in this way by the devil!

These souls think that all such fears stem from humility. And there are many others I could mention. The fears come from our not understanding ourselves completely. They distort self-knowledge; and I'm not surprised if we never get free from ourselves, for this lack of freedom from ourselves, and even more, is what can be feared. So I say, daughters, that we should set our eyes on Christ, our Good, and on His saints. There we shall learn true humility, the intellect will be enhanced, as I have said,[11] and self-knowledge will not make one base and cowardly. Even though this is the first dwelling place, it is very rich and so precious that if the soul slips away from the vermin within it, nothing will be left to do but advance. Terrible are the wiles and deceits used by the devil so that souls may not know themselves or understand their own paths.

12. I could give some very good proofs from experience of the wiles the devil uses in these first dwelling places. Thus I say that you should think not in terms of just a few rooms but in terms of a million;[12] for souls, all with good intentions, enter here in many ways. But since the devil always has such a bad intention, he must have in each room many legions of devils to fight off souls when they try to go from one room to the oter. Since the poor soul doesn't know this, the devil plays tricks on it in a thousand ways. He's not so successful with those who have advanced closer to where the King dwells. But since in the first rooms souls are still absorbed in the world and engulfed in their pleasures and vanities, with their honors and pretenses, their vassals (which are these senses and faculties) don't have the strength God gave human nature in the beginning. And these souls are easily conquered, even though they may go about with desires not to offend God and though they do perform good works. Those who see themselves in this state must approach His Majesty as often as possible. They must take His Blessed Mother and His saints as intercessors so that these intercessors may fight for them, for the soul's vassals have little strength to defend themselves. Truly, in all states it's necessary that strength come to us from God. May His Majesty through His mercy give it to us, amen.

13. How miserable the life in which we live! Because

elsewhere I have said a great deal about the harm done to us by our failure to understand well this humility and self-knowledge,[13] I'll tell you no more about it here, even though this self-knowledge is the most important thing for us. Please God, I may have now said something beneficial for you.

14. You must note that hardly any of the light coming from the King's royal chamber reaches these first dwelling places. Even though they are not dark and black, as when the soul is in sin, they nevertheless are in some way darkened so that the soul cannot see the light. The darkness is not caused by a flaw in the room—for I don't know how to explain myself—but by so many bad things like snakes and vipers and poisonous creatures that enter with the soul and don't allow it to be aware of the light. It's as if a person were to enter a place where the sun is shining but be hardly able to open his eyes because of the mud in them. The room is bright but he doesn't enjoy it because of the impediment of things like these wild animals or beasts that make him close his eyes to everything but them. So, I think, must be the condition of the soul. Even though it may not be in a bad state, it is so involved in worldly things and so absorbed with its possessions, honor, or business affairs, as I have said,[14] that even though as a matter of fact it would want to see and enjoy its beauty these things do not allow it to; nor does it seem that it can slip free from so many impediments. If a person is to enter the second dwelling places, it is important that he strive to give up unnecessary things and business affairs. Each one should do this in conformity with his state in life. It is something so important in order for him to reach the main dwelling place that if he doesn't begin doing this I hold that it will be impossible for him to get there. And it will be even impossible for him to stay where he is without danger even though he has entered the castle, for in the midst of such poisonous creatures one cannot help but be bitten at one time or another.

15. Now then, what would happen, daughters, if we who are already free from these snares, as we are, and have entered much further into the castle to other secret dwelling places should turn back through our own fault and go out to this tumult? There are, because of our sins, many persons to whom

God has granted favors who through their own fault have fallen back into this misery. In the monastery we are free with respect to exterior matters; in interior matters may it please the Lord that we also be free, and may He free us. Guard yourselves, my daughters, from extraneous cares. Remember that there are few dwelling places in this castle in which the devils do not wage battle. True, in some rooms the guards (which I believe I have said are the faculties)[15] have the strength to fight; but it is very necessary that we don't grow careless in recognizing the wiles of the devil, and that he not deceive us by changing himself into an angel of light.[16] There's a host of things he can do to cause us harm; he enters little by little, and until he's done the harm we don't recognize him.

16. I've already told you elsewhere[17] that he's like a noiseless file, that we need to recognize him at the outset. Let me say something that will explain this better for you.

He gives a Sister various impulses toward penance, for it seems to her she has no rest except when she is tormenting herself. This may be a good beginning; but if the prioress has ordered that no penance be done without permission, and the devil makes the Sister think that in a practice that's so good one can be rightly daring, and she secretly gives herself up to such a penitential life that she loses her health and doesn't even observe what the rule commands, you can see clearly where all this good will end up.

He imbues another with a very great zeal for perfection. Such zeal is in itself good. But it could follow that every little fault the Sisters commit will seem to her a serious breach; and she is careful to observe whether they commit them, and then informs the prioress. It could even happen at times that she doesn't see her own faults because of her intense zeal for the religious observance. Since the other Sisters don't understand what's going on within her and see all this concern, they might not accept her zeal so well.

17. What the devil is hereby aiming after is no small thing: the cooling of the charity and love the Sisters have for one another. This would cause serious harm. Let us understand, my daughters, that true perfection consists in love of God and

neighbor; the more perfectly we keep these two commandments the more perfect we will be. All that is in our rule and constitutions serves for nothing else than to be a means toward keeping these commandments with greater perfection. Let's forget about indiscreet zeal; it can do us a lot of harm. Let each one look to herself. Because I have said enough about this elsewhere,[18] I'll not enlarge on the matter.

18. This mutual love is so important that I would never want it to be forgotten. The soul could lose its peace and even disturb the peace of others by going about looking at trifling things in people that at times are not even imperfections, but since we know little we see these things in the worst light; look how costly this kind of perfection would be. Likewise, the devil could tempt the prioress in this way; and such a thing would be more dangerous. As a result much discretion is necessary. If things are done against the rule and constitutions, the matter need not always be seen in a good light. The prioress should be cautioned, and if she doesn't amend, the superior informed. This is charity. And the same with the Sisters if there is something serious. And to fail to do these things for fear of a temptation would itself be a temptation. But it should be carefully noted—so that the devil doesn't deceive us—that we must not talk about these things to one another. The devil could thereby gain greatly and manage to get the custom of gossiping started. The matter should be discussed with the one who will benefit, as I have said. In this house, glory to God, there's not much occasion for gossip since such continual silence is kept; but it is good that we be on guard.

THE SECOND DWELLING PLACES

This Section Has Only One Chapter

Chapter 1

Discusses the importance of perseverance if one is to reach the final dwelling places; the great war the devil wages; and the importance of taking the right road from the beginning. Offers a remedy that has proved very efficacious.

NOW LET US SPEAK about the type of soul that enters the second dwelling places and what such a soul does in them. I'd like to say only a little, for I have spoken at length on this subject elsewhere.[1] And it would be impossible to avoid repeating much of it, for I don't remember a thing of what I said. If I could present the matter for you in a variety of ways I know well that you wouldn't be annoyed since we never tire of books—as many as there are—that deal with it.

2. This stage pertains to those who have already begun to practice prayer and have understood how important it is not to stay in the first dwelling places. But they still don't have the determination to remain in this second stage without turning back, for they don't avoid the occasions of sin. This failure to avoid these occasions is quite dangerous. But these persons have received a good deal of mercy in that they sometimes do strive to escape from snakes and poisonous creatures, and they understand that it is good to avoid them.

These rooms, in part, involve much more effort than do the first, even though there is not as much danger, for it now seems that souls in them recognize the dangers, and there is great hope they will enter further into the castle. I say that these rooms involve more effort because those who are in the first dwelling places are like deaf-mutes and thus the difficulty of not speaking is more easily endured by them than it is by those who hear but cannot speak. Yet, not for this reason does one have greater desire to be deaf, for after all it is a wonderful thing to hear what is being said to us. So these persons are able to hear the Lord when He calls. Since they are getting closer to where His Majesty dwells, He is a very good neighbor. His mercy and goodness are so bountiful; whereas we are occupied in our pastimes, business affairs, pleasures, and worldly buying and selling, and still falling into sin and rising again. These beasts are so poisonous and their presence so dangerous and noisy that it would be a wonder if we kept from stumbling and falling over them. Yet this Lord desires intensely that we love Him and seek His company, so much so that from time to time He calls us to draw near Him. And His voice is so sweet the poor soul dissolves at not doing immediately what He commands. Thus, as I say, hearing His voice is a greater trial than not hearing it.

3. I don't mean that these appeals and calls are like the ones I shall speak of later on.[2] But they come through words spoken by other good people, or through sermons, or through what is read in good books, or through the many things that are heard and by which God calls, or through illnesses and trials, or also through a truth that He teaches during the brief moments we spend in prayer; however lukewarm these moments may be, God esteems them highly. And you, Sisters, don't underestimate this first favor, nor should you become disconsolate if you don't respond at once to the Lord. His Majesty knows well how to wait many days and years, especially when He sees perseverance and good desires. This perseverance is most necessary here. One always gains much through perseverance. But the attacks made by devils in a thousand ways afflict the soul more in these rooms than in the previous ones. In the previous ones the soul was deaf and dumb—at least it heard very little and resisted less, as one who has partly lost hope of

conquering. Here the intellect is more alive and the faculties more skilled. The blows from the artillery strike in such a way that the soul cannot fail to hear. It is in this stage that the devils represent these snakes (worldly things) and the temporal pleasures of the present as though almost eternal. They bring to mind the esteem one has in the world, one's friends and relatives, one's health (when there's thought of penitential practices, for the soul that enters this dwelling place always begins wanting to practice some penance) and a thousand other obstacles.

4. O Jesus, what an uproar the devils instigate here! And the afflictions of the poor soul: it doesn't know whether to continue or to return to the first room. Reason, for its part, shows the soul that it is mistaken in thinking that these things of the world are not worth anything when compared to what it is aiming after. Faith, however, teaches it about where it will find fulfillment. The memory shows it where all these things end, holding before it the death of those who found great joy in them. Through the memory it sees how some have suffered sudden death, how quickly they are forgotten by all. Some whom it had known in great prosperity are under the ground, and their graves are walked upon. This soul itself has often passed by these graves. It reflects that many worms are swarming over the corpses, and thinks about numerous other things. The will is inclined to love after seeing such countless signs of love; it would want to repay something; it especially keeps in mind how this true Lover never leaves it, accompanying it and giving it life and being. Then the intellect helps it realize that it couldn't find a better friend, even were it to live for many years, that the whole world is filled with falsehood, and that so too these joys the devil gives it are filled with trials, cares, and contradictions. The intellect tells the soul of its certainty that outside this castle neither security nor peace will be found, that it should avoid going about to strange houses since its own is so filled with blessings to be enjoyed if it wants. The intellect will ask who it is that finds everything he needs in his own house and, especially, has a guest who will make him lord over all goods provided that he wills to avoid going astray like

the prodigal son and eating the husks of swine.[3]

5. These are reasons for conquering the devils. But, oh, my Lord and my God, how the whole world's habit of getting involved in vanities vitiates everything! Our faith is so dead that we desire what we see more than what faith tells us. And, indeed, we see only a lot of misfortune in those who go after these visible vanities. But these poisonous things we are dealing with are the cause of this misfortune, for just as all is poisoned if a viper bites someone and the wound swells, so we will be poisoned if we do not watch ourselves. Clearly many remedies are necessary to cure us, and God is favoring us a good deal if we do not die from the wound. Certainly the soul undergoes great trials here. If the devil, especially, realizes that it has all it needs in its temperament and habits to advance far, he will gather all hell together to make the soul go back outside.

6. Ah, my Lord! Your help is necessary here; without it one can do nothing.[4] In Your mercy do not consent to allow this soul to suffer deception and give up what was begun. Enlighten it that it may see how all its good is within this castle and that it may turn away from bad companions. It's a wonderful thing for a person to talk to those who speak about this interior castle, to draw near not only to those seen to be in these rooms where he is but to those known to have entered the ones closer to the center. Conversation with these latter will be a great help to him, and he can converse so much with them that they will bring him to where they are. Let the soul always heed the warning not to be conquered. If the devil sees that it has the strong determination to lose its life and repose and all that he offers it rather than return to the first room, he will abandon it much more quickly. Let the soul be manly and not like those soldiers who knelt down to drink before going into battle (I don't remember with whom),[5] but be determined to fight with all the devils and realize that there are no better weapons than those of the cross.

7. Even though I've said this at other times,[6] it's so important that I repeat it here: it is that souls shouldn't be thinking about consolations at this beginning stage. It would be a very poor way to start building so precious and great an edifice. If

the foundation is on sand, the whole building will fall to the ground. They'll never finish being dissatisfied and tempted. These are not the dwelling places where it rains manna; those lie further ahead, where a soul finds in the manna every taste it desires;[7] for it wants only what God wants. It's an amusing thing that even though we still have a thousand impediments and imperfections and our virtues have hardly begun to grow—and please God they may have begun—we are yet not ashamed to seek spiritual delights in prayer or to complain about dryness. May this never happen to you, Sisters. Embrace the cross your Spouse has carried and understand that this must be your task. Let the one who can do so, suffer more for Him; and she will be rewarded that much more. As for other favors, if the Lord should grant you one, thank Him for it as you would for something freely added on.

8. It will seem to you that you are truly determined to undergo exterior trials, provided that God favors you interiorly. His Majesty knows best what is suitable for us. There's no need for us to be advising Him about what He should give us, for He can rightly tell us that we don't know what we're asking for.[8] The whole aim of any person who is beginning prayer—and don't forget this, because it's very important—should be that he work and prepare himself with determination and every possible effort to bring his will into conformity with God's will. Be certain that, as I shall say later,[9] the greatest perfection attainable along the spiritual path lies in this conformity. It is the person who lives in more perfect conformity who will receive more from the Lord and be more advanced on this road. Don't think that in what concerns perfection there is some mystery or things unknown or still to be understood, for in perfect conformity to God's will lies all our good. Now then, if we err in the beginning, desiring that the Lord do our will at once and lead us according to what we imagine, what kind of stability will this edifice have? Let us strive to do what lies in our power and guard ourselves against these poisonous little reptiles, for the Lord often desires that dryness and bad thoughts afflict and pursue us without our being able to get rid of them. Sometimes He even permits these

reptiles to bite us so that afterward we may know how to guard ourselves better and that He may prove whether we are greatly grieved by having offended Him.

9. Thus, if you should at times fall don't become discouraged and stop striving to advance. For even from this fall God will draw out good, as does the seller of an antidote who drinks some poison in order to test whether his antidote is effective. Even if we didn't see our misery—or the great harm that a dissipated life does to us—through any other means than through this assault that we endure for the sake of being brought back to recollection, that would be enough. Can there be an evil greater than that of being ill at ease in our own house? What hope can we have of finding rest outside of ourselves if we cannot be at rest within. We have so many great and true friends and relatives (which are our faculties) with whom we must always live, even though we may not want to. But from what we feel, these seem to be warring against us because of what our vices have done to them. Peace, peace, the Lord said, my Sisters; and He urged His apostle so many times.[10] Well, believe me, if we don't obtain and have peace in our own house we'll not find it outside. Let this war be ended. Through the blood He shed for us I ask those who have not begun to enter within themselves to do so; and those who have begun, not to let the war make them turn back. Let these latter reflect that a relapse is worse than a fall; they already see their loss. Let them trust in the mercy of God and not at all in themselves, and they will see how His Majesty brings them from the dwelling places of one stage to those of another and settles them in a land where these wild animals cannot touch or tire them, but where they themselves will bring all these animals into subjection and scoff at them. And they shall enjoy many more blessings than one can desire—blessings even in this life, I mean.

10. Since, as I've said in the beginning,[11] I've written to you about how you should conduct yourselves in these disturbances set up here by the devil and how you cannot begin to recollect yourselves by force but only by gentleness, if your recollection is going to be more continual, I will not say anything else here

than that in my opinion it is very important to consult persons with experience; for you will be thinking that you are seriously failing to do some necessary thing. Provided that we don't give up, the Lord will guide everything for our benefit, even though we may not find someone to teach us. There is no other remedy for this evil of giving up prayer than to begin again; otherwise the soul will gradually lose more each day—and please God that it will understand this fact.

11. Someone could think that if turning back is so bad it would be better never to begin but to remain outside the castle. I have already told you at the beginning—and the Lord Himself tells you—that anyone who walks in danger perishes in it[12] and that the door of entry to this castle is prayer. Well now, it is foolish to think that we will enter heaven without entering into ourselves, coming to know ourselves, reflecting on our misery and what we owe God, and begging Him often for mercy. The Lord Himself says: *No one will ascend to My Father but through Me*[13] (I don't know if He says it this way—I think He does) and *whoever sees Me sees My Father.*[14] Well, if we never look at Him or reflect on what we owe Him and the death He suffered for us, I don't know how we'll be able to know Him or do works in His service. And what value can faith have without works and without joining them to the merits of Jesus Christ, our Good? Or who will awaken us to love this Lord?

May it please His Majesty to give us understanding of how much we cost Him, of how the servant is no greater than his master,[15] and that we must work in order to enjoy His glory. And we need to pray for this understanding so that we aren't always entering into temptation.[16]

THE THIRD DWELLING PLACES

Contains Two Chapters

Chapter 1

Treats of what little security we can have while living in this exile, even though we may have reached a high state, and of how we should walk with fear. This chapter has some good points.

WHAT SHALL WE SAY to those who through perseverance and the mercy of God have won these battles and have entered the rooms of the third stage, if not: *Blessed is the man who fears the Lord*?[1] His Majesty has done no small thing in giving me understanding right now of what this verse means in the vernacular, for I am ignorant in matters like this. Certainly we are right in calling such a man blessed, since if he doesn't turn back he is, from what we can understand, on the secure path to his salvation.[2] Here you will see, Sisters, how important it was to win the previous battles. I am certain the Lord never fails to give a person like this security of conscience, which is no small blessing. I said "security" and I was wrong, for there is no security in this life; so always understand that I mean "if he doesn't abandon the path he began on."

2. It is a great misery to have to live a life in which we must always walk like those whose enemies are at their doorstep; they can neither sleep nor eat without weapons and without being always frightened lest somewhere these enemies might be able to break through this fortress. O my Lord and my Good, how is it that You want us to desire so miserable a life, for it isn't

possible to stop wanting and asking You to take us out of it unless there is hope of losing it for You or of spending it very earnestly in Your service or, above all, of understanding what Your will is? If it is Your will, my God, may we die with You, as St. Thomas said;[3] for living without You and with these fears of the possibility of losing You forever is nothing else than dying often. That's why, daughters, I say that the blessedness we must ask for is that of being already secure with the blessed. For with these fears, what happiness can anyone have whose whole happiness is to please God? Consider that this happiness was had—and in much greater degree—by some saints who fell into serious sins and that we are not sure that God will help us to get free from these sins and to do penance for them.

3. Certainly, my daughters, I am so fearful as I write this that I don't know how I'm writing it or how I live when I think about it, which is very often. Pray, my daughters, that His Majesty may live in me always. If He doesn't, what security can a life as badly spent as mine have? And do not become sad in knowing that this life has been badly spent, as I have sometimes observed you become when I tell this to you; you continue to desire that I might have lived a very holy life—and you are right. I too would want to have so lived, but what can I do if I have lost holiness through my own fault! I will not complain about God who gave me enough help to carry out your desires. I cannot say this without tears and being very ashamed that I am writing something for those who can teach me. Doing so has been a hard command to obey! May it please the Lord that since it is being done for Him it may be of some benefit to you so that You may ask Him to pardon this miserable and bold creature. But His Majesty well knows that I can boast only of His mercy, and since I cannot cease being what I have been, I have no other remedy than to approach His mercy and to trust in the merits of His Son and of the Virgin, His Mother, whose habit I wear so unworthily, and you wear. Praise Him, my daughters, for you truly belong to our Lady. Thus you have no reason to be ashamed of my misery since you have such a good Mother. Imitate her and reflect that the grandeur of our Lady and the good of having her for your patroness must be in-

deed great since my sins and being what I am have not been enough to tarnish in any way this sacred order.

4. But one thing I advise you: not because you have such a Mother or Patroness should you feel secure, for David was very holy, and you already know who Solomon was. Don't pay any attention to the enclosure and the penance in which you live or feel safe in the fact that you are always conversing with God and practicing such continual prayer and being so withdrawn from the world of things and, in your opinion, holding them in abhorrence. These practices are all good, but not a sufficient reason, as I have said,[4] for us to stop fearing. So, continue to say this verse and often bear it in mind: *Beatus vir qui timet Dominum.*[5]

5. I don't remember what I was speaking about, for I have digressed a great deal and in thinking of myself I feel helpless, as a bird with broken wings, when it comes to saying anything good. So I want to leave this matter aside for now. Let me get back to what I began telling you[6] concerning souls that have entered the third dwelling places, for the Lord has done them no small favor, but a very great one, in letting them get through the first difficulties. I believe that through the goodness of God there are many of these souls in the world. They long not to offend His Majesty, even guarding themselves against venial sins; they are fond of doing penance and setting aside periods for recollection; they spend their time well, practicing works of charity toward their neighbors; and are very balanced in their use of speech and dress and in the governing of their households—those who have them. Certainly, this is a state to be desired. And, in my opinion, there is no reason why entrance even into the final dwelling place should be denied these souls, nor will the Lord deny them this entrance if they desire it; for such a desire is an excellent way to prepare oneself so that every favor may be granted.

6. O Jesus, and who will say that he doesn't want a good so wonderful, especially after having passed through the most difficult trial? No, nobody will. We all say that we want this good. But since there is need of still more in order that the soul possess the Lord completely, it is not enough to say we want it;

just as this was not enough for the young man whom the Lord told what one must do in order to be perfect.[7] From the time I began to speak of these dwelling places I have had this young man in mind. For we are literally like him; and ordinarily the great dryness in prayer comes from this, although it also has other causes. And I'm leaving aside mention of some interior trials that many good souls undergo (unbearable trials and not at all due to their own fault), from which the Lord always frees them to their own great benefit, and mention of those who suffer from melancholy and other illnesses. Briefly, in all things we have to let God be the judge. What I've said, I believe, is what usually happens; for since these souls realize that they wouldn't commit a sin for anything—many wouldn't even advertently commit a venial sin—and that they conduct their lives and households well, they cannot accept patiently that the door of entry to the place where our King dwells be closed to them who consider themselves His vassals. But even though a king here on earth has many vassals, not all enter his chamber. Enter, enter, my daughters, into the interior rooms; pass on from your little works. By the mere fact that you are Christians you must do all these things and much more. It is enough for you to be God's vassals; don't let your desire be for so much that as a result you will be left with nothing. Behold the saints who entered this King's chamber, and you will see the difference between them and us. Don't ask for what you have not deserved, nor should it enter our minds that we have merited this favor however much we may have served—we who have offended God.

7. Oh, humility, humility! I don't know what kind of temptation I'm undergoing in this matter that I cannot help but think that anyone who makes such an issue of this dryness is a little lacking in humility. I said that I've omitted mention of those great interior trials I've referred to,[8] for those involve much more than just a lack of devotion. Let us prove ourselves, my Sisters, or let the Lord prove us, for He knows well how to do this even though we often don't want to understand it. Let us speak now of those souls whose lives are so well ordered; let us recognize what they do for God, and we shall at once see

how we have no reason for complaining of His Majesty. If, like the young man in the Gospel, we turn our backs and go away sad[9] when the Lord tells us what we must do to be perfect, what do you want His Majesty to do? For He must give the reward in conformity with the love we have for Him. And this love, daughters, must not be fabricated in our imaginations but proved by deeds. And don't think He needs our works; He needs the determination of our wills.

8. We seem to think that everything is done when we willingly take and wear the religious habit and abandon all worldly things and possessions for Him—even though these possessions may amount to no more than the nets St. Peter possessed,[10] for he who gives what he has thinks he gives enough. This renunciation is a good enough preparation if one perseveres in it and doesn't turn back and become involved with the vermin in the first rooms, even if it be only in desire. There is no doubt that if a person perseveres in this nakedness and detachment from all worldly things he will reach his goal. But this perseverance includes the condition—and note that I am advising you of this—that you consider yourselves useless servants, as St. Paul, or Christ, says;[11] and believe that you have not put our Lord under any obligation to grant you these kinds of favors. Rather, as one who has received more, you are more indebted.[12] What can we do for a God so generous that He died for us, created us, and gives us being? Shouldn't we consider ourselves lucky to be able to repay something of what we owe Him for His service toward us? I say these words "His service toward us" unwillingly; but the fact is that He did nothing else but serve us all the time He lived in this world. And yet we ask Him again for favors and gifts.

9. Reflect a great deal, daughters, on some of the things that are here pointed out, even though in a jumbled way, for I don't know how to explain them further. The Lord will give you understanding of them so that out of dryness you may draw humility—and not disquiet, which is what the devil aims after. Be convinced that where humility is truly present God will give a peace and conformity—even though He may never give consolations—by which one will walk with greater con-

tentment than will others with their consolations. For often, as you have read,[13] the divine Majesty gives these consolations to the weaker souls; although I think we would not exchange these consolations for the fortitude of those who walk in dryness. We are fonder of consolations than we are of the cross. Test us, Lord—for You know the truth—so that we may know ourselves.

Chapter 2

Continues on the same topic; deals with dryness in prayer; with what, in her opinion, might take place at this stage; how it is necessary to test ourselves; and with the fact that the Lord does try those who are in these dwelling places.

I HAVE KNOWN SOME SOULS and even many—I believe I can say—who have reached this state and have lived many years in this upright and well-ordered way both in body and soul, insofar as can be known. After these years, when it seems they have become lords of the world, at least clearly disillusioned in its regard, His Majesty will try them in some minor matters, and they will go about so disturbed and afflicted that it puzzles me and even makes me fearful. It's useless to give them advice, for since they have engaged so long in the practice of virtue they think they can teach others and that they are more than justified in feeling disturbed.

2. In sum, I have found neither a way of consoling nor a cure for such persons other than to show them compassion in their affliction—and, indeed, compassion is felt on seeing them subject to so much misery—and not contradict their reasoning. For everything in their minds leads them to think they are suffering these things for God, and so, they don't come to realize that their disturbance is an imperfection. This is another mistake of persons so advanced. There is no reason for us to be surprised at what they experience; although I do think the feeling stirred by such things should pass quickly. For God

often desires that His chosen ones feel their wretchedness, and He withdraws His favor a little. No more is necessary, for I would wager that we'd then soon get to know ourselves. The nature of this trial is immediately understood, for they recognize their fault very clearly. Sometimes, seeing their fault distresses them more than the thing that disturbs them, for unable to help themselves they are affected by earthly happenings even though these may not be very burdensome. This distress, I think, is a great mercy from God; and although it is a defect, it is very beneficial for humility.

3. As for the persons I am speaking about, this is not so. But, as I have said, they canonize these feelings in their minds and would like others to do so. I want to mention some of these feelings so that we may understand and test ourselves before the Lord tests us. It is very important to be prepared and to have understood ourselves beforehand.

4. A rich person without children or anyone to whom he might want to leave his possessions happens to lose his wealth, but not to such an extent that he lacks necessities for himself and for the management of his household; he even has a surplus. If he should go about as worried and disturbed as he would be if not even a piece of bread were left, how can our Lord ask him to leave all for Him?[1] Here the person makes the excuse that he feels the way he does because he wants these things for the poor. But I believe that God has a greater desire that such a person conform to the divine will and that, though this person may try to procure such wealth, he keep his soul at rest rather than worry about charity of such a kind. And if the person doesn't do this, because the Lord has not brought him so far, well and good; but he should understand that he lacks this freedom of spirit. And because the Lord will ask him for it, he should prepare himself so that the Lord may give it to him; he will be asking His Majesty for it.

A person has plenty to eat and even a surplus; the opportunity presents itself for him to acquire more wealth; all right, let him do so if it is offered to him. But if he strives for wealth and after possessing it strives for more and more, however good the intention may be (for he should have a good intention because, as

I have said,[2] these are virtuous persons of prayer), he need have no fear of ascending to the dwelling places closest to the King.

5. There is a similar occurrence when an opportunity presents itself for these persons to be despised or to lose a little honor. God often grants them the favor of enduring such a thing; for He is very fond of favoring virtue publicly so that virtue itself will not undergo a loss of esteem. Or He will also do so because they have served Him, for this Beloved of ours is very good. But now they are left in such disquiet they cannot help themselves, nor can they quickly get rid of this disturbance. God help me! Aren't these the ones who for a long while now have considered how the Lord suffered and how good suffering is, and who have desired it? They would like everyone to live a life as well ordered as they do; and please God they will not think their grief is for the faults of others and in their minds turn it into something meritorious.

6. It must seem to you, Sisters, that I'm not staying on the subject or not speaking to you, for these things don't take place here. Neither do we have wealth nor do we desire or strive for it, nor does anyone do injury to us. As a result the examples are not relevant to us. But from these examples many lessons can be learned about things which it would not be good to single out, nor would there be reason to do so. Through the above examples you will understand whether or not you are truly stripped of what you have left behind. For little things happen even though not of this kind, in which you can very well test and know whether or not you are the rulers of your passions. And believe me the whole affair doesn't lie in whether or not we wear the religious habit but in striving to practice the virtues, in surrendering our will to God in everything, in bringing our life into accordance with what His Majesty ordains for it, and in desiring that His will not ours be done.[3] Since we may not have reached this stage—humility, as I have said![4] Humility is the ointment for our wounds because if we indeed have humility, even though there may be a time of delay, the surgeon, who is our Lord, will come to heal us.

7. The penance these souls do is well balanced, like their lives. They desire penance a great deal so as to serve our Lord

by it. Nothing of this is wrong, and thus they are very discreet in doing it in a way so as not to harm their health. Have no fear that they will kill themselves, for their reason is still very much in control. Love has not yet reached the point of overwhelming reason. But I should like us to use our reason to make ourselves dissatisfied with this way of serving God, always going step by step, for we'll never finish this journey. And since, in our opinion, we are continually walking and are tired (for, believe me, it is a wearisome journey), we will be doing quite well if we don't go astray. But does it seem to you, daughters, that if we could go from one land to another in eight days, it would be good to take a year through wind, snow, rain, and bad roads? Wouldn't it be better to make the journey all at once? For all these obstacles are present, as well as danger from snakes. Oh what good proofs I could give of these things. And please God I may have passed beyond this stage, for often enough it seems to me I haven't.

8. Since we are so circumspect, everything offends us because we fear everything; so we don't dare go further—as if we could reach these dwelling places while leaving to other persons the trouble of treading the path for us. Since this is not possible, let us exert ourselves, my Sisters, for the love of the Lord; let's abandon our reason and our fears into His hands; let's forget this natural weakness that can take up our attention so much. Let the prelates take care of our bodily needs; that's their business. As for ourselves, we should care only about moving quickly so as to see this Lord. Even though the comfort you have is little or none at all, we could be deceived by worry about our health. Furthermore, worry over our health will not improve our health. This I know. And I also know that the whole affair doesn't lie in what pertains to the body, for this is what is the least important. The journey I am speaking of must be taken with great humility. For if you have understood, it is in regard to humility, I believe, that there is an obstacle for those who do not go forward. It should seem to us that we have gone but a few steps, and we should believe this to be so, and that those our Sisters have taken are rapid ones; and not only should we desire but we should strive that they consider us the most miserable of all.

9. With humility present, this stage is a most excellent one. If humility is lacking, we will remain here our whole life—and with a thousand afflictions and miseries. For since we will not have abandoned ourselves, this state will be very laborious and burdensome. We shall be walking while weighed down with this mud of our human misery, which is not so with those who ascend to the remaining rooms. But in these rooms of which we're speaking, the Lord, as one who is just or even merciful, does not fail to pay; for He always gives much more than we deserve by giving us consolations far greater than those we find in the comforts and distractions of life. But I don't think He gives much spiritual delight unless sometimes in order to invite souls by the sight of what takes place in the remaining dwelling places and so that they will prepare themselves to enter them.

10. It will seem to you that consolations and spiritual delights are the same, so why should I make this distinction? To me it seems there is a very great difference between the two. Now I can be wrong. I'll say what I understand about this when I speak of the fourth dwelling places which come after these. For since something will have to be explained about the spiritual delights the Lord gives there, the discussion will be more appropriate at that time. And although the explanation may seem to be useless it might help somewhat so that in understanding the nature of each thing you will be able to strive for what is best. Great solace comes to souls God brings there, and confusion to those who think they have everything. If souls are humble they will be moved to give thanks. If there is some lack in humility, they will feel an inner distaste for which they will find no reason. For perfection as well as its reward does not consist in spiritual delights but in greater love and in deeds done with greater justice and truth.

11. You will wonder, if this is true—as it is—what use it serves to explain and treat of these interior favors. I don't know. Ask him who ordered me to write, for I am not obliged to dispute with superiors but to obey—nor would disputing with them be right. What I can truthfully say to you is that at one time I didn't have or even know about these favors through experience or think that I would ever in my life know about

them in this way—and rightly so, for it was happiness enough for me to know, or by conjecture understand, that I was pleasing God in something. But when I read in books about these delights and favors the Lord grants souls that serve Him, I was very much consoled and moved to give great praise to God. Well, if my soul which was so wretched did this, those souls that are good and humble will praise Him much more. And if one alone is led to praise Him even once, it is in my opinion very good that the subject be mentioned so that we know about the happiness and delight we lose through our own fault. Moreover, if these favors are from God they come brimming over with love and fortitude by which you can journey with less labor and grow in the practice of works and virtues. Don't think that it matters little to lose such favors through our own fault; when it isn't our fault, the Lord is just.[5] His Majesty will give you through other paths what He keeps from you on this one because of what He knows, for His secrets are very hidden; at least what He does will without any doubt be what is most suitable for us.

12. What it seems to me would be highly beneficial for those who through the goodness of the Lord are in this state (for, as I have said,[6] He grants them no small mercy because they are very close to ascending higher) is that they study diligently how to be prompt in obedience. And even if they are not members of a religious order, it would be a great thing for them to have—as do many persons—someone whom they could consult so as not to do their own will in anything. Doing our own will is usually what harms us. And they shouldn't seek another of their own making, as they say—one who is so circumspect about everything; but seek out someone who is very free from illusion about the things of the world. For in order to know ourselves, it helps a great deal to speak with someone who already knows the world for what it is. And it helps also because when we see some things done by others that seem so impossible for us and the ease with which they are done, we become very encouraged. And it seems that through the flight of these others we also will make bold to fly, as do the bird's fledglings when they are taught; for even though they do not begin to soar immediately, little by little they imitate the

parent. Receiving this help is most beneficial; I know. However determined they are to keep from offending the Lord, these persons will be right not to place themselves in the occasion of offending Him. Since they are close to the first dwelling places, they could easily return to them. Their fortitude is not founded on solid ground, as is the case with those who are tried in suffering, for these latter know about the storms of the world and what little reason there is to fear them or desire the world's consolations. But it would be possible for the former in a great persecution to return to these consolations. The devil knows well how to stir up tempests so as to do us harm, and these persons would be unable to bear the trials that would come from their zeal to prevent others from committing sin.

13. Let us look at our own faults and leave aside those of others, for it is very characteristic of persons with such well-ordered lives to be shocked by everything. Perhaps we could truly learn from the one who shocks us what is most important even though we may surpass him in external composure and our way of dealing with others. Although good, these latter things are not what is most important; nor is there any reason to desire that everyone follow at once our own path, or to set about teaching the way of the spirit to someone who perhaps doesn't know what such a thing is. For with these desires that God gives us, Sisters, about the good of souls, we can make many mistakes. So it is better to carry out what our rule says, to strive to live always in silence and hope,[7] for the Lord will take care of these souls. If we ourselves are not negligent in beseeching His Majesty to do so, we shall, with His favor, do much good. May He be blessed forever.

THE FOURTH DWELLING PLACES

Contains Three Chapters

Chapter 1

Discusses the difference between consolations (or feelings of tenderness) in prayer and spiritual delights.[1] *Tells of her happiness on learning the difference between the mind and the intellect. This knowledge is very beneficial for anyone who is greatly distracted in prayer.*

IN ORDER TO BEGIN to speak of the fourth dwelling places I really need to entrust myself, as I've already done, to the Holy Spirit and beg Him to speak for me from here on that I may say something about the remaining rooms in a way that you will understand. For supernatural experiences begin here. These are something most difficult to explain, if His Majesty doesn't do so, as was said in another book I wrote fourteen years ago, more or less, in which I dealt with these experiences to the extent of my knowledge of them at that time. Although I think I now have a little more light about these favors the Lord grants to some souls, knowing how to explain them is a different matter.[2] May His Majesty help me to do so if it will be of some benefit; and if not, then no.

2. Since these dwelling places now are closer to where the King is, their beauty is great. There are things to see and understand so delicate that the intellect is incapable of finding words to explain them, although something might turn out to be well put and not at all obscure to the unexperienced; and anyone who has experience, especially when there is a lot of it, will understand very well.

It will seem that to reach these dwelling places one will have had to live in the others a long while. Although it is usual that a person will have to have stayed in those already spoken about, there is no certain rule, as you will have often heard. For the Lord gives when He desires, as He desires, and to whom He desires. Since these blessings belong to Him, He does no injustice to anyone.[3]

3. Poisonous creatures rarely enter these dwelling places. If they enter they do no harm; rather, they are the occasion of gain. I hold that the situation is much better in this stage of prayer when these creatures do enter and wage war, for the devil could deceive one with respect to the spiritual delights given by God if there were no temptations, and do much more harm than when temptations are felt. The soul would not gain so much; at least all the things contributing to its merit would be removed, and it would be left in a habitual absorption. For when a soul is in one continual state, I don't consider it safe, nor do I think it is possible for the spirit of the Lord to be in one fixed state during this exile.

4. Well now, in speaking about what I said I'd mention here[4] concerning the difference in prayer between consolations and spiritual delights, the term "consolations," I think, can be given to those experiences we ourselves acquire through our own meditation and petitions to the Lord, those that proceed from our own nature—although God in the end does have a hand in them; for it must be understood, in whatever I say, that without Him we can do nothing.[5] But the consolations arise from the virtuous work itself that we perform, and it seems that we have earned them through our own effort and are rightly consoled for having engaged in such deeds. But if we reflect upon this, we see that we experience the same joyful consolations in many of the things that can happen to us on earth; for example: when someone suddenly inherits a great fortune; when we suddenly see a person we love very much; when we succeed in a large and important business matter and of which everyone speaks well; when you see your husband or brother or son alive after someone has told you he is dead. I have seen the flow of tears from great consolations, and this has even

happened to me at times. I think that just as these joyful consolations are natural so are those afforded us by the things of God, but these latter are of a nobler kind, although the others are not bad. In sum, joyful consolations in prayer have their beginning in our own human nature and end in God.

The spiritual delights begin in God, but human nature feels and enjoys them as much as it does those I mentioned—and much more. O Jesus, how I long to know how to explain this! For I discern, I think, a very recognizable difference, but I don't have the knowledge to be able to explain myself. May the Lord do so.

5. Now I remember a line that we say at Prime, in the latter part of the verse at the end of the last psalm: *Cum dilatasti cor meum.*[6] For anyone who has had much experience these words are sufficient to see the difference between consolations and spiritual delights; for anyone who has not, more words are needed. The consolations that were mentioned do not expand the heart; rather, they usually seem to constrain it a little—although there is the greatest consolation at seeing what is done for God. But some anxious tears come that in a way, it seems, are brought on by the passions. I don't know much about these passions of the soul—knowledge of them might perhaps have enabled me to explain—and what proceeds from sensuality and from our human nature, for I am very dull. If only I knew how to explain myself, for since I have undergone this I understand it. Knowledge and learning are a great help in everything.

6. My experience of this state (I mean of this joy and consolation that comes during meditation) is that if I began to weep over the Passion I didn't know how to stop until I got a severe headache; if I did so over my sins, the same thing happened. Our Lord granted me quite a favor. Yet I don't want to examine now whether the one or the other is better, but I would like to know how to explain the difference there is between the one and the other. It is for these reasons sometimes that these tears flow and desires come, and they are furthered by human nature and one's temperament; but finally, as I have said,[7] they end in God regardless of their nature. They

are to be esteemed if there is the humility to understand that one is no better because of experiencing them, for it cannot be known whether they are all effects of love. When they are, the gift is God's.

For the most part, the souls in the previous dwelling places are the ones who have these devout feelings, for these souls work almost continually with the intellect, engaging in discursive thought and meditation. And they do well because nothing further has been given them; although they would be right if they engaged for a while in making acts of love, praising God, rejoicing in His goodness, that He is who He is, and in desiring His honor and glory. These acts should be made insofar as possible, for they are great awakeners of the will. Such souls would be well advised when the Lord gives them these acts not to abandon them for the sake of finishing the usual meditation.

7. Because I have spoken at length on this subject elsewhere,[8] I will say nothing about it here. I only wish to inform you that in order to profit by this path and ascend to the dwelling places we desire, the important thing is not to think much but to love much;[9] and so do that which best stirs you to love. Perhaps we don't know what love is. I wouldn't be very surprised, because it doesn't consist in great delight but in desiring with strong determination to please God in everything, in striving, insofar as possible, not to offend Him, and in asking Him for the advancement of the honor and glory of His Son and the increase of the Catholic Church. These are the signs of love. Don't think the matter lies in thinking of nothing else, and that if you become a little distracted all is lost.

8. I have been very afflicted at times in the midst of this turmoil of mind. A little more than four years ago I came to understand through experience that the mind (or imagination, to put it more clearly) is not the intellect. I asked a learned man and he told me that this was so; which brought me no small consolation.[10] For since the intellect is one of the soul's faculties, it was an arduous thing for me that it should be so restless at times. Ordinarily the mind flies about quickly, for only God can hold it fast in such a way as to make it seem that we are somehow loosed from this body. I have seen, I think,

that the faculties of my soul were occupied and recollected in God while my mind on the other hand was distracted. This distraction puzzled me.[11]

9. O Lord, take into account the many things we suffer on this path for lack of knowledge! The trouble is that since we do not think there is anything to know other than that we must think of You, we do not even know how to ask those who know nor do we understand what there is to ask. Terrible trials are suffered because we don't understand ourselves, and that which isn't bad at all but good we think is a serious fault. This lack of knowledge causes the afflictions of many people who engage in prayer; complaints about interior trials, at least to a great extent, by people who have no learning; melancholy and loss of health; and even the complete abandonment of prayer. For such persons don't reflect that there is an interior world here within us. Just as we cannot stop the movement of the heavens, but they proceed in rapid motion, so neither can we stop our mind; and then the faculties of the soul go with it, and we think we are lost and have wasted the time spent before God. But the soul is perhaps completely joined with Him in the dwelling places very close to the center while the mind is on the outskirts of the castle suffering from a thousand wild and poisonous beasts, and meriting by this suffering. As a result we should not be disturbed; nor should we abandon prayer, which is what the devil wants us to do. For the most part all the trials and disturbances come from our not understanding ourselves.

10. While writing this, I'm thinking about what's going on in my head with the great noise there that I mentioned in the beginning.[12] It makes it almost impossible for me to write what I was ordered to. It seems as if there are in my head many rushing rivers and that these waters are hurtling downward, and many little birds and whistling sounds, not in the ears but in the upper part of the head where, they say, the higher part of the soul is. And I was in that superior part for a long time, for it seems this powerful movement of the spirit is a swift upward one. Please God I'll remember to mention the cause of this in discussing the dwelling places that come further on, for this is not a fitting place to do so, and I wouldn't be surprised if

the Lord gave me this headache so that I could understand these things better. For all this turmoil in my head doesn't hinder prayer or what I am saying, but the soul is completely taken up in its quiet, love, desires, and clear knowledge.

11. Now then if the superior part of the soul is in the superior part of the head, why isn't the soul disturbed? This I don't know. But I do know that what I say is true. The pain is felt when suspension does not accompany the prayer. When suspension does accompany prayer, no pain is felt until the suspension passes. But it would be very bad if I were to abandon everything on account of this obstacle. And so it isn't good for us to be disturbed by our thoughts, nor should we be concerned. If the devil causes them, they will cease with this suspension. If they come, as they do, from one of the many miseries inherited through the sin of Adam, let us be patient and endure them for the love of God since we are likewise subject to eating and sleeping without being able to avoid it, which is quite a trial.

12. Let us recognize our misery and desire to go where no one will taunt us, for sometimes I recall having heard these words the bride says in the *Song of Songs*.[13] And indeed I don't find in all of life anything about which they can be more rightly said. It seems to me that all the contempt and trials one can endure in life cannot be compared to these interior battles. Any disquiet and war can be suffered if we find peace where we live, as I have already said.[14] But that we desire to rest from the thousand trials there are in the world and that the Lord wants to prepare us for tranquillity and that within ourselves lies the obstacle to such rest and tranquillity cannot fail to be very painful and almost unbearable. So, Lord, bring us to the place where these miseries will not taunt us, for they seem sometimes to be making fun of the soul. Even in this life, the Lord frees the soul from these miseries when it reaches the last dwelling place, as we shall say if God wills.[15]

13. These miseries will not afflict or assail everyone as much as they did me for many years because of my wretchedness. It seems that I myself wanted to take vengeance on myself. And since the experience was something so painful for me, I think

perhaps that it will be so for you too. And I so often speak of it here and there that I might sometime succeed in explaining to you that it is an unavoidable thing and should not be a disturbance or affliction for you but that we must let the millclapper go clacking on, and must continue grinding our flour and not fail to work with the will and the intellect.

14. There is a more and a less to this obstacle in accordance with one's health and age. Let the poor soul suffer even though it has no fault in this; we have other faults, which makes it right for us to practice patience. And since our reading and the counsels we receive (that is, to pay no attention to these thoughts) don't suffice, I don't think that the time spent in explaining these things for those of you with little knowledge and consoling you in this matter is time lost. But until the Lord wants to enlighten us, these counsels will be of little help. Yet, it is necessary and His Majesty wishes us to take the means and understand ourselves; and let's not blame the soul for what a weak imagination, human nature, and the devil cause.

Chapter 2

Continues on the same subject and explains through a comparison the nature of spiritual delight and how this is attained by not seeking it.

GOD HELP ME with what I have undertaken! I've already forgot what I was dealing with, for business matters and poor health have forced me to set this work aside just when I was at my best; and since I have a poor memory everything will come out confused because I can't go back to read it over. And perhaps even everything else I say is confused; at least that's what I feel it is.

It seems to me I have explained the nature of consolations in the spiritual life.[1] Since they are sometimes mixed with our own passions, they are the occasion of loud sobbing; and I have heard some persons say they experience a tightening in the chest and even external bodily movements that they cannot restrain. The force of these passions can cause nosebleeds and other things just as painful. I don't know how to explain anything about these experiences because I haven't had any. But they must nonetheless be consoling, for, as I'm saying,[2] the whole experience ends in the desire to please God and enjoy His Majesty's company.

2. The experiences that I call spiritual delight in God, that I termed elsewhere the prayer of quiet,[3] are of a very different kind, as those of you who by the mercy of God have experienced them will know. Let's consider, for a better understanding, that we see two founts with two water troughs. (For I don't find anything more appropriate to explain some spiritual experiences than water; and this is because I know little and have no helpful cleverness of mind and am so fond of this element that I have observed it more attentively than other things. In all the things that so great and wise a God has created there must be many beneficial secrets, and those who understand them do benefit, although I believe that in each little thing created by God there is more than what is understood, even if it is a little ant.)

3. These two troughs are filled with water in different ways; with one the water comes from far away through many aqueducts and the use of much ingenuity; with the other the source of the water is right there, and the trough fills without any noise. If the spring is abundant, as is this one we are speaking about, the water overflows once the trough is filled, forming a large stream. There is no need of any skill, nor does the building of aqueducts have to continue; but water is always flowing from the spring.

The water coming from the aqueducts is comparable, in my opinion, to the consolations I mentioned[4] that are drawn from meditation. For we obtain them through thoughts, assisting ourselves, using creatures to help our meditation, and tiring the intellect. Since, in the end, the consolation comes through our own efforts, noise is made when there has to be some replenishing of the benefits the consolation causes in the soul, as has been said.[5]

4. With this other fount, the water comes from its own source which is God. And since His Majesty desires to do so—when He is pleased to grant some supernatural favor—He produces this delight with the greatest peace and quiet and sweetness in the very interior part of ourselves. I don't know from where or how, nor is that happiness and delight experienced, as are earthly consolations, in the heart. I mean there is no similarity at the beginning, for afterward the delight fills everything; this water overflows through all the dwelling places and faculties until reaching the body. That is why I said[6] that it begins in God and ends in ourselves. For, certainly, as anyone who may have experienced it will see, the whole exterior man enjoys this spiritual delight and sweetness.

5. I was now thinking, while writing this, that the verse mentioned above, *Dilatasti cor meum,*[7] says the heart was expanded. I don't think the experience is something, as I say, that rises from the heart, but from another part still more interior, as from something deep. I think this must be the center of the soul, as I later came to understand and will mention at the end.[8] For certainly I see secrets within ourselves that have often caused me to marvel. And how many more there must be! Oh, my Lord and my God, how great are Your grandeurs! We go about here below like foolish little shepherds, for while it seems that we are getting some knowledge of You it must amount to no more than nothing; for even in our own selves there are great secrets that we don't understand. I say "no more than nothing" because I'm comparing it to the many, many secrets that are in You, not because the grandeurs we see in You are not extraordinary; and that includes those we can attain knowledge of through Your works.

6. To return to the verse, what I think is helpful in it for explaining this matter is the idea of expansion. It seems that since that heavenly water begins to rise from this spring I'm mentioning that is deep within us, it swells and expands our whole interior being, producing ineffable blessings; nor does the soul even understand what is given to it there. It perceives a fragrance, let us say for now, as though there were in that interior depth a brazier giving off sweet-smelling perfumes. No

light is seen, nor is the place seen where the brazier is; but the warmth and the fragrant fumes spread through the entire soul and even often enough, as I have said,[9] the body shares in them. See now that you understand me; no heat is felt, nor is there the scent of any perfume, for the experience is more delicate than an experience of these things; but I use the examples only so as to explain it to you. And let persons who have not experienced these things understand that truthfully they do happen and are felt in this way, and the soul understands them in a manner clearer than is my explanation right now. This spiritual delight is not something that can be imagined, because however diligent our efforts we cannot acquire it. The very experience of it makes us realize that it is not of the same metal as we ourselves but fashioned from the purest gold of the divine wisdom. Here, in my opinion, the faculties are not united but absorbed and looking as though in wonder at what they see.

7. It's possible that in dealing with these interior matters I might contradict something of what I said elsewhere. That's no surprise, because in the almost fifteen years[10] since I wrote it the Lord may perhaps have given me clearer understanding in these matters than I had before. Now, as then, I could be completely mistaken—but I would not lie, because by God's mercy I'd rather suffer a thousand deaths. I speak of what I understand.

8. It seems clear to me the will must in some way be united with God's will. But it is in the effects and deeds following afterward that one discerns the true value of prayer; there is no better crucible for testing prayer. It is quite a great favor from our Lord if the person receiving the favor recognizes it, and a very great one if he doesn't turn back.

You will at once desire, my daughters, to obtain this prayer; and you are right, for, as I have said,[11] the soul will never understand the favors the Lord is granting there or the love with which He is drawing it nearer to Himself. It is good to try to understand how we can obtain such a favor; so I am going to tell you what I have understood about this.

9. Let's leave aside the times when our Lord is pleased to grant it because He wants to and for no other reason. He knows why; we don't have to meddle in this. After you have done what should be done by those in the previous dwelling places: humility! humility! By this means the Lord allows Himself to be conquered with regard to anything we want from Him. The first sign for seeing whether or not you have humility is that you do not think you deserve these favors and spiritual delights from the Lord or that you will receive them in your lifetime.

You will ask me how then one can obtain them without seeking them. I answer that for the following reasons there is no better way than the one I mentioned, of not striving for them. First, because the initial thing necessary for such favors is to love God without self-interest. Second, because there is a slight lack of humility in thinking that for our miserable services something so great can be obtained. Third, because the authentic preparation for these favors on the part of those of us who, after all, have offended Him is the desire to suffer and imitate the Lord rather than to have spiritual delights. Fourth, because His Majesty is not obliged to give them to us as He is to give us glory if we keep His commandments. (Without these favors we can be saved, and He knows better than we ourselves what is fitting for us and who of us truly loves Him. This is certain, I know. And I know persons who walk by the path of love as they ought to walk, that is, only so as to serve their Christ crucified; not only do these persons refuse to seek spiritual delights from Him or to desire them but they beseech Him not to give them these favors during their lifetime. This is true.) The fifth reason is that we would be laboring in vain; for since this water must not be drawn through aqueducts as was the previous water, we are little helped by tiring ourselves if the spring doesn't want to produce it. I mean that no matter how much we meditate or how much we try to squeeze something out and have tears, this water doesn't come in such a way. It is given only to whom God wills to give it and often when the soul is least thinking of it.

10. We belong to Him, daughters. Let Him do whatever He likes with us, bring us wherever He pleases. I really believe that

whoever humbles himself and is detached (I mean in fact because the detachment and humility must not be just in our thoughts—for they often deceive us—but complete) will receive the favor of this water from the Lord and many other favors that we don't know how to desire. May He be forever praised and blessed, amen.

Chapter 3

Deals with the prayer of recollection which for the most part the Lord gives before the prayer just mentioned. Tells about its effects and about those that come from that spiritual delight, given by the Lord, that was discussed in the previous chapter.

THE EFFECTS OF THIS PRAYER are many. I shall mention some. But first, I want to mention another kind of prayer that almost always begins before this one. Since I have spoken of such a prayer elsewhere,[1] I shall say little. It is a recollection that also seems to me to be supernatural because it doesn't involve being in the dark or closing the eyes, nor does it consist in any exterior thing, since without first wanting to do so, one does close one's eyes and desire solitude. It seems that without any contrivance the edifice is being built, by means of this recollection, for the prayer that was mentioned. The senses and exterior things seem to be losing their hold because the soul is recovering what it had lost.

2. They say that the soul enters within itself and, at other times, that it rises above itself.[2] With such terminology I wouldn't know how to clarify anything. This is what's wrong with me: that I think you will understand by my way of explaining, while perhaps I'm the only one who will understand myself. Let us suppose that these senses and faculties (for I have already mentioned that these powers are the people of this castle,[3] which is the image I have taken for my explanation) have gone outside and have walked for days and years with strangers—enemies of the well-being of the castle. Having

seen their perdition they've already begun to approach the castle even though they may not manage to remain inside because the habit of doing so is difficult to acquire. But still they are not traitors, and they walk in the environs of the castle. Once the great King, who is in the center dwelling place of this castle, sees their good will, He desires in His wonderful mercy to bring them back to Him. Like a good shepherd, with a whistle so gentle that even they themselves almost fail to hear it, He makes them recognize His voice and stops them from going so far astray so that they will return to their dwelling place. And this shepherd's whistle has such power that they abandon the exterior things in which they were estranged from Him and enter the castle.

3. I don't think I've ever explained it as clearly as I have now. When God grants the favor it is a great help to seek Him within where He is found more easily and in a way more beneficial to us than when sought in creatures, as St. Augustine says after having looked for Him in many places.[4] Don't think this recollection is acquired by the intellect striving to think about God within itself, or by the imagination imagining Him within itself. Such efforts are good and an excellent kind of meditation because they are founded on a truth, which is that God is within us. But this isn't the prayer of recollection because it is something each one can do—with the help of God, as should be understood of everything. But what I'm speaking of comes in a different way. Sometimes before one begins to think of God, these people are already inside the castle. I don't know in what way or how they heard their shepherd's whistle. It wasn't through the ears, because nothing is heard. But one noticeably senses a gentle drawing inward, as anyone who goes through this will observe, for I don't know how to make it clearer. It seems to me I have read where it was compared to a hedgehog curling up or a turtle drawing into its shell.[5] (The one who wrote this example must have understood the experience well.) But these creatures draw inward whenever they want. In the case of this recollection, it doesn't come when we want it but when God wants to grant us the favor. I for myself hold that when His Majesty grants it, He does so to persons who

are already beginning to despise the things of the world. I don't say that those in the married state do so in deed, for they cannot, but in desire; for He calls such persons especially so that they might be attentive to interior matters. So I believe that if we desire to make room for His Majesty, He will give not only this but more, and give it to those whom He begins to call to advance further.

4. May whoever experiences this within himself praise God greatly because it is indeed right to recognize the favor and give thanks, for doing so will dispose one for other greater favors. And this recollection is a preparation for being able to listen, as is counselled in some books,[6] so that the soul instead of striving to engage in discourse strives to remain attentive and aware of what the Lord is working in it. If His Majesty has not begun to absorb us, I cannot understand how the mind can be stopped. There's no way of doing so without bringing about more harm than good, although there has been a lengthy controversy on this matter among some spiritual persons. For my part I must confess my lack of humility, but those in favor of stopping the mind have never given me a reason for submitting to what they say. One of them tried to convince me with a certain book by the saintly Friar Peter of Alcántara[7] — for I believe he is a saint — to whom I would submit because I know that he knew. And we read it together, and he says the same thing I do; although not in my words. But it is clear in what he says that love must be already awakened. It could be that I'm mistaken, but I have the following reasons.

5. First, in this work of the spirit the one who thinks less and has less desire to act does more. What we must do is beg like the needy poor before a rich and great emperor, and then lower our eyes and wait with humility. When through His secret paths it seems we understand that He hears us, then it is good to be silent since He has allowed us to remain near Him; and it will not be wrong to avoid working with the intellect — if we can work with it, I mean. But if we don't yet know whether this King has heard or seen us, we mustn't become fools. The soul does become quite a fool when it tries to induce this prayer, and it is left much drier; and the imagination perhaps

becomes more restless through the effort made not to think of anything. But the Lord desires that we beseech Him and call to mind that we are in His presence; He knows what is suitable for us. I cannot persuade myself to use human diligence in a matter in which it seems His Majesty has placed a limit, and I want to leave the diligence to Him. What He did not reserve to Himself are many other efforts we can make with His help, such as: penance, good deeds, and prayer—insofar as our wretchedness can do these things.

6. The second reason is that these interior works are all gentle and peaceful; doing something arduous would cause more harm than good. I call any force that we might want to use "something arduous"; for example, it would be arduous to hold one's breath. Leave the soul in God's hands, let Him do whatever He wants with it, with the greatest disinterest about your own benefit as is possible and the greatest resignation to the will of God.

The third reason is that the very care used not to think of anything will perhaps rouse the mind to think very much.

The fourth is that what is most essential and pleasing to God is that we be mindful of His honor and glory and forget ourselves and our own profit and comfort and delight. How is a person forgetful of self if he is so careful not to stir or even to allow his intellect or desires to be stirred to a longing for the greater glory of God, or if he rests in what he already has? When His Majesty desires the intellect to stop, He occupies it in another way and gives it a light so far above what we can attain that it remains absorbed. Then, without knowing how, the intellect is much better instructed than it was through all the soul's efforts not to make use of it. Since God gave us our faculties that we might work with them and in this work they find their reward, there is no reason to charm them; we should let them perform their task until God appoints them to another greater one.

7. What I understand to be most fitting for the soul the Lord has desired to put in this dwelling place is that which has been said.[8] And without any effort or noise the soul should

strive to cut down the rambling of the intellect—but not suspend either it or the mind; it is good to be aware that one is in God's presence and of who God is. If what it feels within itself absorbs it, well and good. But let it not strive to understand the nature of this recollection, for it is given to the will. Let the soul enjoy it without any endeavors other than some loving words, for even though we may not try in this prayer to go without thinking of anything, I know that often the intellect will be suspended, even though for only a very brief moment.

8. But as I said elsewhere[9] the reason why in this kind of prayer—that is, the kind that is like the flowing spring in which the water does not come through aqueducts—the soul restrains itself or is restrained is its realization that it doesn't understand what it desires; and so the mind wanders from one extreme to the other, like a fool unable to rest in anything. (I am referring to the kind of prayer this dwelling place began with, for I have joined the prayer of recollection, which I should have mentioned first, with this one. The prayer of recollection is much less intense than the prayer of spiritual delight from God that I mentioned. But it is the beginning through which one goes to the other; for in the prayer of recollection, meditation, or the work of the intellect, must not be set aside.) The will has such deep rest in its God that the clamor of the intellect is a terrible bother to it. There is no need to pay any attention to this clamor, for doing so would make the will lose much of what it enjoys. But one should leave the intellect go and surrender oneself into the arms of love, for His Majesty will teach the soul what it must do at that point. Almost everything lies in finding oneself unworthy of so great a good and in being occupied with giving thanks.

9. In order to deal with the prayer of recollection I postponed mention of the effects or signs in souls to whom God, our Lord, gives this prayer of quiet. What an expansion or dilation of the soul is may be clearly understood from the example of a fount whose water doesn't overflow into a stream because the fount itself is constructed of such material that the more water there is flowing into it the larger the trough becomes. So it seems is the case with this prayer and many other marvels

that God grants to the soul, for He enables and prepares it so that it can keep everything within itself. Hence this interior sweetness and expansion can be verified in the fact that the soul is not as tied down as it was before in things pertaining to the service of God, but has much more freedom. Thus, in not being constrained by the fear of hell (because although there is even greater fear of offending God it loses servile fear here), this soul is left with great confidence that it will enjoy Him. The fear it used to have of doing penance and losing its health has disappeared, and it now thinks it will be able to do all things in God[10] and has greater desire for penance than previously. The fear it used to have of trials it now sees to be tempered. Its faith is more alive; it knows that if it suffers trials for God, His Majesty will give it the grace to suffer them with patience. Sometimes it even desires them because there also remains a strong will to do something for God. Since its knowledge of God's grandeur grows, it considers itself to be more miserable. Because it has already experienced spiritual delight from God, it sees that worldly delights are like filth. It finds itself withdrawing from them little by little, and it is more master of itself for so doing. In sum, there is an improvement in all the virtues. It will continue to grow if it doesn't turn back now to offending God; because if it does, then everything will be lost however high on the summit the soul may be. Nor should it be understood that if God grants this favor once or twice to a soul all these good effects will be caused. It must persevere in receiving them, for in this perseverance lies all our good.

10. One strong warning I give to whoever finds himself in this state is that he guard very carefully against placing himself in the occasion of offending God. In this prayer the soul is not yet grown but is like a suckling child. If it turns away from its mother's breasts, what can be expected for it but death? I am very afraid that this will happen to anyone to whom God has granted this favor and who withdraws from prayer—unless he does so for a particularly special reason—or if he doesn't return quickly to prayer, for he will go from bad to worse. I know there is a great deal to fear in this matter. And I know some persons for whom I have felt quite sorry—and I've seen what

I'm speaking about—because they have turned away from One who with so much love wanted to be their friend and proved it by deeds. I advise them so strongly not to place themselves in the occasions of sin because the devil tries much harder for a soul of this kind than for very many to whom the Lord does not grant these favors. For such a soul can do a great deal of harm to the devil by getting others to follow it, and it could be of great benefit to God's Church. And even though the devil may have no other reason than to see who it is to whom His Majesty shows particular love, that's sufficient for him to wear himself out trying to lead the soul to perdition. So these souls suffer much combat, and if they go astray, they stray much more than do others.

You, Sisters, are free of dangers, from what we can know. From pride and vainglory may God deliver you. If the devil should counterfeit God's favors, this will be known by the fact that these good effects are not caused, but just the opposite.

11. There is one danger I want to warn you about (although I may have mentioned it elsewhere)[11] into which I have seen persons of prayer fall, especially women, for since we are weaker there is more occasion for what I'm about to say. It is that some have a weak constitution because of a great amount of penance, prayer, and keeping vigil, and even without these; in receiving some favor, their nature is overcome. Since they feel some consolation interiorly and a languishing and weakness exteriorly, they think they are experiencing a spiritual sleep (which is a prayer a little more intense than the prayer of quiet)[12] and they let themselves become absorbed. The more they allow this, the more absorbed they become because their nature is further weakened, and they fancy that they are being carried away in rapture. I call it being carried away in foolishness[13] because it amounts to nothing more than wasting time and wearing down one's health. These persons feel nothing through their senses nor do they feel anything concerning God. One person happened to remain eight hours in this state. By sleeping and eating and avoiding so much penance, this person got rid of the stupor, for there was someone who understood her. She had misled both her confessor and other persons, as well as herself—for she hadn't intended to deceive.

I truly believe that the devil was trying to gain ground, and in this instance indeed he was beginning to gain no small amount.

12. It must be understood that when something is truly from God there is no languishing in the soul, even though there may be an interior and exterior languishing, for the soul experiences deep feelings on seeing itself close to God. Nor does the experience last so long, but for a very short while—although one becomes absorbed again. In such prayer, if the cause of it is not weakness, as I said,[14] the body is not worn down nor is any external feeling produced.

13. For this reason let them take the advice that when they feel this languishing in themselves they tell the prioress and distract themselves from it insofar as they can. The prioress should make them give up so many hours for prayer so that they have only a very few and try to get them to sleep and eat well until their natural strength begins to return, if it has been lost through a lack of food and sleep. If a Sister's nature is so weak that this is not enough, may she believe me that God does not want her to practice anything but the active life, which also must be practiced in monasteries. They should let her get busy with different duties; and always take care that she not have a great deal of solitude, for she would lose her health completely. It will be quite a mortification for her; in how she bears this absence is the way the Lord wants to test her love for Him. And He will be pleased to give her strength back after some time. If He doesn't, she will gain through vocal prayer and through obedience and will merit what she would have merited otherwise, and perhaps more.

14. There could also be some persons with such weak heads and imaginations—and I have known some—to whom it seems that everything they think about they see. This is very dangerous. Because I shall perhaps treat of it later on, I'll say no more here. I have greatly enlarged upon this dwelling place because it is the one which more souls enter. Since it is, and since the natural and the supernatural are joined in it, the devil can do more harm. In those dwelling places still to be spoken of, the Lord doesn't give him so much leeway. May His Majesty be forever praised, amen.

THE FIFTH DWELLING PLACES

Contains Four Chapters

Chapter 1

Begins to deal with how the soul is united to God in prayer. Tells how one discerns whether there is any illusion.

O SISTERS, HOW CAN I explain the riches and treasures and delights found in the fifth dwelling places? I believe it would be better not to say anything about these remaining rooms, for there is no way of knowing how to speak of them; neither is the intellect capable of understanding them nor can comparisons help in explaining them; earthly things are too coarse for such a purpose.

Send light from heaven, my Lord, that I might be able to enlighten these Your servants—for You have been pleased that some of them ordinarily enjoy these delights—so that they may not be deceived by the devil transforming himself into an angel of light.[1] For all their desires are directed toward pleasing You.

2. And although I have said "some," there are indeed only a few who fail to enter this dwelling place of which I shall now speak. There are various degrees, and for that reason I say that most enter these places. But I believe that only a few will experience some of the things that I will say are in this room. Yet even if souls do no more than reach the door, God is being very merciful to them; although many are called few are chosen.[2] So I say now that all of us who wear this holy habit of Carmel are called to prayer and contemplation. This call explains our origin; we are the descendants of men who felt this call, of

those holy fathers on Mount Carmel who in such great solitude and contempt for the world sought this treasure, this precious pearl of contemplation that we are speaking about. Yet few of us dispose ourselves that the Lord may communicate it to us. In exterior matters we are proceeding well so that we will reach what is necessary; but in the practice of the virtues that are necessary for arriving at this point we need very, very much and cannot be careless in either small things or great. So, my Sisters, since in some way we can enjoy heaven on earth, be brave in begging the Lord to give us His grace in such a way that nothing will be lacking through our own fault; that He show us the way and strengthen the soul that it may dig until it finds this hidden treasure.[3] The truth is that the treasure lies within our very selves. This is what I would like to know how to explain, if the Lord would enable me to do so.

3. I said "strengthen the soul" so that you will understand that bodily strength is not necessary for those to whom God does not give it. He doesn't make it impossible for anyone to buy His riches. He is content if each one gives what he has. Blessed be so great a God. But reflect, daughters, that He doesn't want you to hold on to anything, so that you will be able to enjoy the favors we are speaking of. Whether you have little or much, He wants everything for Himself; and in conformity with what you know you have given you will receive greater or lesser favors. There is no better proof for recognizing whether our prayer has reached union or not.

4. Don't think this union is some kind of dreamy state like the one I mentioned before.[4] I say "dreamy state" because it only seems that the soul is asleep; for neither does it really think it is asleep nor does it feel awake. There is no need here to use any technique to suspend the mind since all the faculties are asleep in this state—and truly asleep—to the things of the world and to ourselves. As a matter of fact, during the time that the union lasts the soul is left as though without its senses, for it has no power to think even if it wants to. In loving, if it does love, it doesn't understand how or what it is it loves or what it would want. In sum, it is like one who in every respect has died to the world so as to live more completely in God.

Thus the death is a delightful one, an uprooting from the soul of all the operations it can have while being in the body. The death is a delightful one because in truth it seems that in order to dwell more perfectly in God the soul is so separated from the body that I don't even know if it has life enough to breathe. (I was just now thinking about this, and it seems to me that it doesn't—at least if it does breathe, it is unaware it is doing so.) Nonetheless, its whole intellect would want to be occupied in understanding something of what is felt. And since the soul does not have the energy to attain to this, it is so stunned that, even if consciousness is not completely lost, neither a hand nor a foot stirs, as we say here below when a person is in such a swoon that we think he is dead.

O secrets of God! I would never tire of trying to explain them if I thought I could in some way manage to do so; thus I will say a thousand foolish things in order that I might at times succeed and that we might give great praise to the Lord.

5. I said that this union was not some kind of dreamy state,[5] because even if the experience in the dwelling place that was just mentioned is abundant the soul remains doubtful that it was union. It doubts whether it imagined the experience; whether it was asleep; whether the experience was given by God; or whether the devil transformed himself into an angel of light.[6] It is left with a thousand suspicions. That it has them is good, for, as I have said,[7] even our own nature can sometimes deceive us in that dwelling place. Though there is not so much room for poisonous things to enter, some tiny lizards do enter; since these lizards have slender heads they can poke their heads in anywhere. And even though they do no harm, especially if one pays no attention to them, as I said,[8] they are often a bother since they are little thoughts proceeding from the imagination and from what I mentioned. But however slender they may be, these little lizards cannot enter this fifth dwelling place; for there is neither imagination, nor memory, nor intellect that can impede this good. And I would dare say that if the prayer is truly that of union with God the devil cannot even enter or do any damage. His Majesty is so joined and united with the essence of the soul that the devil will not dare approach nor will he even

know about this secret. And this is obvious. Since as they say, he doesn't know our mind, he will have less knowledge of something so secret; for God doesn't even entrust this to our own mind. Oh what a great good, a state in which this accursed one does us no harm! Thus the soul is left with such wonderful blessings because God works within it without anyone disturbing Him, not even ourselves. What will He not give, who is so fond of giving and who can give all that He wants?

6. It seems I have left you confused by saying "if it is union" and that there are other unions. And indeed how true it is that there are! Even though these unions regard vain things, the devil will use such things to transport us when they are greatly loved. But he doesn't do so in the way God does, or with the delight and satisfaction of soul, or with the peace and joy. This union is above all earthly joys, above all delights, above all consolations, and still more than that. It doesn't matter where those spiritual or earthly joys come from, for the feeling is very different as you will have experienced. I once said[9] that the difference is like that between feeling something on the rough outer covering of the body or in the marrow of the bones. And that was right on the mark, for I don't know how to say it better.

7. It seems to me that you're still not satisfied, for you will think you can be mistaken and that these interior things are something difficult to examine. What was said will be sufficient for anyone who has experienced union. Yet, because the difference between union and the previous experience is great, I want to mention a clear sign by which you will be sure against error or doubts about whether the union is from God. His Majesty has brought it to my memory today, and in my opinion it is the sure sign. In difficult matters even though it seems to me I understand and that I speak the truth I always use this expression "it seems to me." For if I am mistaken, I am very much prepared to believe what those who have a great deal of learning say. Even though they have not experienced these things, very learned men have a certain "I don't know what"; for since God destines them to give light to His Church, He enlightens them that they might acknowledge a truth when presented

with it. And if they do not live a dissipated life but are God's servants, they are never surprised by His grandeurs; they have come to understand well that He can do ever more and more. And, finally, even though some things are not so well explained, these learned men will find other things in their books that will show that these things could take place.

8. I have had a great deal of experience with learned men, and have also had experience with half-learned, fearful ones; these latter cost me dearly.[10] At least I think that anyone who refuses to believe that God can do much more or that He has considered and continues to consider it good sometimes to communicate favors to His creatures, has indeed closed the door to receiving them. Therefore, Sisters, let this never happen to you, but believe that God can do far more and don't turn your attention to whether the ones to whom He grants His favors are good or bad; for His Majesty knows this, as I have told you.[11] There is no reason for us to meddle in the matter, but with humility and simplicity of heart we should serve and praise Him for His works and marvels.

9. Well then, to return to the sign that I say is the true one,[12] you now see that God has made this soul a fool with regard to all so as better to impress upon it true wisdom. For during the time of this union it neither sees, nor hears, nor understands, because the union is always short and seems to the soul even much shorter than it probably is. God so places Himself in the interior of that soul that when it returns to itself it can in no way doubt that it was in God and God was in it. This truth remains with it so firmly that even though years go by without God's granting that favor again, the soul can neither forget nor doubt that it was in God and God was in it. This certitude is what matters now, for I shall speak of the effects of this prayer afterward.[13]

10. Now, you will ask me, how did the soul see this truth or understand if it didn't see or understand anything? I don't say that it then saw the truth but that afterward it sees the truth clearly, not because of a vision but because of a certitude remaining in the soul that only God can place there. I know a person who hadn't learned that God was in all things by

presence, power, and essence, and through a favor of this kind that God granted her she came to believe it. After asking a half-learned man of the kind I mentioned[14]—he knew as little as she had known before God enlightened her—she was told that God was present only by grace. Such was her own conviction that even after this she didn't believe him and asked others who told her the truth, with which she was greatly consoled.[15]

11. Don't be mistaken by thinking that this certitude has to do with a corporal form, as in the case of the bodily presence of our Lord Jesus Christ in the Most Blessed Sacrament even though we do not see Him. Here the matter isn't like that; it concerns only the divinity. How, then, is it that what we do not see leaves this certitude? I don't know; these are His works. But I do know I speak the truth. And I would say that whoever does not receive this certitude does not experience union of the whole soul with God, but union of some faculty, or that he experiences one of the many other kinds of favors God grants souls. In regard to all these favors we have to give up looking for reasons to see how they've come about. Since our intellect cannot understand this union why do we have to make this effort? It's enough for us to see that He who is the cause of it is almighty. Since we have no part at all to play in bringing it about no matter how much effort we put forth, but it is God who does so, let us not desire the capacity to understand this union.

12. Now I recall, in saying that we have no part to play, what you have heard the bride say in the *Song of Songs: He brought me into the wine cellar* (or, placed me there, I believe it says).[16] And it doesn't say that she went. And it says also that she went looking about in every part of the city for her Beloved.[17] I understand this union to be the wine cellar where the Lord wishes to place us when He desires and as He desires. But however great the effort we make to do so, we cannot enter. His Majesty must place us there and enter Himself into the center of our soul. And that He may show His marvels more clearly He doesn't want our will to have any part to play, for it has been entirely surrendered to Him. Neither does He want the door of the faculties and of the senses to be opened, for

they are all asleep. But He wants to enter the center of the soul without going through any door, as He entered the place where His disciples were when He said, *pax vobis;*[18] or as He left the tomb without lifting away the stone. Further on you will see in the last dwelling place[19] how His Majesty desires that the soul enjoy Him in its own center even much more than here.

13. O daughters, how much we shall see if we don't want to have anything more to do with our own lowliness and misery and if we understand that we are unworthy of being servants of a Lord who is so great we cannot comprehend His wonders! May He be forever praised, amen.

Chapter 2

Continues on the same topic. Explains the prayer of union through an exquisite comparison. Tells about the effects it leaves in the soul. The chapter is very important.

IT WILL SEEM TO YOU that everything has already been said about what there is to see in this dwelling place. Yet a lot is missing; for, as I said,[1] there are various degrees of intensity. With regard to the nature of union, I don't believe I'd know how to say anything more. But when souls to whom God grants these favors prepare themselves, there are many things to say about the Lord's work in them. I shall speak of some of these and tell about the state the soul is left in. To explain things better I want to use a helpful comparison; it is good for making us see how, even though we can do nothing in this work done by the Lord, we can do much by disposing ourselves so that His Majesty may grant us this favor.

2. You must have already heard about His marvels manifested in the way silk originates, for only He could have invented something like that. The silkworms come from seeds about the size of little grains of pepper. (I have never seen this but heard of it, and so if something in the explanation gets distorted it won't be my fault.) When the warm weather comes

and the leaves begin to appear on the mulberry tree, the seeds start to live, for they are dead until then. The worms nourish themselves on mulberry leaves until, having grown to full size, they settle on some twigs. There with their little mouths they themselves go about spinning the silk and making some very thick little cocoons in which they enclose themselves. The silkworm, which is fat and ugly, then dies, and a little white butterfly, which is very pretty, comes forth from the cocoon. Now if this were not seen but recounted to us as having happened in other times, who would believe it? Or what reasonings could make us conclude that a thing as nonrational as a worm or a bee could be so diligent in working for our benefit and with so much industriousness? And the poor little worm loses its life in the challenge. This is enough, Sisters, for a period of meditation even though I may say no more to you; in it you can consider the wonders and the wisdom of our God. Well now, what would happen if we knew the property of every created thing. It is very beneficial for us to busy ourselves thinking of these grandeurs and delighting in being brides of a King so wise and powerful.

3. Let's return to what I was saying. This silkworm, then, starts to live when by the heat of the Holy Spirit it begins to benefit through the general help given to us all by God and through the remedies left by Him to His Church, by going to confession, reading good books, and hearing sermons, which are the remedies that a soul, dead in its carelessness and sins and placed in the midst of occasions, can make use of. It then begins to live and to sustain itself by these things, and by good meditations, until it is grown. Its being grown is what is relevant to what I'm saying, for these other things have little importance here.

4. Well once this silkworm is grown—in the beginning I dealt with its growth[2]—it begins to spin the silk and build the house wherein it will die. I would like to point out here that this house is Christ. Somewhere, it seems to me, I have read or heard that our life is hidden in Christ or in God (both are the same), or that our life is Christ.[3] Whether the quotation is exact or not doesn't matter for what I intend.

5. Well see here, daughters, what we can do through the help of God: His Majesty Himself, as He does in this prayer of union, becomes the dwelling place we build for ourselves. It seems I'm saying that we can build up God and take Him away since I say that He is the dwelling place and we ourselves can build it so as to place ourselves in it. And, indeed, we can! Not that we can take God away or build Him up, but we can take away from ourselves and build up, as do these little silkworms. For we will not have finished doing all that we can in this work when, to the little we do, which is nothing, God will unite Himself, with His greatness, and give it such high value that the Lord Himself will become the reward of this work. Thus, since it was He who paid the highest price, His Majesty wants to join our little labors with the great ones He suffered so that all the work may become one.

6. Therefore, courage, my daughters! Let's be quick to do this work and weave this little cocoon by getting rid of our self-love and self-will, our attachment to any earthly thing, and by performing deeds of penance, prayer, mortification, obedience, and of all the other things you know. Would to heaven that we would do what we know we must; and we are instructed about what we must do. Let it die; let this silkworm die, as it does in completing what it was created to do! And you will see how we see God, as well as ourselves placed inside His greatness, as is this little silkworm within its cocoon. Keep in mind that I say "see God," in the sense of what I mentioned[4] concerning that which is felt in this kind of union.

7. Now, then, let's see what this silkworm does, for that's the reason I've said everything else. When the soul is, in this prayer, truly dead to the world, a little white butterfly comes forth. Oh, greatness of God! How transformed the soul is when it comes out of this prayer after having been placed within the greatness of God and so closely joined with Him for a little while—in my opinion the union never lasts for as much as a half hour. Truly, I tell you that the soul doesn't recognize itself. Look at the difference there is between an ugly worm and a little white butterfly; that's what the difference is here. The soul doesn't know how it could have merited so much

good—from where this good may have come I mean, for it well knows that it doesn't merit this blessing. It sees within itself a desire to praise the Lord; it would want to dissolve and die a thousand deaths for Him. It soon begins to experience a desire to suffer great trials without its being able to do otherwise. There are the strongest desires for penance, for solitude, and that all might know God; and great pain comes to it when it sees that He is offended. I shall treat of these things more particularly in the next dwelling place[5]; although what is in this dwelling place and the next are almost identical, the force of the effects is very different. As I have said,[6] if after God brings a soul here it makes the effort to advance, it will see great things.

8. Oh, now, to see the restlessness of this little butterfly, even though it has never been quieter and calmer in its life, is something to praise God for! And the difficulty is that it doesn't know where to alight and rest. Since it has experienced such wonderful rest, all that it sees on earth displeases it, especially if God gives it this wine often. Almost each time it gains new treasures. It no longer has any esteem for the works it did while a worm, which was to weave the cocoon little by little; it now has wings. How can it be happy walking step by step when it can fly? On account of its desires, everything it can do for God becomes little in its own eyes. It doesn't wonder as much at what the saints suffered now that it understands through experience how the Lord helps and transforms a soul, for it doesn't recognize itself or its image. The weakness it previously seemed to have with regard to doing penance it now finds is its strength. Its attachment to relatives or friends or wealth (for neither its actions, nor its determination, nor its desire to withdraw were enough; rather, in its opinion, it was more attached to everything) is now so looked upon that it grieves when obliged to do what is necessary in this regard so as not to offend God. Everything wearies it, for it has learned through experience that creatures cannot give it true rest.

9. It seems I have been lengthy, but I could say much more; and whoever has received this favor from God will see that I've been brief. So, there is no reason to be surprised that this little

butterfly seeks rest again since it feels estranged from earthly things. Well then, where will the poor little thing go? It can't return to where it came from; as was said,[7] we are powerless, however much we do, to bring about this favor until God is again pleased to grant it. O Lord, what new trials begin for this soul! Who would say such a thing after a favor so sublime? Briefly, in one way or another, there must be a cross while we live. And with respect to anyone who says that after he arrived here he always enjoyed rest and delight I would say that he never arrived but that perhaps he had experienced some spiritual delight—if he had entered into the previous dwelling place—and his experience had been helped along by natural weakness or perhaps even by the devil who gives him peace so as afterward to wage much greater war against him.

10. I don't mean to say that those who arrive here do not have peace; they do have it, and it is very deep. For the trials themselves are so valuable and have such good roots that although very severe they give rise to peace and happiness. From the very unhappiness caused by worldly things arises the ever so painful desire to leave this world. Any relief the soul has comes from the thought that God wants it to be living in this exile; yet even this is not enough, because in spite of all these benefits it is not entirely surrendered to God's will, as will be seen further on[8]—although it doesn't fail to conform itself. But it conforms with a great feeling that it can do no more because no more has been given it, and with many tears. Every time it is in prayer this regret is its pain. In some way perhaps the sorrow proceeds from the deep pain it feels at seeing that God is offended and little esteemed in this world and that many souls are lost, heretics as well as Moors; although those that grieve it most are Christians. Even though it sees that God's mercy is great—for, however wicked their lives, these Christians can make amends and be saved—it fears that many are being condemned.

11. Oh, greatness of God! A few years ago—and even perhaps days—this soul wasn't mindful of anything but itself. Who has placed it in the midst of such painful concerns? Even were we to meditate for many years we wouldn't be able to feel

them as painfully as does this soul now. Well, God help me, wouldn't it be enough if for many days and years I strove to think about the tremendous evil of an offense against God and that those souls who are condemned are His children and my brothers and about the dangers in which we live and how good it is for us to leave this miserable life? Not at all, daughters; the grief that is felt here is not like that of this world. We can, with God's favor, feel the grief that comes from thinking about these things a great deal, but such grief doesn't reach the intimate depths of our being as does the pain suffered in this state, for it seems that the pain breaks and grinds the soul into pieces, without the soul's striving for it or even at times wanting it. Well, what is this pain? Where does it come from? I shall tell you.

12. Haven't you heard it said of the bride—for I have already mentioned it elsewhere here but not in this sense[9]—that God brought her into the inner wine cellar and put charity in order within her?[10] Well, that is what I mean. Since that soul now surrenders itself into His hands and its great love makes it so surrendered that it neither knows nor wants anything more than what He wants with her (for God will never, in my judgment, grant this favor save to a soul that He takes for His own), He desires that, without its understanding how, it may go forth from this union impressed with His seal. For indeed the soul does no more in this union than does the wax when another impresses a seal on it. The wax doesn't impress the seal upon itself; it is only disposed—I mean by being soft. And even in order to be disposed, it doesn't soften itself but remains still and gives its consent. Oh, goodness of God; everything must be at a cost to You! All You want is our will and that there be no impediment in the wax.

13. Well now, you see here, Sisters, what our God does in this union so that this soul may recognize itself as His own. He gives from what He has, which is what His Son had in this life. He cannot grant us a higher favor. Who could have had a greater desire to leave this life? And so His Majesty said at the Last Supper: *I have earnestly desired.*[11]

Well then, how is it, Lord, that You weren't thinking of the laborious death You were about to suffer, so painful and frightful? You answer: "No, my great love and the desire I have that souls be saved are incomparably more important than these sufferings; and the very greatest sorrows that I have suffered and do suffer, after being in the world, are not enough to be considered anything at all in comparison with this love and desire to save souls."

14. This is true, for I have often reflected on the matter. I know the torment a certain soul of my acquaintance[12] suffers and has suffered at seeing our Lord offended. The pain is so unbearable that she desires to die much more than to suffer it. If a soul with so little charity when compared to Christ's—for its charity could then be considered almost nonexistent—felt this torment to be so unbearable, what must have been the feeling of our Lord Jesus Christ? And what kind of life must He have suffered since all things were present to Him and He was always witnessing the serious offenses committed against His Father? I believe without a doubt that these sufferings were much greater than were those of His most sacred Passion. At the time of His Passion He already saw an end to these trials and with this awareness as well as the happiness of seeing a remedy for us in His death and of showing us the love He had for His Father in suffering so much for Him, His sorrows were tempered. These sorrows are also tempered here below by those who with the strength that comes from love perform great penances, for they almost don't feel them; rather they would want to do more and more—and everything they do seems little to them. Well, what must it have been for His Majesty to find Himself with so excellent an occasion for showing His Father how completely obedient He was to Him, and with love for His neighbor? Oh, great delight, to suffer in doing the will of God! But I consider it so difficult to see the many offenses committed so continually against His Majesty and the many souls going to hell that I believe only one day of that pain would have been sufficient to end many lives; how much more one life, if He had been no more than man.

Chapter 3

Continues on the same subject. Tells about another kind of union the soul can reach with God's help and of how important love of neighbor is for this union. The chapter is very useful.

WELL NOW LET US get back to our little moth[1] and see something about what God gives it in this state. It must always be understood that one has to strive to go forward in the service of our Lord and in self-knowledge. For if a person does no more than receive this favor and if, as though already securely in possession of something, she grows careless in her life and turns aside from the heavenly path, which consists of keeping the commandments, that which happens to the silkworm will happen to her. For it gives forth the seed that produces other silkworms, and itself dies forever. I say that it "gives forth the seed" because I hold that it is God's desire that a favor so great not be given in vain; if a person doesn't herself benefit, the favor will benefit others. For since the soul is left with these desires and virtues that were mentioned, it always brings profit to other souls during the time that it continues to live virtuously; and they catch fire from its fire. And even when the soul has itself lost this fire, the inclination to benefit others will remain, and the soul delights in explaining the favors God grants to whoever loves and serves Him.

2. I know a person to whom this happened.[2] Although she had gone far astray, she enjoyed helping others through the favors God had granted her and showing the way of prayer to those who didn't understand it; and she did a great deal of good. Afterward the Lord again gave her light. It's true that she still hadn't experienced the effects that were mentioned; but how many there must be, like Judas, whom the Lord calls to the apostolate by communing with them, and like Saul, whom He calls to be king, who afterward through their own fault go astray! Thus we can conclude, Sisters, that, in order to merit more and more and avoid getting lost like such persons, our security lies in obedience and refusal to deviate from God's

law. I'm speaking to those to whom He has granted similar favors, and even to everyone.

3. It seems to me that despite all I've said about this dwelling place, the matter is still somewhat obscure. Since so much gain comes from entering this place, it will be good to avoid giving the impression that those to whom the Lord doesn't give things that are so supernatural are left without hope. True union can very well be reached, with God's help, if we make the effort to obtain it by keeping our wills fixed only on that which is God's will. Oh, how many of us there are who will say we do this, and it will seem to us that we don't want anything else and that we would die for this truth, as I believe I have said![3] Well I tell you, and I will often repeat it, that if what you say is true you will have obtained this favor from the Lord, and you needn't care at all about the other delightful union that was mentioned. That which is most valuable in the delightful union is that it proceeds from this union of which I'm now speaking; and one cannot arrive at the delightful union if the union coming from being resigned to God's will is not very certain. Oh, how desirable is this union with God's will! Happy the soul that has reached it. Such a soul will live tranquilly in this life, and in the next as well. Nothing in earthly events afflicts it unless it finds itself in some danger of losing God or sees that He is offended: neither sickness, nor poverty, nor death —unless the death is of someone who will be missed by God's Church—for this soul sees well that the Lord knows what He is doing better than it knows what it is desiring.

4. You must note that there are different kinds of sufferings. Some sufferings are produced suddenly by our human nature, and the same goes for consolations, and even by the charity of compassion for one's neighbor, as our Lord experienced when He raised Lazarus.[4] Being united with God's will doesn't take these experiences away, nor do they disturb the soul with a restless, disquieting passion that lasts a long while. These sufferings pass quickly. As I have said concerning consolations in prayer,[5] it seems they do not reach the soul's depth but only the senses and faculties. They are found in the previous dwelling places; but they do not enter the last ones still to be explained,

since the suspension of the faculties is necessary in order to reach these, as has been said.[6] The Lord has the power to enrich souls through many paths and bring them to these dwelling places, without using the short cut that was mentioned.

5. Nonetheless, take careful note, daughters, that it is necessary for the silkworm to die, and, moreover, at a cost to yourselves. In the delightful union,[7] the experience of seeing oneself in so new a life greatly helps one to die; in the other union,[8] it's necessary that, while living in this life, we ourselves put the silkworm to death. I confess this latter death will require a great deal of effort, or more than that; but it has its value. Thus if you come out victorious the reward will be much greater. But there is no reason to doubt the possibility of this death any more than that of true union with the will of God. This union with God's will is the union I have desired all my life; it is the union I ask the Lord for always and the one that is clearest and safest.

6. But alas for us, how few there must be who reach it; although whoever guards himself against offending the Lord and has entered religious life thinks he has done everything! Oh, but there remain some worms, unrecognized until, like those in the story of Jonah that gnawed away the ivy,[9] they have gnawed away the virtues. This happens through self-love, self-esteem, judging one's neighbors (even though in little things), a lack of charity for them, and not loving them as ourselves. For even though, while crawling along, we fulfill our obligation and no sin is committed, we don't advance very far in what is required for complete union with the will of God.

7. What do you think His will is, daughters? That we be completely perfect. See what we lack to be one with Him and His Father as His Majesty asked.[10] I tell you I am writing this with much pain upon seeing myself so far away—and all through my own fault. The Lord doesn't have to grant us great delights for this union; sufficient is what He has given us in His Son, who would teach us the way. Don't think the matter lies in my being so conformed to the will of God that if my father or brother dies I don't feel it, or that if there are trials or sicknesses I suffer them happily. Such an attitude is good, and

sometimes it's a matter of discretion because we can't do otherwise, and we make a virtue of necessity. How many things like these the philosophers did, or even, though not like these, other things, such as acquiring much learning. Here in our religious life the Lord asks of us only two things: love of His Majesty and love of our neighbor. These are what we must work for. By observing them with perfection, we do His will and so will be united with Him. But how far, as I have said, we are from doing these two things for so great a God as we ought! May it please His Majesty to give us His grace so that we might merit, if we want, to reach this state that lies within our power.

8. The most certain sign, in my opinion, as to whether or not we are observing these two laws is whether we observe well the love of neighbor. We cannot know whether or not we love God, although there are strong indications for recognizing that we do love Him; but we can know whether we love our neighbor.[11] And be certain that the more advanced you see you are in love for your neighbor the more advanced you will be in the love of God, for the love His Majesty has for us is so great that to repay us for our love of neighbor He will in a thousand ways increase the love we have for Him. I cannot doubt this.

9. It's important for us to walk with careful attention to how we are proceeding in this matter, for if we practice love of neighbor with great perfection, we will have done everything. I believe that, since our nature is bad, we will not reach perfection in the love of neighbor if that love doesn't rise from love of God as its root. Since this is so important to us, Sisters, let's try to understand ourselves even in little things, and pay no attention to any big plans that sometimes suddenly come to us during prayer in which it seems we will do wonders for our neighbor and even for just one soul so that it may be saved. If afterward our deeds are not in conformity with those plans, there will be no reason to believe that we will accomplish the plans. I say the same about humility and all the virtues. Great are the wiles of the devil; to make us think we have one virtue—when we don't—he would circle hell a thousand times. And he is right because such a notion is very harmful, for these feigned virtues never come without some vainglory since they

rise from that source; just as virtues from God are free of it as well as of pride.

10. I am amused sometimes to see certain souls who think when they are at prayer that they would like to be humiliated and publicly insulted for God, and afterward they would hide a tiny fault if they could; or, if they have not committed one and yet are charged with it—God deliver us! Well, let anyone who can't bear such a thing be careful not to pay attention to what he has by himself determined—in his opinion—to do. As a matter of fact the determination was not in the will—for when there is a true determination of the will it's another matter—but a work of the imagination; it is in the imagination that the devil produces his wiles and deceits. And with women or unlearned people he can produce a great number, for we don't know how the faculties differ from one another and from the imagination, nor do we know about a thousand other things there are in regard to interior matters. Oh, Sisters, how clearly one sees the degree to which love of neighbor is present in some of you, and how clearly one sees the deficiency in those who lack such perfection! If you were to understand how important this virtue is for us you wouldn't engage in any other study.

11. When I see souls very earnest in trying to understand the prayer they have and very sullen when they are in it—for it seems they don't dare let their minds move or stir lest a bit of their spiritual delight and devotion be lost—it makes me realize how little they understand of the way by which union is attained; they think the whole matter lies in these things. No, Sisters, absolutely not; works are what the Lord wants! He desires that if you see a Sister who is sick to whom you can bring some relief, you have compassion on her and not worry about losing this devotion; and that if she is suffering pain, you also feel it; and that, if necessary, you fast so that she might eat—not so much for her sake as because you know it is your Lord's desire. This is true union with His will, and if you see a person praised, the Lord wants you to be much happier than if you yourself were being praised. This, indeed, is easy, for if you have humility you will feel sorry to see yourself praised. But this

happiness that comes when the virtues of the Sisters are known is a very good thing; and when we see some fault in them, it is also a very good thing to be sorry and hide the fault as though it were our own.

12. I have said a lot on this subject elsewhere,[12] because I see, Sisters, that if we fail in love of neighbor we are lost. May it please the Lord that this will never be so; for if you do not fail, I tell you that you shall receive from His Majesty the union that was mentioned. When you see yourselves lacking in this love, even though you have devotion and gratifying experiences that make you think you have reached this stage, and you experience some little suspension in the prayer of quiet (for to some it then appears that everything has been accomplished), believe me you have not reached union. And beg our Lord to give you this perfect love of neighbor. Let His Majesty have a free hand, for He will give you more than you know how to desire because you are striving and making every effort to do what you can about this love. And force your will to do the will of your Sisters in everything even though you may lose your rights; forget your own good for their sakes no matter how much resistance your nature puts up; and, when the occasion arises, strive to accept work yourself so as to relieve your neighbor of it. Don't think that it won't cost you anything or that you will find everything done for you. Look at what our Spouse's love for us cost Him; in order to free us from death, He died that most painful death of the cross.

Chapter 4

Continues with the same subject, explaining further this kind of prayer. 1 Tells how important it is to walk with care because the devil himself uses a great deal of care in trying to make one turn back from what was begun.

IT SEEMS TO ME you have a desire to see what this little moth is doing and where it rests since as was explained it rests neither in spiritual delights nor in earthly consolations. Its flight is higher, and I cannot satisfy your desire until the last dwelling place. May it please God that I then remember or have the time to write of this. About five months have passed since I began,[2] and because my head is in no condition to read over what I've written, everything will have to continue on without order, and perhaps some things will be said twice. Since this work is for my Sisters, the disorder won't matter much.

2. Nonetheless, I want to explain more to you about what I think this prayer of union is. In accordance with my style, I shall draw a comparison. Later on we'll say more about this little butterfly. Although it is always bearing fruit by doing good for itself and for other souls, it never stops to rest, because it fails to find its true repose.

3. You've already often heard that God espouses souls spiritually. Blessed be His mercy that wants so much to be humbled! And even though the comparison may be a coarse one I cannot find another that would better explain what I mean than the sacrament of marriage. This spiritual espousal is different in kind from marriage, for in these matters that we are dealing with there is never anything that is not spiritual. Corporal things are far distant from them, and the spiritual joys the Lord gives when compared to the delights married people must experience are a thousand leagues distant. For it is all a matter of love united with love, and the actions of love are most pure and so extremely delicate and gentle that there is no way of explaining them, but the Lord knows how to make them very clearly felt.

4. It seems to me that the prayer of union does not yet reach the stage of spiritual betrothal. Here below when two people are to be engaged, there is discussion about whether they are alike, whether they love each other, and whether they might meet together so as to become more satisfied with each other. So, too, in the case of this union with God, the agreement has been made, and this soul is well informed about the goodness of her Spouse and determined to do His will in everything and in as many ways as she sees might make Him happy. And His Majesty, as one who understands clearly whether these things about His betrothed are so, is happy with her. As a result He grants this mercy, for He desired her to know Him more and that they might meet together, as they say, and be united.[3] We can say that union is like this, for it passes in a very short time. In it there no longer takes place the exchanging of gifts, but the soul sees secretly who this Spouse is that she is going to accept. Through the work of the senses and the faculties she couldn't in any way or in a thousand years understand what she understands here in the shortest time. But being who He is, the Spouse from that meeting alone leaves her more worthy for the joining of hands, as they say. The soul is left so much in love that it does for its part all it can to avoid disturbing this divine betrothal. But if it is careless about placing its affection in something other than Him, it loses everything. And the loss is as great as the favors He was granting her, and cannot be exaggerated.

5. For this reason, I ask Christian souls whom the Lord has brought to these boundaries that for His sake they not grow careless but withdraw from occasions. Even in this state the soul is not so strong that it can place itself in the occasions as it will be after the betrothal is made. The betrothal belongs to the dwelling place we shall speak of after this one. This present communication amounts to no more than a meeting, as they say. And the devil will go about very carefully in order to fight against and prevent this betrothal. Afterward, since he sees the soul entirely surrendered to the Spouse he doesn't dare do so much, because he fears it. He has experienced that if sometimes he tries he is left with a great loss; and the soul, with further gain.

6. I tell you, daughters, that I have known persons who had ascended high and had reached this union, who were turned back and won over by the devil with his deep cunning and deceit. All hell must join for such a purpose because, as I have often said,[4] in losing one soul of this kind, not only one is lost but a multitude. The devil already has experience in this matter. Look at the multitude of souls God draws to Himself by means of one. He is to be greatly praised for the thousands converted by the martyrs: for a young girl like St. Ursula; for those the devil must have lost through St. Dominic, St. Francis, and other founders of religious orders, and those he now loses through Father Ignatius, the one who founded the Society. Clearly, all of these received, as we read, similar favors from God. How would this have come about if they hadn't made the effort not to lose through their own fault so divine an espousal? Oh, my daughters, how prepared this Lord is to grant us favors now just as He has granted them to others in the past. And, in part, He is even more in need that we desire to receive them, for there are fewer now who care about His honor than there were then. We love ourselves very much; there's an extraordinary amount of prudence we use so as not to lose our rights. Oh, what great deception! May the Lord through His mercy enlighten us so that we do not fall into similar darknesses.

7. You will ask me or be in doubt concerning two things: First, if the soul is as ready to do the will of God as was mentioned,[5] how can it be deceived since it doesn't want to do anything but His will in all? Second, what are the ways in which the devil can enter so dangerously that your soul goes astray? For you are so withdrawn from the world, so close to the sacraments, and in the company, we could say, of angels, and through the Lord's goodness you have no other desire than to serve God and please Him in everything. With those who are already in the midst of worldly occasions such a turn backward would not be surprising. I say that you are right about this, for God has granted us a great deal of mercy. But when I see, as I have said,[6] that Judas was in the company of the Apostles and conversing always with God Himself and listening to His words, I understand that there is no security in these things.

8. In answer to the first, I say that if this soul were always attached to God's will it is clear that it would not go astray. But the devil comes along with some skillful deception and, under the color of good, confuses it with regard to little things and induces it to get taken up with some of them that he makes it think are good. Then little by little he darkens the intellect, cools the will's ardor, and makes self-love grow until in one way or another he withdraws the soul from the will of God and brings it to his own.

Thus, we have an answer to the second doubt. There is no enclosure so fenced in that he cannot enter, or desert so withdrawn that he fails to go there. And I still have something more to say: perhaps the Lord permits this so as to observe the behavior of that soul He wishes to set up as a light for others. If there is going to be a downfall, it's better that it happen in the beginning rather than later, when it would be harmful to many.

9. The diligence on our part that comes to my mind as being the most effective is the following. First, we must always ask God in prayer to sustain us, and very often think that if He abandons us we will soon end in the abyss, as is true; and we must never trust in ourselves since it would be foolish to do so. Then, we should walk with special care and attention, observing how we are proceeding in the practice of virtue: whether we are getting better or worse in some areas, especially in love for one another, in the desire to be considered the least among the Sisters, and in the performance of ordinary tasks. For if we look out for these things and ask the Lord to enlighten us, we will soon see the gain or the loss. Don't think that a soul that comes so close to God is allowed to lose Him so quickly, that the devil has an easy task. His Majesty would regret the loss of this soul so much that He gives it in many ways a thousand interior warnings, so that the harm will not be hidden from it.

10. Let this, in sum, be the conclusion: that we strive always to advance. And if we don't advance, let us walk with great fear. Without doubt the devil wants to cause some lapse, for it is not possible that after having come so far, one will fail to grow. Love is never idle, and a failure to grow would be a very

bad sign. A soul that has tried to be the betrothed of God Himself, that is now intimate with His Majesty, and has reached the boundaries that were mentioned, must not go to sleep.

That you, daughters, may see what He does with those He now considers to be His betrothed ones, we shall begin to speak of the sixth dwelling places. And you will see how little it all is that we can do to serve and suffer and accomplish so as to dispose ourselves for such great favors. It could be that our Lord ordained that they command me to write so that we might forget our little earthly joys because we will have our eyes set on the reward and see how immeasurable is His mercy—since He desires to commune with and reveal Himself to some worms—and because we will have these eyes set also on His greatness, and thus run along enkindled in His love.

11. May He be pleased that I manage to explain something about these very difficult things. I know well that this will be impossible if His Majesty and the Holy Spirit do not move my pen. And if what I say will not be for your benefit, I beg Him that I may not succeed in saying anything. His Majesty knows that I have no other desire, insofar as I can understand myself, but that His name be praised and that we strive to serve a Lord who even here on earth pays like this. Through His favors we can understand something of what He will give us in heaven without the intervals, trials, and dangers that there are in this tempestuous sea. If there were no danger of losing or offending Him, it would be easy to endure life until the end of the world so as to labor for so great a God and Lord and Spouse.

May it please His Majesty that we may merit to render Him some service; without as many faults as we always have, even in good works, amen.

THE SIXTH DWELLING PLACES

Contains Eleven Chapters

Chapter 1

Discusses how greater trials come when the Lord begins to grant greater favors. Mentions some and how those who are now in this dwelling place conduct themselves. This chapter is good for souls undergoing interior trials.

WELL THEN, LET US, with the help of the Holy Spirit, speak of the sixth dwelling places, where the soul is now wounded with love for its Spouse and strives for more opportunities to be alone and, in conformity with its state, to rid itself of everything that can be an obstacle to this solitude.

That meeting[1] left such an impression that the soul's whole desire is to enjoy it again. I have already said that in this prayer nothing is seen in a way that can be called seeing, nor is anything seen with the imagination. I use the term "meeting" because of the comparison I made.[2] Now the soul is fully determined to take no other spouse. But the Spouse does not look at the soul's great desires that the betrothal take place, for He still wants it to desire this more, and He wants the betrothal to take place at a cost; it is the greatest of blessings. And although everything is small when it comes to paying for this exceptional benefit, I tell you, daughters, that for the soul to endure such delay it needs to have that token or pledge of betrothal that it now has. Oh, God help me, what interior and exterior trials the soul suffers before entering the seventh dwelling place!

2. Indeed, sometimes I reflect and fear that if a soul knew beforehand, its natural weakness would find it most difficult to have the determination to suffer and pass through these trials, no matter what blessings were represented to it—unless it had arrived at the seventh dwelling place. For once it has arrived there, the soul fears nothing and is absolutely determined to overcome every obstacle for God.[3] And the reason is that it is always so closely joined to His Majesty that from this union comes its fortitude. I believe it will be well to recount some of those trials that I know one will certainly undergo. Perhaps not all souls will be led along this path, although I doubt very much that those persons who sometimes enjoy so truly the things of heaven will live free of earthly trials that come in one way or another.

3. Although I hadn't intended to treat of these, I thought doing so would bring great consolation to some soul going through them, for it would learn that these trials take place in souls to whom God grants similar favors; for truly, when one is suffering the trials, it then seems that everything is lost. I will not deal with them according to the order in which they happen, but as they come to mind. And I want to begin with the smallest trials. There is an outcry by persons a Sister is dealing with and even by those she does not deal with and who, it seems to her, would never even think of her; gossip like the following: "she's trying to make out she's a saint; she goes to extremes to deceive the world and bring others to ruin; there are other better Christians who don't put on all this outward show." (And it's worth noting that she is not putting on any outward show but just striving to fulfill well her state in life.) Those she considered her friends turn away from her, and they are the ones who take the largest and most painful bite at her: "that soul has gone astray and is clearly mistaken; these are things of the devil; she will turn out like this person or that other that went astray, and will bring about a decline in virtue; she has deceived her confessors" (and they go to these confessors, telling them so, giving them examples of what happened to some that were lost in this way); a thousand kinds of ridicule and statements like the above.

4. I know a person who had great fear that there would be no one who would hear her confession because of such gossip[4] —so much gossip that there's no reason to go into it all here. And what is worse these things do not pass quickly, but go on throughout the person's whole life including the advice to others to avoid any dealings with such persons.

You will tell me that there are also those who will speak well of that soul. Oh, daughters, how few there are who believe in such favors in comparison with the many who abhor them! Moreover, praise is just another trial greater than those mentioned! Since the soul sees clearly that if it has anything good this is given by God and is by no means its own—for just previously it saw itself to be very poor and surrounded by great sins—praise is an intolerable burden to it, at least in the beginning. Later on, for certain reasons, praise is not so intolerable. First, because experience makes the soul see clearly that people are as quick to say good things as bad, and so it pays no more attention to the good things than to the bad. Second, because it has been more enlightened by the Lord that no good thing comes from itself but is given by His Majesty; and it turns to praise God, forgetful that it has had any part to play, just as if it had seen the gift in another person. Third, if it sees that some souls have benefited from seeing the favors God grants it, it thinks that His Majesty used this means, of its being falsely esteemed as good, so that some blessings might come to those souls. Fourth, since it looks after the honor and glory of God more than its own, the temptation, which came in the beginning, that these praises will destroy it, is removed; little does dishonor matter to it if in exchange God might perhaps thereby just once be praised—afterward, let whatever comes come.

5. These reasons and others mitigate the great pain these praises cause; although some pain is almost always felt, except when one is paying hardly any attention. But it is an incomparably greater trial to see oneself publicly considered as good without reason than the trials mentioned. And when the soul reaches the stage at which it pays little attention to praise, it pays much less to disapproval; on the contrary, it rejoices in

this and finds it a very sweet music. This is an amazing truth. Blame does not intimidate the soul but strengthens it. Experience has already taught it the wonderful gain that comes through this path. It feels that those who persecute it do not offend God; rather that His Majesty permits persecution for the benefit of the soul. And since it clearly experiences the benefits of persecution, it acquires a special and very tender love for its persecutors. It seems to it that they are greater friends and more advantageous than those who speak well of it.

6. The Lord is wont also to send it the severest illnesses. This is a much greater trial, especially when the pains are acute. For in some way, if these pains are severe, the trial is, it seems to me, the greatest on earth—I mean the greatest exterior trial, however many the other pains. I say "if the pains are severe," because they then afflict the soul interiorly and exteriorly in such a way that it doesn't know what to do with itself. It would willingly accept at once any martyrdom rather than these sharp pains; although they do not last long in this extreme form. After all, God gives no more than what can be endured; and His Majesty gives patience first. But other great sufferings and illnesses of many kinds are the usual thing.

7. I know a person who cannot truthfully say that from the time the Lord began forty years ago to grant the favor that was mentioned she spent even one day without pains and other kinds of suffering (from lack of bodily health, I mean) and other great trials.[5] It's true that she had been very wretched and that everything seemed small to her in comparison with the hell she deserved. Others, who have not offended our Lord so much, will be led by another path. But I would always choose the path of suffering, if only to imitate our Lord Jesus Christ if there were no other gain; especially, since there are always so many other benefits.

Oh, were we to treat of interior sufferings these others would seem small if the interior ones could be clearly explained; but it is impossible to explain the way in which they come to pass.

8. Let us begin with the torment one meets with from a confessor who is so discreet and has so little experience that there is

nothing he is sure of: he fears everything and finds in everything something to doubt because he sees these unusual experiences. He becomes especially doubtful if he notices some imperfection in a soul that has them, for it seems to such confessors that the ones to whom God grants these favors must be angels—but that is impossible as long as they are in this body. Everything is immediately condemned as from the devil or melancholy. And the world is so full of this melancholy that I am not surprised. There is so much of it now in the world, and the devil causes so many evils through this means, that confessors are very right in fearing it and considering it carefully. But the poor soul that walks with the same fear and goes to its confessor as to its judge, and is condemned by him, cannot help but be deeply tormented and disturbed. Only the one who has passed through this will understand what a great torment it is. For this is another one of the terrible trials these souls suffer, especially if they have lived wretched lives; thinking that because of their sins God will allow them to be deceived. Even though they feel secure and cannot believe that the favor when granted by His Majesty, is from any other spirit than from God, the torment returns immediately since the favor is something that passes quickly, and the remembrance of sins is always present, and the soul sees faults in itself, which are never lacking. When the confessor assures it, the soul grows calm, although the disturbance will return. But when the confessor contributes to the torment with more fear, the trial becomes something almost unbearable—especially when some dryness comes between the times of these favors. It then seems to the soul that it has never been mindful of God and never will be; and when it hears His Majesty spoken of, it seems to it as though it were hearing about a person far away.

9. All this would amount to nothing if it were not for the fact that in addition comes the feeling that it is incapable of explaining things to its confessors, that it has deceived them. And even though it thinks and sees that it tells its confessors about every stirring, even the first ones, this doesn't help. The soul's understanding is so darkened that it becomes incapable of seeing the truth and believes whatever the imagination represents

to it (for the imagination is then its master) or whatever foolish things the devil wants to represent. The Lord, it seems, gives the devil license so that the soul might be tried and even be made to think it is rejected by God. Many are the things that war against it with an interior oppression so keen and unbearable that I don't know what to compare this experience to if not to the oppression of those that suffer in hell, for no consolation is allowed in the midst of this tempest. If they desire to be consoled by their confessor, it seems the devils assist him to torment it more. Thus, when a confessor was dealing with a person after she had suffered this torment (for it seems a dangerous affliction since there are so many things involved in it), he told her to let him know when she was in this state; but the torment was always so bad that he came to realize there was nothing he could do about it.[6] Well then, if a person in this state who knows how to read well takes up a book in the vernacular, he will find that he understands no more of it than if he didn't know how to read even one of the letters, for the intellect is incapable of understanding.[7]

10. In sum, there is no remedy in this tempest but to wait for the mercy of God. For at an unexpected time, with one word alone or a chance happening, He so quickly calms the storm that it seems there had not been even as much as a cloud in that soul, and it remains filled with sunlight and much more consolation. And like one who has escaped from a dangerous battle and been victorious, it comes out praising our Lord; for it was He who fought for the victory. It knows very clearly that it did not fight, for all the weapons with which it could have defended itself are seen to be, it seems, in the hands of its enemies. Thus, it knows clearly its wretchedness and the very little we of ourselves can do if the Lord abandons us.

11. It seems the soul has no longer any need of reflection to understand this, for the experience of having suffered through it, having seen itself totally incapacitated, made it understand our nothingness and what miserable things we are. For in this state grace is so hidden (even though the soul must not be without grace since with all this torment it doesn't offend God nor would it offend Him for anything on earth) that not even a

very tiny spark is visible. The soul doesn't think that it has any love of God or that it ever had any, for if it has done some good, or His Majesty has granted it some favor, all of this seems to have been dreamed up or fancied. As for sins, it sees certainly that it has committed them.

12. O Jesus, and what a thing it is to see this kind of forsaken soul; and, as I have said,[8] what little help any earthly consolation is for it! Hence, do not think, Sisters, if at some time you find yourselves in this state, that the rich and those who are free will have a better remedy for these times of suffering. Absolutely not, for being rich in this case seems to me like the situation of a person condemned to die who has all the world's delights placed before him. These delights would not be sufficient to alleviate his suffering; rather, they would increase the torment. So it is with this torment; it comes from above, and earthly things are of no avail in the matter. Our great God wants us to know our own misery and that He is king; and this is very important for what lies ahead.

13. Well then, what will this poor soul do when the torment goes on for many days? If it prays, it feels as though it hasn't prayed—as far as consolation goes, I mean. For consolation is not admitted into the soul's interior, nor is what one recites to oneself, even though vocal, understood. As for mental prayer, this definitely is not the time for that, because the faculties are incapable of the practice; rather, solitude causes greater harm—and also another torment for this soul is that it be with anyone or that others speak to it. And thus however much it forces itself not to do so, it goes about with a gloomy and ill-tempered mien that is externally very noticeable.

Is it true that it will know how to explain its experiences? They are indescribable, for they are spiritual afflictions and sufferings that one cannot name. The best remedy (I don't mean for getting rid of them, because I don't find any, but so that they may be endured) is to engage in external works of charity and to hope in the mercy of God who never fails those who hope in Him. May He be forever blessed, amen.

14. Other exterior trials the devils cause must be quite unusual; and so there's no reason to speak of them. Nor are

they, for the most part, so painful; for, however much the devils do, they do not, in my opinion, manage to disable the faculties or disturb the soul in this way. In sum, there's reason for thinking that they can do no more than what the Lord allows them to do; and provided one doesn't lose one's mind, everything is small in comparison with what was mentioned.

15. We shall be speaking in these dwelling places of other interior sufferings, and dealing with different kinds of prayer and favors from the Lord. For even though some favors cause still more severe suffering than those mentioned, as will be seen from the condition in which the body is left, they do not deserve to be called trials. Nor is there any reason for us to write of them since they are such great favors from the Lord. In the midst of receiving them the soul understands that they are great favors and far beyond its merits. This severe suffering comes so that one may enter the seventh dwelling place. It comes along with many other sufferings, only some of which I shall speak of[9] because it would be impossible to speak of them all, or even to explain what they are; for they are of a different, much higher level than those mentioned in this chapter. And if I haven't been able to explain any more than I did about those of a lower kind, less will I be able to say of the others. May the Lord give His help for everything through the merits of His Son, amen.

Chapter 2

Deals with some of the ways in which our Lord awakens the soul. It seems there is nothing in these awakenings to fear even though the experience is sublime and the favors are great.

SEEMINGLY WE HAVE LEFT the little moth far behind; but we have not, for these are the trials that make it fly still higher. Well let us begin, then, to discuss the manner in which the Spouse deals with it and how before He belongs to it completely He makes it desire Him vehemently by certain delicate means the soul itself does not understand. (Nor do I believe I'll be successful in explaining them save to those who have experienced them.) These are impulses so delicate and refined, for they proceed from very deep within the interior part of the soul, that I don't know any comparison that will fit.

2. They are far different from all that we can acquire of ourselves here below and even from the spiritual delights that were mentioned.[1] For often when a person is distracted and forgetful of God, His Majesty will awaken it. His action is as quick as a falling comet. And as clearly as it hears a thunderclap, even though no sound is heard, the soul understands that it was called by God. So well does it understand that sometimes, especially in the beginning, it is made to tremble and even complain without there being anything that causes it pain. It feels that it is wounded in the most exquisite way, but it doesn't learn how or by whom it was wounded. It knows clearly that the wound is something precious, and it would never want to be cured. It complains to its Spouse with words of love, even outwardly, without being able to do otherwise. It knows that He is present, but He doesn't want to reveal the manner in which He allows Himself to be enjoyed. And the pain is great, although delightful and sweet. And even if the soul does not want this wound, the wound cannot be avoided. But the soul, in fact, would never want to be deprived of this pain. The wound satisfies it much more than the delightful and painless absorption of the prayer of quiet.[2]

3. I am struggling, Sisters, to explain for you this action of love, and I don't know how. For it seems a contradiction that the Beloved would give the soul clear understanding that He is with it and yet make it think that He is calling it by a sign so certain that no room is left for doubt and a whisper so penetrating that the soul cannot help but hear it. For it seems that when the Spouse, who is in the seventh dwelling place, communicates in this manner (for the words are not spoken), all the people in the other dwelling places keep still; neither the senses, nor the imagination, nor the faculties stir.

O my powerful God, how sublime are your secrets, and how different spiritual things are from all that is visible and understandable here below. There is nothing that serves to explain this favor, even though the favor is a very small one when compared to the very great ones You work in souls.

4. This action of love is so powerful that the soul dissolves with desire, and yet it doesn't know what to ask for since clearly it thinks that its God is with it.

You will ask me: Well, if it knows this, what does it desire or what pains it? What greater good does it want? I don't know. I do know that it seems this pain reaches to the soul's very depths and that when He who wounds it draws out the arrow, it indeed seems, in accord with the deep love the soul feels, that God is drawing these very depths after Him.[3] I was thinking now that it's as though, from this fire enkindled in the brazier that is my God, a spark leapt forth and so struck the soul that the flaming fire was felt by it. And since the spark was not enough to set the soul on fire, and the fire is so delightful, the soul is left with that pain; but the spark merely by touching the soul produces that effect. It seems to me this is the best comparison I have come up with. This delightful pain—and it is not pain—is not continuous, although sometimes it lasts a long while; at other times it goes away quickly. This depends on the way the Lord wishes to communicate it, for it is not something that can be procured in any human way. But even though it sometimes lasts for a long while, it comes and goes. To sum up, it is never permanent. For this reason it doesn't set the soul on fire; but just as the fire is about to start, the spark goes out and the soul is left with the desire to suffer again that loving pain the spark causes.

5. Here there is no reason to wonder whether the experience is brought on naturally or caused by melancholy, or whether it is some trick of the devil or some illusion. It is something that leaves clear understanding of how this activity comes from the place where the Lord who is unchanging dwells. The activity is not like that found in other feelings of devotion, where the great absorption in delight can make us doubtful. Here all the senses and faculties remain free of any absorption, wondering what this could be, without hindering anything or being able, in my opinion, to increase or take away that delightful pain.

Anyone to whom our Lord may have granted this favor — for if He has, that fact will be recognized on reading this — should thank Him very much. Such a person doesn't have to fear deception. Let his great fear be that he might prove ungrateful for so generous a favor, and let him strive to better his entire life, and to serve, and he will see the results and how he receives more and more. In fact, I know a person[4] who received this favor for some years and was so pleased with it that had she served the Lord through severe trials for a great number of years she would have felt well repaid by it. May He be blessed forever, amen.

6. You may wonder why greater security is present in this favor than in other things. In my opinion, these are the reasons: First, the devil never gives delightful pain like this. He can give the savor and delight that seem to be spiritual, but he doesn't have the power to join pain — and so much of it — to the spiritual quiet and delight of the soul. For all of his powers are on the outside, and the pains he causes are never, in my opinion, delightful or peaceful, but disturbing and contentious. Second, this delightful tempest comes from a region other than those regions of which he can be lord. Third, the favor brings wonderful benefits to the soul, the more customary of which are the determination to suffer for God, the desire to have many trials, and the determination to withdraw from earthly satisfactions and conversations and other similar things.

7. That this favor is no fancy is very clear. Although at other times the soul may strive to experience this favor, it will not be able to counterfeit one. And the favor is something so manifest that it can in no way be fancied. I mean, one cannot think it is imagined, when it is not, or have doubts about it. If some doubt should remain, one must realize that the things experienced are not true impulses; I mean if there should be doubt about whether the favor was experienced or not. The favor is felt as clearly as a loud voice is heard. There's no basis for thinking it is caused by melancholy, because melancholy does not produce or fabricate its fancies save in the imagination. This favor proceeds from the interior part of the soul.

Now it could be that I'm mistaken, but until I hear other

reasons from someone who understands the experience I will always have this opinion. And so I know a person who was quite fearful about being deceived but who never had any fear of this prayer.[5]

8. The Lord also has other ways of awakening the soul: unexpectedly, when it is praying vocally and not thinking of anything interior, it seems a delightful enkindling will come upon it as though a fragrance were suddenly to become so powerful as to spread through all the senses. (I don't say that it is a fragrance but am merely making this comparison.) Or the experience is something like this, and it is communicated only for the sake of making one feel the Spouse's presence there. The soul is moved with a delightful desire to enjoy Him, and thereby it is prepared to make intense acts of love and praise of our Lord. This favor rises out of that place I mentioned;[6] but there is nothing in it that causes pain, nor are the desires themselves to enjoy God painful. Such is the way the soul usually experiences it. Neither does it seem to me, for some of the reasons mentioned,[7] there is anything to fear; but one should try to receive this favor with gratitude.

Chapter 3

Deals with the same subject and tells of the manner in which God, when pleased, speaks to the soul. Gives counsel about how one should behave in such a matter and not follow one's own opinion. Sets down some signs for discerning when there is deception and when not. This chapter is very beneficial.[1]

GOD HAS ANOTHER WAY of awakening the soul. Although it somehow seems to be a greater favor than those mentioned,[2] it can be more dangerous, and therefore I shall pause a little to consider it. There are many kinds of locutions given to the soul. Some seem to come from outside oneself; others, from deep within the interior part of the soul; others, from the superior part; and some are so exterior that they come through the sense of hearing, for it seems there is a spoken word. Sometimes, and often, the locution can be an illusion, especially in persons with a weak imagination or in those who are melancholic, I mean who suffer noticeably from melancholy.

2. In my opinion no attention should be paid to these latter two kinds of persons even if they say they see and hear and understand. But neither should one disturb these persons by telling them their locutions come from the devil; one must listen to them as to sick persons. The prioress or confessor to whom they relate their locutions should tell them to pay no attention to such experiences, that these locutions are not essential to the service of God, and that the devil has deceived many by such means, even though this particular person, perhaps, may not be suffering such deception. This counsel should be given so as not to aggravate the melancholy, for if they tell her the locution is due to melancholy, there will be no end to the matter; she will swear that she sees and hears, for it seems to her that she does.

3. It is true that it's necessary to be firm in taking prayer away from her and to insist strongly that she pay no attention to locutions; for the devil is wont to profit from these souls that are sick in this way, even though what he does may not be to their harm but to the harm of others. But for both the sick and the healthy there is always reason to fear these things until the spirit of such persons is well understood. And I say that in the beginning it is always better to free these persons from such experiences, for if the locutions are from God, doing so is a greater help toward progress, and a person even grows when tested. This is true; nonetheless, one should not proceed in a way that is distressing or disturbing to a soul, because truly the soul can't help it if these locutions come.

4. Now then, to return to what I was saying about locutions, all the kinds I mentioned[3] can be from God or from the devil or from one's own imagination. If I can manage to do so, I shall give, with the help of the Lord, the signs as to when they come from these different sources and when they are dangerous; for there are many souls among prayerful people who hear them.

My desire, Sisters, is that you realize you are doing the right thing if you refuse to give credence to them, even when they are destined just for you (such as, some consolation, or advice about your faults), no matter who tells you about them, or if they are an illusion, for it doesn't matter where they come from. One thing I advise you: do not think, even if the locutions are from God, that you are better because of them, for He spoke frequently with the Pharisees. All the good comes from how one benefits by these words; and pay no more attention to those that are not in close conformity with Scripture than you would to those heard from the devil himself. Even if they come from your weak imagination, it's necessary to treat them as if they were temptations in matters of faith, and thus resist them always. They will then go away because they will have little effect on you.

5. Returning, then, to the first of the different kinds of locutions; whether or not the words come from the interior part of the soul, from the superior part, or from the exterior part doesn't matter in discerning whether or not they are from God. The surest signs they are from God that can be had, in my opinion, are these: the first and truest is the power and authority they bear, for locutions from God effect what they say. Let me explain myself better. A soul finds itself in the midst of all the tribulation and disturbance that was mentioned,[4] in darkness of the intellect and in dryness; with one word alone of these locutions from the Lord ("don't be distressed"), it is left calm and free from all distress, with great light, and without all that suffering in which it seemed to it that all the learned men and all who might come together to give it reasons for not being distressed would be unable to remove its affliction no matter how hard they tried. Or, it is afflicted because its confessor and others have told it that its spirit is from the devil, and it is all full of fear; with one word alone ("it is I, fear not"), the fear is taken away completely, and the soul is most comforted, thinking that nothing would be sufficient to make it believe anything else. Or, it is greatly distressed over how certain serious business matters will turn out; it hears that it should be calm, that everything will turn

out all right. It is left certain and free of anxiety. And this is the way in many other instances.[5]

6. The second sign is the great quiet left in the soul, the devout and peaceful recollection, the readiness to engage in the praises of God. O Lord, if a word sent to be spoken through one of Your attendants (for the Lord Himself does not speak the words—at least not in this dwelling place—but an angel) has such power, what will be the power You leave in the soul that is attached to You, and You to it, through love?

7. The third sign is that these words remain in the memory for a very long time, and some are never forgotten, as are those we listen to here on earth—I mean those we hear from men. For even if the words are spoken by men who are very important and learned, or concern the future, we do not have them engraved on our memory, or believe them, as we do these. The certitude is so strong that even in things that in one's own opinion sometimes seem impossible and in which there is doubt as to whether they will or will not happen, and the intellect wavers, there is an assurance in the soul itself that cannot be overcome. Even though it seems that everything is going contrary to what the soul understood, and years go by, the thought remains that God will find other means than those men know of and that in the end the words will be accomplished; and so they are. Although, as I say, the soul still suffers when it sees the many delays, for since time has passed since it heard the words, and the effects and the certitude that were present about their being from God have passed, these doubts take place. The soul wonders whether the locutions might have come from the devil or from the imagination. Yet, none of these doubts remain in the soul, but it would at present die a thousand deaths for that truth. But, as I say, what won't the devil do with all these imaginings so as to afflict and intimidate the soul, especially if the words regard a business matter which when carried out will bring many blessings to souls, and works that will bring great honor and service to God, and if there is great difficulty involved? At least he weakens faith, for it does great harm not to believe that God has the power to do things that our intellects do not understand.

8. Despite all these struggles and even the persons who tell one that the locutions are foolishness (I mean the confessors with whom one speaks about these things), and despite the many unfortunate occurrences that make it seem the words will not be fulfilled, there remains a spark of assurance so alive—I don't know from where—that the words will be fulfilled, though all other hopes are dead, that even should the soul desire otherwise, that spark will stay alive. And in the end, as I have said,[6] the words of the Lord are fulfilled. And the soul is so consoled and happy it wouldn't want to do anything but always praise His Majesty, and praise Him more for the fact that what He had told it was fulfilled than for the work itself, no matter how important the work is to the soul.

9. I don't know why it is so important to the soul that these words turn out to be true, for if that soul were itself caught in some lies, I don't think it would regret the fact as much. And yet, there is nothing else it can do, for it merely says what it hears. Countless times, in this regard, a certain person thought of how the prophet Jonah feared that Nineveh would not be destroyed.[7] In sum, since the spirit is from God, it is right that the soul be faithful in its desire that the words be considered true, for God is the supreme truth. And so its happiness is great when through a thousand roundabout ways and in most difficult circumstances it sees them fulfilled. Even though great trials should come to the person herself from them, she would rather suffer such trials than the trial of seeing that what she knows for certain the Lord told her fails in fact to happen. Perhaps not all persons will have this weakness—if it is a weakness, for I cannot condemn it as bad.

10. If the locutions come from the imagination, there are none of these signs; neither certitude, nor peace, nor interior delight. But it could happen—and I even know some persons to whom it has happened—that while these imaginings come a person may be very absorbed in the prayer of quiet and spiritual sleep. Some have such a weak constitution and imagination, or I don't know the cause, that indeed in this deep recollection they are so outside themselves (for they don't feel anything exteriorly and all the senses are put to sleep) that they

think as when they are asleep and dreaming (and perhaps it is true that they are asleep) that these locutions are spoken to them and even that they see things. And they think these things are from God, but in the end the effects are like those of sleep. It can also happen that while with affection they are begging our Lord for something, they think the locution is telling them what they want to hear; this sometimes happens. But anyone who has had much experience of God's locutions will not be deceived by these that come, in my opinion, from the imagination.

11. With those locutions coming from the devil there is more to fear. But if the signs mentioned[8] are present, there can be a great deal of certainty that the locutions are from God. But the certainty shouldn't be so strong that if the locution concerns something serious about oneself and has to be carried out in deed, or business affairs involving third parties, anything should ever be done or pass through one's mind without the opinion of a learned and prudent confessor and servant of God. This is so even if the soul increasingly understands and thinks the locution is clearly from God. His Majesty wants the soul to consult in this way; and that it does so does not mean it is failing to carry out the Lord's commands, for He has told us, where the words are undoubtedly His, to hold the confessor in His place.[9] And these words of His help to give courage if the task is a difficult one, and our Lord when He so desires will make the confessor believe that the locution comes from His spirit. If He doesn't, the confessor and the soul are no longer under obligation. To do otherwise and follow nothing but your own opinion in this, I hold to be very dangerous. And so, Sisters, I warn you, on the part of our Lord, that you never let this happen to you.

12. There is another way in which the Lord speaks to the soul—for I hold that it is very definitely from Him—with a certain intellectual vision, the nature of which I will explain further on.[10] The locution takes place in such intimate depths and a person with the ears of the soul seems to hear those words from the Lord Himself so clearly and so in secret that this very way in which they are heard, together with the acts that the vi-

sion itself produces, assures that person and gives him certitude that the devil can have no part to play in the locution. Wonderful effects are left so that the soul may believe; at least there is assurance that the locution doesn't come from the imagination. Furthermore, if the soul is attentive, it can always have assurance for the following reasons: First, there is a difference because of the clarity of the locution. It is so clear that the soul remembers every syllable and whether it is said in one style or another, even if it is a whole sentence. But in a locution fancied by the imagination the words will not be so clear or distinct but like something half-dreamed.

13. Second, in these locutions one often is not thinking about what is heard (I mean that the locution comes unexpectedly and even sometimes while one is in conversation), although many times it is a response to what passes quickly through the mind or to what did so previously. But it often refers to things about the future that never entered the mind, and so the imagination couldn't have fabricated it in such a way that the soul could be deceived in fancying what was not desired or wanted or thought of.

14. Third, the one locution comes as in the case of a person who hears, and that of the imagination comes as in the case of a person who gradually composes what he himself wants to be told.

15. Fourth, the words are very different, and with one of them much is comprehended. Our intellect could not compose them so quickly.

16. Fifth, together with the words, in a way I wouldn't know how to explain, there is often given much more to understand than is ever dreamed possible without words.

I shall speak more about this mode of understanding elsewhere,[11] for it is something very delicate and to the praise of our Lord. For in regard to these different kinds of locutions, there have been persons who were very doubtful and unable to understand themselves. A certain person, especially, experienced this doubt,[12] and so there will be others. And thus I know that she observed the differences with close attention because the Lord has often granted her this favor, and the greatest doubt she had in the beginning was whether she had imagined the locution. That the words come from the devil can be more quickly understood; even though his wiles are so many, for he knows well how to counterfeit the Spirit of light. In my opinion the devil will say the words very clearly so that there will be certitude about their meaning, as is so with those coming from the Spirit of truth. But he will not be able to counterfeit the effects that were mentioned[13] or leave this peace or light in the soul; on the contrary he leaves restlessness and disturbance. But he can do little harm or none if the soul is humble and does what I have mentioned,[14] that is, doesn't make a move to do a thing of what it hears.

17. If the locutions contain words of favor and consolation from the Lord, let the soul look attentively to see if it thinks that because of them it is better than others. The more it hears words of favor the more humble it should be left; if it isn't, let it believe that the spirit is not from God. One thing very certain is that when the spirit is from God the soul esteems itself less, the greater the favor granted, and it has more awareness of its sins and is more forgetful of its own gain, and its will and memory are employed more in seeking only the honor of God, nor does it think about its own profit, and it walks with greater fear lest its will deviate in anything, and with greater certitude that it never deserved any of those favors but deserved hell. Since all the favors and things it experienced in prayer produce these effects, the soul does not walk fearfully but with confidence in the mercy of the Lord, who is faithful[15] and will not let the devil deceive it; although walking with fear is always good.

18. It could be that those whom the Lord does not lead along this path think such souls could refuse to listen to these words spoken to them—and if the words are interior distract themselves in such a way that they not be admitted—and as a result go about free of these dangers.

To this, I reply that it is impossible. I'm not speaking of imaginary locutions, for by not being so desirous of a thing or wanting to pay attention to their imaginings souls have a remedy. In locutions from the Lord, they have none. For the very spirit that speaks puts a stop to all other thoughts and makes the soul attend to what is said. It does this in such a way that I think, and I believe truly, that somehow it would be more possible for a person with very good hearing not to hear someone else speaking in a loud voice. In this latter instance the person would be able to turn his attention away and center his mind and intellect on something else. But in the locution we are speaking about this cannot be done; there are no ears to stop, nor is there the power to think of anything but what is said to the soul. For He who was able to stop the sun (through Joshua's prayer, I believe)[16] can make the faculties and the whole interior stop in such a way that the soul sees clearly that another greater Lord than itself governs that castle. And this brings it deep devotion and humility. So there's no remedy for this kind of locution. May the divine Majesty provide a remedy that will enable us to place our eyes only on pleasing Him and to be forgetful of ourselves, as I said, amen.

Please God that I may have succeeded in explaining what I set out to; may it be helpful for whoever has had such experience.

Chapter 4

Treats of when God suspends the soul in prayer with rapture or ecstasy or transport, which are all the same in my opinion,[1] *and how great courage is necessary to receive sublime favors from His Majesty.*

WITH THESE TRIALS and the other things that were mentioned, what kind of calm can the poor little butterfly have? All these sufferings are meant to increase one's desire to enjoy the Spouse. And His Majesty, as one who knows our weakness, is enabling the soul through these afflictions and many others to have the courage to be joined with so great a Lord and to take Him as its Spouse.[2]

2. You will laugh at my saying this and will think it's

foolishness; it will seem to any one of you that such courage is unnecessary and that there's no woman so miserable who wouldn't have the courage to be married to the king. I believe this is true with respect to kings here on earth; but with respect to the King of heaven, I tell you there is need for more courage than you think. Our nature is very timid and lowly when it comes to something so great, and I am certain that if God were not to give the courage, no matter how much you might see that the favor is good for us, it would be impossible for you to receive that favor. And thus you will see what His Majesty does to conclude this betrothal, which I understand comes about when He gives the soul raptures that draw it out of its senses. For if it were to see itself so near this great majesty while in its senses, it would perhaps die. Let it be understood that I mean true raptures and not the weaknesses women experience here below, for everything seems to us to be a rapture or an ecstasy. And, as I believe I have said,[3] some have constitutions so weak that the prayer of quiet is enough to make them die.

I want to put down here some kinds of rapture that I've come to understand because I've discussed them with so many spiritual persons. But I don't know whether I shall succeed as I did when I wrote elsewhere about them[4] and other things that occur in this dwelling place. On account of certain reasons it seems worthwhile to speak of these kinds of rapture again, and, if for no other reason, so that everything related to these dwelling places will be put down here together.

3. One kind of rapture is that in which the soul even though not in prayer is touched by some word it remembers or hears about God. It seems that His Majesty from the interior of the soul makes the spark we mentioned[5] increase, for He is moved with compassion in seeing the soul suffer so long a time from its desire. All burnt up, the soul is renewed like the phoenix, and one can devoutly believe that its faults are pardoned. Now that it is so pure, the Lord joins it with Himself, without anyone understanding what is happening except these two; nor does the soul itself understand in a way that can afterward be explained. Yet, it does have interior understanding, for this ex-

perience is not like that of fainting or convulsion; in these latter nothing is understood inwardly or outwardly.

4. What I know in this case is that the soul was never so awake to the things of God nor did it have such deep enlightenment and knowledge of His Majesty. This will seem impossible, for if the faculties are so absorbed that we can say they are dead, and likewise the senses, how can a soul know that it understands this secret? I don't know, nor perhaps does any creature but only the Creator. And this goes for many other things that take place in this state—I mean in these two dwelling places, for there is no closed door between the one and the other. Because there are things in the last that are not revealed to those who have not yet reached it, I thought I should divide them.

5. When the soul is in this suspension, the Lord likes to show it some secrets, things about heaven, and imaginative visions. It is able to tell of them afterward, for these remain so impressed on the memory that they are never forgotten. But when the visions are intellectual, the soul doesn't know how to speak of them. For there must be some visions during these moments that are so sublime that it's not fitting for those who live on this earth to have the further understanding necessary to explain them. However, when the soul is again in possession of its senses, it can say many things about these intellectual visions.

It could be that some of you do not know what a vision is, especially an intellectual one. I shall explain at the proper time,[6] for one who has the authority ordered me to do so.[7] And although the explanation may not seem pertinent, it will perhaps benefit some souls.

6. Well now you will ask me: if afterward there is to be no remembrance of these sublime favors granted by the Lord to the soul in this state, what benefit do they have? Oh, daughters, they are so great one cannot exaggerate! For even though they are unexplainable, they are well inscribed in the very interior part of the soul and are never forgotten.

But, you will insist, if there is no image and the faculties do not understand, how can the visions be remembered? I don't understand this either; but I do understand that some truths about the grandeur of God remain so fixed in this soul, that even if faith were not to tell it who God is and of its obligation to believe that He is God, from that very moment it would adore Him as God, as did Jacob when he saw the ladder. By means of the ladder Jacob must have understood other secrets that he didn't know how to explain, for by seeing just a ladder on which angels descended and ascended he would not have understood such great mysteries if there had not been deeper interior enlightenment.[8] I don't know if I'm guessing right in what I say, for although I have heard this story about Jacob, I don't know if I'm remembering it correctly.

7. Nor did Moses know how to describe all that he saw in the bush, but only what God wished him to describe.[9] But if God had not shown secrets to his soul along with a certitude that made him recognize and believe that they were from God, Moses could not have entered into so many severe trials. But he must have understood such deep things among the thorns of that bush that the vision gave him the courage to do what he did for the people of Israel. So, Sisters, we don't have to look for reasons to understand the hidden things of God. Since we believe He is powerful, clearly we must believe that a worm with as limited a power as ours will not understand His grandeurs. Let us praise Him, for He is pleased that we come to know some of them.

8. I have been wanting to find some comparison by which to explain what I'm speaking about, and I don't think there is any that fits. But let's use this one: you enter into the room of a king or great lord, or I believe they call it the treasure chamber, where there are countless kinds of glass and earthen vessels and other things so arranged that almost all these objects are seen upon entering. Once I was brought to a room like this in the house of the Duchess of Alba where, while I was on a journey, obedience ordered me to stay because of this lady's insistence with my superiors.[10] I was amazed on entering and wondered what benefit could be gained from that conglomeration of things, and I saw that one could praise the Lord at seeing so many different kinds of objects, and now I laugh to

myself upon realizing how the experience has helped me here in my explanation. Although I was in that room for a while, there was so much there to see that I soon forgot it all; none of those pieces has remained in my memory any more than if I had never seen them, nor would I know how to explain the workmanship of any of them. I can only say in general that I remember seeing everything. Likewise with this favor, the soul, while it is made one with God, is placed in this room of the empyreal heaven that we must have interiorly. For clearly, the soul has some of these dwelling places since God abides within it. And although the Lord must not want the soul to see these secrets every time it is in this ecstasy, for it can be so absorbed in enjoying Him that a sublime good like that is sufficient for it, sometimes He is pleased that the absorption decrease and the soul see at once what is in that room. After it returns to itself, the soul is left with that representation of the grandeurs it saw; but it cannot describe any of them, nor do its natural powers attain to any more than what God wished that it see supernaturally.

9. You, therefore, might object that I admit that the soul sees and that the vision is an imaginative one. But I'm not saying that, for I'm not dealing with an imaginative vision but with an intellectual one. Since I have no learning, I don't know how in my dullness to explain anything. If what I have said up to now about this prayer is worthwhile, I know clearly that I'm not the one who has said it.

I hold that if at times in its raptures the soul doesn't understand these secrets, its raptures are not given by God but caused by some natural weakness. It can happen to persons with a weak constitution, as is so with women, that any spiritual force will overcome the natural powers, and the soul will be absorbed as I believe I mentioned in reference to the prayer of quiet.[11] These experiences have nothing to do with rapture. In a rapture, believe me, God carries off for Himself the entire soul, and, as to someone who is His own and His spouse, He begins showing it some little part of the kingdom that it has gained by being espoused to Him. However small that part of His kingdom may be, everything that there is in this great God is magnificent. And He doesn't want any hindrance from anyone, neither from the faculties nor from the senses, but He immediately commands the doors of all these dwelling places to be closed; and only that door to His dwelling place remains open so that we can enter. Blessed be so much mercy; they will be rightly cursed who have not wanted to benefit by it and who have lost this Lord.

10. Oh, my Sisters, what nothingness it is, that which we leave! Nor is what we do anything, nor all that we could do for a God who thus wishes to communicate Himself to a worm! And if we hope to enjoy this blessing even in this present life, what are we doing? What is causing us to delay? What is enough to make us, even momentarily, stop looking for this Lord as the bride looked for Him in the streets and in the squares?[12] Oh, what a mockery everything in the world is if it doesn't lead us and help us toward this blessing even if its delights and riches and joys, as much of them as imaginable, were to last forever! It is all loathsome dung compared to these treasures that will be enjoyed without end. Nor are these anything in comparison with having as our own the Lord of all the treasures of heaven and earth.

11. Oh, human blindness! How long, how long before this dust will be removed from our eyes! Even though among ourselves the dust doesn't seem to be capable of blinding us completely, I see some specks, some tiny pebbles that if we allow them to increase will be enough to do us great harm. On the contrary, for the love of God, Sisters, let us benefit by these faults so as to know our misery, and they will give us clearer vision as did the mud to the blind man cured by our Spouse.[13] Thus, seeing ourselves so imperfect, let us increase our supplications that His Majesty may draw good out of our miseries so that we might be pleasing to Him.

12. I have digressed a great deal without realizing it. Pardon me, Sisters, and believe me that having reached these grandeurs of God (I mean, reached the place where I must speak of them), I cannot help but feel very sorry to see what we lose through our own fault. Even though it is true that these are blessings the Lord gives to whomever He wills, His Majesty would give them all to us if we loved Him as He loves us. He

doesn't desire anything else than to have those to whom to give. His riches do not lessen when He gives them away.

13. Well now, to get back to what I was saying,[14] the Spouse commands that the doors of the dwelling places be closed and even those of the castle and the outer wall. For in desiring to carry off this soul, He takes away the breath so that, even though the other senses sometimes last a little longer, a person cannot speak at all; although at other times everything is taken away at once, and the hands and the body grow cold so that the person doesn't seem to have any life; nor sometimes is it known whether he is breathing. This situation lasts but a short while, I mean in its intensity; for when this extreme suspension lets up a little, it seems that the body returns to itself somewhat and is nourished so as to die again and give more life to the soul. Nevertheless so extreme an ecstasy doesn't last long.

14. But it will happen that even though the extreme ecstasy ends, the will remains so absorbed and the intellect so withdrawn, for a day and even days, that the latter seems incapable of understanding anything that doesn't lead to awakening the will to love; and the will is wide awake to this love and asleep to becoming attached to any creature.

15. Oh, when the soul returns completely to itself, what bewilderment and how intense its desires to be occupied in God in every kind of way He might want! If the effects that were mentioned were produced by the former kinds of prayer what will be the effects of a favor as sublime as this? The soul would desire to have a thousand lives so as to employ them all for God and that everything here on earth would be a tongue to help it praise Him. The desires to do penance are most strong, but not much help comes from performing it, because the strength of love makes the soul feel that all that is done amounts to little and see clearly that the martyrs did not accomplish much in suffering the torments they did because with this help from our Lord, such suffering is easy. Hence these souls complain to His Majesty when no opportunity for suffering presents itself.

16. When this favor is granted them in secret, their esteem for it is great; when it is given in the presence of other persons,

their embarrassment and shame are so strong that the pain and worry over what those who saw it will think somehow take the soul away from what was being enjoyed.[15] For these persons know the malice of the world, and they understand that the world will not perhaps regard the experience for what it is, but that what the Lord should be praised for will perhaps be the occasion for rash judgments. In some ways it seems to me that this pain and embarrassment amount to a lack of humility, for if this person desires to be reviled, what difference does it make what others think? But the soul cannot control such feelings. One who was in this affliction heard from the Lord: "Don't be afflicted, either they will praise Me or criticize you; and in either case you gain."[16] I learned afterward that this person was very much consoled and encouraged by these words, and I put them down here in case one of you might find herself in this affliction. It seems that our Lord wishes all to understand that that soul is now His, that no one should touch it. Well and good if its body, or honor, or possessions are touched for this soul draws honor for His Majesty out of everything. But that one touch the soul—absolutely not; for if the soul does not withdraw from its Spouse through a very culpable boldness, He will protect it from the whole world and even from all hell.

17. I don't know if anything has been explained about the nature of rapture, for to explain it is completely impossible, as I have said.[17] But I don't believe anything has been lost by trying. For there are effects that are very different in feigned raptures. I do not say "feigned" because the one who has the experience wants to deceive but because that person is deceived. And since the signs and effects of the feigned raptures are not in conformity with such a great blessing, the true rapture is looked upon unfavorably; and afterward the one to whom the Lord grants it, justifiably is not believed. May He be blessed and praised forever, amen, amen.

Chapter 5

Continues on the same subject and deals with a kind of rapture in which God raises up the soul through a flight of the spirit, an experience different from that just explained. Tells why courage is necessary. Explains something about this delightful favor the Lord grants. The chapter is a very beneficial one.

THERE IS ANOTHER KIND of rapture—I call it flight of the spirit—which, though substantially the same as other raptures, is interiorly experienced very differently.[1] For sometimes suddenly a movement of the soul is felt so swift that it seems the spirit is carried off, and at a fearful speed especially in the beginning. This is why I have told you[2] that strong courage is necessary for the one to whom God grants these favors, and even faith and confidence and a full surrender to our Lord so that He may do what He wants with the soul. Do you think it is a small disturbance for a person to be very much in his senses and see his soul carried off (and in the case of some, we have read, even the body with the soul) without knowing where that soul is going, what or who does this, or how? At the beginning of this swift movement there is not so much certitude that the rapture is from God.[3]

2. Well, now, is there some means by which one can resist it? None at all; rather, to resist makes matters worse, for I know this was so with a certain person.[4] It seems God wishes that the soul that has so often, so earnestly, and with such complete willingness offered everything to Him should understand that in itself it no longer has any part to play; and it is carried off with a noticeably more impetuous movement. It is determined now to do no more than what the straw does when drawn by the amber—if you have noticed—and abandon itself into the hands of the One who is all powerful, for it sees that the safest thing to do is to make a virtue of necessity. And that I

mentioned a straw is certainly appropriate, for as easily as a huge giant snatches up a straw, this great and powerful Giant of ours carries away the spirit.[5]

3. It seems the trough of water we mentioned (I believe it was in the fourth dwelling place, for I don't recall exactly)[6] filled so easily and gently, I mean without any movement. Here this great God, who holds back the springs of water and doesn't allow the sea to go beyond its boundaries,[7] lets loose the springs from which the water in this trough flows. With a powerful impulse, a huge wave rises up so forcefully that it lifts high this little bark that is our soul. A bark cannot prevent the furious waves from leaving it where they will; nor does the pilot have the power, nor do those who take part in controlling the little ship. So much less can the interior part of the soul stay where it will, or make its senses or faculties do other than what they are commanded; here the soul doesn't care what happens in the exterior senses.

4. It is certain, Sisters, that just from writing about it I am amazed at how the immense power of this great King and Emperor is shown here. What will be the amazement of the one who experiences it! I hold that if His Majesty were to reveal this power to those who go astray in the world as He does to these souls, the former would not dare offend Him; this out of fear if not out of love. Oh, how obliged, then, will those persons be who have been informed through so sublime a path to strive with all their might not to displease this Lord! For love of Him, Sisters, I beg you, those of you to whom His Majesty has granted these favors, or others like them, that you don't grow careless and do nothing but receive. Reflect that the one who owes a lot must pay a lot.[8]

5. In this respect, too, great courage is necessary, for this favor is something frightening. If our Lord were not to give such courage, the soul would always go about deeply distressed. For it reflects on what His Majesty does for it and turns back to look at itself, at how little it serves in comparison with its obligation, and at how the tiny bit it does is full of faults, failures, and weaknesses. So as not to recall how imperfectly it

performs some work—if it does—it prefers striving to forget its works, keeping in mind its sins, and placing itself before the mercy of God. Since it doesn't have anything with which to pay, it begs for the pity and mercy God has always had toward sinners.

6. Perhaps He will respond as He did to a person who before a crucifix was reflecting with deep affliction that she had never had anything to give to God, or anything to give up for Him. The Crucified, Himself, in consoling her told her He had given her all the sufferings and trials He had undergone in His Passion so that she could have them as her own to offer His Father.[9] The comfort and enrichment was such that, according to what I have heard from her, she cannot forget the experience. Rather, every time she sees how miserable she is, she gets encouragement and consolation from remembering those words.

I could mention here some other experiences like this, for since I have dealt with so many holy and prayerful persons, I know about many such experiences; but I want to limit myself lest you think I am speaking of myself. What I said seems to me very beneficial to help you understand how pleased our Lord is that we know ourselves and strive to reflect again and again on our poverty and misery and on how we possess nothing that we have not received. So, my Sisters, courage is necessary for this knowledge and for the many other graces given to the soul the Lord has brought to this stage. And when there is humility, courage, in my opinion, is even more necessary for this knowledge of one's own misery. May the Lord give us this humility because of who He is.

7. Well, now, to return to this quick rapture of the spirit.[10] It is such that the spirit truly seems to go forth from the body. On the other hand, it is clear that this person is not dead; at least, he cannot say whether for some moments he was in the body or not. It seems to him that he was entirely in another region different from this in which we live, where there is shown another light so different from earth's light that if he were to spend his whole life trying to imagine that light, along with the other things, he would be unable to do so. It happens

that within an instant so many things together are taught him that if he were to work for many years with his imagination and mind in order to systematize them he wouldn't be able to do so, not with even one thousandth part of one of them. This is not an intellectual but an imaginative vision, for the eyes of the soul see much better than do we with bodily eyes here on earth, and without words understanding of some things is given; I mean that if a person sees some saints, he knows them as well as if he had often spoken with them.

8. At other times, along with the things seen through the eyes of the soul by an intellectual vision, other things are represented, especially a multitude of angels with their Lord. And without seeing anything with the eyes of the body or the soul, through an admirable knowledge I will not be able to explain, there is represented what I'm saying and many other things not meant to be spoken of. Anyone who experiences them, and has more ability than I, will perhaps know how to explain them; although doing so seems to me very difficult indeed. Whether all this takes place in the body or not, I wouldn't know; at least I wouldn't swear that the soul is in the body or that the body is without the soul.[11]

9. I have often thought that just as the sun while in the sky has such strong rays that, even though it doesn't move from there, the rays promptly reach the earth, so the soul and the spirit, which are one,[12] could be like the sun and its rays. Thus, while the soul remains in its place, the superior part rises above it. In a word, I don't know what I'm saying. What is true, is that with the speed of a ball shot from an arquebus, when fire is applied, an interior flight is experienced—I don't know what else to call it—which, though noiseless, is so clearly a movement that it cannot be the work of the imagination. And while the spirit is far outside itself, from all it can understand, great things are shown to it. When it again senses that it is within itself, the benefits it feels are remarkable, and it has so little esteem for all earthly things in comparison to the things it has seen that the former seem like dung. From then on its life on earth is very painful, and it doesn't see anything good in those things that used to seem good to it. The experience causes it to

care little about them. It seems the Lord, like those Israelites who brought back signs from the promised land,[13] has desired to show it something about its future land so that it may suffer the trials of this laborious path, knowing where it must go to get its final rest. Even though something that passes so quickly will not seem to you very beneficial, the blessings left in the soul are so great that only the person who has this experience will be able to understand its value.

10. Wherefore, the experience, obviously, is not from the devil; it would be impossible for the imagination or the devil to represent things that leave so much virtue, peace, calm, and improvement in the soul. Three things, especially, are left in it to a very sublime degree: knowledge of the grandeur of God, because the more we see in this grandeur the greater is our understanding; self-knowledge and humility upon seeing that something so low in comparison with the Creator of so many grandeurs dared to offend Him (and neither does the soul dare look up at Him); the third, little esteem of earthly things save for those that can be used for the service of so great a God.

11. These are the jewels the Spouse begins to give the betrothed, and their value is such that the soul will not want to lose them. For these meetings[14] remain so engraved in the memory that I believe it's impossible to forget them until one enjoys them forever, unless they are forgotten through one's own most serious fault. But the Spouse who gives them has the power to give the grace not to lose them.

12. Well to get back to the courage that is necessary,[15] does it seem to you that this is so trivial a thing? For it truly seems that because the soul loses its senses, and doesn't understand why, that it is separated from the body. It's necessary that He who gives everything else give the courage also. You will say that this fear is well paid. So do I. May it please His Majesty to give us the courage so that we may merit to serve Him, amen.

Chapter 6

Tells about an effect of the prayer discussed in the previous chapter. How to understand whether this effect is true rather than deceptive. Discusses another favor the Lord grants so that the soul might be occupied in praising Him.

AS A RESULT of these wonderful favors the soul is left so full of longings to enjoy completely the One who grants them that it lives in a great though delightful torment. With the strongest yearnings to die, and thus usually with tears, it begs God to take it from this exile. Everything it sees wearies it. When it is alone it finds some relief, but soon this torment returns; yet when the soul does not experience this pain, something is felt to be missing. In sum, this little butterfly is unable to find a lasting place of rest; rather, since the soul goes about with such tender love, any occasion that enkindles this fire more makes the soul fly aloft. As a result, in this dwelling place the raptures are very common and there is no means to avoid them even though they may take place in public. Hence, persecutions and criticism. Even though the soul may want to be free from fears, others do not allow this freedom. For there are many persons who cause these fears, especially confessors.

2. And even though, on the one hand, the soul seems to feel very secure in its interior part, especially when it is alone with God, on the other hand, it goes about in deep distress because it fears the devil may in some way beguile it into offending the One whom it loves so much. Little does it suffer over criticism, unless the confessor himself distresses it, as if it could do more. It does nothing but ask prayers from all and beg His Majesty to lead it by another path, for they all tell it to take another; they say that the path it is on is very dangerous. But since the soul has found this path to be so greatly beneficial, it sees that such a path is leading it along the way to heaven, according to what

it reads, hears, and knows about God's commandments. Even if it wanted to, it could not really desire anything else but to abandon itself into God's hands. And even this powerlessness distresses it, for it thinks it is not obeying its confessor. Obeying and not offending our Lord, it thinks, is the complete remedy against deception. Thus, in its opinion, it would not commit knowingly a venial sin even were others to crush it to pieces. It is intensely afflicted upon seeing that it cannot free itself from unknowingly committing many venial sins.

3. God gives these souls the strongest desire not to displease Him in anything, however small, and the desire to avoid if possible every imperfection. For this reason alone, if for no other, the soul wants to flee people, and it has great envy of those who have lived in deserts. On the other hand, it would want to enter into the midst of the world to try to play a part in getting even one soul to praise God more. A woman in this stage of prayer is distressed by the natural hindrance there is to her entering the world, and she has great envy of those who have the freedom to cry out and spread the news abroad about who this great God of hosts is.

4. Oh, poor little butterfly, bound with so many chains which do not let you fly where you would like! Have pity on it, my God! Ordain that it might somehow fulfill its desires for your honor and glory. Do not be mindful of the little it deserves and of its lowly nature. You have the power, Lord, to make the great sea and the large river Jordan roll back and allow the children of Israel to pass.[1] Yet, do not take pity on this little butterfly! Helped by your strength, it can suffer many trials; it is determined to do so and desires to suffer them. Extend Your powerful arm,[2] Lord, that this soul might not spend its life in things so base. Let Your grandeur appear in a creature so feminine and lowly, whatever the cost to her, so that the world may know that this grandeur is not hers at all and may praise You. This praise is what she desires, and she would give a thousand lives—if she had that many—if one soul were to praise You a little more through her; and she would consider such

lives very well spent. She understands in all truth that she doesn't deserve to suffer for You a tiny trial, much less die.

5. I don't know what my goal was in saying this, Sisters, nor why I said it, for these words were not planned. Let us realize that such effects are undoubtedly left by these suspensions and ecstasies. The desires are not passing but remain, and when an occasion arises to manifest their presence, one sees that they are not feigned. Why do I say they remain? Sometimes the soul feels, and in the smallest things, that it is a coward and so timid and frightened it doesn't think that it has the courage to do anything. I understand that the Lord leaves it then to its own human nature for its own greater good. It then sees that if it had been able to do something, the power was given by His Majesty. This truth is seen with a clarity that leaves the soul annihilated within itself and with deeper knowledge of God's mercy and grandeur—attributes the Lord desired to show to something so low. But usually its state is like that we've just mentioned.

6. Note one thing, Sisters, about these great desires to see our Lord: they sometimes afflict so much that you must necessarily avoid fostering them and must distract yourselves; if you can, I mean, for in other instances which I shall mention further on,[3] this cannot be done, as you will see. As for these initial desires, it's sometimes possible to distract oneself from them because there is every reason to be conformed to the will of God and say what St. Martin said.[4] A person can reflect upon St. Martin's words if the desires afflict a great deal. Since it seems these desires are characteristic of very advanced persons, the devil could instigate them so that we might think we are advanced. It is always good to walk with fear. But my opinion is that he would not be able to give the quiet and peace this suffering gives the soul; he would be stirring some passion, as happens when we suffer over worldly things. But a person who has no experience of the authentic and the inauthentic desires will think his desires are something great and will help them

along as much as he can and will do serious harm to his health. For this suffering is continual, or at least very habitual.

7. Also note that a weak constitution is wont to cause these kinds of suffering, especially in the case of tender persons who will weep over every little thing. A thousand times they will be led to think they weep for God, but they will not be doing so. And it can even happen, when tears flow in abundance (I mean, that for a time every little word the soul hears or thinks concerning God becomes the cause of tears), that some humor has reached the heart thereby contributing more to the tears than does love for God; for seemingly these persons will never finish weeping. Since they have already heard that tears are good, they will not restrain themselves nor would they desire to do anything else; and they help the tears along as much as they can. The devil's aim here is that these persons become so weak they will afterward be unable either to pray or to keep their rule.

8. It seems to me I can see you asking what you should do since I mark danger everywhere and in something as good as tears I think there can be deception; you are wondering if I may be the one who is deceived. And it could be that I am. But believe me, I do not speak without having seen that these false tears can be experienced by some persons; although not by me, for I am not at all tender. Rather, I have a heart so hard that sometimes I am distressed; although when the inner fire is intense, the heart, no matter how hard, distills like an alembic. You will indeed know when this fire is the source of the tears, for they are then more comforting and bring peace not turbulence, and seldom cause harm. The good that lies in the false tears—when there is any good—is that the damage is done to the body (I mean when there is humility) and not to the soul. But even if there is no harm done to the body, it won't be wrong to be suspicious about tears.

9. Let's not think that everything is accomplished through much weeping but set our hands to the task of hard work and virtue. These are what we must pay attention to; let the tears come when God sends them and without any effort on our part to induce them. These tears from God will irrigate this dry

earth, and they are a great help in producing fruit. The less attention we pay to them the more there are, for they are the water that falls from heaven. The tears we draw out by tiring ourselves in digging cannot compare with the tears that come from God, for often in digging we shall get worn out and not find even a puddle of water much less a flowing well. Therefore, Sisters, I consider it better for us to place ourselves in the presence of the Lord and look at His mercy and grandeur and at our own lowliness, and let Him give us what He wants, whether water or dryness. He knows best what is suitable for us. With such an attitude we shall go about refreshed, and the devil will not have so much chance to play tricks on us.

10. In the midst of these experiences that are both painful and delightful together, our Lord sometimes gives the soul feelings of jubilation and a strange prayer it doesn't understand. I am writing about this favor here so that if He grants it to you, you may give Him much praise and know what is taking place. It is, in my opinion, a deep union of the faculties; but our Lord nonetheless leaves them free that they might enjoy this joy—and the same goes for the senses—without understanding what it is they are enjoying or how they are enjoying. What I'm saying seems like gibberish, but certainly the experience takes place in this way, for the joy is so excessive the soul wouldn't want to enjoy it alone but wants to tell everyone about it so that they might help this soul praise our Lord. All its activity is directed to this praise. Oh, how many festivals and demonstrations the soul would organize, if it could, that all might know its joy! It seems it has found itself and that, like the father of the prodigal son, it would want to prepare a festival and invite all[5] because it sees itself in an undoubtedly safe place, at least for the time being. And I hold that there is reason for its desires. The devil cannot give this experience, because there is so much interior joy in the very intimate part of the soul and so much peace; and all the happiness stirs the soul to the praises of God.

11. To be silent and conceal this great impulse of happiness, when experiencing it, is no small pain. St. Francis must have

felt this impulse when the robbers struck him, for he ran through the fields crying out and telling the robbers that he was the herald of the great King; and also other saints must feel it who go to deserts to be able to proclaim as St. Francis these praises of their God. I knew a saint named Friar Peter of Alcántara—for I believe from the way he lived that he was one—who did this very thing,[6] and those who at one time listened to him thought he was crazy. Oh, what blessed madness, Sisters! If only God would give it to us all! And what a favor He has granted you by bringing you to this house where, when the Lord gives you this favor and you tell others about it, you will receive help rather than the criticism you would receive in the world. This proclamation is so unusual there that one is not at all surprised at the criticism.

12. Oh, how unfortunate the times and miserable the life in which we now live; happy are they whose good fortune it is to remain apart from the world. Sometimes it is a particular joy for me to see these Sisters gathered together and feeling such great joy at being in the monastery that they praise our Lord as much as possible. It is seen very clearly that their praises rise from the interior of the soul. I would want you to praise Him often, Sisters; for the one who begins, awakens the others. In what better way can you, when together, use your tongues than in the praises of God since we have so many reasons for praising Him?

13. May it please His Majesty to give us this prayer often since it is so safe and beneficial; to acquire it is impossible because it is something very supernatural. And it may last a whole day. The soul goes about like a person who has drunk a great deal but not so much as to be drawn out of his senses; or like a person suffering melancholy who has not lost his reason completely but cannot free himself from what is in his imagination—nor can anyone else.

These are inelegant comparisons for something so precious, but I can't think up any others. The joy makes a person so forgetful of self and of all things that he doesn't advert to, nor can he speak of anything other than the praises of God which proceed from his joy.

Let us all help this soul, my daughters. Why do we want to have more discretion? What can give us greater happiness? And may all creatures help us forever and ever, amen, amen, amen!

Chapter 7

Discusses the kind of suffering those souls to whom God grants the favors mentioned feel concerning their sins. Tells what a great mistake it is, however spiritual one may be, not to practice keeping the humanity of our Lord and Saviour Jesus Christ present in one's mind; also His most sacred Passion and life, His glorious Mother, and the saints. The chapter is very helpful.

YOU WILL THINK, Sisters, that these souls to whom the Lord communicates Himself in this unusual way will already be so sure of enjoying Him forever that they will have nothing to fear nor sins to weep over. Those especially who have not attained these favors from God will think this, for if they had enjoyed them, they would know what I'm going to say. But to think the above would be a great mistake because suffering over one's sins increases the more one receives from our God. And, for my part, I hold that until we are there where nothing can cause pain this suffering will not be taken away.

2. True, sometimes there is greater affliction than at other times; and the affliction is also of a different kind, for the soul doesn't think about the suffering it will undergo on account of its sins but of how ungrateful it has been to One to whom it owes so much and who deserves so much to be served. For in these grandeurs God communicates to it, it understands much more about Him. It is astonished at how bold it was; it weeps over its lack of respect; it thinks its foolishness was so excessive that it never finishes grieving over that foolishness when it recalls that for such base things it abandoned so great a Majes-

ty. Much more does it recall this foolishness than it does the favors it receives, though these favors are as remarkable as the ones mentioned or as those still to be spoken of. These favors are like the waves of a large river in that they come and go; but the memory these souls have of their sins clings like thick mire. It always seems that these sins are alive in the memory, and this is a heavy cross.

3. I know a person[1] who, apart from wanting to die in order to see God, wanted to die so as not to feel the continual pain of how ungrateful she had been to One to whom she ever owed so much and would owe. Thus it didn't seem to her that anyone's wickedness could equal her own, for she understood that there could be no one else from whom God would have had so much to put up with and to whom He had granted so many favors. As for the fear of hell, such persons don't have any. That they might lose God, at times—though seldom—distresses them very much. All their fear is that God might allow them out of His hand to offend Him, and they find themselves in as miserable a state as they were once before. In regard to their own suffering or glory, they don't care. If they don't want to stay long in purgatory, the reason comes from the fact of their not wanting to be away from God—as are those who are in purgatory—rather than from the sufferings undergone there.

4. I wouldn't consider it safe for a soul, however favored by God, to forget that at one time it saw itself in a miserable state. Although recalling this misery is a painful thing, doing so is helpful for many. Perhaps it is because I have been so wretched that I have this opinion and am always mindful of my misery. Those who have been good will not have to feel this pain, although there will always be failures as long as we live in this mortal body. No relief is afforded this suffering by the thought that our Lord has already pardoned and forgotten the sins. Rather, it adds to the suffering to see so much goodness and realize that favors are granted to one who deserves nothing but hell. I think such a realization was a great martyrdom for St. Peter and the Magdalene. Since their love for God had grown so deep and they had received so many favors and come to know the grandeur and majesty of God, the remembrance of

their misery would have been difficult to suffer, and they would have suffered it with tender sentiments.

5. It will also seem to you that anyone who enjoys such lofty things will no longer meditate on the mysteries of the most sacred humanity of our Lord Jesus Christ. Such a person would now be engaged entirely in loving. This is a matter I wrote about at length elsewhere.[2] They have contradicted me about it and said that I don't understand, because these are paths along which our Lord leads, and that when souls have already passed beyond the beginning stages it is better for them to deal with things concerning the divinity and flee from corporeal things. Nonetheless, they will not make me admit that such a road is a good one. Now it could be that I'm mistaken and that we are all saying the same thing. But I myself see that the devil tried to deceive me in this matter, and thus I have so learned my lesson from experience that I think, although I've spoken on this topic at other times,[3] I will speak of it again here that you will proceed very carefully in this matter. And take notice that I dare say you should not believe anyone who tells you something else. I'll try to explain myself better than I did elsewhere. If anyone perhaps has written what a certain person told me, this would be good if the matter is explained at length, but to speak of it so summarily could do much harm to those of us who are not well informed.[4]

6. It will also seem to some souls that they cannot think about the Passion, or still less about the Blessed Virgin and the lives of the saints; the remembrance of both of these latter is so very helpful and encouraging. I cannot imagine what such souls are thinking of. To be always withdrawn from corporeal things and enkindled in love is the trait of angelic spirits not of those who live in mortal bodies. It's necessary that we speak to, think about, and become the companions of those who having had a mortal body accomplished such great feats for God. How much more is it necessary not to withdraw through one's own efforts from all our good and help which is the most sacred humanity of our Lord Jesus Christ. I cannot believe that these souls do so, but they just don't understand; and they will do harm to themselves and to others. At least I assure them that

they will not enter these last two dwelling places. For if they lose the guide, who is the good Jesus, they will not hit upon the right road. It will be quite an accomplishment if they remain safely in the other dwelling places. The Lord Himself says that He is the way; the Lord says also that He is the light and that no one can go to the Father but through Him, and "anyone who sees me sees my Father."[5] They will say that another meaning is given to these words. I don't know about those other meanings; I have got along very well with this one that my soul always feels to be true.

7. There are some souls—and there are many who have spoken about it to me—who brought by our Lord to perfect contemplation would like to be in that prayer always; but that is impossible. Yet this favor of the Lord remains with them in such a way that afterward they cannot engage as before in discursive thought about the mysteries of the Passion and life of Christ. I don't know the reason, but this inability is very common, for the intellect becomes less capable of meditation. I believe the reason must be that since in meditation the whole effort consists in seeking God and that once God is found the soul becomes used to seeking Him again through the work of the will, the soul doesn't want to tire itself by working with the intellect. Likewise, it seems to me that since this generous faculty, which is the will, is already enkindled, it wants to avoid, if it can, using the other faculty; and it doesn't go wrong. But to avoid this will be impossible, especially before the soul reaches these last two dwelling places; and the soul will lose time, for the will often needs the help of the intellect so as to be enkindled.

8. And note this point, Sisters; it is important, and so I want to explain it further: The soul desires to be completely occupied in love and does not want to be taken up with anything else, but to be so occupied is impossible for it even though it may want to; for although the will is not dead, the fire that usually makes it burn is dying out, and someone must necessarily blow on the fire so that heat will be given off. Would it be good for a soul with this dryness to wait for fire to come down from heaven to burn this sacrifice that it is making

of itself to God, as did our Father Elijah?[6] No, certainly not, nor is it right to expect miracles. The Lord works them for this soul when He pleases, as was said and will be said further on.[7] But His Majesty wants us to consider ourselves undeserving of them because of our wretchedness, and desires that we help ourselves in every way possible. I hold for myself that until we die such an attitude is necessary however sublime the prayer may be.

9. It is true that anyone whom the Lord places in the seventh dwelling place rarely, or hardly ever, needs to make this effort. (I will give the reason for this fact when speaking of that dwelling place, if I remember.)[8] But such a person walks continually in an admirable way with Christ, our Lord, in whom the divine and the human are joined and who is always that person's companion. As for the above, when the fire in the will that was mentioned[9] is not enkindled and God's presence is not felt, it is necessary that we seek this presence. This is what His Majesty wants us to do, as the bride did in the *Song of Songs,*[10] and He wants us to ask creatures who it is who made them—as St. Augustine says, I believe, in his *Meditations or Confessions*[11]—and not be like dunces wasting time waiting for what was given us once before. At the beginning of the life of prayer it may be that the Lord will not give this fire in a year, or even in many years. His Majesty knows why; we must not desire to know nor is there any reason why we should. Since we know the path by which we must please God, which is that of the commandments and counsels, we should follow it very diligently, and think of His life and death and of the many things we owe Him; let the rest come when the Lord desires.

10. At this point, someone may respond that he cannot dwell on these things, and, because of what was said,[12] perhaps he will in a certain way be right. You already know that discursive thinking with the intellect is one thing and representing truths to the intellect by means of the memory is another. You may say, perhaps, that you do not understand me, and indeed it could be that I don't know how to explain the matter; but I shall do the best I can. By meditation I mean much discursive reflection with the intellect in the following way: we begin to

think about the favor God granted us in giving us His only Son, and we do not stop there, but go on to the mysteries of His whole glorious life; or we begin to think about the prayer in the garden, but the intellect doesn't stop until He is on the cross; or we take a phase of the Passion like, let us say, the arrest, and we proceed with this mystery considering in detail the things there are to think of and feel about the betrayal of Judas, the flight of the apostles, and all the rest; this kind of reflection is an admirable and very meritorious prayer.

11. This prayer is the kind that those whom God has brought to supernatural things and to perfect contemplation are right in saying they cannot practice. As I have said,[13] I don't know the reason, but usually they cannot practice discursive reflection. But I say that a person will not be right if he says he does not dwell on these mysteries or often have them in mind, especially when the Catholic Church celebrates them. Nor is it possible for the soul to forget that it has received so much from God, so many precious signs of love, for these are living sparks that will enkindle it more in its love for our Lord. But I say this person doesn't understand himself, because the soul understands these mysteries in a more perfect manner. The intellect represents them in such a way, and they are so stamped on the memory, that the mere sight of the Lord fallen to the ground in the garden with that frightful sweat is enough to last the intellect not only an hour but many days, while it looks with a simple gaze at who He is and how ungrateful we have been for so much suffering. Soon the will responds even though it may not do so with tender feelings, with the desire to serve somehow for such a great favor and to suffer something for One who suffered so much, and with other similar desires relating to what the memory and intellect are dwelling upon. I believe that for this reason a person cannot go on to further discursive reflection on the Passion, and this inability makes him think that he cannot think about it.

12. If he doesn't dwell on these mysteries in the way that was mentioned, it is good that he strive to do so, for I know that doing so will not impede the most sublime prayer. I don't think it's good to fail to dwell often on these mysteries. If as a result

the Lord suspends the intellect, well and good; for even though the soul may not so desire He will make it abandon what it was dwelling on. And I am very certain that this procedure is not a hindrance but a very great help toward every good; the hindrance would come from a great deal of work with the discursive reflection I mentioned in the beginning. I hold that one who has advanced further along cannot practice this discursive reflection. It could be that one can, for God leads souls by many paths. But let not those who can travel by the road of discursive thought condemn those who cannot, or judge them incapable of enjoying the sublime blessings that lie enclosed in the mysteries of our good, Jesus Christ. Nor will anyone make me think, however spiritual he may be, that he will advance by trying to turn away from these mysteries.

13. There are some principles and even means that certain souls use, by which it is thought that when a person begins to experience the prayer of quiet and to relish the enjoyment and spiritual delights given by the Lord, the important thing is to remain always in that state of delight. Well, now, let them believe me and not be so absorbed, as I have said elsewhere.[14] Life is long, and there are in it many trials, and we need to look at Christ our model, how He suffered them, and also at His apostles and saints, so as to bear these trials with perfection. Jesus is too good a companion for us to turn away from Him and His most blessed Mother, and He is very pleased that we grieve over His sufferings even though we sometimes leave aside our own consolation and delight. Moreover, daughters, enjoyment in prayer is not so habitual that there is not time for everything. I would be suspicious of anyone who says this delight is continual; I mean, who can never do what was mentioned. And you should be suspicious too, and strive to free yourselves from this error and avoid such absorption with all your strength. If your efforts aren't enough, tell the prioress so that she might give you some task demanding such care that this danger is removed. For if this absorption continues, it is extremely dangerous at least for the brain and the head.

14. I believe I've explained that it is fitting for souls, however spiritual, to take care not to flee from corporal things

to the extent of thinking that even the most sacred humanity causes harm. Some quote what the Lord said to His disciples that it was fitting that He go.[15] I can't bear this. I would wager that He didn't say it to His most Blessed Mother, because she was firm in the faith; she knew He was God and man, and even though she loved Him more than they did, she did so with such perfection that His presence was a help rather than a hindrance. The apostles must not have been as firm then in the faith as they were afterward and as we have reason to be now. I tell you, daughters, that I consider this a dangerous path and think the devil could make one lose devotion for the most Blessed Sacrament.

15. The mistake it seemed to me I was making wasn't so extreme, rather it consisted of not delighting so much in the thought of our Lord Jesus Christ but in going along in that absorption, waiting for that enjoyment. And I realized clearly that I was proceeding badly. Since it wasn't possible for me to experience the absorption always, the mind wandered here and there. My soul, it seems to me, was like a bird flying about that doesn't know where to light; and it was losing a lot of time and not making progress in virtue or improving in prayer. I didn't understand the reason, nor would I have understood it, in my opinion, because it seemed to me that what I was doing was very correct, until a person with whom I was discussing my prayer, who was a servant of God, warned me. Afterward, I saw clearly how wrong I had been, and I never stop regretting that there had been a time in which I failed to understand that I could not gain much through such a great loss. And even if I could gain, I wouldn't want any good save that acquired through Him from whom all blessings come to us. May He be always praised, amen.

Chapter 8

Discusses how God communicates Himself to the soul through an intellectual vision; gives some counsels. Tells about the effects such a vision causes if it is genuine. Recommends secrecy concerning these favors.

FOR YOU TO SEE, SISTERS, that what I have told you is true and that the further a soul advances the more it is accompanied by the good Jesus, we will do well to discuss how, when His Majesty desires, we cannot do otherwise than walk always with Him. This is evident in the ways and modes by which His Majesty communicates Himself to us and shows us the love He bears us. He does this through some very wonderful apparitions and visions. That you might not be frightened if He grants you some of these, I want briefly to mention something about these visions—if the Lord be pleased that I succeed—so that we might praise Him very much even though He may not grant them to us. We would be praising Him because though He is filled with majesty and power He nonetheless desires to communicate thus with a creature.

2. It will happen while the soul is heedless of any thought about such a favor being granted to it, and though it never had a thought that it deserved this vision, that it will feel Jesus Christ, our Lord, beside it. Yet, it does not see Him, either with the eyes of the body or with those of the soul. This is called an intellectual vision; I don't know why. I saw the person[1] to whom God granted this favor, along with other favors I shall mention further on, quite worried in the beginning because since she didn't see anything she couldn't understand the nature of this vision. However, she knew so certainly that it was Jesus Christ, our Lord, who showed Himself to her in that way that she couldn't doubt; I mean she couldn't doubt the vision was there. As to whether it was from God or not, even though she carried with her great effects to show that it was, she nonetheless was afraid. She had never heard of an intellectual vision, nor had she thought there was such a kind. But she

understood very clearly that it was this same Lord who often spoke to her in the way mentioned.[2] For until He granted her this favor I am referring to, she never knew who was speaking to her, although she understood the words.

3. I know that since she was afraid about this vision (for it isn't like the imaginative one that passes quickly, but lasts many days and sometimes even more than a year), she went very worried to her confessor. He asked her how since she didn't see anything she knew that it was our Lord; what kind of face He had.[3] She told him she didn't know, that she didn't see any face, and that she couldn't say any more than what she had said, that what she did know was that He was the one who spoke to her and that the vision had not been fancied. And although some persons put many fears in her, she was still frequently unable to doubt, especially when the Lord said to her: "Do not be afraid, it is I."[4] These words had so much power that from then on she could not doubt the vision, and she was left very much strengthened and happy over such good company. She saw clearly that the vision was a great help toward walking with a habitual remembrance of God and a deep concern about avoiding anything displeasing to Him, for it seemed to her that He was always looking at her. And each time she wanted to speak with His Majesty in prayer, and even outside of it, she felt He was so near that He couldn't fail to hear her. But she didn't hear words spoken whenever she wanted; only unexpectedly when they were necessary. She felt He was walking at her right side, but she didn't experience this with those senses by which we can know that a person is beside us. This vision comes in another unexplainable, more delicate way. But it is so certain and leaves much certitude; even much more than the other visions do because in the visions that come through the senses one can be deceived, but not in the intellectual vision. For this latter brings great interior benefits and effects that couldn't be present if the experience were caused by melancholy; nor would the devil produce so much good; nor would the soul go about with such peace and continual desires to please God, and with so much contempt for everything that does not bring it to Him. Afterward she understood clearly that

the vision was not caused by the devil, which became more and more clear as time went on.

4. Nonetheless, I know that at times she went about very much frightened; at other times, with the most intense confusion, for she didn't know why so much good had come to her. We were so united, she and I, that nothing took place in her soul of which I was ignorant; so I can be a good witness. And believe me, all I have said of this matter is the truth.

It is a favor from the Lord that she bears in herself the most intense confusion and humility. If the vision were from the devil, the effects would be contrary. And since the vision is something definitely understood to be a gift from God and human effort would not be sufficient to produce this experience, the one who receives it can in no way think it is his own good but a good given through the hand of God. And even though, in my opinion, some of those favors that were mentioned are greater, this favor bears with it a particular knowledge of God. This continual companionship gives rise to a most tender love for His Majesty, to some desires even greater than those mentioned[5] to surrender oneself totally to His service, and to a great purity of conscience because the presence at its side makes the soul pay attention to everything. For even though we already know that God is present in all we do, our nature is such that we neglect to think of this. Here the truth cannot be forgotten, for the Lord awakens the soul to His presence beside it. And even the favors that were mentioned[6] became much more common since the soul goes about almost continually with actual love for the One who it sees and understands is at its side.

5. In sum, with respect to the soul's gain, the vision is seen to be a most wonderful and highly valuable favor. The soul thanks the Lord that He gives the vision without any merits on its part and would not exchange that blessing for any earthly treasure or delight. Thus, when the Lord is pleased to take the vision away, the soul feels very much alone. But all the efforts it could possibly make are of little avail in bringing back that companionship. The Lord gives it when He desires, and it can-

not be acquired. Sometimes also the vision is of some saint, and this too is most beneficial.

6. You will ask how if nothing is seen one knows that it is Christ, or a saint, or His most glorious Mother. This, the soul will not know how to explain, nor can it understand how it knows, but it does know with the greatest certitude. It seems easier for the soul to know when the Lord speaks; but what is more amazing is that it knows the saint, who doesn't speak but seemingly is placed there by the Lord as a help to it and as its companion. Thus there are other spiritual things that one doesn't know how to explain, but through them one knows how lowly our nature is when there is question of understanding the sublime grandeurs of God, for we are incapable even of understanding these spiritual things. But let the one to whom His Majesty gives these favors receive them with admiration and praise for Him. Thus He grants the soul particular graces through these favors. For since the favors are not granted to all, they should be highly esteemed; and one should strive to perform greater services since God in so many ways helps the soul to perform these services. Hence the soul doesn't consider itself to be any greater because of this, and it thinks that it is the one who serves God the least among all who are in the world. This soul thinks that it is more obligated to Him than anyone, and any fault it commits pierces to the core of its being, and very rightly so.

7. These effects from the vision that were mentioned[7] and that are left in the soul can be recognized by anyone of you whom the Lord has brought by this road. Through them you can know that the vision is not an illusion or a fancy. As I have said,[8] I hold that it would be impossible for a vision caused by the devil to last so long and benefit the soul so remarkably, clothing it with so much interior peace. It is not customary for something so evil to do something so good, nor can the devil even though he may want to. If he could, there would at once be some outward show of self-esteem and thought of being better than others. But that the soul goes about always so attached to God and with its thoughts so occupied in Him, causes the devil such rage that even though he might try he would not

often return. And God is so faithful[9] that He will not allow the devil much leeway with a soul that doesn't aim for anything else than to please His Majesty and spend its life for His honor and glory; He will at once ordain how it may be undeceived.

8. My theme is and will be that since, as a result of these favors from God, the soul walks in the way here mentioned, His Majesty will make it be the one to gain. And if He sometimes permits the devil to tempt the soul, He will so ordain that the evil one will be defeated. As a result, daughters, if someone should walk along this road, as I have said, do not be astonished. It is good that there be fear and that we walk with more care. Nor should you be self-confident, for since you are so favored you could grow more careless. If you do not see in yourselves the effects that were mentioned,[10] it will be a sign the favor is not from God. It is good that at the beginning you speak about this vision under the seal of confession with a very learned man, for learned men will give us light. Or, with some very spiritual person, if there be one available; if there isn't, it's better to speak with a very learned man. Or with both a spiritual person and a learned man if both are at hand. And should they tell you the vision is fancied, do not be concerned, for the fancy can do little good or evil. Commend yourself to the divine Majesty that He not let you be deceived. If they should tell you your vision is from the devil, it will be a greater trial, although no one will say this if he is indeed learned and the effects mentioned are present. But if he says so, I know that the Lord Himself who walks with you will console you, assure you, and give the confessor light that he may give it to you.

9. If the confessor is a person whom, although he practices prayer, the Lord has not led by this path, he will at once be frightened and condemn it. For this reason I advise you to have a confessor who is very learned and, if possible, also spiritual. The prioress should give permission for such consultation. Even though, judging by the good life you live, you may be walking securely, the prioress will be obligated to have you speak with a confessor so that both you and she may walk securely. And once you have spoken with these persons, be quiet and don't try to confer about the matter with others; at

times the devil causes some fears so excessive that they force the soul, without its having anything really to fear, not to be satisfied with one consultation. If, especially, the confessor has little experience, and the soul sees that he is fearful, and he himself makes it continue to speak of the matter, that which by rights should have remained very secret is made public, and this soul is persecuted and tormented. For while it thinks the matter is secret, it finds out that the visions are publicly known. As a result many troublesome things happen to it and could happen to its religious order, the way these times are going.[11] Hence a great deal of discretion is necessary in this matter, and I highly recommend it to the prioresses.

10. A prioress should not think that since a Sister has experiences like these she is better than the others. The Lord leads each one as He sees is necessary. This path is a preparation for becoming a very good servant of God, provided that one cooperate. But sometimes God leads the weakest along this path. And so there is nothing in it to approve or condemn. One should consider the virtues and who it is who serves our Lord with greater mortification, humility, and purity of conscience; this is the one who will be the holiest. Yet, little can be known here below with certitude; we must wait until the true Judge gives to each one what is merited. In heaven we will be surprised to see how different His judgment is from what we can understand here below. May He be forever praised, amen.

Chapter 9

Treats of how the Lord communicates with the soul through an imaginative vision; gives careful warning against desiring to walk by this path and the reasons for such a warning. The chapter is very beneficial.

NOW LET US COME to imaginative visions, for they say the devil meddles more in these than in the ones mentioned,[1] and it must be so. But when these imaginative visions are from our Lord, they in some way seem to me more beneficial because they are in greater conformity with our nature. I'm excluding from that comparison the visions the Lord shows in the last dwelling place; no other visions are comparable to those.

2. Well now let us consider what I have told you in the preceding chapter[2] about how this Lord is present. It is as though we had in a gold vessel a precious stone having the highest value and curative powers. We know very certainly that it is there although we have never seen it. But the powers of the stone do not cease to benefit us provided that we carry it with us.[3] Although we have never seen this stone, we do not on that account cease to prize it, because through experience we have seen that it has cured us of some illnesses for which it is suited. But we do not dare look at it or open the reliquary, nor can we, because the manner of opening this reliquary is known solely by the one to whom the jewel belongs. Even though he lent us the jewel for our own benefit, he has kept the key to the reliquary and will open it, as something belonging to him when he desires to show us the contents, and he will take the jewel back when he wants to, as he does.

3. Well, let us say now that sometimes he wants to open the reliquary suddenly in order to do good to the one to whom he has lent it. Clearly, a person will afterward be much happier when he remembers the admirable splendor of the stone, and hence it will remain more deeply engrained in his memory. So it happens here: when our Lord is pleased to give more delight to this soul, He shows it clearly His most sacred humanity in the way He desires; either as He was when He went about in the world or as He is after His resurrection. And even though the vision happens so quickly that we could compare it to a streak of lightning, this most glorious image remains so engraved on the imagination that I think it would be impossible to erase it until it is seen by the soul in that place where it will be enjoyed without end.

4. Although I say "image" let it be understood that, in the opinion of the one who sees it, it is not a painting but truly alive, and sometimes the Lord is speaking to the soul and even revealing great secrets. But you must understand that even

though the soul is detained by this vision for some while, it can no more fix its gaze on the vision than it can on the sun. Hence this vision always passes very quickly, but not because its brilliance is painful, like the sun's, to the inner eye. It is the inner eye that sees all of this. I wouldn't know how to say anything about a vision that comes through the exterior sense of sight, because this person mentioned, of whom I can speak so particularly,[4] had not undergone such a vision, and one cannot be sure about what one has not experienced. The brilliance of this inner vision is like that of an infused light coming from a sun covered by something as transparent as a properly-cut diamond. The garment seems made of a fine Dutch linen. Almost every time God grants this favor the soul is in rapture, for in its lowliness it cannot suffer so frightening a sight.

5. I say "frightening" because although the Lord's presence is the most beautiful and delightful a person could imagine even were he to live and labor a thousand years thinking about it (for it far surpasses the limitations of our imagination or intellect), this presence bears such extraordinary majesty that it causes the soul extreme fright. Certainly it's not necessary here to ask how the soul knows, without having been told, who the Lord is, for it is clearly revealed that He is the Lord of heaven and earth. This is not true of earthly kings, for in themselves they would be held in little account were it not for their retinue, or unless they tell who they are.

6. O Lord, how we Christians fail to know you! What will that day be when You come to judge, for even when You come here with so much friendliness to speak with your bride, she experiences such fear when she looks at You? Oh, daughters, what will it be like when He says in so severe a voice, *depart you who are cursed by My Father*?[5]

7. As a result of this favor granted by God, let us keep in mind the above thought, for it will be no small blessing. Even St. Jerome, though he was a saint, kept it in mind. And thus all that we suffer here in the strict observance of the religious life will seem to us nothing; for, however long it lasts, it lasts but a moment in comparison with eternity. I tell you truthfully that as wretched as I am I have never had fear of the torments of

hell, for they would be nothing if compared to what I recall the condemned will experience upon seeing the anger in these eyes of the Lord, so beautiful, meek, and kind. It doesn't seem my heart could suffer such a sight. I've felt this way all my life. How much more will the person fear this sight to whom the Lord has thus represented Himself since the experience is so powerful that it carries that person out of his senses. The reason the soul is suspended must be that the Lord helps its weakness which is joined to His greatness in this sublime communication.

8. When the soul can remain a long while gazing upon this Lord, I don't believe it will be experiencing a vision but some intense reflection in which some likeness is fashioned in the imagination; compared with a vision this likeness is similar to something dead.

9. It happens to some persons (and I know this is true, for they have spoken with me—and not just three or four but many) that their imagination is so weak, or their intellect so effective, or I don't know what the cause is, that they become absorbed in their imagination to the extent that everything they think about seems to be clearly seen. Yet, if they were to see a real vision, they would know without any doubt whatsoever their mistake, for they themselves are composing what they see with their imagination. This imagining doesn't have any effect afterward, but they are left cold—much more than if they were to see a devotional image. It's very wise not to pay any attention to this kind of imagining and thus what was seen is forgotten much more than a dream.

10. In the vision we are dealing with the above is not so: rather, while the soul is very far from thinking that anything will be seen, or having the thought even pass through its mind, suddenly the vision is represented to it all at once and stirs all the faculties and senses with a great fear and tumult so as to place them afterward in that happy peace. Just as there was a tempest and tumult that came from heaven when St. Paul was hurled to the ground,[6] here in this interior world there is a great stirring; and in a moment, as I have said,[7] all remains calm, and this soul is left so well instructed about so many

great truths that it has no need of any other master. For without any effort on the soul's part, true Wisdom has taken away the mind's dullness and leaves a certitude, which lasts for some time, that this favor is from God. However much the soul is told the contrary, others cannot then cause it fear that there could be any deception. Afterward, if the confessor puts fear in it, God allows it to waver and think that because of its sins it could possibly be deceived. But it does not believe this; rather, as I have said concerning those other things,[8] the devil can stir up doubts, as he does with temptations against matters of faith, that do not allow the soul to be firm in its certitude. But the more the devil fights against that certitude, the more certain the soul is that the devil could not have left it with so many blessings, as they really are, for he cannot do so much in the interior of the soul. The devil can present a vision, but not with this truth and majesty and these results.

11. Since the confessors cannot witness this vision—nor, perhaps, can it be explained by the one to whom God grants this favor—they fear and rightly so. Thus it's necessary to proceed with caution, wait for the time when these apparitions will bear fruit, and move along little by little looking for the humility they leave in the soul and the fortitude in virtue. If the vision is from the devil, he will soon show a sign, and will be caught in a thousand lies. If the confessor has experience and has undergone these experiences, he needs little time for discernment; immediately in the account given he will see whether the vision is from God or the imagination or the devil, especially if His Majesty has given him the gift of discernment of spirits. If he has this latter as well as learning, even though he may have no experience, he will recognize the true vision very well.

12. What is necessary, Sisters, is that you proceed very openly and truthfully with your confessor. I don't mean in regard to telling your sins, for that is obvious, but in giving an account of your prayer. If you do not give such an account, I am not sure you are proceeding well, nor that it is God who is teaching you. He is very fond of our speaking as truthfully and clearly to the one who stands in His place as we would to Him

and of our desiring that the confessor understand all our thoughts and even more our deeds however small they be. If you do this you don't have to go about disturbed or worried. Even if the vision is not from God, it will do you no harm if you have humility and a good conscience. His Majesty knows how to draw good from evil, and the road along which the devil wanted to make you go astray will be to your greater gain. Thinking that God grants you such wonderful favors, you will force yourselves to please Him more and be always remembering His image. As a very learned man said,[9] the devil is a great painter and that if the devil were to show him a living image of the Lord, he wouldn't be grieved but allow the image to awaken his devotion, and that he would thereby wage war on the devil with that evil-one's own wickedness. Even though a painter may be a very poor one, a person shouldn't on that account fail to reverence the image he makes if it is a painting of our every Good.

13. That learned man was strongly opposed to the advice some gave about making the fig[10] when seeing a vision, for he used to say that wherever we see a painting of our King we must reverence it. And I see that he is right, because even here below a similar action would be regretted: If a person knew that before a portrait of himself another whom he loved manifested such contempt, he would be unhappy about the act. Well how much greater reason there is always to have respect for any crucifix or portrait we see of our Emperor? Although I have written of this elsewhere,[11] I am glad to write of it here, for I saw that a person went about in distress when ordered to use this remedy.[12] I don't know who invented a thing that could so torment a person who wasn't able to do anything else than obey, if the confessor gave her this counsel, because she thought she would go astray if she didn't obey. My counsel is that even though a confessor gives you such advice, you should humbly tell him this reason and not accept his counsel. The good reasons given me by that learned man I found very acceptable.

14. A wonderful benefit the soul draws from this favor of the Lord is that when it thinks of Him or of His life and Passion

it remembers His most meek and beautiful countenance. This remembrance is the greatest consolation, just as here below it would be far more consoling to see a person who has done a great deal of good for us than someone we had never met. I tell you that so delightful a remembrance brings much consolation and benefit.

Many are the other blessings these visions bring, but since so much has been said about such effects, and more will be said, I don't want to tire myself, or tire you, but advise you strongly that when you learn or hear that God grants these favors to souls you never beseech Him or desire Him to lead you by this path.

15. Although this path may seem to you very good, one to be highly esteemed and reverenced, desiring it is inappropriate for certain reasons: First, the desire to be given what you have never deserved shows a lack of humility, and so I believe that whoever desires this path will not have much humility. Just as the thoughts of a lowly workman are far from any desire to be king since such a thing seems impossible to him, and he thinks he doesn't deserve it, so too with the humble person in similar matters. I believe that these favors will never be given to those who desire them, because before granting them God gives a deep self-knowledge. For how will he who has such desires understand in truth that he is being granted a very great favor at not being in hell? Second, such a person will very certainly be deceived or in great danger because the devil needs nothing more than to see a little door open before playing a thousand tricks on us. Third, the imagination itself, when there is a great desire, makes a person think that he sees what he desires and hears it, as with those who desiring something during the day and thinking a great deal about it happen to dream of it at night. Fourth, it would be extremely bold to want to choose a path while not knowing what suits me more. Such a matter should be left to the Lord who knows me—for He leads me along the path that is fitting—so that in all things I might do His will. Fifth, do you think the trials suffered by those to whom the Lord grants these favors are few? No, they are ex-

traordinary and of many kinds. How do you know you would be able to bear them? Sixth, by the very way you think you will gain, you will lose, as Saul did by being king.[13]

16. In sum, Sisters, besides these reasons there are others; believe me, the safest way is to want only what God wants. He knows more than we ourselves do, and He loves us. Let us place ourselves in His hands so that His will may be done in us, and we cannot err if with a determined will we always maintain this attitude. And you must note that greater glory is not merited by receiving a large number of these favors; rather, on the contrary the recipients of these favors are obliged to serve more since they have received more. The Lord doesn't take away from us that which, because it lies within our power, is more meritorious. So there are many holy persons who have never received one of these favors; and others who receive them but are not holy. And do not think the favors are given continually; rather, for each time the Lord grants them there are many trials. Thus, the soul doesn't think about receiving more but about how to serve for what it has received.

17. It is true that this vision must be a powerful help toward possessing the virtues with higher perfection, but the person who has gained them at the cost of his own labors will merit much more. I know a person or two persons—one was a man—to whom the Lord had granted some of these favors, who were so desirous of serving His Majesty at their own cost, without these great delights, and so anxious to suffer that they complained to our Lord because He bestowed the favors on them, and if they could decline receiving these gifts they would do so.[14] I am speaking not of the delights coming from these visions—for in the end these persons see that the visions are very beneficial and to be highly esteemed—but of those the Lord gives in contemplation.

18. It is true that these desires also, in my opinion, are supernatural and characteristic of souls very much inflamed in love. Such souls would want the Lord to see that they do not serve Him for pay. Thus, as I have said,[15] they never, as a motive for making the effort to serve more, think about receiv-

ing glory for anything they do. But their desire is to satisfy love, and it is love's nature to serve with deeds in a thousand ways. If it could, love would want to discover ways of consuming the soul within itself. And if it were necessary to be always annihilated for the greater honor of God, love would do so very eagerly. May He be praised forever, amen. For in lowering Himself to commune with such miserable creatures, He wants to show His greatness.

Chapter 10

Tells about other favors God grants the soul, in a way different from those just mentioned, and of the great profit that comes from them.

IN MANY WAYS does the Lord communicate Himself to the soul through these apparitions. He grants some of them when it is afflicted; others, when a great trial is about to come; others, so that His Majesty might take His delight in the soul and give delight to it. There's no reason to go into further detail about each, since my intention is only to explain the different favors there are on this road, insofar as I understand them. Thus you will know, Sisters, their nature and their effects, lest we fancy that everything imagined is a vision. When what you see is an authentic vision, you won't go about disturbed or afflicted if you understand that such a thing is possible. The devil gains much and is extremely pleased to see a soul afflicted and disquieted, for he knows that disturbance impedes it from being totally occupied in loving and praising God.

His Majesty communicates Himself in other ways that are more sublime, and less dangerous because the devil, I believe, will be unable to counterfeit them. Thus, since these latter are something very secret, it is difficult to explain them, whereas the imaginative visions are easier to explain.

2. It will happen, when the Lord is pleased, that while the soul is in prayer and very much in its senses a suspension will suddenly be experienced in which the Lord will reveal deep

secrets. It seems the soul sees these secrets in God Himself, for they are not visions of the most sacred humanity. Although I say the soul sees, it doesn't see anything, for the favor is not an imaginative vision but very much an intellectual one. In this vision it is revealed how all things are seen in God and how He has them all in Himself.[1] This favor is most beneficial. Even though it passes in a moment, it remains deeply engraved in the soul and causes the greatest confusion. The evil of offending God is seen more clearly, because while being in God Himself (I mean being within Him) we commit great evils. I want to draw a comparison—if I succeed—so as to explain this to you. For although what I said is true, and we hear it often, either we do not pay attention to this truth or we do not want to understand it. If the matter were understood, it doesn't seem it would be possible to be so bold.

3. Let's suppose that God is like an immense and beautiful dwelling or palace and that this palace, as I say, is God Himself.[2] Could the sinner, perhaps, so as to engage in his evil deeds leave this palace? No, certainly not; rather, within the palace itself, that is within God Himself, the abominations, indecent actions, and evil deeds committed by us sinners take place. Oh, frightful thought, worthy of deep reflection, and very beneficial for those of us who know little. We don't completely understand these truths, for otherwise it wouldn't be possible to be so foolishly audacious! Let us consider, Sisters, the great mercy and compassion of God in not immediately destroying us there, and be extremely thankful to Him, and let us be ashamed to feel resentment about anything that is said or done against us. The greatest evil of the world is that God, our Creator, suffers so many evil things from His creatures within His very self and that we sometimes resent a word said in our absence and perhaps with no evil intention.

4. Oh, human misery! When, daughters, will we imitate this great God? Oh, let us not think we are doing anything by suffering injuries, but we should very eagerly endure everything, and let us love the one who offends us since this great God has not ceased to love us even though we have offended Him very

much. Thus the Lord is right in wanting all to pardon the wrongs done to them.[3]

I tell you, daughters, that even though this vision passes quickly it is a great favor from our Lord if one desires to benefit from it by keeping it habitually present.

5. It also happens very quickly and ineffably that God will show within Himself a truth that seems to leave in obscurity all those there are in creatures, and one understands very clearly that God alone is Truth, unable to lie.[4] What David says in a psalm about every man being a liar is clearly understood.[5] However frequently the verse may be heard, it is never understood as it is in this vision. God is everlasting Truth. I am reminded of Pilate, how he was often questioning our Lord when during the Passion he asked Him, "What is truth?"[6] and of the little we understand here below about this supreme Truth.

6. I would like to be able to explain more about this, but it is unexplainable. Let us conclude, Sisters, that in order to live in conformity with our God and Spouse in something, it will be well if we always study diligently how to walk in this truth. I'm not merely saying that we should not tell lies, for in that regard, glory to God, I already notice that you take great care in these houses not to tell a lie for anything. I'm saying that we should walk in truth before God and people in as many ways as possible. Especially, there should be no desire that others consider us better than we are. And in our works we should attribute to God what is His and to ourselves what is ours and strive to draw out the truth in everything. Thus, we shall have little esteem for this world, which is a complete lie and falsehood, and as such will not endure.

7. Once I was pondering why our Lord was so fond of this virtue of humility, and this thought came to me—in my opinion not as a result of reflection but suddenly: It is because God is supreme Truth; and to be humble is to walk in truth, for it is a very deep truth that of ourselves we have nothing good but only misery and nothingness. Whoever does not understand this walks in falsehood. The more anyone understands it the more he pleases the supreme Truth because he is walking in

truth. Please God, Sisters, we will be granted the favor never to leave this path of self-knowledge, amen.

8. Our Lord grants these favors to the soul because, as to one to whom He is truly betrothed, one who is already determined to do His will in everything, He desires to give it some knowledge of how to do His will and of His grandeurs. There's no reason to deal with more than these two things I mentioned[7] since they seem to me very beneficial. In similar things there is nothing to fear; rather, the Lord should be praised because He gives them. The devil, in my opinion, and even one's own imagination have little capacity at this level, and so the soul is left with profound satisfaction.

Chapter 11

Treats of some desires God gives the soul that are so powerful and vehement they place it in danger of death. Treats also of the benefits caused by this favor the Lord grants.

DO YOU THINK THAT all these favors the Spouse has bestowed on the soul will be sufficient to satisfy the little dove or butterfly—don't think I have forgotten it—so that it may come to rest in the place where it will die? No, certainly not; rather this little butterfly is much worse. Even though it may have been receiving these favors for many years, it always moans and goes about sorrowful because they leave it with greater pain. The reason is that since it is getting to know ever more the grandeurs of its God and sees itself so distant and far from enjoying Him, the desire for the Lord increases much more; also, love increases in the measure the soul discovers how much this great God and Lord deserves to be loved. And this desire continues gradually growing in these years so that it reaches a point of suffering as great as that I shall now speak of. I have said "years" so as to be in line with the experience of that person I've mentioned here,[1] for I well understand that one must not put limits on God; in a moment He can bring a soul to the lofty experience mentioned here. His Majesty has the power to do whatever He wants and is eager to do many things for us.

2. Well, here is what happens sometimes to a soul that experiences these anxious longings, tears, sighs, and great impulses that were mentioned[2] (for all of these seem to proceed from our love with deep feelings, but they are all nothing in comparison with this other experience that I'm going to explain, for they resemble a smoking fire that though painful can be endured). While this soul is going about in this manner, burning up within itself, a blow is felt from elsewhere (the soul doesn't understand from where or how). The blow comes often through a sudden thought or word about death's delay. Or the soul will feel pierced by a fiery arrow.[3] I don't say that there is an arrow, but whatever the experience, the soul realizes clearly that the feeling couldn't come about naturally. Neither is the experience that of a blow, although I said "blow"; but it causes a sharp wound. And, in my opinion, it isn't felt where earthly sufferings are felt, but in the very deep and intimate part of the soul, where this sudden flash of lightning reduces to dust everything it finds in this earthly nature of ours; for while this experience lasts nothing can be remembered about our being. In an instant the experience so binds the faculties that they have no freedom for anything except those things that will make this pain increase.

3. I wouldn't want what I say to appear to be an exaggeration. Indeed, I see that my words fall short because the experience is unexplainable. It is an enrapturing of the faculties and senses away from everything that is not a help, as I said, to feeling this affliction. For the intellect is very alive to understanding the reason why the soul feels far from God; and His Majesty helps at that time with a vivid knowledge of Himself in such a way that the pain increases to a point that makes the one who experiences it begin to cry aloud. Though she is a person who has suffered and is used to suffering severe pains, she cannot then do otherwise. This feeling is not in the body, as was said,[4] but in the interior part of the soul. As a result, this person understood how much more severe the feelings of the soul are than those of the body, and she reflected that such must be the nature of the sufferings of souls in

purgatory, for the fact that these souls have no body doesn't keep them from suffering much more than they do through all the bodily sufferings they endure here on earth.

4. I saw a person in this condition; truly she thought she was dying, and this was not so surprising because certainly there is great danger of death.[5] And thus, even though the experience lasts a short while, it leaves the body very disjointed, and during that time the heart beat is as slow as it would be if a person were about to render his soul to God. This is no exaggeration, for the natural heat fails, and the fire so burns the soul that with a little more intensity God would have fulfilled the soul's desires. This is true not because a person feels little or much pain in the body; although it is disjointed, as I said, in such a way that for three or four days afterward one feels great sufferings and doesn't even have the strength to write. And it even seems to me always that the body is left weaker. The reason one doesn't feel the pain must be that the interior feeling of the soul is so much greater that one doesn't pay any attention to the body. When one experiences a very sharp bodily pain, other bodily pains are hardly felt even though there may be many. I have indeed experienced this. With the presence of this spiritual pain, I don't believe that physical pain would be felt, little or much, even if the body were cut in pieces.

5. You will tell me that this feeling is an imperfection and ask why the soul doesn't conform to the will of God since it is so surrendered to Him. Until now it could do this, and has spent its life doing so. As for now, the reasoning faculty is in such a condition that the soul is not the master of it, nor can the soul think of anything else than of why it is grieving, of how it is absent from its Good, and of why it should want to live. It feels a strange solitude because no creature in all the earth provides it company, nor do I believe would any heavenly creature, not being the One whom it loves; rather, everything torments it. But the soul sees that it is like a person hanging, who cannot support himself on any earthly thing; nor can it ascend to heaven. On fire with this thirst, it cannot get to the water; and the thirst is not one that is endurable but already at such a point that nothing will take it away. Nor does the soul desire

that the thirst be taken away save by that water of which our Lord spoke to the Samaritan woman.[6] Yet no one gives such water to the soul.

6. Oh, God help me! Lord, how You afflict Your lovers! But everything is small in comparison with what You give them afterward. It's natural that what is worth much costs much. Moreover, if the suffering is to purify this soul so that it might enter the seventh dwelling place—just as those who will enter heaven must be cleansed in purgatory—it is as small as a drop of water in the sea. Furthermore, in spite of all this torment and affliction, which cannot be surpassed, I believe, by any earthly afflictions (for this person had suffered many bodily as well as spiritual pains, but they all seemed nothing in comparison with this suffering), the soul feels that the pain is precious; so precious—it understands very well—that one could not deserve it. However, this awareness is not of a kind that alleviates the suffering in any way. But with this knowledge, the soul suffers the pain very willingly and would suffer it all its life, if God were to be thereby served; although the soul would not then die once but be always dying, for truly the suffering is no less than death.

7. Well, let us consider, Sisters, those who are in hell, who do not have this conformity or this consolation and spiritual delight which is placed by God in the soul; nor do they see that their suffering is beneficial, but they always suffer more and more. The torments of the soul are so much more severe than those of the body, and the torment souls in hell suffer is incomparably greater than the suffering we have here mentioned, and must, it is seen, last forever and ever. What, then, will the suffering of these unfortunate souls be? And what can we do or suffer in so short a life that would amount to anything if we were thereby to free ourselves of those terrible and eternal torments? I tell you it would be impossible to explain how keenly felt is the suffering of the soul, and how different it is from that of the body, if one had not experienced these things. And the Lord Himself desires that we understand this so that we may know the extraordinary debt we owe Him for bringing us to a state in which through His mercy we hope He will free us and pardon our sins.

8. Well, to return to what we were dealing with[7]—for we left this soul with much pain—this pain lasts only a short while in such intensity. At the most it will last three or four hours, in my opinion, because if it were to last a long while natural weakness would not be able to endure it unless by a miracle. It has happened that the experience lasted no more than a quarter of an hour but left the soul in pieces. Truly, that time the person lost her senses completely, and the pain came in its rigor merely from her hearing a word about life not ending. This happened while she was engaged in conversation during Easter week, the last day of the octave, after she had spent all of Easter in so much dryness she almost didn't know it was Easter. In no way can the soul resist. It can no more do so than it can, if thrown in a fire, stop flames from having heat and burning it. This feeling is not one that can be concealed from others, but those who are present are aware of the great danger in which the person lies, although they cannot be witnesses to what is taking place interiorly. True, they provide some company, as though they were shadows; and so, like shadows, do all earthly things appear to that person.

9. And that you realize, in case you might sometime have this experience, what is due to our weakness, it happens at times that while in that state, as you have seen, the soul dies with the desire to die. For the fire afflicts so much that seemingly hardly anything keeps the soul from leaving the body. The soul truly fears and lest it end up dying would want the pain to abate. The soul indeed understands that this fear is from natural weakness, because on the other hand its desire to die is not taken away. Nor can a remedy be found to remove this pain until the Lord Himself takes it away, usually by means of a great rapture, or with some vision, where the true Comforter consoles and strengthens the soul that it might desire to live as long as God wills.

10. This experience is a painful one, but the soul is left with the most beneficial effects, and fear of the trials that can come its way is lost. When compared to the painful feeling experienced in the soul, the trials don't seem to amount to anything. The benefits are such that one would be pleased to

suffer the pain often. But one can in no way do this, nor is there any means for suffering the experience again. The soul must wait until the Lord desires to give this favor, just as there is no way to resist it or remove it when it comes. The soul is left with greater contempt for the world than before because it sees that nothing in the world was any help to it in that torment, and it is much more detached from creatures because it now sees that only the Creator can console and satisfy it. And it has greater fear of offending Him, taking more care not to do so, because it sees that He can also torment as well as console.

11. Two experiences, it seems to me, which lie on this spiritual path, put a person in danger of death: the one is this pain, for it truly is a danger, and no small one; the other is overwhelming joy and delight, which reaches so extraordinary a peak that indeed the soul, I think, swoons to the point that it is hardly kept from leaving the body—indeed, its happiness could not be considered small.

Here you will see, Sisters, whether I was right in saying that courage is necessary,[8] and whether when you ask the Lord for these favors He is right in answering as He did the sons of Zebedee, *are you able to drink the chalice?*[9]

12. I believe all of us, Sisters, will answer yes; and very rightly so, for His Majesty gives strength to the one He sees has need of it. He defends these souls in all things; when they are persecuted and criticized He answers for them as He did for the Magdalene[10]—if not through words, through deeds. And in the very end, before they die, He will pay for everything at once, as you will now see. May He be blessed forever, and may all creatures praise Him, amen.

THE SEVENTH DWELLING PLACES

Contains Four Chapters

Chapter 1

Treats of the great favors God grants souls that have entered the seventh dwelling places. Tells how in her opinion there is a certain difference between the soul and the spirit, although the soul is all one. The chapter contains noteworthy doctrine.

YOU WILL THINK, SISTERS, that since so much has been said about this spiritual path it will be impossible for anything more to be said. Such a thought would be very foolish. Since the greatness of God is without limits, His works are too. Who will finish telling of His mercies and grandeurs? To do so is impossible, and thus do not be surprised at what was said, and will be said, because it is but a naught in comparison to what there is to tell of God. He grants us a great favor in having communicated these things to a person through whom we can know about them. Thus the more we know about His communication to creatures the more we will praise His grandeur and make the effort to have esteem for souls in which the Lord delights so much. Each one of us has a soul, but since we do not prize souls as is deserved by creatures made in the image of God we do not understand the deep secrets that lie in them.

May it please His Majesty, if He may thereby be served, to move my pen and give me understanding of how I might say something about the many things to be said and which God reveals to the one whom He places in this dwelling place. I have earnestly begged this of His Majesty since He knows that my intention is to make known His mercies that His name may be more praised and glorified.

2. I hope, not for myself but for you, Sisters, that He may grant me this favor. Thus you will understand how important it is for you not to impede your Spouse's celebration of this spiritual marriage with your souls, since this marriage brings so many blessings, as you will see. O great God! It seems that a creature as miserable as I should tremble to deal with a thing so foreign to what I deserve to understand. And, indeed, I have been covered with confusion wondering if it might not be better to conclude my discussion of this dwelling place with just a few words. For it seems to me that others will think I know about it through experience. This makes me extremely ashamed; for, knowing what I am, such a thought is a terrible thing. On the other hand, the thought of neglecting to explain this dwelling place seemed to me to be a temptation and weakness on my part, no matter how many of the above judgments you make about me. May God be praised and understood a little more, and let all the world cry out against me; how much more so in that I will perhaps be dead when what I write is seen. May He be blessed who lives, and will live, forever, amen.

3. When our Lord is pleased to have pity on this soul that He has already taken spiritually as His spouse because of what it suffers and has suffered through its desires, He brings it, before the spiritual marriage is consummated, into His dwelling place which is this seventh. For just as in heaven so in the soul His Majesty must have a room where He dwells alone. Let us call it another heaven. It's very important for us, Sisters, not to think the soul is something dark. Since we do not see the soul, it usually seems that there is no such thing as interior light but only the exterior light which we all see, and that a certain darkness is in our soul. As for the soul that is not in grace, I confess this is so, but not through any fault of the Sun of Justice who dwells within it giving it being but because such a soul is incapable of receiving the light, as I believe I have said in the first dwelling place, according to what a certain person

understood.[1] For these unfortunate souls are as though in a dark prison, bound hands and feet, in regard to doing anything good that would enable them to merit, and blind and deaf. We can rightly take pity on them and reflect that at one time we were ourselves in this condition and that the Lord can also have mercy on them.

4. Let us take special care, Sisters, to beg this mercy of Him and not be careless, for it is a most generous alms to pray for those who are in mortal sin. Suppose we were to see a Christian with his hands fastened behind his back by a strong chain, bound to a post, and dying of hunger, not because of lack of food, for there are very choice dishes beside him, but because he cannot take hold of the food and eat, and even has great loathing for it; and suppose he sees that he is about to breathe his last and die, not just an earthly death but an eternal one. Wouldn't it be a terrible cruelty to stand looking at him and not feed him? Well, then, what if through your prayer the chains could be loosed? The answer is obvious. For the love of God I ask you always to remember in your prayers souls in mortal sin.

5. We are not speaking about them now but about those who already by the mercy of God have done penance for their sins and are in the state of grace. Thus we are not reflecting on something restricted to a corner but on an interior world where there is room for so many and such attractive dwelling places, as you have seen; and indeed it is right that the soul be like this since within it there is a dwelling place for God.

Now then, when His Majesty is pleased to grant the soul this divine marriage that was mentioned,[2] He first brings it into His own dwelling place. He desires that the favor be different from what it was at other times when He gave the soul raptures. I really believe that in rapture He unites it with Himself, as well as in the prayer of union that was mentioned.[3] But it doesn't seem to the soul that it is called to enter into its center, as it is here in this dwelling place, but called to the superior part. These things matter little; whether the experience comes in one way or another, the Lord joins the soul to Himself. But He does so by making it blind and deaf, as was St. Paul in his conversion,[4] and by taking away perception of the nature and kind of favor enjoyed, for the great delight the soul then feels is to see itself near God. Yet when He joins it to Himself, it doesn't understand anything; for all the faculties are lost.

6. In this seventh dwelling place the union comes about in a different way: our good God now desires to remove the scales from the soul's eyes and let it see and understand, although in a strange way, something of the favor He grants it. When the soul is brought into that dwelling place, the Most Blessed Trinity, all three Persons, through an intellectual vision, is revealed to it through a certain representation of the truth. First there comes an enkindling in the spirit in the manner of a cloud of magnificent splendor; and these Persons are distinct, and through an admirable knowledge the soul understands as a most profound truth that all three Persons are one substance and one power and one knowledge and one God alone. It knows in such a way that what we hold by faith, it understands, we can say, through sight—although the sight is not with the bodily eyes nor with the eyes of the soul, because we are not dealing with an imaginative vision. Here all three Persons communicate themselves to it, speak to it, and explain those words of the Lord in the Gospel: that He and the Father and the Holy Spirit will come to dwell with the soul that loves Him and keeps His commandments.[5]

7. Oh, God help me! How different is hearing and believing these words from understanding their truth in this way! Each day this soul becomes more amazed, for these Persons never seem to leave it any more, but it clearly beholds, in the way that was mentioned,[6] that they are within it. In the extreme interior, in some place very deep within itself, the nature of which it doesn't know how to explain, because of a lack of learning, it perceives this divine company.

8. You may think that as a result the soul will be outside itself and so absorbed that it will be unable to be occupied with anything else. On the contrary, the soul is much more occupied than before with everything pertaining to the service of God; and once its duties are over it remains with that enjoyable

company. If the soul does not fail God, He will never fail, in my opinion, to make His presence clearly known to it. It has strong confidence that since God has granted this favor He will not allow it to lose the favor. Though the soul thinks this, it goes about with greater care than ever not to displease Him in anything.

9. It should be understood that this presence is not felt so fully, I mean so clearly, as when revealed the first time or at other times when God grants the soul this gift. For if the presence were felt so clearly, the soul would find it impossible to be engaged in anything else or even to live among people. But even though the presence is not perceived with this very clear light, the soul finds itself in this company every time it takes notice. Let's say that the experience resembles that of a person who after being in a bright room with others finds himself, once the shutters are closed, in darkness. The light by which he could see them is taken away. Until it returns he doesn't see them, but not for that reason does he stop knowing they are present. It might be asked whether the soul can see them when it so desires and the light returns. To see them does not lie in its power, but depends on when our Lord desires that the window of the intellect be opened. Great is the mercy He shows in never departing from the soul and in desiring that it perceive Him so manifestly.

10. It seems that the divine Majesty desires, through this wonderful company, to prepare the soul for more. Clearly, the soul will be truly helped in every way to advance in perfection and to lose the fear it sometimes had of the other favors He granted it, as was said.[7] Such was the experience of this person,[8] for in everything she found herself improved, and it seemed to her, despite the trials she underwent and the business affairs she had to attend to, that the essential part of her soul never moved from that room. As a result, it seemed to her that there was, in a certain way, a division in her soul. And while suffering some great trials a little after God granted her this favor, she complained of that part of the soul, as Martha complained of Mary,[9] and sometimes pointed out that it was there always enjoying that quietude at its own pleasure while

leaving her in the midst of so many trials and occupations that she could not keep it company.

11. This will seem to you, daughters, to be foolishness, but it truly happens in this way. Although we know that the soul is all one, what I say is no mere fancy; the experience is very common. Wherefore I said[10] that interior things are seen in such a way that one understands with certitude that there is some kind of difference, a difference clearly recognized, between the soul and the spirit, even though they are both one. So delicate a division is perceived that sometimes it seems the one functions differently from the other, and so does the savor the Lord desires to give them seem different. It also seems to me that the soul and the faculties are not one but different. There are so many and such delicate things in the interior that it would be boldness on my part to set out to explain them. In heaven we will see all this, if the Lord in His mercy grants us the favor of bringing us there where we shall understand these secrets.

Chapter 2

Continues on the same subject. Explains the difference between spiritual union and spiritual marriage. Describes this difference through some delicate comparisons.

NOW THEN LET US deal with the divine and spiritual marriage, although this great favor does not come to its perfect fullness as long as we live; for if we were to withdraw from God, this remarkable blessing would be lost.

The first time the favor is granted, His Majesty desires to show Himself to the soul through an imaginative vision of His most sacred humanity so that the soul will understand and not be ignorant of receiving this sovereign gift. With other persons the favor will be received in another form. With regard to the one of whom we are speaking, the Lord represented Himself to her, just after she had received Communion, in the form of shining splendor, beauty, and majesty, as He was after His resurrection, and told her that now it was time that she consider as her own what belonged to Him and that He would take care of what was hers, and He spoke other words destined more to be heard than to be mentioned.[1]

2. It may seem that this experience was nothing new since at other times the Lord had represented Himself to the soul in such a way. The experience was so different that it left her indeed stupefied and frightened: first, because this vision came with great force; second, because of the words the Lord spoke to her; and also because in the interior of her soul, where He represented Himself to her, she had not seen other visions except the former one.[2] You must understand that there is the greatest difference between all the previous visions and those of this dwelling place. Between the spiritual betrothal and the spiritual marriage the difference is as great as that which exists between two who are betrothed and two who can no longer be separated.[3]

3. I have already said[4] that even though these comparisons are used, because there are no others better suited to our purpose, it should be understood that in this state there is no more thought of the body than if the soul were not in it, but one's thought is only of the spirit. In the spiritual marriage, there is still much less remembrance of the body because this secret union takes place in the very interior center of the soul, which must be where God Himself is, and in my opinion there is no need of any door for Him to enter. I say there is no need of any door because everything that has been said up until now seems to take place by means of the senses and faculties, and this appearance of the humanity of the Lord must also.[5] But that which comes to pass in the union of the spiritual marriage is very different. The Lord appears in this center of the soul, not in an imaginative vision but in an intellectual one, although more delicate than those mentioned,[6] as He appeared to the apostles without entering through the door when He said to them *pax vobis.*[7] What God communicates here to the soul in an instant is a secret so great and a favor so sublime—and the delight the soul experiences so extreme—that I don't know what to compare it to. I can say only that the Lord wishes to

reveal for that moment, in a more sublime manner than through any spiritual vision or taste, the glory of heaven. One can say no more—insofar as can be understood—than that the soul, I mean the spirit, is made one with God. For since His Majesty is also spirit, He has wished to show His love for us by giving some persons understanding of the point to which this love reaches so that we might praise His grandeur. For He has desired to be so joined with the creature that, just as those who are married cannot be separated,[8] He doesn't want to be separated from the soul.

4. The spiritual betrothal is different, for the two often separate. And the union is also different because, even though it is the joining of two things into one, in the end the two can be separated and each remains by itself. We observe this ordinarily, for the favor of union with the Lord passes quickly, and afterward the soul remains without that company; I mean, without awareness of it. In this other favor from the Lord, no. The soul always remains with its God in that center. Let us say that the union is like the joining of two wax candles to such an extent that the flame coming from them is but one, or that the wick, the flame, and the wax are all one. But afterward one candle can be easily separated from the other and there are two candles; the same holds for the wick. In the spiritual marriage the union is like what we have when rain falls from the sky into a river or fount; all is water, for the rain that fell from heaven cannot be divided or separated from the water of the river. Or it is like what we have when a little stream enters the sea, there is no means of separating the two. Or, like the bright light entering a room through two different windows; although the streams of light are separate when entering the room, they become one.

5. Perhaps this is what St. Paul means in saying *He that is joined or united to the Lord becomes one spirit with him,*[9] and is referring to this sovereign marriage, presupposing that His Majesty has brought the soul to it through union. And he also says: *For me to live is Christ, and to die is gain.*[10] The soul as well, I think, can say these words now because this state is the place where the little butterfly we mentioned[11] dies, and with

the greatest joy because its life is now Christ.

6. And that its life is Christ is understood better, with the passing of time, by the effects this life has. Through some secret aspirations the soul understands clearly that it is God who gives life to our soul. These aspirations come very, very often in such a living way that they can in no way be doubted. The soul feels them very clearly even though they are indescribable. But the feeling is so powerful that sometimes the soul cannot avoid the loving expressions they cause, such as: O Life of my life! Sustenance that sustains me! and things of this sort. For from those divine breasts where it seems God is always sustaining the soul there flow streams of milk bringing comfort to all the people of the castle. It seems the Lord desires that in some manner these others in the castle may enjoy the great deal the soul is enjoying and that from that full-flowing river, where this tiny fount is swallowed up, a spurt of that water will sometimes be directed toward the sustenance of those who in corporeal things must serve these two who are wed. Just as a distracted person would feel this water if he were suddenly bathed in it, and would be unable to avoid feeling it, so are these operations recognized, and even with greater certitude. For just as a great gush of water could not reach us if it didn't have a source, as I have said, so it is understood clearly that there is Someone in the interior depths who shoots these arrows and gives life to this life, and that there is a Sun in the interior of the soul from which a brilliant light proceeds and is sent to the faculties. The soul, as I have said,[12] does not move from that center nor is its peace lost; for the very One who gave peace to the apostles when they were together[13] can give it to the soul.

7. It has occurred to me that this greeting of the Lord must have amounted to much more than is apparent from its sound. So, too, with the Lord's words to the glorious Magdalene that she go in peace.[14] Since His words are effected in us as deeds, they must have worked in such a manner in those souls already disposed that everything corporeal in the soul was taken away and it was left in pure spirit. Thus the soul could be joined in this heavenly union with the uncreated Spirit. For it is very certain that in emptying ourselves of all that is creature and

detaching ourselves from it for the love of God, the same Lord will fill us with Himself. And thus, while Jesus our Lord was once praying for His apostles—I don't remember where—He said that they were one with the Father and with Him, just as Jesus Christ our Lord is in the Father and the Father is in Him.[15] I don't know what greater love there can be than this. And all of us are included here, for His Majesty said: *I ask not only for them but for all those who also will believe in me;* and He says: *I am in them.*[16]

8. Oh, God help me, how true these words are! And how well they are understood by the soul who is in this prayer and sees for itself. How well we would all understand them if it were not for our own fault, since the words of Jesus Christ, our King and Lord, cannot fail.[17] But since we fail by not disposing ourselves and turning away from all that can hinder this light, we do not see ourselves in this mirror that we contemplate, where our image is engraved.

9. Well, to return to what we were saying.[18] The Lord puts the soul in this dwelling of His, which is the center of the soul itself. They say that the empyreal heaven where the Lord is does not move as do the other heavens; similarly, it seems, in the soul that enters here there are none of those movements that usually take place in the faculties and the imagination and do harm to the soul, nor do these stirrings take away its peace.

It seems I'm saying that when the soul reaches this state in which God grants it this favor, it is sure of its salvation and safe from falling again. I do not say such a thing, and wherever I so speak that it seems the soul is secure, this should be taken to mean as long as the divine Majesty keeps it in His hand and it does not offend Him. At least I know certainly that the soul doesn't consider itself safe even though it sees itself in this state and the state has lasted for some years. But it goes about with much greater fear than before, guarding itself from any small offense against God and with the strongest desires to serve Him, as will be said further on,[19] and with habitual pain and confusion at seeing the little it can do and the great deal to which it is obliged. This pain is no small cross but a very great penance. For when this soul does penance, the delight will be greater in the measure that the penance is greater. The true penance comes when God takes away the soul's health and strength for doing penance. Even though I have mentioned elsewhere[20] the great pain this lack causes, the pain is much more intense here. All these things must come to the soul from its roots, from where it is planted. The tree that is beside the running water is fresher and gives more fruit. What is there, then, to marvel at in the desires this soul has since its true spirit has become one with the heavenly water we mentioned?[21]

10. Now then, to return to what I was saying,[22] it should not be thought that the faculties, senses, and passions are always in this peace; the soul is, yes. But in those other dwelling places, times of war, trial, and fatigue are never lacking; however, they are such that they do not take the soul from its place and its peace; that is, as a rule.

This center of our soul, or this spirit, is something so difficult to explain, and even believe in, that I think, Sisters, I'll not give you the temptation to disbelieve what I say, for I do not know how to explain this center. That there are trials and sufferings and that at the same time the soul is in peace is a difficult thing to explain. I want to make one or more comparisons for you. Please God, I may be saying something through them; but if not, I know that I'm speaking the truth in what I say.

11. The King is in His palace and there are many wars in his kingdom and many painful things going on, but not on that account does he fail to be at his post. So here, even though in those other dwelling places there is much tumult and there are many poisonous creatures and the noise is heard, no one enters that center dwelling place and makes the soul leave. Nor do the things the soul hears make it leave; even though they cause it some pain, the suffering is not such as to disturb it and take away its peace. The passions are now conquered and have a fear of entering the center because they would go away from there more subdued.

Our entire body may ache; but if the head is sound, the head will not ache just because the body aches.

I am laughing to myself over these comparisons for they do not satisfy me, but I don't know any others. You may think what you want; what I have said is true.

Chapter 3

Deals with the wonderful effects of this prayer that was mentioned. It is necessary to pay attention and heed to these effects, for the difference between them and the previous ones is remarkable.

NOW, THEN, WE ARE SAYING that this little butterfly has already died, with supreme happiness for having found repose and because Christ lives in it. Let us see what life it lives, or how this life differs from the life it was living. For from the effects, we shall see if what was said is true. By what I can understand these effects are the following.[1]

2. The first effect is a forgetfulness of self, for truly the soul, seemingly, no longer is, as was said.[2] Everything is such that this soul doesn't know or recall that there will be heaven or life or honor for it, because it employs all it has in procuring the honor of God. It seems the words His Majesty spoke to her produced the deed in her. They were that she look after what is His and that He would look after what is hers.[3] Thus, the soul doesn't worry about all that can happen. It experiences strange forgetfulness, for, as I say, seemingly the soul no longer is or would want to be anything in anything, except when it understands that there can come from itself something by which the glory and honor of God may increase even one degree. For this purpose the soul would very willingly lay down its life.

3. Don't think by this, daughters, that a person fails to remember to eat and sleep—doing so is no small torment—and to do all that he is obliged to in conformity with his state in life. We are speaking of interior matters, for there is little to say about exterior works. Rather, the soul's pain lies in seeing that what it can now do by its own efforts amounts to nothing. For

no earthly thing would it fail to do all it can and understands to be for the service of our Lord.

4. The second effect is that the soul has a great desire to suffer, but not the kind of desire that disturbs it as previously. For the desire left in these souls that the will of God be done in them reaches such an extreme that they think everything His Majesty does is good. If He desires the soul to suffer, well and good; if not, it doesn't kill itself as it used to.

5. These souls also have a deep interior joy when they are persecuted, with much more peace than that mentioned, and without any hostile feelings toward those who do, or desire to do, them evil. On the contrary, such a soul gains a particular love for its persecutors, in such a way that if it sees these latter in some trial it feels compassion and would take on any burden to free them from their trial, and eagerly recommends them to God and would rejoice to lose the favors His Majesty grants it if He would bestow these same gifts on those others so that they wouldn't offend our Lord.

6. You have already seen the trials and afflictions these souls have experienced in order to die so as to enjoy our Lord.[4] What surprises me most of all now is that they have just as great a desire to serve Him and that through them He be praised and that they may benefit some soul if they can. For not only do they not desire to die but they desire to live very many years suffering the greatest trials if through these they can help that the Lord be praised, even though in something very small. If they knew for certain that in leaving the body the soul would enjoy God, they wouldn't pay attention to that; nor do they think of the glory of the saints. They do not desire at that time to be in glory. Their glory lies in being able some way to help the Crucified, especially when they see He is so offended and that few there are who, detached from everything else, really look after His honor.

7. It is true that sometimes these things are forgotten, and the loving desires to enjoy God and leave this exile return, especially when the soul sees how little it serves Him. But soon it turns and looks within itself and at how continually it ex-

periences His presence, and with that it is content and offers His Majesty the desire to live as the most costly offering it can give Him.

It has no more fear of death than it would of a gentle rapture. The fact is that He who gave those desires that were so excessive a torment, now gives these others. May He be always blessed and praised.

8. The desires these souls have are no longer for consolations or spiritual delight, since the Lord Himself is present with these souls and it is His Majesty who now lives. Clearly, His life was nothing but a continual torment, and He makes ours the same; at least with the desires, for in other things He leads us as the weak, although souls share much in His fortitude when He sees they have need of it.

There is a great detachment from everything and a desire to be always either alone or occupied in something that will benefit some soul. There are no interior trials or feelings of dryness, but the soul lives with a remembrance and tender love of our Lord. It would never want to go without praising Him. When it becomes distracted the Lord Himself awakens it in the manner mentioned,[5] for one sees most clearly that that impulse, or I don't know what to call the feeling, proceeds from the interior depths of the soul, as was said of the impulses in the previous dwelling place.[6] Here, in this dwelling place, these impulses are experienced most gently, but they do not proceed from the mind or the memory, nor do they come from anything that would make one think the soul did something on its own. This experience is an ordinary and frequent one, for it has been observed carefully. Just as a fire does not shoot its flames downward but upward, however great a fire is enkindled, so one experiences here that this interior movement proceeds from the center of the soul and awakens the faculties.

9. Certainly, if there were no other gain in this way of prayer except to understand the particular care God has in communicating with us and beseeching us to remain with Him—for this experience doesn't seem to be anything else—it seems to me that all the trials endured for the sake of enjoying

these touches of His love, so gentle and penetrating, would be well worthwhile.

This you will have experienced, Sisters. For I think that when one has reached the prayer of union the Lord goes about with this concern if we do not grow negligent in keeping His commandments. When this impulse comes to you, remember that it comes from this interior dwelling place where God is in our soul, and praise Him very much. For certainly that note or letter is His, written with intense love and in such a way that He wants you alone to understand it and what He asks of you in it. By no means should you fail to respond to His Majesty, even though you may be externally occupied or in conversation with some persons. For it will often happen that our Lord will want to grant you this secret favor in public, and it is very easy—since the response is interior—to do what I'm saying and make an act of love, or say what St. Paul said: *Lord, what will You have me do?*[7] In many ways He will teach you there what will be pleasing to Him and the acceptable time. I think it is understood that He hears us, and this touch, which is so delicate, almost always disposes the soul to be able to do what was said with a resolute will.

10. The difference in this dwelling place is the one mentioned:[8] There are almost never any experiences of dryness or interior disturbance of the kind that were present at times in all the other dwelling places, but the soul is almost always in quiet. There is no fear that this sublime favor can be counterfeited by the devil, but the soul is wholly sure that the favor comes from God; for, as I have said,[9] the faculties and senses have nothing to do with what goes on in this dwelling place. His Majesty reveals Himself to the soul and brings it to Himself in that place where, in my opinion, the devil will not dare enter, nor will the Lord allow him to enter. Nor does the Lord in all the favors He grants the soul here, as I have said,[10] receive any assistance from the soul itself, except what it has already done in surrendering itself totally to God.

11. Every way in which the Lord helps the soul here, and all He teaches it, takes place with such quiet and so noiselessly that, seemingly to me, the work resembles the building of

Solomon's temple where no sound was heard.[11] So in this temple of God, in this His dwelling place, He alone and the soul rejoice together in the deepest silence. There is no reason for the intellect to stir or seek anything, for the Lord who created it wishes to give it repose here and that through a small crevice it might observe what is taking place. At times this sight is lost and the other faculties do not allow the intellect to look, but this happens for only a very short time. In my opinion, the faculties are not lost here;[12] they do not work, but remain as though in amazement.

12. I am amazed as well to see that when the soul arrives here all raptures are taken away. Only once in a while are they experienced and then without those transports and that flight of the spirit. They happen very rarely and almost never in public as they very often did before. Nor do the great occasions of devotion cause the soul concern as previously. Nor, if souls in this dwelling place see a devout image or hear a sermon—previously it was almost as though they didn't hear it—or music, are they worried as was the poor little butterfly that went about so apprehensive that everything frightened it and made it fly. Now the reason could be that in this dwelling place either the soul has found its repose, or has seen so much that nothing frightens it, or that it doesn't feel that solitude it did before since it enjoys such company. In sum, Sisters, I don't know what the cause may be. For when the Lord begins to show what there is in this dwelling place and to bring the soul there, this great weakness is taken away. The weakness was a severe trial for the soul and previously was not taken away. Perhaps the reason is that the Lord has now fortified, enlarged, and made the soul capable. Or it could be that His Majesty wished to make known publicly that which He did with these souls in secret for certain reasons He knows, for His judgments are beyond all that we can imagine here below.

13. These effects, along with all the other good ones from the degrees of prayer we mentioned, are given by God when He brings the soul to Himself with this kiss sought by the bride,[13] for I think this petition is here granted. Here an abundance of water is given to this deer that was wounded. Here one delights

in God's tabernacle. Here the dove Noah sent out to see if the storm was over finds the olive branch as a sign of firm ground discovered amid the floods and tempests of this world. O Jesus! Who would know the many things there must be in Scripture to explain this peace of soul! My God, since You see how important it is for us, grant that Christians will seek it; and in Your mercy do not take it away from those to whom You have given it. For, in the end, people must always live with fear until You give them true peace and bring them there where that peace will be unending. I say "true peace," not because this peace is not true but because the first war could return if we were to withdraw from God.

14. But what will these souls feel on seeing that they could lack so great a blessing? Seeing this makes them proceed more carefully and seek to draw strength from their weakness so as not to abandon through their own fault any opportunity to please God more. The more favored they are by His Majesty the more they are afraid and fearful of themselves. And since through His grandeurs they have come to a greater knowledge of their own miseries, and their sins become more serious to them, they often go about like the publican[14] not daring to raise their eyes. At other times they go about desiring to die so as to be safe; although, with the love they have, soon they again want to live in order to serve Him, as was said.[15] And in everything concerning themselves they trust in His mercy. Sometimes the many favors make them feel more annihilated, for they fear that just as a ship too heavily laden sinks to the bottom they will go down too.

15. I tell you, Sisters, that the cross is not wanting but it doesn't disquiet or make them lose peace. For the storms, like a wave, pass quickly. And the fair weather returns, because the presence of the Lord they experience makes them soon forget everything. May He be ever blessed and praised by all His creatures, amen.

Chapter 4

Concludes by explaining what she thinks our Lord's purpose is in granting such great favors to the soul and how it is necessary that Martha and Mary join together. This chapter is very beneficial.

YOU MUST NOT THINK, Sisters, that the effects I mentioned[1] are always present in these souls. Hence, where I remember, I say "ordinarily." For sometimes our Lord leaves these individuals in their natural state, and then it seems all the poisonous creatures from the outskirts and other dwelling places of this castle band together to take revenge for the time they were unable to have these souls under their control.

2. True, this natural state lasts only a short while, a day at most or a little more. And in this great disturbance, usually occasioned by some event, the soul's gain through the good company it is in becomes manifest. For the Lord gives the soul great stability and good resolutions not to deviate from His service in anything. But it seems this determination increases, and these souls do not deviate through even a very slight first movement. As I say this disturbance is rare, but our Lord does not want the soul to forget its being, so that, for one thing, it might always be humble; for another, that it might better understand the tremendous favor it receives, what it owes His Majesty, and that it might praise Him.

3. Nor should it pass through your minds that, since these souls have such determination and strong desires not to commit any imperfection for anything on earth, they fail to commit many imperfections, and even sins. Advertently, no; for the Lord must give souls such as these very particular help against such a thing. I mean venial sins, for from what these souls can understand they are free from mortal sins, although not immune. That they might have some sins they don't know about is no small torment to them. They also suffer torment in seeing souls go astray. Even though in some way they have great hope

that they themselves will not be among these souls, they cannot help but fear when they recall some of those persons Scripture mentions who, it seems, were favored by the Lord, like Solomon, who communed so much with His Majesty, as I have said.[2] The one among you who feels safest should fear more, for *blessed is the man who fears the Lord,*[3] says David. May His Majesty protect us always. To beseech Him that we not offend Him is the greatest security we can have. May He be praised forever, amen.

4. It will be good, Sisters, to tell you the reason the Lord grants so many favors in this world. Although, if you have paid attention, you will have understood this in learning of their effects, I want to tell you again here lest someone think that the reason is solely for the sake of giving delight to these souls; that thought would be a serious error. His Majesty couldn't grant us a greater favor than to give us a life that would be an imitation of the life His beloved Son lived. Thus I hold for certain that these favors are meant to fortify our weakness, as I have said here at times,[4] that we may be able to imitate Him in His great sufferings.

5. We have always seen that those who were closest to Christ our Lord were those with the greatest trials. Let us look at what His glorious Mother suffered and the glorious apostles. How do you think St. Paul could have suffered such very great trials? Through him we can see the effects visions and contemplation produce when from our Lord, and not from the imagination or the devil's deceit. Did St. Paul by chance hide himself in the enjoyment of these delights and not engage in anything else? You already see that he didn't have a day of rest, from what we can understand, and neither did he have any rest at night since it was then that he earned his livelihood.[5] I like very much the account about St. Peter fleeing from prison and how our Lord appeared to him and told him "I am on my way to Rome to be crucified again." We never recite the office of this feast, where this account is, that I don't find particular consolation.[6] How did this favor from the Lord impress St. Peter or what did he do? He went straight to his death. And it was no small mercy from the Lord that Peter found someone to provide him with death.

6. O my Sisters! How forgetful this soul, in which the Lord dwells in so particular a way, should be of its own rest, how little it should care for its honor, and how far it should be from wanting esteem in anything! For if it is with Him very much, as is right, it should think little about itself. All its concern is taken up with how to please Him more and how or where it will show Him the love it bears Him. This is the reason for prayer, my daughters, the purpose of this spiritual marriage: the birth always of good works, good works.

7. This is the true sign of a thing, or favor, being from God, as I have already told you.[7] It benefits me little to be alone making acts of devotion to our Lord, proposing and promising to do wonders in His service, if I then go away and when the occasion offers itself do everything the opposite. I was wrong in saying it profits little, for everything having to do with God profits a great deal. And even though we are weak and do not carry out these resolutions afterward, sometimes His Majesty will give us the power to do so, even though, perhaps, doing so is burdensome to us, as is often true. Since He sees that a soul is very faint-hearted He gives it a severe trial, truly against its will, and brings this soul out of the trial with profit. Afterward, since the soul understands this, the fear lessens and one can offer oneself more willingly to Him. I meant "it benefits me little" in comparison with how much greater the benefit is when our deeds conform with what we say in prayer; what cannot be done all at once can be done little by little. Let the soul bend its will if it wishes that prayer be beneficial to it, for within the corners of these little monasteries there will not be lacking many occasions for you to do so.[8]

8. Keep in mind that I could not exaggerate the importance of this. Fix your eyes on the Crucified and everything will become small for you. If His Majesty showed us His love by means of such works and frightful torments, how is it you want to please Him only with words? Do you know what it means to be truly spiritual? It means becoming the slaves of God. Marked with His brand, which is that of the cross, spiritual persons, because now they have given Him their liberty, can be sold by Him as slaves of everyone, as He was. He doesn't

thereby do them any harm or grant them a small favor. And if souls aren't determined about becoming His slaves, let them be convinced that they are not making much progress, for this whole building, as I have said,[9] has humility as its foundation. If humility is not genuinely present, for your own sake the Lord will not construct a high building lest that building fall to the ground. Thus, Sisters, that you might build on good foundations, strive to be the least and the slaves of all, looking at how or where you can please and serve them. What you do in this matter you do more for yourself than for them and lay stones so firmly that the castle will not fall.

9. I repeat, it is necessary that your foundation consist of more than prayer and contemplation. If you do not strive for the virtues and practice them, you will always be dwarfs. And, please God, it will be only a matter of not growing, for you already know that whoever does not increase decreases. I hold that love, where present, cannot possibly be content with remaining always the same.

10. It will seem to you that I am speaking with those who are beginning and that after this beginner's stage souls can rest. I have already told you[10] that the calm these souls have interiorly is for the sake of their having much less calm exteriorly and much less desire to have exterior calm. What, do you think, is the reason for those inspirations (or to put it better, aspirations) I mentioned, and those messages the soul sends from the interior center to the people at the top of the castle and to the dwelling places outside the center where it is? Is it so that those outside might fall asleep? No, absolutely not! That the faculties, senses, and all the corporeal will not be idle, the soul wages more war from the center than it did when it was outside suffering with them, for then it didn't understand the tremendous gain trials bring. Perhaps they were the means by which God brought it to the center, and the company it has gives it much greater strength than ever. For if here below, as David says, in the company of the saints we will become saints,[11] there is no reason to doubt that, being united with the Strong One through so sovereign a union of spirit with spirit, fortitude will

cling to such a soul; and so we shall understand what fortitude the saints had for suffering and dying.

11. It is very certain that from that fortitude which clings to it there the soul assists all those who are in the castle, and even the body itself which often, seemingly, does not feel the strength. But the soul is fortified by the strength it has from drinking wine in this wine cellar, where its Spouse has brought it[12] and from where He doesn't allow it to leave; and strength flows back to the weak body, just as food placed in the stomach strengthens the head and the whole body. Thus the soul has its share of misfortune while it lives. However much it does, the interior strength increases and thus, too, the war that is waged; for everything seems like a trifle to it. The great penances that many saints—especially the glorious Magdalene, who had always been surrounded by so much luxury—performed must have come from this center. Also that hunger which our Father Elijah had for the honor of his God[13] and which St. Dominic and St. Francis had so as to draw souls to praise God. I tell you, though they were forgetful of themselves, their suffering must have been great.

12. This is what I want us to strive for, my Sisters; and let us desire and be occupied in prayer not for the sake of our enjoyment but so as to have this strength to serve. Let's refuse to take an unfamiliar path, for we shall get lost at the most opportune time. It would indeed be novel to think of having these favors from God through a path other than the one He took and the one followed by all His saints. May the thought never enter our minds. Believe me, Martha and Mary must join together in order to show hospitality to the Lord and have Him always present and not host Him badly by failing to give Him something to eat. How would Mary, always seated at His feet, provide Him with food if her sister did not help her? His food is that in every way possible we draw souls that they may be saved and praise Him always.[14]

13. You will make two objections: one, that He said that Mary had chosen the better part. The answer is that she had already performed the task of Martha, pleasing the Lord by washing His feet and drying them with her hair.[15] Do you think

it would be a small mortification for a woman of nobility like her to wander through these streets (and perhaps alone because her fervent love made her unaware of what she was doing) and enter a house she had never entered before and afterward suffer the criticism of the Pharisee and the very many other things she must have suffered? The people saw a woman like her change so much—and, as we know, she was among such malicious people—and they saw her friendship with the Lord whom they vehemently abhorred, and that she wanted to become a saint since obviously she would have changed her manner of dress and everything else. All of that was enough to cause them to comment on the life she had formerly lived. If nowadays there is so much gossip against persons who are not so notorious; what would have been said then? I tell you, Sisters, the better part came after many trials and much mortification, for even if there were no other trial than to see His Majesty abhorred, that would be an intolerable one. Moreover, the many trials that afterward she suffered at the death of the Lord and in the years that she subsequently lived in His absence must have been a terrible torment. You see she wasn't always in the delight of contemplation at the feet of the Lord.

14. The other objection you will make is that you are unable to bring souls to God, that you do not have the means; that you would do it willingly but that not being teachers or preachers, as were the apostles, you do not know how. This objection I have answered at times in writing, but I don't know if I did so in this *Castle.*[16] Yet since the matter is something I believe is passing through your minds on account of the desires God gives you I will not fail to respond here. I already told you elsewhere[17] that sometimes the devil gives us great desires so that we will avoid setting ourselves to the task at hand, serving our Lord in possible things, and instead be content with having desired the impossible. Apart from the fact that by prayer you will be helping greatly, you need not be desiring to benefit the whole world but must concentrate on those who are in your company, and thus your deed will be greater since you are more obliged toward them. Do you think such deep humility, your mortification, service of all and great charity toward

them, and love of the Lord is of little benefit? This fire of love in you enkindles their souls, and with every other virtue you will be always awakening them. Such service will not be small but very great and very pleasing to the Lord. By what you do in deed—that which you can—His Majesty will understand that you would do much more. Thus He will give you the reward He would if you had gained many souls for Him.

15. You will say that such service does not convert souls because all the Sisters you deal with are already good. Who has appointed you judge in this matter? The better they are the more pleasing their praises will be to our Lord and the more their prayer will profit their neighbor.

In sum, my Sisters, what I conclude with is that we shouldn't build castles in the air. The Lord doesn't look so much at the greatness of our works as at the love with which they are done. And if we do what we can, His Majesty will enable us each day to do more and more, provided that we do not quickly tire. But during the little while this life lasts—and perhaps it will last a shorter time than each one thinks—let us offer the Lord interiorly and exteriorly the sacrifice we can. His Majesty will join it with that which He offered on the cross to the Father for us. Thus even though our works are small they will have the value our love for Him would have merited had they been great.

16. May it please His Majesty, my Sisters and daughters, that we all reach that place where we may ever praise Him. Through the merits of His Son who lives and reigns forever and ever, may He give me the grace to carry out something of what I tell you, amen. For I tell you that my confusion is great, and thus I ask you through the same Lord that in your prayers you do not forget this poor wretch.

[Epilogue[1]]

JHS.

ALTHOUGH WHEN I BEGAN writing this book I am sending you I did so with the aversion I mentioned in the beginning,[2] now that I am finished I admit the work has brought me much happiness, and I consider the labor, though I confess it was small, well spent. Considering the strict enclosure and the few things you have for your entertainment, my Sisters, and that your buildings are not always as large as would be fitting for your monasteries, I think it will be a consolation for you to delight in this interior castle since without permission from the prioress you can enter and take a walk through it at any time.

2. True, you will not be able to enter all the dwelling places through your own efforts, even though these efforts may seem to you great, unless the Lord of the castle Himself brings you there. Hence I advise you to use no force if you meet with any resistance, for you will thereby anger Him in such a way that He will never allow you to enter them. He is very fond of humility. By considering that you do not deserve even to enter the third you will more quickly win the favor to reach the fifth. And you will be able to serve Him from there in such a way, continuing to walk through them often, that He will bring you into the very dwelling place He has for Himself. You need never leave this latter dwelling place unless called by the prioress, whose will this great Lord desires that you comply with as much as if it were His own. Even though you are frequently outside through her command, you will always find the door open when you return. Once you get used to enjoying this

castle, you will find rest in all things, even those involving much labor, for you will have the hope of returning to the castle which no one can take from you.

3. Although no more than seven dwelling places were discussed, in each of these there are many others, below and above and to the sides, with lovely gardens and fountains and labyrinths, such delightful things that you would want to be dissolved in praises of the great God who created the soul in His own image and likeness.[3] If you find something good in the way I have explained this to you, believe that indeed His Majesty said it so as to make you happy; the bad that you might find is said by me.

4. Through the strong desire I have to play some part in helping you serve my God and Lord, I ask that each time you read this work you, in my name, praise His Majesty fervently and ask for the increase of His Church and for light for the Lutherans. As for me, ask Him to pardon my sins and deliver me from purgatory, for perhaps by the mercy of God I will be there when this is given you to read—if it may be seen by you after having been examined by learned men. If anything is erroneous it is so because I didn't know otherwise; and I submit in everything to what the holy Roman Catholic Church holds, for in this Church I live, declare my faith, and promise to live and die.

May God our Lord be forever praised and blessed, amen, amen.

5. This writing was finished in the monastery of St. Joseph of Avila in the year 1577, the eve before the feast of St. Andrew,[4] for the glory of God who lives and reigns forever and ever, amen.

Notes

NOTES

THE WAY OF PERFECTION

INTRODUCTION

1. See *The Collected Works of St. Teresa of Avila,* tr. K. Kavanaugh and O. Rodriguez, vol. I (I.C.S. Publications: Washington, D.C., 1976), pp. 17-19.
2. See *Life,* epilogue, no. 2.
3. See *Way of Perfection,* ch. 42, no. 6.
4. Ibid., prologue, no. 1.
5. See ibid., ch. 16, nos. 3-6; ch. 24, nos. 1-2; ch. 30, no. 7.
6. Ibid., prologue, no. 1.
7. Ibid., ch. 15, no. 1.
8. Ibid., ch. 42, no. 6.
9. Ibid.
10. Ibid., prologue, no. 1.
11. See *Camino de Perfección, Reproducción en facsímil del autógrafo de Valladolid,* ed. Tomás de la Cruz et al., vol. 2 (Tipografia Poliglotta Vaticana: Rome, 1965), pp. 15-30.
12. See ibid.
13. Ibid., ch. 16, no. 6.
14. See *Life,* ch. 39, no. 22.
15. Ibid., ch. 38, no. 6.
16. See ibid., ch. 20, no. 13.
17. *Way of Perfection,* ch. 1, no. 2.
18. Cf. ibid., ch. 1, nos. 2, 5; ch. 3, nos. 1, 8; ch. 35, no. 3.
19. *Life,* ch. 25, no. 12.
20. Ibid., ch. 25, no. 13.
21. *Spiritual Testimonies,* 3, no. 13.
22. Cf. *Way of Perfection,* ch. 21, no. 10; ch. 30, no. 4.
23. Ibid., ch. 3, no. 9.
24. Ibid., ch. 1, no. 2.
25. Ibid., ch. 3, no. 1.
26. Ibid., ch. 1, no. 2.
27. Ibid. For further details about Teresa and the Church, see Tomás de la Cruz, "Santa Teresa De Avila Hija De La Iglesia," *Ephemerides Carmeliticae* 17 (1966): 305-367.

28. For further information about these times, see my introduction to the *Life* in the *Collected Works of St. Teresa*, vol. l, pp. 21-41.
29. Francisco de Osuna, *Norte de Estados* (Seville, 1531), as quoted by D. De Pablo Maroto in *Dinámica de la Oracion* (Madrid: Espiritualidad, 1973), p. 109.
30. See *Biblioteca Mística Carmelitana,* ed., Silverio de Santa Teresa, vol. 18 (Burgos: El Monte Carmelo 1934), p. 10.
31. *Obras Completas de Santa Teresa de Jesús,* ed., Efrén de La Madre de Dios and O. Steggink (Madrid: BAC, 1967), p. 190.
32. *Way of Perfection,* ch. 3, no. 7.
33. See J. Ignacio Tellechea Idígoras, "Textos Inéditos Sobre El Fenomeno De Los Alumbrados," *Ephemerides Carmeliticae* 13 (1962): 768-774.
34. See P. Tommaso della Croce, "Santa Teresa E I Movimenti Spirituali Del Suo Tempo," *Santa Teresa Maestra De Orazione* (Rome: Teresianum, 1963), pp. 30-36. Cf. D. De Pablo Maroto, *Dinámica De La Oracion,* p. 106.
35. See *Life,* ch. 26, no. 5.
36. See D. De Pablo Maroto, *Dinámica De La Oracion,* p. 107.
37. *Way of Perfection,* ch. 21, no. 2.
38. Ibid., ch. 22, no. 2.
39. Ibid., ch. 21, no. 8.
40. *Camino de Perfección, Reproducción en facsímil del autógrafo de Valladolid,* vol. 2, p. 76.
41. *Way of Perfection,* ch. 3, no. 7.
42. See ibid.
43. See ibid., ch. 11, no. 4.
44. Cf. *Rule of St. Albert,* eds. H. Clarke and B. Edwards (Aylesford: Carmelite Priory, 1973).
45. *Way of Perfection,* ch. 13, no. 6.
46. Ibid., ch. 4, no. 9.
47. For a glimpse of life at the Incarnation, see P. Tomás Alvarez, "La visita del padre Rubeo a las carmelitas de La Encarnación de Avila (1567)," *Monte Carmelo* 86 (1978): 5-25. Cf. also D. De Pablo Maroto, "Camino De Perfección," *Introducción A La Lectura De Santa Teresa* (Madrid: Espiritualidad, 1978): 285-288.
48. *Way of Perfection,* ch. 27, no. 6.
49. Ibid., ch. 2, no. 8.
50. Ibid., no. 6.
51. Ibid., ch. 4, no. 7.
52. See ibid., ch. 1, no. 2.

53. See ibid., ch. 4, nos. 1-2.
54. See ibid., no. 4.
55. Ibid., prologue, no. 2.
56. See ibid., ch. 4, no. 12, note 8.
57. Ibid., ch. 41, no. 5.
58. Ibid., ch. 2, no. 8, note 4.
59. Ibid., ch. 7, no. 5.
60. Ibid., ch. 10, no. 2.
61. See ibid., ch. 11, no. 3.
62. Ibid., ch. 12, no. 5.
63. Ibid., ch. 13, no. 5, note 2.
64. Ibid., ch. 10, no. 3.
65. Ibid., ch. 16, no. 2.
66. Ibid., ch. 39, no. 2.
67. Ibid., ch. 38, no. 7.
68. Ibid., ch. 19, no. 1.
69. Ibid., ch. 19, no. 2.
70. Ibid.
71. Ibid., ch. 28, no. 4.
72. Ibid., ch. 29, no. 5.
73. Ibid., ch. 26, no. 3.
74. Ibid., ch. 29, no. 5.
75. Ibid., ch. 26, no. 3.
76. See ibid., ch. 29, no. 4.
77. Ibid., ch. 28, no. 7.
78. Ibid., no. 4.
79. Ibid., ch. 29, no. 7.
80. Ibid., no. 6.
81. See ibid., ch. 26, nos. 4, 5, 8.
82. Ibid., ch. 30, nos. 6-7.
83. Ibid., ch. 31, no. 6.
84. Ibid., ch. 42, no. 5.
85. Ibid., ch. 21, no. 2.

FOREWORD

1. Although St. Joseph's in Avila was founded by Teresa, she was not the first prioress. The first prioress was an older nun from the Incarnation, Ana de San Juan (Dávila), who was severe with Teresa, mortifying and humiliating her. After a short while this nun returned to the Incarnation because of bad health, and Teresa, near the beginning of March, 1563, was appointed prioress. She remained so until 1568, and certainly held office while writing this book.

2. This declaration of submission to the Roman Church was written later by Teresa in the copy of Toledo, which was sent for publication in 1579 to Don Teotonio de Braganza, archbishop of Evora.

PROLOGUE

1. An academic title, the equivalent of licentiate.
2. According to Teresa, Fr. Bañez was her confessor for six years, approximately from 1562 to 1568 (see *Spir. Test.*, 58, no. 8).
3. A reference to her *Life*, the second redaction of which was finished at St. Joseph's in Avila toward the end of 1565, before she started *The Way of Perfection.*

CHAPTER 2

1. Allusion to Lk. 21:33.
2. Here Teresa alludes to the social attitude in sixteenth-century Spain in which honor was reserved for people of the upper class or nobility. According to Philip II's *Pragmática*, titles were to be used only by the nobility. Poor people had no right to titles, and so were not honored or esteemed.
3. Teresa might have read such words, attributed to St. Clare, in St. Bonaventure's *Leyenda mayor de S. Francisco y S. Clara* (Toledo, 1526).
4. In the first redaction she wrote more emphatically: ". . . may such a building fall to the ground and kill you all the day you desire one. Moreover, I say this without remorse, and I'll beg it of God."
5. In the mind of Teresa the number of nuns in each community should be small. In 1561 she thought of fifteen (see *Letters*, to Lorenzo de Cepeda, Dec. 23, 1561). Later she spoke of thirteen (see *Life*, ch. 32, no. 13), that is, twelve nuns, representing the number of apostles, and the prioress, standing in the place of Christ. Initially, the monastery of the Incarnation at Avila was to have only fourteen nuns, twelve for the apostles, and two others for our Lord and our Lady. When Teresa, following that early tradition of the Incarnation, added the fifteenth it was to recall St. Joseph. In 1576, Fr. Gratian, as the apostolic commissary, established in accord with Teresa that there be thirteen or fourteen nuns, excluding the lay Sisters, in houses founded in poverty and twenty in those having an income. See *Biblioteca Mística Carmelitana*, ed. P. Silverio de Santa Teresa, O.C.D., 20 vols. (Burgos: El Monte Carmelo, 1915-35), 6:525 (hereafter cited a BMC).

CHAPTER 3

1. Namely, the two mentioned in the preceding paragraph, wherein is contained the apostolic element of the Teresian charism.
2. This paragraph was deleted in the first redaction by Fr. García de Toledo, who thought it was too daring for the attitude toward women that was characteristic of the times. Teresa complied and omitted the passage in the second redaction. Nevertheless, it is a stirring statement in favor of women and of what they can contribute to the Church and the world.
3. Lk. 9:58.
4. A reference to the Bishop of Avila, Don Alvaro de Mendoza (see *Life,* ch. 33, no. 16). In the Toledo manuscript she added in her own hand: ". . . and this order of the Blessed Virgin, and all the other orders."

CHAPTER 4

1. In the autograph (Valladolid) this chapter was divided so that a new chapter began after no. 4. Teresa decided to join them when preparing the copy of Toledo for printing. The chapter heading consists of what originally had been two different headings.
2. The rule states: "Each one of you is to stay in his own cell or nearby, pondering the Lord's law day and night and keeping watch at his prayers unless attending to some other duty." See *The Rule of St. Albert*, eds. H. Clarke, O. Carm. and B. Edwards, O.C.D. (Aylesford: Carmelite Priory, 1973), p.83.
3. See ch. 2, note 5.
4. This strong expression is a kind of Teresian anathema indicating a serious and contagious moral evil. See no. 8.
5. Biblical allusion to 1 P. 1:18-19.
6. See note 2.
7. Jn. 13:34.
8. Teresa was not satisfied with the way she wrote in her first redaction about this second type of love; in her second redaction she rewrote this part. But then she tore out the whole sheet and wrote what is contained in no. 13. The following is what she wrote in her first redaction: ". . . the other is spiritual and mixed with it our own sensuality and weakness. The important thing is that these two kinds of love are unaffected by any passion, for where passion is present the good order is thrown into complete

disorder. And if we love discreetly and moderately with the love I mentioned, all will be meritorious, for what seems to us to be sensuality will be converted into virtue. But the sensuality is so intermingled with the spiritual love that at times there is no one who understands this love, especially if it is for some confessor. For if persons who practice prayer see that he is holy and understands their mode of procedure, they will get to love him deeply. And here the devil batters one with scruples that disturb the soul very much, which is what the devil wants to do. If, especially, the confessor is leading the soul to higher perfection, the devil afflicts it so much that it abandons the confessor. And neither if it goes to another confessor nor again to another does the devil cease to torment it with that temptation.

What souls can do in this situation is to try not to think about whether they love the confessor or don't love him; but if they do love him, let them love him. For since we experience love for one who takes care of our bodies, shouldn't we also love one who always strives and works to care for our souls? Rather, I hold that a great principle for making much progress is to love the confessor, if he is holy and spiritual and if I see that he is diligent about my soul's progress. For our weakness is such that sometimes this love helps us very much to perform great deeds in the service of God. If the love is not of this kind, as I have said, there is danger; and the mere fact that he knows he is loved can do very serious harm, and in houses where there is a great deal of enclosure much more than in others. Because it is difficult to know which confessor is so good, there is need for much caution and prudence. The best advice is that the confessor not know that there is such affection and that no one tell him there is. But the devil so urges the soul to tell the confessor about this love that such advice becomes useless. It seems to the soul that all it has to confess is this affection and that it is obliged to confess it. For this reason I would like the Sisters to realize that this love doesn't amount to anything and pay no attention to it.

Let them take this counsel: if they know that the confessor directs all his words to the profit of their souls and they do not see or know of any other vanity (for this is soon understood by anyone who doesn't want to become a fool), and they know that he is God-fearing, they should not weary themselves over any temptation they may have about their great attachment; when the devil is worn out he will go away. But if they should become aware that the confessor is turning toward some vanity in what he says to them, they should be suspicious about it all and in no way carry on conversations with him even though these may concern prayer or God; but they should make their confession briefly and bring it to a conclusion. And it would be best to tell the Mother prioress that your soul doesn't get on well with him and change confessors. That would be the most proper thing to do, if there is the opportunity to do so, and I hope in God there will be. And you should do what you can to avoid speaking with him—even suffer death."

9. In no. 14.

CHAPTER 5

1. It is worth noting that this Teresian teaching on freedom for cloistered nuns with regard to confessors was later accepted by Church law.
2. The first redaction has a somewhat different slant: "Let her always try to speak to someone with learning; and her nuns should do so as well. May God deliver them from being ruled in everything by the confessor if he is not learned, no matter how spiritual he may seem to be or in fact is."
3. In her *Life* Teresa mentions several instances in which she received bad counsel: ch. 4, no. 7; ch. 5, no. 3; ch. 6, no. 4; ch. 8, no. 11; ch. 26, no. 3.
4. The first redaction continues: "And do not take away their freedom to confess at times with learned men and to discuss their prayer with them even though there are confessors. For many reasons I know that this is fitting and that the harm that might arise is nothing in comparison with the deception and great harm, almost without remedy, so to speak, that comes with the opposite practice. For what happens in monasteries is that good soon suffers a decline if it is not preserved with great care, and evil once it gets started is extremely difficult to get rid of because very quickly the custom becomes a habit and imperfections become natural."
5. In Teresa's time the vicar of a cloistered monastery of nuns was a priest appointed by the local bishop or provincial with special instructions concerning the government of the monastery.
6. The first redaction continues, with insistence: "For as I have said, after everything was considered, grave reasons were found for deciding that this was the best course of action, that is: that the chaplain, if there be one, serve as the ordinary confessor and that when a soul feels the need, confession may be made to per-

sons like the ones mentioned. These may be named by the bishop, or if the Mother prioress is such that the bishop entrusts this task to her, she may name them on her own. Since there are few nuns, they will take little of anyone's time. This practice was decided upon after much prayer by many persons including myself—although wretched—and among many persons of great learning, intelligence, and prayer. So I hope in the Lord it is the most fitting thing to do.

7. The reason the first monastery founded by Teresa was subject to the jurisdiction of the local bishop at Avila can be found in her *Life*, ch. 33, no. 16. See also the original petition to the Holy See in the latter part of 1561 as well as the brief "ex parte vestra" (Feb. 7, 1562) in *Monumenta Historica Carmeli Teresiani*, ed., *Institutum Historicum Teresianum* (Rome: Teresianum, 1973—), 1:5, 10.

CHAPTER 6

1. See ch. 4, no. 12. She intended to explain two kinds of love: one, purely spiritual; the other, mixed. She continues here the topic of purely spiritual love.

CHAPTER 7

1. See ch. 6, nos. 6, 9.
2. See ch. 6, no. 9.
3. In no. 4.
4. See ch. 2, note 5.
5. The first redaction concludes in the following way: "Because I shall treat of this elsewhere, I'll say no more about it here, except that even though your love may not be as perfect as that just mentioned, provided that it goes out toward all in general, I would rather you love one another with tenderness and delight than that there be a moment of discord. May the Lord not permit such discord because of who His Majesty is. Amen."

CHAPTER 8

1. See ch. 2, note 5.
2. Our Lord called Teresa from the monastery of the Incarnation in Avila where there were more than 180 nuns to found the little monastery of St. Joseph where the number was lowered to thirteen.

CHAPTER 9

1. In no. 2.

CHAPTER 10

1. Allusion to Ex. 16; Wis. 16:20.
2. The first redaction puts it more strongly: "Sometimes they feel a frenzy for doing penance without rhyme or reason, a frenzy that lasts only a couple of days, so to speak. Subsequently, the devil makes them imagine that the penances did them harm. No more penance! Not even, after some attempts, what the order commands."

CHAPTER 12

1. In ch. 11, no. 5.
2. See ch. 11, no. 4.
3. See no. 1; ch. 11, no. 5.
4. The first redaction adds: "Perform some public mortification also since they are practiced in this house. Flee these temptations of the devil as you would a plague, and don't allow him to stay with you."
5. In no. 6.
6. Jb. 2:9-13.

CHAPTER 13

1. Allusion to Lk. 1:48-52; 14:11.
2. The first redaction goes on at greater length and is put more strongly: "Oh, what a great act of charity and what a great service to God a nun would perform if when she sees that she cannot follow the practices of perfection and customs of this house she would recognize the fact and go, and leave the others in peace! And they shouldn't keep her in any of the monasteries—at least if they believe me—nor allow her to make profession until after many years of trial to see if she makes amends. I am not referring to failures in the penance and fasts. Even though these are faults, such failures are not things that cause so much harm. But I am speaking about persons who by temperament like to be esteemed and honored and who look at the faults of others and never at their own, and other similar things that truly arise from lack of humility. If God doesn't favor her with a great spiritual gift and if after many years you don't see her make amends, may He free you so that she doesn't remain in your company. Realize that she won't be at peace nor will she allow anyone else to be. Since you do not accept a dowry, God grants you the freedom to send a nun away. What I pity about monasteries is that often, so as not to return the money, they allow the thief to steal the treasure from them, or they do so for the sake of the relatives' honor. In

this house you have risked and lost the honor of this world, for the poor receive no honor. Don't desire that others have it at such a cost to yourselves. Our honor, Sisters, must be to serve God. If someone becomes a hindrance to your doing this, she should remain at home with her honor. For this reason our fathers ordained a one-year probation, and in our order we have the faculty to delay the profession for four years. And in this house I would like to delay it even ten years. A humble nun will not mind a delay of profession. She already knows that if she is good they will not dismiss her; if she is not good, why does she desire to do harm to this college of Christ? In saying 'not good,' I am not speaking of some vanity; for, with God's help, I hope such a thing will stay far from this house. In saying 'not good,' I mean not being mortified but being attached to worldly things or to oneself in the matters I have mentioned. And the nun who doesn't see much detachment in herself should believe me and not make profession, if she doesn't want to have a hell here below. And please God she will not have another in the next life, for there are many things in her that could cause such a misfortune; and perhaps those in the house will not understand them, nor perhaps will she, as I have understood them."

CHAPTER 14

1. In sixteenth-century Spain only the first-born male was entitled to the inheritance. Convent life, as a result, provided a secure future for many girls, and they often entered a monastery without a vocation.

CHAPTER 15

1. See ch. 11, no. 5; ch. 16, nos. 1-2.
2. The first redaction goes on in greater detail: "These false accusations, no matter how serious, did not disturb me. But in little things I followed my nature—and continue to follow it—without paying attention to what is more perfect. Hence I would like each of you to begin early to understand and reflect upon the much that is gained through all the various ways, and that no one, in my opinion, loses by following any of them. The main thing gained is that in some manner we follow the Lord. I say 'in some manner,' because, as I have mentioned, we are never blamed without our having faults."
3. Allusion to Prv. 24:16; 1 Jn. 1:8-10.
4. 1 Cor. 14:34.

5. Lk. 7:36-40; 10:38. Mary Magdalene, the repentant sinner, and Mary of Bethany were generally in Teresa's surroundings thought to be the same person.
6. Lk. 23:41.

CHAPTER 16

1. The first four paragraphs constituted a separate chapter in the first redaction under the heading: "Treats of how necessary it was to mention the things above in order to begin explaining prayer." Teresa copied the four paragraphs in her second redaction but then tore them out, perhaps after having had second thoughts about the advisability of using a "vanity" like the game of chess as an example. After tearing out this short chapter she failed to revise the numbering; thus, a number is missed in the enumeration of the chapters. This chapter 16, then, of the second redaction begins with the fifth paragraph, or number 5. But all editors, from Luis de León to those of the present day, have included these delightful paragraphs in which the chess game provides Teresa with an opportunity for some profound insights and illustrations.
2. These virtues are humility and keeping silent when falsely accused. See ch. 15, nos. 2-3.
3. Allusion to Sg. 4:9.
4. See *Life*, ch. 8, no. 4.
5. The first redaction contains some important differences: "It often happens that the Lord favors a soul that is in a very wretched state. It should be understood that it is not then in mortal sin, in my opinion. God will permit someone who is in mortal sin to see a vision—even a very good one—so as to bring that person back to Himself. But I cannot believe that He would place such a person in contemplation. For in that divine union the Lord delights in the soul and the soul in Him. It's incongruous that the purity of heaven would delight in a soul stained with sin or that the delight of the angels would find comfort in what is not His. Now we know that by sinning mortally a soul belongs to the devil; it can delight in him since it has satisfied him, and we already know that his delights are a continual torment even in this life. The Lord will always have devoted sons in whom He can be consoled. He has no need to go about taking those who do not belong to Him, although His Majesty will do what He often does: snatch them from the devil's hands."
6. See Mt. 4:5.

7. In the first redaction Teresa wrote and then crossed out the following: "...and how well he deserved on account of his boldness that God should create a new hell for him."
8. In no. 6.
9. Allusion to Mt. 21:3.
10. See Ep. 6:9; Ac. 10:34.
11. In no. 6.

CHAPTER 17

1. The monastery of St. Joseph in Avila.
2. In ch. 12, nos. 6-7.
3. Lk. 14:10.
4. In ch. 5, no. 5.
5. The first redaction is more explicit: "I know an elderly nun—please God my life were as good as hers—who is very holy and penitential. She is a great nun and recites much vocal and very ordinary prayer."
6. See *Life*, ch. 15, no. 14; ch. 17, no. 3; ch. 20, nos. 7, 29.
7. Lk. 10:38-40.
8. Allusion to Lk. 10:41-42.
9. In no. 2.

CHAPTER 18

1. Allusion to Lk. 10:42, of which she spoke in ch. 17, no. 5.
2. The first redaction is more strongly worded: "And how much better is the pay than that of those who serve the king! The poor soldiers are continuously in danger of death, and then only God knows how they are paid." Some authors think this passage reveals Teresa's worries about her brothers who were among the conquistadors.
3. In ch. 30, no. 7.
4. In chapter one of her *Constitutions*, Teresa sets aside two hours daily for mental prayer in common, one in the morning and one in the evening.
5. In the first redaction the military metaphor is preserved: "You don't know when the captain will call you and give you more work, disguised in delight. If he doesn't, you should understand that you are not suited for it and that such a situation is what is fitting for you."
6. Allusion to Mt. 25:1-13.
7. See no. 4 and ch. 17, no. 6.
8. Allusion to Mt. 20:22.

CHAPTER 19

1. She no doubt has in mind the very popular book by Fray Luis de Granada, O.P., *Libro de Oración y Meditación*, published in Salamanca in 1554 and included in the brief list of books she recommended for the library of each of her convents. See *Constitutions*, ch. 2.
2. Jn. 4:14.
3. Allusion to Sg. 8:7.
4. See Ps. 8:7. The censor, disagreeing with Teresa's interpretation, crossed out this section and noted in the margin: "This is not the meaning of the scriptural passage; it refers to Christ and to Adam as he was in the state of innocence."
5. In ch. 16, nos. 6-13.
6. Note that for Teresa the "living water" refers to contemplation, in contrast to the "muddy water" which refers to discursive prayer.
7. She is speaking of herself. See *Life*, ch. 20; *Spir. Test.*, 1. The first redaction reads as follows: "So great was her thirst, so much was her desire increasing that she understood clearly it would have been possible to die of love if the raptures hadn't soothed the thirst. Blessed be He who in His Gospel invites us to drink! Thus, since in our Lord and our Good there cannot be anything imperfect, He gives us what we need; it belongs to Him alone to give us this water."
8. In no. 8.
9. See Ph. 1:23.
10. This account can be found in Cassian's *Conferences.* See Philip Schaff and Henry Wace, gen. ed., *The Nicene and Post-Nicene Fathers*, Series Two, 14 vols. (Grand Rapids: Eerdmans, 1964), vol. 11: *The Second Conference of Abbot Moses*, p. 310. Most probably Teresa knew of this story from the *Vida de los Santos Padres* published in Zaragosa, 1511. In the process of beatification Petronila Bautista tells of Teresa's enthusiasm for the conferences of Cassian. "She was very devoted to the *Conferences* of Cassian and of the Fathers of the Desert, and so when this witness was with her the Holy Mother asked her to read two or three accounts of those saints each day and at night tell her about them since she herself didn't have the time to do so because of her just and holy occupations . . ." BMC, 19:591.
11. In no. 2.
12. This quotation probably amounts to a combination of Jn. 7:37 and Mt. 11:28.

CHAPTER 20

1. In ch. 17, no. 2.
2. Allusion to Jn. 14:2.
3. Allusion to Pr. 1:20; Jn. 7:37.

CHAPTER 21

1. She returns to the theme she began to deal with in ch. 19, nos. 1-2.
2. Allusion to Jn. 4:14.
3. In the first redaction she refers to certain books she had read: ". . . and although I have read in some books, and even in several, how good it is to begin with such an attitude, nothing will be lost, in my opinion, by mentioning it here."
4. A reference to ch. 19, no. 2.
5. In the first redaction she refers to her *Life*: "I will deal only briefly with the more sublime things, for, as I say, I have already written about them."

   The last line of the text alludes to the prohibition in 1559 by the Inquisitor, Don Fernando Valdés, of spiritual books written in the vernacular. See *Life*, ch. 26, no. 5; also below, note 8 and ch. 38, no. 1.
6. In the beginning she had the intention of writing about both the Our Father and the Hail Mary. See ch. 24, no. 2; ch. 42, no. 4.
7. Mt. 11:12.
8. A new reference to the matter mentioned in note 5 of this chapter. One of the censors objected to the statement by commenting in the margin: "It seems here that she is reprimanding the Inquisitors who prohibited books on prayer." Teresa excluded the sentence from her second redaction and crossed it out in her first redaction.
9. In no. 5.
10. "Each of you is to remain in his cell or nearby day and night meditating on the law of the Lord and watching in prayer. . ." See *The Rule of Saint Albert*, Eds. H. Clarke, O. Carm. and B. Edwards, O.C.D. (Aylesford: Carmelite Priory, 1973), pp. 82-83.

CHAPTER 22

1. In her visit to Doña Luisa de la Cerda. See *Life*, ch. 34.
2. The first redaction adds: "For, though being what I am, I would like to shout and argue with those who say mental prayer is not necessary."

3. The first redaction concludes: "Don't let anyone frighten you with these fears. Praise God, for He is all powerful and will not let them take mental prayer away from you. On the contrary, anyone who cannot pray vocally with this attention should realize that he isn't fulfilling his obligation. He must strive for this attention with every effort—if he wants to pray with perfection—under pain of not doing what is required of the bride of so great a King. Beg Him, daughters, to give me the grace to do what I am counseling you to do, for I fail very much in this matter. May His Majesty provide because of who He is."

CHAPTER 23

1. Allusion to Jn. 4:14.
2. In ch. 19, no. 15.
3. Allusion to Mt. 19:29.
4. Lk. 11:9.
5. The first redaction concludes as follows: "This is absolutely true; I know it is so. If they don't find this is true, they shouldn't believe me in anything I say. Sisters, you already know it through experience; and, through the goodness of God, I can present you as witnesses. What has been said is good for those who are to come."

CHAPTER 24

1. She takes up once more the subject mentioned in ch. 19, no. 2 and also in ch. 21, no. 3.
2. In ch. 5, no. 5; ch. 17, no. 2; ch. 20, no. 1. See also *Life*, ch. 13, no. 13; ch. 22, no. 2; *Interior Castle*, VI, ch. 7, no. 12; *Foundations*, ch. 5, no. 1.
3. Mt. 6:6.
4. Allusion to Lk. 6:12.
5. In ch. 22, no. 8.

CHAPTER 25

1. A reference to *The Book of Her Life*. See also above, prol., no. 4. In the *Life* she explains at length the nature of contemplation. See chs. 14-21 and chs. 22-31. See especially ch. 14, nos. 2,6; ch. 18, no. 14.
2. In the first redaction this number reads quite differently: "It is all explained well in the book I mentioned I wrote, and thus there is no reason to deal with it here in any particular way. There, I said everything I knew. If God brings any among you to

this state of contemplation—for, as I said, some of you are in it—you should strive to obtain that book after I die; it will mean a lot to you. Those of you who are not in this state will have no reason to do anything but struggle to carry out what is mentioned in this book I'm writing now, to make progress in as many ways as you can, and to use diligence; for the Lord will grant you the ability to do these things if you beg Him for it and adopt the proper measures. As for the rest, the Lord Himself will give it and not deny it to anyone who reaches the end of the journey by fighting as has been said."

CHAPTER 26

1. In ch. 24, no. 2.
2. Sg. 2:14.
3. Allusion to Ru. 1:16.
4. The first redaction reads: ". . . grow accustomed to recalling that the Lord is present within you and to speaking with Him often . . ."

CHAPTER 27

1. Mt. 6:9.
2. The expressions "to enter within itself" and "to rise above itself" were current among writers of the time. As used here, the first refers to the act of interior recollection; the second to mystical prayer. In other places Teresa criticizes the theory which urges the soul to rise above itself through its own efforts. See *Life*, ch. 22, nos. 1-7; *Interior Castle*, IV, ch. 3, nos. 2, 6.
3. Allusion to Mt. 24:35; Mk. 13:31; Lk. 21:33.
4. Allusion to Lk. 15:11-32.
5. Allusion to Ep. 3:15; 2 P. 1:4.
6. Allusion to Jn. 17:21; 10:30; 8:29.
7. One of the censors wrote in the margin: "I don't know where she got this." She could have read it in the *Flos Sanctorum* of her time. From the etymology *Bar-tholomaeus*, son of Ptolemaeus, it was deduced that the Apostle was a descendant of the Ptolemies.
8. The first redaction reads: "And if something of this attitude is present in one of the nuns, don't consent to having her in the house; she is a Judas among the apostles. Do all you can to free yourselves from such bad company. And if you cannot do this, punish her with more severe penances than you would use for any other fault, until she recognizes that she doesn't deserve to be made from even a very wretched kind of mud. The good Jesus

gives you a good Father. Let no one in this house speak about any other father than the one your Spouse has given you."

CHAPTER 28

1. Mt. 6:9
2. A reference either to pseudo-Augustinian *Soliloquies,* ch. 31; or to the *Confessions,* X, ch. 27. See *Life,* ch. 40, no. 6.
3. Allusion to Ps. 55:7.

CHAPTER 29

1. In ch. 28, no. 2.
2. Ps. 34:19.
3. She takes up again the theme of ch. 28, nos. 2, 11-13, mentioned in the heading of this chapter.
4. Allusion to Jn. 15:5.
5. She is probably alluding to *The Ascent of Mount Sion* by Bernardino de Laredo, trans. E. A. Peers (London: Faber and Faber, Ltd., 1950).

CHAPTER 30

1. Mt. 26:39.
2. Mt. 6:9-10.
3. In the revised manuscript of Toledo, Teresa states more specifically: ". . . the holy Roman Church."
4. In ch. 25, no. 1.
5. In the first redaction she adds the detail that this person was an elderly nun.

CHAPTER 31

1. In ch. 30, no. 6.
2. Lk. 2:29
3. Mt. 17:4
4. Teresa is speaking of herself. According to an annotation she made in the ms. of Toledo, the "great contemplative" she consulted was St. Francis Borgia, S.J.
5. Lk. 18:13; actually ". . . the publican would not even lift up his eyes to heaven. . ."
6. The two faculties are the intellect and the memory. See no. 3. It is the will alone that is in the state of quiet. The intellect that is "so distracted" includes the imagination. In the ms. of Toledo above the word "intellect" Teresa wrote "or imagination." A little further on when speaking of paying no more attention to the

intellect than to a madman, she wrote, in the ms. of Toledo, above the word "intellect," "or mind or imagination, for I don't know what it is." And again in no. 10 of the ms. of Toledo, to "that which torments the will is the intellect," she added "or imagination."

7. In no. 6.
8. In no. 4.

CHAPTER 32

1. In the first redaction this passage reads: "Don't be like some nuns that do nothing but promise; and since they don't keep anything, they say they didn't understand what they promised when they made profession. I believe this because it is easy to talk and difficult to act. And if they thought that words are equal to deeds, they certainly didn't understand. Make those who will profess vows here learn through a long trial period not to think their life will amount to words alone, without deeds also. So I want you to know whom you are dealing with, as they say, and what the good Jesus offers the Father through you and what you are giving when you pray that His will be done in you, for you are giving nothing else than that."
2. Mt. 26:39.
3. In ch. 19.
4. In ch. 29, no. 4.

CHAPTER 33

1. In the preceding chapter.
2. In no. 1.
3. Mt. 3:15.
4. In the Castilian version of the Our Father the order in the petition would literally be: "Give us our daily bread this day."
5. Mt. 26:15.

CHAPTER 34

1. The first redaction contains some further thoughts: "In writing this I have felt the desire to know why, after the Lord said 'daily,' He then repeated by saying 'this day.' I want to tell you of my foolish reflections. If they are foolish, so be it because it is foolish enough of me to get involved in this explanation. But since we are learning about what we are asking for, let us think carefully about what it is so that, as I have said, we may appreciate its value and be thankful to Him who with so much care is teaching us."

2. In the first redaction she went on more at length: "With regard to the unfortunate ones who will be condemned, who will not enjoy Him in the next life, He did all He could for their profit and to be with them on 'this day' of this life to strengthen them. If they let themselves be conquered, it will not be His fault. And so as to win consent from the Father, He reminds Him that it will be for only a day."
3. Allusion to Ex. 16:3-4.
4. In chs. 2 and 8.
5. Teresa is referring to herself. See *Life,* ch. 30, no. 14; *Spir. Test.,* 1, no. 23
6. Allusion to Lk. 7:36-48. See also *Life,* ch. 22, note 20 in *The Collected Works of St. Teresa of Avila,* vol. 1, p. 296.
7. Allusion to Mt. 9:20-22; Lk. 8:43-44.
8. Allusion to Mt. 20:22.
9. The first redaction adds: "reflect that this is a most advantageous hour for the soul, during which Jesus is very pleased if you keep Him company. Take great care, daughters, not to lose it."
10. Here Teresa left out an interesting remark from the first redaction: "I don't say that you shouldn't recite vocal prayers (don't take me literally and say that I am dealing with contemplation—unless the Lord places you in it), but that if you recite the Our Father you should understand how truly you are present with Him who taught it to you, kiss His feet in gratitude for it, and beg Him not to leave you."
11. In the first redaction she was more explicit: "It is a wonderful comfort to see an image of our Lady or of some saint to whom we are devoted—how much more of Christ—and something that greatly awakens devotion and that I would like to see at every turn of my head and glance of my eyes."
12. In nos. 5, 10.

CHAPTER 35

1. In ch. 3, nos. 8-10.
2. Allusion to Lk. 11:9.
3. The first redaction contains a further lament: "For it seems they want to cast Him out of the world by tearing down sacred buildings, killing so many priests, profaning so many churches—even Christians sometimes go to church more with the intention of offending Him than of worshiping Him."
4. Allusion to Mt. 8:25-26.

CHAPTER 36

1. Mt. 6:12.
2. In the manuscript of Toledo Teresa wrote in the margin: "Blessed be God! Such a thing does not apply to this house. To say it does would be untrue because the one who has been prioress is the one who afterward humbles herself most. But I say this because it is so common in other monasteries that I fear the devil will tempt us in this way. I consider it so dangerous that, please God, no soul. . ."
3. In no. 2.
4. In chs. 25 and 26.
5. In ch. 18.
6. In nos. 8-9.

CHAPTER 37

1. In the first redaction she alludes to her *Life*: ". . .for if I had not written about it elsewhere—and also so as not to go on at greater length, which would be a bother—a large book on prayer could be written. . ."
2. In no. 2.
3. In the first redaction, instead of the preceding passage and the previous number, we read: "Blessed be His name forever and ever, amen! And I ask the Eternal Father through Him to forgive my debts and great sins—for I have had no one nor anything to forgive, and every day I have something that needs to be forgiven—and give me grace so that one day I may have something to offer with my petition. That we might in some way appear to be sons of such a Father and brothers of such a Brother, Jesus taught us this sublime way of prayer and petitioned that we be angelic beings in this exile—provided that we strive with every effort to make our deeds conform to our words. We may thus know that if, as I mention, we do what we say, the Lord will not fail to accomplish what we ask, will give us His kingdom, and help with supernatural things (the prayer of quiet and perfect contemplation and the other favors the Lord grants us in such prayer in return for our efforts). Everything is small as far as what we can strive for and obtain on our own. But since this is what we ourselves can do, very certainly the Lord will help us because His Son asks this for us."

CHAPTER 38

1. In ch. 36, nos. 8-10.

2. Allusion to 2 Co. 11:14.
3. Allusion to 1 Co. 10:13.
4. The first redaction goes into more detail, but the Spanish of the passage is obscure and confusing. Here is an attempt at translation: "For without our realizing it, while it seems to us that we are proceeding safely, we cause ourselves to fall into a pit we cannot escape from. Although it may not always be a matter of a known mortal sin which would bring us to hell, it will weaken our legs along this road I began to tell you about—for I have not forgotten. Well you know how a person advances when he's bogged in a pit: his life ends there, and he will be doing enough if he doesn't keep from sinking lower, on into hell; he never improves. Since he doesn't improve, being there is of benefit neither to himself nor to others; rather, it does harm. For since the pit is dug out, many others who go along the way can also fall into it. If he gets out and covers it over with dirt, he does no harm to himself or to others. But I tell you that this temptation is very dangerous; I know much about it through experience, and so I am able to tell you about it; although not as well as I should like.

   The devil makes you think you are poor and makes even others who practice prayer think this of themselves. And he is somewhat right because you have promised poverty—orally, that is. I say orally, for it is impossible that, if with the heart we understand what we promise and then promise it, the devil could draw us for twenty years and even our whole lives into this temptation; 'impossible,' because we would see that we are deceiving the world and our own selves.

   Well now, someone thinking he is poor or after having promised poverty will say: 'I don't want anything; I have this because I can't get along without it; the fact is I have to live in order to serve God. God wants us to care for these bodies.' The devil, like an angel, teaches a thousand different kinds of things here—for all these things are good—and so he makes the soul think it is already poor and has this virtue, that everything is accomplished. Now let us come to the test; for this deception of the devil is not recognized in any other way than by always checking carefully one's attitudes; and if care is taken a sign will be given very soon: the person has more income than he needs (I mean than he really needs, that if he can manage with one servant he not have three); someone brings a lawsuit against him for some of it, or a poor peasant fails to pay his rent, and the person becomes so disturbed and makes such a big issue of it that one would think he couldn't live without the money. He will say that he has to be a good administrator—for there is always some excuse. I don't say that he should give everything up but that he should strive to know whether what he is doing is good or not. For the truly poor person holds these things in so little esteem that, though for some reason he obtains them, they are never the cause of disturbance; he never thinks he will be in want. And if he does lack something, he doesn't care much; he considers this an accessory and not the main thing. Since he has higher thoughts, only reluctantly does he become involved with money.

If he is a religious, whether man or woman (for it is already verified that such a person is religious, at least should be), he may not have anything because sometimes nobody gives him anything. But if somebody gives him something, it's a wonder if he thinks it to be more than enough. He always likes to hold on to something. If he can have a habit made out of fine cloth he doesn't ask for one from rough cloth. He keeps some little things he can pawn or sell, even though they may be books; for if a sickness comes he will need more comfort than usual.

Sinner that I am! Here now; is that what you promised? Forget yourselves and surrender to God come what may. If you go about providing for the future, it would be better for you to have a fixed revenue. Even though this may be done without sin, it's good that we understand these imperfections so as to see that we are far from having this virtue; and we may then ask for it from God and strive for it. In thinking that we have it, we become careless and mistaken, which is worse.

This also happens to us in regard to humility: it seems to us we don't want honor or that we couldn't care less about anything. The occasion arises in which a point of honor is at stake, and at once, in what you feel and do, you realize that you are not humble. For if something brings you more honor, you do not renounce it—nor do those we mentioned even who are poor in spirit—for the sake of growing more in humility. And please God they will not go seeking out honor! And so often do some repeat that they don't want anything or care about anything that as a matter of fact they think this is so. Even the habit of saying it makes them believe it more."

5. Allusion to Mk. 14:38-39; see also Mt. 6:13.
6. In nos. 6-7.

CHAPTER 39

1. For Teresa's own experience in this matter see *Life*, ch. 7, nos. 1, 11; ch. 8, no. 5.
2. In place of the above paragraphs the first redaction has the following: "Well be on guard, daughters, against some humble thoughts, caused by the devil, with their great disquiet over the seriousness of past sins, about whether I deserve to approach Communion or whether I have prepared myself well or about my unworthiness to live with good people; things of this sort. When such thoughts come with quiet, calm, and delight, they should be esteemed because they bring self-knowledge. But if they come with agitation, disquiet, and oppression of soul, and if the mind cannot be quieted, believe that they are a temptation and don't consider yourselves humble; humility doesn't come in this way."

CHAPTER 40

1. In ch. 38, nos. 3-4.
2. She writes about it in ch. 41.
3. Allusion to Ps. 89:50.
4. In ch. 16, nos. 6-8; ch. 25, nos. 1-4.
5. Teresa expressed herself more strongly in the first redaction: "As I say, then, this love is recognized when it is present, just as the love between a man and woman cannot be concealed; the more it is hidden the more it seems to reveal itself. However, since the love is for nothing but a worm, it doesn't even deserve the name 'love'; for it is founded on nothing—it's disgusting to make this comparison. And could one conceal a love so strong as is love of God, founded on such cement, having so much to love and so many reasons for loving? In sum, it is love and merits the name 'love,' for where it is present the vanities of the world must be shunned."
6. After "the bad inn lasts for only a night," the first redaction ends briefly with: "Let us praise God and always beseech Him to keep us in His hands, and all sinners as well, and not lead us into these hidden temptations."

CHAPTER 41

1. The first redaction continues thus: "Now let us deal with the fear of God, although I feel badly about not speaking for a while of this love of the world, for I know it well—on account of my sins—and I should like to teach you about it so that you might free yourselves from it forever. But because I am getting off the subject I will have to let this go."

2. See ch. 40, note 2.
3. In ch. 40, no. 3; ch. 16, nos. 6-9.
4. In nos. 1,3.
5. In no. 3.
6. In nos. 5-6.
7. The first redaction has a richer conclusion: "Here you see how with these two virtues—love and fear of God—you can advance on this road with calm and not think that at every step you see a ditch you could fall into; that way you would never arrive. But since we cannot even know with certitude that we in truth have these two virtues that are necessary, the Lord, taking pity on us because we live in so uncertain a life and among so many temptations and dangers, teaching us to ask—and asking for us—says with good reason: *But deliver us from evil. Amen.*"

CHAPTER 42
1. Lk. 22:15.
2. Allusion to 1 Jn. 1:10.
3. In Ph. 4:13.
4. Allusion to Ml. 3:20.
5. She speaks at length of this fount of living water in ch. 19.
6. She is referring to *The Book of her Life*.

MEDITATIONS ON THE SONG OF SONGS

INTRODUCTION
1. See Prologue and ch. 1, no. 8.
2. Ch. 1, no. 8.
3. See ibid.
4. Ch. 1, no. 4.
5. Ch. 1, no. 6.
6. Ch. 1, no. 8.
7. Prologue, no. 1.
8. Ch. 6, no. 8.
9. Ch. 1, no. 8.
10. *Life*, ch. 15, no. 8.
11. Ch. 1, no. 11.
12. See ch. 1, no. 8.
13. Ch. 1, no. 2.
14. See ch. 6, no. 7.

15. Cf. *Interior Castle*, VI, ch. 10, no. 5; *Life*, ch. 23, nos. 1-5.
16. Cf. *Interior Castle*, VII, ch. 1, nos. 6-7; *Spiritual Testimonies*, 13; 65, no. 9.
17. Cf. *Spiritual Testimonies*, 3, no. 10; *Life*, ch. 6, no. 9; ch. 18, no. 14; *Interior Castle*, V, ch. 2, no. 4; VII, ch. 2, no. 5.
18. Cf. *Interior Castle*, VII, ch. 2, nos. 6-7; VII, ch. 3, no. 13.
19. See ch. 6, no. 8.
20. See *Biblioteca Mística Carmelitana*, ed. Silverio de Santa Teresa, vol. 18 (Burgos: El Monte Carmelo 1934), p. 320.
21. See ibid., vol. 20 (1935), p. 349.
22. In ch. 1, no. 8.
23. See ch. 3, no. 8.
24. In ch. 7, no. 2.
25. In ch. 4, no. 1.
26. For further details on some of these matters see D. De Pablo Maroto, "Meditaciones Sobre Los Cantares," *Introducción A La Lectura De Santa Teresa* (Madrid: Espiritualidad, 1978), pp. 383-391; Pietro della Madre di Dio, "La Sacra Scrittura nelle Opere di S. Teresa di Gesu," *Rivista Di Vita Spirituale* 18 (1964): 41-102; and Tomás De La Cruz, "Santa Teresa De Jesús Contemplativa," *Ephemerides Carmeliticae* 13 (1962): 9-62.

PROLOGUE

1. About five lines are missing from the first page which is torn.
2. The prologue is incomplete for the same reason given in note 1.

CHAPTER 1

1. The liturgy on Holy Thursday recalls Jesus' washing of the disciples' feet and the *mandatum novum* (the new commandment of love). See Jn. 13:1-17, 34.
2. In no. 5; she is referring to herself.
3. In no. 1.
4. In no. 2.
5. Allusion to the *Life* and the *Way of Perfection*.
6. In ch. 2. no. 16.

CHAPTER 2

1. Allusion to Jb. 7:1.
2. In chs. 4-7.
3. In no. 2.
4. Allusion to Mt. 25:1-14.
5. Allusion to Lk. 12:16-21.

6. In no. 7.
7. The "discipline" is a term used to refer to the practice of self-scourging with knotted cords, a method of physical penance commonly performed in monastic orders. According to Teresa's *Constitutions* the discipline of cords is to be taken on Monday, Wednesday, and Friday.
8. In Teresa's *Constitutions* the woolen tunics are to be made of coarse material.
9. The *Constitutions* of Teresa also state that the Sisters, as the rule commands, are never to eat meat except out of necessity.
10. The topic begun in no. 6, and then set aside.
11. In ch. 1, no. 2.
12. See *Way of Perfection*, ch. 18, no. 2; ch. 32, no. 7; ch. 41, no. 8; *Interior Castle*, II, ch. 1, no. 6; VI, ch. 4; ch. 5, nos. 1, 6 and 12.
13. See *Foundations*, ch. 6, nos. 9-13, 18-19.
14. The first has to do with the world, its comforts and enjoyments (no. 22); the second with honor and esteem (no. 26).
15. Mt. 14:29.
16. See *Way of Perfection*, ch. 42, nos. 3-4; *Life*, ch. 13, nos. 3-6; *Interior Castle*, I, ch. 2, no. 10.
17. St. Diego of Alcalá (d. 1463) was a popular saint in Teresa's time because of the miraculous cure of Prince Charles in 1563 which was attributed to him.

CHAPTER 3

1. In no. 1.
2. She is speaking of St. Paulinus of Nola (353-431).
3. This person was Alonso de Cordobilla. He sailed from Cádiz and died in Gibraltar October 28, 1566.
4. Mk. 14:38.
5. Mt. 26:38.
6. Sg. 1:2.

CHAPTER 4

1. She alludes to *Life*, chs. 14-15 and *Way of Perfection,* chs. 30-31, where she deals with the prayer of quiet.
2. See above note 1.
3. See this same comparison made in *Way of Perfection,* ch. 31, no. 9.
4. Rm. 8:18.
5. Sg. 6:3; 2:16.
6. See the corresponding locutions relative to the spiritual marriage in *Interior Castle,* VII, ch. 2, no. 1, ch. 3, no. 2; *Spir. Test.*, 31.

7. See *Confessions of St. Augustine,* X, ch. 29.
8. Sg. 2:16.

CHAPTER 5
1. Sg. 2:3-4.
2. Allusion to Wis. 16:20.
3. Lk. 1:35.
4. Ac. 9:3-11.
5. Allusion to Sg. 2:5.
6. See ch. 4, nó. 1; she is alluding to either the *Life* or the *Way of Perfection.*

CHAPTER 6
1. Allusion to Sg. 2:3.
2. In her monastery where she is writing; possibly in Avila.
3. Lk. 1:34-35.
4. Sg. 4:7.
5. Sg. 6:10.
6. Sg. 2:5.

CHAPTER 7
1. She is referring to her experience in Salamanca, 1571, described in *Spir. Test.,* 12; see also *Interior Castle,* VI, ch. 11, nos. 8-10.
2. See *Life,* ch. 30, no. 19.
3. Allusion to Jn. 4:39-43.
4. Sg. 8:4.
5. In ch. 4, nos. 4-5.
6. She is alluding probably to her *Life,* ch. 13, nos. 8-10.

THE INTERIOR CASTLE

INTRODUCTION
1. Antonio De San Joaquin, "Anotaciones al P. Ribera," *Año Teresiano,* 12 vols. (Madrid, 1733-1769), 8:149-150.
2. I, ch. 2, no. 7; see also IV, ch. 1, no. 1; ch. 2, no. 7.
3. Prologue, no. 1.
4. For a detailed treatment of this whole question, cf. Efrén de La Madre de Dios and Otger Steggink, *Tiempo Y Vida De Santa Teresa* (Madrid: BAC, 1977), pp. 701-805; cf. also Ildefonso Moriones, *El Carmelo Teresiano* (Vitoria: Ediciones El Carmen, 1978), pp. 97-180. For a treatment of these questions from a

different perspective, cf. Joachim Smet, *The Carmelites: The Post Tridentine Period,* vol. 2 (Darien, Ill.: Carmelite Spiritual Center, 1976), pp.1-131.

5. *Letters,* October 22, 1577.
6. IV, ch. 2, no. 1.
7. V, ch. 4, no. 1.
8. Prologue, no. 1.
9. Ibid.
10. Epilogue, no. 1.
11. VI, ch. 4, no. 9.
12. IV, ch. 1, no. 1; see also V, ch. 4, no. 11.
13. *Biblioteca Mística Carmelitana,* ed., Silverio de Santa Teresa, vol. 18 (Burgos: El Monte Carmelo 1934), p. 315.
14. I, ch. 1, no. 1.
15. *Way of Perfection,* ch. 28, no. 9.
16. *Biblioteca Mística,* vol. 18, pp. 276-278.
17. Ibid., vol. 2 (1915), p. 493.
18. *Life,* ch. 40, no. 5.
19. Cf. no. 10.
20. Cf. I, ch. 1, nos. 2-3.
21. Epilogue, no. 3.
22. Cf. I, ch. 1, no. 7.
23. Cf. ibid., nos. 6, 8.
24. I, ch. 2, no. 14.
25. Cf. VII, ch. 4, no. 9.
26. Cf. III, ch. 1, no. 5
27. Cf. III, ch. 2, nos. 4-5,7,8.
28. Cf. III, ch. 2, no. 13; ch. 1, no. 7.
29. Cf. III, ch. 2, no. 9.
30. I, ch. 2, no. 7.
31. Cf. Tomás de la Cruz, "Santa Teresa de Jesús Contemplativa," *Ephemerides Carmeliticae* 13(1962): 9-62.
32. Cf. IV, ch. 1, no. 1.
33. Cf. ibid., no. 4.
34. Ibid., no. 7.
35. Ibid.
36. Cf. IV. ch. 3, nos. 1-3.
37. Cf. ibid., no. 8.
38. IV, ch. 2, nos. 3, 8, 9.
39. Cf. V, ch. 1, nos. 3-5, 9-10.
40. Cf. ibid., nos. 5, 11.
41. Cf. V, ch. 2, nos. 2-5.
42. Cf. V, ch. 4, no. 4.

43. Cf. ibid., no. 9.
44. Cf. VI, ch. 1, no. 1.
45. Cf. VI, ch. 2, no. 1; ch. 4, no. 1.
46. VI, ch. 4, no. 1.
47. Cf. VI, ch. 1, nos. 3, 4, 6, 7, 8, 9.
48. Cf. VI, ch. 2.
49. VI, ch. 4, no. 2.
50. Cf. ibid., nos. 3-4.
51. Cf. ibid., nos. 5,8.
52. Cf. VI, ch. 5, no. 10.
53. Cf. VI, ch. 6, nos. 10-13.
54. VI, ch. 7, no. 13.
55. Cf. ibid., nos. 6, 7, 11, 12.
56. VI, ch. 11, nos. 1,6.
57. Cf. ibid., nos. 2, 4, 11.
58. Cf. VI, ch. 4, no. 4.
59. Cf. VII, ch. 1, no. 5.
60. Ibid., no. 6.
61. Ibid., no. 8.
62. Ibid., nos. 8-9.
63. VII, ch. 2, no. 1.
64. Ibid., no. 3.
65. Cf. ibid., no. 4.
66. Ibid., no. 5.
67. Cf. VII, ch. 4, nos. 4, 6, 9, 12.
68. Ibid., nos. 14-15.
69. Cf. Jose Vicente Rodriguez, "Castillo Interior O Las Moradas," *Introducción A La Lectura De Santa Teresa* (Madrid: Espiritualidad, 1978): 368-371.
70. See III, ch. 1, no. 1, note 2.
71. See "Castillo Interior O Las Moradas," p. 318.

PROLOGUE

1. An allusion to her *Life* and *The Way of Perfection.*
2. This is a veiled reference to her *Life.* The autograph of this work was requested by the Inquisition in 1576 and kept in its archives until 1588.
3. It was June 2, 1577. She completed the work in Avila on November 29 of the same year.
4. These were Fr. Jerome Gratian and her confessor Dr. Alonso Velázquez, future bishop of Osma and later archbishop of Santiago de Compostela.

THE FIRST DWELLING PLACES

CHAPTER 1

1. Allusion to Jn. 14:2. Teresa uses the Spanish words *moradas, aposentos,* and *piezas* in approximately the same sense; they refer to rooms or dwelling places within the castle. The fundamental text of Jn. 14:2 has led previous translators to speak of these rooms as mansions. Most people today think of a mansion as a large stately house, not what Teresa had in mind with the term *moradas.* New versions of Scripture render Jn. 14:2 as "in my Father's house there are many dwelling places." "Dwelling places" turns out to be a more precise translation of Teresa's *moradas* than is the classic "mansions," and more biblical and theological in tone.
2. Allusion to Pr. 8:31.
3. Gn. 1:26-27.
4. In no. 1.
5. Jn. 9:2-3.
6. She is probably alluding to Osuna's *Third Spiritual Alphabet* and Laredo's *Ascent of Mount Sion,* favorite books of hers. See *Life,* ch.4, no. 7; ch. 23, no. 12.
7. She also received in an intellectual vision mystical understanding of this truth. See *Spir. Test.,* 20.
8. Gn. 19:26.
9. Fr. Gratian added "and eight" after "thirty years," in accordance with Jn. 5:5.
10. Allusion to Mt. 6:21.

CHAPTER 2

1. Allusion to Ps. 1:3.
2. The person is Teresa herself. See *Spir. Test.,* 20.
3. For similar comparisons see *Life,* ch. 40. no. 5; *Spir. Test.,* 52.
4. Allusion to Ps. 127:1.
5. In no. 2.
6. See her *Constitutions,* nos. 2,7.
7. Teresa laments the fact there are few books that explain mystical (supernatural) prayer in depth. In no. 1 of the following chapter she asserts that there are many books dealing with ascetical matters. Thus her orientation in this book is toward the mystical.
8. She is referring to the *Life* and the *Way of Perfection,* and alludes to a divine influence in the composition of her mystical

writings. See *Life,* ch. 39, no. 8: "...many of the things I write about here do not come from my own head, but my heavenly Master told them to me."

9. In no. 7.
10. A plant about a foot in height, which grows in Andalusia and Valencia, resembling the palm tree. Only the center or heart, the tender part, is eaten.
11. In no. 10.
12. See no. 8. Teresa avoids any arrangement of these dwelling places into neatly structured rows with set numbers. She thereby in her allegory makes it easy for us to imagine a marvelous depth and abundance of inner riches.
13. In the *Way of Perfection,* ch. 39, no. 5. See also *Life,* ch. 13, no. 15.
14. In ch. 1, no. 8.
15. In nos. 4, 12.
16. Allusion to 2 Co. 11:14.
17. In the *Way of Perfection,* ch. 38, no. 2; ch. 39 passim.
18. See *Life,* ch. 13, nos. 8, 10; *Way of Perfection,* ch. 4; *Method for the Visitation of Monasteries,* nos. 17, 20, 21.

THE SECOND DWELLING PLACES

CHAPTER 1

1. See *Life,* chs. 11-13; *Way of Perfection,* passim.
2. In VI, ch. 3.
3. Lk. 15:16.
4. Allusion to Jn. 15:5.
5. Allusion to Jgs. 7:5.
6. See *Life,* ch. 4, no. 2; ch. 11, nos. 10-15; *Way of Perfection,* ch. 20, no. 2; ch. 21, no. 2; chs. 23, 36, 41.
7. Allusion to Wis. 16:20.
8. Allusion to Mt. 20:22.
9. In V, ch. 3, nos. 3-12.
10. Jn. 20:19-21.
11. In no. 1.
12. Allusion to Sir. 3:25.
13. Jn. 14:6.
14. Jn. 14:9.
15. Allusion to Mt. 10:24.
16. Allusion to Mt. 26:41.

THE THIRD DWELLING PLACES

CHAPTER 1

1. Ps. 112:1.
2. Teresa commissioned Fr. Jerome Gratian to review her work. Gratian did so scrupulously and made corrections here and there throughout the manuscript. For example, in this passage he crossed out the word "secure" and substituted "right." In fact this whole chapter has a number of corrections by Gratian who was fearful lest the Saint affirm any certitude about the state of grace, or security about one's own salvation, that would have gone contrary to the teaching of the Council of Trent or have been similar to certain theories of the *Alumbrados.* Fortunately, Gratian made the deletion marks so as to leave the original completely legible. The Jesuit Ribera, in turn, corrected Gratian's corrections with marginal comments such as the following: "One doesn't have to cross out any of the holy Mother's words." A futher example of the skirmish that went on in the margins of Teresa's manuscript can be found in no. 8 of this chapter. In that delicate passage Teresa wrote: "Shouldn't we consider ourselves lucky to be able to repay something of what we owe Him for His service toward us? I say these words 'His service toward us' unwillingly; but the fact is that He did nothing else but serve us all the time He lived in this world." Gratian changed "His service toward us" to "having died for us" and crossed out what followed. Ribera again noted: "Nothing should be deleted; what the Saint said has been very well said." All of this led to Ribera's written admonition on the first page of the autograph of *The Interior Castle*: "What the holy Mother wrote in this book is frequently crossed out, and other words are added or a gloss is made in the margin. Usually the cancellation is poorly conceived and the text is better the way it was first written. . . And since I have read and looked over this work with a certain amount of care, I think I should advise anyone reading it to read it as the holy Mother wrote it, for she understood and said things better, and to pay no attention to what was added or changed unless the correction was made by the Saint herself in her own hand, which is seldom. And I ask out of charity anyone who reads this book to reverence the words and letters formed by so holy a hand and try to understand her correctly; and you will see that there is nothing to correct. Even if you do not understand, believe that she who wrote it knew better and that the words cannot be cor-

rected well unless their meaning is fully understood. If their meaning is not grasped, what is very appropriately said will seem inappropriate. Such is the way books are ruined and lost."

3. Jn. 11:16.
4. In no. 2.
5. Ps. 112:1.
6. In no. 1.
7. Mt. 19:16-22.
8. In no. 6.
9. Mt. 19:22.
10. Mt. 19:27.
11. Teresa first wrote "as St. Paul says," then added between the lines "or Christ." Gratian crossed out both and wrote: "St. Luke says it in chapter 17." See Lk. 17:10.
12. Allusion to Lk. 12:48.
13. This is a vague reference, perhaps to *The Way of Perfection*, ch. 17, nos. 2, 7.

CHAPTER 2

1. Allusion to the young man in the Gospel. See III, ch. 1, no. 6.
2. In no. 1. See III, ch. 1, no. 5.
3. Allusion to Lk. 22:42.
4. In no. 4. See III, ch. 1, no. 7.
5. Allusion to Ps. 119:137. For a similar use of this text see *Life*, ch. 19, no. 9. On the following theme about God's different ways with souls, see *Way of Perfection*, chs. 16-18, especially ch. 17, no. 7.
6. In III, ch. 1, nos. 1, 5, 8.
7. Words from the Carmelite Rule (*The Rule of St. Albert*) and taken from Is. 30:15.

THE FOURTH DWELLING PLACES

CHAPTER 1

1. Teresa uses the Spanish word *contentos* (here rendered in English as consolations) to denote experiences (such as joy, peace, satisfaction) that are not infused; that is, experiences perceived as a result of prayer and virtue but similar to those derived from everyday events. On the other hand, she uses the Spanish word *gustos* (here rendered in English as spiritual delights) to denote infused experiences. Infused, "supernatural," or mystical prayer begins in these fourth dwelling places with the

prayer of infused recollection (ch. 3) and quiet, or spiritual delight (ch. 2). Actually Teresa presents the fourth dwelling places as a stage of transition in which the natural and the supernatural (or the acquired and the infused) are intermingled.

2. In her *Life*. She is alluding to the many chapters there that deal with mystical experiences. See chs. 14-32 and 37-40. When Teresa wrote the *Life* she had not yet come to the stage she describes in the seventh dwelling places. What she explains in her *Life* under the symbol of the fourth water corresponds to the sixth dwelling places. As a result, she points out that she has a better understanding of some matters concerning the spiritual life than she did in that book. See I, ch. 2, no. 7; IV, ch. 2, no. 5.
3. Allusion to Mt. 20:13. The absolute divine freedom in the granting or denying of mystical favors is frequently insisted upon in Teresa's writings. In this work see IV, ch. 2, no. 9; V, ch. 1, no. 12; VI, ch. 4, no. 12; ch. 7, no. 9; ch. 8, no. 5.
4. In III, ch. 2, no. 10.
5. Allusion to Jn. 15:5.
6. Ps. 119:32.
7. In no. 4.
8. In *Life,* ch. 12; *Way of Perfection,* chs. 16-20.
9. One of Teresa's cherished maxims. See the *Foundations,* ch. 5, no. 2.
10. We do not know who the learned man was. Some suggest that it may have been St. John of the Cross who was Teresa's director and confessor from 1572-1575. But Teresa's ignorance of the difference between the imagination (*pensamiento,* or mind, as she often refers to it) and the intellect was not total ignorance. See *Life,* ch. 17, no. 5.
11. For many years this wandering of the mind deeply troubled the Saint. See *Life,* ch. 17, no. 7; *Way of Perfection,* ch. 31, no. 8. In this work she has come to a definite doctrinal position on the matter. The instability and rebellion of the imagination is a consequence of the disorder produced in us through original sin. See no. 11 of this chapter.
12. In the prologue, no. 1.
13. Sg. 8:1.
14. In II, no. 9.
15. See VII, ch. 2, no. 11.

CHAPTER 2

1. In ch. 1, nos. 4-6.

2. See ch. 1, no. 5.
3. See *Life*, chs. 14-15.
4. In III, ch. 2, nos. 9-10; IV, ch. 1, nos. 4-6.
5. In ch. 1, nos. 5, 6, 10.
6. In ch. 1, no. 4.
7. Ps. 119:32. See ch. 1, no. 5.
8. In VII, ch. 1, nos. 3, 7, 10; ch. 2, nos. 3, 9.
9. In no. 4.
10. In ch. 1, no. 1, she says fourteen years. She finished the first redaction of her *Life* in 1562 and is writing these pages in the latter part of 1577.
11. In no. 5.

CHAPTER 3

1. She spoke of the prayer of recollection in various places: *Life*, chs. 14-15; *Way of Perfection*, chs. 28-29; *Spiritual Testimonies*, 59, no. 3. But Teresa is not consistent in her terminology. Sometimes she speaks of a recollection that is not infused (in the *Way of Perfection*); at other times of a recollection that is infused: in the *Life*, using the term indiscriminately with "quiet" to designate the first degree of infused prayer, and in the *Spiritual Testimonies* to designate the first faint experience of mystical prayer that prepares the way for the prayer of quiet. See no. 8 of this chapter.
2. She is alluding to works such as Osuna's *Third Spiritual Alphabet*, IX, ch. 7; and Laredo's *Ascent of Mount Sion*, III, ch. 41. See *Life*, ch. 12, nos. 1, 4, 5, 7; ch. 22, nos. 13, 18.
3. In I, ch. 2, nos. 4, 12, 15.
4. In *Confessions*, X, ch. 27; or in the pseudo-Augustine's *Soliloquies*, ch. 31. See *Life*, ch. 40, no. 6; *Way of Perfection*, ch. 28, no. 2.
5. In Osuna's *Third Spiritual Alphabet*, VI, ch. 4.
6. See Laredo's *Ascent of Mount Sion*, III, ch. 27.
7. Treatise on *Prayer and Meditation* by Granada and at that time attributed to St. Peter of Alcántara.
8. In nos. 4-6; see ch. 2, no. 9.
9. Perhaps she is referring to a parallel passage in the *Way of Perfection* ch. 31, nos. 3, 7.
10. Allusion to Ph. 4:13.
11. In the book of *Foundations*, ch. 6. She will insist on this again in VI, ch. 7, no. 13.
12. See *Life*, chs. 16-17, where Teresa dwells at greater length on

this *sleep of the faculties* as though dealing with a special stage in the degrees of mystical prayer.
13. Teresa makes a pun here with the Spanish words *arrobamiento* (rapture) and *abobamiento* (foolishness).
14. In nos. 11-12.

THE FIFTH DWELLING PLACES

CHAPTER 1

1. Allusion to 2 Co. 11:14.
2. Allusion to Mt. 22:14.
3. Allusion to Mt. 13:44.
4. In IV, ch. 3, no. 11.
5. In no. 3.
6. Another allusion to 2 Co. 11:14.
7. In IV, ch. 3, nos. 11-14.
8. In IV, ch. 1, nos. 8-12.
9. She made a similar observation in the *Way of Perfection*, ch. 31, no. 10.
10. See *Life*, ch. 5, no. 3; ch. 13, no. 19; ch. 25, no. 22.
11. In IV, ch. 1, no. 2; ch. 2, no. 9.
12. See no. 7.
13. She speaks of them in the next chapter, nos. 7-14.
14. In no. 8.
15. See *Life*, ch. 18, no. 15; *Spir. Test.*, 49.
16. Sg. 2:4.
17. Sg. 3:2.
18. Jn. 20:19.
19. See VII, ch. 2, no. 3.

CHAPTER 2

1. In ch. 1, no. 2.
2. In the Dwelling Places I-IV.
3. See Col. 3:3-4.
4. In ch. 1, nos. 10-11.
5. In VI, ch. 6, no. 1; ch. 11 *passim*.
6. In ch. 1, nos. 2, 3, 13.
7. In ch. 1, no. 12; IV, ch. 2, no. 9.
8. In VI, ch. 10, no. 8; VII, ch. 3, no. 4.
9. In ch. 1, no. 12.
10. Allusion to Sg. 2:4.

11. Lk. 22:15.
12. She is referring to herself. See *Life*, ch. 38, no. 18.

CHAPTER 3

1. For Teresa the little moth is equivalent to the little butterfly; she uses these images interchangeably. See ch. 4, no. 1; VI, ch. 2, no. 1; ch. 4, no. 1; ch. 6, no. 1; ch. 11, no. 1; VII, ch. 3, no. 1.
2. She is referring to herself. See *Life*, ch. 7, no. 10.
3. In ch. 2, nos. 6-7.
4. See Jn. 11:33-36.
5. In ch. 1, no. 6; IV, ch. 1, nos. 4-5; ch. 2, nos. 3-5.
6. In ch. 1, nos. 3-4.
7. The delightful union is the infused prayer of union.
8. The union that arises from conformity of wills.
9. Jon. 4:6-7.
10. Jn. 17:22.
11. Allusion to 1 Jn. 4:20.
12. In the *Way of Perfection*, ch. 7; *Foundations*, ch. 5.

CHAPTER 4

1. The prayer of union.
2. Having begun this work in Toledo, June 2, 1577, Teresa in less than a month and a half had got as far as chapter three of the fifth dwelling place. About the middle of July she moved to Avila where she probably wrote chapter three. She then abandoned all work on her book until the beginning of November. And by November 29, 1577, her task was completed.
3. In her comparison, Teresa makes use of the stages that were followed in her day for the arrangement of a marriage: 1) meetings between the young man and woman; 2) exchanging of gifts; 3) falling in love; 4) the joining of hands; 5) betrothal; 6) marriage.
4. See, e.g., IV, ch. 3, nos. 9-10.
5. In no. 4.
6. In ch. 3, no. 2.

THE SIXTH DWELLING PLACES

CHAPTER 1

1. Allusion to the meeting referred to in V, ch. 4, no. 4.
2. See V, ch. 1, nos. 9-11; V, ch. 4, nos. 3-4.

3. See VII, ch. 3, nos. 4-5.
4. She is referring to herself. See *Life*, ch. 28, no. 14.
5. The "favor that was mentioned" is the prayer of union or the "meetings" between the two who will be betrothed, the prayer characteristic of the fifth dwelling place. The person Teresa refers to is herself. "Forty years ago" would have been 1537. For an account of these sufferings and trials see *Life*, chs. 4-6; for her first experiences of union, see *Life*, ch. 4, no. 7.
6. The person here is Teresa, and the confessor is Father Baltasar Alvarez, S.J. See *Life*, ch. 30, no. 13.
7. See *Life*, ch. 30, no. 12.
8. In nos. 9-10.
9. She does so in VI, ch. 11.

CHAPTER 2

1. In the fourth dwelling places.
2. See IV, ch. 3, nos. 11-14.
3. For a parallel passage from her personal experience see her *Life*, ch. 29, no. 10; in no. 13 of that same chapter she describes her experience of the transverberation.
4. She is alluding to herself. See *Spir. Test.*, 59, no. 13.
5. In *Spir. Test.*, 59, no. 15 she speaks of how even the learned men she consulted were free of fears about this prayer. St. John of Avila wrote to her assuring her that the prayer was good. For a description of her personal experience of this grace see also her *Life*, chs. 29 and 30.
6. See nos. 1, 3, and 5. These favors proceed "from very deep within the interior part of the soul," from "the Spouse, who is in the seventh dwelling place," there, "where the Lord who is unchanging dwells."
7. In no. 6.

CHAPTER 3

1. This chapter restates what was said in ch. 25 of the *Life*. In both places the prevailing effort is to distinguish between genuine locutions (coming from God or His saints) and false ones (from the imagination or the devil). In this chapter Teresa deals first with locutions in general (nos. 1-11); then she goes on to treat of a more subtle kind of mystical locution accompanied by "a certain intellectual vision" (nos. 12-18).
2. In ch. 2, nos. 1-4, 8.
3. In no. 1.

4. In ch. 1, nos. 7-15.
5. In a veiled way she is alluding to her own experience described in her *Life*, ch. 25, nos. 14-19.
6. In no. 7.
7. See Jon. chs. 1 and 4. Though Teresa refers to Jonah about six times in her writings and could be referring to herself, she might, on the other hand, be thinking of Teresa Layz the benefactress of Alba about whom she speaks in the *Foundations*, ch. 20, and especially in no. 12.
8. In nos. 5-7.
9. Allusion to Lk. 10:16.
10. She speaks of intellectual visions in chs. 8 and 10; see also ch. 5, nos. 8-9.
11. In ch. 10; also in ch. 4.
12. A reference to herself. See *Life*, ch. 25, nos. 14-19.
13. In nos. 12-16.
14. In no. 11.
15. Allusion to 1 Co. 10:13.
16. Jos. 10:12-13. See *Life*, ch. 25, no. 1.

CHAPTER 4

1. In regard to this terminology see *Life*, ch. 20, no. 1; *Spir. Test.*, 59, no. 9.
2. The need for great courage in order to receive these mystical graces is often stated by Teresa. See *Life*, ch. 13, no. 2; ch. 20, no. 4; ch. 39, no. 21; *Spir. Test.*, 59, no. 9; *Way of Perfection*, ch. 18; and in these sixth dwelling places, ch. 5, nos. 1, 5, 12; ch. 11, no. 11.
3. In IV, ch. 3, nos. 11-12; VI, ch. 3, no. 10.
4. In *Life*, ch. 20, *Spir. Test.*, 59, no. 9.
5. In ch. 2, no. 4.
6. In ch. 8 she will deal with intellectual visions and in ch. 9, with imaginative ones.
7. Fr. Gratian; see Introduction.
8. See Gn. 28:12.
9. See Ex. 3:1-16.
10. This happened sometime during the first months of 1574. See *Foundations*, ch. 21, nos. 1-2.
11. In IV, ch. 3, nos. 11-13.
12. Allusion to Sg. 3:2.
13. Allusion to Jn. 9:6-7.
14. In no. 9.

15. See *Life*, ch. 20, no. 5.
16. She is alluding to herself. See *Life*, ch. 31, no. 13.
17. In nos. 4-5.

CHAPTER 5

1. On the difference between rapture and flight of the spirit see *Life*, ch. 18, no. 7; ch. 20, no. 1; *Spir. Test.*, 59, nos. 9-10.
2. In ch. 4, no. 1.
3. See the account of her personal experience in *Life*, ch. 20, nos. 3-7.
4. She is speaking of herself; see *Life*, ch. 20, nos. 5-6.
5. For parallel passages see *Life*, ch. 22, no. 13; ch. 20, no. 4.
6. In IV, ch. 2, nos. 2-5.
7. Allusion to Pr. 8:29.
8. Allusion to Lk. 12:48.
9. She is speaking of herself. See *Spir. Test.*, 46.
10. She returns to the theme taken up in no. 1.
11. Allusion to 2 Co. 12:2-4.
12. Concerning the distinction between the soul and the spirit, see VII, ch. 1, no. 11; *Spir. Test.*, 59, no. 11; 25, no. 1; *Life*, ch. 20, no. 14.
13. Nb. 13:18-27.
14. She continues to use the symbolic language (jewels and meetings) introduced in V, ch. 4, no. 3.
15. See nos. 1-5; ch. 4, nos. 1-2.

CHAPTER 6

1. Ex. 14:21-22; Jos. 3:13-17.
2. Allusion to Gn. 8:8-9, used again in VII, ch. 3, no. 13.
3. In ch. 11.
4. "Lord, if I am still necessary to your people I don't refuse to live; may Your will be done." See the liturgical office for St. Martin in the Roman Breviary.
5. Lk. 15:22-32.
6. She tells about St. Peter of Alcántara's manner of life in *Life*, ch. 27, nos. 16-20; ch. 30, nos. 2-7.

CHAPTER 7

1. She is referring to herself. See *Life*, ch. 26, no. 2; ch. 34, no. 10; *Spir. Test.*, 1, no. 26; 48, no. 1; 59, no. 12.
2. In *Life*, ch. 22.
3. In *Life*, ch. 22, nos. 2-3.

4. The person to whom Teresa refers is unknown. The passage is intentionally somewhat enigmatic.
5. See Jn. 8:12; 14:6, 9.
6. 1 K. 18:30-39.
7. In VI, ch. 11, no. 8.
8. In VII, ch. 2, nos. 3, 9, 10; ch. 3, nos. 8, 10, 11; ch. 4, nos. 1-2.
9. At the end of no. 7.
10. Sg. 3:1-3.
11. See *The Confessions of St. Augustine*, X, ch. 6, nos. 9-10.
12. In no. 7.
13. In nos. 9-10.
14. In ch. 4, nos. 2, 9; *Life*, ch. 22, no. 10.
15. Jn. 16:7.

CHAPTER 8

1. This person is Teresa herself. See *Life*, ch. 27, nos. 2-5.
2. In ch. 3.
3. See *Life*, ch. 27, no. 3.
4. See *Life*, ch. 25, no. 18; *Spir. Test.*, 22, no. 1; 31; 48; 58, no. 16; *Int. Castle*. VI, ch. 3, no. 5.
5. In ch. 6, nos. 1-6.
6. The series of favors mentioned in the preceding chapters.
7. In nos. 3-5.
8. In no. 3.
9. Allusion to 1 Co. 10:13. See ch. 3, no. 17. She also refers to this statement of St. Paul in her *Life*, ch. 23, no. 15.
10. In no. 1.
11. She is alluding probably to interventions of the Spanish Inquisition.

CHAPTER 9

1. In ch. 8; the intellectual visions.
2. In nos. 2-3.
3. A popular belief in Teresa's time was that certain stones had curative powers; for example, the bezoar.
4. Teresa is referring to herself. See *Life*, ch. 28, especially no. 4; *Spir. Test.*, 58, no. 15, in which she states that "she never saw anything with her bodily eyes."
5. Mt. 25:41.
6. Ac. 9:3-4.
7. In ch. 8, no. 3.
8. In ch. 8, nos. 4, 8.

9. She is referring to Fr. Domingo Báñez, O.P. See her *Book of Foundations*, ch. 8, no. 3.
10. See *Life*, ch. 25, nos. 5-6.
11. In *Foundations*, ch. 8, no. 3.
12. This person is herself. See *Life*, ch. 29, nos. 5-6.
13. See 1 S. 15:10-11.
14. She is speaking of herself. The man could have been St. John of the Cross who was confessor at the monastery of the Incarnation in Avila when St. Teresa was prioress there from 1571-1574.
15. In no. 16; IV, ch. 2, no. 9.

CHAPTER 10

1. See *Life*, ch. 40, no. 9.
2. For the origin of this comparison see *Life*, ch. 40, no. 10.
3. Allusion to Mt. 6:12, 15; Lk. 6:37.
4. Teresa gives a personal account of this experience in *Life*, ch. 40, nos. 1-4.
5. Ps. 116:11.
6. Jn. 18:36-38.
7. In nos. 2 and 5.

CHAPTER 11

1. The person is herself. See ch. 10, nos. 2-5.
2. In ch. 2, no. 1; ch. 6, no. 6; ch. 8, no. 4.
3. Teresa describes an equivalent experience of hers that took place at Salamanca in 1571. See *Spir. Test.*, 12, nos. 1-5.
4. In no. 2.
5. She is speaking of herself. See *Spir. Test.*, 59, no. 14; *Life*, ch. 20, nos. 12-13.
6. Jn. 4:7-14.
7. In nos. 2 and 4.
8. See ch. 4.
9. Mt. 20:22.
10. Lk. 7:40-48.

THE SEVENTH DWELLING PLACES

CHAPTER 1

1. In I, ch. 2, nos. 1-3.
2. In no. 3.
3. In the fifth dwelling place.

4. Ac. 9:8.
5. Jn. 14:23. For another description of this grace see *Spir. Test.*, 13.
6. Through an intellectual vision; see no. 6.
7. In VI, ch. 3, nos. 3 and 17; ch. 6, no. 6; ch. 7, no. 3; ch. 8, nos. 3-4.
8. Teresa is referring to herself.
9. Lk. 10:40.
10. In VI, ch. 5, nos. 1 and 9.

CHAPTER 2

1. See her corresponding account in *Spir. Test.*, 31.
2. The one referred to in ch. 1, nos. 6-7.
3. Teresa first wrote: "between two who have consummated marriage." She then changed it to the present reading.
4. In V, ch. 4, no. 3.
5. See no. 1; *Spir. Test.*, 31.
6. See VI, ch. 8.
7. Jn. 20:19-21. See V, ch. 1, no. 12.
8. Again she changed what she had previously written, "those who have consummated marriage," to the present reading.
9. 1 Co. 6:17. This text from St. Paul and the application were written between the lines. Teresa first wrote and then crossed out: ". . . we are made one spirit with God if we love Him; he doesn't say that we are joined with Him . . . but are made one spirit with Him."
10. Ph. 1:21. Teresa cited the passage in her own form of Latin: *Mi bivere Cristus es mori lucrum.*
11. See V, ch. 3, note 1.
12. In no. 4.
13. Jn. 20:19-21.
14. Lk. 7:50.
15. Jn. 17:21.
16. Jn. 17:20, 23.
17. Allusion to Lk. 21:33.
18. In no. 3.
19. In ch. 3, nos. 3 and 6; ch. 4, no. 2.
20. Probably in V, ch. 2, nos. 7-11.
21. In no. 4; see also IV, ch. 2.
22. In no. 9.

CHAPTER 3

1. Teresa numbers only the first two effects; the others are present in the midst of a series of digressions and commentary. Here is a list of these effects: 1) forgetfulness of self (in no. 2); 2) desire to suffer (no. 4); 3) deep interior joy in persecution (no. 5); 4) desire to serve (no. 6); 5) great detachment (no. 8); 6) no fear of the devil's deceits (no. 10); and finally a recapitulation in no. 13.
2. In ch. 2, nos. 4-5.
3. An allusion to the grace of spiritual marriage. See ch. 2, no. 1; *Spir. Test.*, 31.
4. She is referring to the experiences spoken of in the sixth dwelling place; see particularly ch. 11.
5. In VI, ch. 2.
6. In VI. ch. 2, no. 1; ch. 11, no. 2.
7. Ac. 9:6.
8. In no. 8.
9. In ch. 2, nos. 3 and 10.
10. In ch. 2, nos. 5-6 and 9.
11. 1 K. 6:7.
12. In Teresa's terminology "not lost" is the equivalent of not being enraptured. In this dwelling place the faculties remain in amazement but not ecstatically suspended.
13. Allusion to Sg.1:2; there follows a series of biblical allusions to: Ps. 42:2; Rv. 21:3; Gn. 8:8-12.
14. Allusion to Lk. 18:13.
15. In no. 6.

CHAPTER 4

1. In ch. 3, nos. 2-10.
2. 1 K. 11. See III, ch. 1, nos. 1-4.
3. Ps. 112:1.
4. In VI, ch. 9, nos. 16-17; see also ch. 1, no. 7.
5. Allusion to 1 Th. 2:9.
6. This *quo vadis* legend appeared in the Carmelite breviary, used in the time of St. Teresa, on the feast of St. Peter (June 29).
7. In V, ch. 3, nos. 11.
8. There is a Teresian proverb that reads in Spanish: *La virtud se ha de ver no en los rincones sino en medio de las ocasiones.* It might go like this in English: "Look for virtue not in corners away from the din but right amidst the occasions of sin." See *Foundations,* ch. 5, no. 15.
9. In I, ch. 2, nos. 8-9, 11 and 13.

10. In ch. 3, nos. 3, 5-8.
11. Ps. 18:26.
12. Allusion to Sg. 2:4.
13. Allusion to 1 K. 19:10. The shield of the Carmelite order takes as its motto the prophet Elijah's words: *Zelo zelatus sum pro Domino Deo exercituum.*
14. Lk. 10:38-42.
15. Allusion to Lk. 7:37-38.
16. See *Way of Perfection,* chs. 1-3; *Meditations,* ch. 7.
17. In III, ch. 2, no. 13.

EPILOGUE

1. This epilogue was sent in the form of a letter along with the original manuscript to the Discalced Carmelite nuns in Seville.
2. In Prologue, no. 1.
3. Allusion to Gn. 1:26. See I, ch. 1, no. 1.
4. That is, Nov. 29, 1577, close to six months after she had begun writing on June 2nd of that same year. See Prologue, no. 3.

Index

INDEX

Abandoned (forsaken) 189, 365: not—by God, 133

Abandonment 36, 81, 150, 161, 187 218, 313, 386, 392

Absorption 154, 184, 243, 244, 253, 325, 329, 330, 331, 333, 334, 367, 368, 374, 380, 382, 384, 403, 404, 430: duration of, 384; which excludes humanity of Christ, 276

Academic: question, 268; rank, 179; titles, 458

Accusations, false 464

Achieve *see* **Acquire**

Acquire (attain) 147, 148, 149, 155, 165, 173, 186, 198, 227, 267, 273, 317, 325, 328, 330, 367, 396, 408, 488

Active life 100, 102, 103, 105, 155, 214, 224, 257, 334

Adam 23, 51, 321, 467

Adoration *see* **PRAYER,** Forms of

Advance 200, 223, 309, 351, 357, 393, 431

Advertence *see* **Sin**

Advice: on a matter of life and death, 166; to non-contemplatives, 106; to nuns of her order, 28, 38, 42, 43, 44, 55, 69, 84, 114, 119, 128, 132, 155, 156, 159, 162, 165, 235, 240, 305, 309, 334, 372, 415, 460; to youngest in community, 44

Affability 199, 200

Affection 63, 64, 375: dominates, 55; earthly, 66, 196; evil, 66; for confessor, 460; for God, 159; other than for God, 355; showing, 68; affectionate words are to be kept for God, 70

Affliction of soul 58, 64, 112, 129, 136, 146, 175, 189, 218, 227, 309, 313, 319, 320, 322, 349, 364, 365, 372, 373, 378, 385, 388, 392, 393, 397, 418, 424, 439, 460

Age: more or less an obstacle, 322; *see also* **Nuns,** elderly

Agitation 31,189, 477

Agreeable 199; *see also* **Affability; Holiness**

Alba de Tormes 212: autograph of *Meditations,* 213; monastery of nuns, 493

Alba, Duchess of 212, 381

Albert, St. 487

Allegory 485; *see* **Figures of speech**

Alms: giving, 44, 47, 74, 225; living from, 43; to pray is to give, 429

Alone with God 174

Alumbrados 24, 486

Alvarez, Baltasar, S.J. 492

Amazement 430, 442, 498

Ambition 70

Amendment 225,232,463

Ana de San Juan (Dávila) 457

Analogy 273, 274; *see also* **Castle imagery; Figures of speech**

Anathemas *see* **TERESA,** her nuns

Andalusia 265, 485

Andrew, St. 452

Angels 19, 49, 86, 98, 123, 124, 135, 151, 210, 223, 248, 253, 295, 356,

363, 373, 381, 389, 465, 474, 475: of light, 335, 337; traits of, 399
Anger 91: of the Lord, 413
Annihilation of the soul 393, 418, 443
Annoyance: easily borne by love, 54
Ant 323: courage to kill an, 187
Antifeminism 23; *see also* **Feminine; Woman**
Antonio de San Joaquin 481
Anxiety 254, 274, 373, 422: and tears, 318
Apathy 22
Aposentos 484
Apostles 56, 92, 139, 200, 241, 275, 285, 302, 356, 402, 403, 404, 433, 435, 436, 445, 449, 458: Christ's appearance to, 433
Apostolate 348, 470
Apostolic element of Teresa's charism 459
Apparitions *see* **Visions**
Appetites 82
Arabic 116
Arévalo 269
Argel 239
Argue 220, 468
Aristotle 23
Arms *see* **Ecclesiastical; Secular**
Asceticism 22, 271, 484
Ask (beseech) 127, 160, 185, 240, 244, 250, 256, 310, 315, 319, 326, 330, 336, 357, 368, 391, 476, 478
Aspirations 435
Assurance regarding favors *see* **Certitude**
Attachment 55, 64, 73, 76, 89, 96, 109, 187, 234, 271, 273, 343, 344, 384, 408, 460, 464
ATTENTION:
to God, in prayer, 124, 130, 469; to God's ways; 250
to self, habitual faults, 225; honor, 89; interior matters, 329; lack of humility, 377; differences in locutions, 376; love, 351; painful praise, 361; progress in virtue, 357; speech, 378; tears, 395
Augustine, St. 67, 140, 246, 328, 401, 495: confessions of, 401; pseudo-Augustine, 471, 489
Austerity 41, 89, 113
Authors 118
Autographs 18, 211, 278, 279, 459, 483, 486: variations in, 35; *see also* **Redactions**
Avila 15, 213, 266, 279, 459, 481, 483, 491; *see also* **Monastery of Incarnation; Monastery of St. Joseph**
Awakening 230, 274, 285, 329, 367, 370, 384, 396, 440: one's companions, 450; awakened soul, 407; to things of God, 380; the will, 319
Awareness 131, 287, 329, 331, 377, 424, 434
Ayala, Doña Constancia de 279
Backbiter 165
Baeza 212
Báñez, Domingo, O.P. 15, 16, 17, 21, 23, 39, 204, 212, 213, 458, 496
Bargaining in prayer 163
Bartholomew, St. 139, 470
Beauty: of the soul, 270, 283, 284, 287, 294; of Teresa's countenance, 267; *see also* **CHRIST; Grandeurs of God**
Beginners 104, 114, 250, 260, 447
Beginning 64, 115, 118, 126, 127, 130, 142, 143, 144, 151, 153, 175, 182, 183, 190, 196, 203, 240, 243, 253, 259, 273, 295, 300, 301, 331, 357, 361, 371, 386, 399, 401, 409: wrong, 179
Beholding God present 430
Belief (believing) 62, 129, 140, 203, 372, 373, 381, 430; believe, 339; in the center of the soul, 437; only those who conform, 121; do not believe, 399; one who does not—experiences no favors, 285
Benefactors 47, 225, 493
Benefit: others, 63, 65, 66, 115,

116, 117, 200, 218, 220, 257, 260, 275, 285, 307, 345, 359, 369, 372, 389, 390, 415, 416, 425, 439; to whole world, 449; to self, 63, 81, 131, 149, 158, 165, 182, 200, 232, 237, 246, 310, 323, 446; disinterest about—to self, 330; to companions, 449, 450; from, obedience, 314, persecution, 362, thinking of creation, 342

Beseech *see* **Ask**

Bethlehem, stable of 46

Betrothal: civil—in Teresa's time 355; *see also* **Spiritual, betrothal**

Bezoar 495

Bible 208, 209; *see also* **Gospel; Scripture**

Biblical terms 484; *see also* listings of persons and scenes

Biblioteca Nacional de Madrid 212

Bishop 61, 89, 145, 146: authority of, 59, 60, 461, 462; responsibility of, 238; pray for, 52, 53

Blame 92, 93, 97, 178, 362, 464

Blessed Virgin: Office of, 209, 253; For **B.V.M.** *see also* **Mary**

Blessing 63, 302, 360, 361, 383, 390, 407: to recognize evil of sin is a, 290

Blindness of soul 63; *see also* **Eyes; Soul**

Body (constitution, flesh) 63, 64, 73, 77, 80, 81, 82, 87, 91, 110, 113, 135, 142, 143, 153, 170, 171, 201, 214, 228, 229, 240, 269, 284, 309, 312, 319, 323, 325, 337, 363, 366, 374, 379, 382, 385, 386, 388, 389, 390, 394, 399, 425, 433, 439, 448, 460, 475: disjointed, 423; natural graces of—not enough, 55; natural heat of, 423; needs of, 43, 169; participates in favors, 324; as prison, 164; rough outer—, 338; strength of—not needed, 336; stuper of, 333; wants no activity, 154; *see also* **Bones; Brain; Ears; Eyes; Head; Heart; Languishing**

Bonaventure, St. 458

Bones, marrow of 338

Book(s) 24, 25, 31, 32, 94, 106, 118, 136, 147, 183, 191, 204, 208, 209, 216, 225, 228, 271, 286, 314, 329, 339, 342, 364, 467, 468, 470, 474, 476, 484: of Hours in Spanish, 209; cannot be understood, 364; on prayer, 468; publication prohibited, 468; we never tire of, 297; Teresa's: *see also* ***Foundations; Interior Castle; Letters; Life; Meditations on the Song of Songs; Method for the Visitation of Monasteries; Spiritual Testimonies***

Braganza, Don Teotonio de 458

Brain 403

Bread (material) 170, 183

Breath, breathing 330, 337, 384

Breviary 209, 494: Carmelite, 498

Bride(s): of Christ 86, 124, 134, 382, 412; of the Judge, 230; of the King, 342, 469; from the Song of Songs, 218, 221, 229, 230, 231, 234, 236, 237, 240, 247, 249, 250, 251, 253, 254, 255, 256, 258, 259, 321, 340, 346, 401, 442; looking in streets and squares, 383

Bridget, St. of Sweden 20

Brief: "Ex Parte Vestra", 462; from Rome, 279

Brussels 211

Buildings 30, 46, 47

Burdens 28, 81, 226, 234, 310, 313, 439, 446

Business: affairs (matters) 42, 48, 49, 174, 373,375, 431; God is our, 116

Cádiz 480

Call *see* **Vocation**

Calm(ness) of soul 31, 151, 189, 226, 235, 243, 248, 249, 278, 372, 378, 390, 413, 477: more—of soul and less exterior calm, 447

Calumnies 264

Cano, Melchior, O.P. 24

Capacity: of individual soul, 270; to

understand union, 340; *see also* **Suffering**

Care 125, 330, 357, 431, 460: about progress, 223; for souls, 315; not to sin, 224

Carelessness 127, 231, 336, 342. 355, 387, 409, 429, 476

Carmelite Fathers (*alias* contemplative, primitive, O.C.D.) 265

Carmelite nuns *see* **Advice** to nuns of her order; **Monasteries; Nuns; TERESA** and her nuns; **Vocation**

Carmelite shield and motto 499

Carranza, Archbishop, O.P. 24, 25, 208

Cassian 113, 467

Castile 19, 265

Castle Imagery *see* **Appendix to Index**

Casuistry 212

Catherine of Siena, St. 20

Caution 414, 460

Cells of the religious 49; *see also* **Rooms**

Censors of Teresa's books 16, 17, 18 21, 25, 29, 278, 467, 468, 486

Center of the castle 270: *see also* **Castle Imagery;** of the soul, 141, 320, 324, 340, 341, 429, 436, 440, 447, 448; the—is the spirit, 437; God is always in, 434; the very interior of the, 433

Centering attention of mind 32, 130: on Christ, 33

Cerda, Doña Luisa de la 468

Ceremonies 24, 122

Cerezo Pardo, Don Pedro 279

Certitude (assurance) about favors 218, 273, 339, 340, 363, 373, 374, 375, 376, 377, 381, 386, 406, 408, 409, 410, 414, 432, 435, 441, 478, 486

Chagrin 63

Change(ableness) 127, 201, 230, 232

Chaplain: to be confessor 461

Charity 30, 68, 70, 79, 112, 145, 201, 239, 253, 255, 258, 271, 296, 310: of compassion, 349; cooling of—is devil's aim, 295; external works of, 365; indiscreet, 85; lack of, 350; to neighbor, 306

Chess *see* **Figures of speech**

Children of God 138, 139; *see also* **Figures of speech**

Chosen ones 310

CHRIST

Actions of: becomes man, 221; calls by sign, 367; by a whisper, 367; by whistle, *see also* **Castle Imagery** nos. 31 and 55; cares for us, 170; gives new commandment, 479; insists upon love, 27; personally relates with soul, 270; presence of, 169, 172, 275, 276, 277, 367, 395, 448, 470, in the Eucharist, 340; purifies us by contact with his person, 276; reveals Himself as Lord of heaven and earth, 412; by a method, 173; readily, 173, 219; serves us, 22, 169; speaks in visions, 411; teaches us to pray, *see also below* Titles: Teacher; washes feet of disciples, 479; words of, 137, 138, 438

Aspects of His Life: agony in garden, 402; kingdom, 86; life, 400; His look, 134; His Passion, 51, 135, 141, 172, 219, 243, 249, 318, 347, 388, 399, 400, 415, 420; His Precious Blood, 249; His Resurrection (Risen Lord), 19, 33, 134, 172, 411

Attitudes of: desires, 347; feelings, 347; He knows us, 163; His love for the Father, 347; His love for us, 51, 166, 347; and degree of, 277; *see also* **Love;** He makes no difference between Himself and us; we make one, 168; His mysteries, 33; peace, 211; sorrow, 347; submission to us, 134;

suffering, 92, 134, 343, 347; trials, 86; His will is one with the Father's, 166
Attributes of: He is most beautiful and delightful in visions, 412; divine, 211, 220, 399; faithful, 436; glorious, 172, 272, 319; honored, 50, 51, 319, 439; humble, 138, 166, 168, 221; powerful, 170, 251; rich, 170
Humanity of: 168, 169, 211, 220, 240, 275, 276, 277, 399, 404, 411, 419, 432; appearance of, 433; countenance of, 416; eyes of, 413; face of, 147; is all of our good, 399; is joined to the divinity (two natures), 220, 275, 401, 404
Relations with us: we can do all things in, 201; companionship with Him, 133, 146, 147, 246, 401, 403, 405, 407; in contemplative presence to Him, 33, 276; His dishonors, share in, 86; finding Christ, 134; forgetting Christ bars entry to last two dwelling places, 276; friends of and friendship with Christ, 22, 24, 28, 41, 42, 51, 101, 174, 175, 214, 232; gift of Father to us, 168, 169; hospitality shown to Christ, 448; He is house wherein the soul will die, 342; we look at Him, He looks at us, 134; He shares mutual love with each individual, 211; His presence is felt, 405; we provide food for Him by drawing others to salvation, 448; Christ receives less regard than is given to men who are husbands, 124; He is rejected by many, 175; Christ was sold but can never be bought, 168; set our eyes on Him, 293; man's treatment of Him, 43, 167, 227; mocking Him, 162; union with Him, 211, 277, 278; vision of Him, 408
Titles given to Christ: Lord and His Majesty *are used throughout;* Ambassador, 161; Beloved, 311, 340, 367; Bridegroom, *see* **Spouse;** Brother, 138, 141, 160, 166, 184, 474: Comforter, 425; Crucified, 388, 439, 446; Emperor, 387; Father, 141; Friend, 74, 133; Giant, 387; God and man, 404; Guest, 172; Guide, 400; Judge, 230, 410; King, 48, 77, 86, 141, 153, 250, 251, 255, 387; Lamb of God, 51, 167; Life, 278, Light, 228, 400; Logos, 278; Master, 118, 129, 133, 136, 139, 140, 141, 146, 149, 150, 151, 160, 163, 164, 166, 173, 177, 179, 183, 184, 185, 186, 192, 204, 244, 245, 414; Model, 179, 228, 275, 403; Redeemer, 308; Savior, 107; Servant, 308; Spouse (Bridegroom), 43, 70, 74, 86, 103, 124, 134, 135, 136, 141, 146, 168, 169, 170, 207, 218, 224, 236, 237, 238, 243, 244, 246, 247, 248, 250, 252, 274, 275, 353, 355, 358, 359, 367, 370, 378, 383, 384, 385, 390, 428, 448, 492; Surgeon, 311; Teacher, 26, 32, 33, 34, 35, 62, 77, 118, 129, 130, 133, 137, 141, 169, 173, 184, 200, 204, 237, 242, 244, 245, 331, 350, 441, 472, 473; Truth, 107, 172; Way, 400; Wisdom, 184; Word Incarnate, 278 *See also* **GOD, TERESA**

Christian(s) 21, 22, 25, 42, 48, 94, 96, 97, 122, 128, 130, 246, 271, 345, 360, 429, 443, 473: Christianity, 20, 21, 52; faith, 272; mystery of sin and grace, 270; prayer, 286
Church 19, 20, 21, 22, 26, 42, 43,

50, 51, 52, 121, 151, 174, 176, 211, 219, 231, 319, 333, 342, 349, 402, 452, 455, 458, 459, 461, 471, 473: defenders of the, 22, 42; good of the, 50

Clare, St. 46, 458

Clarity 393: of words in locutions, 376, 377

Class distinction in monasteries 27; *see also* **Social Situations**

Clerics *see* **Preachers; Priests**

Cloister *see* **Enclosure**

Clothing 46, 226, 480: of rough or fine cloth, 476; poverty of, 27; *see also* **Habit of the Order**

Cloud: of Divinity, 249; of magnificent splendor, 430

College of Christ 464

Column (pillar) of the Agony 134, 141; *see also* **CHRIST**: Aspects

Comfort: bodily or material, 30, 41, 53, 63, 73, 78, 80, 86, 112, 165, 214, 228, 231, 233, 234, 239, 241, 245, 248, 271, 313, 473, 476; from God, 372, 388; from Scripture, 260; interior and exterior, 243; *see also* **Consolation**

Command: from forefathers to us, 89; from soul to God, 164

Commandments of God 49, 54, 296, 326, 348, 392, 401, 430, 441

Commentaries on prayer 118, 498

COMMUNICATION:

Between God and soul 164, 218, 219, 243, 244, 250, 270, 336, 348, 355, 358, 367, 368, 383, 397, 405, 413, 418, 427, 433, 440

Between God and Teresa 20

Of each of the Three Persons of the Trinity, with a soul, 430

Of person to person, 136, 193; in the family, 74, 136

Community of religious 26, 28, 54, 89: harm in, 87; number of nuns in, 46, 72, 458, 462

Companion (company): bad, 196, 198: divine, 430, 447; good, 356; *see also* **CHRIST, GOD**

Comparison in spiritual matters: helpful, 290; inelegant, 396; not possible, 335

Compassion 30, 50, 68, 79, 96, 309, 352, 439

Complain 79, 80, 240, 241, 264, 308, 320, 367, 384, 431: about favors, 417; those condemned cannot, 168

Compliments 201; *see also* **Praise of others**

Composing words of locution 376

Compunction *see* **Tears**

Conceptions of the Love of God 212

Concern for human needs 170, 171

Condemned 168, 363, 473: being —without fault, 91

Confessors 15, 39, 40, 57, 58, 59, 60, 61, 78, 105, 132, 190, 193, 204, 209, 211, 220, 230, 232, 269, 274, 360, 361, 364, 371, 372, 374, 375, 391, 392, 406, 409, 410, 414, 415, 458, 460, 461, 462, 483, 488, 496: condemnation by, 363; timorous, 363; too discreet and without experience, 362

Confidence: in God, 190, 198, 241, 377, 386, 431; of soul, 332; *see also* **Trust**

Conformity: between Sisters, 70; to God's will, 271, 301, 308, 310, 345, 350, 351, 423, 424; of locutions to Scripture, 372

Confused (confusion) 313, 357, 407, 419

Conquistadors 466

Conscience 46, 54, 57, 58, 59, 121, 152, 159, 173, 222, 231, 232, 304, 415: examination of, 133; purity of, 407, 410

Consciousness 275, 337

Consent in receiving favors 346

Conservatism in Teresa's time 24

Consolation(s) 60, 63, 73, 83, 96,

112, 114, 138, 140, 146, 148, 157, 169, 170, 190, 202, 203, 204, 207, 215, 219, 241, 258, 259, 271, 272, 284, 300, 308, 309, 313, 314, 317, 319, 324, 333, 338, 340, 349, 360, 364, 372, 374, 377, 385, 388, 403, 409, 416, 424, 425, 426, 440, 445, 451, 487: —begin in human soul and end in God, 318; earthly, 354, 365; false, 186; physical phenomena related to, 322, 323; Christ and soul console one another, 134, 135; *see also* ***Contentos***

Constitution *see* **Body**

Constitutions 30, 31, 53, 54, 223, 290, 296, 466, 480, 484

Constraint 318: to be avoided, 29, 175, 198, 200; keeps others from following, 199; *see also* **Restraint**

Consuegra 212, 213

Consultation regarding favors 410: God wants, 375

Contemplation 16, 18, 22, 24, 25, 26, 32, 33, 34, 94, 95, 96, 100, 101, 102, 105, 121, 131, 132, 137, 143, 152, 163, 169, 180, 183, 185, 190, 196, 223, 248, 259, 268, 271, 335, 336, 400, 402, 417, 436, 443, 449, 465, 467, 469, 470, 473, 474: for carpenters' wives, 24; is a gift, 99; hindrances to, 163; Lord judges who is to receive, 101; not necessary to salvation, 99

Contemplative(s) 53, 99, 103, 104, 105, 114, 155, 182, 193, 202, 214, 447: new manner of — life, 28, 257; trials of, 181

Contempt 336, 426: one must endure, 321; for worldly things, 121, 237, 252

Contention 369

Contentment 87, 101, 155, 157, 202, 226, 308

Contentos 272, 487; *see also* **Consolation; *Gustos***

Contradiction 113, 126

Contrition, act of 133

Convents 467; *see also* **Monasteries; Nuns**

Conversation 115: earthly, 369; favors received during, 425; is no bar to receiving locutions, 376; with the confessor, 57, 461; with a farm worker, 123; with God, 356; with a prince, 123; with the world, 49; of the sort to be avoided, 116, 198

Conversion of souls 450

Convulsion 380

Copies of Teresa's *Meditations* 212

Cordobilla, Alonso de, Friar 213, 480

Corporal: form, 340; things, 354, 399, 435; *see also* **Body**

Correction of Teresa's writings 278

Council *see* **Trent**

Counsel 57, 60, 89: bad, 461; which we receive, 322; *see also* **Evangelical counsels**

Counterfeit *see* **False**

Courage 34, 63, 102, 107, 113, 117, 120, 127, 162, 166, 200, 230, 274, 343, 375, 378, 379, 381, 386, 387, 388, 390, 393, 426, 493: enough to kill an ant, 187; *see also* **Fortitude; Strength**

Cowards 103, 393

Creation 71, 323

Creator 62, 64, 71, 157, 163, 220, 249, 270, 283, 284, 308, 380, 390: difference between—and creature, 284; union of—with creature, 164; *see also* **GOD**

Creature(s) 62, 87, 163, 194, 285, 328, 344, 380, 392, 397, 401, 405, 420, 426, 427, 428, 434, 435, 443: attachment to, 384; cannot be a companion, 423; forgetting, 245; this castle is a, 284; that are not prized are not understood, 427

Creed 122

Criterion for judging experience 210

Criticism 34, 117, 122, 385, 391, 396, 426, 449
Cross, the 75, 86, 104, 259, 301, 309, 443: carrying one's, 135, 345, 436; Christ on, 93, 96, 162, 241, 353, 450; embracing one's, 234; loving—makes it easy, 234; poverty on, 46; remembering one's sins is a heavy, 398; is the brand of God's slaves, 446
Curative powers 495
Cure of Prince Charles 480
Curiosity 219
Custom(s) 69: bad, 87; becomes a habit, 461; complaining becomes, 79; of dismissal, 89; gossip becomes, 296; in prayer, 142; in the religious life, 72, 87, 463; in society, 122; *see also* **Etiquette; Honor; Manners**
Danger 25, 61, 83, 84, 86, 100, 104, 105, 110, 119, 120, 184, 189, 190, 192, 194, 198, 200, 232, 235, 238, 256, 260, 285, 289, 296, 297, 298, 333, 334, 346, 349, 356, 358, 364, 370, 371, 375, 377, 391, 394, 403, 404, 416, 418, 423, 425, 426, 460, 474, 475, 478
Daring 98, 208, 211, 215, 221, 247, 459
Daughters of God 140, 141; *see also* **Children of God; Sons of God**
David, King 146, 217, 306, 420, 445, 447
Day *see* **Judgment**
Death (dying) 19, 82, 87, 111, 202, 257, 273, 299, 349, 365, 379, 384, 388, 391, 393, 398, 421, 423, 426, 439, 440, 443, 445, 448, 461: constantly, 424; danger of dying in prayer, 276; delay of, 422; delightful, 337; desire for, 256; dying from desire to die, 425; fear of, 81; from love, 256; of the silkworm, 350; to die for Christ, 78; in Christ, 274
Deception 36, 192, 193, 225, 229, 233, 335, 356, 357, 363, 369, 370, 371, 375, 376, 377, 385, 392, 394, 399, 406, 409, 414, 416, 445, 461, 475: *see also* **False**
Decorum 61
Deeds (doing) 53, 92, 104, 163, 164, 230, 235, 236, 240, 241, 245, 247, 252, 254, 257, 273, 308, 313, 317, 325, 329, 330, 332, 343, 344, 351, 352, 358, 373, 374, 375, 383, 388, 415, 418, 420, 426, 435, 438, 440, 446, 449, 450, 460, 472, 474: not words, 218, 307; —teach, 69; *see also* **Works**
Defence, God will inspire 93
Definitory General 265
Delight 31, 82, 96, 100, 103, 104, 110, 122, 124, 139, 140, 141, 154, 157, 162, 169, 184, 186, 189, 190, 193, 195, 196, 207, 209, 215, 217, 218, 242, 245, 246, 249, 252, 253, 256, 257, 259, 272, 275, 285, 301, 313, 314, 317, 319, 323, 324, 325, 326, 331, 335, 338, 345, 347, 348, 352, 354, 365, 367, 368, 370, 383, 403, 407, 411, 416, 417, 418, 424, 427, 430, 433, 436, 440, 442, 445, 449, 477, 487, 488: begins in God and nature shares, 272, 318; called *Gustos*, 272, 487; differs from consolation, 318; false, 222; in loving others, 462; delightful pain, 369; passive reception of, 272; of world vs that of spirit, 332; *see also* **Spiritual; Union**
Deliverance from deception 36, 201
Delusions 193
Demand from God 104
Derangement 112
Desert 357, 392, 396: fathers of the, 467; envy of—fathers, 392
Desire 36, 39, 41, 42, 50, 52, 65, 82, 96, 111, 112, 113, 118, 119, 120, 126, 129, 131, 134, 143, 146, 147, 154, 157, 158, 159, 160, 164, 173, 174, 175, 178, 180, 181, 183, 185, 188, 192, 195, 201, 202, 221, 235,

236, 237, 240, 241, 247, 248, 249, 250, 251, 255, 257, 270, 272, 274, 276, 293, 298, 300, 306, 308, 311, 315, 318, 321, 323, 326, 327, 329, 330, 331, 332, 335, 344, 348, 349, 353, 356, 357, 359, 366, 368, 370, 374, 377, 378, 379, 384, 392, 393, 395, 401, 402, 406, 407, 416, 420, 423, 428, 436, 439, 444, 447, 448, 498: authentic, 393; feigned, 393; growing for years, 421; impedes serving, 449; less—to act, 329; to live, 440; never—favors, 416; supernatural, 417

Detachment 27, 28, 30 31, 35, 36, 49, 54, 71, 72, 73, 74, 76, 83, 87, 88, 93, 94, 100, 101, 163, 187, 202, 308, 327, 426, 436, 439, 440, 464, 498

Determination 34, 41, 75, 78, 81, 82, 88, 97, 102, 105, 114, 115, 117, 125, 126, 127, 137, 144, 145, 163, 164, 197, 198, 202, 235, 236, 238, 239, 241, 246, 247, 251, 271, 272, 297, 300, 301, 308, 319, 344, 352, 355, 359, 360, 369, 386, 392, 417, 421, 444, 447: of the imagination, 352; of the will, 352

Devil (demon, Satan) 18, 39, 40, 42, 54, 57, 58, 59, 60, 68, 71, 77, 78, 80, 84, 85, 86, 87, 95, 99, 100, 105, 111, 113, 119, 120, 136, 138, 175, 177, 179, 182, 185, 186, 187, 188, 189, 190, 191, 192, 193, 195, 200, 214, 223, 225, 227, 228, 233, 235, 239, 288, 289, 292, 293, 296, 298, 299, 300, 302, 308, 315, 317, 320, 321, 322, 333, 334, 335, 337, 338, 345, 355, 356, 357, 360, 363, 364, 365, 366, 368, 369, 371, 372, 373, 375, 376, 377, 390, 393, 394, 399, 404, 406, 407, 408, 409, 410, 414, 415, 418, 421, 441, 449, 460, 463, 465, 474, 475, 477, 498: aim of, 295; cannot join pain to delight, 369; deception of, 445; favors from, 194; is friend of sinners, 222; legions, 293; pain from —never peaceful, 369; powers are all on outside, 369; snares of, 197; is traitor and coward, 127; tricks of 395, 416; vision from, 408; weapons of, 40; wiles of, 293, 351

Devotion 46, 105, 118, 165, 172, 175, 232, 243, 251, 307, 319, 352, 353, 368, 378, 404, 442, 446, 473: books of, 215; devotional image, 413

Diego of Alcalá, St., Friar 236, 480

Difference between spirit and soul 432

Difficulties in the spiritual life 164

Dignity 230, 284; *see also* **Persons**

Digression 29, 47, 61, 98, 383, 498

Diligence 357, 470

Director *see* **Master (spiritual)**

Disapproval 361

Disbelief: a bar to favors, 339

Discernment 157, 275, 318, 372, 414

Disciple 118, 129, 341, 404

Discipline: instrument of penance, 52, 53, 229, 480

Discord 120, 462

Discouragement 136, 229, 241

Discretion 69, 78, 91, 113, 229, 234, 237, 239, 257, 296, 312, 351, 397, 410, 460

Discursive: meditation 31, 329; reflection, 133, 401; thought, 276, 400; *see also* **Meditation; Prayer; Reflection; Thought**

Dishonor 180, 361; *see also* **CHRIST**

Disposition of soul 341

Disputes 139

Disquiet 31, 189, 308, 311, 321, 418, 477

Dissipation 199, 339

Distaste, inner 313

Distraction 120, 129, 133, 142, 156, 159, 271, 273, 313, 319, 320, 334, 440, 471: necessary, 393

Distress at having plenty 44
Distrust *see* **GOD; Self; Trust**
Disturbances 31, 58, 59, 66, 71, 73, 116, 119, 120, 122, 146, 154, 156, 189, 193, 223, 309, 310, 311, 320, 321, 322, 338, 349, 363, 366, 369, 371, 372, 377, 386, 394, 415, 418, 437, 439, 441, 444, 460, 475, 476
Diversion 65
Diversity: in contemplative communities, 35; of ways in spiritual life, 270
Division in the soul 431
Doctors: of the Church, 219; of medicine, 79
Doctrine 60, 63, 203, 204, 228, 267
Dominic, St. 356, 448
Dominican Fathers 15, 16, 18, 24, 31, 39, 204, 278; of College of St. Thomas, Avila, 15
Dominion: over elements, 108, 109; over faculties, 143; *see also* **Power**
Dormitories 27; *see also* **Rooms**
Doubt 99, 172, 189, 194, 247, 253, 285, 337, 350, 356, 357, 368, 369, 373, 376, 377, 405, 406, 414: inability to—is a sign, 339
Dove: sent from the ark, 443; *see also* **Figures of speech**
Dowry 71, 90
Dream 375, 376, 413, 416: dreamy state of soul, 336, 337
Dress 271, 306; *see also* **Clothing; Habit of Order**
Dryness 126, 173, 271, 301, 307, 308, 309, 329, 363, 395, 400, 425, 440, 441
Duty of religious to pray 119, 430, 459; *see also* **Obligation**
Dwelling places 154, 156, 263, 267, 269, 400, 484, 490: the most-entered, 335; *see also* **Castle Imagery**
Dying from love of God 221; *see also* **Death**
Earning one's livelihood 170; *see also* **St. Paul**
Ears (hearing) 328, 371, 374, 376, 377, 378, 379, 392, 406, 416, 425, 430: of the soul, 375; make self deaf to inspiration, 159; —words of Scripture, 221; *see also* **Castle Imagery** nos. 29, 30, 55
Earth 19, 131, 137, 138, 142, 160, 161, 166, 169, 336, 358, 380, 383, 389: conversations of, 369; things of, 275, 365; *see also* **World**
Ease 180; *see also* **Rest**
Easter grace *see* **TERESA**
Eating 321, 333, 334, 438; *see also* **Food; Sacrament**
Ecclesiastical arm 22, 48; *see also* **Church; Secular arm**
Ecstasy 275, 276, 379, 382, 393, 498: extreme, 384
Edification 90
Editing of Teresa's writing 34
Effects of favors 182, 183, 184, 214, 237, 240, 244, 252, 257, 273, 319, 323, 325, 327, 331, 332, 333, 339, 344, 348, 357, 368, 372, 373, 375, 376, 377, 384, 385, 393, 405, 406, 407, 408, 409, 413, 414, 416, 425, 435, 438, 442, 444, 445, 498; *see also* **Consolation; Contemplatives; Signs**
Effort (fight, labor, strive, work) in prayer 32, 33, 34, 53, 95, 105, 107, 109, 117, 129, 135, 143, 149, 153, 155, 157, 163, 165, 216, 235, 248, 255, 258, 259, 267, 272, 273, 297, 303, 317, 322, 323, 326, 328, 329, 330, 331, 340, 341, 343, 344, 348, 349, 353, 356, 369, 388, 394, 400, 401, 404, 407, 417, 427, 438, 447, 451, 469, 470, 474: disguised in delight, 103; can be a hindrance, 403; one who owes much must make, 387; what can be achieved through, 267
Elderly *see* **Age; Nuns; Persons**
Elijah: our Father, 401; his hunger for God's glory, 448; his words, 499

Eloquence 124
Embarrassment 385
Emotions *see* **Feelings**
Empty the soul 145, 435
Enclosure 20, 40, 49, 76, 82, 92, 306, 357, 451, 460, 461: of Christ in womb of B.V.M., 144; of God's grandeur in the soul, 144; of poverty and humility, 46; of the self in the heaven of the soul, 141; Council of Trent on, 26
Encouragement 169, 217, 220, 240, 385, 388
Encumbrance of the soul 165
Endurance 311, 321
Enemies 184, 186: of Christ, 41; of God, 230; love of one's, 255
Enjoy *see* **Joy**
Enkindling, of love 131, 221, 255, 358, 368, 370, 391, 399: in souls of companions, 450; of the spirit, 430; of the will, 400, 401
Enlightenment 275; *see also* **Light from God**
Enraptured faculties 498; *see also* **Rapture**
Entertainment: few opportunities for, 451
Enumeration of chapters 465
Envy, a holy 105
Equal, nuns are all to be 27, 139
Erasmus 24
Eremitical spirit 26; *see also* **Desert; Hermit**
Error 57, 185, 445, 452; *see also* **Faults, Sin**
Escorial: library of, 18; text of *The Way of Perfection,* 35
Espousal *see* **Betrothal; Spiritual**
Essence: of God, 340; of the soul 337,431
Esteem 30, 31, 45, 83, 91, 180, 227, 233, 237, 311, 319, 361, 389, 420, 446, 458, 463, 480: of earthly things, 390; for souls in whom God delights, 427
Estrangement 136
Eternal: life, 36; things, 49
Etiquette 122, 123, 139, 149, 178, 179; *see also* **Custom; Honor; Manners**
Etymology 470
Eucharist *see* **Sacraments**
Europe 19
Evangelical: counsels, 22, 28, 41, 46; prayer, 183, 203
Evangelists 219
Evil 116, 192, 201, 222, 228, 235, 346, 419: caused by the devil, 363; forces, 271; good from, 415; incurable, 88; love, 54; in monasteries, 70, 71, 83, 461; mortal sin is the only, 289; remedied, 47
Evora 458: text of *Way of Perfection,* 35
Exaggeration 219, 227, 256, 422
Example 87, 104, 311: obligation to give good, 165
Excess: of delight, 256; of love 54, 55
Exceptions, God makes 255
Excommunication 266
Exchange of gifts 491
Excuse 90, 91, 93: no—for the condemned, 168; *see also* **Self**
Exile 317, 345, 391, 439
Expansion: of heart, 318, 324; of soul, 331, 332
Experience(s) 15, 19, 21, 31, 32, 43, 44, 45, 46, 61, 62, 65, 67, 70, 72, 74, 83, 108, 111, 112, 116, 121, 127, 129, 132, 140, 142, 147, 148, 149, 151, 152, 154, 155, 157, 158, 161, 171, 181, 182, 191, 196, 207, 210, 211, 213, 218, 224, 227, 229, 243, 248, 249, 255, 260, 264, 269, 272, 273, 275, 277, 281, 287, 293, 303, 309, 313, 316, 317, 318, 319, 322, 323, 324, 328, 329, 332, 333, 334, 335, 337, 338, 340, 344, 345,

348, 349, 353, 361, 362, 364, 368, 369, 370, 371, 375, 376, 377, 378, 379, 380, 382, 385, 386, 387, 388, 389, 390, 391, 393, 395, 399, 403, 404, 406, 410, 411, 412, 413, 414, 418, 421, 422, 423, 424, 425, 426, 428, 429, 431, 432, 433, 438, 439, 440, 441, 442, 443, 460, 469, 475, 488, 489, 492: delicate, 325; dependent on having faith, 285; indescribable, 365; infused, 487; an inner—of the content of Revelation, 20; value of, 104; of union, 274; *see also* **Mystical; Supernatural**

Exterior things 134; *see also* **Senses**

Extraordinary mystical phenomena 274; *see also* **Mystical**

Eyes: of body or of soul, (seeing), 62, 142, 153, 170, 171, 172, 173, 327, 358, 371, 378, 389, 405, 419, 430, 440, 442; inner, 412; not in its power to see or not, 431, 436; *see also* **Blindness; GOD**

Eyewitness to evil 54, 55

Factions 55, 70

Faculties 32, 33, 34, 141, 148, 151, 153, 155, 156, 157, 158, 243, 249, 253, 273, 277, 283, 292, 293, 299, 301, 319, 320, 325, 327, 330, 340, 349, 350, 352, 355, 366, 367, 368, 378, 380, 383, 387, 400, 413, 433, 436, 437, 441, 471, 498: are amazed, 442; awakened, 440; bound, 422; dead or asleep, 252; enclosure of, 147; enrapturing of, 422; freedom of, 154, 395; incapability of, 365; lost, 430; silence of, 147; sleep of, 336, 490; and soul are not one, but different, 432; suspension of, 131, 157; union of, 157, 395; *see also* **Absorption; Imagination; Intellect; Memory; Will**

Failure 136, 398

Faintheartedness 141, 235, 246, 446

Fainting 380

Faith 20, 21, 25, 50, 127, 150, 171, 172, 216, 219, 221, 235, 237, 238, 240, 241, 252, 253, 284, 300, 303, 332, 372, 374, 381, 386, 404, 414, 430: mysteries of, 20; and reason teach the soul, 299; truths of, 20; weakened, 373

Fall 120

False (counterfeit, fancied, feigned, suspect) *see these listed under* **Accusation; Consolation; Delight; Desire; Favors; Freedom; Friendship; Humility; Joy; Locutions; Mystics; Peace; Pity; Prophet; Quiet; Rapture; Security; Tears; Virtue;** *see also* **Deception; Delusion; Illusion; Lies**

Falsehood: to walk in, 420

Family: members visit or stay in monastery, 27; relating to one's, 74; ties, 136; *see also* **Relatives**

Fasting 30, 52, 53, 82, 180, 352, 463: and abstaining from meat, 480

Father(s): of prodigal son, 395; all—on earth, 138; *see also* ***God***

Fathers: of the Desert, 467; of the order, 54, 89, 336, 464; mortification of, 81; poverty of, 46

Fatigue 130

Faults 30, 41, 68, 72, 77, 83, 88, 91, 92, 100, 110, 130, 158, 177, 178, 182, 190, 191, 197, 201, 223, 224, 229, 232, 234, 240, 258, 284, 289, 307, 311, 314, 315, 320, 322, 336, 348, 350, 352, 353, 356, 358, 363, 372, 379, 383, 387, 390, 408, 436, 443, 464, 470: distress over, 310; habitual, 225; insensitivity to, 223; of others, 69, 271, 295, 463; repeated, 230; rooted, 230; true friends correct one another's, 67

Favors (gifts) received in prayer 34, 41, 81, 87, 88, 102, 107, 110, 127, 137, 138, 141, 149, 151, 152, 154,

155, 157, 158, 159, 160, 164, 180, 181, 183, 184, 185, 186, 189, 190, 194, 196, 202, 207, 215, 217, 218, 220, 221, 223, 224, 225, 236, 237, 238, 240, 241, 244, 245, 246, 247, 248, 250, 251, 253, 255, 258, 259, 272, 276, 284, 285, 301, 306, 307, 308, 310, 311, 313, 314, 315, 316, 318, 319, 325, 327, 328, 329, 332, 336, 337, 339, 340, 341, 345, 346, 348, 349, 355, 356, 358, 360, 361, 366, 368, 369, 370, 374, 379, 380, 383, 386, 395, 396, 397, 400, 402, 405, 406, 407, 409, 414, 415, 417, 418, 419, 421, 426, 427, 429, 430, 431, 432, 433, 434, 436, 439, 441, 443, 444, 445, 446, 447, 448, 463, 465, 474, 492: with admiration, 408; analyses of, 275; authenticity of, 275; the body participates in, 324; the call to Carmel is a, 72; counterfeit, 333, 377; distress over, 372, 387, 391, 398; duration of, 363; extraordinary, 257; fancied, 365; from God always enrich, 182; granted publicly, 384, 442; never ask for, 416; not necessary for salvation, 326; by those in sin, 18, 95; sovereign, 252; stupefaction from, 251; *see also* **Benefits; Effects; Effort**

Favoritism 146

Fear (fright) 59, 79, 81, 82, 91, 97, 98, 100, 106, 109, 110, 112, 114, 115, 117, 119, 120, 121, 122, 126, 127, 161, 170, 182, 184, 185, 186, 188, 190, 191, 192, 193, 194, 195, 197, 203, 217, 218, 220, 221, 222, 223, 224, 227, 228, 233, 235, 236, 237, 238, 239, 240, 241, 246, 252, 274, 296, 305, 306, 309, 312, 315, 345, 357, 360, 363, 369, 370, 371, 372, 374, 375, 377, 387, 390, 391, 393, 397, 398, 406, 407, 409, 413, 414, 421, 425, 426, 431, 436, 440, 441, 443, 445, 446, 469, 492, 498: distorts self-knowledge, 293; of everything, 271; excessive, 410; of extremes, 199; that is extreme, 412; from false humility, 293; of sin, 289

Fear: of God 77, 196, 198, 200, 223, 304, 332, 477, 478; of offending God, 289

Feeling(s) 62, 157, 161, 173, 199, 225, 249, 252, 274, 277, 309, 310, 318, 319, 331, 333, 334, 337, 338, 345, 350, 361, 363, 368, 370, 393, 399, 400, 402, 405, 430, 431, 435, 440: cannot be controlled, 385; Christ's, 347; cannot be hidden, 425; hostile, 439; in the intimate depth of soul, 422, 423; rejected by God, 274, 364; of the soul are more severe than those of the body, 422, 423; *see also* **Annihilation**

Feminine, a creature so 392; *see also* **Antifeminism**

Fervor: initial, 259; helping others despite loss of, 348

Fidelity 44, 274: *see also* **GOD**

'Fig', the 415

FIGURES OF SPEECH (*Terms of analogy, allegory, metaphor, sign and symbol; see also* **Castle Imagery**)

abyss, 114
adobe, 139
air, 64
alembic, 394
animals, wild (in subjection), 302
annuity, 104
antidote to poison, 302
apples, 250, 259
apple tree, 248, 249
aqueducts, 323, 326, 331
arquebus, ball from, 389
arrival, 117
arrow(s), 252, 368, 435: fiery, 422
assault, 192

Figures of Speech (cont'd)
banner, 181
bark (ship), 387
battle, 49, 81, 103, 113, 127, 134, 169
bed of roses, 224
beehive, 143, 291
bees, 143, 291
beg, 329
betrothed, 124
bird (fledglings), 314, 404
bird with broken wings, 306
black cloth, 289
black vs white, 292
blindness, 119, 120, 150, 192, 227
blows, 127, 422
blowing: on candle, 156; on fire, 400
body, 448
borrowing, 125
boundaries, 387
branches, 71, 249
brazier, 325, 368
breasts (divine), 435
bride and bridegroom, 126, 211
bricks, 139
brute beasts, 286
burning, 425
butterfly, 273,276, 277, 343, 344, 345, 354, 378, 391, 392, 421, 434, 438, 442, 491
candle, 156
captains, 48, 103, 104, 466
captives, 143, 237, 238
carats, 254
caress, 245
castle, in air, 450
castle, fortified, 48, 142, 192
chains, 392
chess, 465: —pieces, 94
child, nursing, 332
children, 97, 114, 196
children's games, 115
chosen people, 48
city, 48
cleansing, 109
clear water, 109
cloud, 120, 364
coat of arms, 46
cocoon, 273, 344
coin, 104
combat, 49, 333
comet falling, 367
conquered, 127
country of the spouse, 124
courage, 107
court, 140, 145
cowards, 48
crazy person, 227
crevice, 442
cripples, 286
crucible, 325
crush devil's head, 120
crystal, 288
cure, 73, 411
custom, 122
danger, 107, 119
deafness, 159
death, 48, 150, 332, 438
death on road, 117
death from thirst, 114, 119, 127
debt, 187, 195
deer, wounded, 442
defense, 104
design, 254
desperado, 127
dew, 249
diamond, 269
digging, 395
disciple, 137
dishonor, 107
ditch, 478
doctor, 73
dove, 348, 354, 366, 421, 491
drink from chalice, 104
drinking, 113, 114, 127, 142, 154, 252, 467
drop of water, 424
drowning, 111
dunces, 401
dung, 383, 389
dust, 110, 383, 422
duty, 103, 104
dwarfs, 447

see also **Dwelling Places**
earth, 108
eat(ing), 88, 111, 158, 169, 258
elements, 108
emperor, 329
enemy, 48, 81, 107, 142, 185, 191, 195, 223, 304, 364
engagement, 274
exile, 284
expenses of trip, 127
falls, 97
farm worker, 123
father, 139
fatigue, 437
feet, clay or leaden, 76
fetters, 164
file, noiseless, 295
fire: 108, 174, 193, 197, 368, 389, 391, 394, 425, 440; of thirst, 423
fire (love of God): 108, 109, 143, 249, 400, 401, 423; dying, 400
flag, 104
flame(s): 108, 425, 434; move upward, 440
flight (fleeing), 120
flowers, 224, 256, 257, 258, 259, 291
flying, 291, 314, 391, 392, 404
foam, 84
food: 51, 88, 97, 150, 157, 158, 170, 248, 448; cut, cooked and chewed, 249
fool, 158, 329, 331
foot of the mount, 230
force of arms, 158
foreign country, 195
fortified city, 48
fountain, crystal-clear, 289
fount of living water, 16, 107, 113, 114, 119, 127, 142, 154, 163, 203, 204, 263, 289, 290, 331, 478; tiny fount, 435
fragrance: 257, 259, 324, 370; powerful, 243
freezing, 109
friend, 238
fruit(s), 248, 258, 259, 289, 354, 395, 437
fumes, fragrant, 325
gain, 119
game(s), 94, 142, 196
gesture of a hand, 171
giant and straw, 387
gifts, 491
giving, 125
glassmaker, 111
go astray, 312
goal, 113, 127
gold: 64, 143, 325; tested, 254
golden vessel, 411
grains of pepper, 341
grinding flour, 322
ground, 121
guards, 123
guest, 144, 156
hair, one, 94
hand, 119, 175, 249
hands: folded, 223; joined, 355, 491
hardship, 107
head, 448
health, 73, 88
healthy persons, 88
heat, 175, 400, 425
hedgehog, 328
honey, 143, 291
honor, 104
hospitality, 172
house: of spouse, 124; of stranger, 156; of straw, 178
hunger, 169
husband, 134, 156
inebriation, 102, 252, 396
infant, nursing, 156, 244
inlays of precious stones and enamels, 254
inn, a bad, 477
insignia, 46
irrigation, 394
jewels, 126, 143, 162, 163, 275, 390, 411, 494
journey, 110, 114, 115, 117, 119, 128, 142, 151, 154, 163, 176,

Figures of Speech (cont'd)
192, 199, 291, 312, 314, 470
journey's end, 117, 142
king(s), 103, 104, 119, 123, 140, 142, 143, 144, 145, 154, 219, 240, 348, 379, 437, 466: in disguise, 172
kingdom, 134, 154, 437
knocking, 224
labor, 107, 314
laborers, 51
lamp, 224
land, 109, 142, 302, 312, 390
land of Egypt, 77
learned men, 123
legs, 475
lender (lending), 125, 126
light, 277, 434
lightning, 422
living water, *see* water
lodging, 172
lord(s), 81, 123, 145
lord's table, 97
lost way, 123, 448
lowered eyes, 329
lowly people, 145
madmen, 156, 472
manna, 77, 169, 248, 301
marriage, 274, 277, 379
married people, 156
master, 137, 170
melancholic, 396
metal, 325
milk, mother's, 156, 157, 260, 435; *see also* mother's
millclapper, 322
millions (revenue), 123
mine, a gold, 64
mire, 398
mirror, 269, 290, 436
mist, 269
mother's: breasts, 332; love, 245
mouth, 157
mud, 109, 110, 139, 470: in eyes, 294
muddy water, 467
music, 132: sweet, 362
nectar, 291
negotiating, 122
obligation, 104
obstacles, 97
odor, bad, 123
offspring, 240
ointment, 243, 311
palace, 142, 143, 144, 145, 154, 437
palmetto, 291
paradise, 146, 252, 283
paralysis, 286
parrots, 281
path, 114, 115, 116, 117, 119, 121, 128, 142, 191, 192, 199, 215, 291, 292, 314, 348, 350, 391, 399, 416, 448
peace, 321, 345
pearl from the Orient, 288
peasant girl, 240
pebbles, 383
penny, 119
perfume, sweet-smelling, 324
pestilence, 55, 71, 83, 186
person: bound 429; hanging 423; starving 429; thirsty 107; uneducated 123;
phoenix, 379
pilot, 387
pinprick, 224
pit, 475
pitch, 108, 289
plague, 463
plants, 230
poison, 185, 198, 217
poisonous creatures, 217
pool, 119
pools for children, 114
poor, 187, 329
portion, 97
price, 117
prince, 123
prison, 151, 164, 187, 429
puddle, 395
pupil, 130
rain, 277, 312, 434
reliquary, 411
rents, 123

respect, 122
rest, 154
retreat, 104
revenue, 104
reward, 113, 117
rich, 127
rider, 107
rivers, 114, 277, 398, 434, 435
road, 110, 114, 117, 132, 291, 399, 400, 478: bad, 312; royal, 119; safe, 191
roots, 71, 257
royal brocade, 219
rudeness, 123
ruler, 158
safe place, 395
salary, 103
scales on eyes, 276, 430
sea, 49, 108, 142, 143, 151, 176, 277, 358, 387, 392, 424, 434
seal, 346
search, 114
seed, 341, 348
serpents, 195
servants, 97, 170, 197
service, 103
shadow, 63, 248, 425
shepherd, 123, 219, 220, 324, 328
ship, 142, 176, 387, 443
sickness, 88
signs, 151, 154
silkworm, 273, 341, 342, 343, 348, 350
simpleton, 122
sips, 151, 202
siren's song, 49
sisters (the virtues), 76
slaves, 197, 447
sleep, 119
smell, foul, 285
smoking fire, painful but endurable, 422
snakes, 312
snow, 312
soldiers, 48, 103, 104, 185, 466
son, 139
sound of building, 442
spark, 143, 365, 368, 379, 402
specks, 383
splendor, 193
spoils, 227
spouses sharing honor and dishonor, 86
springs, 323, 324, 326, 387: flowing 331
standard-bearer, 103
starvation, 48
statues of salt, 286
stealing, 119, 463
step, 115
stomach, 448
stones, precious, 143, 411
stooping, 113
stopping movement of the heavens, 320
storm, 443: calmed 364
straw, 64, 386, 387: drawn by amber, 386
stream, 119, 277, 289, 323, 331, 434
strength, 107, 114
struggle, 119
stumbling block, 192
subjects, 143
sun, 248, 249, 288, 290, 412
sunburn, 248
sunlight, 364
sun's rays, 389
sunrise, 155
sunset, 155
surgeon, 311
surrender, 48
swallowing, 157
sword-in-hand, 227
table: gaming, 142, Lord's, 97
taste, 248, 249
teacher, 130
tempest, 176, 315, 358, 364, 369
tempestuous sea, 194
tenant farmers, 123
thief, 90, 463
thieves, 76
thirst, 32, 110, 111, 204, 424, 467

Figures of Speech (cont'd)
thorn, 224
thread, 112
throne, 144
thunderclap, 367
tired, 312
titles, 123
toxin, 84
traitor, 48
travel(er), 117, 122, 142, 143, 151, 191
treasure, 90, 117, 159, 187, 383, 463
treasure chamber, 381
tree, 257, 259, 289, 290, 437: of life, 288
trifle, 126, 145
turtle, 328
unconquered, 48
vassals, 123, 307
vessels, 111
victors, 185
victory, 48, 127
vineyard, 97
viper's bite, 300
wages, 185
walk, 110, 114, 115, 312
war, 81, 103, 185, 192, 222, 223, 224, 227, 228, 236, 321, 345, 364, 437, 443, 447, 448
warm, 174, 325
water (*see also* **Prayer**) 102, 107, 108, 109, 110, 114, 142, 323, 324, 326, 331, 395, 423, 424, 435, 442, 467: from heaven, 395; running, 437
water, living, 16, 34, 109, 110, 111, 117, 119, 127, 163, 203, 288, 467
water troughs, 273, 323, 331, 387
wave, 387, 398, 443
wax, 346: candles, 434
way, 97, 119, 120, 151, 203, 401
weakness, 113
weaned, 260
weapons, 364
wedding, 124
well, flowing, 395
whistle, 328
wicks, 434
wife, 134, 156
wild horses, 32, 107
wind, 64, 142, 312
wine, 102, 251, 344, 448
wine cellar, 251, 340, 346, 448
wings, 291, 344
wobbly building, 60
worm, 52, 220, 240, 247, 285, 344, 350, 358, 381, 383, 477
wounds, 311
wretched inn, 195

Flesh *see* **Body**
Flight: bodily, 75; of the spirit, 386, 442, 494; from the world, 75
Food 43, 47, 226; *see also* **Eating; Fasting**
Foolishness: of soul, 220, 333, 364, 379, 397, 398, 432, 490; of spirit, 45
Force of arms 22; *see also* **Ecclesiastical arm; Secular arm**
Forgetfulness: of creatures, 245; of the world, 67
Forgiveness 177, 180, 182, 183
Formula for prayer 33
Fortitude 89, 142, 182, 197, 238, 239, 244, 248, 272, 274, 278, 309, 314, 315, 360, 414, 440, 442, 445, 447, 448; in face of opposition, 187, 274
Foundations (*Teresa's book*) 21, 480, 488, 489, 493, 496, 498
Foundation: of monasteries 17, 38, 469; of St. Joseph's, Avila, 15, 41; motives for, 41
Founders of religious orders 356
France 19, 20, 41
Francis of Assissi, St. 108, 356, 395, 396, 448
Francis Borgia, St. 471
Franciscans 17
Freedom 82, 110, 165, 234, 365, 391, 392, 422, 463: of Carmelite

nuns, 48, 57, 59, 60, 61, 89; of cloistered nuns, 461; from distress, 372; from evil, 201; from experiences like locutions, 371; from exterior matters, 295; of the faculties, 154; false, 120; God gives, 295; of hell, 332; from illusion, 314; inner, 30, 63, 73, 93, 161, 198, 241, 295, 321; to be 'mad' in religious community, 396; no—exteriorly, 374; in prayer, 33; from self, 293; of soul, 332; of spirit, 76, 238, 310; of the will from earthly things, 252

FRIENDSHIP
27, 29, 56, 79, 271, 344, 360, 362:
Kind of: dangerous, 57; false, 85; great, 55; suspect, 231; true, 67, 115
Relations in and for: communication an essential in, 136, 214; true—will not dissimulate, 67, 115; excess of love in, 55; fear in, 66; one who needs no one has many friends, 45; partiality in, 55; with the world, 42, 116; *see also* **Love**
With God 25, 26, 102, 104, 127, 133, 164, 175, 195, 221, 225, 229, 230, 231, 232, 234, 236, 240, 242, 243, 333, 449; *see also* **CHRIST**

Frustration 226
Fulfillment 299
Future 373, 376, 390, 476
Garden (of olives) 134, 141, 150, 162, 240, 241
Generosity 63, 126, 163
Genetic laws 22
Gentleness 302, 330
Geography 20
Gibraltar 480
Gift: sovereign, 432; of discernment of spirits, 414; of Holy Spirit, 215; of self, 163; giving of God and the soul is mutual, 254; giving versus receiving, 64
Gloom 365
Glory: one's own, 326, 398; here below, 195; increased, 44; *see also* **CHRIST; GOD**

GOD
Blessed Trinity: indwelling of, 141, 211, 382, 428; Feast of—in 1577, 266; Teresa's vision of, 277, 430
the Father 51, 135, 137, 138, 139, 140, 141, 143, 148, 150, 153, 158, 160, 161, 163, 164, 165, 166, 167, 168, 169, 170, 175, 177, 182, 184, 186, 191, 200, 201, 303, 350, 388, 400, 412, 430, 436, 450, 471, 472, 473, 474; better than all fathers on earth, 138
the Son 137, 138, 140, 141, 153, 166, 167, 168, 169, 177, 272, 277, 303, 350, 430, 436, 445, 450, 474; His love for the Father, 175; *See also* **CHRIST**
the Holy Spirit 26, 109, 112, 140, 185, 207, 209, 215, 217, 219, 242, 253, 267, 316, 317, 342, 358, 359, 375, 377, 378, 430; as mediator, 249
His Actions: activity, 346, 367, 368; afflicts His lovers, 424; has different way with souls, 487; —holds the mind, 319; makes the soul a fool, 339; pardons easily, 126; reveals His love for us, 242; repays, 218; sets seal on soul, 346; shows His Kingdom to soul, 150; will not abandon, 133; one word of His contains a thousand mysteries, 217
His Attributes: arms of, 97, 244, 246, 392; compassion, 419; delight in the soul, 418; divinity, 340; essence, 340; fidelity, 44, 112, 146, 186, 211, 239, 254, 377, 409; mutual fidelity of God and soul, 431; generosity, 126, 285, 308; glory, 50, 140, 258, 272, 285, 319, 330,

God (cont'd)
361, 392, 418, 438, 452; goodness, 51, 285; greatness, 427; has a hand in all our experiences, 317; honor, 51, 138, 235, 258, 272, 319, 330, 356, 361, 377, 385, 392, 418, 438, 448; humility, 123, 133, 218, 354; interests, 234; joy, 164; judgments, 442; justice, 51, 52, 314; knowledge, 430; mercy, 52; mysteries, 216; nearness, 32; power, 340, 430; presence, 133, 153, 173, 175, 269, 273, 289, 330, 331, 340, 395, 401, 407, 411; presence made known clearly to soul, 431; presence never departs from soul, 431; presence is felt, 440, 443; purity, 123; riches, 220; tabernacle, 443; things of, 318; hidden things of, 381; truth, 211; voice, 328; will, 112, 138, 160, 161, 163, 164, 165, 166, 167, 169, 170, 177, 202, 203, 236, 240, 242, 305, 311, 325, 345, 347, 349, 350, 351, 355, 356, 357, 393, 416, 417, 419, 423, 425, 439, 472; His will is the deed, 97; wisdom, 325, 342; wonders, 84, 342; word of, 219, 242, 258; works of, 219

He is: companion, 431, 444, 447; Emperor, 122, who is ignored, 141; free to give or deny favors, 488; little esteemed, 345; living waters of life, 288; Master, 131; not fastidious, 126; not to be limited, 421; not to be separated from the soul, 434; our business and our language, 116; a palace in which the soul sins, 419; patient, 298; source of all our good, 31, 290; sun in the center of the soul, 289; Truth, 113

Soul's Relations with God: slaves of, 446; dealing with, 89; delights begin in Him, 318; delight mutual between – and soul, 418; displeasing, 45, 77, 92, 254, 392; divine milk from, 244; dwelling in, 337; fearing, 460; feeling rejected by Him, 274, 364; finding, 400; impeding the action of, 346; intimacy with, 164, 358; limiting, 285; locutions from, 372; longing for, 391, 422; losing, 358; we must know – before we can know ourselves, 292; offending, 91; pleasing, 26, 42, 43, 45, 47, 50, 51, 54, 87, 133, 150, 193, 230, 234, 238, 239, 253, 254, 258, 259, 272, 288, 319, 323, 330, 335, 356, 378, 383, 388, 401, 406, 409, 415, 419, 431, 441, 443, 446, 450; seeing, 339, 343, 359; soul sees – at its side, 407; seeking, 328, 400; speaking to, 123, 124, 129, 130, 131, 136, 140, 147, 148, 173, 217, 220; speaking to a friend of – is a good way of having, 67; *see also* **CHRIST; Creator; Friendship; Grandeur**

Good 55, 115: not to be an occasion of wrong, 231; goodness, 61, 113

Gospels 27, 33, 118, 127, 467: explained to souls by the Persons of the Trinity, 430; *See also* **Scripture**

Gossip 187, 296, 360, 361, 449

Grace 71, 192, 195, 268, 271, 272, 289, 332, 336, 340, 351, 364, 388, 390, 408, 428, 450: state of, 429, 486

Granada, Luis de, Fray, O.P. 24, 31, 467, 489

Grandeurs of God 124, 131, 144, 174, 244, 248, 250, 252, 253, 275, 285, 324, 332, 339, 342, 381, 382, 383, 390, 392, 393, 395, 397, 398, 408, 419, 427, 434, 443

Gratian, Jerome 211, 212, 263, 265, 278, 279, 458, 483, 484, 486, 487, 493: his edition of *Meditations,* called *Conceptions,* 213
Gratitude (giving thanks) 34, 47, 63, 126, 146, 156, 186, 226, 246, 313, 331, 369, 370, 419, 473: pain at not having, 398
Greek 217
Grief 66, 73, 311, 344, 346, 397: over offending God, 302; over others' faults, 69
Growth, spiritual 104, 332, 357
Guilt *see* **Feelings**
Gustos *see* **Delight**
Habit of the order 38, 50, 86, 308, 311, 335, 476
Habits 91, 93, 130, 136, 148, 198, 300: bad, 83, 90
Hail Mary, the 25, 118, 120, 128, 132, 203, 468
Happiness 87, 244, 245, 257, 305, 314, 324, 345, 353, 374, 397, 426: habitual and interior, 224; impulse of, 395
Harm 58, 59, 63, 68, 71, 73, 74, 87, 89, 90, 97, 104, 110, 113, 115, 116, 122, 127, 131, 147, 165, 186, 194, 199, 227, 228, 260, 314, 315, 317, 329, 330, 338, 357, 365, 371, 373, 377, 383, 394, 399, 415, 436, 447, 460, 461, 464, 475
Head 320, 403, 437: aches from tears, 318; prayer omitted because —aches, 78
Health 77, 78, 79, 80, 81, 91, 111, 126, 129, 163, 171, 201, 228, 251, 271, 274, 295, 307, 312, 320, 322, 332, 333, 334, 349, 350, 362, 371, 394, 437; *see also* **Teresa**: health
Hearing *see* **Ear**
Heart: prayer from, 121, 135, 475; slows up beat, 423; feels earthly consolations, 324; fire of love distills the, 394; *see also* **Expansion**
Heaven 19, 87, 101, 109, 117, 131, 137, 138, 140, 142, 145, 147, 160, 161, 166, 169, 179, 228, 234, 239, 276, 292, 336, 343, 358, 360, 380, 383, 391, 400, 410, 424, 432, 434, 436, 438, 465: many dwelling places in, 283
Hebrew 217
Hell 47, 57, 66, 67, 77, 86, 87, 99, 106, 116, 136, 139, 177, 189, 195, 197, 222, 300, 347, 351, 356, 362, 364, 377, 385, 398, 413, 416, 424, 464, 466, 475
Heresy 120
Heretics 22, 47, 51, 345: no longer use images, 173
Hermit 26, 81, 87, 113
Hermitage 46
Historical context 19, 20, 208; *see also* **Social Situation; Spain**
Holiness 199, 410: and favors, 417
Holy See 462
Honor 27, 30, 36, 51, 59, 65, 70, 83, 84, 86, 89, 97, 123, 162, 178, 179, 181, 182, 187, 193, 214, 226, 227, 233, 234, 235, 239, 241, 257, 271, 272, 311, 385, 438, 446, 458, 463, 464, 476, 480: afflicts, 180; concern for—is a pestilence, 71; and profit do not go together, 178; Teresa's anathema regarding, 71; *see also* **CHRIST; Etiquette; God**
Honorius III 26
Hope 151, 184, 202, 298, 315, 349, 365, 444
House(s) 27, 46, 47
Household affairs, duties, management 24, 70, 101, 183, 271, 306
Huguenots 20
HUMAN
Condition 30, 273, 276
Nature 43, 57, 63, 64, 66, 84, 85, 89, 105, 107, 110, 112, 118, 123, 129, 132, 166, 169, 223, 238, 241, 255, 272, 281, 286, 300, 317, 318, 322, 333, 334, 337, 349, 351, 353, 379, 393, 407, 408, 444: consolation

Human (cont'd)
begins in, 318; 'in the beginning' God gave strength to, 293
Race is made the friend of God 221
Schemes 43
Spirit 371
Humiliation 352
Humility 27, 28, 30, 31, 35, 46, 52, 54, 69, 77, 83, 84, 86, 91, 92, 94, 98, 99, 100, 101, 103, 104, 105, 106, 112, 113, 118, 119, 121, 123, 141, 146, 158, 161, 165, 179, 181, 186, 187, 188, 189, 191, 193, 204, 210, 217, 227, 228, 231, 236, 238, 241, 253, 270, 274, 275, 285, 290, 293, 294, 307, 308, 310, 311, 312, 313, 314, 319, 327, 329, 339, 351, 352, 377, 378, 385, 388, 390, 394, 407, 410, 414, 415, 416, 420, 444, 447, 449, 463, 464, 465, 474, 476, 477: and detachment are sisters, 76; false, 141, 239; sign of, 326
Hundredfold 127
Hunger 43, 81, 165, 170
Idigoras, J. Ignacio Tellechea 456
Ignatius of Loyola, St., S.J. 356
Ignorance 284
Iliterate persons 203
Illnss *See* **Health**
Ill-temper 365
Illumination *See* **Light from God**
Illusion(s) 36, 105, 182, 185, 193, 255, 314, 368, 371, 372, 408: involving sin, 197
Image 136, 173, 380, 411, 415, 436, 442, 473
Imagery 268, 273: *see also* **Castle Imagery** (*in Appendix*); **Figure of speech**
Imagination 131, 136, 165, 172, 226, 308, 319, 322, 325, 328, 329, 337, 352, 359, 363, 364, 367, 369, 373, 374,375, 376, 377, 388, 389, 390, 396, 412, 414, 416, 421, 436, 445, 471, 472: being absorbed in, 413; devil produces wiles in, 352; engraved on the, 411; instability of, 488; rebellion of, 488; a weak, 334, 371, 372, 413; not everything imagined is a vision, 418; imagining is necessary, 144; imaginary pain, 80; *see also* **Faculties**
Imaginative visions *see* **Visions**
Imitation of Christ 46, 65, 66, 86, 91, 135, 238, 259, 326, 362, 419, 445
Impediments *see* **God (Actions); Prayer; Religious life**
Imperfections 73, 79, 182, 200, 201, 257, 301, 309, 363, 387, 423, 444, 476: become natural, 461; seeming, 199; in teachers, 49
Impulse *see* **Happiness; Love**
Incarnation of the Second Person of the Trinity *see* **CHRIST; GOD**
Incarnation, Avila *see* **Monastery**
Inclination to base things 166
Income 27, 41, 43, 44, 458, 475
Index of forbidden books 24: includes Bible, 208
Indies 17
Individual capacities for spiritual life 270
Indulgences 115
Inebriation (intoxication): heavenly, 244, 245, 258; *see also* **Prayer**
Infidelity to God 231, 436
Inflamed in love 417: *see also* **Enkindling; Love**
Infused experiences (i.e. not acquired) 268, 327, 487, 488, 489: *see also* **Prayer; Recollection; Supernatural**
Inheritance 464
Inner: life, 148; oppression, 274, 477; *see also* **Freedom; Interior; Light**
Innocence, state of 467
Innocent IV, Pope 26
Inquisition, Spanish 24, 208, 263, 279, 495: archives of, 483
Inquisitor 25: General, 24, 208, 468
Intellect 106, 110, 131, 134, 137,

139, 141, 143, 154, 158, 172, 216, 236, 237, 239, 245, 252, 253, 254, 273, 283, 292, 293, 299, 319, 322, 323, 328, 329, 331, 335, 337, 340, 373, 376, 378, 384, 400, 401, 402, 403, 412, 413, 442, 471, 472, 488: clamor of, 331; darkened, 357, 372; is in frenzy, 129; incapable of understanding, 364; is instructed, 330; restlessness of, 319; window of—opened by God, 431; *see also* **Faculties**

Intellectual visions *see* **Visions**

Intensity *see* **Love for God; Union**

Intention 43, 186, 200, 251, 310: bad, 227, 288; no evil, 419; of new members, 88; purity of, 69

Intercessors 293

Interior Castle (*Teresa's book*) 21, 264, 269, 274, 278, 279, 449, 469, 470, 479, 480, 481, 486, 495

Interior 53, 290, 325, 329, 338, 352, 369, 378, 379, 380, 387, 391, 395, 396, 414, 438, 492: battles, 321; benefits, 406; delight, 374; empyreal heaven in, 382; experience, 386; the extreme, 277, 430, 440; flight, 389; stirrings, 83, 84; strength, 448; words, 377; works, 330; world, 320; *see also* **Castle Imagery; Joy; Trials**

Intimacy 211: *see also* **God**: Soul's Relations

Intimidation 51, 127, 362, 373

Intoxication, heavenly *see* **Inebriation; Prayer**: Supernatural

Invitation to all 113, 114

Israel(ites) 381: bring back sign, 390; cross the Jordan, 392

Jacob and the ladder 381

Jealousy 125

Jerome, St. 59, 412

Jesuits 356

Jewelry 27; *see also* **Figures of speech**

Jews 135

Job's wife and friends 85

John of Avila, St. 492

John the Baptizer, St. 227

John of the Cross, St. 488, 496

Jonah 374, 493: his ivy and the worm, 350

Jordan River turns back 392

Joshua 378

Journey: inward, 274; spiritual, 278; *see also* **Figures of speech**

Joy (enjoy, rejoicing) 12, 33, 131, 134, 151, 169, 193, 199, 202, 207, 210, 216, 217, 218, 220, 225, 232, 237, 241, 244, 245, 246, 251, 255, 275, 276, 317, 318, 319, 323, 331, 332, 335, 338, 354, 360, 367, 370, 378, 382, 383, 385, 390, 391, 396, 397, 399, 403, 404, 435, 442, 448, 487: annihilates pain, 181; excessive, 395; interior, 439, 498; overwhelming, 426; suspect, 403; of the world, 234

Jubilation 395

Judas 70, 139, 227, 348, 356, 402, 470

Judges are all men 23, 51

Judgment 106, 195: by the One we have loved, 194; Day, 47, 50, 226; of others, 199, 231, 350; on day of death, 230; rash, 385

Justice 104, 313

Kings 45, 52, 67: *see also* **Figures of speech**

Kingdom of God 151, 153, 158, 159, 163, 164, 181, 201, 202: *see also* **GOD; Figures of Speech:** kingdom

Knowledge 22, 62, 63, 144, 151, 157, 165, 170, 171, 199, 207, 253, 254, 275, 318, 321, 322, 324, 329, 330, 332, 355, 380, 386, 388, 389, 390, 392, 393, 421, 422, 424, 430, 443: can be a consolation, 284; of self and of the other, 274; *see also* **Intellect; Self; Castle Imagery** nos. 9, 16

Knowledge of God: all—is equiva-

lent to knowing nothing, 124; particular, 407; of His indescribable closeness, 249; of His grandeurs, 275; *see also* **GOD; Grandeurs**
Labor *see* **Livelihood; Work**
Labor: for the Lord 48; for souls, 64; *see also* **Effort; Figures of speech**
Land 46; *see also* **Figures of spech**
Language: God is our, 116; of heaven, 58, 116; of love, used by the Holy Spirit, 217, 221, 256; of the world, 116
Languages *see* **Arabic; Greek; Hebrew; Latin; Spanish**
Languishing: exterior and interior, 333, 334; *see also* **Prayer; Quiet; Swoon**
Laredo, Bernardino de 471, 484, 489
Las Nieves 212, 213
Last Supper, the 200, 346
Latin 209, 210, 215, 217, 497
Laugh 378: at self, 64; at others, 171; at trials, 135; *see also* **TERESA:** laughs
Law: of the Church, 461; of God, 60, 65, 459
Lawsuit 475
Laxity 232: in observance, 225; in small things, 222; do not rest in, 229
Lay Sisters 458
Layz, Teresa 493
Lazarus 349
Learning 22, 48, 61, 199, 216, 318, 320, 351, 382, 414, 445, 461, 462: lack of 430; *see also* **Men** *and* **Persons** (learned)
Legend of *quo vadis* 445, 497
León, Fray Luis de, O.S.A. 35, 279, 465: imprisonment of, 208
Letters (*Teresa's book*) 482
Library 467: of the Escorial, 18
Licentiate 458
Lies 374, 420; *see also* **False**
Life (*Teresa's book*) 15, 16, 17, 19, 23, 40, 41, 132, 204, 213, 243, 263, 264, 269, 279, 455, 456, 458, 461, 462, 465, 468, 469, 470, 473, 474, 477, 479, 480, 481, 492, 483, 484, 485, 487, 488, 489, 490, 491, 492, 493, 494, 495, 496
Life: new—in Christ, 273; style, 87; wearisome, 237
Light from God 106, 113, 115, 120, 159, 185, 191, 204, 215, 225, 229, 233, 234, 244, 257, 276, 294, 316, 322, 330, 335, 338, 340, 348, 356, 357, 361, 372, 377, 380, 381, 388, 431: infused, 412; interior and exterior, 428
Lineage 139; *see also* **Honor**
Listening 148; *see also* **Ear**
Liturgy 82, 174; *see also* **PRAYER,** Liturgical
Livelihood 235; *see also* **St. Paul; Work** (labor)
Locutions 20, 22, 275, 371, 373, 374, 375, 376, 378, 406, 480: authority of—from God, 372; comprehending, 376; false, 492; from deep within, 370; from outside, 370; genuine, 492; imagined, 377; kinds of, 372; mystical, 492; *see also* **Ear; PRAYER,** Supernatural
Lords 45, 67; *see also* **Figures of speech**
Loss: of everything, 355; of souls, 87
Lost souls receive favors 96
Lot's wife 286

LOVE

God's love for us 56, 97, 138, 139, 144, 166, 182, 190, 195, 217, 219, 243, 244, 245, 246, 247, 248, 249, 254, 255, 325, 333, 346, 373, 383, 402, 405, 417, 419, 434, 446, 450: actions of —are felt, 354; arms of, 331; as Father, and as Son, 167; He reveals it, 242; touches of, 441; *see also* **GOD**

Love for God, 25, 31, 50, 54, 56, 63, 82, 94, 108, 112, 129, 140, 143, 151, 154, 161, 164, 166, 180, 181, 182, 192, 194, 196, 198, 200, 201, 217, 218, 220, 222, 223, 227, 237, 238, 239, 241, 247, 249, 250, 254, 255, 257, 259, 272, 273, 276, 308, 312, 313, 314, 319, 321, 326, 329, 334, 336, 348, 351, 355, 365, 373, 383, 384, 387, 391, 394, 398. 399, 400, 418, 421, 436, 446, 450, 477, 478: acts of, 319, 441; intense acts of, 370; actual, 407; as an arrow, wounds Him, 252; cannot be hidden, 193; death from, 111, 252, 467; default of, 54; has degrees, 193, 229; effects of acts of, 319; *see also* **Enkindling;** heals, 96; impulse of, 19, 111, 251, 255, 274, 367, 369, 387, 422, 440, 441; intensity of, 423; longing of, 19; madness of, 221, 244; manifestations of, 116; is the measure of our suffering, 162; need for genuine, 64; and of others, 447; is love of the neighbor, 63; involves one in Scripture, 210, 221; sick with, 193; most tender, 407, 440; words of, 116; *see also* **Wound of love**

Love of Neighbor 28, 29, 35, 56, 58, 63, 64, 65, 67, 115, 165, 200, 255, 258, 274, 285, 347, 351, 353, 460, 479: for all in general, 462; beneficial, 67; cannot be hidden, 477; for confessors, 460; of creatures, 194; deficiency in, 352; disordered, 57; earthly only, 65; must be equal, 55, 67; falling in, 491; imperfect, 69; impossible to love one who does not love God, 64; make others love you, 199; love between man and woman, 477; mutual among nuns, 296; having none, 350; of one another, 79, 180, 211, 357; passion affecting, 459; *see also* **Passions;** perfect, 462; for persecutors, 362, 439; *see also* **Relatives;** repaying, 63, 64; sensual, 29, 56, 62; shown in deeds, 70; sinful, 66; sisterly, 27, 54, 71; spiritual, 29, 56, 62, 66, 67, 459, 460, 462; spiritual mixed with sensual, 56, 62, 459, 462; love united with love, 354; of the world, 477

Luke, St. 487

Lukewarmness 201, 231

Lutherans 19, 20, 41, 452

Madness, blessed 396

Madrid 264: monastery of nuns in, 19

Maldonado, Fr. Alonso, O.F.M. 17

Malice 89, 223: of the world, 385

Malicious talk 85

Mancio de Corpus Christi, O.P. 21, 25

Manner of life, new 28

Manners 123, 139, 286: *see also* **Custom; Etiquette; Honor; Social Relations**

Mansions 484; *see* ***Dwelling Places***

Margaret Mary Alacoque, St. 20

María del Nacimiento 267

María de San José (Salazar) 265, 279

Marriage 354, 491: arranged, 491; consummated, 497; *see also* **Figures of speech; Persons; Sacraments; Social Relations; Spiritual Marriage**

Martha, St. 100, 101, 155, 257, 431, 448

Martin of Tours, St. 108, 393, 494

Martyrdom 44, 52, 82, 362, 398

Martyrs 258, 356, 384

Mary of Bethany 155, 257, 431, 448, 465

Mary Magdalene, St. 93, 100, 136, 171, 193, 285, 398, 426, 448, 449, 465

Mary, the Mother of God 19, 31, 37, 38, 50, 52, 86, 94, 136, 144, 210, 211, 241, 248, 253, 293, 305, 399, 403, 404, 408, 445, 458, 473: the carpenter's wife, 25; her merits, 50
Masters 226: spiritual, 117; we are to love, be proud of and not forget spiritual, 129, 314
Maundy Thursday 218, 478
Medicine for body 171: *see also* **Body; Health**
Meditations on the Song of Songs (*Teresa's book*) 211, 212, 499
Meditation 31, 32, 106, 115, 217, 248, 317, 318, 319, 323, 326, 328, 331, 342, 345, 399, 401: basis for acquiring virtues, 94; day and night, 468; inability for, 400; method for, 402; reading with, 99; *see also* **PRAYER**
Meeting with the Spouse 355, 359, 390, 491, 492, 494
Melancholy 129, 255, 307, 320, 363, 368, 369, 371, 406: *see also* **Teresa,** reflections related to psychology
Memory 154, 231, 252, 299, 373, 377, 379, 380, 382, 390, 398, 401, 402, 411, 440, 471: *see also* **TERESA,** memory
Men 23, 48, 50, 51, 54, 216, 373: blind, 285, cured with mud, 383; covetous, rich, 225; fearful, 339; a gentleman, 226; half-learned, 339, 340; learned, 20, 21, 38, 40, 42, 49, 50, 57, 59, 123, 128, 209, 210, 219, 220, 253, 266, 282, 286, 290, 319, 338, 339, 372, 375, 409, 415, 452, 461, 488, 492; must be as angels, 49; rich young, 271, 307, 308, 487; at pool, 287; Teresa criticizes, 210; the Lord will make women so strong—will be astonished, 70; *see also* **Persons; Sons of God**
Mendicants 26
Mendoza, Bishop Don Alvaro de 61, 459
Mental prayer *see* **Prayer**
Mercy 48, 72, 96, 114, 146, 165, 174, 178, 180, 189, 190, 194, 215, 230, 231, 241, 243, 246, 249, 285, 287, 293, 298, 302, 303, 304, 310, 314, 323, 328, 335, 345, 355, 356, 358, 364, 365, 377, 383, 388, 393, 395, 419, 424, 427, 429, 432, 443, 445, 452: *see also* **Christ; God**
Merit 244, 251, 253, 311, 317, 334, 343, 344, 348, 351, 358, 390, 407, 410, 417, 429, 450, 460: opportunity to, 251
Messiah, Baptizer is not the 227
Method *see also* **Meditation; Prayer**
Method for the Visitation of Monasteries (*Teresa's book*) 485
Mind 121, 130, 133, 140, 190, 310, 311, 319, 320, 329, 330, 338, 352, 375, 376, 378, 389, 404, 413, 414, 440, 477, 488: absurdities make restless, 99; cleverness of, 323; losing one's, 366; only God can hold the, 319; Teresa's synonym for intellect, 158; wandering of, 488; *see also* **Intellect**
Miracles 172, 401, 425: miraculous cure, 480
Misery (misfortune) 190, 217, 223, 240, 246, 250, 291, 292, 304, 309, 313, 321, 332, 346, 364, 365, 379, 383, 388, 398, 399, 420, 428, 443, 448
Mistakes 38, 191, 309, 315, 325, 329, 338, 341, 397, 399, 404
Misunderstandings 264, 274
Mitigation 80
Moderation 80, 460
Monasteries 38, 40, 59, 72, 78, 80, 82, 83, 86, 87, 89, 105, 178, 179, 212, 215, 224, 228, 233, 234, 263, 265, 278, 279, 282, 334, 396, 446, 451, 461, 463, 474, 481: entrance into—a solution to social problem, 464; government of, 461;

poverty in building, 27; *see also* **Alba; Avila; Madrid; Salamanca; Segovia; Toledo; Valladolid**
Monastery of the Incarnation, Avila 19, 26, 265, 456, 457, 458, 462, 496: rooms bought and sold in, 27
Monastery of St. Joseph, Avila 15, 18, 20, 38, 39, 41, 43, 56, 108, 265, 452, 457, 458, 462, 466: observance in, 41, 50
Money 27, 42, 44, 45, 46, 51, 90, 225, 463, 476: for administration, 476; *see also* **Income**
Monica, St. 67
Moors 237, 238, 345
Moradas 484
Mortification 30, 77, 82, 88, 93, 100, 101, 105, 112, 201, 224, 234, 235, 334, 343, 410, 449, 464: public, 463
Moses and the burning bush 381
Motto of Carmelite order 499
Mount Calvary 141
Mount Carmel 26, 336
Movement of the soul 389, 440: first, 444; impetuous, 386; *see also* **Happiness; Love; Impulse**
Music 442; *see also* **Figures of speech**
Mysteries 118, 207, 217, 219, 260, 270, 275, 276, 277, 381, 399, 402, 403: of the Passion, 400; a thousand in one word of Scripture, 210
Mystical: elements of spiritual life, 268; experiences, 15, 210, 211, 213, need to be explained, 215; graces, 493; phenomena, 274; pseudo-mystical, 275; sense of Scripture, 211; understanding the, 484; *see also* **Prayer, Supernatural**
Mysticism: in Spain, 22; phenom-ena accessory to, 22
Mystics, false 22
Natural graces 55
Necessity made a virtue 161, 351, 386
Need(s) 44, 69, 79, 80, 81, 169, 183, 187, 198, 312: of the neighbor, 259; having—of no one, 45
Neighbor: charity to, 251; helping one's, 235; *see also* **LOVE,** of neighbor
Nineveh 374
Noah 443
Nobility 122, 139, 449, 458
Noise: poverty makes no, 47; in soul, 330
Nonsense 86, 96
Nothingness 420
Nourishment: of body, 171; of soul, 169; *see also* **Eating; Food; Sacrament**
Nuncio *see* **Papal**
Nuns 15, 18, 19, 27, 28, 30, 37, 42, 50, 73, 77, 78, 79, 80, 81, 85, 86, 87, 89, 108, 116, 130, 212, 215, 279, 458, 461, 462, 463, 470, 472, 499: discontented, 88; elderly, 466, 471; taken to be hypocrite, 116; as synonym for obedience, 105; unsophisticated, 116; who cannot follow Rule, 463; *see also* **TERESA** and Nuns
Obedience 16, 39, 60, 61, 69, 105, 173, 175, 179, 190, 215, 260, 264, 266, 268, 281, 282, 283, 313, 314, 334, 343, 347, 348, 392, 415
Obligation: going against, 224; of state in life, 438; of the worldly, 49; regarding locutions, 375; TO: account for riches, 226; avoid displeasing God, 387; be attentive in prayer, 130; to believe, 381; confess is felt, 460; give good example, 165; pray, 469; pray for benefactors, 47; pray for Church, 52, 53; serve God, 186, 227, 250, 258, 387, 408, 417, 436; serve the neighbor, 449; share goods, 226; speak of God, 116; suffer, 250
Observance 28, 37, 46, 53, 78, 80, 91, 166, 179, 225, 295, 412; 419;

see also **Monastery of St. Joseph, Avila**
Obstacles *see* **Peace; Perseverance; PRAYER; Progress**
Occasions *see* **Sin**
Occupation 48, 126, 147, 174, 224, 331, 430, 432: in God, 384; for benefit of others, 440
Offending: Christ, 134; God, 138, 197, 198, 201, 223, 231, 232, 306, 307, 315, 319, 326, 332, 344, 345, 346, 347, 350, 358, 362, 364, 387, 390, 391, 392, 398, 426, 436, 439, 445, 473; by abominations, 134
Offering 33: self to God, 446; *see also* **PRAYER Forms**
Opinion of crowd 121
Order of Our Lady 28, 37, 46, 53, 61, 78, 179, 306, 459, 499: *see also* **Carmelite Fathers; Nuns**
Orientation 484
Ormaneto, Nicolás 265
Orthodoxy 21
Osma 483
Osuna, Fray Francisco de, Franciscan 23, 484, 489
Our Father, the 25, 31, 32, 33, 34, 35, 118, 120, 121, 128, 129, 130, 131, 132, 137, 148, 149, 150, 152, 154, 158, 159, 161, 162, 185, 191, 192, 203, 204, 263, 468, 473: Castilian version of, 472
Pain 31, 112, 275, 344, 345, 346, 347, 361, 362, 367, 370, 385, 389, 391, 397, 398, 422, 423, 426, 436, 437, 438: delightful, 395; duration of, 423, 425; loving, 368; precious, 424; rapture remedies, 425; reaches depths of soul, 368; relieved by Sacrament, 171; spiritual, 421, 424; when there is no suspension, 321; sweet, 111, 189, 367; undeserved, 424; *see also* **Suffering**
Painting of the Lord 415; *see also* **Images**
Palm Sunday 227
Palmetto 291
Papal Nuncio 265; *see also* **Holy See**
Pardon 36, 379, 398, 424
Parents, be good to 74
Particular fondness for friend 56
Passage of the Lord: to center of soul 341; Risen Christ from the tomb, 341
Passions 55, 57, 65, 311, 318, 322, 323, 349, 393, 437: *see also* **LOVE,** affected by passion
Passive element of spiritual life 268
Passive quiet 33: *see also* **PRAYER; Quiet**
Path to God, not all are on same 99, 224
Patience 80, 130, 188, 230, 251, 287, 290, 321, 322, 332, 362: of a loved one, 66
Paul, St. 112, 193, 201, 212, 245, 248, 276, 277, 285, 308, 434, 441, 487, 495, 497: conversion, 430; hurled to ground, 413; working day and night for livelihood, 445
Paulinus of Nola, St. 480
Peace 28, 31, 54, 55, 58, 59, 70, 73, 116, 119, 151, 153, 154, 155, 189, 193, 195, 214, 216, 221, 222, 224, 225, 228, 229, 232, 236, 238, 240, 241, 250, 271, 273, 296, 299, 302, 308, 324, 330, 338, 345, 373, 374, 377, 390, 393, 394, 395, 406, 408, 413, 436, 437, 439, 443, 463, 487: in comfort, 228; dangerous, 225, 228; false, 214, 222, 227; obstacles to, 322; practices to possess, 28; from sensuality, 225; from the world, 225, 236
Peasant 475
Penances 30, 65, 78, 91, 139, 180, 195, 228, 236, 295, 305, 306, 311, 330, 332, 333, 343, 344, 347, 384, 429, 436, 437, 448, 470, 480: excessive, 190; frenzy for, 463; indiscreet, 111; *see also* **Persons; Sacraments**

Pensamiento 488
Perception 165, 430, 431
Perfect: love 54, 55; souls, 63; seek that which is, 50, 59, 86
Perfection 48, 58, 60, 61, 62, 63, 67, 68, 74, 83, 85, 88, 90, 99, 100, 105, 115, 146, 151, 179, 182, 183, 184, 185, 190, 191, 224, 234, 239, 301, 313, 350, 351, 403, 417, 431, 460, 463, 469: killed, 84; Lord continues process of, 115; less important than following the Lord, 464; true—consists in love of God and neighbor, 295; vitiated, 58
Permissions 220, 295: used as excuse, 78
Persecution 91, 162, 163, 169, 177, 185, 240, 251, 257, 259, 315, 362, 391, 410, 426, 439, 498
Persecutors: love and recommend—to God, 439
Perseverance 103, 117, 127, 222, 271, 304, 308, 332, 450: devil causes obstacles to, 127; one always gains much through, 298
Persistence in small faults 222
Persons (people): dignity of, 230; elderly, 99, 466, 471; impatient, 130; learned, 57, 60, 61; married, 30, 80, 86, 124, 134, 156, 329, 354; penitential, 234; of prayer, 82, 311, 333, 388; religious, 82, the holier they are, the more sociable, 199; rich, 165, 226, 365; sick, 371; spiritual, 39, 60, 73, 159, 379, 409, 461; unlearned, 208, 352; of the village, 258; worldly, 222; worth of, 123; *see also* **Children; Daughters *and* Sons of God; Men; Woman**
Pestilence *see* **Figures of speech; Friend; Honor; Rank; Virtue**
Peter of Alcántara, St. 239, 329, 396, 489, 494
Peter, St. 139, 154, 308, 398, 498: legend about, 445; threw himself into sea, 235
Petition (supplication) 33, 34, 42, 50, 51, 52, 130, 151, 159, 160, 183, 184, 186, 222, 229, 237, 243, 251, 257, 317; *see also* **Prayer,** Forms
Petronila Bautista 467
Pets 27
Pharisee 93, 172, 372
Philip II 24, 458
Philosophy 108, 351
Physical Phenomena *see* **Body; Consolations**
Piacenza 265
Piezas 484
Pilate 420
Pilgrims 19
Pity: from others 47; false, 85
Pleasing: creatures, 92; people, 257; *see also* **GOD; Rulers; Self**
Pleasure 65, 75, 232, 234, 244
Pledge of betrothal 359
Pondering of the Lord's law 459
Poor 27, 46, 47, 80, 225, 226, 227, 310, 464, 476; *see also* **Poverty**
Portugal 265
Possessions 55, 234, 308, 310, 385: of a soul that loves God, 217
Poverty 43, 44, 45, 46, 47, 60, 166, 200, 225, 226, 349, 458, 475: of spirit, 27, 30, 45, 187, 188, 388, 476; natural—of the soul, 382; *see also* **St. Clare; Fathers of order; Income; Silence; Thought**
Power (dominion): of the poor in spirit 45; of a word from God, 373, 406
Practices: for peace, 28; of prayer, 306; of virtue, 314, 357; *see also* **Penances**
Praise of God 33, 59, 62, 70, 71, 72, 99, 122, 123, 124, 150, 151, 152, 153, 158, 159, 161, 183, 194, 195, 198, 204, 218, 225, 226, 227, 228, 233, 236, 244, 249, 260, 270, 272, 275, 282, 284, 285, 290, 305, 314, 319, 327, 329, 334, 337, 339, 341,

344, 358, 361, 364, 370, 373, 374, 376, 381, 384, 385, 392, 395, 396, 404, 405, 408, 410, 418, 426, 428, 439, 440, 441, 443, 444, 445, 448, 450, 469, 477: prayer of, 396

Praise: of others, 352, 361; of us, becomes a trial, 274

PRAYER 31, 35, 39, 42, 48, 52, 53, 58, 59, 60, 63, 65, 68, 73, 83, 98, 99, 100, 104, 106, 109, 110, 113, 115, 116, 118, 119, 120, 121, 122, 126, 129, 130, 131, 132, 135, 137, 138, 160, 170, 173, 180, 183, 185, 186, 190, 191, 193, 202, 203, 214, 215, 220, 223, 224, 225, 229, 230, 232, 236, 243, 248, 253, 259, 270, 271, 278, 281, 282, 291, 292, 297, 298, 301, 303, 318, 321, 324, 330, 331, 334, 335, 336, 343, 345, 349, 352, 357, 359, 366, 371, 377, 379, 384, 394, 401, 402, 404, 406, 418, 429, 436, 439, 440, 446, 447, 448, 449, 459, 460, 461, 462, 465, 466, 468, 472, 474, 475, 487, 492:

Conditions related to Prayer: abandoning, 320, 321; absence from, 334; account of, 414; answered, 49; asked, 391; beginning of, 106, 118; degrees of, 442; devil causes terror of, 194; end of, 106, 118; foundation for, 28, 35, 60, 93, 149, 183; habit of, 136; helps to, 46; hours of, 103, 466; impediments to, 163, 164, 174, 294, 301, 383, 418; inducing, 329; manner of, 148; means of, 118; method of, 31, 32, 33, 106, 133, 141, 143, 147, 148, 149, 271; objections to, 118; obstacles to, 321; persistent, 150; private, 189; reading for and with, 103, 118; return to, 332; sharing—between friends, 25; no need to shout, 130; skill in, 118; spontaneity, 33; testing, 325; unceasing, 28, 53, 121, 306; what not to pray for, 43; withdrawal from, 332; teaching prayer to others, 348

Contemplative, 15, 22, 33, 101, 122, 128, 132, 183, 272, 273: impossible to remain always in, 400; infused, 268, 272, 273; value of, 273; *see also* **Contemplation; Contemplatives**

Effects of Prayer: apostolic efficacy of, 26; most profit for neighbor, 450; progress in variety of ways, 223; value of, 325

Forms of Prayer: adoration, 33, 381; *see also* **Grandeurs of God;** colloquy with God, 103; liturgical, 24; of offering, 33; petition, 33; for own soul, 50; for those who receive favors, 194; praise, 33, 396; thanksgiving, 33; *see also* **Petition; Praise of God**

Mental, 24, 25, 94, 97, 101, 103, 119, 121, 122, 123, 125, 128, 130, 131, 132, 147, 152, 183, 286, 466, 468, 469: practice of, 95

Mystical, 34, 267, 272, 470, 484, 487, 490; *see also* **Mystical**

Natural Prayer, 273: acquired, 273; active, 273; discursive, 467; *see also* **Acquire; Active life; Discursive**

Passive, 15, 272, 273

Quiet, of, 18, 33, 36, 141, 151, 152, 153, 154, 155, 156, 157, 158, 159, 183, 214, 243, 273, 331, 333, 353, 367, 374, 379, 382, 403, 474, 480: spiritual sleep, 333; *see also* **Quiet mind**

Recollection, of, 18, 32, 33, 34, 36, 141, 147, 174, 175, 331, 489: infused, 488, 489; struggle for, 148; *see also* **Recollection**

Supernatural Prayer, 132, 153, 155, 158, 182, 252, 268, 272, 273, 290, 349, 396, 474, 484, 487
Union, of, 34, 152, 153, 157, 182, 183, 214, 255, 273, 276, 337, 339, 343, 354, 355, 356, 382, 429, 441, 491, 492: proof of genuine, 336; *see also* **Union**
Vocal, 16, 22, 23, 24, 25, 32, 33, 99, 101, 103, 119, 121, 122, 123, 125, 128, 129, 130, 131, 132, 133, 136, 139, 141, 147, 151, 152, 158, 159, 203, 232, 286, 334, 365, 370, 466, 472: Mass and—are enough, 24; obliging oneself to, 159
Waters (prayer), 326, 327: fourth, 488
See also **Apostolate; Books; Heart; Persons; Progress; TERESA; Torment; Woman**

Preachers 22, 42, 48, 49, 92, 211, 218, 449
Predictions 373
Prelates 52; *see also* **Bishop; Superior**
Preparation to receive God's gifts 308, 310, 313, 326, 341, 410
Presence to God 32, 33, 147; *see also* **CHRIST; GOD**
Presumption 98
Pride 100, 333, 352
Priests 20, 176, 473; *see also* **Confessors; Preachers**
Prioress 56, 83, 84, 128, 179, 190, 295, 334, 371, 403, 451, 458, 461, 462, 474: admonishing one's, 44, 296; advice to, 70; and confessor, 58, 59; to be discreet, 410; to encourage one's, 90; the—should give freedom, 57, 60, 67, 409; if—seems to be harsh, 69; problems of being, 78; *see also* **Teresa as Prioress; Nuns.**
Prison cell 71
Privileges 83
Prodigal son 138, 300, 395
Progress in spiritual life 84, 87, 88, 105, 115, 181, 243, 371, 447, 470: falters, 235; of the house, 61; of a loved one, 65; in three months, 255; obstacles to, 223; principle for making, 460; in the young, 255
Promises: making, 161, 475; to God, 446; nothing but, 472; *see also* **Deeds; Words**
Properties: of things, 108; of water, 109
Prophet, false 203
Protection of the Lord 248, 385
Protestantism 20, 24
Providence 170, 187, 226, 260
Provinces of the order 265
Provincials 59, 461
Prudence 234, 356, 460
Psalmist 109
Psalms 217, 318, 420
Pseudo-mystical phenomena 275
Psychology perceived by Teresa *see* **TERESA**
Publican, the 156, 443, 471
Punishment 69, 71, 150, 180, 231, 470
Purgatory 50, 195, 276, 398, 423, 424, 452
Purification 276, 424: of soul, 379
Purpose of amendment 232
Purpose of Teresian Carmelite call 35, 52, 83, 335
Pusillanimity 235, 238
Quiet 271, 321, 323, 324, 333, 369, 373, 393, 441, 471, 477, 488, 489: enjoyed at pleasure, 431; false, 222, 223; *see also* **Prayer of Quiet**
Quiet mind 190
Rank: in Carmelite communities, 27, 84, 139, 179: concern about—is a pestilence, 83

Rapture(s) 104, 111, 164, 275, 276, 333, 379, 382, 385, 391, 412, 429, 440, 442, 467, 490, 494: duration of, 389; feigned, 385; kinds of, 379; quick, 388; resistance to, 386; fearful speed of, 386; superabundant knowledge gained in, 389; true, 385
Rationality 210, 253
Readiness to love 64, 149; *see also* **LOVE**
Reading 322, 342, 392; *see also* **Books; Meditation; PRAYER**
Reason 110, 112, 216, 309, 312: faculty of, 423
Recollection 46, 61, 118, 128, 130, 133, 135, 136, 140, 141, 142, 143, 144, 147, 148, 149, 171, 215, 271, 273, 302, 306, 320, 328, 329, 331, 373, 374: interior, 470; supernatural, 327; not supernatural, 147; *see also* **PRAYER,** of Recollection
Recreation 46, 56, 65, 69, 73, 101
Redaction of Teresa's writings 458, 459, 461, 462, 463, 465, 468, 469, 470, 472, 473, 475, 477, 478, 489
Reflection 83, 92, 128, 130, 133, 134, 150, 230, 249, 253, 272, 286, 364, 402, 403, 413, 420, 464; *see also* **Discursive**
Reform of Carmelite life 265
Regret, painful 345
Relatives 27, 57, 73, 74, 75, 76, 79, 89, 116, 136, 344, 463: friendship among, 55, 115; love for, 255
Relationships to others, to self and to world 29; *see also* **Friendship; LOVE**
Religious life 46, 48, 49, 59, 61, 83, 87, 97, 119, 161, 163, 165, 235, 236, 350, 351, 412, 476: entrance into—an answer to social problem, 27
new members: acceptance, 88; information on, 89; intelligence needed in, 88, 89, 462; impediments to entering, 83; probation of, 89
professed: 224, 463, 472; admission to profession, 89; delay of, 464
dismissal from, 89
Religious orders 48, 55, 59, 314, 410, 459, 463
Reliquary for the book *Interior Castle* 279
Remedies for evil or temptation 39, 56, 57, 58, 68, 71, 106, 191, 201, 218, 228, 231, 259, 300, 303, 342, 364, 365, 378, 392
Remembrance: habitual—of God, 406, 416: of sins, 363
Remorse for faults 225
Rent 475
Renunciation 74, 97, 142, 308
Repaying *see* **God; LOVE**
Repentance 230, 232
Reputation 233; *see also* **Honor**
Resentment 419
Resignation 330, 349: *see also* **Conformity; GOD; Will**
Resistance 353: to favor impossible, 425, 426
Resolutions 41, 125, 177, 188, 200, 232, 235, 240, 441, 444, 446
Respect 397
Response, interior, 441
Rest (repose) 82, 106, 111, 170, 181, 226, 227, 237, 248, 249, 250, 302, 321, 331, 344, 345, 354, 390, 391, 421, 438, 442, 445, 446, 447; *see also* **Ease**
Restlessness 107, 377
Restraint 331; *see also* **Constraint**
Restrictions 59
Resurrection of Christ 278; *see also* **CHRIST**
Revelation(s) 19, 20, 22, 276: divine, 20, 21; of the glory in heaven, 434
Revenue, fixed 476; *see also* **Income**
Reward 137, 146, 150, 230, 246,

258, 308, 313, 330, 343, 350, 358, 450
Ribera, Francisco de, S.J. 279, 486
Riches 65, 162, 192, 214, 225, 234; *see also* **Persons**
Ridicule 360
Rights 85, 86, 353, 356; *see also* **Wrongs**
Rituals 24
Rodríguez, José Vicente 279
Roman Catholic Church 21, 38, 282; *see also* **Church; TERESA**
Rome 264, 279
Room(s) 484: of self-knowledge, 291, 292; where disciples were, 341; *see also* **Castle Imagery; Cells; *Dwelling Places;* Monastery of the Incarnation, Avila**
Roots: of faults, 230: of the soul, 437
Rosary 123
Rule of the Carmelite order 24, 26, 28, 37, 38, 50, 53, 56, 69, 78, 121, 215, 225, 295, 296, 315, 394, 459, 487
Rulers 45; *see also* **Figures of Speech; Kings; Lords**
Rules 223: of discernment on favors, 275
Sacraments 21, 42, 176, 356:
  Eucharist 20, 36, 51, 70, 120, 168, 169, 170, 172, 173, 174, 175, 176, 189, 232, 241, 246, 267, 340, 404, 477: Jesus is ours in—since Father has given Him, 167; as medicine, 171; true Presence in the, 171; routine reception of, 241; Spiritual Communion, 174
  Matrimony 354
  Penance (Confession) 57, 70, 230, 231, 342, 409, 461
Sacramentals: crucifix, 388, 415; holy water, 231; portrait of our Emperor, 415; sign of the cross, 133; *see also* **Images**
Sacrifice 400: interior and exterior, 450
Sadness 33, 134
Saint(s) 19, 44, 52, 75, 98, 100, 119, 129, 136, 146, 177, 201, 219, 227, 228, 235, 238, 248, 275, 293, 305, 307, 329, 344, 389, 396, 399, 403, 408, 412, 447, 448, 449, 467, 473: does not speak but is companion, 408; glory of the, 439; is necessary to speak to, think about and become companions of, 399; those who are—in own opinion cause more fear than do sinners, 233; fortitude of saintly girls, 238
Salamanca 467: edition of the *Way of Perfection,* 35; monastery of nuns, 19, 481, 496
Salvation 304, 436, 448, 486
Samaritan woman 107, 258, 424
Sanctity 200: of recipients of favors not greater than of those who do not receive them, 285
Santiago de Compostela 483
Satan *see* **Devil**
Satisfaction 63, 110, 151, 154, 155, 157, 189, 232, 246, 257, 258, 259, 338, 367, 369, 418, 421, 426, 487: from tears, 243
Saul, King 417: goes astray, 348
Savor of soul (differs from that of spirit) 432
Scandal 91, 166
Scholastics 23
Sciences *see* **TERESA**: Reflections
Scripture 20, 21, 118, 208, 209, 215, 216, 218, 443, 445, 467: accommodated, literal and mystical sense of, 211; love and, 210; majesty of words of, 221; publication, reading of—in Spain, 208; *see also* **Gospels**
Scruples 99, 224, 460
Seclusion *see* **Enclosure**
Secrets 34, 159, 164, 242, 253, 275, 314, 324, 329, 337, 338, 355, 367, 375, 380, 381, 382, 384, 410, 418,

419, 427, 432, 435, 442: beneficial, 323
Secular arm 22, 47, 48; *see also* **Ecclesiastical arm; Force of arms**
Security 83, 88, 100, 106, 184, 191, 192, 200, 218, 227, 228, 235, 236, 299, 306, 348, 356, 363, 369, 391, 398, 436, 445, 464, 486: of conscience is never certain, 304, 305; false, 76; in love of God, 195
Seeing *see* **Eyes**
Sega, Felipe 265
Segovia 278
Self: advantage to, 69; asleep to, 336; assurance, 190; concern, 82; confidence, 198, 409; control, 148; deception, 201, 475; denial, 83, 93; detachment, 93; discipline, 30; distrust of, 21, 189, 241, 357; dominion over, 81; enter into, 286, 470; esteem, 31, 179, 181, 350, 408; excuse of, 90, 93; faculties employed with, 292; fearful of, 443; forgetfulness of, 100, 157, 179, 181, 245, 247, 258, 330, 377, 378, 396, 438, 448, 476, 498; giving, 163; indulgence, 79, 195; interest, 66, 119, 161, 233, 257, 259, 326; knowledge, 184, 190, 270, 275, 284, 287, 291, 293, 294, 309, 310, 314, 348, 388, 390, 416, 421, 477; love, 79, 246, 255, 343, 350, 356, 357; pleasing, 82; rise above, 470; satisfaction, 82, 88; surrender, 163; thinking of, 290, 291; treasure hidden in, 336; understanding, 293, 320, 322; will, 343
Selfish intentions 239
Seniority 83, 179
Senses 164, 171, 221, 252, 275, 327, 333, 336, 340, 349, 355, 367, 368, 370, 379, 383, 384, 386, 389, 390, 395, 406, 413, 418, 433, 437, 441: exterior and interior, 142, 147, 153; are dead, 380; duration of loss of 425; enrapturing of, 422; obey the soul, 143; are put to sleep, 374; surrender to soul, 143; use the—for sake of the inner life, 148; withdrawal of, 142; *see also* **Ears; Eyes; Figures of Speech**: fragrance; **Taste**
Sensitivity 68, 93
Sensuality 116, 245, 251, 259, 318, 459, 460
Separation from God 288
Sermons 92, 216, 217, 218, 257, 271, 342, 442; *see also* **Preachers**
Servants: should have attitude of, 170, 303; and slaves in monasteries, 27; not greater than Master, 303; useless—of the Gospel, 308
SERVING:
- Christ and the Church, 22; *see also* **CHRIST, Church**
- God, 53, 82, 84, 98, 100, 101, 103, 112, 120, 129, 131, 155, 159, 160, 163, 164, 170, 181, 186, 187, 189, 197, 198, 201, 204, 222, 226, 236, 238, 246, 247, 248, 251, 256, 257, 258, 259, 275, 303, 305, 307, 311, 312, 314, 326, 332, 339, 341, 348, 356, 358, 369, 371, 373, 384, 387, 390, 397, 402, 407, 408, 410, 417, 424, 430, 436, 439, 443, 444, 446, 450, 460, 463, 464, 475, 498; hindrance to, 464; motive for, 413; in possible things, 449
- Neighbor, 99, 103, 104, 109, 257, 498; acts of service of, 277; obligation of, 449, 450; one's Sisters, 450; being slaves to others, 447; those who are good, 450; the sick, 101

Seville, Carmelites of 279, 499
Shadow of the Divinity 249
Shame 63, 385
Sharing wealth 225
Shepherds 123; *see also* **Figures of speech**
Sickness *see* **Health; Persons**

Sighs, anxious 422
Signs 158, 188, 229, 237: against error, 338, 339; that favors are from God, 202, 409, 446; of growth in grace, 192, 193, 196, 358; of authentic locutions, 371-377; of loving truly, 351; regarding rapture, 385; of vision from devil, 414
Silence 27, 33, 34, 53, 56, 78, 82, 91, 296, 315, 329, 395, 442: when falsely accused, 465; as poverty of words, 27, 46
Silverio de Santa Teresa, Fr., O.C.D. 35
Simeon 153
Simple people are not to read Scripture 221
Simplicity 89, 165, 216, 339
Sin 59, 83, 84, 86, 92, 94, 189, 191, 197, 201, 221, 223, 224, 225, 227, 230, 231, 233, 239, 240, 243, 259, 269, 271, 288, 305, 306, 307, 318, 321, 361, 363, 365, 377, 388, 392, 397, 398, 414, 429, 443, 444, 465, 475, 476, 477: advertence in, 197, 444; consequences of, 488; and contemplation, 18; deliberate, 197; disorder of original, 488; no immunity from, 444; is an obstacle to understanding Scripture, 210; occasions of, 48, 55, 77, 142, 143, 190, 196, 198, 223, 232, 288, 315, 332, 333, 342, 355, 498; weeping over, 232
Sinners 136, 175, 194, 201, 233, 388, 419, 477
Slave(s): attitude of—compared to that of Jesus, 168; being—to others, 447; the cross is the brand of God's, 446; of the devil, 99; of God, 446; in the monastery of the Incarnation, Avila, 27; the rich are, 226
Sleep (sleeping) 321, 333, 334, 375, 438: of soul, 244, 245, 336
Sobbing 322
Social Relations described by Teresa 123, 125, 134, 139, 145, 149, 165, 178, 226, 240, 257, 286, 355, 381, 412, 458, 464, 491
Society of Jesus *see* **Jesuits**
Solace 313; *see also* **Comfort; Consolation**
Soldiers, who knelt to drink 300; *see also* **Figures of speech**
Solitude 26, 27, 56, 81, 129, 130, 140, 146, 156, 233, 327, 334, 336, 344, 359, 365, 423, 440, 442, 446: relief in, 391
Solomon 209, 213, 215, 306, 442, 445: noiseless building of his temple, 441-2
Sons of God 227, 465, 474; *see also* **Children** *and* **Daughters of God**
Song of Songs, 207 *passim to* 260; 321, 340, 401; *see also* **Bride; Scripture; Biblical Index**
Sophistication 116
Sorrow 112, 154, 224, 241, 353
Soto, Domingo 24
Soul (*used throughout book, principal themes given here*): is in command of God, 164; depth of, 349; is different from spirit, 432; dignity of, 284; distinction of—from spirit, 435; fixed state is unsafe, 317; functions differ from those of spirit, 432; imperfect, 18; improvement, 390, 431; informed, 355; instructed, 343, 413; interior part, 370; joined with God, 497; liberty of, 446; made to God's image and likeness, 270, 284; noise in, 330; is not something dark, 428; pain in depth of, 368; passion, 349; *see also* **Passions;** profit of, 237; spacious, 291; and spirit, 434, 437; stability of, 444; stinginess of, 163; first stirring, 363; stirring, 436; strength over body, 142; *see also* **Strength;** sun in interior of, 435; superior part of, 320, 321, 370, 429; type of,

297; value of, 284; wealth of, 164; *see also* **Affliction; Annihilation; Blindness; Spirit**
Sound, of Lord's greeting 435; *see also* **Ears**
Spain: in Teresa's time, 20, 24, 208, 264, 279, 410; mysticism in, 22; political situation of, 19
Spanish language 209, 475
Speech 271, 306, 384
Spirit: from God, 374; other than from God, 363; human, 240; freedom of, 29, 74; made one with God, 497; and soul, 389, 432, 433; work of, 329; *see also* **Soul**

SPIRITUAL (*used throughout book, principal themes are given here*):
Betrothal (espousal) 275, 277, 354, 355, 356, 358, 359, 379, 382, 390, 421, 433, 434: preparation for, 274, 491
Communion 174
Delights 317; *see also* **Delight**
Depths 270; *see* **Soul**
Life 270, 271, 488: tested in, 371
Man 289
Marriage 277, 278, 354, 428, 429, 432, 433, 434, 446, 480, 498: fruit of, 278; is more than union, 434; union of, 354
Sleep 333, 374
Things 367
Vision 434
Ways 270
Writers 211
see also **Love; Persons; Union**

Spirituality 30, 61, 89: true, 446; types and variations of, 270
Spiritual Testimonies (*Teresa's book*) 455, 473, 479, 481, 484, 489, 490, 492, 493, 494, 495, 496, 497, 498
Stability 151: instability, 127
State of Life 224: obligations of, 438
Stewards 226: of the Lord, 225
Stillness 346
Strength of soul 40, 68, 76, 91, 105, 107, 108, 142, 154, 162, 164, 165, 185, 246, 251, 254, 259, 260, 278, 293, 334, 336, 344, 355, 362, 425, 426, 437, 443, 447: comes from humility, 241; of love in the soul, 384; of body and soul to serve, 448; *see also* **Soul**
Strife 193
Struggle(s) 127, 148, 185, 271
Stupidity 284
Submission to others 234; *see also* **TERESA** to Church
Subterfuge 166
Suffering 20, 30, 50, 54, 68, 80, 86, 104, 112, 130, 131, 136, 161, 175, 177, 181, 188, 189, 195, 201, 225, 235, 238, 241, 246, 251, 259, 274, 276, 301, 309, 311, 315, 322, 326, 333, 344, 349, 350, 352, 358, 360, 362, 364, 365, 369, 372, 373, 374, 378, 379, 384, 391, 393, 394, 397, 398, 399, 402, 403, 407, 417, 418, 419, 421, 426, 428, 431, 437, 439, 445, 448, 498: of body versus that of soul, 423, 424; capacity for, 161, 162; earthly, 422; habitual, 394; interior, 366; of loved one, 66, 68
Sullenness 352
Supernatural experiences 316, 324, 334, 382, 402; *see also* **Experiences; PRAYER**
Superior 44, 61, 105, 161, 223, 296: leads strong and weak in same way, 161; *see also* **Bishop; Prioress**
Supplication *see* **Petition**
Surprise at experience of God's acts and love, 219, 221, 309, 339, 344, 410, 439
Surrender 82, 143, 253, 331, 345, 346, 386, 423, 441, 476: of will to God, 311; entire, 340; to the Spouse, 355
Suspension 131, 244, 256, 257, 259, 321, 331, 336, 350, 353, 380, 393,

403, 413, 418, 498: even exterior, 252; extreme, 384; duration of, 331, occasioned by singing, 256
Suspicions 337, 461; *see also* **False**
Sustenance 43, 102, 171, 249
Sweetness in interior 243, 253, 256, 324, 332
Swoon: interior and exterior, 153, 218, 244, 337, 426; *see also* **Languishing**
Symbol *see* **Imagery**
Sympathy 68; *see also* **Feelings**
Synthesis of *Dwelling Places*: first, 270; second, 270, 271; third, 271, 272; fourth, 272, 273; fifth, 273, 274; sixth, 274, 275, 276; seventh 276; Teresa's—of the spiritual life, 267, 269
Talk is easy 472; *see also* **Deeds; Words**
Tasks: performance of, 357; from God, 103; Mary had already performed—of Martha, 448; *see also* **Works**
Taste: spiritual, 434; of God's favors, 245, 249
Teacher (teaching) 118, 129, 309; not our business, 117, 315, 449; *see also* **Christ; Teresa**
Tears 52, 65, 100, 109, 232, 236, 243, 317, 318, 326, 345, 391, 395, 422: anxious, 318; false, 394; refreshment from, 108, 395; suspect, 394; weeping, 394, 397
Temperament 30, 233, 300, 318, 463
Temptation(s) 39, 59, 68, 84, 108, 111, 129, 155, 185, 186, 188, 189, 190, 191, 192, 193, 195, 197, 199, 201, 223, 296, 301, 303, 307, 317, 361, 372, 409, 414, 437, 460, 463, 474, 475, 477, 478; *see also* **Remedies**
Tenderness 68, 96, 232, 394, 399, 402, 462
Tense 198; *see also* **Feelings**

TERESA:
age, 40; asks for prayer, 450, 452; her biographers, 268; champions women, 23, 25, 26, 50; criticizes learned men, 210; on her own death, 19, 44, 132; determination, 271; education in Scripture, 209; freedom, 29; handwriting, 17; is hard-hearted, 394; health, 78, 264, 281, 320, 321, 354, 362, 492; laughs, 42, 97, 122, 196, 227, 381, 438; her memory, 220, 281, 338; a 'restless gad-about,' 265; sarcasm, 329; self-deprecation, 56, 305; suffering, 20; is not tender, 394; vivacity, 468; wit, 313, 490; worry about her brother, 466
and Christ: defends Christ before the Father, 167, 175, 176; *see also* **CHRIST; GOD**
and the Church: daughter of, 20, 22; doctrinal position of Teresa, 488; her ministry, 20; her missionary spirit, 17; Scripture, 209; her submission of her writings, 21, 282, 452, 458; burns her *Meditations,* 212
and her Nuns: she is foundress, 15; mother, 94, 128; prioress, 38, 128, 457, 496; her anathemas regarding honor, 71, love, 55, 459 and poverty, 46, 458; her ideal envisioned, 22, 27, 41; her love for the Sisters, 40; her obedience, 15, 16, 37 and occupations, 467; a proverb, 498; her role of teacher, 28, 30, 31, 128; her work threatened, 265
and her Prayer: approved, 492; Easter grace, 425; experience of the mystical life, 20, 275, 467; goal of her interior journey, 278; locutions, 20; longing, 41; meditations, 220; prayed 20 years before contemplation, 95;

read for prayer, 99; her spiritual marriage, 432, 433; her spontaneity, 29, 33; her terminology, 33; visions, 20, 269
and her reflections related to Sciences: Biology, 341, 350; natural science, 108, 109, 323; philosophy, 108; physiology (includes anatomy and medicine) 320, 321, 322, 334; psychology, 55, 125, 134, 145, 149, 163, 165, 166, 169, 170, 173, 191, 198, 199, 226, 233, 237, 241, 243, 244, 257, 258, 260, 310, 315, 317, 318, 334, 379, 394, 396, 415, 416, 423, 449; sociology, *see* **Social Relation**
and her Writing: 16, 17, 18, 21, 28, 29, 32, 34, 35, 39, 62, 72, 90, 98, 106, 117, 132, 208, 213, 215, 219, 220, 225, 243, 263, 266, 267, 268, 270, 271, 272, 273, 274, 275, 276, 277, 278, 290, 297, 306, 322, 327, 338, 354, 358, 389, 393, 427, 428, 451, 452, 465, 472, 484, 485; intended it for, 37; imagery, 268; *see also* **Castle Imagery; Figures of speech;** lapse of time between books, 358, 381; had no strength for writing, 423; wrote in obedience, 316, 325, 489; her work corrected by Gratian, 486; defended by Ribera, 486
Test: by God, 96, 309, 310, 315, 334; He observes soul's behavior, 357; by ourselves, 229, 310, 311, 475
Thanksgiving 33; *see also* **Gratitude; Praise of God; PRAYER**
Theology and theologians 16, 21, 22, 23, 24, 48, 49, 59, 208, 272: terminology of, 484
Thieves on cross 93
Thirst for God: exteriorly manifested, 111; spiritual, 107; *see also* **Figures of speech**
Thomas Aquinas, St. 305
Thought(s) (thinking) 62, 118, 126, 128, 133, 147, 154, 185, 190, 216, 217, 227, 229, 239, 248, 249, 272, 321, 322, 323, 331, 370, 372, 376, 378, 397, 402, 403, 404, 413, 415, 423, 445, 448, 476, 477: about saints necessary, 399; brave—important, 230; is not contemplation, 95; consoling, 112; deceive, 327; discursive, 319; less, 329; lofty, 53; poverty in, 46; no power for, 336; taken to be seeing, 334; of the world, 110
Time 90, 93, 126: all of—but one day, 168; before favors granted, 401; lost in ignoring intellect, 400; wasting, 333
Titles in monasteries 27, 458; *see also* **Nobility**
Toledo 263, 267, 491; copy of *Interior Castle,* 266, 458, 459, 471, 472, 474; monastery of St. Joseph, 17, 35, 282
Toledo, García de, O.P. 15, 16, 18, 21, 28, 35, 459
Tomb: passage from, 341
Torment: spiritual, 276, 362, 363, 364, 365, 384, 410, 415, 423, 426, 438, 444, 446, 460, 472; delightful, 391; excessive, 440; of soul versus of body, 424
Tostado, Jerónimo, Fr. 264, 265
Touches of God's love 441; *see also* **GOD; LOVE**
Touchiness *see* **Honor**
Tranquillity 116, 222, 226, 228, 232, 236, 321, 349
Transformation: in God, 164; of soul, 343, 344
Transition from natural to supernatural 488
Translation 34
Transport 442; from devil, 338; of love, 254; *see also* **Rapture**
Transverberation 492

Treasure 336; *see also* **Figures of speech; Self**
Trent (Tridentine), Council 24, 26, 208, 266, 482, 486
Trials 33, 34, 50, 73, 74, 82, 83, 102, 112, 113, 117, 122, 126, 131, 133, 134, 136, 141, 162, 163, 169, 175, 181, 185, 201, 215, 232, 237, 238, 240, 246, 251, 259, 271, 276, 298, 300, 301, 306, 307, 310, 315, 320, 321, 332, 344, 345, 358, 360, 364, 369, 374, 378, 381, 390, 392, 393, 403, 416, 417, 418, 425, 431, 432, 437, 439, 445, 446, 447, 449, 463, 472; asking for, 160; exterior or interior, 440; extraordinary, 417; having to eat and sleep is a, 321; of loved one, 66; unbearable, 363
Tribulations of contemplatives 102
Trinity *see* **GOD**
Truth(s) 51, 75, 91, 110, 115, 116, 120, 125, 136, 140, 141, 146, 162, 165, 184, 185, 192, 193, 202, 216, 218, 227, 244, 245, 248, 258, 290, 309, 313, 325, 328, 336, 338, 339, 340, 349, 363, 373, 374, 381, 393, 400, 401, 407, 409, 414, 420, 437, 469, 478, 484: God alone is, 420; most profound, 430
Trust 175: in God, 248; in superior, 229; *see also* **Confidence**
Tumult in senses and faculties 413
Understanding 38, 45, 48, 49, 54, 55, 62, 65, 69, 74, 88, 99, 102, 104, 108, 110, 117, 121, 123, 124, 125, 128, 129, 130, 131, 136, 137, 140, 141, 142, 143, 147, 148, 149, 150, 152, 153, 154, 155, 157, 158, 165, 178, 179, 181, 183, 185, 187, 191, 193, 198, 199, 203, 207, 215, 216, 217, 218, 219, 221, 223, 224, 226, 228, 229, 232, 234, 235, 237, 242, 243, 244, 245, 248, 249, 250, 251, 252, 253, 254, 255, 257, 258, 260, 264, 269, 275, 276, 284, 289, 290, 291, 301, 303, 304, 305, 307, 310, 311, 312, 316, 319, 320, 321, 323, 324, 325, 327, 328, 329, 331, 332, 334, 335, 336, 339, 340, 344, 346, 348, 351, 355, 358, 363, 364, 365, 371, 373, 375, 376, 377, 379, 381, 382, 384, 385, 386, 388, 390, 393, 395, 399, 404, 405, 406, 407, 408, 410, 416, 419, 420, 422, 424, 427, 430, 432, 434, 435, 436, 438, 439, 444, 445, 446, 448, 460, 464, 465, 472, 473, 475, 476, 484: inward and outward, 380; received in prayer, 40; and sin, 210
Unhappiness 226
Union: of bride and bridegroom, 237; from conformity of wills, 491; delightful, 349, 350, 491; duration of, 254, 334, 339, 343, 355, 434; error about, 338; of faculties, 325; of some of the faculties, 340; with God, 211, 221, 240, 242, 246, 252, 254, 274, 276, 277, 320, 337, 338, 339, 343, 346, 353, 355, 360, 367, 368, 379, 395, 429, 430; *see also* **CHRIST; GOD;** infused, 491; intensity of, 341; nature of, 341; oneness is more than, 434; prayer of, 109, 155; *see* **PRAYER;** secret, 433; of soul with uncreated Spirit, 435; of the whole soul, 340; of spirit with spirit, 447; with will of God, 236; of will to God's will, 325, 349, 350, 352; *see also* **Will**
Ursula, St. 356
Vainglory 85, 186, 333, 351
Valdés, Fernando de, Inquisitor General, 24, 208, 468
Valencia: editions of *Way of Perfection,* 35, 485
Valladolid: autograph of *Way of Perfection,* 35, 459; monastery of nuns at, 18
Values *see* **Soul**
Vanity 57, 58, 76, 83, 144, 192, 226, 237, 244, 289, 300, 338, 460, 464, 465, 477

Variety: modes of presence to Christ, 33; of ways to proceed in prayer, 223; *see also* **Diversity**
Velásquez, Dr. Alonso 483
Vernacular for Scripture in Teresa's time 208, 209, 215, 217, 304, 468
Vicar 461; right of, 61; *see also* **Superior**
Victory 364
Vigil, keeping 333
Violence 22; spiritual, 119
Virgins, foolish 103
Virtue(s) 31, 42, 45, 46, 51, 54, 55, 56, 62, 69, 71, 74, 75, 76, 77, 87, 90, 91, 92, 93, 94, 95, 100, 105, 119, 120, 130, 143, 161, 180, 182, 185, 187, 188, 189, 192, 196, 227, 232, 235, 236, 238, 239, 240, 244, 245, 252, 254, 255, 274, 288, 291, 301, 309, 311, 314, 317, 332, 336, 348, 350, 351, 352, 353, 357, 386, 390, 394, 404, 410, 414, 417, 450, 460, 465, 475, 476, 478, 487, 498: feigned, 351; imagined—is a pestilence, 186; of a loved one, 66; practice of, 447
Visions (apparitions) 22, 104, 268, 339, 381, 405, 407, 408, 409, 410, 411, 414, 415, 416, 418, 420, 425, 430, 445, 465, 484: acts produced by, 375; authentic, 418; basis of symbol for *The Interior Castle,* 268, 269; beneficial, 417; came with great force, 433; holland linen garment in, 412; differ in seventh Dwelling Places, 433; duration of, 406, 411, 412, 413, 419; engraved in soul, 419; fancied, 409; imaginative, 275, 277, 380, 382, 389, 406, 410, 419, 430, 432, 433, 493; intellectual, 275, 277, 375, 380, 382, 389, 405, 406, 419, 430, 433, 484, 492, 493, 495, 497; *see also* **TERESA** her Prayer
Visitator 264
Vocal Prayer *see* **PRAYER**
Vocation of Carmelite nuns 42, 53: appreciation of, 72; a special call, 248; criteria of, 87; lack of, 87; other vocations, 43; *see also* **Religious life**
Vows 105, 166, 472
Walls of poverty 46
Warning 300, 332, 333: interior, 357
Watch in prayer 468
Water: element, 323; properties of, 108, 109; as prayer, 324; *see also* **PRAYER**
Way of Perfection (*Teresa's book*) 17, 18, 19, 21, 23, 28, 30, 37, 213, 243, 263, 268, 455, 456, 458, 480, 481, 482, 483, 484, 485, 487, 488, 489, 490, 491, 493, 499: divisions of, 35; texts, 35
Weakness 40, 43, 57, 66, 68, 80, 85, 87, 104, 114, 118, 120, 129, 161, 165, 172, 198, 201, 228, 229, 238, 239, 240, 241, 242, 252, 255, 257, 309, 333, 334, 344, 345, 360, 374, 378, 379, 382, 387, 394, 410, 413, 423, 425, 440, 442, 443, 445, 446, 459, 460
Wealth 27, 30, 83, 123, 225, 271, 311, 344: striving for, 310
Weariness 64, 116, 164, 201, 202, 249, 391
Will 76, 82, 105, 131, 137, 140, 143, 154, 155, 156, 157, 159, 161, 162, 163, 164, 165, 169, 183, 198, 200, 202, 234, 235, 236, 240, 242, 249, 252, 292, 299, 301, 308, 314, 319, 322, 331, 332, 346, 349, 352, 353, 377, 384, 387, 400, 402, 417, 446, 471, 472: ardor cooled, 357; enslaved, 55; inquiry of, 249; laughs, 158; cannot love, 64; plays no part, 340; resolute, 441; of the Sisters, 353; no strength, 54; entirely surrendered, 340; union of, 349; willingness, 386
Wisdom 65, 105, 124, 253
Withdrawal 26, 42, 224, 306, 308, 332, 356: actions toward, 344;

from all things, 344; from God, 432, 443; happy, 396

Woman 22, 23, 24, 26, 40, 41, 50, 51, 54, 80, 86, 105, 118, 144, 207, 212, 216, 217, 232, 235, 238, 258, 282, 333, 352, 379, 382, 392, 449, 459: argue, 220; dullness of mind, 290; mistrust of, 25; and prayer, 22, 26; strength of—will astonish men, 70; teach, 220; womanish behavior, 70; write, 220; in Scripture: in Pharisee's house, 449; touched garment of Christ, 172; washed feet of Christ, 448

Words 22, 27, 34, 46, 69, 70, 97, 156, 163, 229, 234, 236, 318, 374, 385, 389, 474: from God are accomplished, 373; in locutions, 371; of loving soul, 259, 331, 367; only, 446; power of—from God, 373; of Scripture, 219; *see also* **CHRIST, Deeds, GOD**

Work (labor) 26, 101, 170, 353, 358: workroom, 56; in prayer, *see also* **Effort**

Works (activities) 59, 218, 278, 293, 314, 446: exterior, 438; fruitless if done in mortal sin, 288; great—performed in service of God and neighbor, 257, 258; our—not needed by God, 308; soul no longer esteems its, 344; *see also* **Deeds**

World 77, 123, 139, 144, 169, 181, 184, 192, 214, 227, 228, 238, 240, 241, 346, 385, 459, 464, 475: is blind, 120; clergy and, 48; collapses, 117; comforts of, 480; consolations, 315, 336; contempt for, 336, 406; delights of, 157, 245; demands perfection in preachers, teachers, theologians, 49; dead to enjoyments of, 336; duration of, 168; false good of, 234; God not esteemed in, 345; in flames, 43; flight from, 75; interests of, 234; an interior, 320; judges in, 51; knowledge of, 62; the—is a lie, 420; love for, 255; Lord battles against—for us, 71; midst of, 392; pleasure of, 190, 222, 245; rank in, 179; relations of religious to, 48, 49, 67, 89; speaking to, 129, 130; storms of—not to be feared, 315; things of, 51, 63, 65, 87, 109, 121, 142, 155, 158, 164, 192, 246, 249, 294, 299, 308, 314, 336, 345, 393, 463; despised, 329; treasure of, 251; worries of, 245; *see also* **Persons; Withdrawal**

Worry 234, 312, 385, 415, 438: about food, 43, 44; about other's financial resources, 43

Wound of love in soul 242, 275, 359, 368, 422; delightful and precious, 367; *see also* **Enkindling; LOVE**

Wretchedness 72, 104, 310, 314, 321, 330, 363, 364, 398, 401, 465: wicked, 398

Wrongs 178, 180, 182; *see also* **Rights**

Yanguas, Diego de, O.P. 212, 278

Yearning for death 391

Yepes, Diego de, Jeronimite 268, 269

Young also receive favors from God 255

Zaragosa 467

Zeal 120: hunger for God's honor, 295; indiscreet, 296; trials from, 315

Zebedee, sons of 426

Appendix to Index

CASTLE IMAGERY: images and applications in Teresa's own words:

	Image	Application	Pages
1)	castle, made of diamond, in which there are many dwelling places	the soul	283, 284, 285, 288, 291, 429
2)	King of the castle	the Lord, His Majesty	283
3)	outer wall of the castle, setting for the diamond	the body	284
4)	main dwelling place	center of the soul where secret exchanges between God and soul take place	284, 291
5)	insects and vermin in wall surrounding the castle	external matters	286
6)	door of entry to castle	prayer and reflection	286, 303, 451
7)	entering the castle	a) have good desires b) entrust self to the Lord c) reflect on self	287
8)	reptiles that enter with those who dwell there	business matters that fill the mind	287

9)	seeing the beauty of the castle	self-knowledge and calmness of soul	287
10)	darkest darkness in castle	mortal sin and the devil	288
11)	sun in all brilliance and beauty in center of soul	God present in the center of the soul	288
12)	water streams coming from crystal-clear fount	works of a soul in grace	288-289
13)	people who live in the rooms within the castle	the senses	289, 327, 367, 448
14)	the custodians, stewards and chief waiters	the faculties	289, 327, 367, 448
15)	blindness and bad management	effects of mortal sin on the faculties	289, 429, 430
16)	a room	self-knowledge	291, 292
17)	flying (free movement) in the rooms	ponder the grandeur and majesty of God	291
18)	mire	our miseries	292
19)	black and foul-smelling streams	works of a soul that is in mortal sin	292

Castle Imagery (Cont'd)

20)	mud	fears, faintheartedness and cowardice	292, 313
21)	vermin within the first dwelling places	wiles and deceits of devil to make souls absorbed in world, and engulfed in pleasures and vanities, with honors, and pretenses so that souls may not know themselves or understand their own paths	293, 295, 308
22)	vassals of the soul	senses and faculties	293
23)	first dwelling places so darkened by presence of snakes, vipers, poisonous creatures which do not allow beauty of room to be seen	involvement in worldly things and absorption with its possessions, honor or business affairs	294, cf 298
24)	entering into second dwelling places	striving to give up unnecessary things and business affairs	294, 297
25)	staying in midst of poisonous creatures and eventually being bitten	turning back through our own fault to go into tumult of worldly things	294, 297
26)	guards of the rooms	the faculties	295, cf 285
27)	living in the second dwelling places	those who have already begun to practice prayer	297

28)	not being determined to stay in the second dwelling places	not avoiding occasions of sin	297, 315
29)	persons who live in the first dwelling places are deaf-mutes	those who cannot pray and do not hear the Lord's call	298, 429, 430
30)	persons who live in the second dwelling places are only mute	those who can hear the Lord's call but cannot pray well	298
31)	the Lord of the castle is a good neighbor, who makes his sweet voice heard, as he calls	God wishes to grant favors because of His mercy and bounty. His voice and call are sermons, words of good people, good books, illness, trial or a truth taught us in prayer.	298
32)	stumbling and falling over poisonous beasts	being so occupied with pastimes, business affairs, pleasures and worldly buying and selling that we fall into sin and rise again	298
33)	blows from artillery in defense of castle against snakes, etc., cannot be ignored	the will is inclined to love and be aware of the true Lover; the intellect is more alive; the faculties, now more skilled, see the world as false; and the soul begins wanting to practice some penance	299
34)	strange houses outside the castle	joys that the devil gives, which are filled with trials, cares and contradictions	299

Castle Imagery (Cont'd)

35)	poisonous things	visible habits that are in and of the world	300
36)	deception to lure one to go back outside the castle	temptations from the devil to go against favorable temperament and good habits and turn to bad companions	300
37)	visiting and talking to others who are in these rooms and even in those closer to the center	conversations with spiritual persons which lead to progress	300
38)	fighting the enemy at the risk of loss of life to prevent going back to the first dwelling places	manly determination to lose life and repose rather than slacken	300
39)	weapons to fight the enemy	the cross	300
40)	a poor way to start building so precious and great an edifice—on sand	thinking about consolations at the beginning, and always being dissatisfied and tempted	300-301
41)	stability of the edifice, the castle	determined effort to bring one's will into conformity with God's will	301
42)	poisonous little reptiles	dryness and bad thoughts which pursue and afflict without our being able to get rid of them	301

43)	being ill at ease in our own house	our own misery and the great harm that a dissipated life does to us	302
44)	many great and true friends and relatives with whom we must always live, even though we may not want to	our faculties	302
45)	the Master of the castle brings one from the dwelling places of one stage to those of another	one trusts in the mercy of God and not at all in oneself	302
46)	winning the battles and entering the rooms of the third dwelling places	work, prayer and perseverance and the mercy of God leading to security of conscience, if one does not abandon the path begun on	303-304
47)	one who will never ascend to the dwelling places closest to the King	one who strives for material wealth and, after possessing it, strives for more and more, no matter how good his intention may be	310-311
48)	walking the path from dwelling place to dwelling place	exerting ourselves to abandon our reason and our fears into the Lord's hands and forgetting our natural weakness for love of Him	312, 313

Castle Imagery (Cont'd)

49)	walking rapidly or on the other hand being weighed down with mud in the walking	having great humility and making progress, or carrying a thousand afflictions and miseries because of not having abandoned ourselves to God's will in humility	312-313
50)	poisonous creatures enter the fourth dwelling places and wage war	temptations are felt which is a gain for it prevents deception by the devil	317, 437
51)	ascending to those dwelling places which we desire	loving much rather than thinking much	319
52)	mind is on the outskirts of the castle, suffering from wild and poisonous beasts, while soul is perhaps completely joined to the King in dwelling places very close to the center	soul perhaps completely joined to God while the mind and faculties are very distracted and are meriting by this suffering	320
53)	the last dwelling place	the state in which we are given rest from the thousand trials in the world and are prepared for tranquillity and freed from the taunts of our miseries	321
54)	the edifice is being built	recollection	327
55)	walking about with strangers and enemies until shepherd's whistle from the King in center dwelling place draws them inside	infused recollection which gently draws souls inward to abandon exterior things in which they were estranged from God	327-328

56)	tiny lizards that poke their slender heads in, to bother but which cannot enter the fifth dwelling places	little thoughts which proceed from the imagination, but which cannot (any more than memory or intellect) impede the prayer of true union with God	337
57)	a dwelling place which we build for ourselves	God Himself in the prayer of union	343
58)	there is no closed door between the last two (the sixth and seventh) dwelling places	similar favors are granted to the soul in both of these stages so near to God	380
59)	the King commands that the doors of all but the last dwelling places be closed. Door of last one alone remains open so we can enter and see some of His kingdom	all hindrances to union with God from faculties and senses are prevented by a rapture by which God carries off for Himself the entire soul	382-383
60)	being brought into the seventh dwelling place	union with God, in which the Most Blessed Trinity is revealed to the soul, all Three Persons, through an intellectual vision	430
61)	streams of milk from the center of the castle bring comfort to all the people of the castle	aspirations that spring up in the soul and sustain the corporeal, giving light to faculties and peace to the soul which does not move from that center	435, 447

Castle Imagery (Cont'd)

62)	the King is in the center dwelling place and no one can enter it to make the soul leave it	the passions are conquered and have a fear of entering the center of the soul	437
63)	the King sends out a secret note or letter from the interior dwelling place which is intended to be understood by one alone	a touch or impulse of love from God in the center of the soul beseeching us to remain with Him	440-441
64)	sometimes all the poisonous creatures from the outskirts and other dwelling places band together to revenge the time they were unable to have the soul under their control	short periods which are permitted by God, when individuals are left in their natural state and so commit many imperfections, though not advertently	444
65)	striving to lay stones so firmly in a good foundation that the castle will not fall	in genuine humility, in addition to prayer and contemplation, striving for virtues, and serving and pleasing others because one is the slave of God whom He can use and sell as slave to everyone	446-447
66)	angering the Lord of the castle so that He will never allow admission to all the dwelling places	trying to use force through one's own efforts and lacking humility	451
67)	going outside the castle but finding that the Lord keeps the door open for one's return	having to leave the center through obedience to the prioress but finding rest in all things, even those involving much labor	451

Biblical Index

Genesis

1:26 452
1:26-27 283
8:8-9 392
8:8-12 443
19:26 286
28:12 381

Exodus

3:1-16 381
14:21-22 392
16 77
16:3-4 169

Numbers

13:18-27 390

Joshua

3:13-17 392
10:12-13 378

Judges

7:5 300

Ruth

1:15 135

1 Samuel

15:10-11 417

1 Kings

6:7 442
11 445
18:30-39 401
19:10 448

Job

2:9-13 85
7:1 223

Psalms

1:3 288
8:7 109
18:26 447
34:19 146
42:2 442
55:7 140
89:50 194
112:1 304, 306, 445
116:11 420
119:32 318, 324
119:137 314
127:1 289

Proverbs

1:20 114
8:29 387
8:31 283
24:16 92

Song of Songs

207-260 *passim*
1:2 216, 236, 242, 442
1:2-3 242
2:3 247, 250
2:3-4 248
2:4 250, 340, 346, 448
2:5 250, 255, 256
2:14 134
2:16 246
3:1-3 401
3:2 340, 383
4:7 254
4:9 94
6:3 246
6:10 255
8:1 321
8:4 259
8:7 108

Wisdom

16:20 77, 248, 301

Sirach

3:25 303

Isaiah

30:15 315

Jonah

1 374
4 374
4:67 350

Malachi

3:20 202

Matthew

3:15 166
4:5 96
6:6 129
6:9 137, 140
6:9-10 150
6:12 420, 177
6:13 186
6:15 420
6:21 287
8:25-26 176
9:20-22 172
10:24 303
11:12 119
11:28 113
13:44 336
14:29 235
17:4 154
19:16-22 307
19:22 308
19:27 308
19:29 127
20:13 317
20:22 104, 172, 301, 426
21:3 97
22:14 335
24:35 138

25:1-13 103
25:1-14 224
25:41 412
26:15 168
26:38 241
26:39 150, 162
26:41 303

Mark

13:31 138
14:38 240
14:38-39 186

Luke

1:35-35 253
1:35 248
1:48-52 86
2:29 153
6:12 129
6:37 420
7:36-40 93
7:36-48 169
7:37-38 448
7:40-48 426
7:50 435
8:43-44 172
9:58 51
10:16 375
10:38 93
10:38-40 100
10:38-42 448
10:40 431
10:41-42 100
10:42 102
11:9 127, 175
12:16-21 225
12:48 308, 387
14:10 99
14:11 86
15:11-32 138
15:16 300
15:22-32 395
17:10 308
18:13 156, 443
21:33 44, 138, 436
22:15 200, 346
22:42 311
23:41 93

John

4:7-14 424
4:14 107, 117, 127
4:39-43 258
5:5 287
7:37 113, 114
8:12 400
8:29 138
9:2-3 285
9:6-7 383
10:30 138
11:16 305
11:33-36 349
13:1-17 218
13:34 56, 218
14:2 114, 283
14:6 303, 400
14:9 303, 400
14:23 430
15:5 147, 300, 317
16:7 404
17:20 436
17:21 138, 436
17:22 350
17:23 436
18:36-38 420
20:19 341
20:19-21 302, 433, 435

Acts of the Apostles

9:3-4 413
9:3-11 248
9:6 441
9:8 430
10:34 98

Romans

8:18 245

1 Corinthians

6:17 434
10:13 186, 377, 409
14:34 92

2 Corinthians

11:14 185, 295, 335, 337
12:2-4 389

Ephesians

3:15 138
6:9 98

Philippians

1:21 434
1:23 112
4:13 201, 332

Colossians

3:3-4 342

1 Thessalonians

2:9 445

1 Peter

1:18-19 55

2 Peter

1:4 138

1 John

1:8-10 92
1:10 201
4:20 351

Revelation

21:3 442

About Us

ICS Publications, based in Washington, D.C., is the publishing house of the Institute of Carmelite Studies (ICS) and a ministry of the Discalced Carmelite Friars of the Washington Province (U.S.A.). The Institute of Carmelite Studies promotes research and publication in the field of Carmelite spirituality, especially about Carmelite saints and related topics. Its members are friars of the Washington Province.

The Discalced Carmelites are a worldwide Roman Catholic religious order comprised of friars, nuns, and laity—men and women who are heirs to the teaching and way of life of Teresa of Avila and John of the Cross, dedicated to contemplation and to ministry in the church and the world.

Information about their way of life is available through local diocesan vocation offices, or from the Discalced Carmelite Friars vocation directors at the following addresses:

Washington Province:
1525 Carmel Road, Hubertus, WI 53033

California-Arizona Province:
P.O. Box 3420, San Jose, CA 95156

Oklahoma Province:
5151 Marylake Drive, Little Rock, AR 72206

Visit our websites at:

www.icspublications.org and *http://ocdfriarsvocation.org*